avorite Recipes of Home Economic Teachers

Too good to be forgotten...

2,000
Favorite
Recipes

MEATS

Favorite Recipes of Home Economic Teachers

FRP
P. O. Box 305142
Nashville, Tennessee 37230
1-800-358-0560

ISBN: 978-0-87197-539-3

Cover and chapter opener design by Rikki Odgen Campbell/pixiedesign, llc

Printed in China

Other books in this series:

DESSERTS

CASSEROLES

SALADS

VEGETABLES

Revised slightly from the version published in 1965.

TABLE OF CONTENTS

ABBREVIATIONS USED IN THIS BOOK

Cup	c.	Large	lge.
Tablespoon	tbsp.	Package	pkg.
Teaspoon	tsp.	Square	sq.
Pound	lb.	Dozen	doz.
Ounce	oz.	Pint	pt.
Gallon	gal.	Quart	qt.

MEASUREMENTS

3 tsp. = 1 tbsp.

2 tbsp. = ⅛ c.

4 tbsp. = ¼ c.

8 tbsp. = ½ c.

16 tbsp. = 1 c.

5 tbsp. + 1 tsp. = ⅓ c.

12 tbsp. = ¾ c.

4 oz. = ½ c.

8 oz. = 1 c.

16 oz. = 1 lb.

1 oz. = 2 tbsp. fat or liquid

2 c. fat = 1 lb.

2 c. = 1 pt.

2 c. sugar = 1 lb.

1 lb. butter = 2 c. or 4 sticks

⅝ c. = ½ c. + 2 tbsp.

⅞ c. = ¾ c. + 2 tbsp.

2 pts. = 1 qt.

1 qt. = 4 c.

A few grains = less than ⅛ tsp.

Pinch = as much as can be taken between tip of finger and thumb

Speck = less than ⅛ tsp.

OVEN TEMPERATURES

Temperature (°F.)	Term
250-300	Slow
325	Moderately slow
350	Moderate
375	Moderately quick
400	Moderately hot
425-450	Hot
475-500	Extremely hot

TERMS AND DEFINITIONS

(For meat, seafood and poultry)

BARBECUE	To cook in a highly seasoned sauce
BASTE	To moisten meats with melted fat, meat drippings, fruit juice or sauce during cooking to prevent drying and to add flavor
BRAISE	To cook slowly by moist heat
BREAD	To coat with crumbs
BROIL	To cook by direct heat
BROTH	A thin soup, or the liquid in which food was cooked
CHOP	To cut coarsely with a knife or cleaver
CROQUETTE	Finely chopped meat, poultry or fish which is shaped, coated and deep-fat fried
CUBE	To cut into small even pieces
DICE	To cut into cubes, about ¼-inch in size
DREDGE	To dip in or sprinkle with flour
DRIPPINGS	The fat and juices collected in a roasting pan or skillet
EN BROCHETTE	Food cooked on a skewer
FILET OR FILLET	A boneless, long shaped piece of meat or fish
LARD	To insert or place strips of fat on surface
MARINATE	To let stand in a mixture of oil and vinegar or lemon juice
PANBROIL	To cook in a skillet kept dry by pouring off accumulated fat
PANFRY	To cook in a small amount of fat in a skillet
PARBOIL	To partially cook in water
POACH	To cook in water just below the boiling point
POT ROAST	To cook slowly by moist heat
ROAST	To cook by dry heat in the oven
ROUX	A smooth blend of fat and flour used for thickening
SAUTE	To cook in a small amount of fat
SCORE	To make shallow cuts in surface or edges of meat
SEAR	To brown quickly
SIMMER	To cook by moist heat at a low temperature
SINGE	To burn the hairs off poultry
STEW	To cook slowly in liquid
STOCK	The liquid in which meat, fish or poultry has been cooked
SUET	The firm white fat of beef
TRUSS	To fasten together with strings or skewers

MEAT, SEAFOOD & POULTRY CALORIE CHART

Food	Amount	Calories
Bacon, broiled or fried crisp	2 slices	95
Beef, trimmed to retail basis, cooked:		
Cuts braised, simmered or pot-roasted:		
Lean and fat	3 oz.	245
Lean only	2.5 oz.	140
Hamburger, broiled:		
Market ground	3 oz.	245
Ground lean	3 oz.	185
Roast, oven-cooked, no liquid added:		
Relatively fat, such as rib:		
Lean and fat	3 oz.	390
Lean only	1.8 oz.	120
Relatively lean, such as round:		
Lean and fat	3 oz.	220
Lean only	2.5 oz.	130
Steak, broiled:		
Relatively fat, such as sirloin:		
Lean and fat	3 oz.	330
Lean only	2 oz.	115
Relatively lean, such as round:		
Lean and fat	3 oz.	220
Lean only	2 oz.	130
Beef, canned:		
Corned beef	3 oz.	180
Corned beef hash	3 oz.	120
Beef, dried or chipped	2 oz.	115
Beef and vegetable stew	1 c.	185
Beef pot pie, baked, about 8 oz. before baking	1 pie	460
Chicken, cooked:		
Flesh and skin, broiled, no bone	3 oz.	185
Breast, fried, with bone	½ breast	215
Leg, fried (thigh and drumstick) with bone	4.3 oz.	245
Chicken, canned, boneless	3 oz.	170
Chile con carne, canned:		
With beans	1 c.	335
Without beans	1 c.	510
Heart, beef, trimmed of fat, braised	3 oz.	160
Lamb, trimmed to retail basis, cooked:		
Chop, thick, with bone, broiled		
Lean and fat	4 oz.	405
Lean only	2.6 oz.	140
Leg, roasted:		
Lean and fat	3 oz.	235
Lean only	2.5 oz.	130
Shoulder, roasted:		
Lean and fat	3 oz.	285
Lean only	2.3 oz.	130

MEAT, SEAFOOD & POULTRY CALORIE CHART

Food	Amount	Calories
Liver, beef, fried	2 oz.	120
Pork, cured, cooked:		
Ham, smoked, lean and fat	3 oz.	290
Luncheon meat:		
Cooked ham, sliced	2 oz.	170
Canned, spiced or unspiced	2 oz.	165
Pork, fresh, trimmed to retail basis, cooked:		
Chop, thick with bone:		
Lean and fat	2.3 oz.	260
Lean only	1.7 oz.	130
Roast, oven-cooked, no liquid added:		
Lean and fat	3 oz.	310
Lean only	2.4 oz.	175
Cuts, simmered:		
Lean and fat	3 oz.	320
Lean only	2.2 oz.	135
Poultry pot pie, about 8 oz.	1 pie	485
Sausage:		
Bologna, slice 4.1x0.1″	8 slices	690
Frankfurter, cooked	1 frank	155
Pork, bulk, canned	4 oz.	340
Tongue, beef, simmered	3 oz.	205
Veal, cooked:		
Cutlet, broiled, no bone	3 oz.	185
Roast, med. fat, medium done, lean and fat	3 oz.	305
Fish and Shellfish:		
Bluefish, baked or boiled	3 oz.	135
Clams:		
Raw, meat only	3 oz.	70
Canned, solids and liquids	3 oz.	45
Crabmeat, canned or cooked	3 oz.	90
Fish sticks, breaded, cooked, frozen	8-oz. pkg.	400
Haddock, fried	3 oz.	135
Mackerel:		
Broiled, Atlantic	3 oz.	200
Canned, Pacific, solids and liquids	3 oz.	155
Ocean perch, breaded, fried	3 oz.	195
Oysters, meat only, raw	1 c.	160
Oyster stew, 1 part oysters, 3 parts milk	1 c.	200
Salmon, pink, canned	3 oz.	120
Sardines, Atlantic type, canned in oil, drained	3 oz.	180
Shad, baked	3 oz.	170
Shrimp, canned, meat only	3 oz.	110
Swordfish, broiled with butter or oleo	3 oz.	150
Tuna, canned in oil, drained	3 oz.	170

HERB, SPICE AND SEASONING CHART

Herbs, spices and seasonings must be used sparingly to enhance, not overpower the flavor of meats, seafood or poultry. The general rule as to quantity is ¼ teaspoon of herbs, spices or seasonings per pound for meats, seafood and poultry, or according to individual taste.

HERB OR SPICE	USE IN
ALLSPICE	Meat ball appetizers, oyster stew, beef stew, pot roast, ham, lamb, oysters
BASIL	Crab spread, turtle soup, lamb liver, meat loaf, heart, venison, bluefish, halibut, mackerel, goose, duck, turkey
BAY LEAF	Beef soup, fish chowders, veal liver, spareribs, beef stew, lamb goulash, pickled fish, shrimp, crab, boiled chicken, seafood casseroles
CARAWAY SEED	Roast pork, kidney, sauerbraten, tuna casseroles, roast goose
CELERY (salt, seeds, flakes)	Ham spread, oyster stew, bouillon, meat loaf, meat stews, pot roasts, codfish, chicken pie or croquettes, tuna salads
CLOVES	Beef soup, ham, pork roasts, boiled tongue, baked fish, chicken a la king, roasted chicken
CURRY POWDER	Clam chowder, chicken soup, lamb, veal, shrimp, baked fish, chicken hash
GARLIC (liquid, salt, powder)	Clam dip, barbecue sauce, steaks, stews, Italian and French meat dishes, chicken, fish
GINGER	Boiled beef, lamb, veal, sauted or baked chicken, Cornish hen, squab
MARJORAM	Oyster stew, pot roasts, stews, lamb, creamed crab, scallops, broiled fish, chicken or seafood salads
MUSTARD	Meat dips, ham sauces, beef-onion soup, pickled meat, ham, kidney, seafood casseroles
NUTMEG	Chopped oyster appetizers, cream of chicken soup, Salisbury steak, meat loaf, chicken
OREGANO	Meat sauces, beef, pork, veal, lamb, Swiss steak, seafood stuffing, fried chicken, seafood salads
ROSEMARY	Turtle, chicken or meat soups, kidney, veal stews, lamb, creamed shellfish, chicken fricassee
SAFFRON	Poultry stuffing, chicken soup stock, lamb, veal, sausage, halibut, sole, chicken, seafood salads
SAGE	Meat sauces and gravies, baked fish stuffing, consomme, chowders, cold roast beef, stews, pork dishes, baked fish, duck
SAVORY	Chicken and fish sauces, liver pastes, fish chowders, hamburgers, lamb roasts, veal, pork, baked or broiled fish
TARRAGON	Meat sauces, meat canape mixtures, veal, sweetbreads, creamed seafood, turkey, game, chicken, chicken salads
THYME	Sauces for meats, chowders, oyster stew

METHODS OF MEAT COOKERY

The basic rule of meat cookery is to always cook meat at low or moderate temperatures. The same rule applies whether meat is cooked by dry heat, moist heat or with fat.

A. ROASTING:

1. Season meat. Place fat-side up on rack in open roasting pan.
2. Insert meat thermometer.
3. Do not add water. Do not cover or baste.
4. Roast in 300 to 350°F. oven to desired doneness.

Cuts To Roast

BEEF—standing ribs, rolled ribs, high quality rump, loaf.

VEAL—leg, loin, rack, bone-in shoulder, cushion-style shoulder, boned and rolled shoulder, loaf.

PORK—center cut loin, blade loin, bone-in sirloin, boneless sirloin, Boston butt, fresh or smoked picnic, fresh or smoked ham, shoulder butt, spareribs, ham loaf.

LAMB—leg, bone-in shoulder, cushion-style shoulder, boned and rolled shoulder, loaf.

B. BROILING:

1. Set oven regulator for broiling. Place meat 2 to 5 inches from source of heat.
2. Broil until top of meat is brown. Season with salt and pepper.
3. Turn meat and cook until done.
4. Season and serve immediately.

Cuts To Broil

BEEF—rib, club, tenderloin (filet mignon), T-bone, porterhouse, tip, sirloin, top round steak, patties.

SMOKED PORK—bacon, Canadian-style bacon, ham slices, sliced smoked shoulder butt.

LAMB—shoulder, rib, loin and sirloin chops, English lamb chops, steaks, patties.

VARIETY MEATS—sweetbreads, brains, veal or lamb liver, kidneys.

C. PANBROILING:

1. Place meat in heavy frying pan.
2. Do not add fat or water. Do not cover.
3. Cook slowly, turning occasionally, pouring off fat as it accumulates.
4. Brown meat on both sides. Season and serve immediately.

Cuts To Panbroil

Same cuts as for broiling.

D. BRAISING:

1. Brown meat on all sides in fat in heavy utensil; season with salt and pepper.
2. Add small amount of liquid if necessary.
3. Cover tightly; cook at low temperature until tender.

Cuts To Braise

BEEF—pot roast, arm, blade, round and flank steaks, short ribs, plate, brisket, cross cut shanks.

VEAL—breast, steaks, rib, loin and kidney chops, cubes.

PORK—shoulder steaks, chops, spareribs, tenderloin, hocks.

LAMB—shoulder chops, breast, neck slices, shanks.

VARIETY MEATS—heart, kidney, brains, liver, sweetbreads.

E. PANFRYING:

1. Brown meat on both sides in small amount of fat. Season with salt and pepper.
2. Do not cover. Cook at moderate temperature until done, turning occasionally.
3. Remove from pan and serve immediately.

Cuts To Panfry

BEEF—thin ribs, club, tenderloin (filet mignon), porterhouse, sirloin and top round steaks, patties.

VEAL—arm, shoulder, sirloin, round steaks, rib, loin, kidney chops.

SMOKED PORK—ham slice, bacon, Canadian-style bacon.

FRESH PORK—thin shoulder steaks, rib, loin chops, tenderloin.

VARIETY MEATS—sweetbreads, brains, liver, veal, lamb kidneys.

LAMB—shoulder, rib and loin chops, patties.

F. COOKING IN LIQUID:

1. Brown meat on all sides in own fat or lard.
2. Season with salt and pepper; cover with liquid.
3. Cover and cook below boiling point until tender.
4. Add vegetables just long enough before serving to be cooked.

Cuts To Cook In Liquid (large cuts and stews)

BEEF—neck, shank, flank, heel of round, plate, brisket, short ribs, corned beef, stew meat.

VEAL—neck, breast, riblets, flank, shoulder, shank, heel of round, stew meat.

SMOKED PORK—ham, picnic, shoulder butt, shank.

LAMB—neck, breast, riblets, flank, shank, stew meat.

VARIETY MEATS—heart, kidney, tongue, brains, sweetbreads.

BEEF

Beef is probaby the favorite meat of most Americans. This favorite meat is sold fresh chilled, cured, cured and smoked, canned, and alone or in combination with other meats as sausages and ready-to-serve meats.

Consider not only the cut, but the quality of the meat itself when buying beef. Young beef, sometimes called "baby beef", may not contain much fat, but it probably will be tender because it is from a young animal. On the other hand, the presence of streaks or spots of fat in the meat is extremely important in judging mature beef.

The lacy network of fat in the lean is called "marbling" and is given top priority by government graders, packers and retailers in determining the grade or brand name that is to appear on the carcass.

AMOUNT TO BUY

For an average serving, allow one-fourth pound of boneless round steak, stew meats, rolled roasts and ground beef per person. For beef with an average amount of bone, such as steaks and bone-in roasts, allow one-third to one-half pound of meat per serving. For beef with more bone, such as short ribs, allow three-fourths to one pound of meat per average serving.

STORING BEEF

Fresh beef should be stored, uncovered or loosely wrapped, in the coldest part of the refrigerator. Loosen the wrapping on pre-packaged beef before placing in the refrigerator unless the meat is to be cooked the same day.

For best results, fresh ground beef should be cooked within 24 hours after purchase. Cured beef should be stored in its original wrapper in the refrigerator. For best results, use within one week.

Cooked beef should be cooled, covered or wrapped tightly, and stored in the coldest part of the refrigerator. Cooked beef will keep better if left in larger pieces and not cut until ready to use. Covering prevents drying of the meat which has lost some moisture during cooking.

FREEZING BEEF

Cut fresh large cuts of beef—rib, round, sirloin and chuck—into convenient sizes for freezing. Package steaks according to the number of servings needed.

Shape ground beef into patties or loaves or package in portions for other dishes. Season ground beef after thawing—seasonings tend to become stronger when frozen. Wrap meat tightly in moisture, vaporproof paper, separating individual servings with a double thickness of the wrapping material. Label packages for easy identification.

Freeze fresh beef quickly and store at 0° F. or lower for three to four months for ground beef and six to twelve months for other fresh beef.

Thaw frozen beef in the refrigerator, at room temperature, or during cooking. Thaw the meat in its original wrapper unless it is defrosted during cooking. Cook frozen beef roasts at 300 to 325°F., allowing one-third to one-half again as long as for cooking thawed roasts.

Corned beef, beef bacon and other cured beef are not recommended for freezing.

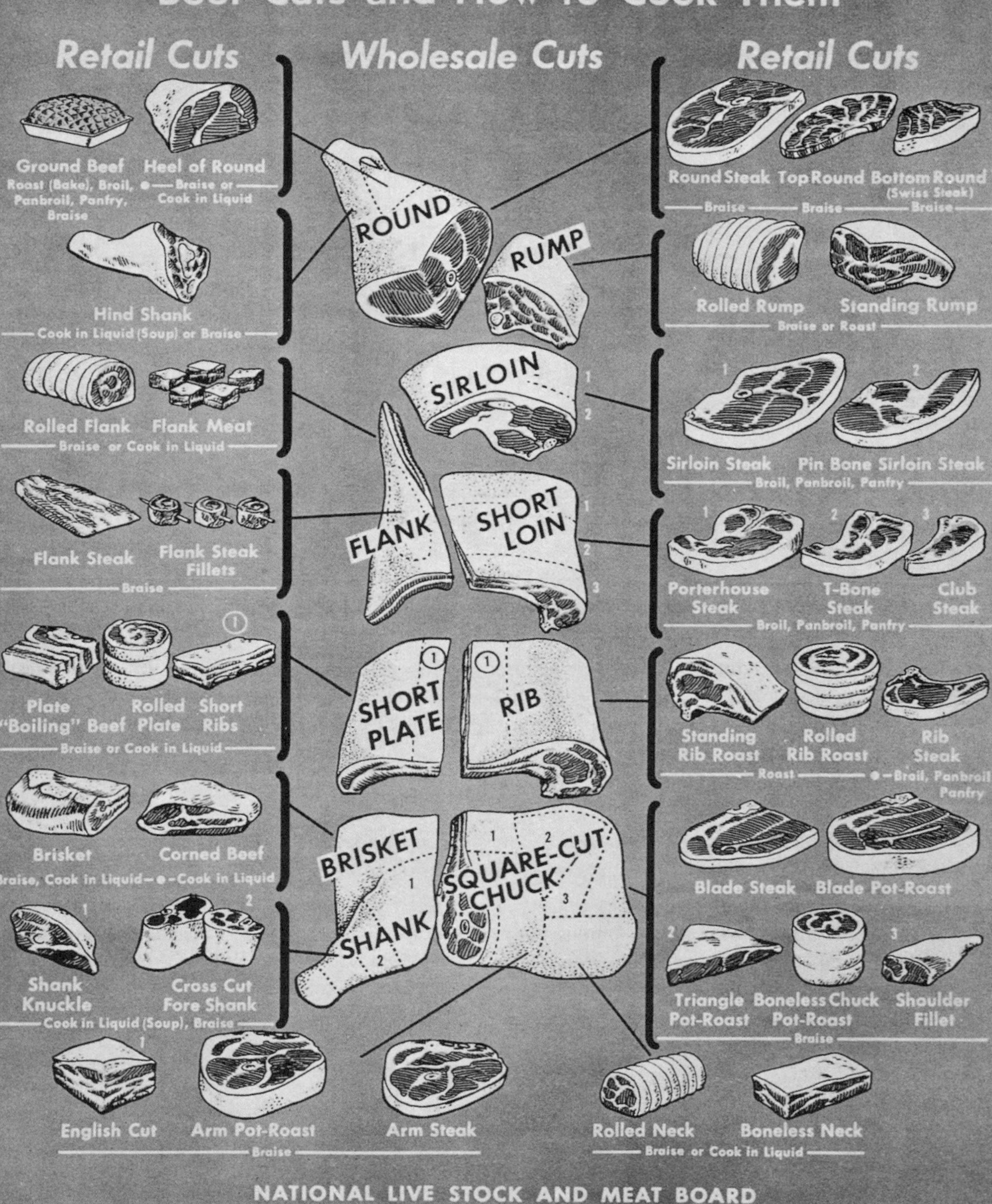
BEEF CHART
Beef Cuts and How to Cook Them
Retail Cuts
Wholesale Cuts
Retail Cuts
Ground Beef
Roast (Bake), Broil, Panbroil, Panfry, Braise
Heel of Round
Braise or Cook in Liquid
Hind Shank
Cook in Liquid (Soup) or Braise
ROUND
RUMP
Round Steak
Top Round
Bottom Round (Swiss Steak)
Braise
Braise
Braise
Rolled Rump
Standing Rump
Braise or Roast
Rolled Flank
Flank Meat
Braise or Cook in Liquid
SIRLOIN
Sirloin Steak
Pin Bone Sirloin Steak
Broil, Panbroil, Panfry
Flank Steak
Flank Steak Fillets
Braise
FLANK
SHORT LOIN
Porterhouse Steak
T-Bone Steak
Club Steak
Broil, Panbroil, Panfry
Plate "Boiling" Beef
Rolled Plate
Short Ribs
Braise or Cook in Liquid
SHORT PLATE
RIB
Standing Rib Roast
Rolled Rib Roast
Rib Steak
Roast
Broil, Panbroil, Panfry
Brisket
Corned Beef
Braise, Cook in Liquid
Cook in Liquid
BRISKET
SQUARE-CUT CHUCK
SHANK
Blade Steak
Blade Pot-Roast
Shank Knuckle
Cross Cut Fore Shank
Cook in Liquid (Soup), Braise
Triangle Pot-Roast
Boneless Chuck Pot-Roast
Shoulder Fillet
Braise
English Cut
Arm Pot-Roast
Arm Steak
Braise
Rolled Neck
Boneless Neck
Braise or Cook in Liquid
NATIONAL LIVE STOCK AND MEAT BOARD

COOKING FRESH BEEF

The method selected for cooking fresh beef depends on the tenderness of the meat, the size and thickness of the cut and the cooking facilities available.

Broil tender steaks, including Delmonico, T-bone, porterhouse, sirloin and filet mignon, cut 1-inch thick or thicker, at moderate temperatures to desired doneness. Tender steaks cut less than 1-inch thick may be panbroiled or panfried.

Ground beef may be roasted (baked) as loaves, broiled, panbroiled or panfried as patties and prepared by a combination of methods in casseroles and similar type dishes.

Less tender cuts including chuck, round and rump should be braised as pot roasts or steaks. Fresh beef brisket, plate, neck, shank and cubes from less tender cuts are usually cooked in liquid, although cross-cut shanks and beef stew meat are also braised. Cuts cooked in liquid or by braising should be cooked well done.

Large cuts, including rib, high-quality rump and high-quality sirloin tip should be roasted at 300 to 325° F. until the meat thermometer registers rare, medium or well done. For easier carving and more attractive servings, it is desirable to let a cooked beef roast "set" for 15 to 30 minutes. Meat continues to cook upon removal from the oven. If the roast is permitted to "set", it should be removed from the oven when the thermometer registers from 5 to 10° F. lower than the desired doneness.

ROASTING TIMETABLE

CUT	APPROXIMATE WEIGHT Pounds	OVEN TEMPERATURE Degrees F.	MEAT THERMOMETER READING Degrees F.	APPROXIMATE COOKING TIME Minutes Per Pound
Standing rib	6 to 8	300 to 325	140 (rare) 160 (medium) 170 (well done)	18 to 20 22 to 25 27 to 30
Rolled rib	5 to 7	300 to 325	140 (rare) 160 (medium) 170 (well done)	32 38 48
Delmonico (rib eye)	4 to 6	350	140 (rare) 160 (medium) 170 (well done)	18 to 20 20 to 22 22 to 24
Standing rump (high quality)	5 to 7	300 to 325	150 to 170	25 to 30
Rolled rump (high quality)	4 to 6	300 to 325	150 to 170	25 to 30
Sirloin tip (high quality)	3½ to 4	300 to 325	150 to 170	35 to 40
Beef Loaf		300 to 325	160 to 170	30 to 45

COOKING FRESH BEEF — CONTINUED

BROILING TIMETABLE

CUT	WEIGHT Pounds	APPROXIMATE TOTAL COOKING TIME Minutes	
		Rare	Medium
Rib steak			
1-inch thick	1 to 1½	12 to 15	18 to 20
1½-inches thick	1½ to 2	20 to 25	25 to 30
2-inches thick	2 to 2½	30 to 35	35 to 45
Club steak			
1-inch thick	1 to 1½	12 to 15	18 to 20
1½-inches thick	1½ to 2	20 to 25	25 to 30
2-inches thick	2 to 2½	30 to 35	35 to 45
Sirloin steak			
1-inch thick	1½ to 3	15 to 20	20 to 30
1½-inches thick	2¼ to 4	25 to 35	35 to 45
2-inches thick	3 to 5	30 to 40	45 to 60
Porterhouse steak			
1-inch thick	1¼ to 2	15 to 20	20 to 30
1½-inches thick	2 to 3	25 to 35	35 to 45
2-inches thick	2½ to 3½	30 to 40	45 to 60
Delmonico (rib eye)			
1-inch thick	10 to 14 oz.	18 to 20	20 to 25
2-inches thick	20 to 24 oz.	30 to 40	35 to 45
Tenderloin (filet mignon)	4 to 8 oz.	10 to 15	15 to 20
Ground beef patties			
1-inch thick x 3 inches	4 oz.	12 to 15	20 to 25

BRAISING TIMETABLE

CUT	APPROXIMATE WEIGHT OR THICKNESS	APPROXIMATE TOTAL COOKING TIME
Pot roast	3 to 5 pounds	3 to 4 hours
Swiss steak	1½ to 2½ inches	2 to 3 hours
Fricassee	2-inch cubes	1½ to 2½ hours
Beef birds	½x2x4 inches	1½ to 2½ hours
Short ribs	2x2x4-inch pieces	1½ to 2½ hours
Round steak	¾ inch	40 to 60 minutes
Stuffed steak	½ to ¾ inch	1½ hours
Flank steak	1½ to 2 pounds	1½ to 2½ hours

PORK

Pork is a very versatile meat. It can be purchased fresh, cured and smoked, pickled or canned. Pork fits into any consumer's food budget. The economy cuts of pork include blade loin and sirloin roasts and other delicious cuts such as salt pork and the butt and shank portions of ham.

Pork is enjoyed for family meals, but becomes very elegant for special occasions in butterfly chops, tenderloin, sliced bacon, roasts, meaty backribs, Canadian bacon and thick center ham slices.

STORING PORK

Fresh Pork:

Store fresh pork, uncovered or loosely wrapped, in the coldest part of the refrigerator. The temperature should be as low as possible without actually freezing the meat. Loosen the wrapping on pre-packaged pork before placing it in the refrigerator unless it is to be used the same day it is purchased.

Cured and Cooked Pork:

Store cured and cooked pork in the refrigerator in its original wrapper. Use within one to two weeks. Unless specified otherwise on the container, canned hams should be refrigerated in the unopened can until ready to use.

Cool cooked pork before refrigerating. Cover tightly after cooling to prevent drying. Store in the coldest part of the refrigerator.

FREEZING PORK

Cut large pieces of pork—loin, shoulder and leg—into convenient sizes for freezing. Shape unseasoned ground pork into patties or loaves. Package chops and steaks according to number of servings. Wrap meat in moisture, vapor-proof freezer paper and seal tightly. Label packages for easy identification, giving date put into freezer, weight or number of servings.

Freeze fresh pork quickly and store at 0° F. for one to three months for ground pork and three to six months for other fresh pork. Cured and smoked pork such as ham, picnics and boneless butts should not be frozen for more than sixty days. Bacon, bologna, frankfurters, fresh pork sausage and canned hams are not recommended for freezing.

COOKING PORK

Pork can be prepared in many delicious ways. Be sure that pork is well done. . . never serve pork rare.

BROILING TIMETABLE

CUT	APPROXIMATE THICKNESS	TOTAL COOKING TIME
Smoked ham slice	½ inch	10 to 12 minutes
Smoked ham slice	1 inch	16 to 20 minutes
Smoked Canadian-style bacon, sliced	¼ inch	6 to 8 minutes
Smoked Canadian-style bacon, sliced	½ inch	8 to 10 minutes
Smoked bacon		4 to 5 minutes

BRAISING TIMETABLE

CUT	APPROXIMATE WEIGHT OR THICKNESS	TOTAL COOKING TIME
Fresh chops	¾ to 1½ inches	45 to 60 minutes
Fresh spareribs	2 to 3 pounds	1½ hours
Fresh tenderloin		
Whole	¾ to 1 pound	45 to 60 minutes
Fillets	½ inch	30 minutes
Fresh shoulder steaks	¾ inch	45 to 60 minutes

COOKING IN LIQUID TIMETABLE

CUT	APPROXIMATE WEIGHT	TOTAL COOKING TIME
Smoked ham (old-style and country cured)		
Large	12 to 16 pounds	4½ to 5 hours
Small	10 to 12 pounds	4½ to 5 hours
Half	5 to 8 pounds	3 to 4 hours
Smoked picnic shoulder	5 to 8 pounds	3½ to 4 hours
Smoked hocks		2 to 2½ hours
Fresh spareribs		2 to 2½ hours
Fresh hocks		2½ to 3 hours

SELECTION OF PORK CUTS

WHOLESALE	RETAIL CUTS	CHARACTERISTICS	COOKING METHODS
Ham — Fresh, pickled, or smoked	Ham, whole	Corresponds to beef round with tail bone and portion of backbone removed. Outer skin or rind is left on the regular ham but it is removed, with excess fat, from the skinned ham.	Roast (bake); cook in liquid
	Ham, shank half	Lower half of ham. Includes shank and half of center section.	Roast (bake); cook in liquid
	Ham shank	Cone - shaped, rind - covered piece containing shank bones.	Cook in liquid
	Ham, butt half	Upper half of ham. Includes butt and half of center section.	Roast (bake); cook in liquid
	Ham butt	Same as above minus most of center section.	Roast (bake); cook in liquid
	Ham, center baking piece	Center section of ham. Both cut surfaces look like center slices.	Roast (bake); cook in liquid
	Ham, center slice	Oval-shape, small round bone, four separate muscles.	Broil; panbroil; panfry
	Ham, boneless	Boneless roll. Fresh, pickled or smoked.	Roast (bake); cook in liquid
Loin — Also tenderloin, boneless back strip, and Canadian-style bacon	Tenderloin	Long tapering round muscle. Weighs ½ to 1 pound.	Roast; braise
	Frenched tenderloin	Piece cut from tenderloin and flattened.	Braise; panfry
	Boneless loin roast	Boneless back strip. Two pieces sometimes tied together.	Roast
	Canadian-style bacon	Boneless back strip, cured and smoked.	Roast; broil; panbroil; panfry
	Butterfly chop	Double chop, hinged together, cut from boneless loin strip.	Braise; panfry
	Sirloin roast	Ham end of loin containing hip bone.	Roast
	Blade loin roast	Shoulder end of loin containing rib bones and blade bone.	Roast
	Loin chop	T-shaped bone and two muscles (back strip and tenderloin).	Braise; panfry
	Rib chop	Alternate chops have rib bone. May be "frenched".	Braise; panfry
	Crown roast	Rib sections "frenched" and formed in shape of crown.	Roast
Picnic shoulder Fresh, pickled or smoked	Picnic shoulder	Includes arm and shank sections of shoulder.	Roast; cook in liquid
	Rolled picnic shoulder	Boneless roll. Fresh, pickled or smoked.	Roast; cook in liquid
	Cushion picnic shoulder	Arm section of fresh picnic with pocket for stuffing.	Roast
	Arm steak	Oval at one end, squared off at other. Small round bone.	Braise; panfry
	Pork hock	Round, tapering, skin - covered piece containing shank bones.	Braise; cook in liquid
Boston butt Also smoked shoulder butt	Boston butt	Upper half of shoulder. Contains part of blade bone.	Roast
	Blade steak	Cut from Boston butt. Most steaks have section of blade bone.	Braise; panfry
	Smoked shoulder butt	Eye of Boston butt. Cured and smoked boneless roll.	Roast; cook in liquid
	Small shoulder butt slices	Round boneless slices. Lean and fat intermixed.	Broil; panbroil; panfry
Side (belly) Fresh, salt, pickled or smoked	Fresh side pork	Usually sliced. Alternating layers of lean and fat.	Braise; panfry
	Pickled side pork	Same as above but cured in sweet pickle solution.	Braise; panfry
	Salt side pork	Same as above but cured with dry salt.	Panfry; cook in liquid
	Sliced bacon	Same as above but cured, dry or in pickle, then smoked.	Broil; panbroil; panfry
Spareribs	Spareribs	Ribs and breastbone which have been removed from the bacon strip.	Roast; braise; cook in liquid
Jowl	Jowl bacon square	Jowl, trimmed square, then cured and smoked. High percentage of fat. May be sliced.	Cook in liquid; broil; panbroil; panfry
Feet	Pig's feet, fresh	Contains bones and tendons of foot and ankle. Little lean meat.	Cook in liquid
	Pig's feet, pickled	Pickled, cook and ready to eat.	No cooking necessary

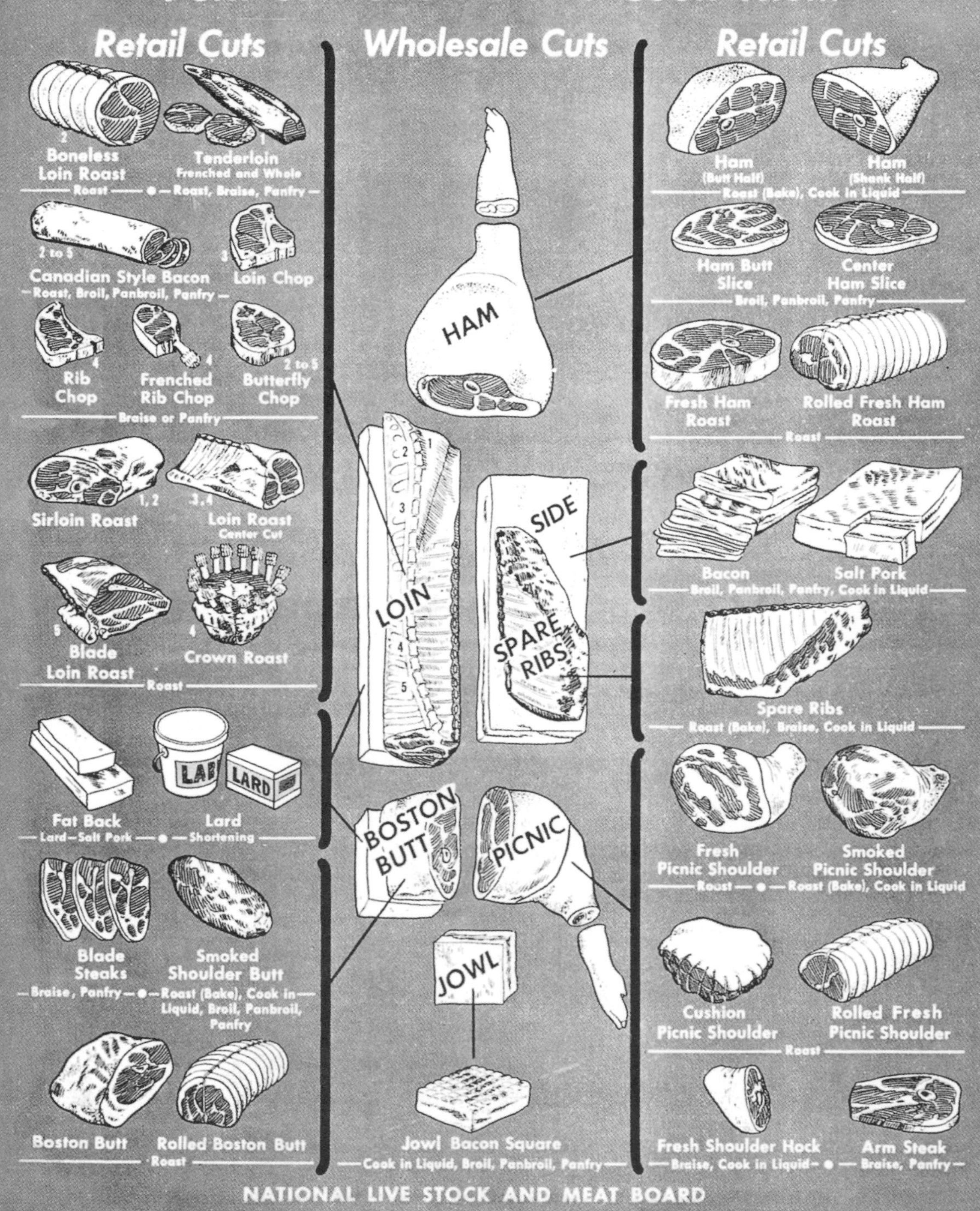

PORK CHART
Pork Cuts and How to Cook Them
Retail Cuts
Wholesale Cuts
Retail Cuts
Boneless Loin Roast
Tenderloin
Frenched and Whole
Roast
Roast, Braise, Panfry
Canadian Style Bacon
Loin Chop
Roast, Broil, Panbroil, Panfry
Rib Chop
Frenched Rib Chop
Butterfly Chop
Braise or Panfry
Sirloin Roast
Loin Roast
Center Cut
Blade Loin Roast
Crown Roast
Roast
Fat Back
Lard
LARD
Lard—Salt Pork
Shortening
Blade Steaks
Smoked Shoulder Butt
Braise, Panfry
Roast (Bake), Cook in Liquid, Broil, Panbroil, Panfry
Boston Butt
Rolled Boston Butt
Roast
HAM
LOIN
SIDE
SPARE RIBS
BOSTON BUTT
PICNIC
JOWL
Jowl Bacon Square
Cook in Liquid, Broil, Panbroil, Panfry
Ham
(Butt Half)
Ham
(Shank Half)
Roast (Bake), Cook in Liquid
Ham Butt Slice
Center Ham Slice
Broil, Panbroil, Panfry
Fresh Ham Roast
Rolled Fresh Ham Roast
Roast
Bacon
Salt Pork
Broil, Panbroil, Panfry, Cook in Liquid
Spare Ribs
Roast (Bake), Braise, Cook in Liquid
Fresh Picnic Shoulder
Smoked Picnic Shoulder
Roast
Roast (Bake), Cook in Liquid
Cushion Picnic Shoulder
Rolled Fresh Picnic Shoulder
Roast
Fresh Shoulder Hock
Arm Steak
Braise, Cook in Liquid
Braise, Panfry
NATIONAL LIVE STOCK AND MEAT BOARD

LAMB

At one time, lamb was considered as a seasonal meat, most readily available in the Spring around Easter time. Now, more and more homemakers are learning that lamb can be prepared in many tasty ways that appeal to the family all year 'round.

The term "lamb" usually refers to sheep that were slaughtered when they were from three months to a year old. "Yearlings" are one year old, but less than two. "Mutton" is usually one and a half to two years of age when slaughtered.

High quality lamb has a smooth covering of clear, pinkish-white, brittle fat over most of the exterior. Over this is a thin, paper-like covering called the "fell". It is usually removed from chops before cooking. Under normal conditions it should not be removed from the legs as this cut will hold its shape better, be more juicy and cook faster when the fell is left on.

METHODS OF COOKING

The method selected for cooking lamb cuts depends on the tenderness, the size and thickness of the cut and available cooking facilities.

All cuts of lamb, regardless of how they are cooked, should be cooked at low temperatures for best results. There are just three rules for cooking lamb: 1) cook at low temperatures; 2) cook according to the cut; 3) avoid overcooking.

The basic methods of cooking lamb are:

1. Dry heat—this method includes roasting, broiling and panbroiling.
2. Moist heat—this includes braising and cooking in liquid.
3. Frying—lamb may be panfried or griddle fried, and in some cases, deep-fat fried.

Chops, including rib, loin and shoulder, and leg steaks, cut 1-inch or more thick, should be broiled at moderate temperatures to desired doneness. Chops and steaks cut less than 1-inch thick are usually panbroiled or fried.

Ground lamb may be roasted (baked) as loaves; broiled, panbroiled or panfried as patties and prepared by a combination of methods in casseroles and similar type dishes.

Less tender cuts, including neck, shank and breast should be braised or cut into small pieces and cooked in liquid for stews. Cuts cooked by braising or in liquid should be cooked well done.

Large cuts, such as leg, loin and shoulder, should be roasted at 300 to 325° F. to the desired doneness. Lamb is usually roasted until the meat thermometer registers 175 to 180° F. (medium to well done). It may be served less well done if desired.

For easier carving and more attractive servings, it is desirable to let a cooked roast "set" for 15 to 30 minutes. Meat continues to cook upon its removal from the oven. If the meat is permitted to "set", it should be removed from the oven when the thermometer registers 5 to 10° F. lower than the desired doneness. Serve lamb hot or cold . . . never lukewarm.

ROASTING TIMETABLE

CUT	APPROXIMATE WEIGHT	MEAT THERMOMETER READING	APPROXIMATE COOKING TIME*
	Pounds	Degrees F.	Minutes Per Pound
Leg	5 to 8	175 to 180	30 to 35
Crown roast	4 to 6	175 to 180	40 to 45
Rack	4 to 5	175 to 180	40 to 45
Shoulder (bone in)	4 to 6	175 to 180	30 to 35
Shoulder (cushion-style)	3 to 5	175 to 180	30 to 35
Shoulder (rolled)	3 to 5	175 to 180	40 to 45

*Roast in a 300 to 325° F. oven.

BROILING TIMETABLE

CUT	APPROXIMATE WEIGHT	APPROXIMATE TOTAL COOKING TIME*
	Ounces	Minutes
Shoulder chops		
1-inch thick	5 to 8	12
1½-inches thick	8 to 10	18
2-inches thick	10 to 16	22
Rib chops		
1-inch thick	3 to 5	12
1½-inches thick	4 to 7	18
2-inches thick	6 to 10	22
Loin chops		
1-inch thick	4 to 7	12
1½-inches thick	6 to 10	18
2-inches thick	8 to 14	22
Ground lamb patties		
1 inch x 3 inches		18

*Broil at moderate temperature.

BRAISING TIMETABLE

CUT	Average Weight or Thickness	Approximate Total Cooking Time
Neck slices	¾ inch	1 hour
Shoulder chops	¾ to 1 inch	45 to 60 minutes
Breast, stuffed	2 to 3 pounds	1½ to 2 hours
Breast, rolled	1½ to 2 pounds	1½ to 2 hours
Riblets		1½ to 2 hours
Shanks	¾ to 1 pound each	1½ to 2 hours
Cubes	1½ inches	1½ to 2 hours

LAMB CHART

Lamb Cuts and How to Cook Them

Retail Cuts

Leg of Lamb
(Three cuts from one leg)
—Roast – ● -Broil, Panbroil, Panfry –● -Braise, Roast

Crown Roast
Rib Chops
Frenched Rib Chops
Roast — ● — Broil, Panbroil, Panfry

Square Cut Shoulder
Arm Chop
Blade Chop
Broil, Panbroil, Panfry, Braise — Roast — ● — Broil, Panbroil, Panfry, Braise

Cushion Shoulder
Saratoga Chops
Roast — ● — Broil, Panbroil, Panfry, Braise

Rolled Shoulder
Boneless Shoulder Chops
Roast, Braise — ● — Broil, Panbroil, Panfry, Braise

Neck Slices
Braise, Cook in Liquid

Wholesale Cuts

LEG
LOIN
RACK
SHOULDER
BREAST
SHANK

Mock Duck
Roast

Retail Cuts

American Leg
Boneless Sirloin Roast
Frenched Leg
Roast

Loin Chop
English Chop
Rolled Loin Roast
Broil, Panbroil, Panfry – ● — Roast

Patties
Loaf
Broil, Panbroil, Panfry — ● — Roast (Bake)

Riblets
Stew Meat
Braise or Cook in Liquid

Rolled Breast
Breast
Braise or Roast

Shanks
Braise or Cook in Liquid

NATIONAL LIVE STOCK AND MEAT BOARD

POULTRY

Chicken and turkey rank among the favorite foods placed on American dining tables. The popularity of poultry lies in the fact that it is economically priced and can be prepared in a wide variety of taste tempting ways.

CHICKEN

Chickens are classified in several ways:

1. BROILERS OR FRYERS. These are young chickens usually nine to twelve weeks old. They are tender-meated, have soft, pliable, smooth-textured skin and flexible breastbone cartilage. These young chickens usually weigh from 1½ to 4 pounds.

2. ROASTING CHICKENS. These are usually three to five months old. They are tender-meated, with soft, pliable, smooth-textured skin. The breastbone cartilage may be somewhat less flexible than that of broilers or fryers. A roasting chicken weighs from 3 to 5¼ pounds or more.

3. STEWING HENS. These are mature birds which are less tender than roasting hens.

AMOUNTS TO BUY

USE	AMOUNT PER SERVING
Frying	¾ to 1 pound
Roasting	¾ to 1 pound
Broiling or barbecuing	½ chicken or 1 pound
Stewing	½ to 1 pound

Each 1 pound of uncooked stewing chicken will yield about 1 cup of cut up, cooked meat. Naturally, you will need more when making sliced chicken sandwiches, a salad plate or cold plate than when fixing a casserole.

Be sure to buy a little more than the chart above suggests if your family members or guests are really big chicken eaters.

STORING CHICKEN

Remove the wrapping from the chicken after you bring it home from the market. Rinse well and pat dry. Wrap loosely in waxed paper. Store in the coldest part of the refrigerator and cook within one to three days.

For freezing, wrap the clean bird tightly in freezer wrap. Keep frozen until ready to use. If the chicken is to be stewed, it can go from the freezer into the pot. No need to thaw it. If you plan to fry, barbecue, broil or roast the chicken, thaw in the refrigerator. Don't unwrap the chicken when transfering from the freezer to the refrigerator for thawing. The skin tends to dry and toughen when exposed to air.

Promptly refrigerate any left-over cooked chicken and gravy in separate containers. Remove any stuffing from stuffed birds and refrigerate separately in covered containers. Properly wrapped meal-size portions of cooked chicken may be frozen for a month.

TURKEY

When buying a turkey, judge the size of the bird by the number of servings you want. Buy ½ pound ready-to-cook turkey per serving. The number of servings depends on the quality of the turkey, correct cooking and carving skill.

READY-TO-COOK TURKEY	NUMBER OF SERVINGS
8 to 10 pounds	16 to 20
10 to 14 pounds	20 to 28
14 to 18 pounds	28 to 36
18 to 20 pounds	36 to 40
20 to 24 pounds	40 to 50

PREPARING A TURKEY FOR ROASTING

GIBLETS: Cook the gizzard, heart and liver promptly after cleaning and washing. They must be cooked tender before being added to the gravy or stuffing. Use giblet broth for liquid in gravy or stuffing.

STUFFING THE TURKEY: Stuff the turkey just before roasting—do not stuff before this time. If the stuffing is prepared in advance, it must be refrigerated. Allow 1 cup stuffing per pound of ready-to-cook turkey or ¾ cup stuffing per pound of dressed weight to fill cavity and neck.

Don't pack stuffing tightly. If you do, the stuffing will be soggy and the bird may burst when stuffing expands during cooking. Turkeys may be roasted without stuffing, but should be trussed.

ROASTING: Follow these simple steps for perfect roasted turkey:

1. Rub cavity lightly with salt.
2. Put enough stuffing in neck to fill it out nicely. Fasten neck skin to back with skewers. Stuff cavity well, but don't pack tightly.
3. Truss the birds and grease skin with softened or melted cooking fat.
4. Place bird on rack in shallow pan with breast down. Have rack at least ½ inch high to raise the bird off the bottom of the pan and keep it out of the juices. When using a flat rack, tip bird so one side of the breast rests on rack. Turn turkey during roasting so other side touches rack and both sides cook evenly.
5. Cover top and sides of turkey with clean, fat-moistened cloth. Cheesecloth is fine for this purpose.
6. Place turkey in preheated oven. Do not sear, cover or add salt.
7. Moisten cloth with fat from bottom of pan if cloth dries slightly during cooking.
8. Cut trussing string between drumsticks and tail after about 1 hour of roasting.
9. Turn bird breast up when about three-fourths done if breast skin needs more browning.
10. To test the doneness of the turkey, move the drumstick up and down. If the leg joint gives readily or breaks, the turkey is done. Or, press down on the fleshy part of the drumstick. If the meat feels soft, the turkey is done.

TIMETABLE FOR ROASTING A TURKEY

READY-TO-COOK WEIGHT	OVEN TEMPERATURE	APPROXIMATE TOTAL COOKING TIME*
8 to 12 pounds	325° F.	4 to 4½ hours
12 to 16 pounds	300° F.	4½ to 5 hours
16 to 20 pounds	300° F.	5 to 5½ hours
20 to 24 pounds	300° F.	5½ to 6 hours

*Unstuffed turkeys require approximately 5 minutes per pound less cooking time.

FISH AND SHELLFISH

One of the keys to successful meal planning is variety. Fish and shellfish offer a wide range of variety to otherwise dull menus. Very few people realize just how many varieties of fish are available to them at the market, for only about seven species of fish are well known to the average customer. There are actually about 160 varieties of fish sold in this country.

Check with your local fish dealer about the availability of different fish in your area.

BASIC FISH COOKERY

The basic rules for cooking most fish are few and easy to follow. The important thing to remember when cooking fish is the amount of fat in the fish you plan to use. As a rule, fat fish, such as salmon or shad, are most desirable for baking, broiling and planking because their fat content will keep them from becoming dry.

Lean fish, such as cod and haddock, are preferred by some for boiling and steaming because their flesh is firm and won't fall apart easily while cooking. Both fat and lean fish are suitable for frying.

SPECIES	FAT OR LEAN	SPECIES	FAT OR LEAN
SALT WATER:			
Bluefish	Lean	Pollock	Lean
Butterfish	Fat	Rockfish	Lean
Cod	Lean	Rosefish	Lean
Croaker	Lean	Salmon	Fat
Flounder	Lean	Scup (Porgy)	Lean
Grouper	Lean	Sea bass	Lean
Haddock	Lean	Sea trout	Lean
Hake	Lean	Shad	Fat
Halibut	Lean	Snapper, red	Lean
Herring, sea	Fat	Spanish mackerel	Fat
Lingcod	Lean	Spot	Lean
Mackerel	Fat	Whiting	Lean
Mullet	Lean		
FRESH WATER:			
Buffalofish	Lean	Sheepshead	Lean
Carp	Lean	Suckers	Lean
Catfish	Fat	Whitefish	Fat
Lake Herring	Lean	Yellow perch	Lean
Lake trout	Fat	Yellow pike	Lean
SHELLFISH:			
Clams	Lean	Oysters	Lean
Crabs	Lean	Shrimp	Lean
Lobsters	Lean		

There are, however, so many exceptions to these rules that actually all fish may be cooked by any of the basic methods with excellent results if allowances are made for the fat content. For example, lean fish, such as halibut, may be broiled or baked if basted frequently with melted fat. If not, they will have a tendency to dry out.

The most important thing to remember in cooking fish is that it is too often overcooked. Just enough cooking to make the flesh turn cream-colored and easily flaked from the bones will leave the fish moist and tender and bring out its delicate flavor.

Handle fish as little as possible during and after cooking. The flesh of fish is tender and delicate. Don't ruin the appearance of the fish by turning too many times during cooking.

FRYING

Protect the fish from the hot fat by coating it in flour, crumbs or batter before frying. After coating the fish, pat it absolutely dry to make sure the coating will stick. This will also prevent splattering.

The temperature of the fat must be hot enough to seal and crisp the surface of the fish immediately. At the same time, it must not get too hot. Watch the fat carefully or you'll find your fish speckled with burnt crumbs and the flavor will be ruined.

Place the fish, flesh-side down, in the hot fat to prevent curling. After the fish is done, drain thoroughly on absorbent paper before serving.

BROILING

This is the fastest way of cooking fish. Broil the fish under full heat during the entire cooking time. Place filets and split fish, skin-side down, on the broiler pan rack and broil without turning. Steaks and whole fish are usually turned only once to brown both sides.

Unless the fish is fat, baste with additional fat as needed to season well and prevent the fish from drying out.

The amount of time required for cooking will depend upon the thickness of the fish and the distance from the heat.

STEAMING AND BOILING

Steaming is cooking by live steam over a small amount of boiling water. A maximum of juices and flavor are retained in fish cooked by this method.

Wrap the fish in cheesecloth, muslin or parchment paper and place on a rack over a small amount of boiling water. Cover the pan tightly and steam until the fish is done.

The exact amount of steaming time will be determined by the weight and thickness of the fish. Fish that are under two inches in thickness require about one minute steaming for each ounce of weight.

Boiling is sometimes used as a way of extracting the flavor and juices for fish stock to be used in soups, chowders and sauces. Boiled fish should be seasoned at the beginning of the cooking period so flavors will blend. The fish may be dropped into boiling water or wrapped as suggested for steaming to make its removal from the stock easier. The fish may also be salted and tied in a square of parchment cooking paper, then punged into enough boiling water to float the bag with its ends above water.

The time required for this method is about 15 minutes per inch of thickness for fresh fish — twice this for frozen. When boiling fish, a sliced lemon or lime added to the water will keep the fish from falling apart and will improve the flavor.

BUYING FISH IN MARKET FORMS

A. Whole or round fish are those marketed just as they come from the water. Before cooking they must be scaled and eviscerated, which means removing the entrails. The head, tail and fins may be removed if desired, and the fish either split or cut into serving pieces, except in fish intended for baking. Some small fish like smelt, are frequently cooked with only the entrails removed.

B. Drawn fish are sold with only the entrails removed. In preparing for cooking they are usually scaled. The head, tail and fins are removed, if desired, and the fish split or cut into serving pieces. Small drawn fish, or larger sizes intended for baking, may be cooked in the form purchased after scaling.

C. Dressed fish are scaled and eviscerated and the head, tail and fins are usually removed, too. The smaller sizes are ready for cooking as purchased (pan dressed). The larger sizes of dressed fish may be baked as purchased, but frequently are cut into steaks or serving pieces.

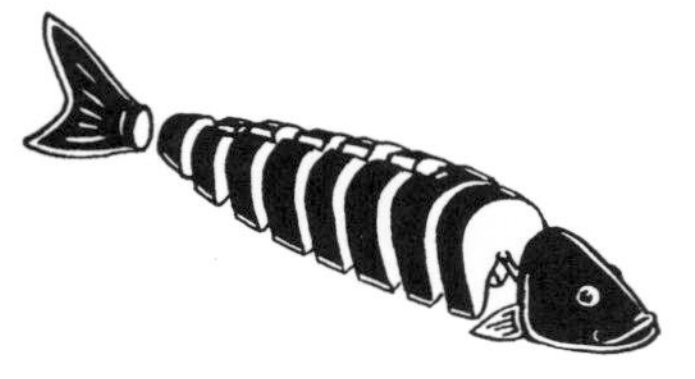

D. Steaks are cross section slices of the larger sizes of dressed fish. They are ready to cook as purchased except for dividing the very large ones into serving portions. A cross section of the backbone is usually the only bone in the steak.

E. Fillets are the sides of the fish cut lengthwise from the backbone. They are practically boneless and require no additional preparation for cooking. Sometimes the skin, with the scales removed, is left on the fillets—others are skinned. A fillet cut from one side of a fish is called a single fillet. This is the type of fillet most generally seen in the market.

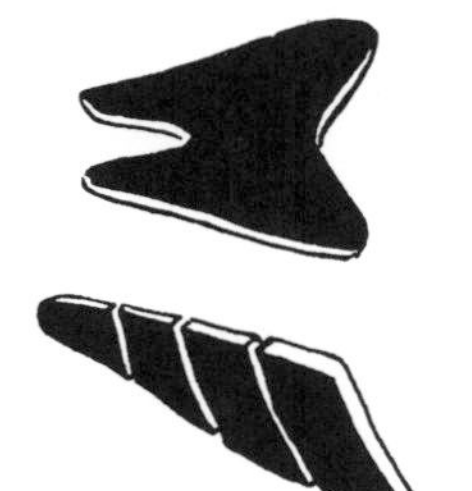

F. Butterfly fillets are the two sides of the fish corresponding to two single fillets held together by uncut flesh and the skin.

G. Sticks are pieces of fish cut lengthwise or crosswise from fillets or steaks into portions of uniform width and length.

WHAT TO LOOK FOR IN FRESH FISH

In buying fish in the round, the following points should be observed to insure freshness:

Eyes—Should be bright, clear, full and bulging

Gills—Should be reddish-pink, free from slime or odor

Scales—Should adhere tightly to the skin and be bright-colored with a characteristic sheen

Flesh—Should be firm and elastic, springing back when pressed, not separating from the bones

Odor—Should be fresh, free from objectionable odors

AMOUNTS TO BUY

Servings of fresh fish are usually based on one-third to one-half pound of the edible flesh per person.

When buying fillets, steaks or sticks, allow one-third pound per person or two pounds for six people. For dressed fish, allow one-half pound per person or three pounds for six people. For whole fish, allow about one pound per person or five pounds for six people.

When buying frozen fish, the amount per person is the same for fresh fish—one-third to one-half pound of the edible flesh per person.

STORING FISH

Fish, like many other foods, will spoil easily if not handled properly. Wrap fresh fish in moisture-proof paper or place in a tightly covered container and store immediately in the refrigerator. If fish is stored in this manner, the odor of the fish will not penetrate other foods. If the fish cannot be thoroughly refrigerated, it should be cooked at once and reheated for serving.

If frozen fish is wrapped in parchment paper or cellophane when it comes from the market, it should be wrapped in additional paper before being placed in the refrigerator. The additional wrapping prevents the absorption of odors by other foods as the fish thaws. Leave packaged frozen fish in the unopened package until time to use.

If you want to keep the fish frozen for several days, place the unopened package in the freezing compartment of your refrigerator. Fish will keep as long as it remains solidly frozen, but once it thaws, it should be used immediately. Never refreeze fish after it thaws.

THAWING FISH

You can cook frozen fillets, steaks and dressed fish as if they were in the unfrozen form —but you must allow additional cooking time. When fish are to be breaded or stuffed, it is more convenient to thaw them first for easier handling. Thawing is necessary for the cleaning and dressing of whole or drawn fish.

Thawing fish in the refrigerator at a temperature of 37 to 40° F. has long been the accepted practice. Hold the fish at this temperature only long enough to permit ease in preparation. Whole or drawn fish may be thawed more readily by immersing them in cold running water.

SHELLFISH

It is very important that shellfish be strictly fresh when purchased and refrigerated properly because they tend to deteriorate quickly.

Shellfish are sold in these forms—in the shell, shucked, cooked meat, canned, and frozen. If purchased in the shell, oysters, crabs, lobsters and clams should be alive. The shells of live hard-shelled clams and oysters should be tightly closed all around or should snap shut when handled. The neck of soft-shelled clams protrudes, but otherwise the shell should be as tightly closed as the neck will permit.

Shucked shellfish is the flesh when it has been removed from the shell. Freshly cooked shellfish meat is the edible portion picked from the cooked shellfish. Since this meat is highly perishable, it should be properly refrigerated and used as soon as possible after purchase.

Oysters

In selecting oysters, those with tightly closed shells should be chosen. Shucked oysters should have a good odor and should not be slimy or bloated when placed in fresh water.

Oysters may be cooked in a variety of ways—baked, broiled, fried, creamed, scalloped, in stews, chowders, poultry stuffings or combination dishes. To keep the delicate flavor and to avoid toughening, cook oysters only enough to heat them through. Cooking them until the "edges curl" is a good test. If oysters are to be fried or broiled, poach them first briefly in their own juices to remove the slippery coating.

For six persons, allow three dozen shell oysters, one quart of shucked oysters or two number 1 cans.

Shrimp

Gulf and Atlantic shrimp are sold according to the size (headless) and number per pound. These are the different counts:

Jumbo	under 25 per pound
Large	25 to 30 per pound
Large Medium	28 to 30 per pound
Medium	30 to 35 per pound
Small	35 and up per pound

Shrimp come in different colors, but all shrimp are pink when cooked. Shrimpers call all raw shrimp "green". Fresh shrimp have a clean sea odor. The parchment like covering should fit close to the body. If the odor is ammoniacal and the color of the shell turned from pearly gray to green with pink shading, the shrimp is stale and should not be used. Uncooked fresh shrimp should be cooked as soon as possible after purchase.

Crabs

Four principal kinds of crabs are commonly marketed in this country—the blue crab, the Dungeness (or market) crab, the Alaska king crab and the rock crab. Other species such as the tanner crab and the stone crab, are chiefly of local importance.

On both coasts and the Gulf of Mexico, there is a large production of fresh cooked crab meat. The classification of this fresh cooked crab meat indicates differences in types of meat. Back-fin lump meat is large lumps of meat removed from only that part of the body of the crab known as the back-fin. Special lump meat is large flakes of meat removed from the body of the crab. White meat is only the fine (small) white meat removed from the body of the crab. Claw meat is the meat removed from only the claws of the Eastern and Gulf crabs.

Lobsters

Lobsters are found in the waters of New England and like most shellfish, must be alive up to the time of cooking.

Live lobsters are naturally dark green in color, not red. In cooking, the normal dark green color of the fresh lobster changes to the distinctive lobster red. The weight usually ranges from three-fourths to three pounds. True lobsters have two large claws.

Beef & Veal Favorites

OVEN POT ROAST

1 4-lb. chuck roast
1 pkg. onion soup mix
1 can cream of mushroom soup

Place roast on aluminum foil; sprinkle both sides of roast with onion soup mix. Spoon mushroom soup over meat. Wrap securely in foil, folding edges to prevent leakage. Place in baking pan. Bake at 350 degrees for 1 hour per pound. Yield: 8-10 servings.

Dorothy E. Brevoort, Retired State Supervisor
Department of Education
Beach Haven, New Jersey

BARBECUED POT ROAST

1 8-oz. can tomato sauce
½ c. beef broth
1 onion, chopped
Paprika to taste
Garlic powder to taste
Salt to taste
1 5-lb. pot roast
Fat
¼ c. vinegar
¼ c. catsup
2 tsp. Worcestershire sauce
1 tsp. mustard

Combine tomato sauce, beef broth and onion; season to taste with paprika, garlic powder and salt. Place roast in refrigerator dish; add tomato sauce mixture. Cover tightly. Refrigerate overnight, or about 12 hours. Remove roast from marinade; brown slowly in hot fat in Dutch oven. Add vinegar, catsup, Worcestershire sauce and mustard to marinade. Stir to blend. Pour over browned roast. Cover and simmer on top of stove or bake at 350 degrees for 2 hours and 30 minutes or until tender. Yield: 8 servings.

Mrs. Linda Knutson, Central Cass H. S.
Casselton, North Dakota

BARBECUED POT ROAST

1 3 to 4-lb. arm or blade roast
Meat tenderizer
½ c. barbecue sauce
1 to 2 tbsp. soy sauce
1 tbsp. Worcestershire sauce
½ clove of garlic, minced
Dash of basil
Dash of oregano
Dash of crushed thyme

Prepare meat with tenderizer according to label directions; place in Dutch oven. Pour mixture of remaining ingredients over roast. Cover and bake at 325 degrees for 3 hours or until tender. Make gravy from pan drippings. Yield: 6-8 servings.

Mrs. Jessye P. MacKay
Pollack Independent H. S., Pollack, South Dakota

BEEF ROAST

1 3 to 5-lb. rump or chuck roast
Salt and pepper (opt.)
1 pkg. dry onion soup mix

Rub meat with salt and pepper; place on aluminum foil. Pour soup mix on top of meat. Close foil airtight around meat. Bake at 250 to 325 degrees for 3 to 5 hours. Yield: 8-10 servings.

Jean Cook, Clarksdale H. S.
Clarksdale, Mississippi
Lois H. Colman, Las Plumas H. S.
Oroville, California
Mrs. Marilyn Orban, Atherton H. S.
Flint, Michigan

BOEFF CHANDLIER

Salt and pepper
1 3-lb. arm roast
White sugar
1 tsp. butter
1 tsp. oil
½ to 1 c. tomato or chili sauce
1 tsp. Tabasco sauce
½ tsp. garlic salt
1 tsp. Worcestershire sauce
1 tbsp. brown sugar
½ tsp. curry powder
½ tsp. pepper
½ c. dry Sherry
¼ tsp. smoked salt

Salt and pepper roast; sprinkle with white sugar. Melt butter and oil in pan; place roast in pan. Brown on both sides. Remove and place in large pan lined with heavy foil. Add remaining ingredients to oil in pan; bring to a boil. Add mixture to roast; seal foil. Bake at 250 degrees for 3 hours to 3 hours and 30 minutes. NOTE: Venison may be prepared in same manner. Yield: 6-8 servings.

Fern S. Zimmerman, Clayton H. S.
Clayton, New Mexico

BARBECUED BRISKET ROAST

1 3 to 4-lb. brisket roast
Meat tenderizer
Monosodium glutamate
Pepper
Garlic salt
Worcestershire sauce
Soy sauce
Seasoned salt
Liquid smoke

Rub roast with meat tenderizer; season to taste with all remaining ingredients. Wrap roast with two sheets of aluminum foil; seal edges. Bake at 300 degrees for 25 minutes per pound. Yield: 6-8 servings.

Mary A. Kirby, Greenville H. S.
Greenville, Texas

BEEF BRISKET AND ONION SAUCE

4 lb. beef brisket
1 carrot, diced
1 sm. onion, diced
2 tsp. salt
4 whole black peppers
4 whole cloves
1 egg, slightly beaten
½ c. dry bread crumbs

Cover meat with boiling water; add vegetables and seasonings. Simmer until tender, about 3 hours. Remove meat from liquid; place in shallow baking dish. Reserve 1 cup stock. Spread egg over meat; sprinkle with crumbs. Bake at 400 degrees for 20 minutes or until brown. Make an onion sauce with reserved stock; serve with meat. Yield: 6-8 servings.

Mrs. Ethel D. Finley, Montgomery Blair H. S.
Silver Spring, Maryland

BARBECUED BEEF BRISKET

1 3-lb. boneless beef brisket
Salt and pepper to taste
Marjoram
Oregano
1 sm. onion, diced
1 egg, slightly beaten
½ c. bread crumbs

Rub meat with seasonings. Place in a large pan; cover with water. Add onion; simmer for 2 hours and 30 minutes to 3 hours or until tender. Remove from liquid; place in shallow baking dish. Spread egg over meat; sprinkle with crumbs. Brown at 400 degrees for about 20 minutes. Yield: 6-8 servings.

Mrs. Variel Garner, Moody H. S.
Moody, Texas

HOST'S DINNER

1 3 to 4-lb. fresh boneless beef brisket
2 tbsp. shortening
⅓ c. vinegar
3 sm. onions
1 bay leaf
1 tbsp. salt
¼ tsp. hickory smoked salt
1 to 2 tbsp. Worcestershire sauce

Brown meat on all sides in shortening; cover meat with water and vinegar. Add whole onions, bay leaf, salts and Worcestershire sauce. Cover and simmer for 3 hours or until tender. Remove meat and cool for about 15 minutes before serving. Yield: 6-8 servings.

Mrs. Jane Lee Froneberger
Frank L. Ashley H. S.
Gastonia, North Carolina

SMOKED BRISKET

1 oz. liquid smoke
1 6-lb. brisket
Salt and pepper to taste
½ 14-oz. bottle barbecue sauce

Pour liquid smoke over brisket. Place in tightly covered container or wrap in foil; store in refrigerator overnight. Place in roasting pan; sprinkle with salt and pepper. Pour barbecue sauce over top of brisket; do not add any liquid. Roast, covered, at 250 degrees for 4 hours. Yield: 12 servings.

Toni Guast, Lackawanna Trail Area School
Factoryville, Pennsylvania

BUSY DAY CHUCK ROAST

1 1½-lb. chuck roast, 1-in. thick
1 envelope dry onion soup mix
3 to 4 carrots, quartered
2 stalks celery, cut into strips
3 to 5 med. potatoes, halved
2 tbsp. butter (opt.)
Salt and pepper to taste (opt.)
1 c. water (opt.)

Place meat on 30 x 18-inch piece of aluminum foil. Cover surface of meat with onion soup mix; place vegetables on top. Dot with butter; sprinkle lightly with salt and pepper. Fold foil tightly to seal. Bake at 350 to 450 degrees for 1 to 2 hours or until done. Yield: 5-6 servings.

Mrs. Jeanne Daugherty, Norwin Jr. H.S., East Irwin, Pennsylvania
Phyllis Wack, Blue Mountain H. S.
Schuylkill Haven, Pennsylvania

COFFEE-FLAVORED POT ROAST

1 pkg. meat marinade
⅔ c. cold coffee
1 med. clove of garlic, minced or pressed
¼ tsp. sweet basil
1 3 to 4-lb. pot roast
1 can cream of mushroom soup
1 lge. onion, sliced

Pour meat marinade into Dutch oven with tight fitting lid. Add coffee; blend thoroughly. Blend in garlic and basil. Place meat in marinade.

(Continued on next page)

Pierce all surfaces of meat deeply and thoroughly with fork. Marinate for 15 minutes, turning serveral times. Add soup and onion; blend into marinade. Bring to a boil; reduce heat. Simmer until tender 2 hours to 2 hours and 30 minutes, turning once. Remove from gravy to hot platter. Thicken gravy, if desired. Yield: 6-8 servings.

Mrs. Ellen S. Racht, Northeast Bradford H. S.
Rome, Pennsylvania

CHUCK ROAST IN FOIL

1 chuck, round or shoulder roast
½ to 1 envelope dry onion soup mix
1 or 2 cans mushroom sauce or cream of mushroom soup or celery soup

Place roast on large piece of aluminum foil; sprinkle with onion soup. Spread mushroom soup on top. Wrap in foil; seal well. Bake in preheated 325 to 350 degree oven for 20 minutes to 1 hour per pound or until done. Remove to heated platter. NOTE: Roast may be cooked on top of stove. Yield: 8 servings.

Dorothy E. Kensman, Ishpeming H. S.
Ishpeming, Michigan
Mrs. Betty Lowrance, Mooresville H. S.
Mooresville, North Carolina
Mrs. Lucy English, Danville Area H. S.
Danville, Pennsylvania
Mrs. Joyce Mauldin Redstone
Vero Beach Jr. H. S.
Vero Beach, Florida
Madge G. Young, Annapolis H. S.
Annapolis, Maryland
Mrs. Myrtle G. Allen, Walterboro H. S.
Walterboro, South Carolina
Mrs. Francys C. Putnam, Phillips Jr. H. S.
Chapel Hill, North Carolina
Janice Wilson Scott, Wauconda H. S.
Wauconda, Illinois
Mrs. Mary Willis, Lawrence Co. H. S.
Lawrenceburg, Tennessee
Dorothea C. Ferrill, Pueblo Co. H. S.
Pueblo, Colorado
Mrs. Myra McBride, Monson H. S.
Monson, Massachusetts
Gwen Edwards, Pine Forest H. S.
Fayetteville, North Carolina
Mrs. Rena D. Marstiller, Valley Mills H. S.
Valley Mills, Texas
Mrs. Barbara D. Ayers, Phil Campbell H. S.
Phil Campbell, Alabama

DELUXE COMPANY ROAST

1 ½ tsp. salt
¼ tsp. pepper
1 6-lb. sirloin roast
¾ lb. Canadian bacon, sliced
2 8-oz. pkg. Swiss cheese

Season meat. Slit roast crosswise deeply. Alternate slices of Canadian bacon and Swiss cheese inside slits made in roast; tie, if needed, to keep flavor inside during cooking. Place on rack. Bake at 325 degrees for 3 hours. Yield: 24 servings.

Mrs. Minta Palmer, Johnston H. S.
Austin, Texas

EASY ROAST BEEF

2 tbsp. Kitchen Bouquet
1 3-lb. shoulder roast
1 tbsp. salt
½ tsp. pepper
3 tbsp. onion flakes
1 c. water

Brush 1 tablespoonful Kitchen Bouquet over top of roast. Sprinkle both sides with salt and pepper. Sprinkle one-half the onion flakes over top; add water. Wrap securely in aluminum foil; Roast at 325 degrees for 45 minutes. Turn roast over; brush top with remaining Kitchen Bouquet; sprinkle with remaining onion flakes. Continue cooking for 45 minutes longer or until tender. Remove roast; add thickening to water and juices to make gravy. Yield: 8-10 servings.

Mrs. Naomi H. Satterfield
Leavelle McCampbell H. S.
Graniteville, South Carolina

EYE OF ROUND ROAST

Suet
1 5-lb. eye of round roast
1 pkg. dry onion soup mix
¼ tsp. pepper

Spread suet over top of roast; sprinkle with soup mix and pepper. Wrap in heavy aluminum foil; seal tightly. Bake at 350 degrees for 12 minutes per pound for rare, 15 minutes for medium and 18 minutes for well done. Remove from aluminum foil. Make gravy from drippings. Yield: 6 servings.

Mrs. Betty Lou Archambault, Merrimack H. S.
Merrimack, New Hampshire

FRANCISCAN BEEF

¼ c. olive oil
¼ c. port wine
4 tsp. onion powder
1 tsp. ground thyme
1 tsp. ground marjoram
½ tsp. crushed rosemary leaves
¼ tsp. garlic powder
1 5-lb. boned and rolled rib roast

Combine all ingredients except meat; mix well. Rub into meat; wrap in aluminum foil and refrigerate overnight. Roast meat in preheated 325 degree oven for 2 hours and 30 minutes or until a meat thermometer inserted in thickest part of meat registers 140 degrees. Remove

(Continued on next page)

from oven; allow to stand in warm place. Yield: 8 servings.

Yola Hudson, Fort Hill H. S.
Cumberland, Maryland

FRUITED POT ROAST

1 3 to 4-lb. pot roast
Fat
1 c. apple cider
2 tbsp. sugar
¼ tsp. cinnamon
¼ tsp. ginger
3 whole cloves
1 ½ c. sliced onions
12 dried apricots
12 prunes

Brown roast on all sides in a small amount hot fat; season. Combine apple cider, sugar, cinnamon, ginger and cloves; pour over meat. Add sliced onions. Cover; simmer for 2 hours and 30 minutes or until meat is tender. Soak dried apricots and prunes. Drain fruit 30 minutes before meat is done; add to meat. Thicken liquid for gravy, if desired. Yield: 6-8 servings.

Mrs. Nancy Jones, Carlisle Co. H. S.
Bardwell, Kentucky

MARINATED POT ROAST

½ tsp. pepper
½ tsp. ground cloves
½ tsp. mace
½ tsp. allspice
1 tbsp. salt
1 4-lb. rump roast
½ c. water
1 med. onion, chopped
1 or 2 cloves of garlic, chopped
¼ c. salad oil
2 tbsp. lemon juice
2 to 3 tbsp. vinegar

Mix pepper, cloves, mace, allspice and salt; rub onto meat. Place in covered roasting pan; add water. Cover meat with onion and garlic. Mix salad oil, lemon juice and vinegar; drizzle over meat. Marinate meat for 4 hours or longer. Bake at 325 degrees for 4 hours. Yield: 6 servings.

Harriet R. Ahlswede, Ramona H. S.
Riverside, California

PEKING ROAST

1 3 to 5-lb. roast
Slivers of garlic
Slivers of onion
1 c. vinegar
Oil
2 c. strong black coffee
2 c. water
Salt and pepper to taste

Cut slits completely through roast; insert garlic and onion in slits. Pour vinegar over meat. Refrigerate for 24 to 48 hours. Place small amount of oil and roast in large pot; brown until almost burned on all sides. Pour black coffee over meat; add water. Cover; simmer on top of stove for 4 to 6 hours. Season with salt and pepper 20 minutes before serving. Yield: 6-8 servings.

Mrs. Carolyn Richards, Commerce Jr. H. S.
Commerce, Georgia

PEPPY POT ROAST

1 3 to 4-lb. pot roast
1 pkg. dry onion soup mix
¾ c. water
2 to 3 tbsp. flour

Brown meat in large heavy pan; pour off fat. Add soup mix and 1/2 cup water. Cover; cook over low heat for 3 hours or until tender. Stir occasionally. Remove meat from pan. Gradually blend remaining water into flour; slowly stir into gravy. Cook, stirring until thickened. Yield: 4-6 servings.

Mrs. Patricia Castle, Ridge Farm H. S.
Ridge Farm, Illinois

POT ROAST NORWAY

1 3 ½-lb. arm or blade pot roast
Flour
1 8-oz. can tomato paste
¾ c. water
1 envelope dry onion soup mix
2 tsp. caraway seed
2 bay leaves

Trim excess fat from roast. Roll meat in flour; brown slowly on all sides in a small amount of hot fat. Combine all remaining ingredients; mix well. Cover; cook slowly for 2 hours and 30 minutes or until tender. Serve on platter with juice from which fat has been skimmed. Yield: 6 servings.

Linda Kay M. Naas, Hazen H. S.
Hazen, North Dakota

ROAST BEEF

1 6 to 8-lb. chuck, shoulder or round roast
Seasoning to taste

Wipe outside of beef with damp cloth; lay meat on broiler rack. Season. Place thermometer in center of meat. Bake at 225 degrees for 15 to 18 hours. NOTE: Low temperature tenderizes the cheaper cuts of meat. Yield: 12 servings.

Mrs. Margaret S. Yoder, Upper Perkiomen H. S.
East Greenville, Pennsylvania

ROAST BEEF

1 tsp. salt
¼ tsp. dried marjoram leaves
¼ tsp. dried basil leaves
¼ tsp. rubbed savory
⅛ tsp. pepper
1 8 to 9-lb. rib roast
1 tsp. liquid gravy seasoning
1 c. Burgundy
¼ c. flour
2 10 ½-oz. cans beef bouillon

Mix 1/2 teaspoonful salt with herbs and pepper. Stand roast, fat-side up, in a shallow roasting pan; rub salt mixture into beef on all sides. Mix gravy seasoning with 1/2 cup Burgundy; spoon some of mixture over beef. Roast, uncovered, at 325 degrees for 3 to 4 hours or until desired doneness. Baste occasionally, while roasting with Burgundy sauce. Remove roast from pan; drain off all but 6 tablespoonfuls drippings. Stir in flour, remaining salt and pepper to taste. Stir until smooth. Gradually add bouillon and remaining Burgundy, stirring until smooth. Bring to a boil; reduce heat. Simmer for 5 minutes. Serve gravy with roast. Yield: 10-12 servings.

Mrs. Betty Addison, Lipan H. S.
Lipan, Texas

ROAST BEEF

1 tsp. salt
⅛ tsp. pepper
4 lb. rolled sirloin
1 tbsp. lard or drippings

Season beef; spread with lard. Place in roaster; cover. Place in preheated 400 degree oven; lower heat to 375 degrees. Bake for 1 hour and 15 minutes for rare, 1 hour and 40 minutes for medium or 2 hours and 5 minutes for well done, removing cover the last 30 minutes of baking. Baste frequently.

YORKSHIRE PUDDING:

½ c. flour
Pinch of salt
1 egg
1 c. milk
Beef drippings

Sift flour and salt into large bowl. Add egg and 1/4 cup milk. Mix on low speed, adding 1/4 cup milk gradually. Mix until smooth; stir in remaining milk. Place 1 teaspoonful drippings in muffin tins or 1/4 cup drippings in 9-inch square pan. Heat at 450 degrees until haze rises from fat. Pour batter into tins, filling each one-half full. Bake at 450 degrees for 20 minutes for muffins, 40 minutes for pan or until puffed and golden brown. Serve with roast and gravy. Yield: 8 servings.

Freda M. Young, Culver City H. S.
Culver City, California

RUMP ROAST

1 3 ½ to 5-lb. rump roast
Cooking oil
⅓ c. salt
1 tbsp. garlic salt
1 can cumin powder
2 tbsp. celery salt
½ tsp. pepper
1 tsp. mustard

Rub surface of roast with cooking oil. Combine all remaining ingredients. Sprinkle roast generously with mixture, using desired amount. Bake at 325 degrees for 25 to 30 minutes per pound. NOTE: Mustard mixture may be stored in a covered jar and refrigerated for future use. Yield: 6-8 servings.

Mrs. May Round, R. H. Watkins H. S.
Laurel, Mississippi

SAUERBRATEN

2 c. vinegar
2 c. water
1 lge. onion, sliced
¼ c. sugar
2 tsp. salt
10 peppercorns or ground pepper
3 whole cloves
2 bay leaves
1 4-lb. blade or other pot roast
1 lemon, cut into ¼-in. slices
3 tbsp. fat

Combine vinegar, water, onion, sugar, salt, pepper, cloves and bay leaves in saucepan; heat. Pour mixture over meat; add lemon slices. Cover and refrigerate in marinade for 4 days, turning each day. Remove meat from marinade; drain. Brown in large skillet in fat; slowly add 2 cups marinade. Reduce heat when marinade simmers. Cover tightly and simmer for 3 hours or until tender. Add marinade when necessary. Make gravy with marinade. Serve over mashed potatoes, if desired. NOTE: Meat may be rubbed with garlic before pouring over marinade. Yield: 8-10 servings.

Mrs. Sue Bevill, Winnfield Jr. H. S.
Winnfield, Louisiana

SAUERBRATEN

1 c. white vinegar
1 c. water
⅓ c. brown sugar
1 tbsp. pickling spices
1 lge. onion, sliced
1 chuck or arm roast
8 to 10 gingersnaps

Mix vinegar, water, brown sugar, spices and onion; pour over roast in a covered container. Refrigerate for 3 to 6 days, turning occasionally. Brown meat in a small amount of vinegar mixture. Strain remaining juice. Slowly cook meat in strained juice until tender. Add water as nec-

(Continued on next page)

essary. Thicken gravy with gingersnaps. Yield: 6-8 servings.

Mrs. Harold Orth, Hawkins H. S.
Hawkins, Wisconsin

SAUERBRATEN

1 4 to 5-lb. chuck, round or rump roast
¼ c. vegetable oil
½ c. chopped onion
2 tsp. salt
2 tbsp. mixed pickling spices
1 c. red wine vinegar
3 c. water
½ c. (firmly packed) brown sugar
12 gingersnaps, crumbled

Brown roast slowly on all sides in oil; pour off excess oil. Add all remaining ingredients except gingersnaps. Simmer for 3 to 4 hours. Remove meat; keep warm. Strain liquid left in kettle to measure 4 cups. Add gingersnaps. Cook, stirring until smooth and slightly thickened. If thicken gravy is desired, add 3 tablespoonfuls flour and 1/3 cup cold water. Yield: 8 servings.

Barbara S. Fifer, Dover Air Force Base School
Dover, Delaware

SAUERBRATEN

1 2-lb. chuck roast
1 c. vinegar
2 bay leaves
5 or 6 peppercorns
6 to 8 cloves
¼ tsp. allspice
¼ c. flour
Salt to taste
¾ tbsp. shortening
2 tsp. sugar

Wipe beef with a damp cloth; place in a deep 10-inch container. Add vinegar and seasonings to beef; add enough water to cover. Place in refrigerator, covered, for 12 to 18 hours. Drain beef; reserve 1 cup liquid. Mix flour with salt; sprinkle over beef. Heat shortening in heavy kettle or skillet. Add beef; cook until lightly browned on all sides, turning. Place rack under beef; add 1/2 cup of reserved liquid. Cover; cook slowly for 3 hours or until tender. Add additional liquid if necessary. Prepare gravy, adding sugar to additional flour. Yield: 4 servings.

Jean Carolyn Leis, Buhler Rural H. S.
Buhler, Kansas

SPICY ORANGE POT ROAST

1 clove of garlic, crushed
1 tsp. salt
½ tsp. ground cumin
½ tsp. ground cloves
⅛ tsp. pepper
1 tbsp. fat
1 4 to 5-lb. chuck roast, 2-in. thick
1 6-oz. can frozen orange juice concentrate, thawed
¾ to 1 c. water or barbecue sauce
1 bay leaf
Cornstarch

Blend garlic, salt, cumin, cloves and pepper. Make small slits in beef with a sharp pointed knife; insert some of garlic mixture into each split until all is used. Melt fat in large Dutch oven; brown meat on both sides. Add orange juice, water and bay leaf. Cover and simmer for 3 hours or until meat is fork tender. Remove meat to warm platter. Measure broth; skim off excess fat. Return broth to Dutch oven; blend in 1 tablespoonful cornstarch for each cup of broth. Cook and stir until gravy is thickened. Serve over roast. Yield: 6-8 servings.

Mary McLarnan, Ashland H. S.
Ashland, Oregon

SUNDAY DINNER ROAST

1 3 to 4-lb. shoulder roast
Salt
Monosodium glutamate
Savory salt

Place meat in heavy 4-quart Dutch oven. Sprinkle with salt, monosodium glutamate and savory salt. Cover tightly. Bake at 275 degrees for 3 to 4 hours. Yield: 12 servings.

Jessie H. Sudweeks, Juab H. S.
Nephi, Utah

BEEF POT ROAST

3 lb. beef, boned
1 tsp. oil
2 med. onions, chopped
1 c. water
2 whole cloves
2 bouillon cubes
2 sm. bay leaves
1 tsp. paprika
2 tsp. salt
1 tsp. celery salt
½ tsp. pepper
Sprig of parsley
Pinch of thyme
Pinch of rosemary
2 ½ c. canned tomatoes

Trim excess fat from meat; brown on all sides in oil in heavy pan. Pour off fat. Add remaining ingredients to meat. Cover pan tightly and simmer for 2 to 3 hours or until meat is very tender. Stir and turn meat very 30 minutes. Yield: 12 servings.

Mrs. Louise B. McIntosh, Tipton H. S.
Tipton, Indiana

TASTY BEEF CHUCK ROAST

1 3 to 4-lb. chuck roast
½ tsp. salt
½ tsp. pepper
2 tsp. mustard
2 to 3 tbsp. flour
2 tbsp. cooking oil or bacon drippings

Rub roast with salt and pepper; spread mustard over entire roast. Sprinkle flour over entire roast. Brown roast on all sides in fat in roaster. Cover and bake in preheated 325 degree oven for 2 hours or until tender. Yield: 6 servings.

Mrs. Virginia S. Sharbutt, Vincent School
Vincent, Alabama

BEEF POT ROAST WITH VEGETABLES

¼ c. salad oil
1 3-lb. chuck or round roast
½ tsp. pepper
4 tsp. salt
3 ½ c. hot water
6 med. onions, peeled
6 med. carrots, scraped
6 med. potatoes, peeled and halved
¼ c. flour

Heat salad oil in large skillet or Dutch oven. Wipe meat with damp cloth; sprinkle with pepper and 2 teaspoonfuls salt. Slowly brown meat in hot fat, about 15 minutes on each side. Reduce heat; add 1/2 cup water. Cover; simmer for 1 hour and 30 minutes. Add water as needed. Add onions; continue to cook for 30 minutes longer, covered. Add carrots and potatoes; sprinkle with remaining salt. Cover; simmer for 30 minutes or until meat and vegetables are tender. Remove to serving platter. Make a paste of flour and remaining water; add to juices. Heat to boiling. Yield: 6-8 servings.

Mrs. Joyce Morehead, Arkadelphia H. S.
Arkadelphia, Arkansas

SAUERBRATEN

4 lb. round or rump, thinly cut
2 tsp. salt
½ tsp. pepper
4 bay leaves
8 peppercorns
8 whole cloves
2 med. onions, sliced
1 sm. carrot, minced
1 stalk celery, chopped
1 ½ c. red wine vinegar
2 ½ c. water
¼ c. butter

Rub meat well with salt and pepper. Place in deep ovenware bowl; add spices and vegetables. Heat vinegar and water to boiling and pour over meat immediately. Let cool. Cover; refrigerate. Marinate for 48 hours, turning meat twice a day. Remove meat from marinade and dry with clean cloth or paper towels. Brown in melted butter on both sides in a heavy deep kettle. Strain marinade and pour over meat. Cover tightly and simmer for 3 hours or until meat is tender. Remove meat to warm platter; slice. Serve warm.

GINGERSNAP GRAVY:

2 tbsp. sugar
1 ½ c. hot marinade
½ c. water
⅔ c. gingersnap crumbs
Salt

Melt sugar in skillet, stirring constantly, until golden brown. Gradually stir in marinade and water. Add gingersnap crumbs; cook, stirring constantly, until mixture thickens. Salt to taste. Spoon part of gravy over Sauerbraten; serve remaining gravy in gravy dish. Yield: 12 servings.

Mrs. Melba M. Sanders, Pike Co. H. S.
Brundidge, Alabama

BELGIAN ROAST BEEF

1 3 to 4-lb. boneless rump roast
½ lb. salt pork
2 tsp. salt
Dash of pepper
2 tbsp. dry mustard
½ c. fat
4 lge. onions, thinly sliced
1 c. beef stock or canned bouillon
3 med. tomatoes, peeled and halved
2 tbsp. red wine vinegar

Lard beef, using thin strips of salt pork in larding needle. Combine salt, pepper and mustard; rub into meat on both sides. Melt fat in skillet or Dutch oven. Brown meat on both sides; remove from skillet. Add onions; cook until golden brown. Place meat on bed of onions; add beef stock. Roast, covered, at 325 degrees for 2 hours and 30 minutes to 3 hours. Add tomatoes and a small amount wine vinegar 30 minutes before end of roasting. Continue cooking until meat is tender. Serve on platter, surrounded by onions. Garnish with parsley or watercress, if desired. Yield: 6-8 servings.

Mrs. Emma S. Thomas, Laurel H. S.
Alexander City, Alabama
Mrs. Doris Gruber, Walsh H. S.
Walsh, Colorado

BRAISED SIRLOIN TIP ROAST

1 3 to 4-lb. sirloin tip or other roast
Flour
Fat
2 tsp. salt
¼ tsp. pepper
1 med. onion, sliced (opt.)
2 bay leaves (opt.)
1 clove of garlic, minced (opt.)
½ c. hot water
4 to 8 sm. onions, peeled
6 to 8 med. carrots, pared
4 to 8 sm. potatoes, pared

(Continued on next page)

Sprinkle meat lightly with flour; rub in. Brown slowly on all sides in a small amount of hot fat in Dutch oven. Season with salt and pepper. Add sliced onion, bay leaves, garlic and water. Cover and bake at 300 to 350 degrees until almost tender. Add vegetables; cook until tender.

Sister Mary Louise, Notre Dame H. S.
Clarksburg, West Virginia
Mrs. Jeanette Wilson, Ralls H. S.
Ralls, Texas

CREOLE POT ROAST

1 3 to 4-lb. rump roast
3 tbsp. salad oil
1 tsp. seasoned salt
¼ tsp. pepper
1 c. onion rings
¼ c. chopped green pepper
½ c. chopped celery
3 ½ c. stewed tomatoes
½ c. sliced stuffed green olives
6 drops of hot pepper sauce

Brown meat in oil in Dutch oven; sprinkle with salt and pepper. Add onion rings, green pepper and celery to skillet; saute until tender. Add all remaining ingredients; stir to break tomatoes. Spoon sauce over meat; cover. Simmer for 2 hours and 30 minutes to 3 hours or until meat is tender. Thicken gravy with flour, if desired. Yield: 6-8 servings.

Mrs. Wanda Brian, Weatherford Jr. H. S.
Weatherford, Texas

FAMILY POT ROAST

1 3 to 4-lb. chuck roast
2 tbsp. fat
¾ c. hot water
½ c. catsup
½ c. V-8 juice
½ tsp. garlic salt
½ tsp. onion salt
½ tsp. pepper
8 med. potatoes, peeled and halved
8 lge. carrots

Brown meat on both sides in hot fat; add hot water. Cover and simmer slowly for 1 hour. Combine catsup, V-8 juice, garlic salt, onion salt and pepper. Slowly pour sauce over meat, covering all of meat. Simmer for 2 hours. Add potatoes and carrots. Simmer for 30 minutes longer or until vegetables are tender. Yield: 6-8 servings.

Mrs. Mary Lodrick, Medina H. S.
Medina, Ohio

HERBED VEGETABLE-BEEF DINNER

1 3-lb. boneless round or chuck roast
3 c. water
½ tsp. basil
¼ tsp. rosemary
10 carrots, scraped and cut into 1-in. pieces
3 med. yellow squash, scrubbed and cut into 1-in. rounds
6 med. potatoes, pared and cut into halves

Brown roast in non-stick Dutch oven; stir in water, basil and rosemary. Simmer for 1 hour and 30 minutes. Chill and remove all fat, if desired. Place carrots, squash and potatoes over meat 1 hour before meat is done. Salt to taste. Simmer for 1 hour or until meat and vegetables are tender. Cut meat into 1/2-inch slices; serve with vegetables on platter. Serve broth to spoon over all. Yield: 10 servings.

Mrs. K. E. Sharp, Houston Jr. H. S.
Borger, Texas

ITALIAN POT ROAST

2 cloves of garlic, minced
3 tbsp. olive oil
1 3-lb. rump roast
1 can tomatoes
3 med. bay leaves
5 cloves
2 peppercorns, chopped
½ green pepper
Salt and pepper

Brown garlic until golden brown in olive oil. Brown meat on both sides; add tomatoes, bay leaves, cloves, peppercorns and green pepper. Season to taste. Simmer slowly in covered kettle for about 3 hours or until tender. NOTE: Potatoes, carrots and onions may be added, if desired. Yield: 4-6 servings.

Mrs. Dorothy Yoh, Boyertown Area Jr. H. S.
Boyertown, Pennsylvania

POT ROAST JARDINIERE

1 3 to 4-lb. pot roast
1 10 ½-oz. can beef broth
1 tsp. salt
¼ tsp. pepper
¼ tsp. crushed rosemary
4 sm. carrots, halved lengthwise
2 med. turnips, quartered
8 sm. white onions
Chopped parsley
¼ c. water
¼ c. flour

Brown meat on all sides in large heavy pan. Add broth; cover. Cook over low heat for 2 hours and 30 minutes. Add seasonings, carrots, turnips and onions. Cook, covered, for 1 hour longer or until meat and vegetables are done. Remove meat and vegetables to heated platter; garnish with parsley. Gradually blend water into flour; slowly stir into gravy. Cook, stirring until thickened. Yield: 6 servings.

Mrs. Ned R. Mitchell, Charleston H. S.
Charleston, South Carolina

POT ROAST

1 4 to 6-lb. chuck roast
1 tsp. meat tenderizer
1 tsp. celery salt
1 tsp. onion salt
Potatoes
Carrots

Place roast in electric fry pan; turn heat to 385 degrees. Cover beef with meat tenderizer; brown. Turn meat; add celery salt and onion salt; brown second side. Reduce heat to 325 degrees; cover. Cook until beef is tender. Add potatoes and carrots. Cook until vegetables are tender; serve. NOTE: Other vegetables may be added, if desired. Yield: 8-12 servings.

Mrs. Kenneth Esch, Holland H. S.
Holland, Michigan

POT ROAST WITH VEGETABLES

1 4-lb. chuck roast
Flour
1 c. water or tomato juice
Salt and pepper
6 to 8 med. potatoes, cut into halves
4 carrots, cut into halves

Trim off a portion of suet; dice. Fry in electric skillet or fry pan. Roll meat in flour; brown in suet drippings. Add water or tomato juice and 1 1/2 teaspoonfuls salt and pepper. Simmer for 1 hour and 30 minutes to 2 hours. Add potatoes and carrots; sprinkle with a small amount of salt and pepper. Cook for 30 minutes longer or until vegetables are tender. Yield: 6 servings.

Mrs. Dorothy Schofield, Marion H. S.
Chesterhill, Ohio

RIB ROAST BRAISED IN WINE

1 5-lb. boned and rolled rib roast
Flour
¼ c. butter
½ c. chopped onion
½ c. chopped leeks
½ c. chopped carrots
1 clove of garlic, crushed
2 c. dry red wine
½ tsp. thyme
8 peppercorns, crushed
1 bay leaf
¼ tsp. marjoram
2 tbsp. Cognac, warmed

Dredge roast with flour; brown in butter on all sides in Dutch oven. Add onion, leeks, carrots and garlic; saute until browned. Add red wine and seasonings. Ignite Cognac; add to roast. Cover and bake until the meat is tender, about 4 hours. If necessary, add more wine. Transfer meat to a warm platter and keep hot. Strain sauce; and additional seasonings, if desired. Pour over beef. NOTE: Five pounds boneless chunk or rump roast may be substituted for rib roast. Yield: 12 servings.

Mrs. Joe H. Rainey, Chester Co. H. S.
Henderson, Tennessee

SMOTHERED BEEF

Flour
Salt and pepper to taste
1 3-lb. rump roast
1 med. onion, sliced
3 tbsp. fat
2 tbsp. prepared mustard
Celery seed
1 c. strained tomatoes or ½ can tomato soup

Season flour with salt and pepper. Dredge meat in flour mixture; brown in a heavy pan. Brown onion in fat; add mustard, celery seed and tomatoes. Pour over meat; simmer for 3 hours. Yield: 6 servings.

Mrs. Diane Bagky, Todd Co. H. S.
Mission, South Dakota

SPECIAL CHUCK POT ROAST

1 5-lb. chuck roast
1 tsp. salt
½ tsp. instant minced onion
½ tsp. garlic salt
½ c. cooking Sherry
½ c. wine vinegar
1 pt. tomatoes
1 tsp. oregano
½ tsp. pepper

Place sheet of aluminum foil in large pan. Place roast on foil. Combine all remaining ingredients; add to roast. Cover with foil. Bake at 325 degrees for 2 hours and 30 minutes or until meat is tender. Make gravy by thickening with a paste of flour and water. Yield: 8-10 servings.

Mrs. Helen Loftin, Denton H. S.
Denton, North Carolina

BARBECUED BEEF RIBS

Salt and pepper to taste
3 ½ lb. short ribs
Flour
1 c. barbecue sauce
2 c. water

Salt and pepper ribs; lightly roll each rib in flour. Brown ribs in a small amount of fat in a deep 4-quart roast pan. Drain off fat, if desired. Pour barbecue sauce over ribs. Add water. Place lid on pan. Bake at 350 degrees for about 3 hours. When ribs are done, place in a shallow loaf pan; pour a small amount of drippings from roaster over ribs. Bake at 400 degrees for 20

(Continued on next page)

minutes longer or until brown. Yield: 4-5 servings.

Mrs. Emma Jewel Goodwin, Bertram H. S.
Bertram, Texas

BARBECUED SHORT RIBS

1 ½ to 2 lb. short ribs
2 stalks celery, chopped
1 med. onion, minced
1 tbsp. sugar
½ c. catsup
1 tbsp. vinegar
¼ tsp. Tabasco sauce
¼ tsp. chili powder
Pepper to taste
½ tsp. salt
1 c. water

Place ribs in roaster. Combine celery, onion, sugar, catsup, vinegar, Tabasco sauce, chili powder, pepper, salt and water; pour over ribs. Add additional water if sauce does not cover ribs. Cover and bake at 350 degrees for 2 to 3 hours or until tender. Yield: 4 servings.

Mrs. Phyllis I. Pope, Rib Lake H. S.
Rib Lake, Wisconsin

BARBECUED SHORT RIBS

3 lb. short ribs, cut into serving pieces
1 onion, chopped
2 tbsp. fat
¼ c. vinegar
2 tbsp. sugar
2 tsp. salt
1 c. catsup
½ c. water
3 tbsp. Worcestershire sauce
1 tsp. prepared mustard
½ c. sliced celery

Brown short ribs with onion in hot fat. Combine remaining ingredients; add to ribs. Cover and cook slowly for 1 hour and 30 minutes to 2 hours or until tender. Yield: 4-5 servings.

Mrs. Della O. Lindsay, Riverside H. S.
Broadman, Oregon

SWEET-SOUR SHORT RIBS

1 No. 2 can pineapple chunks
2 lb. short ribs
2 tbsp. fat
¾ c. water
⅓ c. brown sugar
2 tbsp. cornstarch
½ tsp. salt
¼ c. vinegar
1 tbsp. soy sauce
½ c. green pepper, cut into strips
½ c. thinly sliced onion

Drain pineapple, reserving 1 cup syrup. Brown ribs in hot fat. Cover and cook slowly for 1 hour and 30 minutes to 2 hours or until tender, adding more water if necessary. Drain off fat. Combine sugar and cornstarch; add salt, reserved pineapple syrup, vinegar and soy sauce. Cook over low heat until thick, stirring constantly. Pour over hot ribs; let stand for 10 minutes. Add green pepper, onion and pineapple; cook for 5 minutes. Serve over hot chow mein noodles or rice, if desired. Yield: 5-6 servings.

Mrs. Enid Cox, Scappoose Union H. S.
Scappoose, Oregon

CANTONESE SHORT RIBS

3 lb. short ribs, cut into serving portions
3 tbsp. oil
1 1-lb. 4-oz. can sliced pineapple
⅓ c. soy sauce
Brown sugar
1 tsp. ginger
Melted butter

Brown ribs on all sides in hot oil in heavy skillet. Drain pineapple, reserving juice. Mix pineapple juice with enough water to make 2 cups; add soy sauce, 1 tablespoonful brown sugar and ginger. Pour over ribs. Cover and simmer for 3 hours or until meat is very tender. Add additional water, if necessary. Brush pineapple slices with melted butter; sprinkle with a small amount of brown sugar. Brown lightly under broiler. Serve ribs on a hot platter surrounded with hot broiled pineapple slices. Yield: 6 servings.

Lucile K. Lawson, Hayfork H. S.
Hayfork, California

BAKED STEAK

1 1 ½-lb. round steak, 1-in. thick
Flour
Pepper
Salt
3 tbsp. fat
1 can cream of chicken soup
1 soup can water
1 tsp. Worcestershire sauce
Onion slices

Pound steak with flour, 1/4 teaspoonful pepper and 1 teaspoonful salt. Brown in fat over medium heat. Place in greased casserole; cover with soup, water, Worcestershire sauce, onion slices and salt and pepper to taste. Cover and bake at 400 degrees for 1 hour. NOTE: One 3-pound chicken may be substituted for steak. Yield: 4 servings.

Sharon A. Anderson, Fosston H. S.
Fosston, Minnesota

APRICOT STEAK

Salt and pepper to taste
1 ½ lb. round steak
¼ c. flour
2 tbsp. chopped onion
¼ c. fat
1 No. 2 can apricot halves

Season steak; cut into serving pieces. Dredge steak in flour; reserve remaining flour. Brown onion and steak in fat; remove to a casserole dish. Drain apricots, reserving juice. Blend reserved flour and juice; add to casserole. Cover. Bake at 350 degrees for 45 minutes or until tender. Add water as needed. Add apricots during last 15 minutes of baking time; bake uncovered. Yield: 6 servings.

Willie Hawkins, Lovelady H. S.
Lovelady, Texas

BAKED THICK STEAK

¼ to ⅓ lb. tallow
1 4 to 5-lb. round steak, 2-in. thick
Salt and pepper to taste
Flour

Melt tallow in large Dutch oven. Trim steak and pound; salt and pepper to taste. Coat thoroughly with flour. Brown steak on both sides in melted fat. Add enough boiling water to cover steak. Bake at 350 degrees until well done, about two hours. Yield: 12 servings.

Mrs. Marian L. Carpenter, Farmersville H. S.
Farmersville, Texas

BARBECUE STEAK

1 c. corn oil
¼ c. red wine
¼ c. vinegar
¼ tsp. rosemary
¼ tsp. garlic salt
¼ tsp. pepper
1 sirloin or tenderloin steak
1 tsp. cornstarch
½ c. sour cream
1 4-oz. can sliced or buttered mushrooms, drained

Combine corn oil, red wine, vinegar, rosemary, garlic salt and pepper. Marinate steak in mixture for several hours or overnight, turning several times. Remove steak from marinade; drain slightly. Broil until done. Stir marinade; measure 1/2 cup into small saucepan. Bring to a boil over medium heat; reduce heat and simmer for 1 minute. Serve over steak.

Photograph for recipe on page 29.

BARBECUED STEAK

2 cloves of garlic
2 1 ½ to 2-lb. chuck steaks
½ c. red wine or wine vinegar

Crush garlic into both sides of meat. Marinate steaks in wine or wine vinegar at toom temperature for 4 to 6 hours, turning occasionally. Place on broiler rack, 4 inches from heat; broil for 6 to 10 minutes on each side. Cut into thin slices, diagonally across the grain. Yield: 4-6 servings.

Mrs. V. C. Ives, Antioch H. S.
Antioch, California

BEEF PARMIGIANA

1 ½ lb. round steak
1 egg, beaten
⅓ c. grated Parmesan cheese
⅓ c. fine dry bread crumbs
⅓ c. cooking oil
1 med. onion, minced
1 tsp. salt
¼ tsp. pepper
½ tsp. sugar
½ tsp. powdered marjoram
1 6-oz. can tomato paste
2 c. hot water
½ lb. Mozzarella cheese, sliced

Cut meat into several pieces; pound to about 1/4-inch thickness. Dip into egg; roll in mixture of Parmesan cheese and crumbs. Brown meat in oil until golden brown. Lay in shallow, wide baking dish. Cook onion over low heat until soft in same skillet. Stir in salt, pepper, sugar, marjoram and tomato paste. Add hot water. Boil for 5 minutes. Pour most of sauce over meat; top with cheese slices and remaining sauce. Cover and bake at 350 degrees for 1 hour or until meat is tender, adding more water if needed. Serve with spaghetti or rice, if desired. Yield: 4-6 servings.

Mrs. Nell Fenoglio, West Covina H. S.
West Covina, California

BEEF PIZZA

1 ½ to 2 lb. round steak
2 tbsp. fat
1 pkg. dry onion soup mix
1 6-oz. can tomato paste
1 tsp. salt
Dash of pepper
1 c. water
1 tsp. oregano
1 tbsp. sugar
2 tbsp. flour

Brown steak in hot fat; add onion soup, tomato paste, salt, pepper, 1/2 cup water, oregano and sugar. Cover and cook over low heat for 1 hour and 30 minutes. Combine remaining water and flour; stir into mixture. Cook until mixture bubbles. Yield: 6 servings.

Mrs. Frances Steube, Groveport-Madison H. S.
Groveport, Ohio

BEEF IN SOUR CREAM

2 lb. shoulder or chuck
Flour
Shortening
2 med. onions, sliced
Salt and pepper
1 c. sour cream
2 tbsp. grated cheese

Cut meat into serving pieces; roll each piece in flour. Brown in hot shortening; add onions, salt and pepper. Pour sour cream around meat; sprinkle grated cheese on top. Cover; cook for 2 hours or until meat is tender. Add water, if necessary. Place in center of a large platter; surround with sour cream sauce from pan. Yield: 6 servings.

Alma Will, Fairview School
Calgary, Alberta, Canada

CHICKEN-FRIED ROUND STEAK

1 ½ lb. round steak, ½-in. thick
1 c. milk
1 c. flour
Seasoned salt
Paprika
Pepper

Cut round steak into serving pieces. Pound steak well; dip into milk. Roll steak in mixture of flour, salt, paprika and pepper. Fry quickly in hot fat. Drain off excess fat; add a small amount of water. Cover; steam for 15 minutes. Yield: 4 servings.

Mrs. Louella R. Pence, Macon H. S.
Macon, Illinois

CHOPPED SIRLOIN STEAKS

2 tbsp. butter
1 4-oz. chopped sirloin steak
Salt and pepper to taste

Butter both sides of steak; salt and pepper to taste. Place in heavy skillet. Cover and cook to desired doneness. Yield: 1 serving.

Mrs. Park Prater, Southeastern H. S.
Richmond Dale, Ohio

CUBED STEAK SUPREME

½ c. flour
⅛ tsp. pepper
1 tsp. salt
¼ tsp. paprika
6 cubed steaks
½ c. shortening or butter
1 can cream of mushroom soup
1 c. water

Mix flour, pepper, salt and paprika; coat steaks with mixture. Brown steaks on both sides in shortening or butter in large skillet. Dilute soup with water; heat to boiling. Add steak. Simmer for 1 hour or until meat is tender. Yield: 6 servings.

Mrs. Elizabeth Carson, Sulphur Springs H. S.
Jonesboro, Tennessee

DEVILED STEAK

¼ c. flour
2 tsp. salt
¼ tsp. pepper
1 ½ tsp. dry mustard
1 3-lb. round steak, cut 1 ½-in. thick
¼ c. cooking oil
½ c. water
1 tbsp. Worcestershire sauce
1 3-oz. can broiled mushroom crowns, drained
Butter or margarine

Combine flour, salt, pepper and dry mustard; sprinkle over steak. Pound into meat with meat mallet. Brown steak slowly on both sides in hot oil in heavy skillet. Combine water and Worcestershire sauce; add to browned meat in skillet. Cover tightly and cook over very low heat for 1 hour and 45 minutes to 2 hours or until tender. Remove steak to serving platter. Heat mushrooms in a small amount of butter. Serve with steak. Garnish with parsley, if desired. Skim excess fat from meat juices; serve juices with steak. Yield: 6-8 servings.

Linda Bland, Luverne H. S.
Luverne, Alabama

FLANK STEAK-TERIYAKI BARBECUE

¼ c. vegetable oil
½ c. soy sauce
4 c. honey
2 tbsp. vinegar
2 tbsp. finely chopped green onion
1 lge. clove of garlic, minced
1 ½ tsp. ground ginger
1 1 ½-lb. flank steak

Combine oil, soy sauce, honey, vinegar, onion, garlic and ginger; pour over steak. Marinate for 4 hours or longer, turning occasionally. Barbecue steak over hot coals, turning once. Cook until desired doneness. Baste occasionally with marinade. Carve into thin slices, cutting on the diagonal from top to bottom of steak. Yield: 4 servings.

Mrs. Elaine Kohl, Mechanicsburg H. S.
Mechanicsburg, Ohio

GRENADINE OF BEEF

2 4-oz. filet steaks, ½-in. thick
Flour
1 tsp. butter
2 lge. mushrooms
Pinch of salt
1 tsp. red wine
3 tbsp. beef broth

(Continued on next page)

Coat steaks with flour. Saute steaks in skillet in butter for 3 minutes on each side. Add mushrooms and salt. Saute for 2 minutes longer. Add red wine and beef broth. Simmer until sauce is slightly thickened. Yield: 1 serving.

Mrs. June Letcher, Mount Shasta H. S.
Mount Shasta, California

HERB STEAK

1 lb. round steak
2 tbsp. flour
1 tsp. seasoned salt
2 tbsp. salad oil
1 10 ½-oz. can cream of mushroom soup
¾ c. water
1 tbsp. herb seasoning

Cut steak into serving pieces. Combine flour and seasoned salt; pound into steak. Brown meat on both sides in hot oil in heavy skillet. Add remaining ingredients; cover. Simmer for 45 minutes or bake at 350 degrees for 1 hour. Serve with hot buttered noodles, if desired. Yield: 3-4 servings.

Margaret N. Phillips, Grant Comm. H. S.
Fox Lake, Illinois

LONDON SOY BROIL

2 lb. flank steak or top round
1 c. salad oil
1 onion, sliced
2 tbsp. vinegar
¼ c. soy sauce

Place a piece of aluminum foil in bottom of shallow pan. Place meat in pan; cover with mixture of remaining ingredients. Cover with foil. Refrigerate overnight, turning several times. Drain off marinade. Broil for 4 to 5 minutes on each side. Slice into thin slices across the grain. Yield: 4 servings.

Mrs. Sally Foley, Winslow H. S.
Winslow, Maine

MARINATED ROUND STEAK

2 lb. round steak, cut ¾-in. thick
¼ c. wine vinegar
1 tbsp. soy sauce
1 tsp. onion salt
¼ tsp. pepper
1 tbsp. catsup
1 sm. clove of garlic, finely minced
2 tbsp. salad or olive oil

Arrange steak in shallow pan. Combine remaining ingredients; pour over steak. Refrigerate for at least 3 hours; drain. Heat broiler. Arrange steak on broiler pan, 5 inches from heat. Broil for 5 minutes on each side or to desired doneness. Yield: 6 servings.

Mrs. Effie G. Hoyle, Warwick H. S.
Newport News, Virginia

MARTHA STEAK

¼ c. flour
1 tsp. salt
¼ tsp. pepper
1 1 ½-lb. round steak
3 tbsp. fat
1 med. onion, sliced
1 lemon, sliced
1 c. catsup
1 green pepper, sliced

Combine flour, salt and pepper. Dredge steak in flour mixture; brown in hot fat. Remove from heat; place in a 9 x 12-inch baking dish. Add onion, lemon, catsup and green pepper. Cover. Bake at 350 degrees for 1 hour. Yield: 6 servings.

Mary Ann Keel, Lorena H. S.
Lorena, Texas

MINUTE STEAK BAKE

6 minute steaks
Salt and pepper to taste
½ can cream of mushroom soup
½ can cream of celery soup
1 soup can water
1 med. onion, chopped
Butter

Season steaks with salt and pepper. Place steaks in casserole; cover with soups and water. Add onion; dot with butter. Bake at 350 degrees for 2 hours. Yield: 6 servings.

Mrs. Magdaline Dhuey, Casco H. S.
Casco, Wisconsin

OVEN BARBECUED STEAKS

3 lb. round steak, ¾-in. thick
2 tbsp. salad oil
½ c. chopped onion
¾ c. catsup
½ c. vinegar
¾ c. water
1 tbsp. brown sugar
1 tbsp. prepared mustard
1 tbsp. Worcestershire sauce
½ tsp. salt
⅛ tsp. pepper

Cut steak into serving pieces. Pour oil in skillet; brown steak on both sides. Transfer steak to roasting pan. Add onion to skillet; brown lightly. Add remaining ingredients. Simmer in skillet for about 5 minutes. Pour sauce over steak in roasting pan; cover. Bake at 350 degrees for 2 hours to 2 hours and 30 minutes or until meat is fork tender. Serve hot. Yield: 10 servings.

Mrs. Delia E. McClurg, Merino H. S.
Merino, Colorado

OVEN ROUND STEAK

1 1 ½ to 2-lb. round steak or 3 T-bone steaks
½ to 1 pkg. dry onion soup mix
Salt and pepper to taste (opt.)

Pound steak well; lay flat in foil-lined pan. Sprinkle meat with onion soup; sprinkle soup with water, if desired. Cover with foil; fasten edges tightly. Bake round steak at 375 degrees for 1 hour to 1 hour and 30 minutes. Bake T-bones at 350 degrees for 1 hour. Season with salt and pepper.

Mary E. Finley, Baker Co. H. S.
Macclenny, Florida
Sandra M. Cuchna, Webb H. S.
Reedsburg, Wisconsin

PEPPER STEAK

2 lb. round steak
1 clove of garlic, cut
Salt
Pepper to taste
¼ c. flour
3 tbsp. oil
1 6-oz. can tomato paste
1 ½ c. water
1 bay leaf
¼ tsp. thyme
1 lge. onion, sliced
1 green pepper, cut into rings

Cut steak into serving pieces. Rub with garlic; sprinkle with salt and pepper. Pound flour into steak. Heat oil in large skillet; brown steak. Remove meat; place in casserole. Drain oil from skillet. Mix tomato paste, water, 1/2 teaspoonful salt, bay leaf and thyme; heat in same skillet. Arrange onion and green pepper rings over meat; pour tomato mixture over all. Cover tightly. Bake at 350 degrees for 1 hour to 1 hour and 30 minutes. Yield: 6 servings.

Mrs. Jewell Spivey, Harmony School
Gilmer, Texas

ROUND STEAK

1 ½ lb. round steak, 1-in. thick
¾ tsp. monosodium glutamate
½ c. flour
2 tbsp. fat
1 sm. onion, sliced
1 ½ tsp. salt
¼ tsp. dry mustard
⅛ tsp. pepper
1 stalk celery, chopped
⅔ c. water

Wipe steak; slash fat edges to prevent curling. Place on meat board; sprinkle with monosodium glutamate. Sprinkle with flour; pound into meat with hammer or back of French knife. Place fat in skillet; add onion and cook. Remove onion. Brown both sides of meat in fat; add seasonings and celery. Pour water slowly into skillet; cover and simmer or bake at 300 degrees for 1 hour and 30 minutes or until tender. Add water if necessary.

V. M. Bradford, Golden Secondary School
Golden, British Columbia, Canada

ROUND STEAK

2 lb. round steak
2 beef bouillon cubes
1 pkg. dry onion soup mix

Cut steak into serving pieces. Brown steak; place in casserole. Dissolve bouillon cubes in hot water; add onion soup. Pour over steak. Cover and bake at 375 degrees for 1 hour. Remove cover; bake for 30 minutes longer. Yield: 6 servings.

Pauline K. Brown, Lone Wolf School
Lone Wolf, Oklahoma

ROUND STEAK CASSEROLE

2 lb. round steak, cut into serving pieces
Oil
3 med. onions, sliced
Salt and pepper to taste
Worcestershire sauce
¼ to ½ c. water

Brown steak in a small amount of oil. Alternate layers of steak and onion slices in casserole. Add seasonings. Add water to meat drippings in skillet; pour over meat and onions. Bake at 300 degrees for 1 hour. Yield: 4-6 servings.

Virginia S. McEwen, Coosa Co. H. S.
Rockford, Alabama

SAUCY STEAK

1 3-lb. round steak, ½-in. thick
¼ c. flour
½ tsp. salt
⅛ tsp. pepper
2 tbsp. fat
1 can onion soup
½ c. water
½ tsp. celery seed
2 tbsp. chili sauce

Pound steak to 1/4-inch thickness. Cut into four to six pieces. Dredge steak in mixture of flour, salt and pepper. Brown in hot fat; pour off drippings. Add soup, water, celery seed and chili sauce. Cover tightly and simmer for 1 hour and 15 minutes to 2 hours or until tender. Yield: 4-6 servings.

Mrs. Joseph Matanich
Mountain Iron School No. 703
Mountain Iron, Minnesota

SEBERN STEAK

1 3 to 4-lb. shoulder steak, 2-in. thick
½ c. catsup
1 pkg. dry onion soup mix
½ c. hot water

Brown steak in 10-inch frying pan; cover with catsup. Sprinkle steak with onion soup. Pour water into bottom of pan. Simmer for 2 hours and 30 minutes or until tender. Yield: 8 servings.

Mrs. Harold W. Severn, Cummings Jr. H. S.
Brownsville, Texas

SMOTHERED STEAKS

6 minute steaks
1 can cream of mushroom soup
1 soup can water
1 tsp. salt
3 tbsp. Kitchen Bouquet

Braise steaks; place in a shallow roaster. Pour soup into saucepan; stir in water. Add salt and Kitchen Bouquet; pour mixture over steaks. Cover. Bake at 350 degrees for about 35 minutes. Yield: 6 servings.

Mrs. Hazel Sargent, Odon H. S.
Odon, Indiana

SOUR BEEF STEAK

2 lb. round steak
3 tbsp. flour
1 ½ c. water
2 tsp. salt
½ c. vinegar
½ c. brown sugar
½ tsp. powdered cloves

Cut meat into serving pieces; coat with flour. Brown meat in greased pan. Remove meat from pan. Make gravy with flour, water and salt; simmer until thick. Mix in vinegar, brown sugar and cloves. Add meat to mixture. Simmer, covered, for 1 hour or longer. Yield: 6 servings.

Mrs. Marilyn Breeding, Prospect H. S.
Mt. Prospect, Illinois

SOUTHSEAS STEAK

1 sirloin steak, 1-in. thick
¼ c. wine vinegar
2 tbsp. salad oil
2 tbsp. soy sauce
2 tbsp. instant onion
1 tbsp. brown sugar
¼ tsp. ground ginger
¼ tsp. dry mustard
⅛ tsp. pepper
1 clove of garlic, finely chopped

Place steak in shallow bowl. Combine all remaining ingredients; pour over steak. Cover; marinate in refrigerator for 2 to 3 hours. Remove steak from marinade; slash edge at 2-inch intervals. Place on rack of broiler pan, about 2 to 3 inches from heat. Broil steak about 5 to 8 minutes on each side. Yield: 2-3 servings.

Mary A. Hugus, Fairless H.S.
Justus, Ohio

SPECIAL STEAK

Flour
1 slice round steak, 1 to 1 ½-in. thick
Fat
Salt to taste
¼ c. brown sugar
1 to 1 ½ c. water

Brown floured steak in hot fat in heavy skillet; brown on both sides. Sprinkle with salt, 3 tablespoonfuls flour and brown sugar. Add water. Cover. Bake at 350 degrees for 2 hours. NOTE: A small can of mushrooms may be added to gravy before serving, if desired. Yield: 6-8 servings.

Mrs. Virginia Smith, North H. S.
Evansville, Indiana

STEAK DELUXE

Salt and pepper to taste
¼ c. flour
3 lb. round steak, cut 1 ½-in. thick
¾ c. french dressing
1 lge. onion, sliced

Pound salt, pepper and flour into steak. Heat dressing in heavy skillet; add meat and brown slowly on both sides. Add onion. Cover and simmer for 2 hours or until tender. Yield: 8 servings.

Mrs. Jessie Wines, Adena H. S.
Frankfort, Ohio

STEAK IN FOIL WITH MUSHROOMS

2 lb. round steak, 1 in. thick
1 c. sliced mushrooms
Butter
½ pkg. dry onion soup mix
⅛ tsp. pepper
2 tbsp. water

Center steak on heavy aluminum foil. Saute mushrooms in a small amount of butter; sprinkle over meat. Add remaining ingredients. Seal carefully. Bake at 450 degrees for 1 hour and 30 minutes or until tender. Yield: 4-5 servings.

Alethea Stewart, Strathcona Composite H. S.
Edmonton, Alberta, Canada

STEAK AND GRAVY

2 lb. round steak, ½-in. thick
4 tbsp. flour
1 tsp. salt
¼ tsp. pepper
4 tbsp. fat
1 med. onion, sliced
1 3-oz. can mushrooms, drained
1 c. water
½ c. sour cream
½ c. shredded sharp process cheese

Cut meat into serving pieces. Combine flour, salt and pepper. Dredge meat in flour. Brown steak in hot fat. Add onion, mushrooms and 1/2 cup water. Cover and simmer for 1 hour or until meat is very tender. Remove steak. Add sour cream, cheese and remaining water to broth; bring to a boil. Serve over steak. Serve while hot. Yield: 6 servings.

Mrs. Annie Fred Wright, Blacksburg H. S.
Blacksburg, Virginia

STEAK WITH ONIONS AND SOUR CREAM

Flour
2 lb. round steak
4 tbsp. melted butter
1 tsp. salt
⅛ tsp. pepper
½ c. diced onion
½ c. diced mushrooms
1 c. sour cream

Pound flour into steak with a meat chopper or heavy plate. Sear steak in melted butter; add salt and pepper. Saute onion and mushrooms. Combine onion, mushrooms, sour cream and 2 tablespoonfuls flour. Place steak in a large casserole or skillet; cover with sour cream mixture. Bake, covered, at 275 degrees for 2 hours. Serve. Yield: 6 servings.

Mrs. Fleta Bruce, Hamburg Comm. H. S.
Hamburg, Iowa

STEAK ORIENTAL

1 c. soy sauce
¼ c. brown sugar
1 tbsp. ground ginger
4 rib steaks, ¾-in. thick

Combine soy sauce, brown sugar and ginger. Marinate steaks for 1 hour and 30 minutes in mixture. Broil for 5 to 10 minutes in broiler, 2 inches from heat. Yield: 4 servings.

Mrs. Dona Louise Greeson, Stonington H. S.
Stonington, Illinois

STEAK WITH MUSHROOMS

5 lb. top sirloin
1 tsp. salt
¼ tsp. pepper
4 tbsp. flour
Fat
2 lge. onions, sliced
1 4-oz. can mushroom stems and pieces
½ tsp. seasoned salt
⅛ tsp. ground cloves
¼ tsp. dried marjoram leaves
¼ tsp. dried thyme
1 tsp. paprika
1 c. wine or 1 can consomme
1 c. sour cream

Sprinkle meat with one-half of salt, pepper and flour; pound well into meat. Turn meat over. Sprinkle with remaining salt, pepper and flour, pound into meat. Brown meat on both sides in a small amount of fat; place on steak. Add remaining ingredients except sour cream. Cover and simmer very slowly for 3 hours or until fork tender. Remove meat; thicken juice for gravy. Add sour cream.

Mrs. Gene Taresh, East Nicolaus H. S.
East Nicolaus, California

STEAK AND MUSHROOM SAUCE

3 lb. round steak, cut into serving pieces
2 tbsp. butter
1 lge. onion, diced
1 can cream of mushroom soup
1 soup can water
1 tsp. salt
Pepper to taste
½ c. sour cream
½ c. creme de cacao

Brown steak in butter; remove steak. Saute onion in same skillet. Add remaining ingredients; stir well. Return meat. Cover and simmer for 45 minutes or until meat is tender, stirring occasionally. More water may be added, if needed. Serve on rice, noodles or potatoes, if desired. Yield: 6 servings.

Mrs. Mae Baker Kelly, Poth H. S.
Poth, Texas

STEAK IN SAUCE

¼ c. seasoned flour
1 ½ lb. round steak
2 tbsp. shortening
1 can cream of mushroom soup
½ soup can water
½ c. sour cream (opt.)

Pound seasoned flour into steak with meat hammer or edge of heavy saucer. Brown steak on both sides in shortening in large skillet. Add soup and water. Cover; cook over low heat for 45 minutes or until steak is tender. Stir often. Just before serving, stir in sour cream, if desired. Yield: 4-6 servings.

Barbara M. Silva, Belen H. S.
Belen, New Mexico

BEST SWISS STEAK

1 lb. round steak
½ tsp. salt
¼ tsp. pepper
2 tbsp. flour
1 tbsp. shortening
¾ c. hot water
½ c. chopped onion
½ c. chopped celery
1 can tomato soup
¼ c. chopped olives (opt.)

Pound steak; sprinkle with salt, pepper and flour. Brown steak in shortening; add hot water. Cover; steam for about 5 minutes. Add chopped onion, chopped celery, tomato soup and chopped olives. Bake at 200 to 250 degrees for 1 hour or until steak is tender. Yield: 4 servings.

Mrs. J. C. Waller, Mt. Enterprise H. S.
Mt. Enterprise, Texas

DELECTABLE SWISS STEAK

1 tbsp. shortening
1 med. onion, sliced
1 slice round steak, 1-in. thick
⅓ c. flour
1 tsp. salt
¼ tsp. pepper
1 pt. tomato juice

Melt shortening in a deep skillet; add onion. Brown. Dredge steak with flour; add to onion and fat. Sear steak on both sides. Add salt, pepper and tomato juice. Cover; cook over low heat for about 1 hour and 30 minutes or until tender. Add additional tomato juice, if desired. Yield: 6 servings.

Mrs. Paul Bishop, Cloudland H. S.
Roan Mountain, Tennessee

DELICIOUS SWISS STEAK

2 lb. round steak, 1-in. thick
¼ tsp. salt
¼ tsp. seasoned salt
Pepper to taste
¼ c. flour
3 tbsp. oil
2 c. canned tomatoes
1 6-oz. can tomato paste
1 onion, chopped
1 paste can water

Wipe meat; cut into serving pieces. Sprinkle with salt, seasoned salt and pepper; pound in flour. Brown meat in hot oil in heavy skillet or Dutch oven. Add tomatoes, tomato paste, onion and water. Cover and simmer for 2 hours or until tender, stirring occasionally. Yield: 6 servings.

Maud Stanton, Red Springs H. S.
Red Springs, North Carolina

GOURMET SWISS STEAK

½ c. flour
1 tsp. salt
½ tsp. pepper
1 round steak, cut up
3 tbsp. lard
1 10 ½-oz. can beef consomme
1 4-oz. can mushroom stems and pieces, undrained
1 tbsp. herb seasoning

Pound flour, salt and pepper into both sides of steak; reserve remaining flour. Brown steak in lard. Pour off drippings; add beef consomme, mushrooms and herb seasoning. Cover tightly. Simmer for 3 hour and 30 minutes or until meat is tender. Thicken liquid with remaining seasoned flour, for gravy. Yield: 6-8 servings.

Mary Wood, Atlanta H. S.
Atlanta, Texas

QUICK SWISS STEAK

1 ½ lb. round steak
Salt and pepper to taste
¾ c. flour
4 tbsp. fat
½ c. chopped onion
¼ c. chopped green pepper
½ c. chopped celery
½ No. 303 can tomatoes
1 c. water

Pound steak; salt and pepper to taste. Roll in flour. Brown in hot fat in pressure saucepan. Brown any remaining flour in fat. Add remaining ingredients. Cook at 10 pounds pressure for 30 minutes. Cool pan for 5 minutes. Place under running water to reduce pressure. Yield: 4 servings.

Mrs. Mildred W. Tate, Henderson City H. S.
Henderson, Kentucky

SAVORY SWISS STEAK

2 tbsp. flour
1 tsp. salt
⅛ tsp. pepper
1 ½ lb. round steak, 1-in. thick
2 tbsp. fat
2 c. sliced onions
1 tsp. dry mustard
½ tsp. chili powder
1 bay leaf
2 tsp. Worcestershire sauce
2 c. canned tomatoes

Combine flour, salt and pepper; pound into meat. Brown meat in hot fat; top with onion slices. Combine seasonings and tomatoes; pour over steak. Cover; cook slowly over low heat for about 1 hour and 30 minutes or until tender. Yield: 6 servings.

Mrs. Caryl Nelson, Glenwood H. S.
Glenwood, Minnesota

SWISS STEAK

⅓ to ½ c. flour
1 to 2 tsp. salt
⅛ to ½ tsp. pepper
2 lb. round or chuck steak, 1 ½ to 2-in. thick
1 sm. onion, chopped
3 tbsp. fat
1 to 2 ½ c. canned tomatoes

Mix flour, salt and pepper; pound thoroughly into steak. Brown meat and onion in hot fat; add tomatoes. Cover; cook over low heat or bake at 300 to 350 degrees for 1 hour and 30 minutes or until tender. Yield: 6 servings.

Mrs. Martha McCormick, Muleshoe H. S.
Muleshoe, Texas
Mrs. Bob Farris, Altus-Denning H. S.
Altus, Arkansas

SWISS STEAK

1 ¼ lb. round steak, 1 to 1 ½-in. thick
¼ c. flour
1 tsp. salt
⅛ tsp. pepper
2 tbsp. fat
½ c. tomato juice
½ onion, sliced

Place steak on bread board. Mix flour, salt and pepper; pound into steak on both sides. Brown steak on both sides in hot fat; add tomato juice and onion. Cover tightly and simmer for 1 hour or until tender. Yield: 4 servings.

Bertha Keller Benthien
Clermont Northeastern H. S., Batavia, Ohio

SWISS STEAK

3 lb. round steak
½ c. flour
2 tsp. salt
¼ tsp. pepper
2 tbsp. oil
3 tbsp. cornstarch
¼ tsp. garlic powder
1 tsp. onion powder
3 tbsp. powdered mushrooms
1 beef bouillon cube
1 c. water
1 8-oz. can tomato sauce
½ c. dry red wine
1 ½ tsp. seasoned salt
½ tsp. crushed oregano
½ tsp. sweet basil
1 med. can stewed tomatoes

Trim excess fat from meat. Combine flour, salt and pepper; pound mixture into meat on both sides with edge of sauce. Heat oil in Dutch oven; brown meat. Remove meat and insert rack in Dutch oven to keep meat from sticking. Dissolve bouillon cube in water. Add to mixture with remaining ingredients; pour over meat. Bake in covered pan at 300 degrees for 3 hours and 30 minutes to 4 hours. Add water if sauce is too thick or another can of stewed tomatoes. Yield: 6-8 servings.

Mrs. Joan Bull, Dallas Jr. H. S.
Dallas, Oregon

SWISS STEAK IN FOIL

1 c. catsup
¼ c. flour
2 lb. round steak, 1-in. thick
1 lge. onion, sliced
2 tbsp. lemon juice or 1 lemon, thinly sliced (opt.)

Combine catsup and flour; spoon one-half of mixture into center of large piece of aluminum foil. Place steak over mixture; season with salt and pepper. Cover meat with onion slices and remaining catsup mixture; sprinkle with lemon juice or top with lemon slices. Fold foil over top; seal edges securely. Place in shallow baking pan. Bake at 450 degrees for 1 hour and 30 minutes or until meat is tender. Remove foil; cut steak into pieces. Yield: 5-6 servings.

Mrs. Sharon Haynes, Magrath H. S.
Magrath, Alberta, Canada

TEXAS ROUND STEAK

2 tbsp. flour
¼ tsp. crushed leaf thyme
Dash of pepper
1 ½ lb. round steak
1 med. onion, sliced
½ med. green pepper, sliced
2 tbsp. shortening
1 10 ¾-oz. can tomato-rice soup
½ soup can water

Combine flour, thyme and pepper; pound into steak. Cut into six pieces. Brown meat, onion and green pepper in shortening at 400 degrees in an electric skillet. Reduce heat to 220 degrees. Stir in soup and water. Cover and simmer for 1 hour and 30 minutes or until meat is tender. Spoon sauce over meat several times during cooking. Yield: 6 servings.

Mrs. Audrey Henderson, Jefferson H. S.
Jefferson, South Dakota

UNCLE RUSS' STEAK SPECIALTY

2 lb. round steak
2 lge. bottles catsup
10 lge. onions, sliced vertically

Place steak in a large skillet. Add catsup and onions. Simmer for 1 hour and 30 minutes or until steak is tender. Serve, using catsup and onion sauce as gravy. Yield: 6 servings.

Mrs. Dawna R. Pitzer, Western Beaver H. S.
Industry, Pennsylvania

BEEF BIRDS

2 c. seasoned bread crumbs
¾ tsp. salt
1 tsp. parsley flakes
¼ c. minced onion
3 tbsp. melted butter
3 cubed steaks
1 ½ tbsp. fat
1 tsp. Worcestershire sauce
1 tbsp. flour

Combine crumbs, salt, parsley flakes, onion and butter; add just enough water to moisten. Spread each steak with some of bread mixture. Roll up; secure with toothpicks or string. Brown in hot fat in heavy skillet. Add 1/2 cup water and Worcestershire sauce. Cover and simmer until tender. Remove meat. Blend flour with 2 tablespoonfuls water; stir into drippings. Serve with meat. Yield: 3 servings.

Mrs. Judy C. Loving, West End School
West End, North Carolina

BEEF 'N' PINEAPPLE PACKETS

1 14-oz. can pineapple chunks
½ c. chopped onion
1 c. grated carrots
¼ tsp. salt
⅛ tsp. pepper
2 tbsp. melted butter
1 c. soft bread crumbs
2 lb. round steak, cut ¼-in. thick
2 tbsp. shortening
1 tbsp. vinegar
1 beef bouillon cube, crumbled
½ c. water
2 med. tomatoes

Drain pineapple, reserving syrup. Combine one-half the chunks with onion, carrots, salt, pepper, butter and crumbs. Pound meat or score with sharp knife. Cut into six serving pieces. Spread with pineapple stuffing; roll like jelly roll. Tie with string. Sprinkle with additional salt and pepper. Brown rolls on all sides in shortening. Drain off excess fat. Add pineapple syrup, vinegar, bouillon cube and water. Cut tomatoes into wedges; add to meat with remaining pineapple chunks. Simmer for a few minutes. If desired, thicken gravy with 2 teaspoonfuls cornstarch mixed with 1 tablespoonful cold water. Yield: 6 servings.

Wanda M. Stacks, Marshfield H. S.
Marshall, Wisconsin

BEEF ROLL UPS

1 2-lb. round steak, thinly cut
Salt and pepper
8 strips bacon
2 med. onions, cut into fourths
2 stalks celery, cut into 3-in. pieces
1 sm. bunch carrots, cut into 3-in. pieces
Seasoned flour
Fat

Cut steak into 3 x 6-inch pieces. Salt and pepper one side. Place a slice of bacon on each piece of meat; place a fourth of onion, a stick of celery and a carrot stick on top of bacon. Roll up; tie with string. Roll in seasoned flour; brown in a small amount of fat. Add enough water to half cover. Simmer for 1 hour and 30 mintues. Thicken gravy. Yield: 8 servings.

Mrs. I. T. Wetzel, Bangor H. S.
Bangor, Wisconsin

BRAJOAL

1 piece salt pork, 1-in. square
2 tbsp. snipped parsley
Pinch of garlic salt
Pinch of salt and pepper
2 lb. round steak
1 can tomato sauce

Place salt pork on board; sprinkle with parsley and seasonings. Score salt pork with knife until paste consistency. Pound steak to tenderize; cut into 4 x 8-inch strips. Spread steak with salt pork mixture; roll up. Wrap with thread. Saute in a small amount of fat until partially cooked; pour in tomato sauce. Continue cooking for about 1 hour and 30 minutes longer. Remove thread; serve steak with pasta. Yield: 4-6 servings.

Mrs. Betty Jean Flocco, West Allegheny H. S.
Imperial, Pennsylvania

FLANK STEAK WITH APPLE STUFFING

1 tbsp. minced onion
2 tbsp. butter or margarine
1 c. small bread cubes
Salt and pepper
2 c. finely chopped tart apples
Beef stock
1 2 to 2 ½-lb. flank steak
2 tbsp. fat or salad oil
1 c. water

Brown onion in butter; add bread cubes, salt and pepper to taste, apples and enough stock to moisten. Spread steak with mixture; roll up. Tie securely. Seat stead in hot fat or salad oil. Add salt, pepper and water. Cover. Bake at 350 degrees for 2 hours. Yield: 6 servings.

Mrs. Norma Kay Isern, Moore H. S.
Moore, Montana

FLANK STEAK ROAST

1 ½ lb. flank steak
1 tsp. salt
⅛ tsp. pepper
¼ tsp. paprika
4 med. potatoes, sliced
1 med. onion, chopped
3 tbsp. shortening
1 bay leaf
1 ½ c. hot water

(Continued on next page)

Cut deep pocket into side of steak. Combine salt, pepper and paprika; sprinkle one-half seasoning mixture over potatoes with onion on top. Stuff steak with potatoes. Skewer or sew pocket. Place steak in shortening in heavy skillet or Dutch oven with lid. Brown; add remaining seasoning mixture, bay leaf and water. Cover. Bake at 350 degrees for 45 minutes to 1 hour or until tender. Thicken gravy; serve with meat. NOTE: Carrots may be added along with water and seasonings. Yield: 6 servings.

Mrs. Louis Weiss, Sedgwick H. S.
Sedgwick, Colorado

HERB-STUFFED FLANK STEAK

⅓ c. chopped onion
2 tbsp. butter or margarine
2 hard-cooked eggs, chopped
1 c. sour cream
2 c. herb-seasoned croutons
½ c. hot water
1 egg, beaten
1 1-lb. flank steak
Meat tenderizer
2 tbsp. hot fat

Cook onion in butter or margarine until tender. Stir in hard-cooked eggs, 1/4 cup sour cream, croutons, water and beaten egg. Pound steak into thin rectangle. Use tenderizer according to package directions. Spread stuffing over meat; roll up from wide edge. Skewer securely. Brown in hot fat; add 1/2 cup water. Cover; simmer for 1 hour and 30 minutes or until tender. Remove meat. Add water to drippings to make 1/2 cup; stir in remaining sour cream. Heat just to boiling. Serve sauce with meat. Yield: 4 servings.

Mrs. Frances Whited, Toledo H. S.
Toledo, Oregon

MICE

1 1 ½-lb. round steak
1 onion, sliced
2 slices bacon
Ground mustard (opt.)
Salt and pepper to taste
Flour (opt.)
Butter
1 c. water

Cut round steak into 4 x 4-inch pieces. Place a slice of onion, 1/3 slice of bacon, ground mustard, salt and pepper in wedge of steak; roll. Fasten with toothpicks. Dredge steak in flour; brown in butter. Add water. Simmer until done. Yield: 6 servings.

Mrs. Ruth Aurin Jennings, Eufaula H. S.
Eufaula, Alabama
Becky Bahnsen, Reed City H. S.
Reed City, Michigan
Mrs. Margaret Hempel, Lennox Public School
Lennox, South Dakota

PORCUPINES

1 lb. round steak
¼ c. flour
1 tsp. prepared mustard
4 oz. 12-in. spaghetti, broken into halves
1 tsp. salt
⅛ tsp. pepper
¼ c. shortening
1 sm. onion, sliced
1 pt. tomato juice

Cut steak into four pieces; pound flour into steak with side of saucer. Spread meat with mustard on one side. Partially cook spaghetti in salted water. Place one-fourth of spaghetti across each piece of meat. Season meat with salt and pepper; wrap meat around spaghetti. Spaghetti will project 1 1/2 inches from the rolled meat. Tie with string. Brown meat rolls lightly in shortening to bring out the flavor. Arrange rolls in a baking dish; place onion slices over rolls. Pour tomato juice over rolls. Cover. Bake at 325 degrees for 1 hour and 30 minutes to 2 hours. Yield: 4 servings.

Mrs. Helen Goska, West Bend H. S.
West Bend, Wisconsin

ROLLED ROUND STEAK

1 1 to 1 ½-lb. thin round steak
Salt and pepper to taste
Flour
1 clove of garlic, minced
Sliced onion
3 tbsp. margarine
1 ½ c. rye bread crumbs
1 tbsp. parsley flakes
2 8-oz. cans spiced tomato sauce
1 sauce can water

Pound steak; season with salt and pepper. Flour steak on one side. Saute garlic and 1/2 cup onion slices in margarine in skillet. Add crumbs; brown slightly. Add parsley flakes. Place crumb mixture down center of steak; roll up tightly. Secure with string. Brown meat on all sides in large skillet; add tomato sauce, water and 2/3 cup onion slices. Simmer for at least 1 hour. Add additional water as needed. Yield: 4-5 servings.

Mrs. Donald Maeker, Moulton H. S.
Moulton, Texas

ROLLED STEAK

1 round steak, ½-in. thick
Salt
Pepper
Ground cloves
1 ½ c. soft bread crumbs
1 sm. onion, chopped
Milk or hot water
Flour
2 to 3 tbsp. shortening

Wipe steak; sprinkle with salt, pepper and ground cloves. Combine bread crumbs, onion, 1/2 teaspoonful ground cloves, 1/2 teaspoonful salt and 1/4 teaspoonful pepper; moisten with milk.

(Continued on next page)

Spread stuffing over steak; roll up. Tie with string. Dredge in flour; brown slowly on all sides in shortening. Add 1/2 cup water. Cover. Bake at 350 degrees for 1 hour and 30 minutes. Yield: 6-8 servings.

Mrs. Geneva Franklin, Powderly H. S.
Paris, Texas

ROLLED STUFFED ROUND STEAK

3 c. soft bread crumbs
¼ c. chopped onion
¼ c. chopped celery
1 tbsp. chopped parsley
½ tsp. powdered sage
½ tsp. salt
Pepper to taste
⅓ c. soup stock or beef bouillon
1 round steak, ½-in. thick
3 tbsp. fat
¼ c. water

Combine bread crumbs, onion, celery, parsley, seasonings and enough stock to moisten. Spread stuffing on steak; roll like a jelly roll. Tie in several places with string. Brown roll on all sides in fat; add water. Cover tightly. Cook slowly for about 1 hour and 30 minutes or until meat is tender. Remove to platter; make gravy with drippings in pan. Yield: 6-8 servings.

Mrs. Eleanor Roberts
Thompsonville Comm. H. S.
Thompsonville, Illinois

SAUCY BEEF ROULADES CONTINENTAL

1 ½ lb. round steak, thinly sliced
1 ½ c. herb-seasoned stuffing mix
¼ c. finely chopped celery
¼ c. minced onion
2 tbsp. shortening
1 10 ¾-oz. can tomato soup
½ c. water
⅛ tsp. crushed oregano
1 sm. clove of garlic, minced

Pound beef; cut into six long pieces. Combine stuffing, celery and onion; place in center of each beef piece. Roll up and fasten with toothpicks or skewers. Brown beef in shortening in skillet. Pour off fat; add remaining ingredients. Cover; cook over low heat for 1 hour and 30 minutes or until tender. Stir occasionally. Serve on platter garnished with whole green beans and white onions, if desired. Yield: 6 servings.

Mrs. Ronald J. Martin, Lascassas H. S.
Lascassas, Tennessee

STEAK ROLL UPS

Minute steak
Mustard
Salt
Pepper
Bacon
Chopped sweet pickle
Flour
1 c. water
Bay leaf

For each serving, spread a piece of minute steak with mustard; season with salt and pepper. Add 1/2 slice of bacon and chopped pickle; roll up. Fasten with toothpicks. Roll in flour; brown in fat in heavy skillet. When brown, add water and bay leaf. Simmer for 20 to 30 minutes. Add more liquid if needed.

Mrs. Paul Beaty, York Institute
Jamestown, Tennessee

STEAK ROLL UPS

½ c. bread crumbs
¼ tsp. salt
⅛ tsp. pepper
4 pieces cubed steak
3 tbsp. fat
1 can cream of mushroom soup
1 c. water

Combine bread crumbs, salt and pepper; place on steak. Roll up; secure with toothpick. Brown in fat; add soup and water. Simmer for 1 hour. Yield: 4 servings.

Mrs. Betty C. Mullins, Forest Park H. S.
Forest Park, Georgia

STUFFED FLANK STEAK

1 ½ to 2 lb. flank steak
2 tsp. mustard
1 tsp. salt
⅛ tsp. pepper
½ tsp. monosodium glutamate
1 ½ c. soft bread crumbs
1 med. onion, chopped
½ c. chopped celery
¾ tsp. poultry seasoning
¼ c. melted shortening
5 tbsp. flour
3 tbsp. suet
1 c. water or beef broth

Score steak. Spread with mustard; sprinkle with salt, pepper and monosodium glutamate. Toss bread crumbs with onion, celery, poultry seasoning and shortening. Spoon mixture evenly over steak; roll as for a jelly roll. Fasten with small skewers along edge and at ends. Roll steak in 2 tablespoonfuls flour. Melt suet in Dutch oven or small roast pan. Place steak in pan. Brown all sides over medium heat. Add 1/2 cup broth to steak. Cover tightly; cook over low heat for 1 hour and 30 minutes or roast in 350 degree oven for 2 hours. Remove steak from pan. Add remaining broth, flour and 1/2 cup water to make gravy. Yield: 6 servings.

Mrs. Esta Lee Bibb, Dyess H. S.
Dyess, Arkansas

STUFFED FLANK STEAK

1 sm. onion
1 c. bread crumbs
¼ tsp. salt
Pepper to taste
Poultry seasoning to taste
1 flank steak
1 tbsp. cooking oil
1 can cream of mushroom soup or consomme

Slice onion into a saucepan; cover with water. Boil for about 15 to 20 minutes or until tender. Drain; add to crumbs. Mix, cutting onion into small pieces; add salt, pepper and pountry seasoning to taste. Pound steak; score. Place stuffing along one edge of steak. Roll up; anchor with skewers and string. Sear steak in oil in hot pan until brown on all sides. Cover with soup. Cover. Bake at 350 degrees for 1 hour or until tender, basting often. Yield: 3-4 servings.

B. Brown, Ft. Langley Jr. Secondary School
Fort Langley, British Columbia, Canada

STUFFED FLANK STEAK

1 flank steak
1 tsp. unseasoned meat tenderizer
¼ c. flour
½ tsp. salt
Pepper
1 tsp. paprika
2 tbsp. shortening
1 onion, chopped
½ c. chopped celery
2 tbsp. butter
2 c. fresh bread cubes
⅛ tsp. garlic salt
Sage to taste
1 egg, well beaten
1 can beef bouillon

Moisten both sides of steak with water; sprinkle all over with tenderizer. Score diagonally. Sprinkle with mixture of flour, 1/2 teaspoonful salt, 1/8 teaspoon pepper and paprika; rub into meat. Brown meat in shortening. Brown onion and celery in butter; add bread cubes, garlic salt, pepper to taste, sage and egg. Add enough water to slightly moisten. Place on meat; roll up. Tie with string. Pour bouillon into casserole; add meat roll. Cover and bake at 325 degrees for 2 hours. Yield: 3-4 servings.

Patricia McKevitt, Morro Bay Jr.-Sr. H. S.
Morro Bay, California

STUFFED ROUND STEAK

2 to 2 ½ lb. round steak
4 slices bacon, diced
1 onion, chopped
1 ½ c. toasted bread cubes
2 tbsp. minced parsley
½ tsp. celery salt
¼ tsp. sage
½ tsp. salt
⅛ tsp. pepper
1 c. bouillon
1 8-oz. can tomato sauce

Cut steak into five portions. Saute bacon with onion; mix in bread cubes, parsley, celery salt and sage. Sprinkle steak with salt and pepper. Spread each portion of steak with stuffing; roll up. Secure with toothpicks. Place in large skillet. Pour bouillon over steaks. Cover and simmer for 1 hour. Pour in tomato sauce. Cover and simmer for 45 minutes or until done. If gravy is too thin, cook, uncovered, until of desired consistency. Garnish with additional minced parsley, if desired. Yield: 5 servings.

Mrs. Alma Hicks, Elverado H. S.
Elkville, Illinois

STUFFED STEAK

1 round steak
1 egg, beaten
2 tbsp. milk
Flour
1 lge. onion, chopped
12 saltine crackers, crumbled
2 c. gravy
2 c. grated cheese

Cut steak into serving pieces. Combine egg and milk; dip steak into mixture. Roll steak in flour; fry until all sides are browned. Place steak in 11 x 13-inch glass casserole dish; cover with onion, crackers and gravy. Water may be added to cover meat. Sprinkle cheese over top. Bake at 350 degrees for 1 hour. Yield: 6 servings.

Mrs. Ann Schroeder, Texas City H. S.
Texas City, Texas

STUFFED STEAK

1 round steak, 1 ½-in. thick
Salt and pepper to taste
1 c. bread crumbs
¼ c. melted butter
1 med. onion, finely chopped
1 green pepper, finely diced
3 lge. stalks celery, finely chopped

Wipe meat; season with salt and pepper. Combine all remaining ingredients. Lay meat flat; spread with dressing. Roll up, starting with smallest end. Fasten with skewers or toothpicks; tie with heavy string. Brown on all sides; add water. Cover; cook until tender. Yield: 6-8 servings.

Vivian J. Ryland, LaFargue, H. S.
Effie, Louisiana

STUFFED STEAK ROAST

1 2-lb. round steak
1 tsp. salt
½ tsp. pepper
2 c. dry bread crumbs
3 tbsp. grated onion
1 tsp. sage
⅓ c. milk
2 tbsp. catsup
1 egg, beaten

(Continued on next page)

Wipe steak with damp cloth; season with salt and pepper. Combine remaining ingredients; spread on steak. Roll as for jelly roll. Tie with a string. Bake at 350 degrees for 45 minutes to 1 hour. Yield: 4-5 servings.

Mrs. Alma M. Scott, Orland H. S.
Madison, South Dakota

BUSY DAY BAKED DINNER

Round steak, ¾-in. thick
Flour
Salt and pepper
Sliced onion, ½-in. thick
Potatoes
1 can tomatoes

Pound each slice of round steak with flour, salt and pepper; brown in a small amount of fat. Cut steak into serving pieces; place in a baking pan. Place an onion slice and 1 potato on each piece. Sprinkle with salt and pepper; cover with tomatoes. Sprinkle again with salt and pepper. Bake, covered, at 350 degrees for 1 hour and 30 minutes or until fork tender.

Mother Martina, F.C.J.
Immaculate Conception Convent School
Edmonton, Alberta, Canada

CHINESE BEEF SKILLET

2 c. sliced celery
3 tbsp. salad oil
1 lb. minute or sandwich beef steaks, thinly sliced
¼ c. chopped onion
1 sm. clove of garlic
4 c. thinly sliced cauliflowerets
1 c. canned beef broth
2 tbsp. cornstarch
¼ c. soy sauce
½ c. cold water
Hot cooked rice

Pour boiling water over celery; cook for 5 minutes. Drain. Add 2 tablespoonfuls salad oil to preheated 410 degree electric skillet. Add one-half of the beef; cook quickly, turning constantly, for 1 or 2 minutes or until browned. Remove meat. Repeat with remaining beef. Add remaining beef. Add remaining oil; cook onion and garlic for a few seconds. Add cauliflowerets; pour broth over all. Cook, stirring gently, for 3 minutes or until cauliflowerets are crisp. Mix cornstarch, soy sauce and water; stir into skillet. Add beef and celery, stirring constantly until sauce thickens. Serve with rice. Yield: 4-6 servings.

Mrs. Joseph O'Leary, Southbury Training School
Southbury, Connecticut

EASY STEAK DINNER

1 1-lb. round steak, ½-in. thick
¼ c. flour
1 tsp. salt
4 sm. carrots, cut into strips
¼ c. shortening
4 sm. onions
4 sm. potatoes
1 can cream of mushroom soup

Cut steak into 3 x 5-inch pieces; dredge in flour seasoned with salt. Place three or four carrot strips on each piece of steak; wrap around carrots. Fasten with toothpicks. Brown rolls slowly in shortening; add onions and potatoes. Pour mushroom soup over all. Cover. Cook over low heat or simmer for 45 minutes. Yield: 4 servings.

Mrs. Ruth Wingo, Kaufman H. S.
Kaufman, Texas

SWISS STEAK WITH VEGETABLES

1 2½-lb. round steak, ¼-in. thick
½ c. flour
1½ tsp. salt
½ tsp. pepper
¼ c. fat or salad oil
2 c. sliced onions
1½ cans tomato soup
1 soup can water
8 new potatoes
6 carrots, quartered
1 pkg. frozen peas

Cut round steak into eight large pieces. Mix flour, salt and pepper; pound into meat. Brown meat in fat; add onions. Brown. Add soup and water. Cover; simmer until meat is tender. Add potatoes and carrots. Simmer, covered, for 30 minutes. Add additional seasonings, if necessary. Break block of frozen peas in one-half; place halves on each side of meat and vegetables in Dutch oven. Cook for 10 minutes. Yield: 8 servings.

Mrs. Marjorie Dye, Homer Comm. School
Homer, Michigan

BACON-WRAPPED FLANK STEAK

1½ lb. flank steak
1 clove of garlic
Salt and pepper
½ lb. bacon, sliced
Flour
1 sm. onion, chopped
1 sm. can tomato puree

Score flank steak; cut into strips the width of bacon strips. Pound steak strips; rub with clove of garlic. Salt and pepper lightly. Place a strip of uncooked bacon over strip of flank steak; roll up. Secure with a toothpick. Dust rolls with flour; brown in hot fat. Place steak in frying pan with onion and tomato puree. Cover fry pan; simmer for 1 hour. Yield: 6 servings.

Mrs. Luella Tupper, Lakeview H. S.
Battle Creek, Michigan

BEEF CUBES WITH MUSHROOMS

1 sm. can mushrooms
4 tbsp. butter
1 onion, sliced
1 ½ lb. round steak, cubed
6 tbsp. flour
1 tsp. salt
¼ tsp. pepper
6 tbsp. shortening
2 tsp. brown gravy seasoning
1 10 ½-oz. can cream of mushroom soup

Drain mushrooms, reserving liquid. Saute mushrooms in butter for 3 minutes. Remove from pan. Saute onion in butter until brown; remove from pan. Dredge meat cubes in flour seasoned with salt and pepper. Add shortening to frying pan; brown. Sprinkle any remaining flour over meat; add enough water to reserved mushroom liquid to equal 2 cups. Add liquid, seasoning, mushrooms and onion to meat mixture. Cover; simmer for 45 minutes. Add mushroom soup; simmer, covered, for 1 hour longer. Add additional water if needed. Serve over buttered noodles or rice. Yield: 6 servings.

Mrs. Merle Brotherton, Lockney H. S.
Lockney, Texas

BEEF CUBES IN SOUR CREAM

2 lb. beef shank, cut into 1-in. cubes
2 med. onions, sliced
½ c. sour cream
½ c. water
2 tbsp. grated American cheese
Salt and pepper

Roll meat in flour; brown in hot fat. Add onion. Combine remaining ingredients; pour over meat. Cover tightly and cook slowly for 2 hours or until tender. Yield: 6 servings.

Mrs. Ethlyn West, Mercedes H. S.
Mercedes, Texas

BEEF CURRY WITH SOUR CREAM

2 lb. beef steak, cut into 1 ½-in. cubes
2 onions, sliced
1 tbsp. curry powder
Salt and pepper to taste
1 c. red wine
1 c. consomme
½ pt. sour cream
1 tbsp. horseradish

Place beef steak, onions, curry powder, salt, pepper, wine and consomme in a pan; bring to a boil. Bake, covered, at 350 degrees for about 2 hours or until meat is tender. Stir in sour cream and horseradish; do not boil. May be served over buttered noodles or steamed rice. Yield: 8 servings.

Mrs. Dorothy Deare O'Rear, Bellevue H. S.
Bellevue, Washington

BEEF KABOBS

1 c. chili sauce or catsup
2 tsp. vinegar
2 tsp. prepared mustard
1 tbsp. Worcestershire sauce
1 tsp. sugar
1 tsp. salt
1 tbsp. steak sauce
1 tsp. meat tenderizer
2 lb. lean beef, cut into 1-in. cubes

Combine all ingredients except beef. Heat sauce to boiling; cool. Pour sauce over beef; marinate. Place beef on skewers 1-inch apart. Broil until brown on both sides. Yield: 4 servings.

Mrs. Claire Shaw, Southern H. S.
Durham, North Carolina

BEEF ON RICE

2 lb. stew meat
2 tbsp. dry onion flakes
Salt and pepper to taste
2 tbsp. Worcestershire sauce
1 can cream of mushroom soup
1 can cream of celery soup
1 soup can water
3 c. cooked rice

Brown meat in heavy skillet; add remaining ingredients except rice. Simmer for 1 hour, adding additional water, if needed. Serve over hot rice. Yield: 6 servings.

Mrs. Layne M. Storment, Kahlotus H. S.
Kahlotus, Washington

BEEF STEW BOURBONNAIS

1 ½ lb. chuck, cut into 1-in. cubes
1 tbsp. shortening
1 clove of garlic, minced
1 med. onion, chopped
½ tsp. salt
⅛ tsp. pepper
1 can tomato soup
¾ c. red wine
¼ c. water
¼ tsp. powdered basil
¼ tsp. powdered thyme
½ c. catsup
3 med. carrots, cut into ½-in. pieces
1 ½ c. celery, cut into 1-in. pieces diagonally
4 med. potatoes, pared and quartered

Lightly brown beef in shortening. Add garlic and onion; saute until transparent. Sprinkle with salt and pepper. Stir in soup, wine and water. Cover and simmer for 30 minutes. Add herbs and catsup. Arrange vegetables on top of meat and in gravy. Cover and simmer for 1 hour and 30 minutes or until meat and vegetables are tender, adding more water if necessary. NOTE: One-half cup lemon juice may be substituted for red wine. Increase water from 1/4 to 3/4 cup. Yield: 4-6 servings.

Michele M. Mixon, Central Jr. H. S.
Eau Gallie, Florida

BEEF STEAK BUNDLES

1 lb. round steak
3 c. cooked rice
1 pkg. dry onion soup mix
½ c. evaporated milk
4 tsp. butter

Cut steak into 1 x 3-inch strips. Place 3/4 cup rice in center of each of four 8 x 12-inch pieces of foil. Sprinkle 1 tablespoonful onion soup mix over each; place steak on rice. Pour 2 tablespoonfuls evaporated milk over each. Add 1 tablespoonful butter to each. Bring foil together; fold tightly. Bake at 350 degrees for 1 hour. Serve in foil. Yield: 4-5 servings.

Marion Drew, Gardiner H. S.
Gardiner, Montana

BEEF TIPS NAPOLI

3 lb. boneless chuck, rump or lean stew beef
1 tsp. salt
¼ tsp. pepper
2 tbsp. cooking oil
2 6-oz. cans tomato paste
1 ½ c. water
2 tbsp. lemon juice
½ tsp. sugar
1 tsp. marjoram or oregano
1 sm. carrot, thinly sliced
⅛ tsp. garlic powder
1 pkg. sea shell or elbow macaroni, cooked and drained
¼ c. grated Parmesan cheese
2 tbsp. parsley

Cut beef into 1 1/2 to 2-inch cubes; sprinkle with salt and pepper. Brown meat in oil in large skillet. Mix tomato paste in water; mix in lemon juice, sugar, marjoram, carrot and garlic. Pour over meat; cover. Simmer for 1 hour and 30 minutes to 2 hours or until beef is tender. Add additional water, if sauce is too thick. Add additional salt to taste. Serve with macaroni blended with Parmesan cheese and parsley. Yield: 6 servings.

Mrs. G. Bruner, Valier H. S.
Valier, Montana

BONELESS BIRDS

1 ½ lb. round steak
Salt and pepper
1 onion, chopped
Bacon strips
Shortening
1 tbsp. flour
1 pt. boiling water

Pound steak; sprinkle with salt and pepper. Cut into 4-inch squares. Place some onion and a half strip of bacon on each square. Roll and fasten with two toothpicks. Brown in shortening. Add flour; stir until browned. Add boiling water and salt and pepper to taste. Cover and simmer for 2 hours. Serve hot. Yield: 4 servings.

Mrs. Hannah Hoff Brown
Consultant Homemaking Education
Texas Education Agency, Waco, Texas

BRAISED BEEF

1 lb. boneless stew beef
½ tsp. salt
¼ tsp. pepper
¼ c. flour
3 tbsp. corn oil
1 tbsp. instant minced onion
1 tbsp. red wine vinegar
2 tbsp. water
½ tsp. Beau Monde seasoning

Sprinkle meat with salt and pepper; sprinkle flour over meat, coating each piece thoroughly. Brown quickly in hot oil. Place meat in baking dish; sprinkle with onion, vinegar, water and Beau Monde seasoning. Cover and bake at 325 degrees for 1 hour and 30 minutes. Yield: 4 servings.

Nancy B. Tyler, Boswell H. S.
Saginaw, Texas

BROWN STEW

2 lb. chuck or stew meat, cut into 1 ½-in. cubes
2 tbsp. fat
4 c. boiling water
1 to 3 tsp. lemon juice
1 tsp. Worcestershire sauce
1 clove of garlic, minced
1 med. onion, sliced
1 to 2 bay leaves (opt.)
1 tbsp. salt
½ tsp. pepper
½ tsp. paprika
Dash of allspice or cloves (opt.)
1 tsp. sugar
Small onions
Celery (opt.)
Carrots
Potatoes
Peas (opt.)
1 can stewed tomatoes (opt.)

Thoroughly brown meat on all sides in hot fat; add water, lemon juice, Worcestershire sauce, garlic, sliced onion and seasonings. Simmer for 2 hours, stirring occasionally. Add vegetables. Cook until vegetables are done, about 30 minutes. Remove meat and vegetables; thicken liquid for gravy. Add meat and vegetables to gravy; carefully blend. Heat for a few minutes. NOTE: Other vegetables may be used. Yield: 6-8 servings.

Mrs. Edna B. Hughes, Goshen Central School
Goshen, New York
Mrs. Charlene Clute, Tolna H. S.
Tolna, North Dakota
Mrs. Ruth F. Gamble, Northern Potter School
Ulysses, Pennsylvania
Mrs. Azalee S. Bowtin, Dacusville H. S.
Daucusville, South Carolina
Mrs. Ruth Riffe, Hobart H. S.
Hobart, Oklahoma

CROCKED STEAK

2 lb. flank steak
1 c. beef consomme

(Continued on next page)

⅓ c. soy sauce
1 ½ tsp. salt
¼ c. grated onion and tops
1 clove of garlic, minced and mashed
3 tbsp. lime juice
2 tbsp. brown sugar

Cut meat into 1-inch diagonal strips. Combine all remaining ingredients. Marinate meat in mixture in refrigerator for 24 hours. Turn occasionally while marinating. Barbecue meat for 2 to 4 minutes on each side, turning only once; brush with marinade while cooking. Yield: 5-6 servings.

Jean Penrose, Juneau H. S.
Juneau, Alaska

DEVILED BEEF STEW

2 tbsp. flour
1 tsp. salt
Dash of paprika
1 ½ lb. stew beef, cubed
1 c. minced onions
2 tbsp. melted butter
1 bouillon cube
1 ½ c. boiling water
1 tsp. prepared mustard
2 tsp. horseradish
½ c. sour cream

Mix flour with salt and paprika. Roll cubed beef in flour mixture. Saute onions in butter. Remove onions; set aside. Brown meat. Dissolve bouillon cube in boiling water; pour over meat. Add onions, mustard and horseradish. Cook at 15 pounds pressure in pressure cooker for 15 minutes. Let cool gradually. Stir in sour cream; serve over rice or toast, if desired. Yield: 4 servings.

Mrs. Wilma Sonne, Plankinton H. S.
Plankinton, South Dakota

EASY INDOOR SHISH KABOBS

½ lb. round steak, cut into squares
½ c. water
½ c. spicy French dressing
1 tsp. salt
1 tsp. pepper
4 sm. white onions
2 green peppers
4 sm. tomatoes
8 lge. mushrooms
8 sm. red potatoes, precooked

Marinate steak in water and dressing for 2 hours or longer. Sprinkle with salt and pepper. Arrange meat, onions, peppers, tomatoes, mushrooms and potatoes on long skewers. Set skewers under medium heated broiler; turn occasionally to allow even baking. Broil for 25 minutes. Yield: 4 servings.

Mrs. Carol Bishop, Manteno H. S.
Manteno, Illinois

GOULASH

1 ½ lb. stew meat, diced
½ c. onion, sliced
1 beef bouillon cube
1 c. hot water
1 can tomato sauce
1 sm. can mushrooms
3 tbsp. shortening
2 tsp. sugar
1 tsp. marjoram
1 tsp. salt
Dash of pepper
Garlic salt (opt.)
2 tbsp. Worcestershire sauce

Brown meat and onion. Dissolve bouillon cube in water; add with all remaining ingredients to meat mixture. Bake at 240 degrees for 2 hours and 30 minutes to 3 hours. Serve over egg noodles. Yield: 6 servings.

Mrs. Flo Brame, Lake Air Jr. H. S.
Waco, Texas

HUNGARIAN GOULASH

¼ c. butter
2 lb. steak trimmings
1 lb. onions, sliced
2 tsp. paprika
1 c. stewed tomatoes
1 c. beef stock
1 clove of garlic
Slice of lemon
½ tsp. caraway seed
2 tbsp. flour
1 lb. uncooked noodles

Melt butter in heavy pot; add steak trimmings and onions. Cook until onions are transparent; add paprika and tomatoes. Add beef stock. Chop garlic and lemon peel; Add to onion mixture with caraway seed. Simmer for about 45 minutes to 1 hour. Thicken with 2 tablespoonfuls additional butter and flour. Cook noodles according to package directions. Serve sauce over noodles. Yield: 4-6 servings.

Mrs. Richard Haas, Memorial Jr. H. S.
Millville, New Jersey

HUNGARIAN GOULASH

1 ½ lb. stew beef or round steak, cut into cubes
2 tbsp. fat
1 tsp. salt
1 tsp. pepper
2 tbsp. flour
1 No. 303 can stewed tomatoes
¼ c. orange juice concentrate
1 c. water
2 tbsp. pickling spices
1 med. onion, sliced (opt.)
2 tbsp. chopped green pepper (opt.)

(Continued on next page)

Brown meat in fat; season with salt and pepper. Sprinkle flour over meat; brown. Cover meat with tomatoes, orange juice and water. Make a spice bag by tying pickling spices in 3-inch square of muslin; place spice bag in liquid. Simmer for 2 hour to 2 hours and 30 minutes or until meat is tender. Add onion and green pepper; cook until done. Remove spice bag before serving. NOTE: Potatoes may be added to liquid with meat, if desired. Yield: 6-8 servings.

Mrs. Dora Clark Fleming, Centerville H. S.
Sand Coulee, Montana

ONE-POT MEAL

2 lb. boneless stew meat
2 tbsp. shortening
6 to 8 carrots, peeled and cut into quarters
6 med. Irish potatoes, peeled and cubed
1 lge. onion
1 tsp. salt
½ tsp. pepper
1 c. water

Brown meat in skillet in shortening; place in bottom of pot. Place carrots over meat; cover with potatoes. Place onion in center. Sprinkle with seasonings; add water. Cook for 1 hour or until tender. Yield: 6-8 servings.

Mrs. B. K. Sanders, Goldonna H. S.
Goldonna, Louisiana

PEPPER STEAK

1 ½ lb. round steak
¾ tsp. meat tenderizer
3 tbsp. salad oil
2 lge. green peppers, cut into 1-in. squares
1 ½ c. sliced celery
3 onions, thinly sliced
1 tbsp. cornstarch
1 ½ c. bouillon
3 tbsp. soy sauce
¾ tsp. salt
1 tsp. garlic salt
1 ½ tsp. monosodium glutamate
1 ½ tsp. ginger
2 tsp. lemon juice
1 sm. can mushroom steak sauce

Cut steak into thin, long slices; sprinkle with tenderizer. Heat oil in skillet over high heat. Add beef slices and cook until brown. Simmer until tender. Add peppers, celery and onions. Cover and cook for 15 minutes. Blend cornstarch with a small amount of water; stir in remaining ingredients. Cook slowly until well blended. Serve with chow mein noodles or rice, if desired. Yield: 6-8 servings.

Mrs. Verna Lensink, Hosterman Jr. H. S.
Minneapolis, Minnesota

SANTA ROSA STEAK

1 c. condensed beef bouillon
1 c. tomato sauce
¼ c. salad oil
2 tbsp. lemon juice
1 tbsp. minced onion
1 tsp. salt
1 tsp. sugar
1 tsp. basil
1 tsp. paprika
1 2-lb. chuck roast, cut into 2-in. strips

Combine all ingredients except roast in a 2-quart pan; simmer for 10 minutes. Cool. Pour cooled marinade over meat; refrigerate overnight. Bake meat in marinade at 325 degrees for 1 hour and 30 minutes. Serve. Yield: 4 servings.

Mrs. Donna Rasmussen, Middle School
Milliken, Colorado

SAUERBRATEN

1 2-lb. rump steak, 2-in. thick
½ c. butter or margarine, melted
1 med. onion, sliced
1 c. red wine
1 tbsp. flour
1 c. beef broth or 1 can consomme

Cut meat into 2-inch squares. Brown meat well in hot butter with onion. Remove meat; add flour to pan. Brown. Add beef broth and 3/4 cup wine; stir until well mixed. Return meat to pan; cover. Cook over low heat for 2 hours to 2 hours and 30 minutes or until tender. Add remaining wine; heat. Serve with potato dumplings or noodles. Yield: 6 servings.

Mrs. Chelsea A. Merritt, Tollesboro H. S.
Tollesboro, Kentucky

ROUND STEAK SAUERBRATEN

1 ½ lb. round steak, ½-in. thick
1 tbsp. fat
1 envelope brown gravy mix
2 c. water
1 tbsp. instant minced onion
2 tbsp. wine vinegar
2 tbsp. brown sugar
½ tsp. salt
¼ tsp. pepper
1 tsp. Worcestershire sauce
1 bay leaf
Hot buttered noodles

Cut meat into 1-inch cubes. Brown meat on all sides in hot fat in large skillet; remove meat from skillet. Add gravy mix and water; bring to a boil, stirring constantly. Stir in remaining ingredients, except noodles. Return meat to skillet; cover and simmer for 1 hour and 30 minutes, stirring occasionally. Remove bay leaf. Serve meat over hot buttered noodles. Yield: 5-6 servings.

Mrs. Marilyn M. Hallisey, Pacifica H. S.
Pittsburg, California

SHERRIED BEEF

3 lb. stew beef
1 can cream of mushroom soup
½ pkg. dry onion soup mix
⅔ c. Sherry

Place beef in a casserole; cover with all remaining ingredients. Cover with aluminum foil; do not seal. Bake at 350 degrees for 3 hours. Yield: 5 servings.

Mrs. Eloise Hearin, Thomas Edison Jr. H. S.
Springfield, Illinois

STEAK BITES

Seasoned meat tenderizer
4 lb. sirloin
1 clove of garlic, split
1 c. cooking Sherry
½ c. margarine
1 tbsp. dry mustard
½ tsp. garlic salt
1 tbsp. Worcestershire sauce
⅛ tsp. pepper
⅛ tsp. Tabasco sauce
1 tbsp. liquid smoke
1 sm. can mushroom steams, undrained

Season sirloin with tenderizer; rub with cut garlic on both sides. Marinate for 30 minutes on each side in cooking Sherry. Reserve marinade. Broil steak, medium well done and cut into bite-sized pieces. Combine 1/3 cup marinade with remaining ingredients; pour over meat. Heat and serve in chafing dish, if desired. NOTE: Steak and sauce may be made the day before serving and heated just before serving. Yield: 5 servings.

Mrs. Pattye Warren, Oxford H. S.
Oxford, Mississippi

BEEF STROGANOFF

1 lb. round steak, 1-in. thick
Flour
Butter
1 tbsp. instant onion
1 med. can mushrooms
1 ½ tsp. soy sauce
1 ½ tsp. Worcestershire sauce
1 tsp. salt
1 ½ c. uncooked rice
1 carton sour cream
Paprika

Cut beef into thin strips; dip in flour. Brown in butter. Place beef in pan with onion, mushrooms, soy sauce, Worcestershire sauce and salt; cover. Simmer until tender. Cook rice in 2 1/2 cups boiling salted water. Pile rice into center of serving dish. Remove meat mixture from heat; add sour cream. Stir until mixed. Arrange meat mixture around rice; dust with paprika. Garnish with parsley or sliced peppers, if desired.

Mrs. Ila Mitchell, Biggs Union H. S.
Biggs, California

BEEF STROGANOFF

8 oz. mushrooms
1 lge. onion, sliced
4 tbsp. butter
1 c. flour
½ tsp. salt
½ tsp. monosodium glutamate
⅛ tsp. pepper
2 lb. flank or round steak, cut into ½-in. pieces
1 tbsp. horseradish
1 tbsp. chili sauce
½ c. water
1 pt. sour cream

Saute mushrooms and onion in butter; remove from pan. Combine flour, salt, monosodium glutamate and pepper in a paper bag. Add meat; shake until well coated. Brown meat in remaining butter in skillet; cover with mushrooms and onion. Dot with horseradish and chili sauce. Add water; simmer until meat is tender. Add additional water, as needed. Cook, covered, over low heat for 2 hours and 30 minutes to 3 hours. Thirty minutes before serving, stir in sour cream. Serve over rice, if desired. Yield: 6 servings.

Mrs. Evelyn Gose Owens, Valley H. S.
Albuquerque, New Mexico

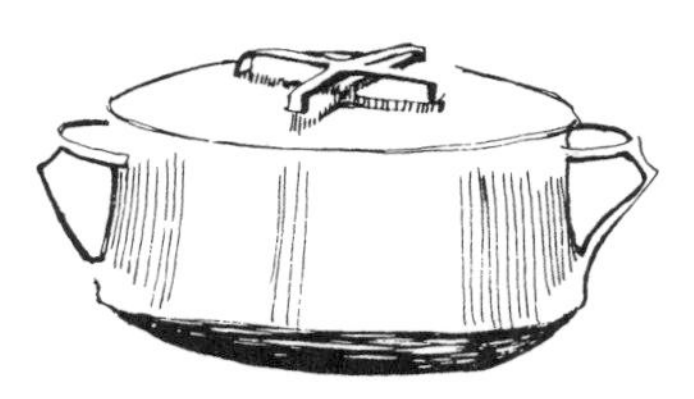

BEEF STROGANOFF

1 lb. onions, thinly sliced
2 lb. top round, cut into strips
¾ c. butter
1 tbsp. chopped parsley
1 tbsp. dry mustard
1 tsp. salt
¼ tsp. pepper
2 bay leaves
1 c. sour cream
1 tbsp. flour

Saute onions slowly in 1/2 cup butter until a light golden brown. Saute strips of top round in remaining butter long enough for meat to lose red color; add onions, parsley, dry mustard, salt, pepper, bay leaves and 1 tablespoonful sour cream. Simmer gently over low heat for about 1 hour or until meat is done. Sprinkle with flour; add remaining sour cream. Continue cooking over very low heat until mixed. Serve over noodles or rice as desired. Yield: 6-8 servings.

Mary Ella Ingram, Wagram H. S.
Wagram, North Carolina

DELICIOUS STROGANOFF

1 lb. round steak, cut into ¾-in. squares
¼ c. flour
½ tsp. salt
⅛ tsp. pepper
4 tbsp. shortening
½ c. chopped onion
½ c. diced green pepper
1 6-oz. can mushrooms
1 clove of garlic, finely chopped
1 No. 2 ½ can tomatoes
1 tbsp. Worcestershire sauce
¼ tsp. Tabasco sauce
1 c. thick sour cream

Dredge meat in flour seasoned with salt and pepper in paper sack. Turn control on electric skillet to 360 degrees to melt shortening. Brown meat on all sides. Add all remaining ingredients except sour cream; mix thoroughly. Cover; continue cooking at 360 degrees until steam escapes; reduce heat to 220 degrees. Cook for 35 minutes longer. Just before serving, stir in sour cream. Heat; do not boil. Serve over steamed rice. Yield: 8-10 servings.

Mrs. Betty Wilson, Panama H. S.
Panama, Oklahoma

DIFFERENT STROGANOFF

2 lb. beef chunks
1 tbsp. fat
2 sm. onions, minced
2 tsp. salt
Dash of pepper
1 or 2 cartons sour cream
1 c. diced American or Cheddar cheese

Brown meat in fat; add remaining ingredients except sour cream and cheese. Cover and cook until done, about 1 hour. Add sour cream and cheese. Cook 10 minutes longer. Serve over rice or mashed potatoes, if desired. Yield: 8-10 servings.

Mrs. Carolyn Dolton, Dunlap H. S.
Dunlap, Illinois

EASY BEEF STROGANOFF

½ c. chopped or sliced onion
1 to 1 ½ lb. round steak, cut into strips
¼ c. butter or margarine
1 can cream of mushroom soup
¼ c. water (opt.)
½ to 1 c. sour cream
1 tsp. paprika (opt.)
Salt and pepper to taste

Brown onion and beef in melted butter; add remaining ingredients. Simmer for 45 minutes to 1 hour. Serve over hot cooked noodles, if desired. Yield: 4 servings.

Mrs. Jacqueline Fanning, Omak Jr. H. S.
Omak, Washington
Mary Virginia Wood, Bluestone H. S.
Skipwith, Virginia

ELEGANT BEEF STROGANOFF

1 lb. sirloin steak, cut into sm. pieces
1 sm. onion, sliced (opt.)
1 can sliced mushrooms
1 can beef bouillon
Salt and pepper
1 c. sour cream
4 tbsp. cooking Sherry

Brown beef and onion in butter; add mushrooms and bouillon. Simmer until tender. Season with salt and pepper. Add sour cream and Sherry; heat thoroughly. Serve over hot fluffy rice. NOTE: Two tablespoonfuls flour may be added, if a thicker sauce is desired. Yield: 4 servings.

Tina Butler, Brantley H. S.
Beantley, Alabama

ELEGANT BEEF STROGANOFF

1 lb. sirloin steak, ½-in. thick
1 clove of garlic, minced
1 med. onion, chopped
2 tbsp. shortening
¼ c. flour
½ tsp. salt
¼ tsp. pepper
1 c. undrained sliced mushrooms
6 tbsp. catsup
1 c. beef bouillon
1 c. sour cream
Cooked rice
Poppy seed

Cut steak into 2-inch square pieces. Saute garlic and onion in shortening; remove from skillet. Dredge beef in mixture of flour, salt and pepper; brown evenly over low heat. Return onion and garlic to skillet; add mushrooms, catsup and bouillon. Cover lightly and cook over low heat for 1 hour or until meat is tender, stirring occasionally. Add additional bouillon if mixture becomes too thick. Add sour cream; mix thoroughly. Serve immediately over hot rice sprinkled with poppy seed. Yield: 4 servings.

Mrs. James D. Skaggs, Bowling Green H. S.
Bowling Green, Kentucky

FAVORITE BEEF STROGANOFF

1 ½ lb. round steak, cut into strips
¼ c. flour
Dash of pepper
¼ c. butter or margarine
1 4-oz. can sliced mushrooms, drained
½ c. chopped onion
1 sm. clove of garlic, minced
1 10 ½-oz. can beef consomme
1 c. sour cream
3 c. cooked noodles

Dust meat with flour and pepper. Brown meat in butter in skillet. Add mushrooms, onion and garlic; brown lightly. Stir in consomme; cover. Cook for 1 hour or until meat is tender, stirring often. Gradually blend in sour cream; cook over

(Continued on next page)

low heat for 5 minutes longer. Serve over noodles. Yield: 4 servings.

Cathy Prihar, Bridgeport H. S.
Bridgeport, Washington

BEEF STROGANOFF

1 1-lb. sirloin or round steak, ¼-in. thick
1 clove of garlic, peeled and cut
3 to 4 tbsp. flour
1 ½ to 1 ¾ tsp. salt
⅛ to ¼ tsp. pepper
1 tsp. paprika (opt.)
4 to 6 tbsp. shortening
½ c. chopped onion
1 can consomme or cream of mushroom soup
¼ to 1 lb. mushrooms, sliced (opt.)
¼ to ½ c. water
½ to 1 c. sour cream
2 tbsp. finely chopped chives or green onion tops
Chopped parsley or dill (opt.)

Rub both sides of meat with garlic; cut into 1 1/2 x 1-inch strips. Mix flour, salt, pepper and paprika. Add meat strips; toss lightly until strips are coated. Reserve remaining flour mixture. Heat shortening in heavy skillet; add meat. Brown well. Add onion; cook until transparent. Add reserved flour mixture, consomme, mushrooms and water; cover. Cook slowly, stirring occasionally, for 45 minutes to 1 hour and 30 minutes or until meat is tender. Remove cover; continue cooking until mixture is slightly thickened. Add sour cream and chives; blend. Serve with rice or wide noodles, if desired. Garnish with parsley. Yield: 6 servings.

Mrs. Martha Wilson, St. Joseph Ogden H. S.
St. Joseph, Illinois
Elda Kaufman, Central Jr. H. S.
Clifton, Illinois
Mrs. Jean P. Driver, Ft. Defiance H. S.
Ft. Defiance, Virginia

CONTINENTAL STROGANOFF

1 lb. round steak, cut into thin strips
1 4-oz. can sliced mushrooms, drained
2 tbsp. butter or margarine
1 can dry onion soup mix
2 tbsp. flour
1 c. milk
1 c. water
½ c. sour cream
3 c. cooked noodles
½ c. finely chopped parsley

Brown meat and mushrooms in butter; add soup mix and flour. Gradually stir in milk and water to blend. Cover; cook over low heat for 45 minutes or until tender. Stir occasionally. Blend in sour cream; heat. Serve over noodles. Sprinkle with parsley. Yield: 4 servings.

Mrs. Gladys Nichols, San Benito H. S.
San Benito, Texas

BEEF STROGANOFF

2 lb. round steak
1 med. onion, sliced
1 c. sour cream
1 tsp. salt

Cut meat into 1 x 2 x 1/2-inch strips; brown with onion. Place meat and onion in baking dish. Season. Roast at 350 degrees for 1 hour and 30 minutes. Pour sour cream over top 30 minutes before removing from oven. Yield: 8-10 servings.

Mrs. Evelyn Altendorf, Warren H. S.
Warren, Minnesota

STROGANOFF

1 lb. beef tenderloin, top round or sirloin, ¼-in. thick
4 to 6 tbsp. flour
½ to 2 ½ tsp. salt
¼ tsp. pepper (opt.)
½ c. finely chopped onion
1 tsp. garlic powder or 1 clove of garlic, finely chopped
½ lb. mushrooms, sliced
¼ c. butter, melted
¾ to 1 ¼ c. beef bouillon
2 to 3 tbsp. Sherry
2 tbsp. Worcestershire sauce (opt.)
1 tbsp. tomato paste
¼ c. sliced stuffed green olives (opt.)
1 c. sour cream

Cut meat into 1/2 to 2-inch strips. Combine 1/4 cup flour, 1 1/2 teaspoonfuls salt and pepper. Dredge meat in flour mixture. Saute onion, garlic and mushrooms in butter for several minutes; add meat. Brown meat on both sides. Remove meat from pan; keep warm. Stir remaining flour into vegetables and drippings; add bouillon slowly. Add Sherry, Worcestershire sauce, tomato paste, olives and remaining salt. Cook until thick, stirring constantly. Add sour cream, a small amount at a time; heat slowly until sauce simmers. Add beef; heat. Yield: 5 servings.

Darlene F. Nauman
Henry-Senachwine Consolidated H. S.
Henry, Illinois
Mrs. Patricia L. Teske, Central Jr. H. S.
Lovington, New Mexico

STROGANOFF

2 lb. lean beef cubes, cut into 1-in. cubes
½ lb. butter
1 onion, diced
1 c. sliced mushrooms
Dash of Tabasco sauce
1 tbsp. Worcestershire sauce
½ green pepper, chopped
1 clove of garlic, diced
1 tbsp. garlic salt
½ can beef sonsomme
1 c. sour cream
1 c. heavy cream
2 tbsp. flour (opt.)
Thin noodles

(Continued on next page)

Saute beef cubes in butter until meat begins to brown. Add onion, mushrooms, Tabasco sauce, Worcestershire sauce, green pepper, garlic and garlic salt. Cook until vegetables begin to soften; add consomme. Cook until beef is fork tender. Add sour cream and heavy cream just before serving. Add flour to thicken, if needed. Cook noodles until tender; drain. Serve stroganoff over noodles. Garnish with parsley or Mandarin orange slices, if desired. Yield: 4 servings.

Mrs. Joanna Partain, Round Rock H. S.
Round Rock, Texas

STROGANOFF

2 lb. beef
Salt and pepper
1 tbsp. flour
5 tbsp. butter
2 c. beef stock
1 carton heavy sour cream
2 tbsp. tomato juice or paste
3 tbsp. grated onion

Cut beef into thin strips; sprinkle with salt and pepper. Let stand for 2 hours in cool place. Blend flour into 2 tablespoonfuls melted butter. Cook over low heat until mixture bubbles and is smooth. Gradually stir beef stock. Cook until mixture begins to thicken. Boil for 2 minutes; strain into saucepan. Add sour cream alternately with tomato juice, stirring constantly. Simmer very gently. Brown beef in remaining butter with onion. Pour into sauce. Taste for seasoning. Simmer gently for 20 minutes. Yield: 10 servings.

Mrs. W. J. Haire, Newman H. S.
Newman, Illinois

STROGANOFF

1 sm. onion, chopped
4 tbsp. olive oil
2 lb. chuck, cut into strips
1 lb. fresh mushrooms, sliced
1 sm. can tomato paste
1 paste can water
1 ½ tsp. salt
⅛ tsp. pepper
½ tsp. Tabasco sauce
1 tsp. Worcestershire sauce
½ pt. sour cream

Saute onion in 2 tablespoonfuls olive oil. Add beef; saute for about 5 minutes. Remove from pan. Add remaining olive oil to pan; saute sliced mushrooms until tender. Add meat, tomato paste, water and seasonings. Cover pan; simmer for 2 hours. Place in casserole; add hot sour cream. May be served with cooked noodles. Yield: 6-8 servings.

Mrs. Anne Stalter, Riverside Park Jr. H. S.
Springfield, Vermont

TERIYAKI STEAK

1 lb. round steak
½ c. oil
½ c. wine or wine vinegar
Meat tenderizer
Salt and pepper to taste

Slice steak into strips 2-inches long and 1/4-inch wide, diagonally across grain of meat. Place in shallow, flat pan. Combine remaining ingredients; pour over meat. Marinate for at least 2 to 3 hours. Drain. Place in frying pan. Panbroil meat for 5 to 10 minutes. Yield: 4 servings.

Mrs. Lenice Chase, Clarksburg H. S.
Clarksburg, California

TERIYAKI

3 lb. round or sirloin steak
½ c. soy sauce
2 tbsp. brown sugar
1 clove of garlic
1 sm. piece ginger root or ½ tsp. ground ginger

Freeze meat for 1 hour; slice thinly across grain. Combine remaining ingredients; marinate meat in sauce for 30 minutes. Drain. Place on broiler rack 4-inches from broiling unit; broil for 7 to 9 minutes. Turn and brown other side. Serve immediately. Yield: 6 servings.

Mrs. Kathryn Whitten, Hanford H. S.
Hanford, California

TERIYAKI KABOB PUPUS

1 lb. sirloin steak, ¾-in. thick
1 can pineapple chunks
¼ c. soy sauce
½ tsp. sugar
½ to 1 tsp. grated ginger root or ¼ tsp. ground ginger
1 clove of garlic, grated
25 water chestnuts
25 stuffed green olives

Cut steak into 25 cubes. Drain pineapple, reserving 1/2 cup syrup. Mix reserved syrup, soy sauce, sugar, ginger and garlic. Add meat cubes; marinate for 1 hour, turning occasionally. Place 1 cube of meat, 1 chunk of pineapple and 1 water chestnut on each bamboo stick. Broil 3 inches from heat for 5 minutes; turn and broil for 5 minutes or until browned. Garnish end of stick with olives. Serve piping hot. Yield: 5 servings.

Bernice Delano, Toppenish H. S.
Toppenish, Washington

VENETIAN BEEF PIE

CRUST:

1 ½ c. flour
1 tsp. garlic

(Continued on next page)

1 tsp. leaf oregano
¼ c. grated Parmesan or Romano cheese
½ c. butter
4 to 5 tbsp. cold water

Sift flour with garlic; add oregano and grated cheese. Cut in butter until crumbly. Sprinkle water over mixture, stirring with fork until dough holds together. Roll out two-thirds of dough onto floured surface to an 11-inch circle; fit into pan.

MEAT FILLING:

1 lb. round steak, cubed
½ c. flour
¼ c. butter
2 c. tomato sauce
¼ c. chopped onion
3 tbsp. grated Parmesan or Romano cheese
1 tbsp. sugar
1 tsp. sweet basil
½ tsp. salt
½ tsp. oregano
½ tsp. garlic
⅛ tsp. pepper
4 slices Cheddar cheese

Coat steak with flour; brown in butter. Stir in all remaining ingredients except Cheddar cheese; cover. Simmer for 30 minutes or until meat is tender. Turn into pastry-lined pan; top with cheese slices. Roll out remaining dough 1/8-inch thick. Cut into 2-inch rounds; place on cheese overlapping slightly. Flute edges. Bake at 400 degrees for 30 to 40 minutes or until golden brown. Yield: 6-8 servings.

Mrs. Jeanette Knox, Decatur H. S.
Decatur, Alabama

WESTERN SPAGHETTI

1 ½ lb. round steak, cubed
5 c. tomato juice
2 c. water
1 tsp. salt
⅛ tsp. pepper
½ c. sliced onion
½ c. sliced stuffed olives
½ c. ripe pitted olives
1 8-oz. pkg. spaghetti
2 c. cubed cheese

Brown beef; add tomato juice and water. Simmer until the meat is tender. Add salt, pepper, onion, olives and spaghetti. Cook until spaghetti is tender. Add cheese; toss until melted. Yield: 6-8 servings.

Emily Truitt Duley, Frederick Sasscer H. S.
Upper Marlboro, Maryland

BAKED VEAL CHOPS

4 veal chops
Salt and pepper to taste
1 egg, beaten
2 slices bread, crumbled
1 med. onion, sliced
1 10 ½-oz. can tomato soup
½ soup can water
1 tsp. oregano

Sprinkle chops with salt and pepper. Dip each chop first in egg. Dip in bread crumbs. Brown slowly on both sides in skillet. Place chops in baking dish with onion slices on top. Mix tomato soup with water and heat until blended; add oregano, salt and pepper. Pour sauce over chops. Bake at 350 degrees for 30 minutes. Yield: 4 servings.

Mrs. Betty Barnes, Beulah H. S.
River View, Alabama

CHERRIED VEAL CHOPS

6 rib veal chops
¾ tsp. salt
Onion salt to taste
3 tbsp. shortening
1 1-lb. 6-oz. can cherry pie filling
½ c. orange juice
3 tbsp. Sherry (opt.)
¼ tsp. dry mustard
¼ tsp. ground ginger
2 tbsp. orange rind
1 8-oz. pkg. broad noodles

Sprinkle chops with salt and onion salt; brown well on both sides in hot shortening in large skillet, turning as needed. Remove from skillet. Gently blend cherry pie filling with orange juice, Sherry, mustard and ginger; pour into a bowl through strainer, separating sauce from cherries. Return chops to skillet; cover with cherry sauce. Sprinkle with one-half of orange rind. Simmer, covered, for 30 minutes or until tender; stir occasionally to prevent scorching. Cook noodles in boiling salted water until tender; drain. Arrange hot noodles on platter; top with veal chops. Fold cherries back into sauce mixture with remaining rind; heat through. Spoon over chops and noodles. Yield: 3-6 servings.

Mrs. Adele Rummell Viales, Alisal H. S.
Salinas, California

VEAL CHOPS DELUXE

4 veal loin chops
Shortening
4 slices onion
4 slices apples

Brown loin chops in a small amount of shortening. On each chop, place 1 slice of onion and 1 thick slice of apple; let simmer-until tender. Yield: 4 servings.

Ella Bang, Yankton H. S.
Yankton, South Dakota

AFRICAN CHOW MEIN

1 ½ lb. veal, cut into cubes
Shortening
2 cans cream of mushroom soup
2 cans cream of chicken soup
3 soup cans water
2 c. diced celery
2 med. onions, chopped
2 4-oz. cans mushrooms, cut into sm. pieces
1 c. uncooked rice

Brown veal in a small amount of shortening until it changes color. Mix soups and water in pan; heat. Place meat, celery, onions, mushrooms and soups in two 9 x 13-inch baking pans. Mix well. Sprinkle uncooked rice on top of meat mixture. Mix slightly. Bake at 325 degrees for 1 hour and 30 minutes. Yield: 18-20 servings.

Bessie M. Orr, Arkansas City, Jr. H. S.
Arkansas City, Kansas

HUNGARIAN GOULASH

3 lb. onions, sliced
½ c. fat
3 lb. veal shoulder, cut into 1-in. cubes
4 tbsp. paprika
1 bay leaf
2 cloves of garlic, finely chopped
2 qt. white stock, consomme or water
2 tomatoes, finely chopped
Salt and pepper
Cooked noodles

Cook onions until yellow in fat in kettle. Add veal; brown. Mix in paprika, bay leaf, chopped garlic, white stock, tomatoes and salt and pepper to taste. Cover. Simmer for 2 hours or until meat is tender. Remove bay leaf. Serve hot with cooked noodles. Yield: 8 servings.

Mary Ann Hribek, Giddings H. S.
Giddings, Texas

VEAL PAPRIKA

1 ½ lb. boneless veal
¼ c. flour
1 tsp. salt
Dash of pepper
¼ c. chopped onion
1 tsp. paprika
3 tbsp. fat
½ c. water
½ c. strained tomatoes
½ c. sour cream

Cut veal into 1-inch cubes. Dredge veal in mixture of flour, salt and pepper. Saute veal, onion and paprika in the fat until meat is well browned. Add water to tomatoes; pour over browned meat and simmer for 1 hour and 30 minutes or until meat is tender. Add sour cream and simmer for 15 minutes longer. Serve on rice, if desired. Yield: 6 servings.

Eleanor Sturman, Blue Ridge School Dist.
New Milford, Pennsylvania

VEAL PAPRIKA

2 lb. veal round, cut into 1 ½-in. cubes
4 tbsp. flour
½ tsp. salt
Pepper
5 tbsp. shortening
1 c. thinly sliced onions
1 c. sour cream
3 c. cooked rice
2 ½ tsp. paprika
Parsley

Dredge meat in mixture of flour, salt and pepper. Brown one-half the meat at a time in shortening. Add onions and simmer for 1 hour and 30 minutes or until tender. Add sour cream and heat for 5 minutes. Serve on a platter surrounded with fluffy rice. Garnish with paprika and parsley. Yield: 6 servings.

Mrs. D. T. Hamilton, Michie H. S.
Michie, Tennessee

VEAL CHEESE

1 lb. veal cubes
1 meaty veal skin bone
3 c. water
1 onion, sliced
Salt and pepper
4 hard-cooked eggs, sliced

Cook veal cubes and bone in water in pressure cooker with onion seasonings or simmer on top of stove until tender. Reserve juice from meat. Remove meat from bone and grind with veal cubes. Place three layers of meat and sliced eggs in a 10 x 12-inch casserole, beginning with meat. Pour reserved juice over layers. Press mixture down with a heavy object. Chill until jelled. Slice and serve cold. Yield: 6 servings.

Frances B. Buzby, Millville Memorial Jr. H. S.
Millville, New Jersey

VEAL PARTY DISH

1 ½ lb. veal, cut into cubes
1 tbsp. chopped onion
2 tbsp. butter
1 c. mushrooms
2 c. diced celery
¼ c. diced green pepper
¾ c. uncooked white rice
1 can cream of mushroom soup
1 can cream of chicken soup
1 ½ soup cans water
1 c. cashew nuts

Brown meat and onion in butter; brown mushrooms. Add all remaining ingredients except cashew nuts; mix well. Pour into a greased 9 x 15 x 2 1/2-inch baking pan. Bake at 350 degrees for 1 hour and 15 minutes. Cover with nuts; bake at 325 degrees for 25 minutes. Yield: 12 servings.

Jeannette M. Carroll, Round Valley H. S.
Covelo, California

BREADED VEAL CUTLETS

3 tbsp. butter
1 egg, slightly beaten
2 tbsp. milk
1 tsp. salt
4 or 5 veal cutlets, ½-in. thick
1 c. fine cracker crumbs

Preheat electric skillet to 320 degrees; add butter. Combine egg, milk and salt. Dip cutlets into egg mixture then into crumbs. Brown in skillet for 10 minutes on each side; continue cooking until tender. Yield: 4-5 servings.

Wilma Quapp, Picture Butte H. S.
Picture Butte, Alberta, Canada

VEAL PAPRIKA

¼ c. very thinly sliced onion
3 tbsp. butter
1 lb. veal cutlets, sliced ¼-in. thick
1 tsp. salt
⅛ tsp. pepper
¼ c. flour
1 ½ c. chicken stock
¾ c. sour cream
1 tsp. paprika

Saute onion in butter. Remove from pan. Cut veal into four serving pieces; roll in seasoned flour. Brown in same pan. Add stock and onion; simmer, covered, for 1 hour. Stir in sour cream and paprika until heated and well blended. Serve with buttered noodles. Yield: 4 servings.

Margaret Morgan, Austin H. S.
Austin, Minnesota

VEAL VERMOUTH

½ c. butter
2 lb. veal cutlets, cut into sm. serving pieces
Salt and pepper to taste
Grated Parmesan cheese
2 lge. onions, chopped
4 or 5 carrots, sliced diagonally
1 c. halved mushrooms
3 chicken bouillon cubes
1 ½ c. boiling water
½ c. Vermouth

Heat one-half of butter in heavy skillet. Sprinkle cutlets with salt, pepper and cheese; place in skillet. Cook over medium heat until lightly browned. Transfer meat to a 3-quart casserole. Heat remaining butter in skillet; add onions, carrots and mushrooms. Cook until almost tender. Dissolve bouillon cubes in boiling water; stir in Vermouth. Pour mixture over vegetables. Combine mixtures and pour over cutlets. Cover and refrigerate. Return cutlets to room temperature. Bake at 325 degrees for 1 hour. Serve juices with rice or noodles. Yield: 5 servings.

Mary Ann Spangler, Johnson Creek H. S.
Johnson Creek, Wisconsin

PARMESAN VEAL

2 veal round steaks, ¾-in. thick
¼ c. flour
1 tsp. salt
2 eggs, beaten
1 c. bread crumbs
½ c. Parmesan cheese
1 clove of garlic, minced
½ c. salad oil

Dredge steaks in flour and salt; dip into eggs. Mix crumbs with cheese and garlic; dip steaks into crumb mixture. Brown in oil; cook for 1 hour and 15 minutes. Yield: 4 servings.

Mrs. Lois Lovos, Mayville H. S.
Mayville, North Dakota

VEAL BIRDS

2 lb. veal round steak, ¼-in. thick
½ c. melted butter
¼ c. chopped parsley
Salt and pepper
½ c. hot water
1 c. sour cream

Pound meat thoroughly with meat mallet; cut into 3 x 4-inch pieces. Brush each piece with melted butter and sprinkle with parsley. Salt and pepper meat lightly. Roll up each piece as for jelly roll and secure with string or toothpicks. Brown a few birds at a time in remaining melted butter in deep skillet. Mix the hot water with the brownings in skillet; blend in sour cream. Place birds in sour cream mixture. Cover and simmer for 1 hour or until meat is tender.

Mrs. Sigrid Reishus Hurley
Belle Plaine Comm. H. S.
Belle Plaine, Minnesota

VEAL DELIGHT

2 veal round steaks, ½-in. thick
2 tbsp. lard
1 green pepper, chopped
2 tbsp. butter or margarine
3 tbsp. flour
1 4-oz. can sliced mushrooms
2 c. milk
1 pkg. dry onion soup mix
¼ c. pimento, cut into 1-in. slices

Cut steaks into six serving pieces. Pound to 1/4-inch thickeness. Brown in lard; pour off fat. Cook green pepper in butter until tender. Stir in flour; drain mushrooms, reserving liquid. Add liquid with milk and onion soup mix to green pepper. Cook, stirring constantly, until thick. Place veal in greased 8 x 12-inch pan. Pour sauce over steaks. Place pimento and mushrooms on top. Bake at 300 degrees for 30 minutes. Uncover; bake for 15 minutes. Yield: 6 servings.

Mrs. Joanne Bloom, Atlanta H. S.
Atlanta, Illinois

VEAL FIESTAS

1 ½ lb. veal steak
Salt and pepper to taste
¼ c. flour
4 tbsp. shortening
3 lge. onions, sliced
½ c. chili sauce
1 ½ c. hot water
½ c. grated cheese
1 ½ c. cooked macaroni

Cut veal into serving pieces; season. Dredge meat with flour. Brown on both sides in hot shortening; cover with onions, chili sauce and hot water. Cover. Bake at 375 degrees for 30 minutes. Remove cover; sprinkle with grated cheese. Bake for 10 minutes longer or until cheese melts. Remove meat to hot platter. Stir cooked macaroni into gravy; heat. Pour mixture around meat. Yield: 4 servings.

Jean Schumacher, Edison Jr. H. S.
Los Angeles, California

VEAL FRICASSEE

2 lb. veal steak, ½-in. thick
Salt and pepper
Flour
1 tsp. paprika
1 c. sour cream
½ c. meat stock or water

Cut veal into serving pieces. Season; dip into flour. Brown in hot fat. Combine 1 tablespoonful flour, paprika, sour cream and stock; pour over meat. Cover and cook slowly for 1 hour. Yield: 6 servings.

Mrs. T. J. Clanton, Jr., Buckatunna H. S.
Buckatunna, Mississippi

VEAL PARMIGIANA

1 slice frozen cubed veal
1 egg, beaten
Seasoned bread crumbs
1 tsp. tomato paste
Parmesan cheese

Dip veal into egg; dip into crumbs. Brown both sides in a small amount of fat in electric skillet. Spread veal with tomato paste. Cover. Turn heat to 300 degrees; cook for 15 minutes. Sprinkle generously with Parmesan cheese. Yield: 1 serving.

Echo P. Schepman, North Bend H. S.
North Bend, Oregon

VEAL ROLLS CONTINENTAL

1 1 ¼-lb. veal steak, ¼-in. thick
1 tbsp. prepared mustard
¼ c. grated Parmesan cheese
2 tbsp. snipped parsley
1 tsp. salt or garlic salt
1 sm. onion, finely diced
¼ c. plus 2 tbsp. butter
4 slices bread, cubed
1 tbsp. flour
1 tsp. paprika
½ c. water

Cut veal into four pieces; spread each with mustard. Sprinkle with cheese, parsley and salt. Saute onion in 2 tablespoonfuls butter until tender; add to cubed bread. Sprinkle bread mixture over meat; roll up. Tie securely with string. Combine flour and paprika; coat rolls on all sides, reserving left-over flour. Brown rolls well in remaining butter in skillet. Add water; simmer, covered, for 30 minutes or until meat is fork tender. Remove rolls to heated platter; remove strings. Sift reserved flour into liquid in skillet; heat, stirring, until thickened and smooth. Pour over rolls; sprinkle with additional parsley, if desired. Yield: 4 servings.

Mrs. E. Wasson, Bridgeton H. S.
Bridgeton, New Jersey

MOCK VEAL SCALLOPINI

3 med. onions, chopped
3 tbsp. shortening
⅔ c. pancake or biscuit mix
1 tsp. salt
½ tsp. pepper
2 lb. veal cutlets, thinly sliced or pounded
1 10 ½-oz. can beef consomme
1 clove of garlic, crushed
¼ tsp. rosemary

Lightly brown onions in shortening; place in shallow casserole. Combine pancake mix, salt and pepper; dredge veal in mixture. Reserve any remaining flour mixture. Brown veal on both sides in small amount of shortening in frying pan and place on onions in casserole. Add consomme, garlic, rosemary and remaining pancake mixture to frying pan; bring to a boil, stirring constantly. Pour over veal. Bake in preheated 350 degree oven for 45 minutes or until veal is tender. Yield: 6 servings.

Grace W. Beaulieu, Dracut H. S.
Dracut, Massachusetts

VEAL STROGANOFF

1 lb. boneless veal, thinly sliced
Seasoned flour
¼ c. butter or margarine
½ c. chopped onion
1 lb. sliced mushrooms
1 10-oz. can cream of celery soup
Salt and pepper to taste
1 c. sour cream

Coat veal with flour. Melt margarine; add veal and onion. Cook until veal is browned. Add mushrooms, soup, salt and pepper. Cover and cook over low heat for 20 minutes, stirring occasionally. Add sour cream; mix well. Serve over cooked rice. Yield: 4 servings.

Muriel Young, Penticton Secondary School
Penticton, British Columbia, Canada

Ground Beef Favorites

BARBECUED MEAT BALLS

1 lb. ground beef
1/8 tsp. pepper
1 tsp. salt
2/3 c. milk
3/4 c. oats
2 tbsp. fat
1/2 c. catsup
2 tbsp. Worcestershire sauce
2 tbsp. vinegar
2 tbsp. brown sugar
2 tbsp. prepared mustard

Combine meat, seasonings, milk and oats. Shape into 12 meat balls. Brown on all sides in hot fat. Combine remaining ingredients. Place meat balls in casserole; pour sauce over top. Cover; bake at 350 degrees for 30 minutes. Yield: 6-8 servings.

Mrs. Julia Read Clark, Grundy Co. H. S.
Tracy City, Tennessee

BEEF AND RICE BALLS

1/2 c. rice
1 lb. hamburger
1 tbsp. finely chopped onion
2 tbsp. chopped green pepper
1 tsp. salt
1/2 tsp. celery salt
1 clove of garlic, finely chopped
2 c. tomato juice
4 whole cloves
1/2 tsp. cinnamon
2 tbsp. sugar
1 tbsp. Worcestershire sauce

Wash rice; drain. Combine rice, hamburger, onion, green pepper, salt, celery salt and garlic. Form into balls about 1 1/2 inches in diameter. Heat tomato juice, cloves, cinnamon, sugar and Worcestershire sauce in heavy skillet. Drop in meat balls. Cover tightly; simmer for 50 minutes. Yield: 5-6 servings.

Mrs. Jo Nita Schwarz, Central H. S.
San Angelo, Texas

BEV'S DISCOVERY

1 lb. hamburger
1 tbsp. Worcestershire sauce
2 tbsp. chopped onion
1/4 c. heavy cream
Salt and pepper to taste
Bacon fat
1 tbsp. flour
1/4 c. catsup
1 c. cold water
1 tsp. Kitchen Bouquet

Mix hamburger, Worcestershire sauce, onion, heavy cream, salt and pepper. Form into 1-inch balls. Brown in bacon fat; remove from fat. Blend flour into fat in skillet; mix well. Add catsup and water; blend in Kitchen Bouquet. Add meat balls. Simmer for 30 minutes. Yield: 4-6 servings.

Mrs. Beverly L. Haas, Elgin H. S.
Elgin, North Dakota

FAVORITE LITTLE MEAT BALLS

1 1/2 lb. ground chuck
2 tsp. salt
1/4 tsp. pepper
1 med. onion, minced
Fat
2 8-oz. cans tomato sauce
1 clove of garlic, minced or 1/8 tsp. garlic powder

Combine ground chuck with 1 teaspoonful salt, 1/8 teaspoonful pepper and onion; shape into small balls 1 inch in diameter. Brown in a small amount of fat in skillet. Mix tomato sauce, 1 teaspoonful salt, 1/8 teaspoonful pepper and garlic; pour over meat balls. Cover and simmer for 1 hour. Serve over rice, if desired. Yield: 6 servings.

Mrs. Margaret H. Meetze, Heath Springs H. S.
Heath Springs, South Carolina

FLOPPY MEAT BALLS

2 lb. ground beef
2 eggs, beaten
1 c. fine bread crumbs
3 c. milk
1 onion, finely chopped
2 tsp. salt
1/4 tsp. pepper
Flour
Fat
1 can cream of mushroom soup
1 c. water

Combine all ingredients except flour, fat, soup and water; shape mixture into balls. Dip into flour; brown in hot fat. Place balls in roaster. Mix soup and water; pour over meat balls. Bake at 350 degrees for 1 hour. Yield: 8-10 servings.

Mrs. Eleanore Dahl, Belgrade H. S.
Belgrade, Minnesota

MEAT BALLS

1 lb. ground beef
2 eggs, well beaten
1 sm. onion, chopped
1 c. bread crumbs
1 tsp. salt
3 1/4 c. water
2 c. tomato paste
2 1/2 tsp. sugar
1 tbsp. diced onion
1/4 tsp. pepper
1/2 tsp. soda

(Continued on next page)

Combine meat, eggs, onion, crumbs, 1/2 teaspoonful salt and 1/4 cup water; form into balls about 1 to 1 1/2 inches in diameter. Brown meat balls in hot fat; drain. Combine remaining salt and water with tomato paste, sugar, onion and pepper; bring to a boil. Add soda. Add browned meat balls. Simmer for 1 hour. Serve with hot cooked rice or spaghetti. Yield: 6 servings.

Mrs. Beulah Hanna, Sardis H. S.
Sardis, Tennessee

MEAT BALLS

1 lb. ground beef
1 tbsp. onion salt
¼ tsp. pepper
½ tsp. chili powder
1 lge. egg, beaten
⅓ c. rice
2 tbsp. oil
3 c. tomato juice

Mix ground beef with seasonings; add egg. Mix well. Stir in rice; mix until well blended. Shape into 1 1/2-inch balls. Heat oil in skillet; brown balls. Add tomato juice to mixture. Simmer for 35 to 40 minutes or until rice is cooked. Yield: 5 servings.

Mrs. L. L. Stewart, Lakeville Comm. School
Otisville, Michigan

MEAT BALLS

4 slices bread
⅔ c. milk
1 lb. ground beef
Salt and pepper to taste
2 tsp. baking powder
2 cans cream of mushroom soup

Cut bread into 1/4 to 1/2-inch squares; mix with milk. Beat to consistency of whipped cream. Combine with meat, seasonings and baking powder. Shape mixture into 1 1/2-inch balls; brown on all sides. Place in casserole; pour soup over all. Cook slowly for 1 hour and 15 minutes. Add water to keep gravy above meat. Yield: 18-20 meat balls.

Patricia Morgan, Laurel H. S.
Laurel, Montana

MEAT BALLS AND RICE IN CONSOMME

1 lb. ground chuck
1 tsp. salt
⅛ tsp. pepper
¼ c. chopped green pepper
2 tbsp. chopped celery and leaves
1 sm. onion, chopped
⅔ c. rice
1 can comsomme
1 can water

Mix ground meat, salt and pepper; shape into 12 balls. Brown slowly on all sides in skillet, using a small amount of fat, if necessary. Add green pepper, celery and onion; cook for 5 minutes longer. Add rice, consomme and water. Bring to a boil; cover and simmer gently, stirring occasionally, for 20 minutes or until rice is tender and liquid is absorbed. NOTE: If desired, 3 bouillon cubes dissolved in 3 cups hot water may be substituted for consomme. Yield: 4 servings.

Mrs. Margaret Deason Randall, Tallulah H. S.
Tallulah, Louisiana

MEAT BALLS AND SAUERKRAUT

1 1-lb. 11-oz. can sauerkraut, drained
½ can water
2 tbsp. uncooked rice
2 lb. ground beef
2 eggs
10 soda crackers, crushed
Salt and pepper to taste
3 8-oz. cans tomato sauce
½ c. raisins
⅔ c. (packed) dark brown sugar

Combine sauerkraut, water and rice. Cook for 45 minutes. Combine ground beef, eggs, cracker crumbs and seasonings; mix well. Shape mixture into balls the size of large marbles. Add tomato sauce, raisins and brown sugar to sauerkraut mixture; stir well. Add meat balls and simmer for 2 hours.

Dorothy Wygant, Columbia H. S.
East Greenbush, New York

MEAT BALLS CREOLE

1 ½ lb. ground beef
¾ c. oats
1 tsp. salt
1 tsp. garlic salt
1 8-oz. can tomato sauce
Flour
Fat

Combine beef, oats, salts and tomato sauce. Shape into balls, using 1 tablespoonful mixture for each ball. Roll in flour; brown in frying pan in a small amount of hot fat.

CREOLE SAUCE:

1 8-oz. can tomato sauce
1 c. chili sauce
1 ½ c. water
4 sm. onions, sliced
½ green pepper, sliced

Combine tomato sauce, chili sauce and water; add onions and green pepper. Pour over meat balls. Simmer for 20 minutes or until done. Yield: 6 servings.

Mrs. Helen H. Wilson, State Supervisor, Home Economics Education, State Board for Vocational Education, Boise, Idaho

MEAT BALLS CON CHILI

1 10 ½-oz. can tomato soup
1 tsp. chili powder
1 lb. ground beef
2 tbsp. fine dry bread crumbs
2 tbsp. minced onion
1 tsp. salt
1 egg, slightly beaten
2 tbsp. shortening
1 sm. clove of garlic, minced
½ c. water

Mix 1/4 cup soup and one-half the chili powder with beef, crumbs, onion, salt and egg; shape into balls about 1 inch in diameter. Brown meat balls in shortening in skillet with garlic and remaining chili powder; stir in remaining soup and water. Cover; cook over low heat for about 20 minutes, stirring occasionally. Yield: 4 servings.

Photograph for this recipe on page 65 .

MEAT BALLS IN CASSEROLE

1 tsp. salt
½ c. applesauce
½ c. crushed corn flakes
1 egg, slightly beaten
1 ¼ lb. lean ground beef
1 can tomato sauce

Add salt, applesauce and corn flakes to egg. Blend. Add ground beef; mix thoroughly. Shape into 12 to 14 small balls; place in casserole. Pour tomato sauce over meat balls. Bake at 350 degrees for 50 minutes to 1 hour. Yield: 6 servings.

Mrs. Gorden Tyra, Marietta H. S.
Marietta, Mississippi

MEAT BALLS WITH MUSHROOM GRAVY

1 ½ lb. ground beef
Seasoning to taste
1 lge. onion
1 can cream of mushroom soup
1 soup can water

Mix ground beef with seasoning to taste; form into balls. Brown in skillet. Place in baking dish; cut up onion over meat balls. Pour mushroom soup and water over balls. Bake at 350 degrees for 1 hour. Yield: 6 servings.

Mrs. Thelma Maxey, Lorenzo H. S.
Lorenzo, Texas

MEAT BALLS WRAPPED IN BACON

1 lb. ground beef
½ tsp. salt
1 tsp. Worcestershire sauce
Dash of pepper
4 slices thin bacon

Combine beef, salt, Worcestershire sauce and pepper. Mix well. Shape beef into four round beef patties. Place a slice of bacon around each meat ball; fasten with a toothpick. Press meat ball and bacon together until meat ball is very firm. Sear on each side; cook slowly in covered skillet until desired doneness. Yield: 4 servings.

Mrs. Daisy Massey, Fredericksburg H. S.
Fredericksburg, Texas

MEAT BALLS WITH SOUP

1 ½ lb. ground chuck
1 tsp. salt
⅛ tsp. seasoned pepper
⅛ tsp. onion salt
1 tsp. monosodium glutamate
2 tbsp. chopped green pepper (opt.)
1 tbsp. Worcestershire sauce
3 tbsp. oil
1 can cream of chicken soup
1 can cream of mushroom soup

Combine meat with remaining ingredients except oil and soups. Form into small balls. Brown in oil in skillet. Remove meat balls from skillet; pour off fat. Return balls to skillet. Cover with undiluted soups. Cover and simmer for 25 minutes. Serve over rice or potatoes. Yield: 6 servings.

Mrs. Trudy Fulmer, Springfield H. S.
Springfield, South Carolina

MISSOURI SKILLET LUAU

1 lb. ground beef
1 egg, beaten
¼ c. dry bread crumbs
½ tsp. salt
¼ tsp. ginger
¼ c. flour
3 tbsp. salad oil
1 No. 2 can pineapple chunks
3 tbsp. brown sugar
¾ tsp. cornstarch
¼ c. vinegar
1 tbsp. soy sauce
2 green peppers, seeded and cut into strips

Mix beef with egg, crumbs and seasonings; form into 16 balls. Dredge balls in flour; brown in salad oil in large frying pan. Remove meat balls from pan. Drain pineapple, reserving liquid; add water to syrup to make 1 cup. Stir into drippings in pan. Mix brown sugar with cornstarch, vinegar and soy sauce. Add to syrup mixture. Cook, stirring constantly, until sauce is thickened and clear. Arrange meat balls, pineapple chunks and pepper strips separately in pan; stir each gently to coat with sauce. Cover; simmer for 10 minutes or until green pepper is tender, but still crisp. Serve with hot buttered noodles or toasted almonds, if desired. Yield: 4 servings.

Mrs. Helen M. Young, Christiansburg H. S.
Christiansburg, Virginia

PARMESAN MEAT BALLS

½ c. soft bread crumbs
½ c. grated Parmesan cheese
1 egg, slightly beaten
½ c. milk
1 tbsp. minced onion
1 tsp. monosodium glutamate
Salt and pepper to taste
1 lb. ground round or chuck
¼ c. flour
1 c. beef bouillon
1 4-oz. can sliced mushrooms or ½-lb. fresh mushrooms

Combine bread crumbs, cheese, egg, milk, onion, monosodium glutamate, salt and pepper with ground beef. Form gently into balls. Place in large non-stick baking pan. Bake at 350 degrees until nicely brown. When browned, remove from pan and set aside. Blend flour into remaining drippings; add bouillon and undrained mushrooms. When all is blended, add seasonings to taste; return meat balls to sauce. Cover and bake at 350 degrees for 30 minutes. Serve with hot rice, if desired. NOTE: If fresh mushrooms are used, add 1/4 cup water. Yield: 5-6 servings.

Mrs. Ruth H. Methvin, Fall River H. S.
McArthur, California

PARSLEY MEAT BALLS

¾ c. dry bread crumbs
½ c. milk
2 onions, chopped
½ c. water
2 lb. ground lean beef
¾ c. finely chopped parsley
3 mint leaves, chopped
2 egg yolks
3 sm. cloves of garlic, minced
1 ½ tsp. salt
¼ tsp. pepper
1 ½ tbsp. olive oil
1 ½ tbsp. butter
¼ c. red wine vinegar or lemon juice
½ tsp. crumbled dried oregano

Soak bread crumbs in milk; beat until mushy. Cook onions, covered in water, until water has evaporated. Mix meat thoroughly with bread crumbs, onions, parsley, mint, egg yolks, garlic, salt and pepper. Shape into balls the size of a walnut. Heat oil and butter in frying pan; slowly brown meat well on all sides. Place meat balls in a serving dish. Pour wine vinegar into pan; heat. Scrape up drippings; pour over meat balls. Sprinkle with oregano. Yield: 3 dozen meat balls.

Eliza Ninmann, Gresham H. S.
Gresham, Wisconsin

PARTY MEAT BALLS

1 ½ c. soft bread crumbs
¼ c. catsup
½ tsp. cumin
½ c. milk
1 egg, slightly beaten
3 tbsp. finely cut onion
1 ½ tsp. salt
⅛ tsp. pepper
1 lb. lean ground beef
3 tbsp. flour
2 tbsp. shortening

Combine all ingredients except flour and shortening; shape into 16 balls with wet hands. Roll balls in flour. Brown meat balls on all sides in shortening over medium heat; cook for 10 minutes. Drain. Yield: 8 servings.

Linda Stevens, Fullerton H. S.
Fullerton, Nebraska

PORCUPINE MEAT BALLS

1 can tomato soup
¼ to ½ c. uncooked rice
2 slices bread, crumbled (opt.)
1 lb. ground beef
½ c. minced onion
1 egg (opt.)
2 tbsp. minced parsley (opt.)
Salt and pepper to taste
2 tbsp. shortening (opt.)
1 to 1 ¼ c. water

Mix 1/4 cup tomato soup, rice, bread, ground beef, onion, egg, parsley, salt and pepper. Shape

(Continued on next page)

into sixteen 1 1/2-inch balls. Brown in shortening. Blend in remaining soup and water. Cover; simmer for about 40 minutes to 1 hour or until rice is tender, stirring occasionally. Yield: 4 servings.

Mrs. Judy Fish, Piketon H. S.
Piketon, Ohio
Virginia Courrier, Grand Meadow Public School
Grand Meadow, Minnesota

NELL'S MEAT BALLS

Chopped onions
Margarine
Chopped parsley
Salt and pepper
1 slice bread
Milk
1 lb. ground beef
Bread crumbs
Caraway seed
1 bouillon cube
1 to 2 c. water

Fry onions in margarine. Add parsley and seasonings. Soak bread slice in milk; add with onion mixture to meat. Form into balls. Mix crumbs with caraway seed. Roll balls in crumbs. Fry until brown. Add bouillon cube dissolved in water. Simmer, covered, for 30 minutes. Yield: 6 servings.

Mrs. Nell Stevens, Indianola H. S.
Indianola, Mississippi

SAUERBRATEN MEAT BALLS

1 lb. ground beef
¼ c. fine dry bread crumbs
⅔ c. chopped onions
1 ½ tsp. salt
Dash of pepper
⅔ c. evaporated milk
2 tbsp. butter
1 c. water
2 tbsp. vinegar
2 tbsp. catsup
1 tbsp. brown sugar
8 peppercorns
1 bay leaf, crumbled
⅓ c. raisins
6 gingersnaps, crushed

Combine beef, bread crumbs, onions, 1 teaspoonful salt, pepper and milk; shape into balls. Brown in butter. Stir in mixture of remaining ingredients. Stir gently to mix well. Bring to a boil over medium heat. Cover skillet tightly and simmer for 15 minutes. Stir. Cover and simmer for 15 minutes longer. Yield: 6 servings.

Virginia Christensen, North Sevier H. S.
Salina, Utah

SCALLOPED MEAT BALLS AND POTATOES

4 c. thinly sliced potatoes
4 tbsp. butter
4 tbsp. flour
2 c. milk
1 c. water
2 tsp. salt
Dash of pepper
1 lb. ground beef
3 tbsp. chili sauce
1 ¼ tsp. prepared mustard
1 ¼ tsp. bottled horseradish
1 ½ tsp. grated onion
1 ¼ tsp. Worcestershire sauce

Cook potatoes in salted water for 10 minutes. Drain; arrange in baking dish. Melt butter in saucepan. Stir in flour; add milk and water, stirring until thickened. Add 1 teaspoonful salt and small amount of pepper. Pour over potatoes. Combine remaining ingredients; shape into 10 balls. Place meat balls on top. Bake, uncovered, at 350 degrees for 45 minutes or until done. Yield: 6 servings.

Mabel Brill, Moorefield H. S.
Moorefield, West Virginia

SPICY MEAT BALLS

1 ½ lb. ground beef
1 med. onion, chopped
1 tbsp. dried parsley
1 slice bread, crumbled
1 tsp. salt
¼ tsp. sage
Pepper to taste
16 oz. tomato sauce or juice
1 sm. onion, grated
¼ tsp. salt
3 bay leaves
⅛ tsp. ground cloves

Combine meat, chopped onion, parsley, bread, 3/4 teaspoonful salt, sage and pepper; form into small balls. Combine all remaining ingredients; bring to a boil. Simmer for 10 to 20 minutes. Add meat balls. Simmer for 15 to 20 minutes longer. Serve on rice, noodles, spaghetti or macaroni. Yield: 6 servings.

Josephine M. Jones, Arickaree H. S.
Anton, Colorado

MEAT BALLS STROGANOFF

1 lb. ground beef
2 tbsp. dry bread crumbs
2 tbsp. finely chopped onion
1 egg, slightly beaten
¼ tsp. salt
1 tbsp. shortening
1 10 ¾-oz. can beef gravy
¼ c. sour cream

(Continued on next page)

Mix beef, crumbs, onion, egg and salt. Shape into 16 meat balls. Brown in shortening; pour off fat. Stir in gravy. Cook over low heat for 15 minutes or until done, stirring occasionally. Blend in sour cream; heat. Serve with cooked noodles. Yield: 4 servings.

Mrs. Ruth C. Bowman, Eagleton Jr. H. S.
Maryville, Tennessee

BEEF BALLS STROGANOFF

1 lb. ground beef
½ c. milk
½ c. dry bread crumbs
1 tsp. salt
⅛ tsp. pepper
1 tbsp. fresh minced parsley
3 tbsp. butter
1 med. onion, finely diced
¼ c. chopped green pepper
1 sm. can mushrooms, sliced
½ tsp. paprika
2 tbsp. flour
1 c. beef bouillon
½ c. sour cream
1 tsp. Worcestershire sauce

Combine ground beef, milk, bread crumbs, salt, pepper and parsley. Blend well; shape into 1-inch balls. Melt butter; brown beef balls well on all sides. Remove; add onion, green pepper and mushrooms. Saute. Sprinkle with paprika and flour; add bouillon, stirring constantly until mixture thickens. Blend in sour cream and Worcestershire sauce. Heat thoroughly over low heat. Serve with buttered noodles or rice, if desired. Yield: 6-8 servings.

Mrs. Kemper R. Russell, Logansport H. S.
Logansport, Louisiana

MEAT BALLS STROGANOFF

2 slices stale bread
¼ lb. onions, sliced
3 tbsp. butter
1 lge. green pepper, cut into rings
1 ½ lb. ground beef
1 ½ c. buttermilk
1 egg
Salt and pepper to taste
Few grains of nutmeg
Dash of monosodium glutamate
3 tbsp. oil
1 can cream of mushroom soup
⅓ c. catsup
1 tbsp. caraway seed

Soak bread in water. Saute onions in butter; remove from pan. Saute green pepper. Combine meat, bread, 1/4 cup buttermilk, egg, salt, pepper, nutmeg, onions and monosodium glutamate; shape into balls. Heat oil in pan; brown meat balls. Combine soup, catsup, remaining buttermilk and caraway seed; simmer. Add green pepper rings. Pour sauce mixture over meat balls. Serve over hot noodles, if desired. Yield: 6 servings.

Mrs. Shirley Susman, Seekonk H. S.
Seekonk, Massachusetts

CREAMED SWEDISH MEAT BALLS

1 c. fine bread crumbs
2 ½ c. milk
2 lb. ground beef
1 c. finely chopped onions
2 eggs, slightly beaten
1 ½ tsp. salt
¼ tsp. pepper
1 tsp. nutmeg
½ c. butter or margarine
¼ c. flour
3 beef bouillon cubes
3 c. hot water
1 ½ c. light cream

Soften bread crumbs in 1 cup milk. Add beef, onions, eggs and seasonings; mix thoroughly. Shape into 1-inch balls. Heat butter in large skillet; add meat balls, a few at a time. Brown on all sides. Remove meat balls; stir flour into drippings. Blend well. Dissolve bouillon cubes in hot water. Gradually add to flour mixture, stirring constantly until smooth. Add remaining milk and cream. Cook over low heat, stirring constantly, for 3 minutes. Add meat balls. Simmer for 10 to 15 minutes, stirring occasionally. Yield: 12 servings.

LaRee Kirby, Delphos H. S.
Delphos, Kansas

SWEDISH MEAT BALLS

1 can cream of celery soup
½ soup can water
1 lb. ground beef
⅔ c. fine dry bread crumbs
1 egg, slightly beaten
2 tbsp. minced onion
1 tbsp. chopped parsley
1 tsp. salt
1 to 2 tbsp. minced dill pickle (opt.)

Blend celery soup with water. Reserve 1/4 cup soup mixture. Combine remaining soup mixture with ground beef, bread crumbs, egg, onion, parsley and salt. Shape into balls 1 inch in diameter; brown in shortening in large skillet. Add reserved soup mixture and dill pickle, if desired. Cover. Cook over low heat for 20 minutes, stirring occasionally. Yield: 4 servings.

Mrs. Jenilee Lemmon, Trent Independent School
Trent, Texas

SWEDISH MEAT BALLS

1 ½ lb. ground round or lean chuck
1 egg
½ c. milk
1 ½ slices bread, finely crumbled
2 tbsp. instant minced onion
1 ½ tsp. salt
1 ½ tsp. sugar
½ tsp. paprika
½ tsp. allspice
¼ tsp. nutmeg
1 tsp. dry mustard
½ tsp. marjoram
½ tsp. thyme
1 tsp. monosodium glutamate
¼ tsp. pepper
Cooking oil or butter
2 c. beef bouillon
¼ tsp. garlic powder
1 tsp. dill weed
Sour cream (opt.)

Combine meat, egg, milk, bread crumbs, onion, salt and sugar with spices. Mix thoroughly but lightly; shape into small balls. Brown on all sides in oil or butter. Mix bouillon with garlic powder and dill weed; pour over meat balls. Cover and simmer for 30 minutes. Add water or additional bouillon if liquid evaporates. Add sour cream to mixture, if desired. Do not boil after adding sour cream. Serve with buttered noodles, if desired. Yield: 6 servings.

Virginia Mullen, Lake Oswego H. S.
Lake Oswego, Oregon

SWEDISH MEAT BALLS

1 lb. ground beef
¼ c. fine dry bread crumbs
¼ c. minced onion
1 egg, slightly beaten
2 tbsp. parsley flakes
1 can cream of mushroom soup
½ soup can water
1 to 2 tbsp. minced dill pickle
Cooked rice

Mix beef, bread crumbs, onion, egg and parsley; shape into 24 meat balls. Brown meat balls; pour off drippings. Stir in soup, water and pickle. Cover; cook over low heat for 20 minutes, stirring often. Serve with rice. Yield: 4 servings.

Mrs. Barbara Reid Wood, Urbandale Jr. H. S.
Urbandale, Iowa

SWEDISH MEAT BALLS

¼ c. chopped onion
¼ c. butter
1 ½ lb. ground chuck
½ lb. ground pork
¼ lb. ground veal
1 c. dried bread crumbs or oats
2 eggs, slightly beaten
1 c. milk
2 tsp. salt
¼ tsp. pepper
Dash of nutmeg
Dash of allspice
¼ c. drippings
¼ c. flour

Saute onion in butter until golden; combine onion and remaining ingredients except drippings and flour in large mixing bowl. Toss lightly until well mixed. With teaspoon, shape into small balls; roll in seasoned flour. Brown meat balls in skillet in butter, turning to brown all sides. Remove meat balls. Make sauce of drippings, flour and 2 cups hot water; cook until thickened. Season. Add meat balls; simmer for 30 minutes.

Myrtle B. Sellie, Ellis Jr. H. S.
Austin, Minnesota

SWEDISH MEAT BALLS

1 lb. ground beef
½ tsp. nutmeg
½ tsp. pepper
2 slices dry bread, crumbled
3 tbsp. oil
3 tbsp. flour
3 bouillon cubes
1 ½ c. water

Combine beef, nutmeg, pepper and bread; shape into meat balls. Brown in oil. Push meat balls aside; combine flour with oil to make a paste. Add bouillon with water. Cover and simmer for 1 hour, basting often. Yield: 6 servings.

Mary Kay Smith, Washington H. S.
Washington, Oklahoma

SWEET AND SOUR BEEF BALLS

1 ½ lb. ground beef
2 eggs
3 tbsp. flour
½ tsp. salt
Cracked black pepper
9 slices canned pineapple, diced
¾ c. oil
1 ½ c. chicken bouillon
3 lge. green peppers, diced
1 sm. can bamboo shoots
2 tbsp. cornstarch
2 tbsp. soy sauce
1 tsp. monosodium glutamate
¾ c. pineapple juice
¾ c. sugar
1 tsp. ginger
¾ c. vinegar

Shape ground beef into walnut-sized balls. Combine eggs, flour, salt and pepper; dip meat balls into batter. Fry until brown. Remove meat balls;

(Continued on next page)

keep warm. Pour out all but 1 tablespoonful fat; add pineapple. Cover; cook over medium heat for 10 minutes. Add all remaining ingredients; mix well. Cook, stirring constantly, until mixture comes to a boil and thickens. Add meat balls; simmer for 15 minutes. Yield: 6 servings.

Jannette Y. Weaver, Talladega H. S.
Talladega, Alabama

SWEETLY DIFFERENT MEAT BALLS

2 eggs
1 c. bread crumbs
1 c. applesauce
Salt
1 tsp. pepper
2 lb. ground beef
2 tbsp. fat
2 tbsp. finely chopped onion
¼ c. finely chopped celery
2 tbsp. diced carrots
2 tbsp. flour
2 c. tomato juice
2 tsp. sugar

Beat eggs; stir in bread crumbs, applesauce, 2 teaspoonfuls salt, pepper and ground beef. Mix well. Form beef mixture into 1/2-inch balls; brown in fat. Drain off all but 2 tablespoonfuls fat; add onion, celery, carrots and flour. Stir in tomato juice, 1/4 teaspoonful salt and sugar. Cook for 1 minute. Place in a baking dish; cover. Bake at 350 degrees for 45 minutes. Yield: 6-8 servings.

Lorene L. Arent, Wausa Public School
Wausa, Nebraska

BARBECUE-STYLE MEAT LOAF

1 ½ lb. ground beef
½ c. fresh bread crumbs
1 onion, chopped
1 egg, beaten
1 ½ tsp. salt
¼ tsp. pepper
2 cans tomato sauce
½ c. water
3 tbsp. vinegar
3 tbsp. brown sugar
2 tbsp. prepared mustard
2 tsp. Worcestershire sauce

Mix ground beef, bread crumbs, chopped onion, egg, seasonings and 1/2 can tomato sauce; form into loaf or individual patties. Combine remaining tomato sauce with water, vinegar, brown sugar, mustard and Worcestershire sauce; pour over loaf or patties. Bake at 350 degrees for 1 hour. Yield: 6 servings.

Mrs. Iris Hendershot, Southern Fulton H. S.
Warfordsburg, Pennsylvania

BEEF AND FRENCH FRY LOAF

1 ½ lb. ground beef
½ c. quick cooking oats
2 eggs, slightly beaten
⅓ c. chopped onion
½ c. chili sauce
2 tsp. salt
⅛ tsp. pepper
1 9-oz. pkg. frozen French fries
1 can cheese soup

Combine all ingredients except French Fries and cheese soup. Divide meat mixture into three equal portions; pack one portion of meat into a layer in bottom of greased 9 x 5 x 3-inch loaf pan. Press one-half of potatoes into meat mixture; cover with a second layer of meat and potatoes. Pack remaining meat onto top to form a loaf. Bake at 350 degrees for about 1 hour or until done. Let stand for 5 to 10 minutes before removing from pan. Top with cheese soup. Yield: 6-8 servings.

Mrs. Frances Moorman, Sterlington H. S.
Sterlington, Louisiana

BUSY DAY MEAT LOAF

2 lb. ground beef
1 c. mashed potatoes
2 eggs
½ c. soft bread crumbs
1 tsp. salt
¼ tsp. pepper
1 tbsp. minced parsley (opt.)

Combine all ingredients. Shape into 6 or 8 individual meat loaves; wrap in foil. Place in shallow baking dish. Bake at 350 degrees for 45 minutes to 1 hour. NOTE: Loaves may be frozen. Yield: 6-8 servings.

Mrs. Marie Della-Penna, Jefferson Union H. S.
Richmond, Ohio

CRANBERRY MEAT LOAF

1 lb. ground beef
1 c. cooked rice
½ c. tomato juice
1 egg, slightly beaten
¼ c. chopped onion
1 ½ tsp. salt
2 c. whole cranberry sauce
⅓ c. sugar
1 tbsp. lemon juice

Combine ground beef, rice, tomato juice, egg, onion and salt. Shape into loaf; put into pan. Mix remaining ingredients; pour over loaf. Bake at 350 degrees for 45 minutes to 1 hour. Yield: 6-8 servings.

Mrs. Ruth N. Powell, Franklinville H. S.
Franklinville, North Carolina

CHEESEBURGER MEAT LOAF

2 eggs
¼ c. light cream
2 slices stale bread, coarsely crumbled
1 sm. onion, finely chopped
¼ c. finely chopped celery
¼ c. chopped green pepper
1 tsp. salt
¼ tsp. pepper
Dash of garlic salt
2 lb. ground beef
3 slices yellow cheese
Tomato sauce or catsup

Beat eggs in medium mixing bowl. Add cream; beat. Add crumbs to egg mixture. Let set until bread becomes soft; stir. Add all remaining ingredients except cheese and tomato sauce. Work mixture until well mixed. Place one-half of mixture into well greased loaf baking dish; shape and flatten top until even. Lay slices of cheese on surface of loaf; do not extend over edge. Place remaining meat mixture on top of cheese; shape loaf with hands, sealing edges well. Bake at 350 degrees for 50 minutes to 1 hour. Remove from oven; spread tomato sauce over top. Bake for 20 to 30 minutes longer or until done. Yield: 6-8 servings.

Mrs. Hazel Huckaby, Fowler H. S.
Fowler, Colorado

CHILI MEAT LOAF

1 c. tomato sauce
2 tbsp. brown sugar
1 tbsp. vinegar
1 tsp. Worcestershire sauce
¼ tsp. mustard
½ tsp. chili powder
1 ½ tsp. salt
1 lb. ground beef
½ c. evaporated milk
⅓ c. oats
¼ c. finely cut onion
⅛ tsp. pepper

Combine tomato sauce with brown sugar, vinegar, Worcestershire sauce, mustard, chili powder and 1/2 teaspoonful salt in saucepan. Cook for 5 minutes over low heat. Combine ground beef, milk, oats, onion, 1 teaspoonful salt and pepper. Remove sauce from heat; mix one-half of sauce with meat mixture. Press meat mixture into an ungreased 9 x 5-inch loaf pan; spoon remaining sauce over meat. Place on center oven rack. Bake at 350 degrees for 50 minutes. Yield: 4 servings.

Mrs. Anita Himbury, Shidler H. S.
Shidler, Oklahoma

DOUBLE MEAT AND RICE LOAF

2 ⅔ c. instant rice
3 tsp. salt
⅔ c. chopped onion
2 ⅔ c. boiling water
2 tbsp. chopped parsley
1 c. bread cubes
1 c. milk
2 lb. ground beef
2 eggs, slightly beaten
Dash of pepper
2 tsp. Worcestershire sauce
¼ c. catsup

Add rice, 1 teaspoonful salt and 2 tablespoonfuls onion to the boiling water in saucepan. Mix just to moisten rice. Cover; remove from heat. Let stand for 5 minutes. Add parsley, mixing lightly with a fork. Soak bread in milk. Add meat, eggs, 2 teaspoonfuls salt, pepper, Worcestershire sauce, catsup and remaining onion. Place a layer of meat mixture in bottom of two greased 10 x 5 x 3-inch loaf pans. Add rice and remaining meat mixture. Repeat layers. Bake at 350 degrees for 45 minutes. Unmold onto platter. Serve with gravy or mustard sauce. Yield: 10 servings.

Edith Flanagan, North Middle School
Westford, Massachusetts

DIFFERENT MEAT LOAF

1 lb. ground beef
1 egg yolk
2 tbsp. chopped parsley
¼ c. plus 1 tbsp. soft butter
1 tbsp. bread crumbs
1 tsp. lemon juice
1 tsp. salt
¼ tsp. pepper
½ tsp. onion juice
¼ c. butter
1 c. vegetable stock or 1 c. boiling water plus ½ pkg. dry soup mix

Combine all ingredients except 1/4 cup butter and stock; shape into a loaf. Place loaf in a lightly greased pan. Bake at 350 degrees for 1 hour. Combine 1/4 cup butter and vegetable stock. Baste loaf every 5 minutes with mixture. Yield: 4 servings.

Hilda Gilleland, Cedartown H. S.
Cedartown, Georgia

ECONOMICAL MEAT LOAF

2 slices white bread
⅔ c. water
⅓ c. dry milk
1 lb. ground meat
Salt and pepper to taste
1 tbsp. minced onion or ½ tsp. onion juice (opt.)
1 tbsp. Worcestershire sauce (opt.)
1 egg, slightly beaten
1 slice bacon or 1 tbsp. fat (opt.)

Soften bread in water. Add dry milk, meat, salt, pepper, onion, Worcestershire sauce and egg;

(Continued on next page)

mix well. Shape into 1 or 2 oblong loaves; place in shallow baking dish. Cut bacon slice into thirds; place on top of loaves. Bake, uncovered, at 350 degrees until done. Serve with catsup, if desired. NOTE: Fresh milk may be substituted for dry milk and water. Yield: 6-8 servings.

Bernice J. Palmer, Lynville H. S.
Preston, Mississippi
Ruth Cooper Humphrey, Wheeler Co. H. S.
Alamo, Georgia

EVERYDAY MEAT LOAF

8 c. bread crumbs
3 qt. milk
18 lb. ground beef
2 doz. eggs
3 c. ground onions (opt.)
¼ c. salt
1 ½ tsp. pepper
2 tbsp. sage

Combine all ingredients; shape into 10 or 12 loaves. Bake at 350 degrees for 45 minutes.

PIQUANT SAUCE:

2 ¼ c. brown sugar
3 c. catsup
1 tbsp. nutmeg
¼ c. dry mustard

Combine all ingredients; pour over meat loaves. Yield: 100 servings.

Mrs. Kathryn I. Starcher, Sunnyside H. S.
Tucson, Arizona

EVERYDAY MEAT LOAF

⅔ c. to ¾ c. quick cooking oats
¾ to 1 c. milk
1 ½ lb. ground beef
1 or 2 eggs, beaten
¼ c. chopped green pepper (opt.)
¼ c. grated onion
1 to 2 tsp. salt
½ tsp. sage (opt.)
⅛ tsp. pepper
3 tbsp. brown sugar (opt.)
¼ c. catsup (opt.)
1 tsp. nutmeg (opt.)
1 tsp. dry mustard or 1 tbsp. prepared mustard (opt.)

Cook oats in milk; add meat, eggs, onion, salt and pepper. Mix well. Form meat mixture into loaf; place in greased pan or casserole. Combine brown sugar, catsup, nutmeg and dry mustard; pour over meat loaf. Bake at 350 degrees for 45 minutes to 1 hour. NOTE: Bread crumbs may be substituted for oats. Soak crumbs in the milk. Yield: 6-8 servings.

Earle H. Vallentine, Edisto H. S.
Cordova, South Carolina
Mrs. Rita Fielder, Biggers-Reyno H. S.
Biggers, Arkansas
Ruth I. Schwarz, Galesburg Sr. H. S.
Galesburg, Illinois
Mrs. Karen Gee, Farragut Comm. Schools
Farragut, Iowa
Mrs. Novell H. Berry, Douglas H. S.
Douglas, Alabama

FAVORITE BEEF LOAF

1 ½ lb. ground beef
1 c. cracker crumbs
2 eggs, beaten
1 8-oz. can seasoned tomato sauce
½ c. finely chopped onion
2 tbsp. chopped green pepper
1 ½ tsp. salt
1 med. bay leaf, crushed
Dash of thyme
Dash of marjoram
2 green pepper rings, (opt.)
1 onion ring (opt.)

Combine all ingredients except green pepper and onion rings; mix well. Shape mixture into a loaf in shallow baking dish. Press green pepper rings and onion ring on meat loaf, if desired. Bake at 350 degrees for 1 hour. Yield: 6-8 servings.

Iona Ross, Freer H. S.
Freer, Texas

INDIVIDUAL BEEF LOAVES

1 3-oz. can chopped mushrooms
1 egg, slightly beaten
¾ c. fine dry bread crumbs
1 lb. ground beef
1 tsp. onion salt
¼ tsp. pepper
⅛ tsp. oregano
¼ c. catsup
1 tsp. Kitchen Bouquet

Drain mushrooms, reserving liquid; combine egg and liquid. Add crumbs, soak for 10 minutes. Add meat, mushrooms, seasonings and 2 tablespoonfuls catsup; mix well. Form into four individual meat loaves. Place in oiled shallow baking pan. Bake at 350 degrees for 30 minutes or until done. When done, brush with mixture of remaining catsup and Kitchen Bouquet. Return to oven for 5 to 10 minutes longer. Serve hot or cold. Yield: 4 servings.

Mrs. Hazel L. Seaton, Twiggs Co. H. S.
Danville, Georgia

FLORENCE'S MEAT LOAF

1 ½ lb. ground beef
1 c. cracker crumbs
1 green pepper, chopped
1 c. tomatoes, drained
1 egg
1 sm. onion, diced
1 can tomato soup
1 c. water
3 tbsp. brown sugar
5 tbsp. catsup
½ tsp. salt
¼ tsp. pepper
½ tsp. dry mustard
2 tbsp. butter

Combine ground beef, cracker crumbs, green pepper and tomatoes; mix well. Form into a loaf in baking dish. Combine remaining ingredients except butter in saucepan; cook for 5 minutes. Add butter. Pour all but 1 cup sauce over meat loaf. Bake at 350 degrees for 1 hour and 30 minutes, basting often. Before serving, pour reserved heated sauce over meat loaf. Yield: 6 servings.

Frances Potter, Salyersville H. S.
Salyersville, Kentucky

INDIAN MEAT LOAF

1 ½ lb. ground beef
1 egg
½ c. corn meal
2 tsp. salt
¼ tsp. pepper
½ tsp. sage
½ c. chopped onion
¼ c. chopped green pepper
½ c. cream-style corn
1 ¼ c. canned tomatoes

Combine all ingredients. Pack into a greased 5 x 9-inch loaf pan. Bake at 300 degrees for 1 hour and 30 minutes. Yield: 6-8 servings.

Mrs. Sharon Doke, Weed H. S.
Weed, California

INDIVIDUAL MEAT LOAVES

½ lb. ground beef
⅓ c. crushed corn flakes
2 tbsp. chopped onion
1 egg
½ tsp. salt
Dash of pepper

Combine all ingredients; mix well. Divide into two parts. Press into two large greased custard or muffin cups. Bake at 325 degrees for 40 to 50 minutes. Yield: 2 servings.

Mrs. Marlene Westby, Sioux Valley H. S.
Volga, South Dakota

INDIVIDUAL MEAT LOAVES

1 ½ lb. ground beef
¾ c. oats
2 eggs, beaten
½ c. chopped onion
2 tsp. salt
½ tsp. pepper
1 c. tomato juice
1 can cream of mushroom soup

Combine all ingredients except mushroom soup; shape into medium-sized oblong meat loaves. Place loaves in a glass baking dish. Spoon mushroom soup over each meat loaf. Bake at 350 degrees for 1 hour. Yield: 8 servings.

Ruth Elizabeth Thompson, Mesquite H. S.
Mesquite, Texas

INDIVIDUAL MEAT LOAVES

3 lb. ground beef
2 c. dry bread crumbs
½ c. chopped onion
½ c. grated carrots
½ c. chopped green pepper
1 tbsp. salt
¼ tsp. pepper
1 egg
1 c. milk
1 ½ tbsp. shortening
1 beef bouillon cube
1 c. hot water
½ lb. fresh mushrooms, sliced

Combine beef, bread crumbs, onion, carrots, green pepper, seasonings, egg and milk. Shape mixture into twelve 5 x 2 1/2-inch loaves. Melt shortening in preheated 350 degree electric skillet. Brown loaves well on all sides in shortening. Dissolve bouillon cube in hot water; add to skillet. Cover, with vent closed, and reduce heat to 225 degrees. Simmer for 40 minutes. Saute mushrooms in skillet juices; use as a garnish. Yield: 10-12 servings.

Mrs. Helen Masters, Shallowater H. S.
Shallowater, Texas

LAURA'S MEAT LOAF

1 ½ lb. ground beef
1 c. cracker crumbs
1 med. onion, chopped
2 eggs, beaten
1 c. milk Cheddar cheese, cubed
Salt and pepper to taste
½ c. water
Dash of chili powder (opt.)
Dash of curry powder (opt.)
1 sm. can tomato sauce

Mix all ingredients except one-half of tomato sauce. Pat into a ball; place in a glass baking

(Continued on next page)

dish. Cover with remaining tomato sauce; strip with bacon across top, if desired. Bake at 325 degrees for about 1 hour and 30 minutes. Yield: 6-8 servings.

Mrs. Jo Ann Gray, Waxahachie, H. S.
Waxahachie, Texas

LAYERED MEAT LOAF

1 ½ lb. ground beef
2 ½ tsp. salt
Pepper
2 eggs
2 ½ c. bread crumbs
½ c. milk
½ c. chopped celery
1 tbsp. instant minced onion
1 tbsp. melted butter
1 tbsp. minced parsley

Combine ground beef, 1 1/2 teaspoonful salt, 1/8 teaspoonful pepper, 1 egg, 1/2 cup bread crumbs and milk in large mixing bowl. Blend well. Combine 2 cups bread crumbs, celery, onion, butter, parsley, 1 teaspoonful salt and 1/8 teaspoonful pepper in a bowl. Layer meat mixture and dressing in a 9 x 5 x 3-inch pan, using two layers of meat mixture to one layer of dressing. Bake at 350 degrees for 50 minutes to 1 hour. Yield: 6 servings.

Anglee Smith, Hazel Green H. S.
East Bernstadt, Kentucky
Mrs. Donna Faye Kuehn, Colfax H. S.
Colfax, Washington

LITTLE CHEDDAR LOAVES

1 ½ lb. ground beef
¾ c. oats
1 tsp. salt
½ c. grated sharp Cheddar cheese
¼ c. chopped onion
1 egg
¾ c. milk
1 tbsp. (firmly packed) brown sugar
1 tbsp. prepared mustard
⅓ c. catsup

Combine all ingredients except brown sugar, mustard and catsup. Shape into 6 small loaves. Place in shallow baking pan. Combine remaining ingredients; spread over top of loaves. Bake at 350 degrees for about 35 minutes. Yield: 6 loaves.

Mrs. Mary Neighbors, Arthur H. S.
Arthur, Illinois

MEAT LOAF

5 or 6 slices toast or 2 c. bread crumbs
Water
3 med. onions, minced
1 ½ can tomato soup
3 lb. ground beef
Salt and pepper to taste

Soak toast in water. Squeeze bread or drain in colander. Mix all ingredients except 1/2 can tomato sauce. Press into a greased loaf casserole. Pour remaining soup over top. Bake at 350 degrees for 2 hours. Yield: 8-10 servings.

Mrs. Ralph Hale, Sequatchie Co. H. S.
Dunlap, Tennessee

MEAT LOAF

2 lb. hamburger
1 c. tomato soup
8 saltine crackers, finely crushed
1 egg
1 tsp. salt
½ tsp. poultry seasoning
1 med. onion, grated
2 tbsp. catsup

Combine all ingredients with a potato masher. Place in a greased loaf bread tin. Bake at 350 degrees for about 1 hour. Yield: 8 servings.

Mrs. Dorothy B. Tobey
Hampton Academy Jr. H. S.
Hampton, New Hampshire

MEAT LOAF

2 lb. ground chuck
1 ½ c. diced cheese
2 eggs
2 tsp. seasoned salt
1 c. dry cracker crumbs
1 c. milk
1 onion, diced (opt.)
1 green pepper, chopped (opt.)

Combine all ingredients; mix well. Form into 2 loaves. Bake at 350 degrees for 1 hour and 30 minutes. Yield: 8-10 servings.

Doris Peterson, Chaffey H. S.
Ontario, California

MEAT LOAF

1 lb. ground beef
⅔ c. evaporated milk
⅓ c. fine dry bread crumbs
¼ c. catsup
1 tsp. salt
2 tsp. Worcestershire sauce
¼ tsp. pepper
½ onion, chopped

(Continued on next page)

Combine all ingredients; pour into greased 1 1/2-quart casserole. Surround top and sides of loaf with additional onion slices. Cover with foil. Bake at 350 degrees for 1 hour. Uncover; remove onion slices. Bake for 10 minutes longer to brown meat. Yield: 4 servings.

Juliet Woods Jenkins
Mayewood Consolidated School
Sumter, South Carolina

MEAT LOAF WITH CHEESE STUFFING

3 lb. ground beef
3 c. fresh bread crumbs
1 c. minced onions
½ c. minced green pepper
4 eggs, slightly beaten
3 tbsp. horseradish
1 tbsp. salt
2 tbsp. prepared mustard
¼ c. evaporated milk
¼ c. catsup
2 8-oz. pkg. sharp cheese slices
Snipped parsley

Lightly mix meat, crumbs, onions and green pepper into eggs. Add remaining ingredients except cheese and parsley. Combine lightly. Divide into three parts; pat one part into 10 x 5 x 3-inch loaf pan. Cover with 5 overlapping cheese slices. Spread with second part of meat mixture. Repeat with 6 more cheese slices. Add remaining meat mixture. Invert loaf onto jelly roll pan or foil-covered cookie sheet. Turn up edges of foil to form rim. Bake in preheated 400 degree oven for 45 minutes. Crumble 2 cheese slices over meat loaf; bake for 5 minutes. Cool for 15 minutes before serving. Garnish with parsley. Slice to serve. Yield: 10-12 servings.

Patricia Irvin, Wells-Easton H. S.
Wells, Minnesota

MEAT LOAF WITH PIQUANT SAUCE

1 lb. ground beef
1 egg, beaten
½ to ¾ c. evaporated milk
¼ c. oats
⅛ tsp. garlic powder
¼ tsp. Worcestershire sauce
1 med. onion, chopped
½ green pepper, chopped
Salt and pepper to taste
1 tbsp. brown sugar
½ c. catsup
½ tsp. nutmeg
1 tsp. dry mustard

Combine all ingredients except brown sugar, catsup, nutmeg and mustard; mold into a loaf. Place loaf in a greased pan. Bake at 350 degrees for about 45 minutes. Remove from oven. Combine brown sugar, catsup, nutmeg and mustard; pour over meat loaf. Continue baking for 10 minutes longer. Yield: 5 servings.

Mrs. Dorothy J. Evans, Ouachita Parish H. S.
Monroe, Louisiana

MY MEAT LOAF

2 eggs, slightly beaten
¾ c. milk
1 ½ c. soft bread crumbs
1 envelope dry onion soup mix
⅓ c. canned tomatoes
2 lb. hamburger

Combine eggs, milk, bread crumbs, soup mix and tomatoes in a mixing bowl. Add meat; mix well. Place mixture in greased loaf pan. Bake at 350 degrees for 1 hour. Yield: 10 servings.

Genevieve Overvaag, Mountain Lake H. S.
Mountain Lake, Minnesota

MEAT LOAF AND POTATOES

1 lb. ground beef
1 egg
1 can tomato soup
Salt and pepper to taste
Corn flakes
Mashed potatoes

Combine beef, egg, 1/2 can soup and seasonings with enough corn flakes to make a firm loaf; shape into a loaf. Place in pan. Bake at 350 degrees for 45 minutes. Place loaf on medium serving platter. Spoon mashed potatoes on top of loaf; pour remaining heated tomato soup over top. Yield: 6 servings.

Nancy Wurmle, Farmington Comm. H. S.
Farmington, Illinois

OLD-FASHIONED MEAT LOAF

1 c. bread crumbs
1 c. milk
¼ lb. salt pork, chopped
1 med. onion, chopped
2 eggs, slightly beaten
2 lb. hamburger
¼ c. catsup
¼ tsp. pepper
1 tbsp. salt

Soak bread crumbs in milk. Panfry chopped salt pork and onion until lightly browned. Combine all ingredients except salt pork slices; pack into 8 x 4-inch loaf pan. Cut pork into 2-inch pieces; place on top of meat loaf. Bake at 350 degrees for 1 hour. Yield: 8-10 servings.

Mrs. Elva Sigrest, Walnut Grove H. S.
Walnut Grove, Mississippi

POPULAR MEAT LOAF

1 lge. egg, slightly beaten
½ c. milk
¼ c. minced parsley
2 tbsp. dry onion soup mix
1 tsp. salt
⅛ tsp. pepper
1 tsp. Worcestershire sauce
½ tsp. prepared mustard
1 c. soft bread crumbs
1 lb. lean ground beef
1 tbsp. chili sauce

Mix all ingredients except beef and chili sauce; and beef and mix thoroughly. Place mixture in an 11 x 7 x 2-inch pan. Shape meat into an 8 x 4-inch loaf; spread surface with chili sauce. Bake at 350 degrees for 50 minutes.

Mrs. Effie G. Fisher, Knox Central H. S.
Barbourville, Kentucky

POT ROAST MEAT LOAF

1 lb. ground beef
1 egg (opt.)
⅓ to 1 c. fine bread or cracker crumbs
Salt and pepper to taste
2 tbsp. minced onion (opt.)
⅔ c. evaporated milk
2 tbsp. minced green pepper (opt.)
¼ c. catsup or chili sauce (opt.)
¼ to 2 tsp. Worcestershire sauce
2 or 3 med. potatoes, sliced ¼-in. thick
2 or 3 med. onions, sliced ¼-in. thick
3 med. carrots, peeled and quartered
2 tsp. parsley flakes (opt.)

Combine meat, egg, crumbs, salt, pepper, minced onion, milk, green pepper, catsup and Worcestershire sauce; shape into loaf in center of 13 x 2 x 9-inch pan. Place vegetables in layers around meat. Mix parsley flakes, salt and a few grains of pepper; sprinkle vegetable layers with mixture. Cover tightly with foil. Bake at 375 degrees for about 1 hour or until vegetables are tender. Uncover; bake for 10 minutes longer or until browned. Yield: 4-6 servings.

Mrs. Dixie Dunn Ruby, Charles Town H. S.
Charles Town, West Virginia
Mrs. Edith Conner, Hooks H. S.
Hooks, Texas
Johnie Sport, Dozier H. S.
Dozier, Alabama

RUSCH MEAT LOAF

1 lb. lean ground beef
1 teacup cracker meal
1 tsp. mustard
1 egg
1 tsp. monosodium glutamate
1 tsp. salt
½ tsp. pepper
1 med. green pepper, finely chopped
1 med. onion, finely chopped
Milk
1 10 ¾-oz. can tomato soup
1 No. 2 ½ can whole peeled tomatoes
2 strips bacon

Combine ground beef, cracker meal, mustard, egg, seasonings, green pepper and onion; mix well with fork. Moisten with milk, about 2 cups, until mixture just holds shape. Turn out into baking pan. Shape into an oval. Pour mixture of soup and tomatoes over meat; place strips of bacon across top. Bake at 375 degrees for 40 minutes. Yield: 8 servings.

Sister Mary Isabel, Marylawn of the Oranges
South Orange, New Jersey

STUDENTS' MEAT LOAF

2 slices bread, crumbled
⅔ c. milk
1 lb. ground beef
2 eggs, beaten
½ c. catsup
2 tbsp. Worcestershire sauce
2 tsp. salt
2 sm. onions, finely chopped

Soak bread in milk until softened. Mix all ingredients thoroughly; press into muffin tins, filling each three-fourths full. Bake at 400 degrees for 25 to 30 minutes. Yield: 8 servings.

Mrs. Betty Coles, Bowling Green H. S.
Bowling Green, Kentucky

SUPERB MEAT LOAF

2 slices bread
¾ c. milk
2 lb. ground meat
2 eggs
1 sm. onion, chopped
Salt to taste
1 tsp. pepper
1 can tomato soup
½ c. water
½ tsp. celery salt
½ tsp. garlic salt
1 tbsp. Worcestershire sauce
1 tbsp. sugar
1 tsp. dry mustard

Soak bread in milk; add meat, eggs, onion, salt and pepper. Mix well. Shape mixture into two molded loaves; place in baking dish. Combine all remaining ingredients; pour over meat loaves. Bake at 350 degrees for 1 hour and 15 minutes. Yield: 10 servings.

Mrs. Eleanor Weathermon, Wink H. S.
Wink, Texas

SURPRISE MEAT LOAF

¾ lb. ground chuck
¾ c. dry bread crumbs
⅓ c. diced process American cheese
¼ c. chopped onion
¼ c. chopped celery
1 tbsp. chopped green pepper
1 tsp. salt
Dash of thyme
Dash of garlic salt
1 egg, beaten
½ c. tomato sauce
1 tbsp. catsup

Combine all ingredients except catsup in bowl; blend thoroughly. Place mixture in a shallow baking pan; mold into a uniform loaf. Bake at 350 degrees for 25 minutes. Remove from oven; score top of loaf diagonally a knife; Fill slits with catsup. Return to oven; bake for 30 minutes longer. Remove loaf from oven; let stand in pan 5 minutes before serving. Place on warm serving dish; garnish with tomato wedges and parsley. Yield: 4 servings.

Mrs. Janet G. Trefry, Duxbury H. S.
Duxbury, Massachusetts

ZESTY MEAT LOAF

1 lb. round steak, ground
1 sm. onion, minced
1 sm. green pepper, minced
1 ⅓ c. soft bread crumbs
½ tsp. salt
½ c. milk
1 egg
2 ½ tsp. horseradish
½ tsp. dry mustard
⅓ c. plus 3 tbsp. catsup

Combine all ingredients except 1/3 cup catsup; blend well. Pack firmly into 9 1/2 x 5 1/4 x 2 3/4-inch casserole. Pour remaining catsup over loaf. Bake at 350 degrees for 1 hour and 30 minutes.

Mrs. Julia Miller Simpson, Troutman H. S.
Troutman, North Carolina

BARBECUED HAMBURGERS

1 lb. ground beef
2 tbsp. fat
2 tbsp. water
½ tsp. chili powder
1 tsp. Worcestershire sauce
1 tbsp. vinegar
2 tbsp. brown sugar
¼ tsp. dry mustard
½ tsp. salt
1 c. tomato sauce

Shape ground beef into six patties; freeze. Brown frozen patties slowly on both sides in hot fat. Combine all remaining ingredients except tomato sauce in a small bowl. Spoon off excess fat from meat; pour in tomato sauce. Cover; cook for 25 to 30 minutes longer. Yield: 6 servings.

Mrs. B. Fred German, Copper Basin H. S.
Copperhill, Tennessee

BARBECUED HAMBURGERS

1 ½ lb. hamburger
½ c. fine dry bread crumbs
½ c. milk
1 ½ tsp. salt
⅛ tsp. pepper
2 tbsp. horseradish
½ c. diced onion
¼ c. vinegar
2 tsp. Worcestershire sauce
½ c. catsup or chili sauce
¾ tsp. chili powder

Combine hamburger with bread crumbs, milk, salt, pepper, horseradish and 1/4 cup diced onion; mix well. Shape into patties; place in shallow baking pan. Mix remaining onion, vinegar, Worcestershire sauce, catsup and chili powder in saucepan. Heat to boiling; pour over hamburger patties. Bake at 350 degrees for 45 minutes. Yield: 6 servings.

Ann Dean Carr, Caverna H. S.
Cave City, Kentucky

BEEF PATTIES

1 ½ lb. ground beef
⅓ c. finely chopped onion
1 tbsp. prepared mustard
1 tbsp. Worcestershire sauce
1 tsp. salt
1 tsp. pepper
4 slices cheese

Combine all ingredients except cheese; shape into four round patties. Circle each pattie with a slice of bacon; secure with a toothpick. Broil about 4 inches from heat for 12 minutes on each side. Place a slice of cheese on each pattie during last few minutes of broiling. Yield: 4 servings.

Nell Criswell, Northwest H. S.
Justin, Texas

HAMBURGER DELIGHT

2 lb. ground beef
2 tsp. salt
½ tsp. pepper
1 tbsp. shortening or oil
8 tbsp. chopped onion (opt.)
1 sm. can mushrooms (opt.)
1 can cream of mushroom soup

Mix ground beef, salt and pepper; shape into eight patties. Brown hamburgers on both sides in hot shortening. Place in shallow baking dish.

(Continued on next page)

Sprinkle 1 tablespoonful chopped onion over each hamburger. Cover with mushrooms and soup. Bake at 350 degrees for 30 to 45 minutes. Yield: 4-6 servings.

Annita Bullock, Satanta Rural H. S.
Satanta, Kansas
Mrs. Peggy Hall, Gosnell H. S.
Blytheville, Arkansas

HAMBURGER STEAKS CREOLE

Seasonings to taste
1 ½ lb. ground beef
½ med. green pepper
½ c. diced onion
½ c. diced celery
1 can tomato sauce

Season ground beef; shape into steaks. Panfry with green pepper, onion and celery until almost done. Add tomato sauce; simmer for 8 to 10 minutes. Yield: 6 servings.

Betty Lou Blackburn, Konawa H. S.
Konawa, Oklahoma

HAWAIIAN HAMBURGER WITH SWEET 'N' SOUR SAUCE

⅔ c. evaporated milk
1 ½ lb. ground beef
½ c. chopped onion
⅔ c. cracker crumbs
1 tsp. seasoned salt
1 15-oz. can pineapple chunks
2 tbsp. cornstarch
¼ c. vinegar
¼ c. brown sugar
2 tbsp. soy sauce

Combine milk ground beef, onion, crumbs and salt. Form mixture into six 4-inch patties, by pressing each between two pieces of waxed paper. Brown patties in skillet in small amount of fat. Drain pineapple; reserve syrup. Add enough water to reserved syrup to equal 1 cup liquid. Combine syrup, cornstarch, vinegar, brown sugar and soy sauce in a saucepan; cook, stirring until thick and clear. Pour excess fat off of patties. Cover patties with sauce. Add pineapple chunks. Cover; simmer over low heat for 15 minutes. Yield: 6 servings.

Mrs. Iris Kozmak, Two Hills H. S.
Two Hills, Alberta, Canada

HOBO DINNER

2 lb. hamburger
3 med. potatoes, sliced
3 carrots, sliced
2 stalks celery, sliced
½ tsp. salt
⅛ tsp. pepper

Shape hamburger patties. Place a layer of potatoes on a pattie; top with another pattie. Seal together. Add carrots, then another pattie. Seal. Add celery, then another pattie. Seal. Repeat with remaining hamburger patties. Salt and pepper. Wrap in foil. Broil for 20 to 25 minutes. Yield: 4 servings.

Kathaleen Hellickson, Harlem H. S.
Harlem, Montana

HOBO DINNER

1 lb. ground beef
2 med. potatoes, quartered
2 med. onions, quartered
2 carrots, sliced
2 pats butter
Salt and pepper to taste

Shape meat into two patties; place on piece of aluminum foil. Top with potatoes, onions and carrots; wrap tightly. Bake at 350 degrees for 1 hour. Butter and season patties and vegetables; serve. Yield: 2 servings.

Jean Bugg, Highland Home H. S.
Highland Home, Alabama

HOBO'S DINNER

¼ lb. hamburger
¾ c. cubed potatoes
½ c. cubed carrots
½ tsp. salt
Dash of pepper
¼ tsp. onion soup mix

Shape hamburger into one pattie. Place potatoes, carrots and hamburger pattie in center of 12-inch piece of foil. Season well with salt and pepper; add soup mix. Fold sides up over food and secure with drugstore wrap. Fold ends over several times so juices do not leak through. Bake in 400 degree oven or over grill for 1 hour. Yield: 1 serving.

Mrs. Nora Estrem, Battle Lake H. S.
Battle Lake, Minnesota

LUMBERJACK HAMBURGERS

⅓ c. butter or margarine
2 c. finely chopped onions
1 c. finely chopped green peppers
3 lb. ground beef chuck
2 eggs, slightly beaten

(Continued on next page)

3 tbsp. Worcestershire sauce
2 tsp. salt
½ tsp. pepper
¾ c. chili sauce
1 ½ tsp. oregano
1 c. grated sharp Cheddar cheese

Melt butter in skillet; add onions and green peppers. Cook for about 5 minutes or until tender. Combine ground beef, eggs, Worcestershire sauce, salt and pepper; mix lightly. Shape mixture into twelve 6 x 3-inch patties. Spoon green pepper mixture onto center of six patties; top each with 2 tablespoonfuls chili sauce and 1/4 teaspoonful oregano. Cover with remaining patties. Press; seal edges securely. Place in refrigerator until ready to cook. Broil 3 inches from heat for about 5 minutes on each side or until desired doneness. Sprinkle cheese over top of patties; broil just until cheese melts. Serve immediately. Yield: 6 servings.

Joanne F. Jordan, H.M. Bailey Jr. H. S.
West Haven, Connecticut

MOCK VEAL CUTLETS

1 ½ lb. ground meat
Salt and pepper to taste
3 eggs
2 c. broken crackers
Shortening

Crumble ground meat into large bowl; season to taste. Beat 2 eggs; add to meat. Mix well. Add 3/4 cup cracker bits to meat mixture; mix well. Shape into firm 4 x 6-inch squares. Place remaining cracker bits on waxed paper. Beat remaining egg in sauce dish. Dip meat into egg; roll in crackers. Fry in hot fat until golden brown and well done. Drain. Yield: 6 servings.

Mrs. Ruth Brown, Tenton H. S.
Tenton, Louisiana

PANBROILED BEEF PATTIES

1 lb. ground beef
1 tsp. salt
½ c. soft bread crumbs
¼ c. half and half
1 tbsp. minced onion
1 tbsp. fat

Mix beef, salt, crumbs, half and half and onion. Shape mixture into 4 patties, 1/2-inch thick. Melt fat in skillet; cook patties over medium heat for about 6 minutes on each side or until browned. Yield: 4 servings.

Shari Leaf, Del Norte H. S.
Del Norte, Colorado

MOCK FILET MIGNON

1 lb. ground beef
1 c. bread crumbs
Milk
1 tsp. salt
½ c. ground raw carrots
1 egg
½ tsp. pepper
1 tbsp. onion juice
6 slices bacon

Combine all ingredients except bacon; shape into patties 3/4-inch thick. Wrap each pattie with one slice of bacon; stick with toothpicks. Place on broiler rack 3 inches from unit. Broil for 15 minutes. Yield: 6 servings.

Mrs. Clara Maples, Sweeny H. S.
Sweeney, Texas

PAUL BUNYAN BURGERS

1 egg
2 lb. hamburger
2 tbsp. Worcestershire sauce
1 ½ tsp. salt
½ tsp. garlic salt
Pepper
Grated cheese
Chopped dill pickle
Chopped onion (opt.)

Mix egg, hamburger, Worcestershire sauce, salt, garlic salt and pepper; divide into 4 balls. Flatten each ball into a round pattie. Mix remaining ingredients. Place filling on half of each pattie; fold pattie and seal edges. Broil for 5 to 8 minutes. Yield: 4 servings.

Colleen Lenz, New Prague H. S.
New Prague, Minnesota

PICNIC MEAT PATTIES

2 lb. onions, peeled and chopped
2 lb. ground beef
½ bunch parsley, minced
1 c. fine dry bread crumbs
2 eggs
2 tbsp. grated Parmesan cheese
½ tsp. thyme
2 tsp. salt
½ tsp. pepper
Oil

Boil onions until tender; drain thoroughly; force through sieve. Combine onions with remaining ingredients except oil. Shape into 48 small patties. Fry in hot shallow oil; drain on absorbent paper. Yield: 8 servings.

Helen Janis Hale, Somerset H. S.
Somerset, Kentucky

POOR MAN'S STEAK

6 ground beef patties
Flour
1 can mushroom soup or 2 c. thin gravy
½ soup can milk
Salt and pepper to taste

Roll beef patties in flour. Brown slightly in a small amount of hot fat. Place in a single layer in a baking dish. Cover with mushroom soup mixed with milk. Season to taste. Bake at 250 degrees for 2 hours and 30 minutes to 3 hours. Serve topped with sauce or gravy. Yield: 6 servings.

Mrs. Maralee H. Garland, Unicoi Co. H. S.
Erwin, Tennessee

SALISBURY STEAK

1 lb. ground beef
½ c. cream or evaporated milk
1 tbsp. grated onion
1 tsp. salt
½ tsp. pepper
2 tbsp. flour
2 tbsp. bacon drippings or margarine
½ c. consomme or 1 beef bouillon cube
¼ to ½ c. dry red wine
1 tsp. Worcestershire sauce
2 tbsp. chopped parsley
1 4-oz. can mushrooms, undrained

Mix beef with cream, onion, salt, and pepper; shape into three or four patties. Brown meat; remove from skillet. Add flour to drippings; blend well. Add consomme and wine; cook, stirring constantly, until mixture boils and thickens. Add Worcestershire sauce, parsley and mushrooms (with liquid). Season to taste. Serve over meat and rice or potatoes. Yield: 3-4 servings.

Mrs. Nancy K. Roop, Dodge City Jr. H. S.
Dodge City, Kansas

POTATO BURGERS

1 med. onion, grated
2 lge. potatoes, grated
1 tsp. salt
1 ½ lb. hamburger
1 No. 2 ½ can tomatoes

Mix onion and potatoes; add salt and hamburger. Mix well; shape into patties. Brown on one side in heavy skillet. Turn; pour tomatoes over patties. Cover. Continue cooking on low heat for 35 to 40 minutes or until done. Yield: 4-6 servings.

Mrs. Audrey Vandenborre
Armstrong Secondary School
Armstrong, British Columbia, Canada

SALISBURY STEAK

1 egg, slightly beaten
½ c. milk
2 slices soft bread, crumbled
1 lb. lean ground beef
1 ½ tsp. salt
½ tsp. pepper
½ tsp. paprika
¼ c. finely chopped green pepper
¼ c. finely chopped celery
¼ c. finely chopped onion
1 c. dry bread crumbs

Beat egg; add milk and crumbled soft bread. Let soak. Mix in all remaining ingredients except dry bread crumbs; shape into patties about 1/2-inch thick. Coat well with dry bread crumbs. Heat cooking oil or shortening in skillet to about half cover steaks; fry on each side until golden brown. Yield: 6 servings.

Mrs. Vada Belle Zellner
South San Antonio H. S.
San Antonio, Texas

SAVORY BEEF BURGERS

1 ½ c. Rice Krispies
1 ½ lb. ground beef
¼ c. chili sauce
1 tsp. salt
1 tsp. Worcestershire sauce
2 tsp. prepared mustard
3 tbsp. grated onion
1 egg, slightly beaten
6 slices bacon

(Continued on next page)

Crush Rice Krispies slightly. Combine with remaining ingredients except bacon; mix well. Divide meat mixture into six patties. Cut each bacon slice into two strips; arrange crosswise. Place a pattie in center. Bring strips together on top of pattie; fasten with toothpick or skewer. Place on broiler rack. Broil for 6 minutes; turn and broil for 6 minutes. Serve immediately. Garnish with tomato wedges. Yield: 6 servings.

Mrs. Virginia T. Darling, Laingsburg H. S.
Laingsburg, Michigan

STEAKBURGER DELUXE

2 lb. lean ground chuck
Garlic salt to taste
Salt and pepper to taste
3 onions, sliced
2 green peppers, sliced
1 stick butter
6 med. potatoes, sliced

Shape meat into six patties; place on a double square of aluminum foil. Season. Place a large slice of onion over top of each pattie; add slice of green pepper and a pat of butter. Place potatoes around meat; season. Wrap in foil. Bake at 300 degrees for about 1 hour and 15 minutes. Yield: 6 servings.

Mrs. Lodena Waggoner, Hickory Att Center
Hickory, Mississippi

STUFFED HAMBURGER PATTIES

1 lb. hamburger
1 tsp. salt
2 tbsp. butter
1 tsp. poultry seasoning
¼ tsp. pepper
Juice of 1 lemon
1 sm. onion
3 tbsp. cracker or bread crumbs

Combine hamburger and salt; divide into eight parts. Form into patties. Mix remaining ingredients. Place mixture on four patties. Cover with remaining patties; seal edges. Brown in skillet until done. Serve while hot. Yield: 4 servings.

Marie Edmunds, Bonners Ferry H. S.
Bonners Ferry, Idaho

TEXAS BURGERS

Seasonings to taste
1 ½ lb. ground beef
4 slices American cheese
4 to 8 slices tomato
1 onion, chopped

Season ground beef; shape into eight thin patties. On top of each of four patties, place a slice of cheese, 1 or 2 slices tomato and 1 teaspoonful chopped onion. Place remaining patties over top; seal edges well. Broil patties 4 inches from heat for 10 minutes on each side. Yield: 4 servings.

Olga Masch Decker, Gunter H. S.
Gunter, Texas

T-BONE STEAKETTES

1 lb. hamburger
¾ c. tomato juice
¼ c. catsup
2 tbsp. minced onion
1 tsp. salt
½ tsp. pepper
1 egg, beaten
4 slices stale bread
Thin carrot strips

Mix meat with tomato juice, catsup, onion, salt, pepper and egg. Place bread in deep bowl; completely cover with cold water. Soak for 1 hour. Squeeze bread gently and crumble. Thoroughly combine bread crumbs with meat mixture. Shape into steakettes. Form T-bone with strips of carrot. Place on broiler pan, carrot-bone down. Broil for 10 minutes. Turn; broil to 10 to 12 minutes or until done. Yield: 8 servings.

Mrs. Louise H. Motes, Laurens H. S.
Laurens, South Carolina

HAMBURGER-ONION PIE

1 c. plus 2 tbsp. prepared biscuit mix
⅓ c. light cream
1 lb. ground beef
2 med. onions, sliced
1 tsp. salt
¼ tsp. pepper (opt.)
¼ tsp. celery seed (opt.)
½ tsp. monosodium glutamate
2 eggs, slightly beaten
1 c. small curd cottage cheese
Paprika (opt.)

Mix 1 cup biscuit mix and cream with fork; knead gently 10 times on lightly floured surface. Roll dough to fit a 9-inch pie pan. Flute edges. Saute ground beef and onions until meat loses color. Add salt, pepper, celery seed, monosodium glutamate and remaining biscuit mix; spread over dough in pan. Blend eggs with cottage cheese; pour over meat mixture. Sprinkle with paprika. Bake at 375 degrees for 30 minutes. Cut into wedges to serve. Yield: 6-8 servings.

Mrs. Mavis Waterman, Elkton Public H. S.
Elkton, Minnesota
Mrs. Carolyn Mueckler, Brethren H. S.
Brethren, Michigan

HAMBURGER PIE

¼ c. minced onion
1 lb. ground beef
⅓ c. plus 2 tbsp. shortening
1 can tomato soup
½ soup can water
1 tsp. salt
¼ tsp. pepper
1 tbsp. Worcestershire sauce
⅓ c. brown sugar
2 c. sifted flour
1 tbsp. baking powder
½ tsp. salt
¾ c. milk

Brown onion and ground beef in skillet with 2 tablespoonfuls shortening. Add tomato soup, water, seasonings and brown sugar. Simmer. Measure and sift flour with baking powder and salt; cut in remaining shortening. Add milk, stirring only until flour is moistened. Turn beef mixture into a 2-quart casserole. Cover with pastry. Bake at 400 degrees for 25 minutes. Turn onto serving plate with topping-side down. Yield: 6 servings.

Mrs. Margaret A. Poling, Bridgman H. S.
Bridgman, Michigan

HAMBURGER PIE

1 lb. hamburger
2 tbsp. butter
½ tsp. salt
⅛ tsp. pepper
⅛ tsp. garlic salt
⅛ tsp. thyme
⅛ tsp. nutmeg
⅛ tsp. marjoram
1 tbsp. minced parsley
1 tbsp. minced onion
1 tbsp. lemon juice
1 can frozen cream of potato soup, thawed
1 8-in. pie shell

Brown meat in butter; stir to crumble. Add salt, pepper, seasonings, parsley, onion and lemon juice. Blend in potato soup; heat thoroughly. Spoon into pie shell; top with pastry strips, if desired. Bake at 400 degrees for 10 minutes or until throughly heated. Yield: 4 servings.

Mrs. Carol Maata, Dye Jr. H. S.
Flint, Michigan

SWISSBURGER PIE

¼ c. fat
½ c. chopped onion
1 lb. ground chuck
¼ c. flour
2 tsp. salt
¼ tsp. pepper
2 ½ c. tomato juice
¼ c. diced green pepper (opt.)
1 c. diced celery
1 recipe pastry or 1 stick packaged pastry

Heat fat in heavy frying pan. Saute onion in fat until golden brown; add ground chuck and brown. Stir in flour, salt and pepper. Add tomato juice, green pepper and celery. Bring to a boil; simmer for 10 minutes. Pour into 1 1/2-quart casserole; cover with pastry topping. Bake for 30 to 35 minutes. Yield: 6 servings.

Daphne Smith, Winnsboro H. S.
Winnsboro, Texas

BEEF BARBECUE

5 lb. hamburger
1 lb. onions, chopped
5 stalks celery, chopped
5 tbsp. brown sugar
1 ½ bottles catsup
3 tbsp. tapioca
8 tbsp. vinegar
1 tsp. poultry seasoning
3 tsp. salt

Saute hamburger, onions and celery; add all remaining ingredients. Simmer for 1 hour and 30 minutes. Yield: 50 servings.

Mrs. Gaynelle C. James, Gardner S.W. H. S.
Gardner, Illinois

ELECTRIC SKILLET BEEF SUPPER

2 lb. ground chuck
1 lge. onion, chopped
1 clove of garlic, minced
2 to 3 stalks celery
1 green pepper, chopped
½ pt. sour cream
1 can mushrooms
1 can cream of mushroom soup
1 tsp. salt

Brown beef with onion and garlic; add remaining ingredients. Simmer for 1 hour. Serve on rice, if desired. Yield: 6 servings.

Mrs. Berniece Gorsuch, Bellingham H. S.
Bellingham, Washington

HAMBURGER STROGANOFF

2 lb. ground beef
Salt and pepper to taste
1 onion, diced
1 can cream of mushroom soup
1 3-oz. can sliced mushrooms
2 tbsp. catsup
2 tsp. Worcestershire sauce
1 c. sour cream

Brown ground beef; season with salt and pepper. Add onion and brown lightly. Add remaining ingredients except sour cream; simmer for 1

(Continued on next page)

hour. Just before serving, add sour cream and heat through. Serve over rice. Yield: 8 servings.

Theresa A. Zettel, Reedsville H. S.
Reedsville, Wisconsin

WEST VIRGINIA SLOPPY JOES

25 lb. hamburger
5 lge. onions, chopped
1 bunch celery, chopped
½ 9-oz. jar prepared mustard
½ lb. light brown sugar
4 cans tomato paste
4 qt. tomato juice
2 tbsp. monosodium glutamate
2 tsp. garlic salt
¼ tsp. pepper
2 tbsp. salt

Brown hamburger; add onions and celery. Remove from heat. Combine mustard, sugar and tomato paste. Mix with tomato juice, monosodium glutamate, garlic salt, pepper and salt. Add sauce to meat. Simmer for 1 to 2 hours or until sauce consistency is reached. Yield: 16 servings.

Mrs. Winifred McCoy, Follansbee H. S.
Follansbee, West Virginia

ITALIAN SURPRISE

1 lb. ground beef
1 clove of garlic, minced
2 tbsp. chopped onion
1 tbsp. oil or butter
1 can tomato soup
1 can tomato paste
1 paste can water
½ tsp. salt
½ tsp. pepper
¼ tsp. chili powder
1 sm. bottle whole mushrooms
1 bottle small stuffed green olives
½ lb. uncooked macaroni

Stir and cook beef, garlic and onion in hot oil until beef is lightly browned; add soup, tomato paste, water and seasonings. Simmer for 20 minutes. Add mushrooms and olives; simmer for 10 minutes longer. Cook macaroni; drain. Add to meat mixture. Heat thoroughly. Yield: 5-6 servings.

Maudie White, Gridley Jr. H. S.
Erie, Pennsylvania

SKILLET MACARONI AND BEEF

1 ½ lb. ground beef
½ c. minced onion
½ lb. uncooked elbow or salad macaroni
½ c. chopped green pepper
Vegetable oil
2 8-oz. cans tomato sauce
1 c. water
1 tsp. salt
¼ tsp. pepper
1 to 1 ½ tbsp. Worcestershire sauce

Cook beef in large skillet until meat loses redness. Remove from skillet; cook onion, macaroni and green pepper in drippings until macaroni is yellow. Add 1 to 2 tablespoonfuls oil, if needed. Return meat to skillet with tomato sauce, water, salt, pepper and Worcestershire sauce. Cover; simmer for 25 minutes or until macaroni is cooked. Yield: 6 servings.

Eldena M. Koger, Pickett Co. H. S.
Byrdstown, Tennessee

BEEF AND DUMPLINGS IN SOUR CREAM

1 lb. ground beef
1 sm. onion
2 tbsp. fat
1 8-oz. pkg. dumplings
3 c. tomato juice
2 tsp. salt
Dash of pepper
2 tsp. Worcestershire sauce
1 c. sour cream

Brown meat and onion in hot fat in heavy saucepan. Place dumplings in a layer over meat. Combine remaining ingredients except sour cream; pour over dumplings to moisten. Bring to a boil. Cover tightly; simmer over low heat for 40 minutes or until dumplings are tender. Stir in sour cream just before serving. Heat thoroughly. Turn into serving dish; sprinkle with buttered crumbs or Parmesan cheese and paprika, if desired. Yield: 4 servings.

Mrs. Madge C. Young, Hiddenite H. S.
Hiddenite, North Carolina

BEEF STROGANOFF

1 lb. ground beef
1 med. onion, chopped
2 c. uncooked noodles
3 c. tomato juice
2 tsp. Worcestershire sauce
2 tsp. salt
⅛ tsp. pepper
½ c. water
1 c. sour cream

Brown beef and onion; add noodles. Mix remaining ingredients except sour cream; pour over beef and noodles. Spread sour cream on top; do not stir. Bring to a boil; simmer for 45 minutes or until noodles are tender. Yield: 6 servings.

Rhonda Trainor, Brewster Vocational School
Tampa, Florida

BEEF-NOODLE CASSEROLE

1 lb. hamburger
1 sm. onion, finely chopped
1 tsp. salt
½ tsp. pepper
1 can onion soup
1 can cream of celery soup
1 tsp. parsley
1 10-oz. pkg. noodles, cooked

Brown meat and onion in skillet. Add salt and pepper. Add soups and parsley; simmer for 30 minutes. Add cooked noodles; heat. Yield: 6 servings.

Mrs. Hazel Oakes Jeane, Bloomington H. S.
Bloomington, Texas

JIFFY BEEF STROGANOFF

1 lb. ground beef
2 tbsp. fat
½ box dry onion soup mix
½ tsp. ginger
3 c. medium noodles
1 3-oz. can sliced mushrooms
3 to 3 ½ c. hot water
2 tbsp. flour
1 c. sour cream

Brown ground beef in fat in electric fry pan at 350 degrees. Sprinkle with dry onion soup mix and ginger. Arrange noodles in layer over meat; add mushrooms with liquid. Pour water over noodles until all are moistened; cover tightly. Reduce heat to 225 degrees; cook for 20 to 25 minutes or until noodles are done. Blend flour into sour cream; stir into stroganoff. Cook for 3 minutes longer. NOTE: If desired, 2 tablespoonfuls cooking Sherry may be added just before serving. Yield: 6-8 servings.

Billie C. Carver, Roxboro H. S.
Roxboro, North Carolina
Mrs. Eunice S. Tate, Malvern H. S.
Malvern, Arkansas

WITCHES BREW

¼ lb. bacon, cut up
1 ½ lb. ground beef
2 lge. onions, chopped
2 green peppers, chopped
1 sm. can mushrooms, cut up
1 can kidney beans
2 c. noodles, cooked
1 No. 2 can tomatoes
Grated cheese

Fry bacon until crisp. Fry hamburger until brown; add onions and peppers. Add mushrooms, kidney beans, noodles and tomatoes; simmer for 1 hour over low heat. Sprinkle with grated cheese; place in oven to blend. Yield: 8 servings.

Mrs. Sara Yowell, Hillcrest Jr. H. S.
Hayetteville, Arkansas

ELECTRIC SKILLET SPAGHETTI

1 lb. hamburger
1 c. chopped onions
1 tbsp. fat
3 c. tomato juice
¼ tsp. mace
¼ tsp. allspice
½ tsp. mustard
1 tsp. salt
¼ tsp. pepper
1 ½ c. broken dry spaghetti

Brown hamburger and onions in fat in electric skillet on medium heat. Add tomato juice and seasonings. Turn heat to high; bring to a boil. Sprinkle spaghetti over top. Cover; cook slowly over low heat for about 25 minutes. Yield: 10 servings.

Mrs. Zula Rowland, Mackville H. S.
Mackville, Kentucky

FAMILY-STYLE SPAGHETTI

1 onion, minced
1 green pepper, finely chopped
2 tbsp. shortening
1 lb. ground beef
3 ½ c. canned tomatoes with liquid
2 cloves of garlic, finely chopped
1 bay leaf, crumbled
1 tsp. salt
⅛ tsp. pepper
1 16-oz. pkg. spaghetti, cooked and drained
Grated Parmesan cheese

Cook onion and green pepper in hot shortening until yellow. Add meat; cook until browned. Add remaining ingredients except spaghetti and cheese. Simmer slowly for 30 minutes to 1 hour. Pour over spaghetti; sprinkle generously with Parmesan cheese. NOTE: One pound ground pork and 1/2 pound ground beef may be substituted for 1 pound ground beef. Yield: 6-8 servings.

Mrs. Mary Hult, Aldergrove Secondary School
Aldergrove, British Columbia, Canada

GROUND BEEF WITH SPAGHETTI

1 green pepper, chopped
1 med. onion, chopped
3 or 4 tbsp. cooking oil
1 lb. ground beef
1 No. 303 can tomatoes
1 sm. can English peas
1 sm. can button mushrooms
1 tsp. salt
Pepper
1 tbsp. Worcestershire sauce
1 10-oz. pkg. spaghetti, cooked and drained

Brown green pepper and onion in hot oil in large skillet; add ground beef. Mix well and cook until done, stirring often. Add tomatoes, English peas, mushrooms and seasonings. Simmer for 15 to 20 minutes. Cook spaghetti as directed on package;

(Continued on next page)

drain. Mix thoroughly with ground beef mixture. Yield: 6-8 servings.

Mrs. Wylodine Reed, Aberdeen H. S.
Aberdeen, Mississippi

HAMBURGER MEAT SAUCE AND SPAGHETTI

2 tbsp. fat
1 lb. hamburger
1 tsp. salt
1 8-oz. can tomato sauce
1 8-oz. can spaghetti sauce
½ c. water
1 lb. spaghetti

Melt fat in medium-sized skillet. Add hamburger; brown. Add salt. Add tomato sauce, spaghetti sauce and water. Simmer for 15 minutes. Cook spaghetti according to directions on package; drain. Mix sauce and spaghetti or serve separate. Yield: 4 servings.

Mrs. Roberta R. Martin, Central H. S.
Shelbyville, Tennessee

HAMBURGER-SPAGHETTI DINNER

½ med. onion, chopped
Shortening
1 ½ lb. hamburger
1 can cream of mushroom soup
1 15-oz. can tomato sauce
½ c. ripe olives
1 12-oz. pkg. spaghetti, cooked and drained
1 c. shredded cheese

Brown onion lightly in small amount of shortening. Add to hamburger; cook in covered frying pan until done. Mix mushroom soup with tomato sauce and olives. Stir mixture thoroughly; add to hamburger. Slowly add hamburger mixture to spaghetti. Place mixture in medium baking dish; cover with shredded cheese. Bake at 350 degrees for 15 minutes. Yield: 8 servings.

Mrs. Edna Crow, Hollis H. S.
Hollis, Oklahoma

ITALIAN SPAGHETTI WITH MEAT BALLS

1 med. onion, chopped
2 cloves of garlic, minced
2 tbsp. cooking oil
1 pt. tomatoes, mashed
1 6-oz. can tomato paste
4 tsp. oregano
2 tsp. salt
¼ tsp. pepper
1 lb. ground beef
4 slices bacon
2 hard-cooked eggs, chopped
1 slice bread, diced
8 oz. spaghetti
Parmesan cheese

Saute onion and garlic in oil; add tomatoes, tomato paste, 3 teaspoonfuls oregano, 1 teaspoonful salt and pepper. Simmer for 1 hour and 30 minutes to 2 hours or until thick. Combine beef, remaining salt and remaining oregano. Fry bacon; drain, reserving drippings. Crumble bacon. Combine eggs, bread, bacon and 2 tablespoonfuls of reserved drippings; form into balls. Press meat mixture around egg balls firmly; fry in bacon drippings for 10 minutes. Add meat balls to tomato sauce; simmer for 10 minutes longer. Cook spaghetti in boiling salted water for 7 minutes or until tender; drain. Cover with meat balls and sauce; sprinkle with cheese. Yield: 6 servings.

Mrs. Velma Cain, Burwell H. S.
Burwell, Nebraska

MEAT AND SPAGHETTI

1 lb. ground beef
2 tbsp. shortening
1 c. diced green peppers
1 c. diced onions
1 c. diced celery
1 clove of garlic, minced
1 box long spaghetti
1 c. catsup
2 cans tomato juice
1 tsp. allspice
1 bay leaf
1 tsp. fresh or dried parsley
½ tsp. thyme
2 tbsp. Worcestershire sauce
2 tbsp. steak sauce
½ lb. cheese, grated

Brown meat in shortening until meat is well seared. Cook green peppers, onions, celery and garlic in a small amount of water until tender; add to meat with remaining ingredients except cheese. Cook slowly until spaghetti is tender. Add cheese about 30 minutes before serving. Yield: 10-12 servings.

Mrs. Mary Anne Power, Sidney H. S.
Sidney, Texas

MEAT SAUCE WITH SPAGHETTI

1 lb. ground beef
1 med. onion, finely chopped
1 tsp. garlic salt
3 tsp. salt
½ tsp. red pepper (opt.)
⅛ tsp. black pepper (opt.)
2 tsp. chili powder
2 tsp. Worcestershire sauce
4 c. tomato sauce
1 lb. long thin spaghetti, cooked

Brown meat; drain off excess fat. Add onion; cook for 1 minute. Add garlic salt, salt, peppers, chili powder, Worcestershire sauce and tomato sauce. Cover; simmer for 2 hours, stirring occasionally. Serve over hot cooked spaghetti; sprinkle with grated cheese. Yield: 8-10 servings.

Mrs. Maxine Sewell, Cordell H. S.
Cordell, Oklahoma

SKILLET SPAGHETTI

1 lb. ground beef
¼ c. corn meal
1 c. chopped onions
1 tsp. salt
¼ c. chopped green pepper
⅔ c. evaporated milk
2 tbsp. flour
¼ c. margarine
2 No. 2 cans tomato juice
1 tsp. chili powder
1 7-oz. pkg. spaghetti

Mix meat, corn meal, 1/2 cup onion, 1/2 teaspoonful salt, one-half of pepper and evaporated milk; mix well. Shape into twelve balls. Roll and coat each ball in flour. Melt margarine in large frying pan over low heat; add meat balls. Brown on all sides. Push balls to sides of pan to form ring; cook until tender. Place remaining onions and green pepper in center of ring; cook until vegetables are tender. Pour tomato juice, 1/2 teaspoonful salt and chili powder over mixture; add spaghetti. Cover. Cook, stirring, for 40 minutes or until done. Yield: 6 servings.

Mrs. Freida K. Wooden, Bremen Comm. H. S.
Midlothian, Illinois

SPAGHETTI

1 clove of garlic, minced
1 green pepper, minced
1 med. onion, minced
1 tbsp. salt
Red pepper
Paprika
7 tbsp. cooking oil
1 ½ lb. ground beef
1 18-oz. pkg. spaghetti, cooked
1 lge. can tomatoes
1 lge. can corn
Grated Parmesan cheese

Cook garlic, green pepper, onion, salt, red pepper and paprika in cooking oil for 10 minutes. Add ground beef; cook for 10 minutes longer or until brown. Add spaghetti; cook for 10 minutes. Add tomatoes and corn; simmer for 30 minutes. Sprinkle with Parmesan cheese. Yield: 12 servings.

Mrs. Irene Bruce, Livingston H. S.
Livingston, Alabama
Peggy T. Raybon, Livingston H. S.
Livingston, Alabama

SPAGHETTI PLATTER DINNER

1 lge. onion, chopped
¼ c. salad oil
1 lb. ground beef
1 8-oz. can tomato sauce
2 ½ c. tomatoes
1 c. water
½ c. chopped celery
1 clove of garlic, minced
½ bay leaf
2 to 3 tsp. chili powder
1 tsp. salt
Dash of pepper
1 8-oz. pkg. long spaghetti
1 3-oz. pkg. grated Parmesan cheese

Brown onion in hot salad oil; add meat and brown. Add remaining ingredients except spaghetti and cheese; simmer for 2 hours, stirring occasionally. Cook spaghetti in boiling salted water until tender. Drain; rinse with hot water and drain. Pour sauce over spaghetti on large platter. Toss with forks to blend. Sprinkle with cheese. Yield: 6 servings.

Broxie C. Stuckey, Gordo School
Gordo, Alabama

BUBU'S CURRIED RICE

1 lb. ground beef
1 lge. onion, chopped
⅛ c. cooking oil
1 c. uncooked rice
1 can tomato soup
2 ½ soup cans water
1 c. chopped potato
1 pkg. frozen peas
¼ tsp. garlic powder
½ tsp. curry powder
½ tsp. salt

Saute beef and onion in oil in large fry pan until onion is lightly browned; add rice, soup and water, stirring well. Add potato and peas. Add garlic powder, curry powder and salt. Cover; bring to a boil. Simmer for 15 minutes. Top with sour cream or yoghurt. Yield: 4 servings.

Niva J. Reddick, Largo H. S.
Largo, Florida

BEEF SCRAMBLE

1 lb. ground beef
1 pkg. dry onion soup mix
1 c. diced celery
2 c. diced celery
2 c. canned tomatoes
½ c. uncooked rice

Saute beef until color changes; drain. Combine in saucepan with remaining ingredients. Cover and heat on high until steam escapes. Reduce to low heat and continue cooking for 30 minutes or until rice is tender. Yield: 4 servings.

Mrs. Laurena Croom Ward, Ashford H. S.
Ashford, Alabama

HAMBURGER STROGANOFF

1 lb. ground beef
½ c. chopped onion
2 tbsp. flour
1 4-oz. can sliced mushrooms
1 10 ½-oz. can cream of mushroom soup
¼ c. chopped pimento
¼ c. shredded cheese
1 tsp. salt
¼ tsp. pepper
1 c. sour cream
3 c. cooked rice

Brown meat in large skillet; add onion, flour, mushrooms, soup, pimento, cheese, salt and pepper. Cook over low heat for 30 to 40 minutes. Add sour cream a few minutes before serving. Serve meat mixture over rice. Yield: 8 servings.

Mrs. W. W. Matthews, Scottsboro H. S.
Scottsboro, Alabama

JAMBALAYA

2 tbsp. fat
1 lb. ground beef
1 can tomato soup
1 soup can water
½ c. chopped onion
⅓ c. chopped green pepper
1 clove of garlic, finely minced
2 tsp. salt
⅛ tsp. pepper
¼ tsp. thyme
⅔ c. uncooked rice

Melt fat in large skillet. Brown meat in hot fat until crumbly. Add soup diluted with water and remaining ingredients; stir well. Cover. When steam appears, reduce heat to simmer. Cook for 35 minutes. Stir well before serving. Garnish with strips of green pepper. Yield: 8 servings.

Annie Lewis Varnell, Dora H. S.
Dora, New Mexico

TEXAS HASH

1 to 3 lge. onions, sliced
1 lge. green pepper, minced
2 to 3 tbsp. fat
1 lb. ground beef
2 c. cooked tomatoes
½ to 1 c. uncooked rice or 2 c. uncooked noodles
½ to 1 ½ tsp. chili powder
1 ¾ to 2 tsp. salt
⅛ to ¼ tsp. pepper
1 tsp. seasoned salt

Cook onions and green pepper in fat until onions are yellow. Add meat and cook until brown. Stir in remaining ingredients. Cook over low heat in a covered skillet until rice is tender. Serve hot. NOTE: May be baked in a greased 2-quart covered casserole at 350 degrees for 1 hour. Remove cover last 15 minutes. One 12-ounce package frozen English peas may be added. Yield: 6 servings.

Carol Coldwell, Jayton H. S.
Jayton, Texas
Opal Carpenter, Mentone H. S.
Mentone, Indiana
Mrs. Johnny Morrow, Waco H. S.
Waco, Texas

BEEF GARDEN CASSEROLE

1 med. onion, chopped
1 lb. ground beef
¾ tsp. salt
¼ tsp. pepper
1 1-lb. can cut green beans, drained
1 can whole kernel corn, undrained
1 10 ½-oz. can tomato soup
2 tbsp. shortening
1 c. sifted self-rising flour
⅓ c. milk
½ c. grated sharp Cheddar cheese

Cook onion in small amount of fat until tender but not brown. Add ground beef and seasonings; brown lightly. Add green beans, corn and tomato soup. Pour into 1 1/2-quart casserole. Cut shortening into flour; stir in milk. Turn out onto floured board or pastry cloth; knead lightly. Roll out into a rectangle. Spread cheese over dough. Roll as for a jelly roll. Cut into 1-inch slices; place on top of casserole. Bake in preheated 425 degree oven for 15 to 20 minutes. Yield: 8 servings.

Miss Callie L. Owen, Madison H. S.
Madison, Tennessee

BETTY'S SPECIAL

1 ½ lb. hamburger
1 lge. onion, chopped
1 tbsp. butter
¼ lb. macaroni or spaghetti
2 qt. water
1 tsp. salt

(Continued on next page)

¼ tsp. pepper
¼ tsp. garlic salt
2 tbsp. catsup
1 can cream of mushroom soup
2 cans tomato soup
1 lge. kidney beans

Saute hamburger and onion in butter until browned. Cook macaroni in boiling, salted water until tender; drain. Add pepper, garlic salt and catsup to meat; stir well. Add soups, beans and macaroni. Heat thoroughly. Yield: 12 servings.

Mrs. Betty Peters, Lincoln H. S.
Ypsilanti, Michigan

CABBAGE ROLLS

1 lge. onion, chopped
1 tbsp. chopped green pepper
1 lb. ground beef
Salt and pepper to taste
Paprika to taste
Worcestershire sauce to taste
1 can tomato-rice soup
1 egg, beaten
2 c. cooked rice
1 lge. cabbage
Butter
1 can tomato soup

Cook onion, green pepper and meat until meat is browned. Add seasonings and tomato-rice soup. Remove from heat; stir in egg. Add rice. Separate cabbage leaves. Place 2 tablespoonfuls meat mixture in each cabbage leaf. Roll up; secure with toothpicks. Place in pan; dot with butter. Add tomato soup. Bake at 250 degrees for 1 hour and 30 minutes. Yield: 6-8 servings.

Mrs. John Okerson, Lowndes Co. H. S.
Valdosta, Georgia

CABBAGE ROLLS

8 lge. cabbage leaves
½ lb. hamburger
½ c. cooked rice
1 egg
1 tsp. salt
¼ tsp. pepper
1 ¼ c. plus 2 tbsp. chopped onion
2 tbsp. fat
½ c. cooked tomatoes of catsup
1 bay leaf (opt.)
4 whole cloves (opt.)

Cook cabbage leaves in salted water for 5 minutes. Combine hamburger, rice, egg, salt, pepper and 2 tablespoonfuls onion. Brown lightly in hot fat. Place a spoonful of meat mixture in each leaf; roll up. Secure with a toothpick. Place in skillet; add tomatoes, remaining onion, bay leaf and cloves. Cover; simmer for 45 minutes. Yield: 4 servings.

Mrs. Nelle McLellan, Smithville H. S.
Smithville, Texas

ONE-DISH MEAL

1 lb. hamburger
1 onion, chopped
1 can tomato soup
½ soup can cold water
1 can peas
4 or 5 potatoes, sliced

Fry hamburger until browned. Add onion, soup, water, peas and potatoes; stir gently. Cover; cook slowly over low heat for 20 to 30 minutes, stirring occasionally. Yield: 4-5 servings.

Mrs. Mayo Neilson, Arlington H. S.
Arlington, South Dakota

RICCI-STUFFED PEPPERS

3 lge. green peppers
3 tbsp. minced white onion
½ c. plus 3 tbsp. water
2 tbsp. butter
1 lb. ground beef
½ c. instant rice, cooked
½ tsp. salt
2 8-oz. cans tomato sauce
½ c. Sherry
1 c. sour cream
¼ lb. sharp Cheddar cheese, grated

Split green peppers into halves lengthwise; remove seed and stems. Wash peppers; drop into a large pot of boiling salted water. Turn off heat; let stand for 5 minutes. Drain and arrange peppers in baking dish. Soften onion in 3 tablespoonfuls water for 5 minutes. Saute onion in butter for 5 minutes. Mix onion, ground beef, rice, salt and 1 can tomato sauce. Fill peppers with meat mixture. Combine 1 can tomato sauce, 1/2 cup water, wine and sour cream; pour over stuffed peppers. Bake at 350 degrees for 40 minutes. Sprinkle with grated cheese; continue baking for 20 minutes longer. Yield: 6 servings.

Mrs. Marion Griffin, Frederick R. Noble School
Willimantic, Connecticut

STUFFED GREEN PEPPERS

6 lge. green peppers
1 lb. ground beef
1 c. dry bread crumbs
1 tsp. salt
¼ tsp. pepper
1 tbsp. chopped onion
1 ½ c. tomato juice

Remove stems and seeds from peppers. Rinse and drain on paper towel. Mix ground beef, bread crumbs, salt, pepper, onion and 1/2 cup tomato juice. Stuff peppers with mixture. Place in a 1 1/2-quart baking dish. Pour remaining juice over stuffed peppers. Bake, covered, at 350 degrees for 45 minutes. Uncover and bake for 15 minutes longer. Yield: 6 servings.

Ann Holman, Juanita Valley H. S.
Alexandria, Pennsylvania

STUFFED GREEN PEPPERS

½ lb. rice
1 med. onion, chopped
2 tbsp. lard
6 to 8 green peppers
1 c. canned tomatoes
1 lb. ground beef
1 tsp. salt
¼ tsp. pepper
1 c. sour cream

Cook rice in covered saucepan for 10 minutes; rinse and drain. Saute chopped onion in lard. Core, seed and wash green peppers; soak in hot water for a few minutes. Drain well. Combine cooked rice, sauted onion, tomato pulp, ground beef, salt and pepper. Mix well. Fill peppers two-thirds full with mixture; place in baking dish. Add hot water around peppers to come up to 2 inches. Cover. Bake at 375 degrees for 1 hour. Add sour cream to liquid around peppers the last 10 minutes of baking. Yield: 6 servings.

Mrs. Mary Soroka, Lackawanna H. S.
Lackawanna, New York

STUFFED PEPPERS

¼ c. rice
Hamburger
½ tsp. salt
4 peppers, cleaned and stemmed
1 can tomato soup or paste

Bring rice to boil in small amount of water; drain. Add rice to 3/8 to 1/2 pound hamburger. Season with salt. Fill cavity of peppers with hamburger-rice mixture. Place in saucepan; cover with tomato sauce. Cook over low heat for 1 hour or until peppers are soft. Yield: 4 servings.

Mrs. Janet Kimmel, S. Huntingdon Co. H. S.
Orbisonia, Pennsylvania

STUFFED TOMATOES OR PEPPERS

6 to 8 tomatoes or green peppers
1 lb. ground chuck
Margarine
½ c. chopped onion
1 No. 2 can tomatoes
1 tsp. parsley flakes
1 tsp. dried mint
1 tsp. salt
½ c. uncooked rice
1 tbsp. brown sugar

Cut tops from vegetables; reserve. Hollow out and wash vegetables; invert to drain. Brown beef in margarine or meat fat; add onion. Cook until transparent. Add remaining ingredients; bring to a boil. Fill vegetables with meat mixture; replace reserved tops. Bake, uncovered, at 350 degrees for 1 hour and 30 minutes. Yield: 6-8 servings.

Cleo Codas, Northern H. S.
Durham, North Carolina

BEEF ON PARADE

1 ½ lb. ground beef
1 ½ tsp. salt
1 ½ tsp. dry mustard
1 ½ tsp. Worcestershire sauce
1 egg
⅓ c. chopped onion
3 tbsp. chopped green pepper
⅓ c. cracker meal
¼ c. shortening or drippings

Combine ground beef, salt, dry mustard, Worcestershire sauce, egg, onion and green pepper. Shape meat mixture onto eight wooden skewers, leaving about 1 1/2 inches of skewers exposed. Roll skewered meat in cracker meal; brown on all sides in shortening or drippings. Cook, turning occasionally, for 30 minutes or until done. Yield: 6-8 servings.

Mrs. Verna Eberhart, Cavalier Public School
Cavalier, North Dakota

COUNTRY PIE

½ c. tomato sauce
1 ½ c. bread crumbs
¼ c. finely chopped onion
2 tsp. salt
⅛ tsp. pepper
⅛ tsp. oregano
1 lb. ground beef
2 tbsp. chopped green pepper
1 ⅓ c. instant rice
1 c. water
1 c. grated Cheddar cheese

Combine tomato sauce crumbs, onion, 1 1/2 teaspoonfuls salt, pepper, oregano, meat and green pepper. Mix well. Pat crust mixture into 9-inch pie pan. Flute edges. Combine remaining ingredients except cheese. Spoon into meat shell. Cover with foil. Bake at 350 degrees for 25 minutes. Uncover; spread with cheese. Bake for 10 to 15 minutes. Cut into pie shapes; serve hot. Yield: 6 servings.

Frieda K. Wooden, Bremen H. S.
Midlothian, Illinois

ENCHILADAS

1 lb. ground beef
2 med. onions, chopped
½ lb. American cheese, grated
½ tsp. salt
⅛ tsp. pepper
1 tsp. chili powder
1 can enchilada sauce
1 pkg. frozen tortillas

Brown ground beef in a skillet; place in a mixing bowl. Add onions, cheese, salt, pepper and chili powder. Mix well; set aside. Heat enchilada sauce. Fry tortillas in deep fat until brown; soak in hot enchilada sauce until soft. Fold tortillas

(Continued on next page)

into half-moon shapes; add meat and cheese mixture to each tortilla. Add remaining sauce; sprinkle grated cheese over top. Bake at 400 degrees for 20 to 25 minutes. Yield: 6-8 servings.

Mrs. Margaret Kemp, Mountain View School
Mountain View, Arkansas

ENCHILADAS

3 tbsp. flour
4 tsp. chili powder
3 tbsp. oil
2 c. water
1 lb. hamburger
½ c. chopped onion
1 tsp. salt
¼ tsp. pepper
½ tsp. garlic salt
1 lb. grated Cheddar cheese
12 tortillas

Brown flour and chili powder in oil. Gradually stir in water; simmer for 30 minutes. Brown hamburger and onion. Season with salt, pepper and garlic salt. Dip tortillas in sauce until softened. Fill center of tortilla with meat and cheese; roll and place in baking dish. Sprinkle remaining cheese over top. Pour sauce over enchiladas. Bake at 350 degrees until cheese is melted. Serve hot. Yield: 4 servings.

Marilyn Finger, Round Rock H. S.
Round Rock, Texas

GERMAN KRAUT BIEROCKS

Bread dough
1 lb. hamburger
Salt and pepper to taste
4 tbsp. fat
1 to 2 c. chopped cabbage
½ c. water
1 med. onion, cut up

Let bread dough rise. Mix hamburger with seasoning to taste. Place 2 tablespoonfuls fat in skillet; add cabbage, water, salt and pepper. Cover and steam until cabbage is limp, stirring occasionally. Add more water if cabbage becomes dry. Place remaining fat in another skillet; add onion. Fry until brown; crumble in hamburger. Fry until redness disappears. Combine hamburger and cabbage. Roll dough medium thin; cut into 3 1/2-inch squares. Place 1 heaping tablespoonful cabbage mixture on each square. Bring opposite corners together, pressing sides down. Place in greased baking dish. Let rise for 20 minutes. Bake at 350 degrees for 20 to 25 minutes. Yield: 8 servings.

Mrs. Louis Weiss, Ovid H. S.
Ovid, Colorado

KRAUT RUNZA

1 lb. ground beef
1 c. chopped cabbage
1 onion, chopped
1 pkg. hot roll mix

Combine ground beef, cabbage and onion; mix well. Steam until done. Prepare hot roll mix as directed on package; roll out to 1/8 to 1/4-inch thickness. Cut and shape as for dumplings. Fill dough with cabbage mixture. Fold dough; seal. Let rise for 1 hour. Bake at 375 degrees for 25 minutes. Yield: 12 servings.

Mrs. Lanell Long, Grand Prairie H. S.
Grand Prairie, Texas

MEAT-CRUST POTATO PIE

3 med. potatoes
Butter
Cream
1 lb. ground round beef
1 tsp. salt
Garlic salt
¼ tsp. pepper
1 med. onion, chopped
1 8-oz. can tomato sauce

Peel, dice and boil potatoes. Whip with butter and cream. Mix remaining ingredients; line an 8-inch pie plate with mixture. Bake at 425 degrees for 20 to 30 minutes. Fill meat crust with potatoes; broil just until peaks of potatoes are browned. Yield: 4 servings.

Martha F. Jenkins, Hildebran H. S.
Hildebran, North Carolina

MEAT-CRUST POTATO PIE

⅓ c. tomato sauce
½ c. bread crumbs
1 lb. ground beef
½ c. chopped onion
1 tsp. salt
⅛ tsp. pepper
Mashed potatoes

Combine all ingredients except potatoes; mix well. Pat into bottom and sides of a 9-inch pie plate. Place mashed potatoes over mixture. Sprinkle top with grated Parmesan cheese, if desired. Bake at 350 degrees for 30 minutes. Yield: 5-6 servings.

Mrs. Glaray Sue Lacy, Kermit H. S.
Kermit, West Virginia

MEAT LOAF CUPS

1 lb. ground beef
¼ c. dry bread crumbs
½ c. milk
1 tsp. salt

(Continued on next page)

1/8 tsp. pepper
1 tbsp. chopped onion

Combine all ingredients thoroughly; divide mixture into 6 to 8 large portions or 12 to 15 medium portions. Line muffin cups with mixture to 1/4-inch thickness. Bake at 350 degrees for 30 minutes. Cups may be filled with green peas, creamed potatoes, carrots or corn after baking. Yield: 6 servings.

Ava L. Torrence, West Point H. S.
West Point, Virginia

MEAT PANCAKES

3 eggs, separated
1/2 lb. ground beef
1/4 tsp. baking powder
1/2 tsp. salt
Dash of pepper
1 tsp. lemon juice
1 tbsp. minced parsley
1 tbsp. grated onion

Lightly beat egg yolks. Add ground beef, baking powder, salt, pepper, lemon juice, parsley and onion. Fold in stiffly beaten egg whites. Drop by spoonfuls onto greased hot griddle. When puffed and brown, turn and brown other side. Serve at once with mushroom sauce or creamed vegetable, if desired. Yield: 6 servings.

Betty Sue Brown, Zama School
Kosciusko, Mississippi

MEAT PUFFS

1/4 c. chopped onion
1 tbsp. butter
2 eggs, beaten
1 lb. ground beef
1/2 c. fine dry bread crumbs
1/2 c. chili sauce
1 tsp. salt
1 tsp. Worcestershire sauce
3/4 c. milk

Cook onion in butter for 3 minutes. Combine eggs, beef, crumbs, 1/4 cup chili sauce, salt, Worcestershire sauce and milk with cooked onion mixture. Mix well but do not knead. Place in greased muffin pan and spread with remaining chili sauce. Bake in preheated 375 degree oven for 30 minutes. NOTE: Freezes well. Yield: 8 meat puffs.

Mrs. Willie Ruth Atchley, Lanier H. S.
Maryville, Tennessee

MEAT TURNOVERS

3 tbsp. flour
3 tbsp. butter
1 c. rich milk
1/4 tsp. salt
1/8 tsp. pepper
Celery salt to taste
1/8 tsp. ginger
2 c. chopped cooked meat
2 tsp. minced onion
1 recipe plain pastry

Blend flour into butter; gradually add milk, then seasonings. Cook until thickened, stirring constantly. Cool. Combine meat, onion and white sauce. Roll out pastry 1/8-inch thick. Cut into six circles or squares. Place heaping tablespoonful of meat mixture over one-half of each circle; cover with remaining half. Seal edges. Place on cookie sheet. Bake at 450 degrees for 20 minutes or until browned. NOTE: Pastry should be based on 2 cups flour. Yield: 6 servings.

Mrs. Natasha Decker, Brick Twp. H. S.
Brick Town, New Jersey

MEATZA PIE

1 lb. ground beef
2/3 c. evaporated milk
1/2 c. fine dry bread crumbs
1/2 to 1 tsp. garlic salt
1/3 c. tomato paste or catsup
1 2 to 3-oz. can sliced mushrooms, drained
1 c. shredded sharp Cheddar cheese
1/4 tsp. oregano
2 tbsp. grated Parmesan cheese
1/2 c. chopped onion
1/2 c. chopped ripe olives (opt.)

Place meat, evaporated milk, bread crumbs and garlic salt in a 9-inch pie plate; mix thoroughly with a fork. Pat evenly onto bottom and over sides of pie plate; rim with fingers, pressing firmly into place. Spread tomato paste over meat mixture. Drain mushrooms; arrange over top of tomato paste. Add cheddar cheese, oregano, Parmesan cheese, onion and olives in layers. Bake in preheated 375 degree oven for 25 minutes or until meat is done and cheese is lightly browned. Yield: 4-6 servings.

Mrs. Barbara Johnston, Conneaut
Lake Area H. S., Conneaut Lake, Pennsylvania
Meroe E. Stanley, Northville H. S.
Northville, Michigan

QUICK AND EASY MEAT LOAF

1 lb. ground beef
3/4 c. cracker crumbs
1 6-oz. can tomato paste
1 egg, beaten
1/4 c. chopped onion
1/4 c. chopped green pepper
1 tsp. salt

Mix all ingredients thoroughly; shape into egg-sized balls. Place balls in greased muffin tins.

(Continued on next page)

Bake at 350 degrees for 25 to 30 minutes. Yield: 8 to 12 servings.

Mrs. Carol Jean Smith, Scott Central H. S.
Forest, Mississippi

BEEF AND BISCUIT

1 lb. ground beef
¼ c. finely chopped onion
½ c. chopped green pepper
2 tbsp. fat
1 tsp. salt
Dash of pepper
2 tbsp. flour
1 c. milk
2 c. prepared biscuit mix
Melted butter
1 10 ½-oz. can tomato soup

Brown beef, onion and green pepper in fat; add seasonings. Blend in flour; add milk. Cook over medium heat until thick. Roll biscuit dough 1/2-inch thick; spread with meat mixture. Roll as for jelly roll; cut into 1 1/4-inch slices. Place slices, cut-side down, in greased baking dish; brush tops with melted butter. Bake at 400 degrees for 20 to 25 minutes. Heat tomato soup; serve as sauce. Yield: 6 servings.

Helen Tussey, Sugar Valley Area School
Loganton, Pennsylvania

BEEF PINWHEELS

1 c. mashed potatoes
½ c. canned peas, drained
1 tbsp. chopped onion
¼ c. chopped green pepper
1 lb. ground beef
1 ½ tsp. salt
¼ tsp. pepper
1 egg, well beaten
Bread crumbs
Butter or margarine

Combine potatoes, peas, onion and green pepper in bowl. In another bowl, combine ground beef, salt, pepper, egg and bread crumbs. Place meat mixture between two sheets of waxed paper; roll out with rolling pin to 6 x 10 inches. Remove top sheet of waxed paper. Spread potato mixture over meat; roll up like a jelly roll. Chill well. Remove paper; cut roll into 1-inch slices. Grease skillet well with butter or margarine; fry slices of meat until well cooked and brown, turning once. Yield: 6 servings.

Lillian Thompson, Salina H. S.
Salina, Oklahoma

MEAT LOAF SWIRL

2 lb. ground beef
¼ c. chopped onion
½ c. milk
1 egg, slightly beaten
2 tsp. salt
Dash of pepper
1 ½ c. soft bread crumbs
1 ½ c. shredded potatoes
2 tbsp. snipped parsley
1 tsp. sage
½ tsp. salt

Combine ground beef, onion, milk, egg, salt and pepper; mix well. Pat beef mixture into 10-inch square on piece of aluminum foil. Combine remaining ingredients; mix well. Spread over meat. Roll meat as for jelly roll; place seam-side down in shallow pan. Bake at 350 degrees for 1 hour and 15 minutes. Yield: 8-10 servings.

Maggie Beth Watts, Era Consolidated School
Era, Texas

MOZZARELLA MEAT WHIRL

1 ½ lb. ground beef
½ c. soft bread crumbs
1 egg, slightly beaten
1 tbsp. mustard
⅛ tsp. pepper
3 tsp. salt
6 oz. Mozzarella cheese, sliced
1 tsp. dry parsley
¾ c. catsup
¾ c. water
1 tbsp. Worcestershire sauce

Mix ground beef, bread crumbs, egg, mustard, pepper and salt. Lightly pat mixture into a 10 x 14-inch rectangle. Place cheese slices on meat; sprinkle with parsley. Starting at short end, roll tightly as for jelly roll, lifting paper with one hand. Press ends to seal. Carefully transfer to shallow baking dish, seam side-down. Combine catsup, water and Worcestershire sauce; pour over meat. Bake at 375 degrees for 1 hour and 10 minutes, basting frequently. Serve sauce separately. Yield: 8 servings.

Mrs. Darlene Freadhoff, Valley City H. S.
Valley City, North Dakota

ROMA BEEF ROLL

1 ½ lb. lean ground beef
1 egg
¾ c. cracker crumbs
½ c. finely chopped onion
2 8-oz. cans tomato sauce with cheese
1 tsp. salt
½ tsp. oregano
⅛ tsp. pepper
2 c. Mozzarella cheese

Combine ground beef, egg, cracker crumbs, onion, 1 can tomato sauce with cheese, salt, oregano and pepper. Mix well; shape into a flat 10 x 12-inch rectangle on waxed paper. Sprinkle cheese evenly over meat mixture. Roll up like a jelly roll; press ends of roll to seal. Place in shallow baking dish. Bake at 350 degrees for 1

(Continued on next page)

hour. Drain off excess fat. Pour on remaining tomato sauce; bake for 15 minutes longer. Yield: 4-6 servings.

Mrs. Lela Jo Goar, Bovina H. S.
Bovina, Texas
Mrs. Cecile L. Herscher, Union H. S.
Dowagiac, Michigan

SLOPPY JOES

1 lb. ground beef
1 egg, beaten
1 sm. onion, minced
1 tsp. salt
1/8 tsp. pepper
2 c. puffed rice
2 c. milk

Mix all ingredients; place in greased casserole. cover and bake at 325 degrees for 1 hour. Remove cover; stir. Bake 2 hours longer, stirring occasionally. Yield: 12 servings.

Mrs. Diana J. Plant, Ashland Jr. H. S.
Ashland, Ohio

STEAK CUPS

1 1/2 lb. ground chuck
3/4 c. milk
1 egg, slightly beaten
2/3 c. quick cooking oats
1/3 c. finely chopped green pepper
1 tsp. salt
1 tbsp. horseradish
1 tbsp. prepared mustard
8 tbsp. catsup or tomato sauce

Combine all ingredients except catsup. Divide meat mixture into 12 equal portions; place in large muffin tins. Mold meat around muffin cups with teaspoon, leaving small hollow in center of meat. Fill centers with catsup or tomato sauce. Bake at 350 degrees for 30 to 40 minutes. NOTE: May be wrapped and frozen in muffin tins. Yield: 12 servings.

Mrs. Zelda Austin, Avery H. S.
Avery, Texas

STUFFED HAMBURGER MEAT ROLL

2 lb. hamburger
Salt and pepper to taste
1 egg, beaten
4 slices bread, toasted
1 3/4 c. grated cheese
1/3 c. finely chopped onion
1/2 tsp. sage

Combine meat, salt, pepper and egg; mix well. Pat out to 10 x 12-inch rectangle. Cube toasted bread; combine with 1 1/2 cups cheese, onion and sage. Spread mixture on meat to within 1 inch of edge. Roll meat around stuffing; press to seal. Bake at 300 degrees for 50 minutes. Sprinkle remaining cheese along top of meat. Bake for 10 minutes longer or until done. Yield: 6 servings.

Mrs. Aleta B. Nelson, Tidehaven H. S.
Blessing, Texas

STUFFED BURGER BUNDLES

1 c. packaged herb-seasoned stuffing mix
1/3 c. evaporated milk
1 lb. ground beef
1 can cream of mushroom soup
2 tsp. Worcestershire sauce
1 tbsp. catsup

Prepare stuffing mix according to package directions. Combine milk and meat; divide into five patties. On waxed paper, pat each to 6-inch circle. Place 1/4 cup stuffing in center of each pattie. Draw meat over stuffing; seal. Place in 1 1/2- quart casserole. Combine remaining ingredients; pour over meat. Bake, uncovered, at 350 degrees for 35 to 40 minutes. Yield: 5 servings.

Mrs. Delene, Barage H. S.
Barage, Michigan

Pork Favorites

BACON PIE

1 ½ c. sifted flour
1 ½ tsp. salt
⅓ c. shortening
3 tbsp. cold water
¼ lb. bacon, cut into 1-in. pieces
2 tsp. parsley, chopped
2 hard-cooked eggs, chopped
½ lemon rind, grated
⅔ c. meat stock

Sift flour with 1/2 teaspoonful salt; cut in shortening. Add water to make a stiff paste; mix thoroughly. Allow to stand for a few minutes. Roll out on a well floured board; cover bottom of greased casserole with one-half of pastry. Arrange bacon in casserole with parsley, egg and lemon rind. Add 1 teaspoonful salt and stock. Cover pie tightly with remaining pastry; brush with milk. Bake at 400 degrees for 30 minutes. Reduce heat to 350 degrees and bake for 1 hour longer. Yield: 6 servings.

Betty Mac Spadden, Salinas H. S.
Salinas, California

BACON ROLLS

1 c. bread crumbs
2 tbsp. butter
¼ c. nuts
¼ c. raisins
½ tsp. salt
Dash of pepper
½ tsp. sage
12 slices Canadian bacon
¾ c. tomato juice

Combine all ingredients except bacon and tomato juice. Spread bacon slices with stuffing; roll and secure with toothpick. Place rolls in muffin tins. Pour 1 tablespoonful tomato juice over each roll. Bake at 350 degrees for 45 minutes. Yield: 6 servings.

Mrs. Ruth Marie Scaggs, Mapletown H. S.
Greensboro, Pennsylvania

CANADIAN BACON WITH ORANGE SAUCE

12 slices Canadian bacon, cut ¼-in. thick
6 thin onion slices
6 orange slices, peeled
2 tsp. sugar
1 tbsp. cornstarch
1 c. orange juice
1 orange, peeled and sectioned
2 tsp. grated lemon rind

Arrange 6 slices Canadian bacon in greased, shallow 1 1/2-quart baking dish. Top each with an onion slice, an orange slice and another slice of bacon. Bake in preheated 300 degree oven for 30 minutes. Mix sugar and cornstarch in saucepan; blend in orange juice, mixing well. Cook, stirring constantly, until thickened and clear. Stir in orange sections and lemon rind. Serve sauce over meat. Yield: 6 servings.

Mrs. Twila Shankland, Iver C. Ranum H. S.
Westminster, Colorado

QUICHE LORRAINE

1 9-in. pastry shell, unbaked
8 slices bacon, diced
½ lb. Swiss cheese, shredded
1 tbsp. flour
½ tsp. salt
Dash of nutmeg
3 eggs, beaten
1 ¾ c. milk

Bake pastry shell at 450 degrees for 7 minutes or until lightly browned. Remove from oven. Fry bacon until crisp; drain and crumble. Place bacon in pie shell, reserving 2 tablespoonfuls; add cheese. Combine remaining ingredients; pour over cheese. Sprinkle reserved bacon on top in circle. Bake at 325 degrees for 35 to 40 minutes; cool for 25 minutes before serving. Yield: 6 servings.

Deborah Mabon, Hughesville H. S.
Hughesville, Pennsylvania

RICE CHILI

6 to 8 slices bacon, diced
1 c. rice
½ c. hot water
4 c. canned tomatoes
¼ lb. Cheddar cheese, grated
1 tbsp. sugar
1 tbsp. chili
½ tsp. salt

Fry bacon tender but not crisp. Add all ingredients to bacon; cook, stirring to blend. Reduce heat; continue cooking until rice is tender. NOTE: May be cooked on top of stove or put in oven. Yield: 4-5 servings.

Mrs. Helen Purvis
Mount Baker Secondary School
Cranbrook, British Columbia, Canada

ARABIAN PORK CHOPS

4 shoulder pork chops
2 onions, sliced
2 tomatoes, sliced
2 tbsp. chopped green pepper
2 tbsp. flour
1 tsp. salt
1 c. hot water

Brown chops on both sides in skillet; place in large shallow casserole. Arrange onion and tomato slices on each chop; sprinkle with green pepper. Drain off all but 2 tablespoonfuls fat from skillet; blend flour and salt into fat in skillet. Cook until brown. Gradually stir in water. Cook, stirring constantly, until thick and smooth. Pour over chops. Cover and bake at 350 degrees for 1 hour and 15 minutes or until tender. Yield: 4 servings.

Mrs. Joanne G. Thomas
Greencastle-Antrim H. S.
Greencastle, Pennsylvania

BAKED LEMON PORK CHOPS

3 or 4 thick lean loin chops
½ tsp. salt
⅛ tsp. pepper
1 c. flour
½ tbsp. shortening
3 or 4 slices lemon
½ c. catsup
½ c. water
1 ½ tbsp. brown sugar

Dredge chops with seasoned flour. Brown on both sides in shortening. Arrange chops in baking dish. Place a slice of lemon on each chop. Mix catsup, water and brown sugar. Pour over chops. Bake, uncovered, at 350 degrees for 45 minutes to 1 hour or until done. Add a small amount of water, if needed, toward end of baking period. Yield: 3-4 servings.

Barbara Waybourn, Patton Springs H. S.
Afton, Texas
Mrs. Gloria Dahl, Warner H. S.
Warner, Alberta, Canada

BAKED PORK CHOPS

4 to 6 lean pork chops, ½ to 1-in. thick
1 egg, beaten
Salt and pepper to taste
Corn flakes or fine cracker crumbs
Butter or oil

Wipe chops; dip into egg seasoned with salt and pepper. Roll in corn flakes. Melt 3 tablespoonfuls butter in baking dish; lay chops in dish. Dot with butter. Bake at 375 degrees for 30 minutes, turning once during baking to brown on both sides or cover with foil, leaving an opening; bake at 350 degrees for 1 hour. Yield: 4-6 servings.

Mary Ann Watters, Herington H. S.
Herington, Kansas
Mrs. Sally Herrington
North Forrest Attendance Center
Hattisburg, Mississippi

BAKED PORK CHOPS

6 pork chops
Fat
Salt and pepper
Garlic salt
2 c. milk
Parsley

Brown pork chops in hot fat; add salt and pepper. Sprinkle lightly with garlic salt. Add milk until chops are barely covered. Bake at 350 degrees for 1 hour. Sprinkle with chopped parsley and serve.

A. Casari, Pewamo-Westphalia H. S.
Pewamo, Michigan

BAKED PORK CHOPS

6 to 8 pork chops
1 tbsp. prepared mustard
Salt and pepper
Paprika
Celery salt
Garlic salt
Flour
2 lge. onions, cut into rings
1 green pepper, cut into rings
2 tsp. grated lemon rind

Rub chops with mustard. Sprinkle with seasonings and flour. Brown in heavy skillet in a small amount of fat. Place in flat baking dish. Cover with onion and green pepper rings, water and lemon rind. Bake at 325 degrees for 45 minutes.

Mrs. Ruth Hardwick, May H. S.
May, Texas

BAKED PORK CHOPS AND SAUERKRAUT

1 can sauerkraut
1 tsp. pepper
½ tsp. salt
4 thick pork chops

Place sauerkraut in bottom of casserole; top with seasoned pork chops. Cover and bake at 350 degrees for 1 hour. Remove cover and bake for 20 minutes longer or until pork chops brown. Yield: 4 servings.

Barbara Ann Dunbury, Woburn, H. S.
Woburn, Massachusetts

CORN AND PORK CHOPS

12 pork chops, ½-in. thick
4 c. soft bread crumbs
2 c. whole kernel corn
2 tsp. salt
4 tsp. chopped green pepper
1 tbsp. chopped onion
4 tbsp. melted butter
2 eggs

Brown chops in hot skillet; place in baking dish. Mix remaining ingredients; beat well. Place a serving of corn on each chop. Add a small amount of water to dish. Bake at 325 degrees for 1 hour.

Mrs. Betsy Hill, Otsego H. S.
Otsego, Michigan

CROWNED PORK CHOPS

1 c. whole kernel corn
1 ½ c. bread crumbs
Milk
1 egg
2 tbsp. chopped green pepper
1 tbsp. chopped onion
¼ tsp. salt
⅛ tsp. pepper
½ tsp. seasoning salt
6 to 8 med. pork chops

Combine corn with crumbs and a small amount of milk; mix in egg, green pepper, onion, salt, pepper and seasoning salt. Place chops in a pan or baking dish; cover each chop with corn mixture. Bake at 375 degrees for 1 hour.

Mrs. Marion Morgan, La Grande H. S.
La Grande, Oregon

PEG'S PORK CHOPS

10 double pork chops
1 sm. can evaporated milk
Bread crumbs
Shortening
2 lemons, sliced
½ c. brown sugar
1 can tomato soup
½ soup can water

Dip chops into milk, then into bread crumbs. Set aside for 1 hour. Brown in a small amount of shortening; place in roasting pan. Place 1 slice of lemon on each chop. Place 1 teaspoonful brown sugar on each lemon slice. Mix soup with water; pour over all. Bake at 325 degrees for 2 hours, basting frequently. Yield: 10 servings.

Mrs. Betty Jane Bower
Francis McClure Jr. H. S.
McKeesport, Pennsylvania

PORK CHOPS AND DRESSING

8 pork chops
Fat
¼ c. water
3 c. croutons
1 can cream of mushroom soup
1 4-oz. can mushrooms
1 ½ c. chopped celery
1 med. onion, chopped
Salt and pepper
¼ tsp. sage

Brown pork chops in fat; place in baking pan. Add water to meat drippings. Mix remaining ingredients into dressing mixture. Place a mound of dressing on each pork chop. Bake at 350 degrees for 1 hour. Yield: 8 servings.

Mrs. Alice Sheppard, South Jr. H. S.
Grand Forks, North Dakota

PORK CHOPS

6 lean pork chops
1 onion, sliced
½ can water
1 can cream of chicken soup
3 tbsp. catsup
3 tsp. Worcestershire sauce
Salt and pepper to taste

Trim fat from pork chops; melt into 3 tablespoons fat. Brown chops in fat. Layer chops and sliced onion in casserole; drain off fat. Mix water, soup, catsup, Worcestershire sauce and seasonings; pour over chops. Bake at 350 degrees for 1 hour and 30 minutes to 2 hours.

Anne E. Derrick, Banff H. S.
Banff, Alberta, Canada

PORK CHOPS

Salt and pepper to taste
6 pork chops, cut ½-in. thick
2 c. chopped celery
9 tbsp. brown sugar
Juice of 1 lemon
1 sm. can tomato sauce

Salt and pepper pork chops; dredge in flour. Brown in fat. Place in baking dish. Cover each pork chop with celery and 1 1/2 tablespoonfuls brown sugar. Squeeze lemon juice over sugar; cover with tomato sauce. Bake at 325 degrees for 45 minutes. Yield: 6 servings.

Mrs. Ione Thompson, Phillips H. S.
Phillips, Texas

PORK CHOPS AND DRESSING

¼ c. chopped celery
1 tbsp. minced onion
¼ c. butter
3 c. croutons
3 med. carrots, coarsely grated
½ tsp. seasoned salt
6 pork chops, browned

Brown celery and onion in melted butter. Stir in croutons, carrots, salt and enough water to moisten. Place mixture in bottom of shallow casserole. Arrange pork chops on top. Cover and bake at 350 degrees for 1 hour and 30 minutes. Yield: 4-6 servings.

Mrs. Ken Armsdorf, Comfrey Public School
Comfrey, Minnesota

PORK CHOPS AND SOUR CREAM

6 pork chops
1 tbsp. chopped green pepper
1 tbsp. minced onion
1 can cream of chicken soup
1 c. sour cream
Salt and pepper to taste

(Continued on next page)

Brown pork chops. Combine remaining ingredients; pour over chops. Bake at 325 degrees for 25 to 30 minutes. Yield: 6 servings.

Sue Chaffin, Ithaca H. S.
Ithica, Michigan

PORK CHOPS AND STUFFING

4 pork chops
3 c. soft bread cubes
2 tbsp. chopped onion
¼ c. melted butter
Water
¼ tsp. poultry seasoning
1 10 ½-oz. can cream of mushroom soup

Brown pork chops on both sides. Pour off grease. Mix bread cubes, onion, butter, 1/4 cup water and poultry seasoning. Place a mound of stuffing on each chop. Blend soup with 1/3 cup water. Pour over chops in baking dish. Bake at 350 degrees for 1 hour. Yield: 4 servings.

Mrs. Barbara A. McCrea, Superior H. S.
Superior, Montana

PORK CHOP CASSEROLE

4 lge. or 8 sm. pork chops
4 c. soft bread crumbs
½ c. melted fat
Salt
¼ tsp. pepper
4 tbsp. chopped onion
4 tbsp. chopped green pepper
2 tbsp. chopped parsley
1 apple, quartered

Brown chops in frying pan over low heat. Place bread crumbs in casserole; stir in melted fat with fork. Stir in 1/2 teaspoonful salt, pepper and vegetables. Place browned chops on dressing. Lay apple on top. Sprinkle with salt. Bake, uncovered, at 350 degrees for 1 hour. Yield: 4 servings.

Nancy B. Willard, East Haven H. S.
East Haven, Connecticut

PORK CHOPS IN CREAM SOUP

4 pork chops, ¾-in. thick
2 tbsp. hot fat
Salt and pepper
1 10 ½-oz. can cream of mushroom or onion soup

Brown chops on both sides in hot fat. Season. Pour soup over chops. Cover tightly; simmer over low heat or bake at 325 degrees for 1 hour. Yield: 4 servings.

Marie B. King, Ligonier Valley School
Ligonier, Pennsylvania

PORK CHOPS IN TOMATO SAUCE

Salt and pepper to taste
½ c. flour
6 pork chops
1 10 ½-oz. can tomato soup

Season and flour pork chops; brown in skillet. Place chops in small baking pan or casserole dish; cover with tomato soup. Bake at 350 degrees for 45 minutes. Yield: 6 servings.

Mrs. Naomi F. Stock, Lakota H. S.
West Chester, Ohio

PORK CHOPS SUPREME

Salt and pepper (opt.)
4 pork chops, 1-in. thick
4 thin slices lemon
4 thin slices onion
4 tbsp. brown sugar
4 tbsp. catsup

Place seasoned chops in deep baking dish. Place a slice of lemon and onion on each chop. Sprinkle brown sugar over onion; spread catsup over all. Cover with lid or tight foil. Bake at 350 degrees for 1 hour. Uncover; bake for 30 minutes. NOTE: Recipe may be doubled. Yield: 4 servings.

Mrs. Ethel Barksdale Teves
East Bakersfield H. S., Bakersfield, California
Mrs. Marlys Cordes, Henning Public School
Henning, Minnesota
Mrs. Lois E. Boy, Syracuse H. S.
Syracuse, Kansas

SMOTHERED PORK CHOPS

6 lean pork chops
2 tbsp. flour (opt.)
Salt and pepper to taste
1 can cream of mushroom soup
½ to ¾ c. water
½ tsp. thyme (opt.)
½ tsp. ginger (opt.)
¼ tsp. crushed rosemary (opt.)
1 tsp. parsley flakes (opt.)
½ c. sour cream (opt.)
1 3 ½-oz. can French-fried onions (opt.)

Brown chops; arrange in baking dish. Sprinkle with flour, salt and pepper. Combine soup, water and seasonings. Heat; add parsley, sour cream and one-half of the onions. Mix thoroughly. Pour over chops. Cover and simmer or bake at 350 degrees for 1 hour or until tender. Remove cover; sprinkle remaining onions over chops. Bake for 5 minutes. Yield: 4-6 servings.

Mary Elizabeth Burns, West Montgomery H. S.
Mt. Gilead, North Carolina
Mrs. Irma Ewing, Mackinaw City H. S.
Mackinaw City, Michigan
Mrs. Jo Nell Baker, Kemp H. S.
Kemp, Texas
Maureen E. Flynn, Parkway Jr. H. S.
Whitesboro, New York
Mrs. Emily Santee, West Greene H. S.
Rogersville, Pennsylvania

QUICK AND EASY PORK DELIGHT

6 pork chops or steaks
1 can cream of mushroom soup

Place pork in casserole. Add soup. Bake at 350 degrees for 1 hour and 30 minutes. Yield: 4-6 servings.

Mrs. Sandra Sugden, Plymouth H. S.
Plymouth, Wisconsin

SWEET AND SOUR PORK CHOPS

4 pork chops, 1-in. thick
Salt and pepper
¾ c. brown sugar
2 tbsp. prepared mustard
4 slices lemon

Place chops in single layer in baking dish; sprinkle with salt and pepper. Mix sugar and mustard to a paste; spread on each chop. Top with a lemon slice; squeeze juice from lemon ends into baking dish. Add 1/4-inch water. Bake in preheated 350 degree oven for 1 hour or until tender. Yield: 4 servings.

Mary Hill, Lawrence Station H. S.
Lawrence Station, New Brunswick, Canada

SWISS PORK CHOPS

8 pork chops
2 tbsp. cooking oil
4 8-oz. cans tomato sauce
1 ½ c. chopped celery
¼ c. minced onion
½ tsp. pepper
2 tsp. salt

Brown pork chops in cooking oil. Combine remaining ingredients in 3-quart casserole. Place pork chops in sauce, covering each chop completely with sauce. Cover and bake at 350 degrees for 1 hour and 30 minutes or until tender. Yield: 4 servings.

Mrs. Ann Lozon, Garden City H. S. East
Garden City, Michigan

BARBECUED PORK CHOPS

6 lean pork chops
Seasonings to taste
2 tbsp. fat
1 green pepper, sliced
1 onion, sliced
1 bottle chili sauce
1 c. water

Fry pork chops in hot fat at 360 degrees for 15 minutes or until nicely browned on both sides. Season to taste. Place ring of green pepper on each chop; place onion slice inside each ring. Pour chili sauce and water over chops. Cover and reduce heat to 220 degrees. Simmer for 25 to 30 minutes or until no trace of pink remains inside and chops are tender. Chops may be garnished with a ring of onion and green pepper, if desired.

Sister M. Isabel, S.S.N.D., Mission Church H. S.
Roxbury, Massachusetts

BARBECUED PORK CHOPS

4 to 6 pork chops
¼ to ¾ c. water
½ to ¾ c. catsup
2 tbsp. vinegar
2 tbsp. Worcestershire sauce
1 to 3 tsp. salt
1 tsp. paprika
½ tsp. pepper
1 tsp. chili powder
Dash of cayenne pepper (opt.)

Brown pork chops on both sides; place in baking dish, overlapping slightly. Combine remaining ingredients; pour over pork chops. Cover; bake at 350 degrees for 40 minutes or until tender. Yield: 4-6 servings.

Monna Smith Miller, Lake City H. S.
Lake City, Tennessee
Mrs. Verneta L. Davy
George Pringle Secondary School
Okanagan Mission, British Columbia, Canada

BARBECUED PORK CHOPS

½ c. water
¼ c. vinegar
2 tbsp. sugar
1 tbsp. prepared mustard
1 ½ tsp. salt
½ tsp. pepper
¼ tsp. cayenne
1 slice lemon
1 med. onion, sliced
½ c. catsup
2 tbsp. Worcestershire sauce
1 to 2 tsp. liquid smoke
6 rib pork chops, ½-in. thick

Mix water, vinegar, sugar, mustard, salt, pepper and cayenne; add lemon and onion. Simmer for 20 minutes. Add catsup, Worcestershire sauce; add liquid smoke. Bring to a boil. Place chops in 11 1/2 x 7 1/2 x 1 1/2-inch baking dish. Pour sauce over chops. Bake, uncovered, at 350 degrees for 1 hour and 25 minutes. Turn chops once. Yield: 6 servings.

Mrs. Lorraine B. Criswell, Prichard H. S.
Grayson, Kentucky

BARBECUED PORK CHOPS

1 ½ tbsp. dry mustard
3 tbsp. brown sugar
3 tbsp. catsup
½ c. vinegar
½ c. water
Salt and pepper
12 pork chops

Blend all ingredients except pork chops. Place chops in baking dish. Pour sauce over chops. Bake, uncovered, at 300 degrees for 1 hour to 1 hour and 30 minutes. NOTE: Sauce may also be used over spareribs, sausage patties or sliced smoked ham. Yield: 12 servings.

Alice Walther, Milbank Public H. S.
Milbank, South Dakota

BEST BARBECUED PORK CHOPS

Salt and pepper
Flour
6 pork chops, ¾-in. thick
½ c. catsup
¼ c. vinegar
2 ½ tbsp. brown sugar
½ c. water
1 tsp. mustard
½ med. onion, sliced
2 tsp. Worcestershire sauce
½ tsp. liquid smoke
¼ tsp. Tabasco sauce
Few drops of garlic juice

Season and flour chops; brown in hot fat. Arrange slightly staggered in flat baking dish. Mix remaining ingredients and pour over chops. Cover tightly with foil and bake at 350 degrees for 1 hour and 30 minutes. Yield: 6 servings.

Margaret Schlotz, Waldport H. S.
Waldport, Oregon

PORK CHOPS IN BARBECUE SAUCE

6 thick pork chops
¼ c. catsup
¼ c. water
2 tbsp. lemon juice
1 tsp. Worcestershire sauce
½ tsp. dry mustard
1 sm. onion, sliced

Brown chops in small amount hot fat; place in casserole. Combine remaining ingredients except onion and pour over chops; top with onion slices. Cover and bake at 350 degrees or cook over low heat for 1 hour or until done. Yield: 6 servings.

Mrs. Lois J. Latteman, Washington H. S.
Washington, New Jersey

PORK CHOPS IN BARBECUE SAUCE

7 to 10 pork chops
½ c. catsup
1 tsp. salt
2 tbsp. cider vinegar
2 tbsp. sugar
2 tbsp. steak sauce
2 tbsp. Worcestershire sauce
¼ c. water

Place pork chops in roaster or pan. Combine remaining ingredients; pour mixture over chops. Bake at 350 degrees for 1 hour, basting every 20 minutes with sauce. Yield: 7-10 servings.

Sharon Sullivan, South Lake H. S.
St. Clair Shores, Michigan

SKILLET BARBECUED PORK CHOPS

6 pork chops
Salt and pepper
½ onion, chopped
1 c. catsup
1 tbsp. Worcestershire sauce
1 ½ tsp. mustard
1 c. water

Brown pork chops lightly on both sides; salt and pepper to taste. Combine 1/4 teaspoonful salt and remaining ingredients; pour over chops. Cover and simmer on top of stove for 20 minutes. Yield: 6 servings.

Dorothy B. Byrd, South Gwinnett H. S.
Snellville, Georgia

SKILLET BARBECUED PORK CHOPS

4 to 6 pork chops
1 tbsp. vegetable oil
⅓ c. chopped celery
2 tbsp. brown sugar
2 tbsp. lemon juice
½ tsp. salt
½ tsp. dry mustard
⅛ tsp. pepper
2 8-oz. cans tomato sauce

Brown chops in oil in large skillet over medium heat for 5 minutes on each side. Drain off excess fat. Sprinkle celery, brown sugar, lemon juice and seasonings evenly over chops. Cover with tomato sauce. Cover and simmer over low heat for 1 hour or until chops are tender. Yield: 4-6 servings.

Carolyn Lloyd, Stillwater Jr. H. S.
Stillwater, Oklahoma
Jeanne Mackie, Milwaukie H. S.
Milwaukie, Oregon

ORIENTAL PORK CHOPS

6 pork chops
½ c. soy sauce
½ c. water
1 clove of garlic, minced

(Continued on next page)

Score fat edges of chops; place in shallow baking dish. Combine remaining ingredients and pour over chops. Refrigerate for several hours or overnight. Arrange marinated chops on broiler pan rack. Broil 3 inches from heat for 10 minutes on each side. Yield: 6 servings.

Carolyn Carpenter, Sam Houston, H. S.
Arlington, Texas

TANGY BARBECUED PORK CHOPS

3 to 4 lb. pork chops
1 lge. onion, finely chopped
2 to 3 tsp. salt
2 tbsp. vinegar
4 tbsp. lemon juice
2 tbsp. brown sugar
1 c. catsup or chili sauce
2 tsp. dry mustard
1 c. water
½ c. chopped celery
1 tsp. paprika

Brown pork chops in skillet over low heat. Remove chops and brown onion. Pour off drippings and return chops to skillet. Mix remaining ingredients and pour over chops. Cover and cook over low heat for 1 hour and 30 minutes to 2 hours or until done. Yield: 6 servings.

Betty Horn, Midland H. S.
Midland, Texas

BRAISED PORK CHOPS WITH MUSTARD CREAM

6 pork chops, cut 1-in. thick
Salt and pepper
½ c. flour
2 tbsp. butter
2 tbsp. vegetable oil
1 ½ c. finely sliced onions
½ tsp. finely chopped garlic
2 tbsp. white wine vinegar
1 lge. bay leaf
1 c. heavy cream
1 tbsp. Dijon mustard
½ tsp. lemon juice

Season pork chops with salt and pepper; dredge in flour, shaking off excess flour. Saute chops in butter and oil in heavy skillet for 3 minutes on each side or until golden brown. Place in bottom of casserole. Pour off all but 2 tablespoonfuls fat; brown onions and garlic slightly in the fat. Remove pan from heat; add white wine vinegar. Scrape bottom and sides of pan; spoon onions and drippings over chops. Crumble in bay leaf and heat casserole on top of stove until bubbly. Cover tightly and bake in preheated 325 degree oven for 10 minutes. Turn and baste chops with casserole juices. Continue baking until chops are done. Skim as much fat as possible from juice in casserole. Add heavy cream to chops and bring sauce to a boil over high heat. Turn off heat. When sauce has reduced one-half, add mustard and lemon juice. Yield: 6 servings.

Mrs. Sue Harrison, Mississippi Co. H. S.
West Ridge, Arkansas

CARAWAY PORK CHOPS

6 lge. pork chops
Salt and pepper
Flour
2 tbsp. caraway seed
Paprika
1 c. water

Roll pork chops in seasoned flour; saute until brown. Sprinkle with caraway seed and enough paprika to color. Add water. Simmer for 45 minutes to 1 hour or until tender. Yield: 6 servings.

Mrs. Lillian Barber, Haines City H. S.
Haines City, Florida

CHICKEN-FRIED PORK CHOPS

3 pork chops, ¾-in. thick
1 egg, beaten
1 tbsp. milk
½ c. fine cracker crumbs
¼ tsp. salt
⅛ c. water

Pound chops thoroughly to 1/2-inch thickness. Mix eggs and milk. Dip meat into egg mixture; dip into crumbs. Brown on both sides in hot fat. Season with salt. Add water. Cover; cook over low heat for 40 minutes to 1 hour. Lift chops occasionally to prevent sticking. For crisp coating, remove cover last 15 minutes. NOTE: Recipe may be doubled. Yield: 3 servings. ings.

Kathryn Sue Hurst, Clarksville H. S.
Clarksville, Arkansas
Mrs. Esta Newman, Bluffs H. S.
Bluffs, Illinois

CHICKEN LICKIN' GOOD PORK CHOPS

½ c. flour
½ tsp. salt
1 tsp. dry mustard
½ tsp. garlic salt
6 loin pork chops, 1-in. thick
1 tbsp. fat
1 10 ½-oz. can chicken with rice soup

Mix flour with salt, dry mustard and garlic salt. Dredge pork chops with blended flour. Brown chops slowly in fat in skillet. Reduce heat; add soup. Cover. Cook over low heat for 1 hour or until chops are thoroughly done. Add 1 can of water during cooking. Add flour mixture to make gravy, 5 minutes before serving. Yield: 6 servings.

Cheryll Nevin, White Sulphur Springs H. S.
White Sulphur Springs, Montana

HARVEST PORK CHOPS

6 pork chops
Fat
½ c. catsup
Grated rind of ½ orange
½ c. orange juice
¼ tsp. salt

Brown chops in fat. Mix remaining ingredients; pour over chops. Cover with tight fitting cover. Simmer for 45 minutes, basting often. Yield:6 servings.

Mrs. Margaret Redman, Graveraet Jr. H. S.
Marquette, Michigan

PORK CHOPS CALIFORNIA

6 loin chops
Salt and pepper
1 tbsp. fat
1 clove of garlic, slit or pinch of garlic salt
2 tbsp. cornstarch
½ tsp. rosemary
1 ¼ c. hot water
2 tbsp. lemon juice
6 lemon slices, ¼-in. thick

Sprinkle pork chops with salt and pepper; brown on each side in hot fat in a heavy skillet. Add garlic just before desired browning is reached. Remove chops and garlic. Mix cornstarch, 1/2 teaspoonful salt and rosemary; add to drippings. Place over low heat; gradually add hot water, stirring constantly to prevent lumping. Cook until thick and glossy; add lemon juice. Add browned pork chops and lemon slices to sauce. Simmer, in covered pan, for 40 to 50 minutes. Yield: 6 servings.

Ruby Jo Bonds, Rancier Jr. H. S.
Killeen, Texas

PORK CHOP DISH

2 tbsp. fat
8 pork chops
Salt and pepper
1 lge. white onion, thinly sliced
2 fresh green sweet peppers, sliced into rings
2 lge. fresh tomatoes

Place fat in large skillet; brown pork chops on both sides. Add salt and pepper to taste. Place onion slice, a pepper ring and tomato slice on each chop. Salt again lightly. Cover skillet tightly; cook at 275 degrees for 20 minutes. If chops become too dry, add 1/4 cup water and continue cooking. NOTE: Chops may be browned and layered with vegetables in a casserole and baked at 275 degrees for 20 minutes. Yield: 8 servings.

Mrs. J. J. Durham, Hereford H. S.
Hereford, Texas

PORK CHOPS PIQUANT

1 egg
3 tbsp. water
4 pork chops
1 c. bread crumbs
Fat
2 tsp. Worcestershire sauce
4 tbsp. cream of mushroom soup
Dash of salt and pepper
4 slices Bermuda onion

Beat egg slightly with water; dip each pork chop into mixture. Dip into bread crumbs. Brown lightly in a small amount of fat in large frying pan. Mix Worcestershire sauce with soup; spread over chops. Sprinkle with salt and pepper; top each chop with a slice of onion. Cover and simmer for 45 minutes. Yield: 4 servings.

Mrs. Barbara Carr, Southside Jr. H. S.
Greenwood, South Carolina

PORK CHOPS WITH TOMATO-OLIVE SAUCE

6 pork chops
4 med. tomatoes, sliced
¼ c. stuffed olives, sliced
1 tbsp. flour
Salt and pepper
3 med. potatoes, pared and sliced

Brown chops on both sides at 350 degrees for 10 to 15 minutes in electric fry pan. Remove chops; place tomatoes and olives in pan. Combine flour, salt and pepper; sprinkle over tomatoes. Place chops on tomatoes. Arrange sliced potatoes on chops. Cover and cook at 200 degrees for 45 minutes. Yield: 6 servings.

Mrs. Marie Harlan, Hamlin Jr. H. S.
Corpus Christi, Texas

PORK SURPRISE

4 lge. lean pork chops
Salad oil
4 thick onion slices
½ 10 ½-oz. can cream of mushroom soup
¼ c. milk or water
¼ c. peanut butter
1 tsp. Worcestershire sauce
1 tsp. salt
⅛ tsp. pepper

Brown chops on both sides in small amount of salad oil in large skillet. Pour off fat when chops are brown. Place onion slice on each chop. Mix soup and milk; blend well. Add peanut butter, Worcestershire sauce and seasonings. Pour over chops. Cover skillet and cook over low heat for 45 minutes. Yield: 4 servings.

Nettie-Adelyn Landau, E. C. Best School
Fallon, Nevada

SKILLET PORKERS WITH FLORIDA SAUERKRAUT

1 onion, sliced
6 pork chops
2 tsp. salt
¼ c. water
1 c. Florida orange juice
½ tsp. grated Florida orange rind
1 tsp. cornstarch
1 ½ lb. sauerkraut, drained
¼ tsp. caraway seed
2 Florida oranges, sectioned

Saute onion in a small amount of fat until onion is tender in large skillet. Add pork chops and sprinkle with salt. Saute chops on both sides until golden brown. Add water. Cover and cook for 1 hour or until tender. Remove chops from skillet to platter. Add orange juice and 1/4 teaspoonful orange rind to skillet; blend with juice in pan. Blend cornstarch with a small amount of water; add to skillet. Bring just to a boil, stirring constantly. Serve over pork chops. Place sauerkraut in saucepan; sprinkle with caraway seed. Cover and cook for about 15 minutes, tossing occasionally until thoroughly blended. Add orange sections and remaining rind. Cover and heat for about 10 minutes. Serve with skillet porkers. Yield: 4-6 servings.

Photograph for this recipe on page 97.

APPLE-STUFFED PORK CHOPS

4 double pork chops, cut ½ to 1-in. thick
Salt and pepper
1 tart apple, sliced
2 tsp. brown sugar (opt.)
1 egg, slightly beaten
1 c. plus 1 tbsp. water (opt.)
Soft bread crumbs or ½ c. crushed corn flakes
Fat

Cut chops along the bone to form pocket; season. Fill with mixture of apple slices and brown sugar. Dip chops into mixture of egg and 1 tablespoonful water. Roll chops in crumbs; brown in hot fat. Add remaining water and cover. Bake at 350 degrees for 30 to 45 minutes or until tender, adding additional water if necessary. Yield: 4 servings.

Mrs. Emma Lou Schwagel, Boonsboro H. S.
Boonsboro, Maryland
Mrs. Rhea DaLee Thomas, Norton H. S.
Norton, Texas

DELUXE STUFFED CHOPS

1 onion, finely diced
3 stalks celery, finely diced
3 tbsp. bacon drippings or butter
Seasoned salt
1 ½ c. fine bread crumbs
½ c. instant rice
1 tsp. poultry seasoning
½ c. warm water
8 loin chops, 1 ½-in. thick
Monosodium glutamate
Pepper

Simmer onion and celery in bacon drippings; season well with seasoned salt. Mix crumbs, rice, poultry seasoning and warm water in a bowl. Add onions and celery; mix well. Slash chops for stuffing. Season on both sides and in pocket with seasoned salt, monosodium glutamate and pepper. Stuff each chop with dressing; place in roasting pan. Bake, uncovered, in preheated 350 degree oven for 30 minutes. Cover; reduce heat to 300 degrees. Bake for 1 hour. Yield: 4-8 servings.

Mrs. Jack Adderson, Colonel Irvine Jr. H. S.
Calgary, Alberta, Canada

EASY STUFFED PORK CHOPS

4 double pork chops
4 tbsp. brown sugar
½ tart apple, cored and sliced
½ tsp. salt

Have pocket cup in each chop. Insert 1 tablespoonful brown sugar, 1 slice apple and 1/8 teaspoonful salt. Place in lightly greased large baking dish without crowding. Bake at 325 degrees for 1 hour. Yield: 4 servings.

Mrs. Doveta Hunt, Pecos H. S.
Pecos, Texas

FRUIT-FILLED PORK CHOPS

1 sm. onion, minced
3 tbsp. fat
1 ½ c. bread crumbs
½ c. canned minced apricots
½ c. canned minced Kadota figs
¼ tsp. salt
Dash of pepper
6 double pork chops with deep pockets

Brown onion in fat; add crumbs, fruit and seasonings. Stuff pockets of chops. Close with toothpicks. Place in shallow pan lined with foil. Bake, uncovered, at 350 degrees for 1 hour and 30 minutes. Yield: 6 servings.

Mrs. Anthony G. Stone
Newell-Providence Comm. School, Newell, Iowa

POCKETBOOK PORK CHOPS

2 tbsp. chopped onion
6 tbsp. fat
Salt and pepper
½ tsp. poultry seasoning
⅛ tsp. celery salt
2 c. soft bread crumbs
4 pork chops, ¾ to 1-in. thick
½ c. flour
¼ c. water

Cook onion slowly in 2 tablespoonfuls fat for 5 minutes. Add 1/2 teaspoonful salt, 1/8 teaspoon-

(Continued on next page)

ful pepper and remaining seasonings to bread crumbs; add crumb mixture to onion-fat mixture. Mix thoroughly. Make a slit along side of pork chop, cutting into meat almost to the bone. Stuff some of dressing into each pocket. Fasten edges with a toothpick. Mix flour with 1/2 teaspoonful salt and 1/8 teaspoonful pepper; roll each chop in mixture. Melt 4 tablespoonfuls fat in skillet. Brown chops, turning once. Add water. Cover skillet; cook over low heat for 30 to 45 minutes or place in baking dish. Bake at 300 degrees for 1 hour. Yield: 4 servings.

Marilyn J. Miller, Spooner H. S.
Spooner, Wisconsin

STUFFED PORK CHOPS

2 c. bread crumbs
2 tbsp. chopped onion
½ tsp. salt
¼ tsp. pepper
¼ tsp. sage
3 tbsp. melted butter
½ c. chopped apple
Hot water to moisten
6 double pork chops

Combine all ingredients except pork chops. Have pocket cut in pork chops and fill with bread stuffing. Bake, uncovered, at 325 degrees for1 hour. Yield: 6 servings.

Mrs. Frances H. Bowyer, Fayetteville H. S.
Fayetteville, North Carolina

PORK CHOPS WITH CURRY STUFFING

4 pork chops or steaks, cut 1-in. thick
3 tbsp. fat
¾ c. diced apple
2 tbsp. diced onion
¼ c. chopped celery
1 ½ c. soft whole wheat bread crumbs
¼ c. milk
1 tsp. curry powder
1 tsp. salt
3 tbsp. flour

Have pockets cut in chops. Melt 1 tablespoonful fat; add apple, onion and celery. Cook over low heat until golden brown. Mix bread crumbs and milk; fold in cooked apple mixture. Sprinkle with 1/2 teaspoonful curry powder and 1/2 teaspoonful salt and toss; stuff chops. Combine flour with remaining curry powder and salt; dredge chops in mix. Brown in remaining fat and arrange in casserole. Cover and bake at 325 degrees to 350 degrees for 45 minutes. Remove cover and bake for 15 minutes longer. Yield: 4 servings.

Mrs. Patsy Steffensen, Lake Norden H. S.
Lake Norden, South Dakota

STUFFED PORK CHOPS

1 tbsp. onion, grated
½ c. chopped celery
½ tsp. salt
½ tsp. poultry seasoning
2 c. bread crumbs
1 tbsp. parsley
½ c. diced apple
1 can chicken with rice soup
6 loin pork chops, butterflied

Combine all ingredients except chops. Stuff chops with mixture. Bake at 375 degrees for 1 hour and 15 minutes. Yield: 6 servings.

Mrs. Helen Alders, Douglass H. S.
Douglass, Texas

PORK CHOPS WITH DRESSING

6 pork chops, cut 1-in. thick
1 c. corn bread crumbs
1 c. bread crumbs
½ c. milk
1 egg, beaten
1 ½ tsp. salt
Dash of pepper
2 tbsp. chopped parsley
1 sm. onion, finely chopped

Have pocket cut in pork chops. Combine crumbs milk, egg, 1/2 teaspoonful salt and seasonings. Stuff chops with dressing. Season chops with remaining salt and brown on both sides in a skillet with a small amount of fat. Bake at 300 degrees for 45 minutes to 1 hour. Yield: 6 servings.

Mrs. Nora Gardner, Floyd Co. H. S.
Floyd, Virginia

STUFFED PORK CHOPS

4 lge. pork chops, 1-in. thick
4 c. dry bread cubes
1 c. chopped celery
½ c. chopped onion
1 ½ tsp. sage
1 ½ tsp. salt
¼ tsp. pepper
⅓ c. melted butter

Slit pockets in chops. Combine all remaining ingredients with just enough water to moisten; mix lightly. Stuff each chop with part of mixture. Fasten pockets together with toothpicks. Place chops in an 8 x 8-inch roasting pan; place additional stuffing over chops. Cover with aluminum foil. Bake at 350 degrees for 1 hour. Uncover the last 10 to 15 minutes of baking. Yield: 4 servings.

Mrs. Carolyn Schelkopf, Elmwood Comm. H. S.
Elmwood, Illinois

STUFFED PORK CHOPS

6 double pork chops
1 c. bread crumbs
½ tsp. salt
½ tsp. monosodium glutamate
½ tsp. dried parsley
½ tsp. celery salt
½ tsp. dried onion
4 very sm. pieces bay leaf

Slash pocket in chops on fatty side. Mix remaining ingredients; lightly stuff dressing into each pocket. Fasten with several toothpicks. Brown chops on both sides in frying pan. Pour off most of the fat, leaving pan juices. Cover tightly; bake in preheated 350 degree oven for 1 hour and 30 minutes. Yield: 6 servings.

Mrs. Marion R. Hessler, Governor Mifflin H. S.
Shillington, Pennsylvania

STUFFED PORK CHOPS

4 pork chops, cut 1-in. thick
2 c. bread crumbs
1 tbsp. sage
1 egg
1 tbsp. chopped onion
¾ c. hot water

Cut pocket in pork chops along edge to bone. Mix remaining ingredients. Add more water if needed as stuffing should be thin. Fill pocket of each pork chop with stuffing. Place in greased pan or cookie sheet with sides. Bake at 375 degrees for 1 hour or until pork is thoroughly cooked. Yield: 4 servings.

Barbara Gilhaus, ABL Comm. Unit No. 6
Broadlands, Illinois

BREADED PORK CHOPS WITH APPLE RINGS

1 egg
2 tbsp. water
1 tsp. salt
¼ tsp. pepper
4 pork chops, ½-in. thick
½ c. cracker crumbs
¼ c. shortening
3 to 4 unpeeled apples

Mix egg with water and seasonings; dip pork chops into mixture. Roll in crumbs; let stand for a few minutes. Brown chops on both sides in hot shortening. Cover; cook slowly for 30 minutes. Remove from pan; keep warm. Core apples; slice into 1/2-inch slices. Fry apple slices in the same pan until tender and lightly browned. Yield: 4 servings.

Mrs. Mary Ruth Wilson, Rule H. S.
Knoxville, Tennessee
Le Nora Hudson, Oklahoma State School for Deaf
Sulphur, Oklahoma

CRANBERRY PORK CHOPS

Salt and pepper
Flour
4 pork chops
2 c. cranberries, washed
1 c. sugar
¼ c. water

Season chops with salt and pepper; dredge in flour. Brown in frying pan with small amount fat. Place browned chops in baking dish. Mix cranberries with sugar and water; cover chops with cranberry mixture. Cover baking dish. Bake at 350 degrees for 45 minutes. Yield: 4 servings.

Mrs. Lois McComber Benson
Mountain Home H. S.
Mountain Home, Idaho

FRUITED PORK CHOPS

6 pork chops, 1-in. thick
2 tbsp. flour
1 tsp. salt
½ tsp. paprika
2 tbsp. butter or margarine
1 13½-oz. can pineapple chunks
1 11-oz. can Mandarin orange sections, drained
2 tbsp. well drained sweet pickle relish
2 tbsp. soy sauce
1 tbsp. cornstarch
1 tbsp. sugar

Coat chops with a mixture of flour, salt, and paprika; brown well on both sides in margarine. Arrange in shallow casserole. Combine undrained pineapple, orange sections, relish, soy sauce, cornstarch and sugar; mix and pour over chops. Cover with foil; crimp securely to edge of casserole. Bake at 350 degrees for 1 hour to 1 hour and 45 minutes or until meat is fork tender. Serve plain or with hot seasoned rice, if desired.

Alice E. Stone, Sherrard H. S.
Sherrard, Illinois

HAWAIIAN BAKED PORK CHOPS

2 c. crushed pineapple
3 med. sweet potatoes, pared and sliced
2 tbsp. brown sugar
4 center-cut pork chops
Salt and pepper
4 strips bacon (opt.)

Place pineapple in large baking dish. Place sweet potatoes over pineapple; sprinkle with brown sugar. Season chops with salt and pepper; place on top of sweet potatoes. Place a strip of bacon on each chop. Cover; bake at 350 degrees for 1 hour or until done. Yield: 4 servings.

Mrs. Zenobia McWaters, Girard H. S.
Girard, Texas
Gail P. Corbett, Murfreesboro H. S.
Murfreesboro, North Carolina

HAWAIIAN PORK CHOPS

6 8-oz. double rib pork chops
Salt and pepper
½ c. honey
12 coriander seed, crushed
½ c. pineapple juice
2 tsp. dry mustard
6 cloves
1 lemon
1 orange
1 lime
Maraschino cherries

Brown chops; season with salt and pepper. Place in shallow baking dish. Combine all remaining ingredients, except fruit; spoon 3 tablespoonfuls mixture over each chop. Bake, uncovered, at 350 degrees for 1 hour and 15 minutes. Baste occasionally. Peg with a toothpick, one slice orange, lemon and lime; place on each chop. Top each chop with a Maraschino cherry. Baste fruit and bake at 350 degrees for 10 minutes longer. Yield: 6 servings.

Mrs. Grace T. Mayhall, Tremont H. S.
Tremont, Mississippi

LUAU PORK CHOPS

4 pork loin chops, thick enough to include 2 rib bones
Salt
Monosodium glutamate
4 slices canned pineapple
4 slices unpeeled Naval orange, cut ¼-in. thick
4 slices unpeeled lemon, cut ⅛-in. thick
4 slices upeeled lime, cut ⅛-in. thick
¾ c. honey
½ c. orange juice
4 Maraschino cherries with stems

Brown chops well; place in baking dish. Season with salt and monosodium glutamate to taste. Add sufficient water to cover bottom of pan 1/4-inch deep. Cover tightly. Bake at 350 degrees for 1 hour. Remove cover. Drain pineapple, reserving 1/2 cup juice. Place slice pineapple, orange, lemon and lime on top of each chop. Combine honey, reserved pineapple juice and orange juice. Pour glaze over chops. Return to oven and bake, uncovered, for 30 minutes longer. Baste every 5 to 10 minutes with glaze. Top each chop with a Maraschino cherry and serve. Yield: 4 servings.

Mrs. J. S. Elsner, Hampton H. S.
Allison Park, Pennsylvania

ORANGE-GLAZED PORK CHOPS

4 loin pork chops
Salt and pepper
Paprika
2 tbsp. water
5 tbsp. sugar
1 ½ tsp. cornstarch
¼ tsp. cinnamon
10 whole cloves
2 tsp. grated orange rind
½ c. orange juice
4 orange slices, cut into halves

Trim a small amount fat from chops; place in skillet. Fry slowly until a thin coating of fat is in skillet. Sprinkle each side of chops with salt, pepper and paprika. Remove pieces of fat from skillet; place chops in. Brown well on each side over medium heat; as fat accumulates, spoon off. Reduce heat to low; add water. Cover skillet. Cook for 45 minutes to 1 hour or until tender and done. Turn occasionally as chops cook. Mix sugar, cornstarch, 1/4 teaspoonful salt, cinnamon, cloves, orange rind and orange juice, stirring until thickened and clear. Add orange slices; cover pan. Remove from heat. Arrange chops on platter; spoon glaze over chops. Garnish with orange slices, if desired. Yield: 4 servings.

Dorothy J. McCabe, Blakely Borough H. S.
Peckville, Pennsylvania

ORANGE PORK CHOPS

4 pork chops or steaks
Salt and pepper to taste
Sage to taste
1 onion, sliced
1 6-oz. can frozen orange juice
1 6-oz. can water

Brown chops or steaks in fat. Arrange in casserole or baking dish. Sprinkle with salt, pepper and sage. Top with onion. Mix orange juice and water; pour over meat. Cover; bake at 350 degrees for 1 hour.

OVEN STEAMED RICE:

1 ½ c. uncooked rice
1 ½ tsp. salt
Dash of pepper
2 tbsp. butter
3 ½ c. boiling water
¼ c. sliced green onions

Mix rice and seasonings in 2-quart casserole. Dot with butter. Add boiling water; stir with fork. Bake, covered, at 350 degrees for 45 minutes. Add onions. Serve with chops. Yield: 4 servings.

Mrs. H. F. Noyes, Davis H. S.
Kaysville, Utah

PORK CHOPS AND APPLES

6 pork chops
Fat
3 or 4 unpeeled apples, cored and sliced
¼ c. (packed) brown sugar
½ tsp. cinnamon
2 tbsp. butter

(Continued on next page)

Brown chops on all sides in hot fat. Place apple slices in greased 1 1/2-quart baking dish; sprinkle with brown sugar and cinnamon. Dot with butter; top with chops. Cover. Bake in preheated 400 degree oven for 1 hour and 30 minutes. Yield: 6 servings.

Mrs. Helen Stone Gardner, South Marshall H. S.
Benton, Kentucky

PINEAPPLE PORK CHOPS

6 loin pork chops, cut ½-in. thick
1 tbsp. butter or margarine
Salt and pepper
6 pineapple slices
¼ c. water
1 tbsp. wine vinegar
1 tbsp. sugar
⅓ c. pineapple syrup
1 tbsp. raisins
1 tbsp. pine nuts or peanuts
2 tsp. candied orange peel, finely chopped
1 tsp. cornstarch

Brown pork chops in butter on one side over medium heat; turn. Salt and pepper chops. Brown for 5 minutes on second side. Place 1 pineapple slice on each chop. Add water; cover pan. Reduce heat; simmer for 30 minutes or until chops are well done. Remove to hot platter. Skim grease from pan. Blend vinegar, sugar and syrup in pan; add raisins, nuts and orange. Simmer, stirring for 2 to 3 minutes. Mix cornstarch with 1 tablespoonful water; stir into sauce and cook, stirring, until thickened and clear. Spoon sauce over chops. Yield: 6 servings.

Louise Bollinger, Sweetwater H. S.
Sweetwater, Texas

PORK CHOPS IN ORANGE SAUCE

¼ c. flour
1 tsp. salt
6 loin or shoulder pork chops
1 tbsp. salad oil or shortening
½ c. orange juice
1 tbsp. grated orange rind
1 tsp. sugar
½ c. water or orange juice

Mix flour with salt; coat chops in mixture. Brown in hot oil or shortening in heavy skillet; pour off all fat. Add orange juice to chops; cook slowly for 25 to 30 minutes. Remove meat from skillet; place in baking dish. Keep warm in oven. Mix orange rind with sugar, a small amount flour, water or orange juice until smooth. Stir into skillet. Cook, stirring constantly, until sauce is thick. Pour over chops and serve. Yield: 4-6 servings.

Mrs. Hazel Janson, Blount Jr. H. S.
Pensacola, Florida

PORK CHOPS SUPREME

Salt and pepper
Dash of garlic salt
6 pork chops, cut 2-in. thick
Graham cracker crumbs
Margarine
2 Winesap apples, sliced and cored
1 lge. onion, sliced
1 can tomato soup

Season chops; roll in crumbs and brown in margarine. Place chops in frying pan; top with an apple slice and onion slice. Pour tomato soup over chops and simmer until tender. Yield: 6 servings.

Ella Bang, Yankton H. S.
Yankton, South Dakota

PORK CHOPS WITH PINEAPPLE-FRUIT SAUCE

Salt and pepper
6 to 8 center-cut pork chops
1 c. drained fruit cocktail
1 c. brown sugar
¼ c. vinegar
2 tbsp. soy sauce
2 tbsp. cornstarch
½ c. pineapple juice
1 c. drained pineapple chunks
½ c. mixed cherries, chopped cooked prunes and raisins

Season pork chops and brown on both sides; place in casserole. Combine fruit cocktail, brown sugar, vinegar, soy sauce, cornstarch and pineapple juice. Bring to a boil over low heat; boil for 4 to 5 minutes. Add remaining fruits; mix well and pour over pork chops. Bake at 350 degrees for 25 to 30 minutes. Serve with cooked rice, if desired. Yield: 6-8 servings.

Mrs. Coral Hawkins, Tehachapi H. S.
Tehachapi, California

CHICKEN-BAKED PORK CHOPS

Salt and pepper to taste
6 pork chops
2 tbsp. bacon fat
3 c. instant rice
1 10 ½-oz. can cream of chicken soup
1 c. water

Sprinkle salt and pepper on pork chops. Fry chops in bacon fat until brown. Pour rice into casserole; place chops on rice. Blend soup with water; pour over chops and rice. Bake at 350 degrees for 30 minutes or until brown. Yield: 6 servings.

Mrs. Eva Pearl Quillen, Central H. S.
Cookeville, Tennessee

PORK CHOPS WITH PRUNE SAUCE

⅔ lb. dried prunes
8 pork chops, cut 1-in. thick
3 tbsp. flour
1 egg, beaten
¾ c. dried bread crumbs
¼ c. butter or margarine
1 tsp. grated lemon rind
¼ tsp. cinnamon
¼ tsp. ground cloves
½ c. water
½ c. Port wine or Sherry
½ tsp. salt
¼ c. sugar

Cook prunes according to package directions; do not add sugar. Pit and mash; Chill 1 cup prunes overnight. Trim fat from chops. Sprinkle chops with flour; dip into egg. Dip into crumbs and brown on both sides in hot butter in large skillet over medium heat. Reduce heat and cook, covered, for 45 minutes, or until tender. Turn chops once and add additional water if necessary. Simmer prunes with rind, cinnamon, cloves and water for 10 minutes; add wine, salt and sugar. Bring to a boil once; keep warm. Spoon prune sauce over chops. Serve with mashed potatoes or fluffy rice, if desired. Yield: 8 servings.

Mrs. Adeline H. Kirk, Central H. S.
San Angelo, Texas

PORK CHOP CASSEROLE

6 pork chops
Salt and pepper
6 tbsp. uncooked rice
1 1-lb. 4½-oz. can tomatoes

Season and brown chops; place in greased casserole. Place 1 tablespoonful uncooked rice on each chop. Pour tomatoes over chops. Cover and bake at 350 degrees for 1 hour and 30 minutes or until rice is done. Yield: 6 servings.

Mrs. Marjorie Joan Mattie, Boscobel H. S.
Boscobel, Wisconsin

PORK CHOPS AND RICE

Seasonings to taste
5 pork chops
⅔ c. uncooked rice
1 can tomatoes
1 lge. onion, sliced
1 green pepper, sliced

Season and brown pork chops. Place uncooked rice on top of chops; add tomatoes. Place an onion slice and green pepper slice on top each chop. Season. Cover and cook for 45 minutes. Yield: 5 servings.

Joyce F. DeVivo, Lee Co. H. S.
Leesburg, Georgia

PORK CHOPS AND WILD RICE

Salt and pepper
6 pork chops
1 tbsp. fat
2 onions, chopped
1 clove of garlic, minced
1 can condensed tomato soup
2 ½ c. hot water
¼ green pepper, diced
¼ c. diced celery
¾ c. uncooked rice
¼ c. chopped green onions
Pinch of marjoram
Pinch of thyme
½ bay leaf, crushed
2 tbsp. parsley
1 tsp. salt

Season chops and brown in fat. Remove chops; drain, reserving 1 tablespoonful fat. Brown onions in reserved fat with garlic. Add soup, water, green pepper, celery, rice, green onions and seasonings. Mix well. Place chops in casserole; cover with mixture. Cover casserole. Bake at 350 degrees for 1 hour and 15 minutes. Yield: 6 servings.

Mrs. Alex Gray, Waynesboro H. S.
Waynesboro, Georgia

PORK CHOPS AND WILD RICE

Seasoning
4 tenderloin pork chops, cut 1-in. thick
Bacon drippings
Garlic
⅓ c. wild rice
1 can tomato soup
1 sm. can mushrooms

Season and brown pork chops in bacon drippings with a small amount of garlic. Arrange chops in loaf pan; spread a thin layer of rice around chops. Pour on tomato soup and enough water to cover. Add mushrooms. Bake at 350 degrees for 1 hour and 30 minutes.

Bonita Carlson, Granite Falls H. S.
Granite Falls, Minnesota

PORK CHOPS, RICE AND MUSHROOM GRAVY

Flour
6 pork chops
Salt and pepper to taste
1 10 ¾-oz. can cream of mushroom soup
1 c. cooked rice

Flour pork chops; brown in own fat in a 12-inch fry pan. Cover; simmer until well done. Remove chops; add 2 tablespoonfuls flour to fat. Add salt and pepper. Add enough water to make thick gravy. Mix in mushroom soup; stir until smooth. Serve gravy over cooked rice with pork chops. Yield: 6 servings.

Berniece M. Cobb, Westminster H. S.
Westminster, Colorado

STUFFED PORK CHOPS

6 pork chops
2 tbsp. shortening
1 ½ c. cooked rice
2 tomatoes, sliced
2 green peppers, sliced
1 onion, sliced
1 ½ c. hot water

Sear chops in shortening and place in broiler pan. Top each chop with rice, tomato, green pepper and onion slices. Pour water in bottom of broiler. Bake at 350 degrees for 45 minutes. Yield: 6 servings.

Constance Day, La Grange H. S.
La Grange, Georgia

BAKED COUNTRY HAM

1 country ham
2 c. brown sugar
1 tbsp. prepared mustard
Sweet pickle juice
Whole cloves

Trim mold from ham; saw off ham hock. Soak ham overnight in cold water. Place in brown paper bag and weigh. Place in large pan. Bake in preheated 260 degree oven for 30 minutes per pound for whole ham or 40 minutes per pound for half. Remove rind. Combine brown sugar, mustard and enough juice to make a thick paste. Spread over ham; stud with cloves. Brown at 450 degrees.

Rosalie Floyd, North Warren H. S.
Smiths Grove, Kentucky

BAKED CURED HAM

1 10 to 12-lb. cured ham

Soak cured ham overnight in enough cold water to cover. Clean and prepare for cooking. Wrap well in two layers of heavy aluminum foil; place in open pan, fat-side up. Add 1 inch water to pan. Bake at 325 degrees for 25 minutes per pound adding water as necessary. Remove from foil; skin and slice. Serve hot or cold.

Josephine M. Grant, Rocky Mount H. S.
Rocky Mount, North Carolina

BAKED HAM

1 shoulder or picnic ham
1 c. brown sugar
1 tbsp. dry mustard
½ c. pickle juice or spiced fruit juice
10 to 15 whole cloves (opt.)

Place ham on rack of roast pan, skin-side up. Bake in preheated 350 degree oven for 30 to 35 minutes per pound. Remove from oven 30 minutes before baking time is up. Remove rind; score fat. Combine remaining ingredients except cloves. Spread on ham. Insert cloves. Bake at 400 degrees for 15 to 20 minutes.

Helen E. Pyle, Christian Co. H. S.
Hopkinsville, Kentucky

BAKED STUFFED HAM

1 lb. saltine crackers, crumbled
1 loaf sliced white bread
3 med. onions, minced
½ lb. suet, ground
2 tbsp. sugar
½ c. minced celery
1 tbsp. mustard seed
2 tbsp. dry mustard
1 9-oz. jar sweet pickle relish
¼ c. snipped parsley
4 eggs, well beaten
4 dashes Tabasco sauce
1 ½ c. cider vinegar
1 wrapped 10 to 12-lb. boned ham, fully cooked
½ c. apricot preserves, melted

Combine fine cracker crumbs and bread, using an electric blender or other method. Place in large bowl or pan; add onions, suet, sugar, celery, mustard seed, dry mustard, pickle relish and parsley. Stir in eggs, Tabasco sauce and vinegar. Unwrap ham; place in large roasting pan. With sharp knife make lengthwise cut through top center of ham halfway; spread halves apart. Fill cut with part of crumb mixture; pat remaining crumb mixture over top of ham. Bake, uncovered, in preheated 350 degree oven for 1 hour. Brush stuffing with melted apricot preserves. Bake for 15 minutes longer. Cool. When cool, refrigerate ham for 2 days before serving. Yield: 20-22 servings.

Mrs. Vaudene Pruitt, Mercedes H. S.
Mercedes, Texas

COUNTRY CURED HAM

1 country cured ham

Soak ham overnight. Wash and remove hock. Place soaked ham in roaster. Add 5 cups water; cover tightly. Place in preheated 375 degree oven. Reduce heat to 500 degrees and bake for 10 minutes. Turn off oven; let ham set in oven for 3 hours. Do not open door. Bake at 500 degrees for 10 minutes. Turn oven off; do not open for 24 hours. For well done ham, heat oven to 375 degrees. Place ham in roaster; add 5 cups water. Cover tightly; bake at 500 degrees for 10 minutes longer. Cool before opening oven door.

Mrs. Martha B. Godwin, Windsor H. S.
Windsor, Virginia

COUNTRY HAM

1 country ham
2 c. dark molasses
1 c. vinegar
Brown sugar
Pickle juice

Scrub ham well with a stiff brush. Place in container; cover with cold water. Add 1 cup molasses and vinegar; allow ham to soak overnight. Remove ham from water; rinse well and cover with fresh water. Add remaining molasses. Cover. Place over high heat; allow to come to rolling boil. Boil for 30 minutes. Remove container from heat. Do not remove cover. Cover with newspapers and blankets. Allow to stand overnight. Remove ham from water; remove skin, if desired. Score; stick a clove in each square. Combine brown sugar and pickle juice to a paste; spread over ham. Bake at 300 degrees for 60 minutes.

Mrs. Thelma L. Fowler, South Side H. S.
Counce, Tennessee

FLAVORFUL BAKED HAM

1 can frozen orange juice concentrate
1 c. Sherry wine or 1 c. pineapple juice
¼ c. brown sugar
1 tsp. mustard
1 tsp. Worcestershire sauce
1 whole ham
Whole cloves
Fruit

Allow orange concentrate to thaw; mix undiluted juice with wine. Blend in brown sugar, mustard and Worcestershire sauce. Place ham on a long sheet of heavy duty foil in a shallow pan. Spoon one-half of mixture over ham, rubbing mixture into ham with back of spoon. Fold foil over ham. Do not seal airtight. Bake at 400 degrees until done. Spoon off fat; score ham. Stud with cloves decorate with desired fruit. Cover with remaining sauce; return to oven for 15 minutes.

Mrs. Kathryn Patrick, Cummings Jr. H. S.
Brownsville, Texas

FRESH HAM

1 4 to 5-lb. fresh ham
2 lge. onions
Salt and pepper
Monosodium glutamate to taste
2 tbsp. flour
Milk

Place ham and onions in open roasting pan. Roast at 300 to 325 degrees for 30 minutes per pound. Season after 1 hour of roasting. Stir flour and milk into drippings to make gravy.

Mrs. Hazel Jacobsen, Highland H. S.
Ault, Colorado

HAM BAKED IN CIDER

1 11-lb. precooked ham
24 whole cloves
1 c. boiling water
1 qt. cider
2 tbsp. brown sugar
2 sm. onions
1 tbsp. lemon juice
1 tbsp. flour, browned

Sear ham and stud with cloves. Combine boiling water, cider, brown sugar and onions; boil for 10 minutes. Strain and pour over ham in roaster. Bake at 350 degrees for 1 hour, basting every 15 minutes. Strain liquid; add lemon juice and thicken with browned flour. Serve with ham.

Mrs. William V. Hadden, Auburn H. S.
Auburn, Kentucky

HAM IN A BLANKET

1 5-lb. canned smoked ham
2 c. sifted flour
½ tsp. salt
½ c. butter or margarine
3 tbsp. cooking oil
1 egg
2 tbsp. ice water

Heat ham in 325 degree oven for 1 hour. Mix flour with salt; cut in butter or margarine. Lightly beat cooking oil with egg; blend into flour mixture. Stir in ice water until dough forms a ball. Wrap in waxed paper; refrigerate for 1 hour. Remove ham from oven; allow to cool slightly. Roll chilled dough to a 12 x 16-inch rectangle about 1/8-inch thick. Wrap dough around ham, tucking edges under and trimming away excess pastry. Place ham on baking sheet; pierce pastry with fork tines. Bake at 425 degrees for 15 minutes. Remove from oven; trim with pastry. Return to oven for 10 to 15 minutes longer. Yield: 10-12 servings.

Harriette McDowell Holton, Shelby H. S.
Shelby, North Carolina

MISSOURI BAKED HAM

1 10 to 12-lb. ham
Cinnamon
Whole cloves
½ lb. brown sugar
1 tbsp. prepared mustard
1 ½ c. boiling water
1 ½ c. vinegar

Boil ham gently for 1 hour. Skin off fat; place ham in baking pan, fat-side up. Score fat. Sprinkle ham with cinnamon; dot thickly with whole cloves. Pack with brown sugar. Add mustard and boiling water to vinegar; pour into bottom of pan. Cover with a tight-fitting lid. Bake at 300 to 350 degrees for 3 hours.

Jane Parnell, Fort Sumner H. S.
Fort Sumner, New Mexico

HONEY-GLAZED HAM

1 6-lb. smoked ham
1/3 c. honey
1/3 c. brown sugar
1/4 c. orange juice concentrate

Score ham. Place fat-side up, on rack in shallow pan. Bake at 325 degrees for 3 hours to 3 hours and 15 minutes. During the last 30 minutes, baste with honey, brown sugar and orange juice concentrate. Yield: 12 servings.

Mrs. Jeanette H. Stabler, St. Matthews H. S.
St. Matthews, South Carolina

SHERRIED HAM

1 8 to 10-lb. canned ham
1 1/2 c. creme Sherry
1/2 c. apricot or peach jam
Dash of nutmeg or cinnamon or combination
1/2 c. honey
1 tbsp. cornstarch

Place ham in shallow pan; cover with 1/2 cup creme Sherry. Bake at 325 degrees for 1 hour and 30 minutes or until done. Combine jam with nutmeg and honey. Stir in cornstarch and add remaining creme Sherry. Cook, stirring until thickened; spoon over ham. Bake ham for 20 minutes longer or until glazed. NOTE: To give added flavor to ham, marinate in 1/2 cup Sherry for several hours or overnight. Yield: 16-20 servings.

Claudine Marie Becker, Lemoore Union H. S.
Lemoore, California

BAKED HAM

1 slice cured ham, 1 to 2-in. thick
Whole cloves
1 tsp. dry mustard
1 to 2 tbsp. brown sugar
1 to 2 tbsp. flour (opt.)
1 to 2 c. milk

Place ham in casserole. Stick cloves in meat. Mix mustard, brown sugar and flour; sprinkle over ham. Let stand for 1 hour, if desired. Pour milk around ham. Cover; bake at 325 degrees for 1 hour. Remove cover and brown. Yield: 4-6 servings.

Mrs. Helen Peckham, Drexel Hill Jr. H. S.
Drexel Hill, Pennsylvania
Mrs. Jack Turner, Bourne H. S.
Bourne, Massachusetts
Elaine L. Smith, Union City Comm. H. S.
Union City, Indiana

SOUTHERN BAKED HAM

1 3 to 4-lb. picnic ham
1 qt. plus 1 c. milk
2 tbsp. butter
6 tbsp. brown sugar
6 tbsp. dry mustard
1 green pepper, shredded
Whole cloves (opt.)

Trim ham; soak in 1 quart milk overnight. Wash ham; spread with a paste of creamed butter, brown sugar and mustard. Spread on both sides of ham. Sprinkle green pepper over top. Stick a few cloves in the fat side. Place ham in roaster; add remaining milk. Bake at 325 degrees for 3 to 4 hours. More milk may be added. Yield: 10-12 servings.

Mrs. H. W. Iverson, Riggs H. S.
Pierre, South Dakota

BAKED HAM SLICES

1 slice center-cut ham
2 tbsp. sugar
1 tbsp. mustard
Milk

Place ham in 9 x 9-inch pan. Combine sugar and mustard, spread over top of ham slice. Pour milk in pan until milk comes to top of ham. Bake in preheated 350 degree oven for 1 hour. Yield: 4 servings.

Mrs. Lucille Weaver, West Jr. H. S.
Gulf Port, Mississippi

BAKED HAM SLICE

1 center slice ham, 1-in. thick
1/4 c. brown sugar
2 tbsp. steak sauce
1 tbsp. mustard
1 tsp. ground cloves
1 pt. milk

Place ham in deep baking dish. Combine brown sugar, steak sauce, mustard and cloves; spread over ham. Pour milk around ham. Bake at 350 degrees for 40 minutes. Yield: 6 servings.

Allene B. Dunn, Valley H. S.
Fairfax, Alabama

BAKED HAM SLICE

4 smoked ham slices
1/2 c. brown sugar
1/2 c. dry bread crumbs
2 tsp. mustard
1/4 c. wine vinegar
1 1/4 c. apple juice

(Continued on next page)

Place ham in baking dish. Combine remaining ingredients except 1 cup apple juice; spread evenly over ham. Pour remaining juice around ham. Bake, uncovered, at 325 degrees for 1 hour and 30 minutes or until topping is crisp. Yield: 4 servings.

Mrs. Charlotte J. Callihan
Greene Central H. S.
Snow Hill, North Carolina

BAKED HAM SLICE

½ tsp. dry or prepared mustard
¼ c. brown sugar
1 1 ½-lb. tenderized ham slice, 1-in. thick
4 slices pineapple
½ c. pineapple juice

Rub mustard and brown sugar over surface of ham; slash edges of fat around ham. Place in baking dish; cover with pineapple slices. Pour juice around ham. Bake at 350 degrees for 1 hour, basting frequently with pineapple juice. NOTE: Precooked sweet potatoes rolled in brown sugar may be placed around ham during last 30 minutes of baking. Yield: 4 servings.

Mrs. Nannie C. Edwards, Oxford Area H. S.
Oxford, Pennsylvania

BROILED HAM AND LIMAS

1 slice smoked ham, 1-in. thick
2 c. hot cooked or canned green lima beans
2 c. shredded process cheese

Score fat edge of ham; broil 3 to 5 inches from heat for 5 minutes on each side for cooked ham or 10 minutes each side for uncooked ham. Drain beans; mound on ham. Sprinkle with cheese. Reduce heat; broil for 1 minute or until cheese melts. Yield: 4-6 servings.

Mrs. Doris M. Beaman, Greene Central H. S.
Snow Hill, North Carolina

CRANBERRY-HAM SLICES

1 3-lb. canned ham
¾ c. white sugar
¾ c. brown sugar
1 ½ tbsp. dry mustard
½ c. vinegar
¼ c. butter, melted
1 8-oz. can whole cranberry sauce

Slice ham into 1/2-inch thick slices; arrange in shallow casserole. Combine sugars and mustard in small saucepan; stir in vinegar and butter. Simmer for 8 minutes, stirring occasionally. Add cranberry sauce and cook for 2 minutes longer. Pour sauce over ham slices. Bake, uncovered, at 350 degrees for 30 minutes. Yield: 6-8 servings.

Mrs. Harriet Okino
Waiakea Intermediate School, Hilo, Hawaii

CHEESE-STUFFED HAM STEAKS

1 No. 2 can crushed pineapple
¾ c. crumbled Bleu cheese
½ c. fine dry bread crumbs
¼ c. chopped celery
¼ c. mayonnaise
2 med. ham steaks, cut ½-in. thick
2 tbsp. vinegar
1 tbsp. cornstarch
2 tbsp. brown sugar

Drain pineapple, reserving syrup. Combine 1/2 cup crushed pineapple, 1/2 cup crumbled Bleu cheese, bread crumbs, celery and mayonnaise; mix well. Spread mixture on 1 ham steak. Top with second ham steak and fasten with toothpicks. Place in baking pan. Bake at 350 degrees for 1 hour and 15 minutes. Heat remaining pineapple and syrup to boiling point. Combine vinegar, cornstarch and brown sugar; add to pineapple mixture. Cook, stirring constantly, until thickened and clear. Add remaining Bleu cheese and cook for 5 minutes, stirring occasionally. Serve sauce over ham steaks. Yield: 6-8 servings.

Eulyn Dynes, Phillips H. S.
Phillips, Texas

CRUNCHY HAM SLICE

1 1-lb. ham steak, ¾-in. thick
¼ c. crunchy peanut butter
¼ c. (packed) brown sugar
½ tsp. dry mustard
1 tbsp. vinegar

Place ham in shallow baking dish; spread peanut butter evenly over ham slice. Mix remaining ingredients; sprinkle over peanut butter. Bake for 25 minutes at 375 degrees.

Mrs. Saralu C. Jenkins, Clarkston H. S.
Clarkston, Georgia

GLAZED HAM SLICE

1 slice ham, cut 1 ½-in. thick
Whole cloves
¼ c. honey
2 tbsp. orange marmalade

Snip fat-edge of ham in several places to prevent curling; stick fat with cloves. Place in 2 to 3 quart-casserole. Combine honey and marmalade; spoon over ham. Cover and bake at 325 degrees for 1 hour to 1 hour and 15 minutes or until tender. Uncover during last 15 minutes of baking time to brown. NOTE: If using cooked ham slice, bake for 30 minutes covered; uncover and brown. Yield: 4-6 servings.

Mrs. Bea Myers, Tulare Western H. S.
Tulare, California

GLAZED HAM SLICE WITH CRANBERRY SAUCE

1 2-lb. cooked ham, sliced 1 ½-in. thick
Whole cloves (opt.)
½ c. brown sugar
2 tbsp. cornstarch
Dash of ground cloves
Dash of salt
1 ½ c. cranberry juice cocktail
½ c. orange juice
½ c. raisins

Slash fat edge of ham at 2-inch intervals. Insert whole cloves in fat. Place ham in shallow baking dish. Bake at 325 degrees for 30 minutes. Mix brown sugar, cornstarch, ground cloves and salt. Add fruit juices and raisins. Cook and stir until mixture is thick and boiling. Spoon part of sauce over ham; bake for 20 minutes or until glazed. Serve with remaining sauce. Yield: 6 servings.

Riette Godbout, Perth Regional H. S.
Perth, New Brunswick, Canada

GOLDEN HAM SLICE

1 smoked ham slice, 1-in. thick
1 8 ¾-oz. can crushed pineapple
1 tbsp. cornstarch
1 tbsp. brown sugar
¼ tsp. cinnamon
⅓ c. finely grated carrots

Place ham slice on rack in open roasting pan. Bake at 300 degrees for 30 minutes. Drain pineapple, reserving liquid. Combine cornstarch, brown sugar and cinnamon in saucepan. Add pineapple liquid; cook, stirring constantly, until thickened and clear. Stir in pineapple and carrots. Spread pineapple mixture over ham slice; bake for 30 minutes. Yield: 4-6 servings.

Mrs. Marilyn Kuhn, Mina H. S.
Bastrop, Texas

HAM BAKED WITH POTATOES

1 2-lb. slice ham, 2-in. thick
4 c. sliced potatoes
1 sm. onion, minced
Mustard
Salt and pepper
2 to 3 c. milk

Brown ham on both sides; cover with potatoes. Season with onion, mustard, pepper and a small amount of salt. Heat in oven for 15 minutes. Pour hot milk on ham. Bake, covered, at 325 degrees for 1 hour or until potatoes and ham are tender. Yield: 6 servings.

Mrs. John Wandell, Eastern Sebanon Co. School
Myerstown, Pennsylvania

HAM CASSEROLE

1 lb. ham, cut into serving pieces
2 tbsp. peanut butter
1 tbsp. mustard
1 ⅔ c. evaporated milk

Spread ham with mixture of peanut butter and mustard. Place in baking dish. Cover with milk. Bake at 350 degrees for 1 hour. Yield: 2-4 servings.

Mrs. Edith Donaldson, Gadsden H. S.
Anthony, New Mexico

HAM WITH CHERRIES

2 tbsp. cornstarch
Water
1 No. 2 can sweetened cherries, undrained
1 cured ham, cooked and sliced

Make a paste of cornstarch and water; add cherries. Cook and stir until thick. Serve on ham.

Jacquelyn S. Howell, Theodore H. S.
Theodore, Alabama

HAM SLICE

1 center slice ham, 1 to 1 ¾-in. thick
1 to 3 tsp. dry mustard
¼ to ½ c. brown sugar
¼ tsp. soda (opt.)
2 c. milk

Cut slashes in edge of ham. Sprinkle with mustard, brown sugar and soda. Place in heavy skillet or baking pan. Pour milk around ham until milk barely reaches top. Bake, uncovered, at 300 to 350 degrees for 1 hour and 15 minutes. Yield: 4 servings.

Florence L. Tackett, Warren School
Vincent, Ohio
Mrs. Marjorie P. Landry, Spring Ford H. S.
Royersford, Pennsylvania
Beulah Riegel, Brookville H. S.
Brookville, Ohio

HAM SLICE DELUXE

1 ham slice, 1-in. thick
½ c. currant jelly
2 tbsp. horseradish
Canned whole green string beans
Boiled white onion rings

Place ham in a shallow baking pan. Beat currant jelly with horseradish; spread over ham. Bake at 325 degrees for 30 minutes per pound. Separate

(Continued on next page)

green beans into bundles; place each bundle through a ring of white onion. Heat in oven for 15 minutes. Serve around ham on hot platter. Yield: 4 servings.

Martha J. Homer, Plum H. S.
Pittsburgh, Pennsylvania

PLANTATION-STYLE HAM SLICE

1 c. brown sugar
1 tsp. dry mustard
1 center slice ham, cut 2-in. thick
1 ¼ c. pineapple juice

Mix 3/4 cup brown sugar with mustard; rub entire mixture into ham on both sides. Place ham in roasting pan or heavy skillet; sprinkle with remaining brown sugar and add pineapple juice. Bake at 350 degrees for 2 hours or until tender, basting occasionally. Serve hot. Yield: 6-8 servings.

Mrs. Sanders McWhorter, Roxboro H. S.
Roxboro, North Carolina

SOUTHWEST-STYLE HAM STEAK

1 2-lb. ham steak
2 tbsp. corn oil
2 tbsp. pickle liquid
4 tbsp. water
2 tbsp. molasses
⅛ tsp. cloves
⅛ tsp. ginger
1 c. sour cream
2 sm. dill pickles, diced

Brown ham steak quickly in oil in skillet; transfer to roasting pan. Mix pickle liquid with water; add with molasses, cloves and ginger to drippings in skillet. Pour mixture over ham. Bake at 350 degrees for 50 minutes. Add sour cream and pickles to drippings in roaster. Blend well. Pour over ham; serve immediately. Yield: 4 servings.

Mrs. Anona Moore, Alvin Jr. H. S.
Alvin, Texas

STUFFED HAM SLICES

¼ c. chopped celery
2 tbsp. chopped parsley
¼ c. butter
1 12-oz. can crushed pineapple
4 c. dry bread cubes
½ tsp. ground marjoram
2 center cut ham slices, ½-in. thick
1 ½ tsp. lemon juice
Dash of ground cloves

Cook celery and parsley in butter until tender. Add 3/4 cup pineapple, bread cubes and marjoram; mix well. Spoon over ham slice. Place second ham slice over first slice. Combine remaining pineapple, lemon juice and cloves. Spread over ham. Pour a small amount of water into baking pan. Bake at 325 degrees for 1 hour. Yield: 6 servings.

Mrs. Cora Ann Coleman, Coffeeville H. S.
Coffeeville, Alabama

STUFFED HAM SLICES

2 c. soft bread crumbs
½ c. raisins
½ c. chopped peanuts
2 tbsp. dark corn syrup
½ tsp. dry mustard
¼ c. butter or margarine
2 slices ham, cut ½-in. thick
Cloves
1 can raisin pie filling (opt.)

Combine all ingredients except ham, cloves and pie filling. Place one slice ham in shallow baking pan; spread stuffing over ham. Top with second slice ham; stick whole cloves in fat. Bake at 300 degrees for 1 hour. Before serving, spread one can raisin pie filling on top. Garnish with fresh parsley and fresh orange slices, if desired. Yield: 6 servings.

Mrs. Marie G. Reid
Rochester Area Jr.-Sr. High
Rochester, Pennsylvania
Vivian Werk, Lebanon H. S.
Lebanon, Ohio
Mrs. Roger R. Adams, Allen H. S.
Allen, Texas
Sister Mary Giovanni, O.S.F., St. Mary's H. S.
North Washington, Iowa

WEST VIRGINIA-STYLE FRIED COUNTRY HAM

3 slices country ham, cut into halves
1 c. milk
½ c. flour
1 tbsp. fat

Place ham in shallow dish; cover with milk. Let stand for 30 minutes. Remove from milk; roll in flour. Melt fat in heavy skillet; cook ham slowly until tender and browned on both sides. Yield: 6 servings.

Mrs. Bess Snyder Mohl, Petersburg, H. S.
Petersburg, West Virginia

HAM-BANANA ROLLS WITH CHEESE SAUCE

4 slices boiled ham, ⅛-in. thick
Prepared mustard
4 firm bananas, peeled
Butter or margarine
1 tbsp. flour
¾ c. milk
1 ½ c. grated sharp Cheddar cheese

(Continued on next page)

Spread each ham slice with mustard. Wrap each banana in a slice of ham. Brush banana tips with 2 to 4 teaspoonfuls melted butter. Place in greased shallow baking dish. Melt 1 tablespoonful butter in saucepan. Blend in flour to a smooth paste. Slowly add milk, stirring constantly until thickened. Remove from heat; add cheese. Stir until cheese is melted. Pour sauce over rolls. Bake in preheated 350 degree oven for 30 minutes or until bananas are easily pierced with a fork. NOTE: Canned cheese soup may be substituted for sauce. Yield: 4 servings.

Leeta G. Adolphe, Fort Vancouver H. S.
Vancouver, Washington

HAM ROLLS WITH COTTAGE CHEESE IN SOUR CREAM SAUCE

2 cans cream of mushroom soup
1 pt. sour cream
2 c. cream-style cottage cheese
2 eggs, slightly beaten
½ c. chopped string onions
1 10-oz. pkg. frozen chopped spinach, cooked and drained
1 tsp. dry mustard
½ tsp. salt
1 ½ lb. cooked ham, sliced

Combine soup and1/2 cup sour cream in a bowl; set aside. Combine remaining sour cream with cottage cheese, eggs, onions, spinach, mustard and salt. Mix well. Spoon 2 tablespoonfuls of cottage cheese filling onto each ham slice. Roll up ham, folding in the edges. Place in shallow baking dish. Cover with sour cream sauce. Bake at 350 degrees for 20 to 25 minutes. Yield: 8 servings.

Mrs. Sylvia Czerwinski
Waltonville Comm. School Unit No. 1
Waltonville, Illinois

ST. LOUIS HAM ROLLS

2 c. cooked rice
1 tbsp. chopped onion
2 tbsp. chopped parsley
2 tbsp. melted butter
½ tsp. salt
⅛ tsp. pepper
1 egg, slightly beaten
2 c. milk
6 slices boiled ham

Mix rice, onion, parsley, butter, seasonings, egg and 1/4 cup milk. Spread on ham slices; roll like a jelly roll. Fasten with toothpick; place in pan. Pour remaining milk over ham slices. Bake in covered pan at 350 degrees for 15 minutes. Uncover and bake for 15 minutes longer. Yield: 6 servings.

Mrs. Patricia Boyle, Giannotti Jr. H. S.
West Haven, Connecticutt

HAM 'N' EGG PUDDING

1 c. diced ham
2 c. milk, scalded
2 tbsp. melted butter or margarine
2 c. soft bread crumbs
1 tsp. salt
¼ tsp. pepper
6 eggs, separated

Combine ham, milk, butter, bread crumbs, salt and pepper; stir in egg yolks. Beat egg whites until stiff but not dry. Fold egg whites into yolk mixture. Pour into buttered 12 x 8 x 2-inch baking dish. Bake at 325 degrees for 20 to 25 minutes until firm to the touch. Serve at once. Yield: 6 servings.

Myrtis L. McAlhany, Saint George H. S.
Saint George, South Carolina

HAM HASH

4 med. potatoes, pared
1 med. onion
½ green pepper, seeded
1 c. diced cooked ham
¼ tsp. monosodium glutamate
¼ tsp. salt
⅛ tsp. pepper
3 tbsp. butter or margarine

Grind potatoes, onion, green pepper and ham on medium fine blade on food chopper. Add monosodium glutamate, salt and pepper, mixing well. Heat butter in large skillet; pour in ham mixture. Cook, covered, over low heat for 15 minutes or until potatoes are cooked and hash is browned on bottom. Remove from heat; uncover. Let stand for 1 minute to dry out; loosen edges with spatula. With pancake turner, turn one-half onto other; turn out onto serving plate. Yield: 3-4 servings.

Shirlie Hodge, Kanloops H. S.
North Surrey, British Columbia, Canada

WAIKIKI KABOBS

1 13-oz. can pineapple chunks
½ c. butter
2 tbsp. lemon juice
3 tbsp. brown sugar
⅛ tsp. ground cloves
⅛ tsp. dry mustard
1 lb. cooked ham
1 lge. orange, sectioned

Drain pineapple, reserving 1/4 cup juice. Melt butter in 1-quart saucepan; add pineapple and lemon juices, brown sugar, cloves and mustard. Cook and stir until heated through. Cut ham into 1 x 1/2-inch chunks. Thread ham, pineapple and orange sections on 5-inch skewers. Place on broiler pan. Broil for 5 minutes, basting with butter and turning kabobs once. Serve over hot buttered rice, if desired. Yield: 8-10 servings.

Mrs. Janet Stark Halvorson
St. Anthony Village H. S.
Minneapolis, Minnesota

HAM BALLS

1 ½ lb. fresh pork
1 lb. smoked ham
2 eggs
1 c. cracker crumbs
1 c. milk
½ tsp. salt
¼ tsp. pepper
1 c. vinegar
1 ½ c. brown sugar
1 ½ tbsp. dry mustard

Grind pork with ham. Mix meats with eggs, crumbs, milk, salt and pepper. Shape into 24 balls. Place in 9 x 13-inch baking dish. Mix vinegar, brown sugar and mustard in saucepan. Boil well; pour over ham balls. Bake at 350 degrees for 1 hour and 30 minutes. Baste with sauce twice during cooking. Yield: 12 servings.

Mrs. Edna Watson, Green Springs H. S.
Green Springs, Ohio

CANDIED HAM BALLS

2 c. ground cooked ham
1 c. bread crumbs
1 egg, beaten
¼ c. milk
1 tbsp. fat
¾ c. brown sugar
¼ c. vinegar
¼ c. water
½ tsp. dry mustard

Combine ham, crumbs and egg with milk; shape into eight balls. Brown in fat in heavy skillet. Heat remaining ingredients in saucepan; pour over ham balls. Bake at 325 degrees for 45 minutes. Yield: 8 servings.

Mrs. Mildred Walters, Eastside H. S.
Nappanee, Indiana

GLAZED HAM BALLS

5 lb. ground ham
6 lb. ground pork
1 lb. oats
10 eggs
Milk
⅔ c. flour
1 ¼ qt. pineapple, apricot or peach juice or water
⅔ c. vinegar
1 ½ tbsp. dry mustard
2 c. brown sugar
1 tbsp. whole cloves
2 c. dark corn syrup

Combine meats, oats, eggs and enough milk to moisten. Mix thoroughly but lightly until well blended. Chill; shape into small balls. Place in shallow pans. Bake at 300 degrees for 1 hour. Drain off drippings. Combine remaining ingredients; cook over low heat until thickened. Pour over ham balls during last 15 minutes of baking. Yield: 50 servings.

Ladonna Stewart, Hardin Northern H. S.
Dola, Ohio

GLAZED HAM BALLS

½ lb. ground ham
¾ lb. ground pork
⅔ c. oats
1 egg, beaten
½ c. milk
⅓ c. brown sugar
2 tbsp. flour
1 tsp. dry mustard
⅔ c. fruit juice
2 tbsp. vinegar
6 whole cloves
⅓ c. dark syrup

Combine ham, pork, oats, egg and milk; blend. Chill thoroughly. Shape into small balls; place in shallow baking pan. Bake at 300 degrees for 1 hour. Drain. Combine remaining ingredients in saucepan; cook over direct heat until slightly thickened. Pour over ham balls. Continue baking for 15 minutes longer. Yield: 6 servings.

Josephine Tupy, New Prague H. S.
New Prague, Minnesota

HAM BALLS ON PINEAPPLE

2 ½ c. ground cooked ham
½ c. quick cooking oats
½ c. milk
1 egg, slightly beaten
⅓ c. plus 1 tbsp. brown sugar
Cloves
6 slices canned pineapple, drained
⅓ c. pineapple syrup
2 tbsp. lemon juice
1 tbsp. vinegar

(Continued on next page)

Combine ham, oats, milk, egg, 1 tablespoonful brown sugar and dash of cloves; mix well. Form into 18 small balls about 1 inch in diameter. Place pineapple slices in large skillet; top each slice with three ham balls. Combine remaining ingredients and dash of cloves. Simmer for 8 to 10 minutes or until mixture becomes syrupy. Pour over ham balls and pineapple slices. Cover and simmer for 10 to 15 minutes, basting with sauce several times. Yield: 6 servings.

Sister M. Juliana, S.S.N.D., Trinity H. S.
Dickinson, North Dakota

CARAMEL-HAM LOAF

1 lb. pork shoulder, ground
1 ½ lb. cured ham, ground
1 tbsp. minced onion
2 eggs, beaten
½ tsp. baking powder
½ c. milk
⅛ tsp. pepper
⅔ c. tomatoes or tomato juice
1 c. cracker or bread crumbs
½ c. brown sugar
1 tsp. dry mustard
¼ c. water
3 tbsp. vinegar

Combine all ingredients except brown sugar, mustard, water and vinegar; place mixture in loaf pan. Bake 375 degrees for 1 hour and 30 minutes. Combine remaining ingredients and boil for a few minutes. At intervals, baste loaf with the sauce. Yield: 6 servings.

Odessa L. Carlson, Wakefield H. S.
Wakefield, Michigan

CHILI-HAM LOAF

1 lb. lean smoked ham
2 lb. lean fresh pork
2 eggs, slightly beaten
1 ½ c. cracker crumbs
½ c. chili sauce

Have butcher grind ham with pork. Combine meats, eggs, crumbs and chili sauce. Mix well. Pack firmly into 5 x 9 x 3-inch loaf pan. Place in pan of hot water. Bake at 350 degrees for 1 hour and 30 minutes. Remove from pan; slice for serving. Yield: 8-10 servings.

Mrs. Hazel Speake, Washington Jr. H. S.
Albuquerque, New Mexico

CRANBERRY-HAM LOAF

2 eggs
¾ c. milk
½ tsp. salt
Pepper
1 c. soft bread crumbs
1 lb. uncooked ground ham
1 lb. ground boned pork shoulder
1 c. canned cranberry sauce
1 tsp. grated orange rind

Place eggs in bowl; beat lightly with fork. Stir in milk, salt, pepper and crumbs; let stand for 5 minutes. Add ham and pork; blend with fork. Shape into oval loaf in shallow 9 x 5-inch baking dish. Mash cranberry sauce; stir in orange rind. Spread on top of loaf. Bake at 400 degrees for 1 hour. Yield: 7-8 servings.

Sharon Marshall, Central Colchester H. S.
Truro, Nova Scotia, Canada

DELICIOUS HAM LOAF

1 lb. ground ham
½ lb. fresh ground pork
2 eggs
½ to ¾ c. milk
1 c. fine bread crumbs
Dash of pepper
2 tbsp. prepared mustard
½ c. pineapple juice
½ c. brown sugar

Combine meats, eggs, milk, bread crumbs and pepper; shape into a loaf. Mix mustard, pineapple juice and brown sugar; pour over loaf in baking pan. Bake at 350 degrees for about 1 hour. Baste several times during baking.

Mrs. Virginia Bradford, Penns Valley H. S.
Spring Mills, Pennsylvania

DELIGHTFUL HAM LOAF

1 lb. smoked ham, ground
1 ½ lb. fresh ham, ground
1 c. cracker crumbs
2 eggs
1 tbsp. horseradish
2 tbsp. chopped onion
2 tbsp. chopped green pepper
1 ½ c. milk
1 tbsp. lemon juice
½ c. chili sauce
½ c. brown sugar

Combine all ingredients except chili sauce and brown sugar. Mix well; form loaf. Bake at 300 degrees for 1 hour and 30 minutes. Combine remaining ingredients and spread over ham loaf. Bake for 30 minutes longer. NOTE: Serve with whipped cream-horseradish sauce, if desired. Do not add salt. Yield: 10-12 servings.

Mrs. Doris Patterson, Shelbyville Jr. H. S.
Shelbyville, Indiana

GLAZED HAMLOAF

1 lb. ground smoked ham
1 ½ lb. ground fresh pork
1 c. bread crumbs or 2 c. cracker crumbs
1 c. milk
2 or 3 eggs, slightly beaten
1 c. brown sugar
½ to 2 tsp. dry mustard
½ c. vinegar
½ c. water (opt.)

Grind ham with pork. Combine with bread crumbs moistened with milk and eggs. Shape into loaf in dripping pan. Combine brown sugar, mustard, vinegar and water. Pour over loaf. Bake at 250 to 350 degrees for 1 hour and 30 minutes to 2 hours. Baste frequently with sauce. Yield: 15 servings.

Mickey Schliefert, Plattsmouth H. S.
Plattsmouth, Nebraska
Ettie Belle Robinson, Dawson H. S.
Dawson, Texas

HAM LOAF

1 lb. smoked ham, ground
2 lb. lean pork, ground
1 c. bread crumbs
1 c. light cream
2 eggs
Salt and pepper to taste
1 can tomato soup

Combine all ingredients except soup. Place in loaf pan. Bake at 350 degrees for 30 minutes or until loaf forms a crust. Add soup. Bake at 325 degrees for 1 hour. Yield: 15 servings.

Mrs. Melba Olverson, Clark H. S.
Clark, South Dakota

HAM LOAF

2 lb. ground ham
2 lb. ground pork
3 eggs
1 c. evaporated milk or 1 ½ c. cream or rich milk
2 c. bread crumbs or crushed soda crackers
1 c. tomato soup
1 c. brown sugar
½ c. vinegar
1 tsp. dry mustard
½ c. water

Combine meats, eggs, milk and crumbs. Shape into loaf. Combine remaining ingredients. Bake loaf at 350 degrees until done, basting occasionally with sauce. Yield: 16 servings.

Grace A. Seanor, Hempfield H. S.
Greensborg, Pennsylvania

HAM LOAF

Bread crusts
½ to ¾ c. milk
2 lb. ground ham
1 lb. ground lean pork
½ tsp. salt
1 tsp. sugar
2 eggs, beaten
Dash of pepper

Soak bread crumbs in milk. Combine all ingredients; pack into loaf pan. Bake at 350 degrees for 2 hours. Yield: 8 servings.

Mrs. Kathryn Joan Keith
Southern Huntingdon Co. H. S.
Orbisonia, Pennsylvania

HAM LOAF

1 ¼ lb. ground smoked ham
2 lb. ground fresh pork steak
3 eggs, beaten
1 c. milk
1 c. ground bread crumbs

Combine ground ham and pork; add eggs. Add milk and crumbs; mix well. Pack into casserole. Bake at 325 degrees for 1 hour. Yield: 6 servings.

Mrs. Wilda Carr, Holdrege H. S.
Holdrege, Nebraska

HAM LOAF

1 ½ lb. ground smoked ham
1 ½ lb. sausage
3 c. soft bread crumbs
2 eggs, well beaten
1 tsp. dry mustard
½ tsp. salt
¼ tsp. pepper
½ c. minced onion
½ c. ginger ale

Combine all ingredients; form into a loaf. Place in a loaf pan. Bake in 300 to 325 degree oven for 45 minutes.

SAUCE:

1 ½ tsp. cloves
½ c. brown sugar
2 tsp. prepared mustard

Combine all ingredients; spread over ham loaf. Bake for 15 minutes longer. Yield: 8-10 servings.

Margaret D. Noller
Colorado Deaf and Blind School
Colorado Springs, Colorado

HAM LOAF AND DRESSING

2 ½ lb. ham, ground
½ lb. pork, ground
1 ½ c. milk
2 c. bread crumbs
4 eggs
1 can tomato soup
½ c. sugar
1 tsp. salt
2 tsp. flour
4 egg yolks
1 pt. cream
1 c. vinegar

Combine meats, milk, bread crumbs and 4 eggs; place in loaf pan. Pour tomato soup over loaf and place in another pan of water. Bake at 325 degrees for 3 hours. Mix sugar, salt and flour; add to 4 lightly beaten egg yolks. Heat cream and add dry mixture to cream. Add vinegar and cook over low heat until thickened. Serve over hot ham loaf. Yield: 12 servings.

Mrs. Vivian L. English, Turkey Creek H. S.
Plant City, Florida

HAM LOAF AND RAISIN SAUCE

1 ½ lb. smoked ham, ground
2 lb. fresh pork, ground
1 c. milk
1 c. cracker crumbs
1 c. tomato juice
1 c. apple cider, peach, pickle or pineapple juice
2 tbsp. flour
2 tbsp. butter
2 tbsp. brown sugar
¼ c. raisins
⅛ tsp. salt

Combine meats, milk, crumbs and tomato juice; shape into a loaf in a 7 x 10-inch pan. Bake at 325 degrees for 2 hours. Gradually add cider or juice with flour and butter; add to remaining ingredients. Mix; spread over ham loaf 20 minutes before end of baking. NOTE: Pineapple slices may be placed on loaf just before loaf is done. Yield: 8-10 servings.

Mrs. Theresa H. Smith, Northside H. S.
Warner Robins, Georgia

HAM LOGS

1 lb. smoked ham, ground
½ lb. pork, ground
1 ½ c. soft fine bread crumbs
1 egg, well beaten
½ tsp. dry mustard
¼ c. brown sugar
1 tsp. prepared mustard

Combine ham, pork, bread crumbs, egg and dry mustard; mix well. Shape into logs; place in shallow pan. Combine brown sugar and prepared mustard, spreading it over top of logs. Bake at 350 degrees for 45 minutes.

CHERRY SAUCE:

1 No. 2 ½ can Bing cherries, drained
2 tbsp. cornstarch
½ c. sugar
1 tsp. salt
1 tsp. grated lemon rind

Drain cherries, reserving juice; cut cherries into halves and set aside. Combine cornstarch, sugar, salt and lemon rind in saucepan. Add enough water to juice to make 2 cups liquid and add to cornstarch mixture. Cool over medium heat until thickened and comes to a boil. Add cherries and serve over ham logs. Yield: 6 servings.

Mrs. Sue Thomas, Atoka H. S.
Atoka, Oklahoma

SUSAN'S HAM LOAF

1 ½ lb. smoked ham, ground
1 ½ lb. fresh pork, ground
4 crackers
2 eggs
½ c. vinegar
1 to 1 ½ qt. water

Combine meats, crackers and eggs; shape into a loaf. Place in small cloth bag and boil for 2 hours in solution of vinegar and water. Serve piping hot. Yield: 8-10 servings.

LaVonne Dupraz, Tracy H. S.
Tracy, Minnesota

UPSIDE-DOWN HAM LOAF

2 tbsp. butter
¼ c. brown sugar
8 to 12 canned pineapple wedges
Whole cloves
4 c. cooked ham
1 tbsp. grated onion (opt.)
½ tsp. dry mustard
1 c. bread crumbs
½ c. pineapple juice
2 eggs, slightly beaten
Dash of pepper

Melt butter in bottom of a greased loaf pan or casserole; sprinkle with brown sugar. Stud pineapple wedges with whole cloves; arrange on top of brown sugar. Combine ham with all remaining ingredients; pack into pan or casserole over pineapple wedges. Bake at 375 degrees for about 30 minutes. Turn out, upside-down, onto a hot platter. Yield: 6-8 servings.

Mrs. Martha Wilson, Ogden Comm. H. S.
Ogden, Illinois

TANGY HAM LOAF

1 ½ lb. fresh pork
1 ½ lb. smoked ham
1 tbsp. horseradish
2 eggs
1 c. quick cooking oats
1 ½ c. milk
1 c. bread crumbs
½ c. brown sugar
⅔ c. vinegar

Combine all ingredients except brown sugar and vinegar; form into roll and place in roaster. Mix brown sugar and vinegar; pour over meat. Cover and bake at 350 degrees for 1 hour and 30 minutes to 2 hours, basting occasionally. Yield: 12 servings.

Florence T. Shaffer, Berwick Area H. S.
Berwick, Pennsylvania

HAM CROQUETTES

2 c. ground cooked ham
1 c. mashed potatoes
1 tbsp. chopped onion
1 tbsp. chopped parsley
Salt and pepper to taste
1 tbsp. water
1 egg, beaten
Fine dry crumbs
Fat or oil

Combine ham, potatoes, onion and parsley; add salt and pepper. Chill. Shape into eight croquettes. Add water to egg; dip croquettes into egg mixture and roll in crumbs. Brown croquettes in small amount hot fat, turning to form a good crust all over. Yield: 4 servings.

Dolores Q. Parks, R. B. Worthy H. S.
Saltville, Virginia

HAM AND RICE CROQUETTES

1 can cream of celery soup
1 c. cooked rice
1 tbsp. finely chopped green pepper
1 lb. ground cooked ham
1 tbsp. finely chopped onion
1 to 2 tbsp. prepared mustard
1 egg, beaten
1 c. fine bread crumbs
2 8-oz. pkg. frozen peas in cream sauce, cooked

Combine soup, rice, green pepper, ham, onion and mustard. Shape into croquettes, using 1/4 cup mixture for each. Dip into mixture of egg and crumbs; let stand for a few minutes. Fry two or three at a time in deep 365 degree fat for 3 to 5 minutes or until brown. Keep temperature constant. Drain croquettes on paper towels. Serve peas in sauce with croquettes. Yield: 8-10 servings.

Mrs. Manona Brewer, Orestimba H. S.
Newman, California

HAM PATTIES ON PINEAPPLE

2 c. ground baked ham
½ c. left-over mashed potatoes
8 slices pineapple
8 Maraschino cherries

Mix ham and mashed potatoes; form into patties. Place pineapple slices on waxed paper-lined cookie sheet; place ham patties on pineapple. Bake at 350 degrees for 20 mintues. Garnish with cherry in center pineapple.

Mrs. Edna Earle Beck, Anson H. S.
Anson, Texas

HAM-SOMES

2 c. sifted flour
3 ½ tsp. baking powder
½ tsp. salt
2 tsp. sugar
½ c. shortening
2 tsp. caraway seed
2 eggs
Milk
2 ½ c. ground cooked ham
1 onion, ground
2 tbsp. chopped parsley
1 tbsp. prepared horseradish
2 tsp. dry mustard
⅛ tsp. pepper

Sift flour, baking powder, salt and sugar. Cut in shortening until particles are fine; stir in caraway seed. Beat 1 egg; add enough milk to make 2/3 cup. Add to dry ingredients all at once. Stir until dough forms ball. Knead gently on floured surface about ten strokes. Roll out to 12 x 10-inch rectangle. Beat remaining egg and mix thoroughly into mixture of remaining ingredients. Spread mixture evenly over dough. Roll as for jelly roll, starting with 12-inch side. Cut into eight slices; place, cut-side down, on ungreased baking sheet 1 inch apart. Bake at 425 degrees for 15 to 20 minutes. Yield: 8 servings.

Mrs. Virginia O. Sheely, Littlestown H. S.
Littlestown, Pennsylvania

HAM TIMBALE

2 c. ground cooked ham
1 c. medium white sauce
2 eggs, beaten
¼ tsp. powdered dry mustard

Mix all ingredients; pour into shallow greased baking dish. Place dish in pan of hot water. Bake at 350 degrees for 50 minutes or until mixture is firm in center. Yield: 4 servings.

Mrs. Kelley Storey, Paris H. S.
Paris, Texas

BARBECUE PORK

1 bottle catsup
½ bottle Worcestershire sauce
1 lge. onion, finely chopped
1 sm. can tomato puree
1 ½ c. vinegar
1 clove of garlic
2 tsp. salt
1 tbsp. sugar
1 tbsp. red pepper
1 tbsp. black pepper
6 lb. fresh pork shoulder

Combine all ingredients except pork. Cook for 15 to 20 minutes or until thick. Cook pork for 4 hours, reserving broth. Cool; tear into shreds. Add 1 pint sauce and 1 pint broth. Place pork in long shallow pan. Bake at 375 degrees for 45 minutes. Yield: 15 servings.

Mrs. Robert C. Sanders, Jones H. S.
Lynnville, Tennessee

ECONOMICAL PORK BARBECUE

1 2 ½ to 3-lb. pork roast
Salt and pepper
1 c. catsup
1 tsp. Tabasco sauce

Place roast on sheet of heavy foil. Salt and pepper; fold foil tightly. Bake at 350 degrees for 45 to 50 minutes per pound. Coarsely chop enough pork to make 2 cups. Skim fat from broth; combine 3/4 cup broth with pork, catsup and 1 teaspoonful Tabasco sauce or more in heavy saucepan. Simmer for 20 minutes. Yield: One quart.

Sarah A. McCreight, Oak Hill H. S.
Morganton, North Carolina

PINEAPPLE-STUFFED PORK ROLL

1 smoked boneless pork butt
1 ½ c. drained crushed pineapple
½ c. chopped celery
1 c. bread crumbs
1 tsp. salt
Apricot juice
Apricot halves

Brown meat in heavy skillet; cool. Mix pineapple, celery, bread crumbs and salt in medium bowl. Make slashes 2 inches deep and 2 inches apart in top of meat to form pockets. Fill pockets with stuffing. Shape into a roll; tie with heavy string. Pour apricot juice over meat. Cover and bake at 325 degrees for 2 hours or until tender. Baste meat with apricot juice and place apricot halves on meat the last hour of baking. Yield: 8 servings.

Mrs. Jack C. Montgomery, Fort Gibson H. S.
Fort Gibson, Oklahoma

ROAST LUAU PIG

1 15 to 20-lb. suckling pig, dressed
2 loaves bread, crumbled
Chopped onion to taste
Chopped celery to taste
Seasonings
1 apple
2 Maraschino or candied cherries

Have pig dressed, leaving head, tail and feet intact; remove eyes. Wash pig thoroughly and dry. Combine bread, onion, celery and seasonings; mix in broth or liquid to dressing consistency. Stuff pig loosely with dressing; close cavity. Place a block of wood in mouth. Cover ears and tail with foil to prevent burning. Place in pan, folding legs under to form rack. Roast, uncovered, at 325 degrees for 6 to 7 hours. If pig browns too quickly, cover with foil or lower temperature. Remove block from mouth and insert apple; place cherries in eye sockets. Arrange a lei or other decoration around neck. Carve along spine, cracking backbone; cut off legs. Cut two ribs plus skin and meat for each serving. Yield: 20 servings.

Margaret K. Shollenberger
Rice Avenue Union H. S.
Girard, Pennsylvania

PORK TENDERLOIN BIRDS

6 pork tenderloins
½ tsp. salt
Dash of pepper
Sage to taste
1 tbsp. chopped onion
2 c. bread crumbs
Fat
¾ c. boiling water
1 egg, slightly beaten
Flour
Milk or water

Split pork or pound until 1/3-inch thick. Add salt, pepper, sage and onion to crumbs. Mix lightly with a fork. Add 2 tablespoonfuls melted fat to boiling water; mix with bread just until moistened, but not soggy. Add egg. Spread split pieces with stuffing and skewer together. Or, spread flattened pieces with stuffing; fold one-half over the other and skewer. Roll in flour; brown in a small amount of fat. Add a small amount of milk or water. Simmer or bake at 350 degrees for 2 hours or until tender. Remove to a hot platter. Thicken liquid for sauce. Yield: 6 servings.

Ruth Bosley, Leavenworth H. S.
Leavenworth, Indiana

ROAST PORK TENDERLOIN

1 c. chicken stock
¼ c. soy sauce
¼ c. honey
2 tbsp. cooking Sherry

(Continued on next page)

1 tbsp. lemon juice
½ clove of garlic
1 tsp. cinnamon
1 tsp. salt
¼ tsp. powdered ginger
3 ¾-lb. pork tenderloins
2 tbsp. cornstarch

Combine chicken stock, soy sauce, honey, Sherry, lemon juice, garlic, cinnamon, salt and ginger; marinate meat for 2 hours in mixture. Drain meat, reserving marinade. Coat meat with with cornstarch; place in shallow roasting pan. Bake at 325 degrees for 1 hour and 30 minutes, basting frequently with marinade. Yield: 8 servings.

Blanche Knott, Lawrence Co. H. S.
Lawrenceburg, Tennessee

BAKED APPLES FILLED WITH SAUSAGE

6 lge. tart apples
1 c. seasoned sausage
1 tsp. salt
2 tbsp. brown sugar

Wash apples; cut slice from top. Scoop out cores and pulp, leaving shells 3/4-inch thick. Chop pulp. Combine pulp with sausage, salt and brown sugar. Fill apples with sausage mixture. Bake at 375 degrees until done. Serve with potatoes or rice.

Mrs. Janice Cabler, East Nashville H. S.
Nashville, Tennessee

BISCUIT PIZZA

½ lb. ground sausage
2 ½ c. packaged biscuit mix
⅔ c. evaporated milk
2 tbsp. melted butter
Salt and pepper
1 6-oz. can tomato paste
2 c. shredded cheese
1 tsp. ground oregano leaves

Cook meat until lightly browned, breaking up meat while cooking. Drain. Blend biscuit mix with milk; chill for 10 minutes. Knead lightly; divide in half. Roll each portion into 9-inch circle; place on pizza pan or cookie sheet. Brush dough with butter; sprinkle with salt and pepper. Spread one-half the tomato paste, cheese and sausage evenly over each. Sprinkle with oregano. Bake at 400 degrees for 10 to 15 minutes. Yield: 4-6 servings.

Mrs. Charles Weems, Hazen H. S.
Hazen, Arkansas

CORN MEAL MUSH

1 lb. sausage
3 c. water
1 c. corn meal
2 tsp. salt
⅛ tsp. pepper

Brown sausage in large skillet; pour off fat. Add 2 cups water; heat to boiling. Combine corn meal, salt, pepper and remaining water; add to boiling liquid, stirring constantly. Reduce heat and simmer for 10 minutes, stirring frequently. Pour into greased loaf pan; chill. Cut into 1/2-inch slices. Saute in hot fat until brown.

Mrs. Violet Shaffner, Marshall H. S.
Marshall, Illinois

ENGLISH SAUSAGE ROLLS

1 lb. pork sausage
2 c. flour
½ tsp. salt
⅔ c. shortening
5 to 6 tbsp. ice water

Partially cook sausage in small skillet. Sift flour with salt; cut in shortening with pastry blender. Add ice water, 1 tablespoonful at a time, using fork to combine water with ingredients. Add only enough water to make ingredients hold together. Divide dough into two equal parts. Roll one part on floured surface into an oblong until dough is 1/8-inch thick. Cut into eight equal pieces. Place a small amount of sausage on each piece. Wet edges of pastry; fold over and press edges together. Place on greased cookie sheet. Bake at 400 degrees for 20 minutes. Surface of pastry may be brushed with melted butter before cooking. Yield: 16 servings.

Heather C. Kelly, Mansfield, H. S.
Mansfield, Louisiana

HOMEMADE SAUSAGE WITH SAGE

2 lb. lean pork, ground
1 tsp. salt
½ tsp. sage
½ tsp. cumin
¼ tsp. ginger
1 bay leaf
½ tsp. pepper

Mix pork thoroughly with all ingredients; shape into 12 to 15 patties. Fry in skillet for 8 minutes on each side or until nicely browned. NOTE: Sausage may be shaped into cakes, wrapped in foil and broiled over coals. Serve in foil casing, if desired. Yield: 8-12 servings.

Mrs. Vivian Steinbauer, Hanover School
Hanover, Illinois

JOHNNY

2 lb. bulk sausage
2 qt. boiling water

(Continued on next page)

1 med. onion, diced
1 46-oz. can tomato juice
1 lge. pkg. noodles

Form sausage into 1-inch balls. Drop into boiling water with onion. Cover; simmer for 15 minutes or until sausage is done. Chill for several hours or overnight; skim off fat. Add tomato juice; bring to a boil and add noodles. Cook until noodles are tender. Yield: 8 servings.

Mrs. Mary Kathryn Lands
Amanda Clear Creek School
Amanda, Ohio

MEXICAN LUNCHEON SKILLET

2 lb. bulk pork sausage
1 c. diced onions
1 c. diced green peppers
1 can tomatoes
2 c. uncooked elbow macaroni
2 tbsp. sugar
1 tbsp. chili powder
1 tsp. salt
1 c. sour cream

Brown sausage, onions and green peppers in skillet. Pour off drippings; add tomatoes, macaroni, seasonings and sour cream. Cover. Cook slowly on low heat for 10 minutes. Uncover; simmer for 15 to 20 minutes. Serve immediately. Yield: 6 servings.

Lou Wigley, Buckhorn H. S.
New Market, Alabama

OLD SOUTH SAUSAGE PIE

½ lb. pork sausage
1 c. chopped celery
⅓ c. chopped onion
¼ c. chopped green pepper
2 tbsp. minced parsley
½ tsp. salt
¾ c. tomato paste
¾ c. water
1 c. kidney beans

Brown sausage in heavy skillet; add celery, onion, green pepper and parsley. Brown lightly; drain off excess fat. Season with salt. Combine tomato paste and water; add to meat mixture in skillet. Add kidney beans, mixing well. Cover; reduce heat. Simmer for 10 minutes. Pour into 1 1/2-quart casserole.

CHEESE PUFFS:

1 c. flour
1 ½ tsp. baking powder
½ tsp. salt
2 tbsp. shortening
½ c. shredded American cheese
½ c. milk

Sift flour with baking powder and salt; cut in shortening until mixture is crumbly. Add cheese and milk, mixing until flour is moistened. Drop by spoonfuls around edge of casserole. Bake at 425 degrees for 20 minutes. Yield: 4 servings.

Mrs. A. Catherine Boshart
Northern Lebannon H. S.
Fredericksburg, Pennsylvania

SAUSAGE-APPLE STACKS

½ c. chopped apples
1 ½ tbsp. chopped onion
¼ c. bread crumbs
1 lb. sausage roll or bulk sausage

Combine apples, onion and crumbs. Make eight sausage patties. Place four patties in bottom of shallow pan. Cover with apple mixture and top with remaining patties. Bake at 350 degrees for 45 minutes. Yield: 4 servings.

June Houchins, Tuslaw H. S.
Massillon, Ohio

SAUSAGE 'N' RICE

12 link sausages
Cooking oil
1 ⅓ c. instant rice
1 can onion soup
Water
Salt and pepper
2 doz. pimento stuffed olives, sliced

Brown sausages in a small amount of cooking oil; mix rice with onion soup and enough water to make 2 cups liquid. Salt and pepper to taste. Pour rice and onion soup mixture over sausages; simmer until rice is done. Top with sliced olives. NOTE: Other type meats may be substituted for sausages. Yield: 6 servings.

Romie Stewart, Jefferson Jr. H. S.
Grand Prairie, Texas

SAUSAGE ROLL-UPS

1 lb. bulk sausage
1 tsp. sausage seasoning
1 recipe biscuit dough

Mix sausage and seasoning; brown in skillet. Drain sausage, reserving drippings. Prepare biscuit dough; roll out to rectangle 1/4-inch thick. Spread browned sausage over dough and roll up as for jelly roll. Slice into 1/2-inch slices; place in greased baking pan. Bake at 450 degrees for 10 to 15 minutes. Serve with gravy made from drippings of browned sausage. Yield: 6 servings.

Norma L. Brown, Comm. Unit H. S.
Beecher City, Illinois

SAUSAGE PIES

2 c. flour
4 tsp. baking powder
½ tsp. salt
2 tbsp. shortening
¼ c. milk or water
¾ lb. sausage
4 tomatoes

Sift flour with baking powder and salt; add shortening. Mix thoroughly with fork or pastry blender. Add enough milk or water to make stiff dough; knead until outside looks smooth. Roll out 1/8-inch thick; cut into eight 4-inch squares. Divide sausage into eight flat cakes; place on each square of dough. Fold in edges to form pie look, so crust will hold in liquids cooked from sausage and still not completely cover sausage. Place one-half tomato, sliced across so tomato covers most of sausage. Sprinkle each pie lightly with salt. Bake at 400 degrees for 25 minutes or until bread or crust is brown and crisp. Yield: 8 servings.

Mrs. Gwendolyn Mote, Lookeba-Sickles School
Lookeba, Oklahoma

BAKED BARBECUED SPARERIBS

3 to 4 lb. ribs, cut into pieces
1 lemon
1 lge. onion, thinly sliced
1 c. catsup
⅓ c. Worcestershire sauce
1 tsp. chili powder
1 tsp. salt
2 dashes Tabasco sauce
2 c. water

Place ribs in shallow roasting pan, meaty-side up. On each piece, place slice of unpeeled lemon and 1 thin slice of onion. Bake at 450 degrees for 30 minutes. Combine remaining ingredients; bring to a boil. Pour over ribs. Continue baking at 350 degrees for 45 minutes to 1 hour or until tender. Baste ribs with the sauce at 15 minute intervals. If sauce gets too thick, add more water. Yield: 4 servings.

Mrs. Shirley Underwood, LaRue Co. H. S.
Hodgenville, Kentucky

BAKED SPARERIBS ALOHA

3 lb. lean spareribs
Salt and pepper
½ c. finely diced onion
¼ c. diced green onion
2 8-oz. cans tomato sauce
1 tbsp. Worcestershire sauce
⅓ c. cider vinegar
¼ c. brown sugar
½ tsp. dry mustard
1 No. 2 can pineapple chunks

Cut meat after every third rib, cutting about halfway through strip. Sprinkle with salt and pepper; place in shallow roasting pan. Bake at 350 degrees for 1 hour and 15 minutes to 1 hour and 30 minutes. Drain off excess fat. Mix remaining ingredients and let stand to blend flavors. Pour over ribs and bake for 45 minutes to 1 hour longer, basting frequently to coat ribs with sauce. Yield: 4-6 servings.

Mary C. Smith, Kress H. S.
Kress, Texas
Mrs. Sofia Birtcil, Chico H. S.
Chico, California

BARBECUED COUNTRY RIBS

4 lb. country-style ribs
2 onions, minced
½ c. vinegar
1 tsp. dry mustard
8 tbsp. catsup
4 tbsp. barbecue sauce
4 tbsp. sugar
4 tbsp. Worcestershire sauce
1 ¼ c. water

Place ribs in baking pan. Combine remaining ingredients; pour over ribs. Roast at 350 degrees for 1 hour and 40 minutes to 1 hour and 55 minutes, basting often. Yield: 5-6 servings.

Joan F. Klingbeil, Cumberland H. S.
Cumberland, Wisconsin

BARBECUED RIBS

2 tbsp. butter
1 med. onion, chopped
1 med. green pepper, chopped
½ c. chopped celery
4 tbsp. lemon juice
2 tbsp. vinegar
2 tbsp. brown sugar
½ tsp. cayenne pepper
3 tbsp. Worcestershire sauce
1 c. catsup
1 c. water
½ tbsp. ground mustard
1 tbsp. celery salt
2 tbsp. fat
4 lb. ribs

Place butter in saucepan; add onion, green pepper and celery. Let simmer for a few seconds. Add all remaining ingredients except ribs. Cook for 10 to 12 minutes. Brown ribs. Pour sauce over ribs. Cook at 350 degrees for 2 hours or until tender. Yield: 6 servings.

Ruth Darnell
Neoga Comm. School Unit Dist. No. 3
Neoga, Illinois

BARBECUED SPARERIBS

3 lb. spareribs
2 lemons, sliced
½ c. chopped onion
2 tbsp. brown sugar
1 tbsp. paprika
1 tsp. salt
1 tsp. chili powder
2 tbsp. Worcestershire sauce
⅛ tsp. cayenne pepper
¼ c. vinegar
½ c. water
1 c. tomato juice
¼ c. catsup

Place ribs on rack in shallow baking pan; do not cover or add water. Place 1 lemon slice on each piece; sprinkle with onion. Bake at 450 degrees for 30 minutes. Combine remaining ingredients in saucepan. Simmer for 15 minutes. Pour over ribs. Bake at 350 degrees for 1 hour and 30 minutes to 2 hours, basting with sauce every 15 minutes. Cover during last 30 minutes of baking. If sauce thickens, add a small amount of water. Yield: 4 servings.

Mrs. Imogene Halcomb, Willimsburg H. S.
Williamsburg, Kentucky

BARBECUED SPARERIBS

3 to 4 lb. ribs, cut into pieces
1 or 2 unpeeled lemons, sliced
1 lge. or 2 sm. onions, thinly sliced
½ to 1 c. catsup
¼ to ⅓ c. Worcestershire sauce
1 tsp. chili powder
1 tsp. salt
2 dashes of Tabasco sauce
1 to 2 c. water

Place ribs in shallow roasting pan, meaty-side up. Place lemon slice and onion slice on each piece. Roast at 450 degrees for 30 minutes. Combine remaining ingredients; bring to a boil and pour over ribs. Bake at 350 degrees for 45 minutes to 1 hour longer or until tender. Baste ribs with sauce every 15 minutes, adding water to sauce if necessary. Yield: 4 servings.

Mrs. Alfrieda Jacobson, Granite Falls H. S.
Granite Falls, Minnesota
Mrs. Connie Tate, Southern H. S.
Durham, North Carolina

BARBECUED SPARERIBS

4 lb. spareribs
Salt and pepper
2 lemons, sliced
2 sm. onions, diced
1 c. diced onions
1 clove of garlic
2 tbsp. fat
2 tbsp. brown sugar
½ tbsp. dry mustard
2 c. meat stock
1 c. chopped tomatoes
1 c. diced green peppers
1 c. diced celery
1 c. catsup or tomato sauce

Season spareribs with salt and pepper; place on baking rack in shallow baking pan. Do not cover; do not add water. Place lemon slice on each piece; add the 2 diced onions. Bake at 450 degrees for 30 minutes. Fry 1 cup diced onions and garlic in fat; add remaining ingredients. Season and cook slowly for 1 hour. Pour sauce over meat. Bake at 350 degrees for 1 hour and 30 minutes to 2 hours, basting with sauce every 15 minutes. Cover for last 30 minutes of baking. Yield: 6 servings.

Bettye R. B. Jones, Oakville H. S.
Tacoma, Washington

BARBECUED SPARERIBS

3 lb. spareribs
1 tbsp. vinegar
1 tbsp. Worcestershire sauce
½ tsp. salt
¼ tsp. pepper
½ tsp. paprika
½ tsp. chili powder
½ c. catsup
½ c. water

Place spareribs in heavy skillet or roaster. Combine remaining ingredients and pour over meat. Bake at 300 to 325 degrees for 2 hours. Yield: 6 servings.

Mrs. Mary Nestande, Fairfax Public School
Fairfax, Minnesota

BARBECUED SPARERIBS

4 lb. spareribs
1 c. sliced onions
1 c. catsup
1 c. water
2 tsp. salt
2 tbsp. Worcestershire sauce
¼ c. vinegar
¼ c. brown sugar
2 tsp. dry mustard

Have spareribs cut into individual portions; arrange ribs in shallow pan. Combine remaining ingredients and cook until onions are tender. Cover and bake ribs at 350 degrees for 1 hour and 30 minutes, basting occasionally with sauce. Pour sauce left from basting over ribs and serve. Yield: 6-8 servings.

Tomasita Madrid, Santa Rosa H. S.
Santa Rosa, New Mexico

BARBECUED SPARERIBS

3 to 4 lb. spareribs, cut into pieces
1 tbsp. lemon juice
1 ½ tbsp. onion flakes
1 c. catsup
⅓ c. Worcestershire sauce
1 tsp. chili powder
1 tsp. salt
2 c. water

Brown spareribs in electric skillet at 325 degrees on each side. Reduce heat to simmer. Combine lemon juice, onion flakes, catsup, Worcestershire sauce, chili powder, salt and water in saucepan. Bring to a boil; pour over ribs. Simmer, covered, in skillet for 1 hour and 30 minutes to 2 hours or until completely done. Add more water if sauce thickens during cooking. Yield: 3-4 servings.

Mrs. Charlotte Russell, Litchfield H. S.
Litchfield, Michigan

DELICIOUS BARBECUED SPARERIBS

4 lb. lean spareribs, cut into serving pieces
1 lge. onion, sliced
½ c. catsup
1 ½ tsp. salt
¼ tsp. Tabasco sauce
⅛ tsp. chili powder
1 c. water
½ tsp. dry mustard
1 tsp. brown sugar

Place a layer of ribs in pan. Cover with layer of onion. Combine remaining ingredients; pour over ribs. Repeat layers. Cover and bake at 325 degrees for 2 hours to 2 hours and 30 minutes or until meat is tender. Uncover 30 minutes before serving; serve hot. Yield: 8 servings.

Verlys N. Malme, Erskine H. S.
Erskine, Minnesota

DELUXE BARBECUED RIBS

3 to 4 lb. spareribs
1 c. catsup
1 tbsp. grated onion
4 tbsp. brown sugar
Juice of 1 lemon
1 tsp. salt
1 tbsp. Worcestershire sauce
1 tbsp. steak sauce
¼ tsp. Tabasco sauce
1 tsp. grated lemon rind

Arrange spareribs, meaty-side up and slightly overlapping, on broiler pan with rack. Mix remaining ingredients; spread sauce over ribs generously. Place ribs 5 inches from broiler; broil until sauce has glazed appearance. Remove from broiler and set oven at 325 degrees. Continue to bake for 2 hours, basting with remaining sauce. NOTE: May be baked at 250 degrees for 4 hours. Yield: 4-5 servings.

Mrs. Thordis K. Danielson, New Rockford H. S.
New Rockford, North Dakota

EASY BARBECUED SPARERIBS

1 c. chopped onions
2 tbsp. butter
2 tsp. paprika
½ tsp. pepper
2 tbsp. brown sugar
1 tsp. dry mustard
2 tbsp. Worcestershire sauce
½ c. catsup
2 tbsp. vinegar
2 lb. spareribs

Cook onions in butter until clear; add remaining ingredients except spareribs. Simmer for 8 to 10 minutes. Simmer spareribs in small amount of water for 1 hour; drain. Cut into portions and cook on grill for 20 minutes, turning and basting frequently. NOTE: Ribs may also be prepared by covering with sauce and baking at 300 degrees for 45 minutes.

Mrs. Evelyn Johnson, North H. S.
Fargo, North Dakota

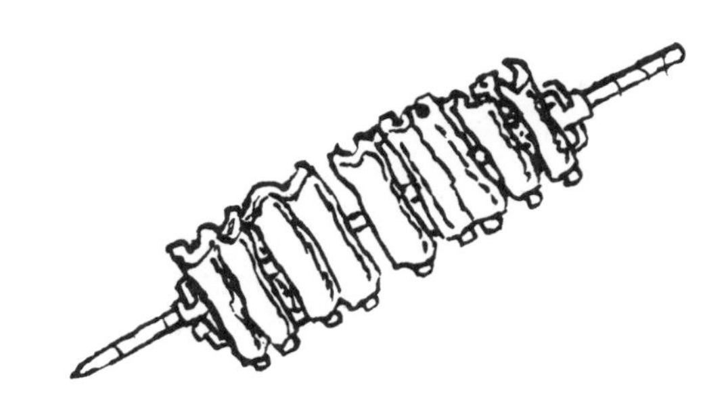

MANDARIN SPARERIBS

1 can beef bouillon
⅓ c. soy sauce
⅓ c. brown sugar or honey
2 cloves of garlic, crushed
½ tsp. ginger
⅓ c. catsup (opt.)
Spareribs

Combine undiluted bouillon with remaining ingredients except ribs. Cover spareribs with sauce; refrigerate for at least 2 hours. Grill 10 inches above coals, basting with sauce. Or, bake at 325 to 350 degrees for 1 hour and 30 minutes. Meat should shrink from bones when done.

Mrs. Alma Martin, St. Maries H. S.
St. Maries, Idaho

OVEN BARBECUED PORK RIBS

3 lb. pork ribs, cut into serving pieces
¼ tsp. Worcestershire sauce (opt.)
1 can tomato sauce
1 sauce can water
1 med. onion, diced
¼ c. sugar
1 tsp. dry mustard
½ c. vinegar

Place ribs on rack in roaster. Cover and bake at 325 degrees for 1 hour. Drain off fat; remove rack and place ribs in bottom of pan. Mix remaining ingredients and boil for 5 minutes. Spoon sauce over ribs. Bake for 1 hour longer, turning and basting. Remove cover and brown if necessary. Yield: 3 servings.

Nina Swindler, Newbern H. S.
Newbern, Tennessee

SPARERIB BARBECUE

½ c. catsup
1 c. water
½ tsp. chili powder
1 ½ tsp. Worcestershire sauce
2 tbsp. vinegar
1 tsp. salt
1 tbsp. sugar
1 tsp. dry mustard
2 sides spareribs, cut into serving pieces
2 med. onions, sliced

Combine catsup, water, chili powder, Worcestershire sauce, vinegar, salt, sugar and mustard; place a layer or ribs in roasting pan. Slice onions over ribs; cover with sauce. Repeat layers. Cover pan; bake at 325 degrees for 2 hours. Uncover the last 30 minutes for ribs to brown. Yield: 8 servings.

Margaret Dickey, Allen Co. H. S.
Scottsville, Kentucky

POLYNESIAN SPARERIBS

4 lb. spareribs
2 cloves of garlic, crushed
2 tsp. salt
¼ c. honey
¼ c. soy sauce
1 c. chicken bouillon
¼ c. catsup

Have butcher cut ribs into small pieces. Marinate ribs for several hours in mixture of garlic, salt, honey, soy sauce, chicken bouillon and catsup. Bake at 450 degrees for 10 minutes. Reduce heat to 325 degrees; bake for 1 hour and 20 minutes or until crisp. Serve with hot mustard. Yield: 8 servings.

Mrs. Ruth Ann Linse, Stillwater H. S.
Stillwater, Minnesota

SPARERIB COMBINATION

2 lb. spareribs, cut into serving pieces
Salt and pepper
1 tbsp. fat
1 med. onion, minced
2 tbsp. barbecue sauce
1 can tomato soup
4 or 5 lge. potatoes

Season ribs with salt and pepper. Sear in hot fat in skillet until golden brown. Sprinkle with onion. Pour barbecue sauce and tomato soup over ribs. Place potatoes on meat. Cook slowly until meat and potatoes are tender. May be cooked in pressure cooker for 15 minutes. Yield: 4-6 servings.

Mrs. Sammy G. Waldrip, Bastrop H. S.
Bastrop, Louisiana

SHERRY-GLAZED SPARERIBS

2 lb. country-style spareribs
Salt and pepper to taste
1 8-oz. can tomato sauce
1 c. Sherry
½ c. honey
2 tbsp. wine vinegar
2 tbsp. minced onion
¼ tsp. Worcestershire sauce

Cut ribs into serving-sized pieces and season. Place ribs in shallow pan. Bake at 400 degrees for 40 minutes. Remove from oven and drain off excess fat. Combine remaining ingredients and pour over ribs. Bake for 1 hour longer. Yield: 4-6 servings.

Patricia A. Wenzel, Mesa H. S.
Mesa, Arizona

SPARERIBS AND SAUERKRAUT

1 ½ lb. country-style spareribs
1 tbsp. shortening
3 med. onions, sliced
1 tbsp. caraway seed
1 No. 2 ½ can sauerkraut, undrained

Brown spareribs in hot shortening in deep kettle. Add 1 slice onion, 1 teaspoonful caraway seed and one-half the sauerkraut. Cover with another sliced onion, 1 teaspoonful caraway seed and remaining sauerkraut. Top with remaining sliced onion and caraway seed. Cover tightly and simmer for 2 hours to 2 hours and 30 minutes. Yield: 8 servings.

Mrs. Pauline M. Hunter, Highland Jr. H. S.
Highland, California

SWEET AND SOUR SPARERIBS

2 lb. spareribs
1 tbsp. melted shortening
2 tbsp. cornstarch
½ tsp. salt
¼ c. vinegar
1 c. pineapple juice and chunks
1 tbsp. soy sauce
¼ c. boiling water

Cover spareribs with water. Simmer for 1 hour or until tender; drain. Brown in melted shortening. Combine remaining ingredients and cook in saucepan until sauce thickens. Pour sauce over spareribs and simmer for 5 minutes. Serve hot with rice, if desired. Yield: 6 servings.

Gaylene Thomson, St. Mary's School
Taber, Alberta, Canada

SWEET AND SOUR SPARERIBS

Salt
¼ tsp. pepper
2 to 3 lb. spareribs or butt ribs
2 tbsp. brown sugar
2 tbsp. cornstarch
¼ c. vinegar
¼ c. cold water
1 c. orange juice
1 tbsp. Worcestershire sauce or ¼ tsp. chili powder

Sprinkle 2 teaspoonfuls salt and pepper on ribs; place in roaster. Bake in preheated 450 degree oven for 1 hour. Stir occasionally. Mix brown sugar, cornstarch and pinch of salt in pan. Stir in vinegar, cold water, juice and Worcestershire sauce. Cook very slowly, stirring vigorously, until mixture becomes transparent. Drain fat from ribs. Place ribs on large platter; pour on sauce. Yield: 4-6 Servings.

Mrs. Mary Ann Goerzen, Sexsmith School
Sexsmith, Alberta, Canada

SWEET 'N' SOUR SPARERIBS

2 ½ to 3 lb. meaty spareribs
Salt and pepper
1 sm. onion, coarsely chopped
½ green pepper, cut into ½-in. squares
¼ c. thinly sliced celery
2 tbsp. butter or margarine
1 tbsp. cornstarch
1 No. 2 can crushed pineapple or chunks
¼ c. vinegar
1 tbsp. soy sauce

Have butcher cut spareribs lengthwise into two strips. Salt and pepper lightly on both sides; cut into small servings. Bake at 300 degrees for 1 hour and 30 minutes, turning pieces and pouring off fat two or three times. Cook onion, green pepper and celery gently in butter for 3 to 4 minutes. Sprinkle with cornstarch; stir well. Add pineapple and syrup; cook, stirring, until slightly thickened and clear. Add vinegar and soy sauce. Drain spareribs again; pour hot sauce over all. Bake for 45 minutes longer, basting occasionally with sauce in pan. Serve hot. Yield: 6 servings.

Charlotte R. Turner, Hendersonville H. S.
Hendersonville, North Carolina

PORK STEAK WITH POTATOES AND GREEN BEANS

2 tbsp. fat
Salt
4 pork steaks
¼ c. flour
6 med. potatoes, peeled
1 qt. green beans, undrained
1 bay leaf (opt.)

Melt fat in pressure saucepan. Salt pork steaks; coat with flour. Brown in pan. Halve potatoes; place on top of meat. Add green beans. Add additional salt and bay leaf, if desired. Cook under pressure for 10 minutes, counting time when proper point is reached, as determined by brand of pressure pan being used. Water cool. If desired, broth may be thickened to a gravy before serving or served as broth over potatoes. Yield: 4 servings.

Mrs. Agnes Kowitz Boulger
Bradley Bourbonnais Comm. H. S.
Bradley, Illinois

CHOP SUEY

1 c. cubed lean pork
1 c. chopped celery
1 med. onion, chopped
2 No. 303 cans bean sprouts
1 c. chopped mushrooms
2 tbsp. soy sauce
1 tsp. salt
Cornstarch
3 c. cooked rice

Cook pork, celery and onion for 20 minutes or until done. Add bean sprouts and a small amount water. Cover; simmer for 15 to 20 minutes or until done. Add mushrooms, soy sauce and salt; stir well. Mix a small amount cornstarch and water; add to mixture. Remove from heat; serve at once over cooked rice. Yield: 6 servings.

Charlotte K. Macy, Ottawa H. S.
Ottawa, Kansas

CURRIED PORK

2 c. fresh chopped pork
1 onion, chopped
2 raw potatoes, diced
2 sticks celery, diced
1 green pepper, finely chopped

(Continued on next page)

1 c. mushrooms
1 tsp. curry powder
1 tsp. salt
Dash of pepper
4 c. tomatoes

Combine pork, onion, potatoes, celery, green pepper and mushrooms in a frying pan. Brown. Add the seasonings and tomatoes. Simmer until mixture becomes thick. Serve over steamed rice, if desired. NOTE: A small amount of sugar may be added to vary taste of tomatoes. Yield: 6 servings.

Lois J. Smeltzer, Eastern Lebanon Co. H. S.
Myerstown, Pennsylvania

HAWAIIAN PORK

1 ½ lb. pork shoulder, cubed
¼ c. fat or shortening
¼ c. water
2 tbsp. cornstarch
⅓ c. vinegar
½ tsp. salt
1 c. pineapple juice
1 tbsp. soy sauce
½ c. chopped green pepper
1 med. onion, chopped
2 ½ c. pineapple chunks

Brown meat in fat; add water. Cover and simmer for 1 hour. Combine remaining ingredients except green pepper, onion and pineapple in saucepan; cook until thickened. Pour sauce over pork; let stand for 10 minutes. Add green pepper, onion and pineapple; cook for 5 minutes. Serve over hot rice. Yield: 4-6 servings.

Mrs. Eleanor Piskorik
Vincent Massey Jr. H. S.
New Westminster, British Columbia, Canada

PORK AND PINEAPPLE PACKAGES

2 lb. fresh pork shoulder, cut into 2-in. pieces
1 ¾ tsp. onion or garlic salt
⅛ tsp. pepper
½ tsp. ground ginger
1 No. 2 can pineapple chunks, drained
2 green peppers, seeded and quartered
8 sm. tomatoes

Place pork on waxed paper; sprinkle with onion salt, pepper and ginger. Place pork, pineapple, green peppers and tomatoes on eight 12-inch pieces of foil. Gather each piece of foil together at top; arrange on shallow baking pan. Bake in preheated 350 degree oven for 2 hours. Yield: 8 servings.

Margaret M. Stouffer, South Western H. S.
Hanover, Pennsylvania

SWEET AND SOUR PORK

1 lb. lean pork, cubed
1 c. water
¼ tsp. salt
1 c. diced celery
½ c. diced onion
1 No. 1 can mushrooms
4 tbsp. butter or margarine
1 No. 2 can crushed pineapple
3 tbsp. sugar
1 tbsp. cornstarch
3 tbsp. vinegar
1 tbsp. soy sauce

Cook pork in salted water until white; drain. Combine celery, onion and mushrooms; cook in 2 tablespoonfuls butter for 5 minutes. Add crushed pineapple; bring to boil. Combine sugar, cornstarch, vinegar and soy sauce; add to vegetable-pineapple mixture. Cook until mixture begins to thicken. Melt remaining butter in large skillet; add pork. Cook for 5 minutes, stirring constantly. Pour pineapple-vegetable mixture over pork; cover. Bake at 350 degrees for 45 minutes. Serve with rice or baked potato, if desired.

Mrs. Georgia Short, Dell City H. S.
Dell City, Texas

SWEET-SOUR PORK

1 egg, beaten
¼ c. flour
1 tsp. salt
Dash of pepper
3 tbsp. milk
1 lb. lean pork, cubed
Oil
1 c. pineapple chunks
1 lge. green pepper, sliced
⅓ c. red wine vinegar
½ c. brown sugar
1 c. water
2 tsp. soy sauce
2 tbsp. cornstarch

(Continued on next page)

Mix egg with flour, salt, pepper and milk; make a thin batter. Dip pork into batter; fry in oil until golden brown. Combine pineapple, green pepper, vinegar, brown sugar, 3/4 cup water and soy sauce; heat to boiling. Mix cornstarch and remaining water; stir into sauce and cook until thickened. Remove green pepper when pepper looses bright green color. Add fried pork. Cook for 2 minutes. Serve immediately with hot cooked rice, if desired. Yield: 6 servings.

Mrs. Ruth Beymer, Vallivue H. S.
Caldwell, Idaho

SWEET-SOUR PORK ON RICE

3 tbsp. salad oil
1 ½ lb. boneless pork, thinly sliced and cut into squares
1 med. onion, thinly sliced
½ c. Russian dressing
1 c. water
2 tbsp. cornstarch
1 tsp. vinegar
1 lge. can pineapple chunks
1 med. green pepper, cut into 1-in. squares
¼ c. slivered almonds
1 ½ c. instant rice

Heat salad oil in large skillet. Brown meat and onion, turning frequently. Combine Russian dressing, water, cornstarch and vinegar. Drain pineapple; mix juice with cornstarch mixture. Pour over meat; stir for 2 minutes or until thickened. Cover; simmer for 30 minutes or until pork is tender. Add green pepper and pineapple chunks; cook for 2 to 3 minutes until green pepper is tender-crisp. Stir in almonds. Prepare rice according to package directions. Serve hot meat mixture over rice. Yield: 6 servings.

Mrs. D. J. Lovely, Walter S. Parker Jr. H. S.
Reading, Massachusetts

SWEET-SOUR PORK

2 lge. green peppers
¾ c. shortening
1 clove of garlic
2 tbsp. salt
1 egg
4 tsp. flour
Dash of pepper
1 lb. lean pork, cut into ½-in. cubes
1 ⅔ c. chicken bouillon
1 c. pineapple chunks
3 tsp. cornstarch
2 tbsp. soy sauce
⅓ c. vinegar
½ c. sugar
Cooked rice

Cut peppers into 12 pieces; cook in boiling water for 8 minutes. Heat shortening with garlic and salt. Make a batter of egg, flour, additional salt and pepper. Dip pork into batter: brown in shortening. Drain all but 2 tablespoonfuls of grease; add 1 cup bouillon, pineapple, green pepper and pork. Cover tightly; simmer for 10 minutes. Blend cornstarch, soy sauce, vinegar, sugar and remaining bouillon. Add pork to mixture; stir until juice thickens. Serve over hot cooked rice. Yield: 8 servings.

Estelle J. Garrison, Fayette Co. H. S.
Fayette, Alabama

SWEET-SOUR PORK ON RICE

1 ½ lb. pork cubes
1 tsp. salt
Pepper to taste
¼ c. flour
2 tbsp. oil
½ c. water
¼ c. vinegar
2 tbsp. soy sauce
1 c. apricot preserves
1 green pepper, cut into strips

Toss pork cubes with seasoned flour; brown in oil. Stir in water, vinegar and soy sauce; cover and simmer for 45 minutes. Add preserves and green pepper; cook for 15 minutes. Serve on hot cooked rice. Yield: 6 servings.

Mrs. Mildred M. Newbold, Sparks Jr. H. S.
Sparks, Nevada

PICKLED PORK HOCKS

4 pork hocks
4 c. vinegar
2 tsp. whole cloves
1 bay leaf
1 tbsp. salt
½ tsp. pepper
1 med. onion

Boil hocks until meat will slip from the bones; drain and place in bowl. Reserve 2 cups broth. Combine vinegar, cloves, bay leaf, salt, pepper and onion. Boil for 30 minutes. Add broth; strain. Pour over hocks; let stand for three days before serving.

Mrs. Beverly Wruck, Clintonville H. S.
Clintonville, Wisconsin

BAKED PORK ROLL-UPS

12 to 14 slices thin pork steaks
Salt and pepper
Prepared mustard
4 c. soft bread crumbs
½ c. raisins
½ c. chopped celery
½ c. chopped apple
1 tsp. salt
2 tsp. sage
Flour
1 c. hot water

Trim fat and remove bone from steaks; fry out fat over low heat. Pound steaks to 1/4-inch thickness; season. Spread lightly with mustard. Combine crumbs, raisins, celery, apple, salt and sage. Spread on meat; roll and fasten with toothpicks or string. Dust with flour; brown. Place in 3-quart casserole; add hot water and cover tightly. Bake at 350 degrees for 1 hour or until tender. NOTE: May be placed in Dutch oven with water to cover. Simmer for 1 hour, adding more water if necessary. Yield: 12 servings.

Mrs. Mann Nutt, Lewis Co. H. S.
Hohenwald, Tennessee

CRISP SALT PORK

6 thick slices lean salt pork
3 c. water

Place pork in uncovered saucepan. Cover with cold water. Slowly bring to boil, moving pork about frequently. Do not boil. Remove pork from water; drain on paper towel. Panbroil until crisp, turning as meat cooks. Yield: 6 servings.

Mrs. Ava Bush, Grapeland H. S.
Grapeland, Texas

PORK SHANKS AND BEANS WITH DUMPLINGS

4 lge. pork shanks
1 lb. navy beans
2 med. onions, sliced
1 tsp. salt
Pepper
2 lge. potatoes
2 c. flour
3 tsp. baking powder
½ tsp. salt
2 tsp. butter or shortening
⅔ c. milk

Place pork shanks in cold water in large kettle. Bring to a boil; skim foam from top. Reduce heat to low and cook until tender. Cut lean meat from shanks, discarding skin and bones. Reserve broth. Wash and soak beans for several hours or overnight. Cook slowly until almost done. Combine broth, beans, lean meat, onions, salt and pepper; simmer. Peel potatoes and cut into medium-sized pieces. Add to meat mixture and cook for 10 minutes. Sift flour, baking powder and salt. Work in butter with tips of fingers. Add milk gradually to make a soft dough. Drop by spoonfuls over meat mixture. Cover kettle tightly and steam for 12 minutes. Yield: 6-8 servings.

Mrs. Mary K. Adams, New Troy H. S.
New Troy, Michigan

Poultry Favorites

BAKED CHICKEN

1 3 to 3 ½-lb. chicken, cut up
Salt to taste
1 c. flour
¼ lb. butter
½ c. shortening
1 tsp. lemon juice
Paprika to taste

Dust chicken with salt and flour. Dip chicken in melted butter, shortening and lemon juice. Place in shallow baking dish; sprinkle with paprika. Bake, covered, at 350 degrees for 1 hour. Uncover; cook for 30 minutes longer. Yield: 5-7 servings.

Carolyn Mullins, Puryear H. S.
Puryear, Tennessee

BAKED CHICKEN

1 2 ½-lb. fryer, cut up
¼ c. oil
2 tsp. salt
1 tsp. dry mustard
1 tsp. paprika

Combine all ingredients except chicken. Dip chicken into mixture; place in shallow 9 1/2 x 13 1/2-inch cake pan. Bake at 400 degrees for 1 hour. Yield: 4 servings.

Karen E. Aznoe, Powell Co. H. S.
Deer Lodge, Montana

BAKED CHICKEN ITALIAN

4 chicken drumsticks or thighs
2 whole chicken breasts, cut into halves
¼ c. flour
1 tsp. salt
¼ tsp. garlic salt
⅛ tsp pepper
¼ c. vegetable oil
1 chicken bouillon cube
½ c. water
1 tsp. vinegar
1 med. onion, sliced
¼ c. chopped celery
1 8-oz. can tomato sauce
¾ c. pizza-flavored catsup

Coat chicken pieces with mixture of flour, salt, garlic salt and pepper. Brown in vegetable oil in skillet. Place chicken pieces in 1 1/2-quart baking dish. Dissolve chicken bouillon cube in 1/2 cup water. Add bouillon and remaining ingredients to skillet. Simmer for 5 minutes; pour over chicken. Bake at 350 degrees for 1 hour. Yield: 4 servings.

Sister St. Anita Marie C.N.D.
Mabou Consolidated School
Mabou, Nova Scotia, Canada

BARBECUED CHICKEN

Salt and pepper
1 stick margarine
½ c. vinegar
1 tbsp. pepper
1 tbsp. celery salt
½ c. tomato sauce
Juice of 1 lemon
¼ tbsp. Tabasco sauce
1 qt. water
¼ c. brown sugar
1 tbsp. garlic salt
2 tbsp. prepared mustard
½ tbsp. paprika
1 tbsp. Worcestershire sauce
2 med. fryers

Combine 1 tablespoonful salt with remaining ingredients except fryers in a saucepan; bring to a boil. Salt and pepper chicken; place in pan or foil. Bake at 350 degrees for 1 hour and 15 minutes, basting with sauce. NOTE: Remaining sauce may be stored in jars for later use. Yield: 8-10 servings.

Mrs. Emily Bierschwale, Junction H. S.
Junction, Texas

BARBECUED CHICKEN

1 3-lb. fryer, cut up
Flour (opt.)
Fat
1 to 2 med. onions
½ to 1 c. catsup
2 to 3 tbsp. Worcestershire sauce
Salt and pepper
½ tbsp. prepared mustard
1 c. water
½ c. chopped celery (opt.)
2 tbsp. vinegar
3 to 4 tbsp. brown sugar
¼ c. lemon juice or vinegar
2 tbsp. light corn syrup (opt.)

Coat chicken with flour, if desired. Brown in hot fat. Brown onion slowly in 2 tablespoonfuls fat; add remaining ingredients. Simmer for 30 minutes, if desired. Place chicken in shallow baking pan; pour sauce over chicken. Bake at 300 to 325 degrees for 1 hour and 30 minutes to 2 hours. Yield: 6 servings.

Mrs. Luana Hutchings, Moapa Valley H. S.
Overton, Nevada
Mrs. Edwin F. Cook, Union Co. H. S.
Blairsville, Georgia

BARBECUED CHICKEN

Salt
Flour
1 fryer, cut up
Fat
1 med. onion, chopped
1 c. catsup
1 c. water
¼ c. vinegar

(Continued on next page)

2 tbsp. brown sugar
¼ tsp. red pepper
½ tsp. black pepper

Salt and flour chicken; brown in hot fat. Brown onion in 2 tablespoonfuls fat; combine 1 teaspoonful salt and onions with remaining ingredients. Simmer for 10 minutes. Pour over browned chicken. Bake at 325 degrees for 1 hour. Yield: 6-8 servings.

Mary E. Roddam, Curry H. S.
Jasper, Alabama

CHICKEN BARBECUE

1 to 6 tsp. catsup
2 to 6 tsp. white vinegar
2 to 6 tsp. butter
2 tsp. Worcestershire sauce
2 to 4 tsp. water
½ tsp. red pepper (opt.)
2 tsp. lemon juice
1 to 2 tsp. mustard
1 tsp. salt (opt.)
1 tsp. paprika
1 tsp. chili powder
1 2-lb. chicken, cut up

Mix all ingredients except chicken; heat. Dip seasoned chicken in hot sauce; place in a well greased paper bag. Place bag in a covered roaster. Bake at 500 degrees for 15 minutes. Decrease temperature to 350 degrees and bake for 1 hour and 15 minutes. NOTE: Chicken may be baked at 375 degrees for 1 hour.

Ruth B. Sweeten, Parrottsville H. S.
Parrottsville, Tennessee
Mrs. Lona Caphaw, Hermitage Springs School
Red Boiling Springs, Tennessee

CHICKEN WITH LEMON BARBECUE SAUCE

3 green onions
3 clove of garlic or garlic salt
¾ c. oil
½ c. Worcestershire sauce
2 lemons
¼ c. vinegar
¼ c. chopped celery
1 tbsp. butter
2 broiler chickens, split into halves
Salt and pepper
Paprika

Combine all ingredients except chicken, salt, pepper and paprika in boiler; warm. Place chickens on broiler pan, cut-side down. Bake at 300 degrees for 10 minutes. Turn chickens; cover with one-half the sauce. Bake for 20 minutes. Turn and add remaining sauce. Sprinkle generously with salt, pepper and paprika. Bake at 325 degrees for 1 hour longer. Yield: 4 servings.

Frances Morton, Tallulah H. S.
Tallulah, Louisiana

CHINESE-STYLE BARBECUED CHICKEN

1 2½-lb. frying chicken
2 tbsp. wine vinegar
1 ⅓ c. soy sauce
3 tbsp. vegetable oil
½ tsp. ground ginger
¼ tsp. pepper
1 clove of garlic, minced
1 tsp. dry mustard

Cut each drumstick and thigh into two pieces; cut breast into five pieces. Cut remaining chicken into small pieces. Combine all remaining ingredients. Brush all sides of chicken with part of mixture; let soak for 30 minutes. Place chicken on rack in shallow pan. Bake at 350 degrees for 15 minutes. Baste chicken with sauce; bake for 15 minutes longer. Turn chicken; baste again. Raise oven temperature to 400 degrees; bake for 15 minutes. Baste chicken with remaining sauce. Bake chicken 15 minutes longer. Serve. Yield: 4-5 servings.

Mrs. Lois Millam, Linden Union H. S.
Linden, California

DELICIOUS OVEN BARBECUED CHICKEN

¾ c. chopped onion
½ c. margarine
¾ c. catsup
¾ c. water
⅓ c. lemon juice or vinegar
3 tbsp. sugar
3 tbsp. Worcestershire sauce
2 tbsp. mustard
1 tsp. pepper
Salt
2 fryers, cut into halves

Cook onion in margarine in pan; add catsup, water, lemon juice, sugar, Worcestershire sauce, mustard and pepper. Cook for 15 minutes. Salt chicken; dip chicken into sauce. Place in baking pan. Bake at 350 degrees for 1 hour and 30 minutes. Baste with sauce several times while baking.

Mrs. Rozanne Aker, Waynetown School
Waynetown, Indiana

EASY BARBECUED CHICKEN

1 onion, finely chopped
¼ c. vinegar
2 tbsp. sugar
1 c. catsup
½ c. water
2 tbsp. Worcestershire sauce
1 tsp. prepared mustard
2 tsp. salt
Dash of pepper
1 lge. fryer, cut into pieces

(Continued on next page)

Combine all ingredients except chicken in small saucepan. Simmer for 10 minutes. Place chicken on large piece of foil in shallow baking pan. Pour sauce over chicken; wrap, using drug store wrap. Bake at 325 degrees for 1 hour. Yield: 4 servings.

Mrs. Pauline R. Cook, Vernon H. S.
Vernon, Florida

OVEN-BARBECUED CHICKEN

1 chicken, cut up
Salt
¼ lb. butter
½ c. catsup
3 tbsp. Worcestershire sauce
1 tbsp. lemon juice
½ c. water

Place chicken pieces in casserole. Season with salt. Combine remaining ingredients; melt and pour over chicken. Cover and bake at 450 degrees for 15 minutes. Reduce heat to 250 degrees and bake for 2 hours. Yield: 6 servings.

Mrs. Sammie Lee Pounds
New Site Attendance Center
New Site, Mississippi

OVEN-BARBECUED CHICKEN

1 frying chicken
¼ c. flour
Salt and pepper
¼ c. fat
3 tbsp. butter or margarine
½ c. sliced onion
½ c. sliced green pepper
1 c. mushrooms
1 c. catsup
⅔ c. water
2 tbsp. Worcestershire sauce
2 drops Tabasco sauce
1 tbsp. brown sugar
½ tsp. paprika

Wash chicken; season with flour, salt and pepper. Brown in fat. Melt butter in saucepan; add onion, green pepper and mushrooms. Cook until tender. Stir in 1/4 teaspoonful salt and remaining ingredients; bring to a boil. Place chicken in 2-quart casserole; pour sauce over chicken. Cover; bake at 350 degrees for 45 minutes or until chicken is tender. Yield: 6 servings.

Margaret Whitley, Caney H. S.
Caney, Oklahoma

OVEN-BARBECUED CHICKEN

2 tbsp. vinegar
½ c. cooking oil
½ tsp. garlic salt
1 tsp. salt
½ tsp. pepper
1 3-lb. fryer, cut up

Combine all ingredients except chicken; blend well. Pour over chicken; let stand overnight. Place chicken in baking dish. Bake at 500 degrees for 20 minutes.

BARBECUE SAUCE:

2 med. onions, finely chopped
2 tsp. dry mustard
1 tbsp. sugar
1 tsp. salt
¼ tsp. pepper
2 tsp. Worcestershire sauce
2 tsp. vinegar
1 c. chili sauce

Combine all ingredients in saucepan. Bring to a boil; cook for 15 minutes. Pour over chicken in baking dish. Bake at 350 degrees for 1 hour, basting after 30 minutes. Yield: 6 servings.

Mrs. Janice M. Kennedy, Troy Area H. S.
Troy, Pennsylvania

OVEN-BARBECUED CHICKEN

¼ c. cooking oil
1 2½ to 3-lb. frying chicken, cut into serving pieces
1 c. chili sauce
¼ c. vinegar
¼ c. water
2 tbsp. sugar
½ tsp. chili powder
½ tsp. salt
⅛ tsp. cayenne pepper
1 tbsp. prepared mustard
1 med. onion
¼ c. cooking oil
Parsley

Pour one-half the cooking oil into flat roasting pan. Place pieces of chicken, skin-side up, in pan; do not overlap. Brush top sides with remaining oil. Bake at 350 degrees for 1 hour. Combine chili sauce with all remaining ingredients, except parsley, in saucepan; heat to boiling. Reduce heat; simmer gently for 10 minutes, stirring frequently. Remove from heat; spoon over chicken at 10 minute intervals for 30 minutes or until chicken is tender. Reserve a small amount of sauce and pour over chicken just before serving. Garnish with parsley. Yield: 4-6 servings.

Mrs. Robert W. Philbeck, Robert E. Lee Jr. H.S.
Orlando, Florida

OVEN-BARBECUED CHICKEN

Salt to taste
1 fryer, cut up

(Continued on next page)

½ c. vinegar
¼ c. water
½ lb. butter or margarine
1 tsp. red pepper

Salt chicken and place in baking dish. Combine remaining ingredients; heat until butter is melted. Baste chicken with vinegar mixture. Bake in preheated 425 degree oven for 45 minutes to 1 hour. Yield: 4 servings.

Pauline Waggener, DuQuoin Twp. H. S.
DuQuoin, Illinois

PAPER BAG BARBECUED CHICKEN

Salt and pepper
1 frying chicken, cut up
3 to 6 tbsp. catsup
2 tbsp. vinegar
1 tbsp. lemon juice or juice of 1 lemon
2 tbsp. Worcestershire sauce
4 tbsp. water
¼ to 1 stick butter
3 to 4 tbsp. brown sugar
1 tsp. salt
1 to 2 tsp. dry mustard
1 to 2 tsp. chili powder
½ tsp. red pepper or 1 tsp. paprika

Salt and pepper chicken lightly. Combine all remaining ingredients in saucepan; bring to boiling. Grease inside of a large paper bag with margarine. Place in roaster. Dip each piece chicken in hot sauce; place in bag. Pour remaining sauce over chicken in bag. Fold bag down from top; fasten with paper clips. Place lid on roaster. Bake at 500 degrees for 15 minutes; reduce heat to 350 and bake for 1 hour and 15 minutes longer. NOTE: Chicken may be baked at 350 degrees for 1 hour and 30 minutes. Yield: 8-10 servings.

Margaret Myrick, Harlan City H. S.
Harlan, Kentucky
Mrs. Beth Nickerson, Nashua H. S.
Nashua, Montana
Mrs. Rosemary K. Harwood, North Stanly H. S.
New London, North Carolina

VARIED BARBECUED CHICKEN

1 stick butter or margarine
Juice of 1 lemon
3 tbsp. Worcestershire sauce
1 sm. frying chicken, cut up
Salt to taste

Combine margarine, lemon juice and Worcestershire sauce in a 9-inch skillet. Cook, covered, over low heat until margarine is melted. Dip each piece of chicken into cooked mixture; arrange in skillet. Salt to taste. Place covered skillet in oven. Bake at 350 degrees for 1 hour. Turn chicken once while baking; baste often. Remove cover; let brown for 15 minutes. Yield: 4 servings.

Phyllis M. Taylor, Trezevant H. S.
Memphis, Tennessee

BREADED CHICKEN

Salt
1 4-lb. fryer, cut into serving portions
Flour
1 egg
1 tbsp. water
Toasted bread crumbs
2 to 3 c. vegetable oil
Poultry seasoning

Salt chicken lightly; let stand for 1 hour. Roll pieces in flour, shaking off excess. Beat egg with water; dip floured chicken into egg mixture. Place pieces in plastic bag containing bread crumbs; shake until coated. Place on rack or tray; let crumbs dry for 1 hour or longer, if desired. Brown chicken lightly in hot oil in large saucepan. Place chicken in single layer in roaster or large pan. Sprinkle with poultry seasoning. Bake at 325 degrees for 1 hour and 30 minutes or until done. Yield: 4 servings.

Mrs. Gloria Lorenz, Prospect H. S.
Mt. Prospect, Illinois

BAKED CHICKEN BREASTS

6 chicken breasts
2 cans cream of chicken soup
1 can cream of mushroom soup
Slivered almonds

Place chicken breasts in glass baking dish. Mix soups in mixing bowl; mix thoroughly. Pour soup mixture over chicken breasts; sprinkle with almonds. Bake at 350 degrees for 1 hour. Remove breasts; dip up soup for gravy. NOTE: Do not season chicken. Yield: 6 servings.

Mrs. Nadine Kaiser, Hydro H. S.
Hydro, Oklahoma

BAKED CHICKEN BREASTS

6 chicken breasts
Seasonings to taste
1 stick margarine, melted
2 c. fine toasted bread crumbs

Soak chicken in ice water for 30 minutes; drain well. Season chicken. Dip chicken into butter and roll in crumbs. Place in broiler pan skin-side up. Bake at 400 degrees for 1 hour. Yield: 6 servings.

Mrs. Nonie Lee Hardage, Carthage H. S.
Carthage, Mississippi

BAKED CHICKEN BREASTS WITH ALMONDS

Salt and pepper to taste
4 or 5 frozen chicken breasts
4 tbsp. cooking oil
1 can cream of mushroom soup
½ c. cooking Sherry
¼ c. sharp Cheddar cheese
3 tbsp. grated onion
2 tbsp. Worcestershire sauce
½ c. slivered almonds

Salt and pepper chicken; brown in oil. Place in baking dish. Combine soup, wine, cheese, onion and Worcestershire sauce; pour over chicken. Place almonds on top; cover with foil. Bake at 350 degrees for 45 minutes. Yield: 4-5 servings.

Patricia Allen, Smyrna H. S.
Smyrna, Tennessee

BAKED CHICKEN BREASTS SUPREME

2 c. sour cream
¼ c. lemon juice
3 to 4 tsp. Worcestershire sauce
3 to 4 tsp. celery salt
2 tsp. paprika
4 cloves of garlic, minced or ½ tsp. instant minced garlic
1 to 4 tsp. salt
½ tsp. pepper
6 12-oz. broiler breasts, cut into halves
1 ¾ c. bread crumbs
½ c. butter
½ c. shortening

Combine sour cream, lemon juice and seasonings. Add chicken, coating each piece well. Cover and refrigerate overnight. Roll chicken breasts in crumbs, coating evenly. Arrange in single layer in large shallow baking pan. Melt butter and shortening; spoon one-half the butter over chicken. Bake, uncovered, in preheated 350 degree oven for 45 minutes. Spoon remaining butter mixture over chicken. Bake for 10 to 15 minutes longer or until chicken is tender and browned. Yield: 12 servings.

Mrs. Allen S. Lawrence
E. Merle Smith Jr. H. S.
Sinton, Texas
Mrs. Norma Macri, Kellogg Jr. H. S.
Kellogg, Idaho

CHICKEN BREASTS IN MUSHROOM SAUCE

Salt and pepper to taste
6 to 8 chicken breasts
1 can cream of mushroom soup
1 can mushroom pieces, drained (opt.)
⅓ to 1 c. milk or cream

Place seasoned breasts in baking dish. Brown in 400 degree oven, if desired. Combine soup, mushroom pieces and milk; pour over chicken breasts. Reduce heat to 350 degrees; bake for 45 minutes to 1 hour or until done. Yield: 6-8 servings.

Mrs. Charles W. Samples, Dawson Co. H. S.
Dawsonville, Georgia
Mrs. Warren Webb, Columbia Jr. H. S.
Columbia, Kentucky

CHICKEN BREAST SUPREME

6 chicken breasts fillets
1 can cream of chicken soup
1 can cream of celery soup
1 pkg. dry onion soup mix
½ c. cooking Sherry

Brown chicken in butter; place in casserole dish. Pour soups over chicken; sprinkle onion soup over top. Add cooking Sherry and small amount of water, if desired. Bake at 350 degrees for 1 hour and 30 minutes. Yield: 4-6 servings.

Shirley H. Travis, Tucker H. S.
Tucker, Georgia

CHICKEN KIEV

Salt and pepper
6 chicken breasts, boned and skinned
Melted butter
Fresh parsley, chopped
Butter
4 eggs, beaten
½ c. light cream or evaporated milk
Flour
2 c. cracker crumbs
Cooking oil

Salt and pepper chicken breasts; pound flat. Dip into melted butter. Place a 1/2-inch piece of cold butter and 1 tablespoonful chopped parsley in center of each breast; fold up and fasten with toothpicks. Mix eggs and cream or evaporated milk. Roll breasts in flour. Roll in beaten egg mixture; roll in cracker crumbs. Brown in melted butter and cooking oil in hot skillet. Bake in 325 degree oven for 1 hour or until tender and crisp. Baste with butter during baking. Yield: 6 servings.

Mrs. Audrey Eckert
Walsh Co. Agricultural School
Park River, North Dakota

CHICKEN KIEV

4 boned chicken breasts, skinned
½ c. butter
½ c. flour
½ c. cold milk
1 tsp. salt
2 eggs, beaten
1 c. bread crumbs
Fat

(Continued on next page)

Place each breast between two pieces of paper; pound to 1/4-inch thickness. Shape butter into bars, allowing 1 1/2 tablespoonfuls per breast; Roll each piece of chicken around a bar. Coat chicken with flour. Dip into cold milk; drain. Dip into salted beaten egg; dip into crumbs and again in egg. Dip again in crumbs. Chill overnight. Fry gently in small amount of fat until golden brown. Place on cookie sheet. Bake at 400 degrees for 30 minutes or until tender. Serve hot or cold. NOTE: Leave a short length of breast-bone attached to chicken to give body. Yield: 4 servings.

Mrs. Margueritte Cook, Bloom-Carroll School
Carroll, Ohio

CHICKEN KIEV

4 med. chicken breasts
Salt
4 tbsp. chopped green onion
4 tbsp. chopped parsley
1 stick butter
1 egg, beaten
Dry bread crumbs

Cut chicken breasts in half lengthwise. Remove skin; cut away bone. Do not tear meat. Place each piece chicken, boned-side up, between two pieces plastic wrap. Pound chicken to about 1/4-inch thickness with wooden mallet, working from center out. Remove plastic wrap; sprinkle meat with salt. Sprinkle 1 tablespoonful onion and 1 tablespoonful parsley over cutlets. Cut the chilled 1/4 pound stick of butter into eight sticks. Place small stick of butter near end of cutlet. Roll as for jelly roll, tucking in sides of meat and pressing to seal well. Dust chicken breasts with flour. Dip into egg, then roll in breast crumbs. Chill chicken rolls for at least 1 hour. Fry in deep fat at 340 degrees for 5 minutes or until golden brown. Yield: 4 servings.

Mrs. Nona Ross, Pratt H. S.
Pratt, Kansas

CHICKEN PARMESAN

1 pkg. saltine crackers, crushed
¾ c. grated Parmesan cheese
6 chicken breasts halves or 12 thighs
1 stick butter, melted

Mix cracker crumbs and Parmesan cheese. Dip chicken pieces in melted butter; roll in cracker mixture to coat chicken. Place chicken in baking pan; bake, uncovered, at 325 degrees to 350 degrees for 1 hour. Yield: 6 servings.

Louise R. Clark, Jacksonville H. S.
Jacksonville, Alabama

CHICKEN AND ORANGE BURGUNDY

2 whole chicken breasts
3 tbsp. cooking oil
⅓ c. Burgundy
⅓ c. orange juice
1 tsp. lemon juice
3 tbsp. orange marmalade
3 tbsp. brown sugar
¼ tsp. salt
1 orange, sliced

Brown chicken in oil; mix remaining ingredients except orange. Bring to a boil. Place chicken in a flat casserole; pour sauce over chicken. Lay slices of orange over chicken. Bake at 350 degrees for 45 minutes to 1 hour, basting occasionally with sauce. Yield: 4 servings.

Mrs. Mildred Rivers, Wilson Jr. H. S.
Charlotte, North Carolina

CHICKEN WITH WINE

8 chicken breasts or legs
1 c. Sauterne
1 c. Sherry
1 c. Vermouth
1 can cream of mushroom soup
1 c. sour cream
Salt and pepper

Place chicken in large flat casserole. Blend remaining ingredients; pour over chicken. Bake, uncovered, at 300 degrees for 3 hours. Yield: 8 servings.

Rosemary Martine, Gridley Jr. H. S.
Erie, Pennsylvania

ORANGE CHICKEN

4 chicken breasts
Juice of 1 orange
1 tbsp. orange rind
½ tsp. salt
½ tsp. paprika
½ tsp. mustard
¼ tsp. Worcestershire sauce
3 tbsp. cooking oil
1 can broken mushroom pieces or ¾ c. fresh sliced mushrooms

Place chicken breasts in baking pan, skin-side down. Combine remaining ingredients except mushrooms. Pour over chicken, coating each piece well. Bake at 375 degrees for 1 hour, basting occasionally. Turn chicken; sprinkle with mushrooms and baste again. Bake for 15 to 30 minutes longer. Remove to hot platter; pour sauce over chicken and serve. Yield: 4 servings.

Mrs. Florence N. Jackson
Belchertown Jr.-Sr. H. S.
Belchertown, Massachusetts

COUNTRY CAPTAIN

4 lb. chicken breasts
1 c. seasoned flour
½ c. shortening
2 onions, chopped
2 green peppers, chopped
1 clove of garlic, minced
1 tbsp. curry powder
1 ½ tsp. salt
½ tsp. white pepper
½ tsp. thyme
2 cans tomatoes
1 tbsp. chopped parsley
6 c. cooked rice
¼ c. currants
¼ lb. toasted almonds

Remove skin from chicken; roll in flour. Fry in shortening until brown. Cook onions, green peppers and garlic in remaining fat. Stir in curry powder, salt, pepper and thyme; mix well. Add tomatoes and parsley; heat until all is heated through. Place chicken in large casserole; pour sauce over chicken. Cover and bake at 350 degrees for 45 minutes. Drain rice; place in center of serving dish. Remove chicken from casserole; place around rice. Sprinkle currants into sauce; pour sauce over rice. Sprinkle almonds over chicken. Yield: 8 servings.

Mrs. Patricia W. Chase, Greensboro H. S.
Greensboro, Florida

OVEN-BAKED CHICKEN

2 chicken breasts, split
½ c. shortening
¼ c. margarine
1 tbsp. lemon juice
½ c. sour cream
¼ c. milk
1 ½ to 2 c. fine bread crumbs
1 tsp. sage
Dash of nutmeg
½ tsp. salt
Dash of freshly ground black pepper

Wash chicken, removing skins, if desired. Melt shortening and margarine with lemon juice in baking dish in 350 degree oven. Dilute sour cream with milk. Mix bread crumbs and seasonings in heavy paper bag. Dip chicken into sour cream mixture, then shake in bag to coat with bread crumb mixture. Place chicken in baking dish, bone-side down; baste. Bake at 350 degrees for 45 minutes to 1 hour, basting occasionally. Yield: 4 servings.

Sallie S. Gates, Pentucket Regional School
West Newbury, Massachusetts

POLYNESIAN BREAST OF CHICKEN

1 c. melted butter
3 to 4 tbsp. lemon juice
Grated lemon rind
8 ½-lb. chicken breasts

Combine butter, lemon juice and rind. Coat breasts with butter mixture. Line up breasts in shallow pan. Place on top rack of oven. Bake at 500 degrees for 20 minutes or until browned.

SAUCE:

4 tbsp. butter
½ c. finely minced onion
4 tbsp. flour
1 tsp. beau monde seasoning
½ tsp. paprika
⅛ tsp. dry mustard
¼ tsp. dry basil
Dash of Tabasco sauce
3 c. water
3 bouillon cubes

Melt butter in skillet; saute onion until light. brown. Blend in flour, beau monde, paprika, mustard, basil and Tabasco sauce. Gradually add water and bouillon cubes. Cook until mixture starts to boil Pour over chicken breasts. Bake at 300 to 325 degrees for 45 minutes or until tender.

Mary Ella Crozier, Elgin H. S.
Elgin, Texas

POTATO CHIP CHICKEN

1 4-oz. pkg. potato chips
¼ tsp. garlic salt
Dash of pepper
4 to 8 chicken breasts or legs or 1 2 ½ to 3-lb. broiler-fryer, cut up
½ c. melted butter

Crush potato chips with rolling pin before opening; mix chips with garlic salt and pepper on waxed paper. Dip chicken in melted butter; roll in potato chip crumbs. Place pieces on pan, skin-side up, so that they do not touch. Pour remaining butter and crumbs over chicken. Bake at 375 degrees for 1 hour. Do not turn chicken. Yield: 4-6 servings.

Joanne K. Peterson, Hayward H. S.
Hayward, Wisconsin

RUSSIAN CHICKEN BAKE

2 lge. chicken breasts, split into 4 pieces
Salt and pepper
4 tbsp. butter
1 lemon, cut in half
1 c. Russian dressing

Wash chicken; remove skin. Salt and pepper chicken lightly; arrange in a 9 x 6 x 2-inch baking pan, skin-side up. Place 1 tablespoonful butter on top of each piece. Squeeze lemon juice over chicken; pour Russian dressing over top. Cover pan with foil; bake at 350 degrees for 1 hour. Remove foil last 10 minutes of baking time. Yield: 4 servings.

Susan E. Connell, Rutherford H. S.
Panama City, Florida

STUFFED CHICKEN BREASTS

2 tbsp. chopped onion
2 tbsp. chopped celery
⅔ c. canned mushroom pieces
¾ c. butter, melted
¼ tsp. pepper
¾ tsp. salt
4 tbsp. lemon juice
½ c. chopped toasted almonds
6 fryer breasts, boned
1 ½ c. finely crushed potato chips
6 strips bacon

Saute onion, celery and mushrooms in 1/4 cup butter. Add pepper, 1/4 teaspoonful salt, lemon juice and almonds. Fill cavities of boned chicken breasts with stuffing. Close and fasten with skewers. Roll chicken in 1/4 cup melted butter, then in potato chips. Place in 13 x 9 x 2-inch pan, skewer-side down. Salt and place bacon strip on each breast. Bake at 350 degrees for 1 hour and 30 minutes or until tender. Yield: 6 servings.

Margaret Landis, Kutztown Area H. S.
Kutztown, Pennsylvania

STUFFED CHICKEN BREASTS

3 chicken breasts, boned and skinned
⅓ c. butter
¼ c. finely minced onion
4 c. coarse or fine bread crumbs or cubes
1 ½ to 2 c. poultry stuffing
½ c. chopped celery stalks and leaves
1 tsp. salt
⅛ tsp. pepper
1 tsp. dried sage, thyme or marjoram
Poultry seasoning to taste
Fat

Cut chicken breasts in halves. Pound each piece between heavy plastic wrap until wafer thin. Melt butter in heavy skillet; add onion and cook until yellow, stirring occasionally. Stir in part of crumbs. Heat, stirring to prevent excessive browning. Turn into deep bowl; mix in remaining ingredients. Mix lightly. For moist dressing, add just enough water to moisten crumbs. Place 2 tablespoonfuls dressing on each piece of chicken. Roll and wrap chicken around stuffing, securing ends with toothpicks. Brown in fat. Place in baking dish. Bake at 350 degrees for 1 hour and 15 minutes. Serve with packaged gravy, cream of mushroom soup or poultry sauce. Yield: 3-6 servings.

Mrs. Camille R. Cambier
Western Beaver H. S.
Industry, Pennsylvania

CALIFORNIA GLAZED CHICKEN WITH BISCUITS

½ c. sifted flour
1 tsp. salt
¼ tsp. pepper
1 3 to 3 ½-lb. fryer, cut up
½ c. shortening
⅔ c. orange marmalade
2 c. prepared biscuit mix
2 tsp. grated orange rind
⅔ c. orange juice

Combine flour, salt and pepper; coat chicken with flour mixture. Brown in hot shortening in heavy skillet. Cover; cook over low heat for 30 minutes or until tender. Place chicken in greased 11 3/4 x 7 1/2-inch baking dish. Spread orange marmalade over chicken, reservings 2 tablespoonfuls for biscuits. Combine biscuit mix, orange rind and orange juice. Roll out and cut into 1 1/2-inch rounds. Place around edge of chicken. Make a dent in top of each biscuit; fill with 1/2 teaspoonful marmalade. Bake at 425 degrees for 15 minutes or until biscuits are browned. Yield: 6 servings.

Marilyn Donnel, Pawnee Comm. H. S.
Pawnee, Illinois

CHICKEN AND BISCUITS

1 2 ½ to 3-lb. frying chicken, cut up
½ c. flour
2 tsp. salt
¼ tsp. pepper
1 tsp. paprika
¼ c. butter or margarine
1 10 ½-oz. can condensed cream of chicken or mushroom soup
½ c. milk
½ tsp. dill seed (opt.)
½ c. sliced olives
1 can biscuits

Roll chicken in mixture of flour, salt, pepper and paprika. Melt butter in 13 x 9-inch pan. Add chicken, skin-side down. Bake at 400 degrees for 40 minutes, turning chicken. Combine soup, milk, dill seed and sliced olives; pour over chicken. Place biscuits on top. Bake for 10 to 12 minutes or until biscuits are golden brown. Serve hot. Yield: 6 servings.

Mrs. Dorothy Smith
Palacios, Texas

CHICKEN CRUNCH

1 can cream of mushroom soup
¾ c. milk
1 tbsp. finely chopped onion or onion salt to taste
1 tbsp. chopped parsley
2 tbsp. melted butter or margarine
2 lb. chicken pieces
1 c. finely crushed packaged herb-seasoned stuffing or potato chips

Mix soup, milk, onion and parsley. Dip chicken into soup mixture; roll in stuffing. Place in shallow foil-lined 12 x 8 x 2-inch baking dish. Drizzle butter on chicken. Bake at 400 degrees for 1 hour. Heat remaining soup and milk; stirring occasionally. Serve over chicken. NOTE:

(Continued on next page)

One cup fine dry bread crumbs may be substituted for stuffing; add 1/2 teaspoonful poultry seasoning and 1/2 teaspoonful salt. Yield: 4-6 servings.

Mrs. Marion Ray, Dunlap Comm. School
Dunlap, Iowa
Mrs. Maude Anders, Winnfield H. S.
Winnfield, Louisiana
Mary Ellen Harrison, O.W. Best Jr. H. S.
Dearborn Heights, Michigan

CHICKEN DIABLE

1 3-lb. broiler-fryer, cut up
4 tbsp. butter
½ c. honey
¼ c. prepared mustard
1 tsp. salt
1 tsp. curry powder

Remove skin from chicken, if desired. Melt butter in shallow baking pan; stir in remaining ingredients. Roll chicken pieces in butter mixture to coat both sides; arrange, meaty-side up, in single layer in same pan. Bake at 375 degrees for 1 hour. Baste once during baking time, if desired. Yield: 4 servings.

Wilma Brereton Gross, Catalina H. S.
Tuscon, Arizona

CHICKEN FOR DIETERS

1 tsp. salt
⅛ tsp. pepper
1 tbsp. minced onion
1 tsp. powdered sage
1 tsp. chopped parsley
1 3-lb. fryer

Mix seasonings. Rub inside and outside of chicken with seasonings. Place in small roaster. Bake at 325 degrees for 2 hours to 2 hours and 30 minutes, adding small amount of water, if necessary. Yield: 6 servings.

Ruth E. Carlson, Donovan H. S.
Donovan, Illinois

CHICKEN FRICASSEE

1 4-lb. chicken, cut into serving pieces
½ c. flour
2 tsp. salt
½ tsp. paprika
1 can cream of chicken soup
1 ¼ c. milk

Dredge chicken pieces in mixture of flour, salt and paprika. Brown slowly in hot fat. Place chicken in casserole; add mixture of chicken soup and milk. Bake in preheated 325 degree oven for 1 hour or until fork tender. Serve hot using liquid as gravy. Yield: 5 servings.

Mrs. Mavis Tom, Saline H. S.
Saline, Louisiana

CHICKEN MARENGO

1 chicken, cut up
Salt and pepper
Paprika
¼ c. salad oil
¼ c. chopped mushrooms
¼ c. chopped onion
1 clove of garlic, crushed
¼ c. Sherry
½ c. canned tomatoes
1 ½ c. Espagnole sauce

Season chicken with salt, pepper and paprika; saute in oil until brown. Place chicken in casserole. Saute mushrooms, onion and garlic; add to casserole. Add remaining ingredients. Bake, uncovered, at 375 degrees for 1 hour.

ESPAGNOLE SAUCE:

1 lb. beef shank, cut up
1 carrot, cut up
1 onion, cut up
1 stalk celery, cut up
½ c. salad oil
½ c. flour
1 tsp. salt
⅛ tsp. pepper
1 sm. bay leaf
1 c. canned tomatoes
2 qt. water

Brown shanks and vegetables in oil. Add flour and mix well. Add salt, pepper, bay leaf, tomatoes and water. Stir and simmer for 2 hours. Strain. Yield: 4 servings.

L. G. MacVicar
Senator Patrick Burns Jr. H. S.
Calgary, Alberta, Canada

CHICKEN WITH LEMON SAUCE

SAUCE:

1 tbsp. soy sauce
½ tsp. salt

(Continued on next page)

½ tsp. pepper
¼ c. salad oil
½ c. lemon juice
2 tbsp. grated lemon peel
1 clove of garlic, crushed

Combine all sauce ingredients; mix well. Refrigerate for at least 1 hour.

FRIED CHICKEN:

½ c. flour
1 tsp. salt
¼ tsp. pepper
2 tsp. paprika
1 2½ to 3-lb. broiler-fryer, cut up
½ c. butter or margarine, melted

Combine flour, salt, pepper and paprika; coat chicken in mixture. Arrange chicken, skin-side down, in single layer in shallow pan. Brush chicken well with butter. Bake, uncovered, at 400 degrees for 30 minutes. Turn; pour sauce over chicken. Bake 30 minutes longer or until chicken is tender. Yield: 4 servings.

Mrs. Judith R. Wisley, Booneville H. S.
Booneville, Arkansas

CHICKEN MARINARA

MARINARA SAUCE:

1 clove of garlic, minced
¼ c. chopped onion
2 tbsp. oil
1 14½-oz. can tomato puree
1 tsp. salt
½ tsp. oregano
¼ tsp. basil
2 tsp. minced parsley

Saute garlic and onion in 2 tablespoonfuls oil; add tomato puree and seasonings. Simmer, uncovered, for 15 minutes.

CHICKEN:

¼ c. butter
Salt and pepper
Flour
1 3 to 3½-lb. fryer, cut up
1 ¾ c. Marinara Sauce
1 tsp. chopped dill weed
⅓ c. grated Parmesan cheese

Melt butter in 9 x 13 x 2-inch pan. Season and flour chicken lightly. Place chicken, skin-side up, in pan. Bake at 450 degrees for 30 to 40 minutes. Combine Marinara sauce with dill weed and spoon over chicken. Top with cheese. Bake at 350 degrees for 30 minutes longer. Yield: 4 servings.

Mrs. Linda Magnuson, Hyre Jr. H. S.
Akron, Ohio

CHICKEN-MUSHROOM A LA NOEL

2 tbsp. butter or margarine
4 tbsp. flour
1 c. evaporated milk
1 c. chicken broth
½ tsp. poultry seasoning
1 tsp. salt
1 3-lb. chicken, stewed and cut into pieces
1 7-oz. can mushrooms
1 c. crushed Rice Krispies

Melt butter or margarine in a heavy saucepan; add flour, milk and broth. Stir and heat until sauce is thickened; add seasonings, chicken pieces and mushrooms. Place in buttered 1-quart casserole; top with crushed Rice Crispies. Bake at 375 degrees for 30 minutes. Note: Casserole may be prepared ahead of time and stored in refrigerator or freezer until needed. If stored in refrigerator, allow 45 minutes in oven. If frozen, allow 1 hour in oven. Yield: 6 servings.

Mrs. D. Jean Zook, Miami Palmetto H. S.
Miami, Florida

CHICKEN ORIENTAL

¼ c. cooking oil
¼ c. soy sauce
¼ c. vinegar
¼ c. dry wine
1 3 to 3½-lb. frying chicken, cut up
Pepper

Mix oil, soy sauce, vinegar and wine. Marinate chicken pieces in mixture for 1 hour, turning pieces over once. Sprinkle pieces with pepper; place in single layer in large baking dish. Pour sauce over chicken. Bake, uncovered, at 325 degrees for 1 hour or until tender. Yield: 4 servings.

Mrs. Emma Lou Leftwich, Mt. Pleasant H. S.
Mt. Pleasant, Texas

CHICKEN IN ORANGE SAUCE

1 2-lb. fryer, cut up
Flour
1 c. cooking oil
⅓ c. chopped onion
¼ c. water
½ 6-oz. can frozen orange juice concentrate

Coat chicken with flour; brown in oil, turning occasionally. Place chicken in a 1 1/2-quart casserole. Brown onions in skillet; add water. Cook and stir to loosen all browned particles. Remove from heat; stir in orange juice concentrate. Pour over chicken in casserole. Cover and bake at 350 degrees for 30 to 45 minutes. NOTE: May be cooked in an electric skillet. Yield: 4-6 servings.

Mrs. Ginny S. Melton, Hermleigh H. S.
Hermleigh, Texas

CHICKEN PAPRIKA

1 2 to 2 ½-lb. chicken
½ c. salad oil
½ c. flour
1 ½ tsp. salt
¼ tsp. pepper
1 tbsp. paprika

Cut chicken into four serving pieces; discard back, neck and giblets. Combine oil, flour, salt, pepper and paprika; dip each chicken piece into mixture. Drain. Place in baking dish. Bake at 400 degrees for 1 hour. Yield: 4 servings.

Frances H. Judy, Richwood H. S.
Richwood, West Virginia

CHICKEN SUPREME

1 fryer, cut into serving pieces
Salt and pepper
2 cans cream of mushroom soup
1 c. milk

Place chicken in baking dish; season with salt and pepper. Cover with aluminum foil; bake at 350 degrees for 20 minutes. Turn chicken; cover and continue baking for 20 minutes. Add soup diluted with milk; bake, uncovered, for 20 minutes.

Mrs. Evelyn Piper, Minnewaukan H. S.
Minnewaukan, North Dakota

CHICKEN-STUFFED CASSEROLE

4 to 6 chicken legs and thighs
3 chicken bouillon cubes
¾ c. water
1 lge. onion, chopped
½ green pepper, chopped
¾ c. diced celery
1 pkg. prepared dressing
1 can chicken gravy or onion sauce

Brown chicken in fat or drippings in Dutch oven. Arrange pieces around side of Dutch oven, using rack to keep chicken from sticking. Dissolve bouillon cubes in the water; bring to boil. Add onion, green pepper and celery. Simmer for 10 minutes. Add to dressing, a spoonful at a time. Toss with fork until all crumbs are moist. Place dressing in center of Dutch oven. Pour gravy over chicken and dressing. Add enough water to reach top of rack. Bake at 325 degrees for 1 hour and 10 minutes. Yield: 4-6 servings.

Betty G. Quick, Barrington H. S.
Barrington, Illinois

CHICKEN TONAKHOKNENLLI

¼ lb. butter or margarine
2 2-lb. chickens
1 lge. onion, chopped
½ c. Sherry
½ c. tomato juice
1 tsp. paprika
1 tsp. salt
Pepper to taste
1 c. water

Melt butter in frying pan; add chickens. Braise until light brown; remove chicken from frying pan. Place in baking pan. Saute onion in remaining butter in pan; add remaining ingredients. Pour over chicken. Bake at 400 degrees for 30 minutes. Turn and bake for 30 minutes longer. Turn again and bake for 15 minutes longer. Yield: 4-6 servings.

Mrs. Estelle Greene, Yreka H. S.
Yreka, California

CHICKEN IN WINE SAUCE

1 stick margarine, melted
½ c. chopped green onions
¼ c. chopped parsley
1 tsp. paprika
3 tsp. salt
1 c. dry white wine
¼ c. lemon juice
1 sm. can mushrooms (opt.)
2 chickens, cut up

Mix all ingredients except chicken in a roaster or large pan. Place chicken, skin-side down, in sauce. Bake, uncovered, at 375 degrees for 1 hour. Turn chicken; bake for 30 minutes longer. Increase heat to 450 degrees; bake for 30 minutes, basting several times. Serve over rice. Yield: 8-10 servings.

Mrs. Dorothy E. Perryman, Alpine H. S.
Alpine, Texas

CRUSTY HERB-FRIED CHICKEN

1 3 to 3 ½-lb. chicken, cut into serving pieces
½ tsp. thyme
½ tsp. marjoram
¾ to 1 c. flour
¾ c. fat or salad oil
½ tsp. rosemary
1 tbsp. minced parsley
½ tsp. salt
¼ tsp. pepper
¾ c. water

Sprinkle chicken with thyme and marjoram; let stand for 30 minutes to 1 hour. Roll in flour; fry in hot fat or salad oil just long enough to brown on both sides. Remove; place in baking pan. Sprinkle with rosemary, parsley, salt and pepper. Pour water into frying pan and stir thoroughly. Pour liquid over chicken. Bake at 375 degrees for 40 to 45 minutes. Yield: 4-5 servings.

Mrs. Richard Comtois, Bellows Falls H. S.
Bellows Falls, Vermont

CORN-CRISP CHICKEN

4 chicken leg quarters
2 chicken breasts, halved
½ c. evaporated milk
1 ½ tsp. salt
¼ tsp. pepper
1 c. corn flake crumbs

Dip chicken into milk; roll in seasoned crumbs. Place chicken, skin-side up, in a shallow foil-lined baking pan. Do not crowd. Bake in a 350 degree preheated oven for 1 hour. Yield: 6-8 servings.

Mary Ida Hoffman, Meridean H. S.
Meridean, Mississippi

EASY BAKED CHICKEN

Salt to taste
1 2 to 3-lb. fryer, cut up
¾ c. cream of celery soup
¾ c. cream of mushroom soup

Salt chicken to taste. Place pieces, skin-side up, in lightly buttered 9 x 12-inch dish. Do not overlap pieces. Combine soups; brush soup mixture on chicken. Bake at 300 degrees for 45 to 50 minutes. Yield: 6 servings.

Mrs. C. T. Spigner, Foreman H. S.
Foreman, Arkansas

EASY OVEN CHICKEN

1 fryer, cut up
3 tbsp. butter or margarine
½ tsp. salt
2 tbsp. flour
¼ c. water
2 tsp. marjoram

Rub chicken with butter. Place in aluminum foil-lined casserole or baking pan. Sprinkle with salt, flour, water and marjoram. Bake at 350 degrees for 1 hour, basting frequently with drippings from pan. Yield: 4-6 servings.

Mrs. Ruth Schaffer, Annville-Cleona H. S.
Annville, Pennsylvania

BAKED CHICKEN WITH PINEAPPLE

½ c. flour
1 tsp. salt
1 tsp. celery salt
¼ tsp. garlic salt
¼ tsp. nutmeg
2 2 to 3-lb. fryers, cut into serving pieces
Butter or oil
1 20-oz. can sliced pineapple
½ c. soy sauce
2 tbsp. sugar

Combine flour, salt, celery salt, garlic salt and nutmeg in paper bag, shaking to mix. Shake several chicken pieces at a time in flour mixture. Brown chicken pieces slowly and evenly in melted butter in skillet, adding more butter if necessary. Transfer browned chicken to 3-quart casserole or baking dish. Drain pineapple, reserving 1 cup syrup. Combine pineapple syrup with soy sauce and sugar; pour over chicken. Cover and bake in preheated 350 degree oven for 1 hour or until chicken is tender, basting with juices occasionally. Saute pineapple slices in butter; serve with chicken. Yield: 6-8 servings.

Reba Wortham, Marlow H. S.
Marlow, Oklahoma

CHICKEN NORMANDY

1 3-lb. broiler-fryer chicken
1 tsp. salt
4 tbsp. melted butter
3 golden Delicious apples, peeled and cut into 8 pieces
1 c. heavy cream
1 ½ tsp. lemon juice
1 pkg. dehydrated scallopini sauce mix
¼ c. water
Chopped parsley

Sprinkle chicken with salt. Brown chicken pieces in melted butter. Remove chicken to an ungreased casserole. Lightly brown apples in pan drippings. Add apples to chicken. Blend heavy cream with lemon juice and scallopini sauce mix blended with water. Pour cream mixture over chicken. Cover casserole; bake at 350 degrees for 45 minutes. Sprinkle chicken with chopped parsley and serve. Yield: 4-5 servings.

Mrs. Juanita Finlayson, Morningside H. S.
Inglewood, California

ORANGE-BAKED CHICKEN

⅓ c. flour
1 tsp. salt
⅛ tsp. pepper
1 2 to 2 ½-lb. fryer or broiler, cut up
⅓ c. shortening
½ tsp. celery seed
½ c. diced onion
¾ c. fresh orange juice
1 orange

Mix flour, salt and pepper in bag. Place chicken in bag and shake to coat. Heat shortening in frying pan; add chicken. Sprinkle with celery seed. Brown on both sides over low to medium heat. Place chicken in greased casserole. Cook onion in frying pan until tender. Add orange juice; bring to a boil. Pour over chicken. Cut orange into eight wedges; arrange around edge of casserole. Cover and bake at 350 degrees until chicken is tender, about 1 hour. Yield: 4 servings.

Mrs. Stanley MacDonald
Guysboro Municipal H. S.
Guysboro, Nova Scotia, Canada

HAWAIIAN CHICKEN

1 2 ½-lb. fryer
¼ c. butter
1 No. 2 can pineapple chunks
2 tbsp. brown sugar
1 tsp. ginger
1 8-oz. can tomato sauce
Dash of salt
¾ c. chicken broth

Brown chicken in the butter; pour off grease. Drain pineapple, reserving 1/2 cup juice. Combine pineapple juice, brown sugar, ginger, tomato sauce, salt and chicken broth; add to browned chicken. Cover and bake at 350 degrees for 20 minutes. Add pineapple chunks and bake, uncovered, for 1 hour. Yield: 6 servings.

Sarah Yates, Hiawatha H. S.
Hiawatha, Kansas

POLYNESIAN BAKED CHICKEN

2 fryers, cut up
1 c. flour
1 tsp. seasoned salt
½ lb. butter or margarine
1 c. diluted frozen orange juice
2 tbsp. lemon juice
½ c. brown sugar
1 tbsp. soy sauce
½ tsp. salt
1 tbsp. cornstarch
2 c. fresh papaya, cubed

Shake chicken parts in paper bag with flour and seasoned salt. Melt margarine, rubbing 2 tablespoonfuls into a large baking dish. Place chicken in dish, brushing remaining fat over each piece. Bake in preheated 350 degree oven for 50 minutes or until crusty brown. Combine juices, brown sugar, soy sauce, salt and cornstarch in a saucepan; bring to a boil, stirring constantly. Remove from heat when clear and thickened. Add papaya. Pour mixture over browned chicken, coating each piece. Bake for 10 minutes longer. Garnish with chopped parsley or a mixture of finely chopped green pepper and sesame seed, if desired. Yield: 8 servings.

Sister Mary Benedict Beehler, O. S. B.
Mount St. Benedict Academy
Crookston, Minnesota

GOLDEN CHICKEN

3 tbsp. butter
1 3 ½-lb. fryer
1 sm. onion
1 tsp. Worcestershire sauce
1 can cream of mushroom soup

Butter roaster on baking dish. Add remaining butter to chicken. Slice onion into dish; place chicken over onion. Mix Worcestershire sauce and mushroom soup; pour over chicken. Bake at 325 degrees for 2 hours. Yield: 6 servings.

Arlene Black, Souk Prairie H. S.
Prairie du Sac, Wisconsin

GOLDEN CHICKEN BAKE

2 lb. chicken pieces
2 tbsp. melted butter or margarine
1 can cream of chicken, celery, vegetable or mushroom soup
1 tbsp. minced parsley

Arrange chicken, skin-side down, in shallow baking dish. Drizzle butter over chicken. Bake at 400 degrees for 20 minutes. Turn chicken; bake for 20 minutes longer. Pour soup over chicken; sprinkle parsley on top. Bake for 20 minutes longer. NOTE: Cream of vegetable, mushroom or Cheddar cheese soup may be used. Yield: 4-6 servings.

Melba M. Hackett, Henrico H. S.
Richmond, Virginia
Mrs. H. A. Hollman, Kenedy H. S.
Kenedy, Texas

HERB-GLAZED CHICKEN

1 3-lb. fryer, cut into serving pieces
Melted margarine
1 ½ tsp. salt
¼ tsp. pepper
¼ tsp. marjoram
1 tsp. grated lemon rind
Juice of 1 lemon
½ c. dark corn syrup
¼ c. water

Brown chicken in melted margarine in large skillet. Sprinkle with seasonings. Blend lemon rind, lemon juice, corn syrup and water; pour over chicken. Bake at 350 for 45 minutes or until chicken is tender. Yield: 4 servings.

Mrs. Dorothy S. Bienski, Waller H. S.
Waller, Texas

JUG CHICKEN

1 chicken, cut up
1 ½ tsp. salt
½ tsp. pepper

Sprinkle chicken with salt and pepper. Place in covered casserole. Bake at 350 degrees for 30 minutes. Reduce heat to 250 degrees; cook for 1 hour. Yield: 4-6 servings.

Mrs. Martha Berryhill, Corner H. S.
Warrior, Alabama

HONEY CHICKEN

1 2 ½ to 3-lb. fryer, cut up
½ tsp. garlic powder
2 tsp. salt
¼ tsp. pepper
1 egg, separated
1 ½ tbsp. honey
4 tbsp. butter or margarine

Rub chicken with mixture of garlic, salt and pepper. Beat egg yolk with honey and one-half of butter; brush over chicken. Place, skin-side up, in greased baking dish. Bake at 325 degrees for 45 minutes to 1 hour, basting with remaining butter. Just before serving, turn and brown for 10 to 15 minutes. Yield: 5 servings.

Mrs. Irene J. Hodges, Camp Laboratory
Cullowhee, North Carolina

LEMONED CHICKEN

2 chickens, quartered
2 fresh lemons
⅔ c. flour
1 tbsp. salt
1 tsp. paprika
½ c. shortening or oil
4 tbsp. brown sugar
2 c. chicken broth or bouillon
1 tbsp. Angostura aromatic bitters

Wash chicken and dry well. Cut 1 lemon in half; squeeze over each chicken piece. Combine flour, salt and paprika in paper bag. Coat chicken by shaking pieces, one at a time, in the bag. Brown chicken parts slowly in shortening or oil. Arrange chicken in baking dish or Dutch oven. Thinly slice remaining lemon and place in layer over chicken. Dissolve brown sugar in chicken broth; add Angostura bitters. Pour over chicken. Cover and bake at 375 degrees or simmer over very low flame until chicken is tender, about 1 hour. Serve hot with juice. Yield: 8 servings.

Photograph for recipe on front cover.

BAKED CHICKEN LOAF

1 4-lb. hen
2 c. soft bread crumbs
1 tbsp. minced parsley
1 pimento, chopped
½ tsp. salt
¼ tsp. pepper
1 c. milk
2 eggs
2 tbsp. melted butter or margarine

Cook hen until tender. Remove meat from bones and finely chop. Mix chicken, 1 3/4 cups bread crumbs, minced parsley, pimento, salt, pepper, milk and eggs. Stir in melted butter of margarine. Place mixture in a loaf pan or oblong baking dish; sprinkle remaining bread crumbs over top. Bake at 325 degrees for 45 minutes. Cut into squares and serve. Serve with hot mushroom sauce. Yield: 8 servings.

Mrs. R. S. Clark, Troup H. S.
LaGrange, Georgia

CHICKEN LOAF

1 4-lb. chicken or hen
3 c. bread crumbs
1 c. cooked rice
3 c. broth
4 eggs, beaten
1 sm. can pimento
1 ½ tbsp. Worcestershire sauce
¼ tsp. Tabasco sauce
Dash of red pepper
Salt to taste
1 sm. onion, chopped

Boil chicken; remove meat from bones. Add remaining ingredients. Place in buttered pan; cook in pan of hot water at 325 degrees for about 45 minutes to 1 hour. Serve with mushroom sauce. Yield: 12 servings.

Sheron Ann Weinberg, Ramer H. S.
Ramer, Tennessee

OVEN-BAKED CHICKEN

1 fryer, split in half lengthwise
Salt and pepper
3 tbsp. melted butter
Juice of 1 lemon

Place aluminum foil in shallow baking pan, leaving enough on sides and ends for wrapping chicken. Sprinkle chicken with salt and pepper. Brush with melted butter and lemon juice. Place chicken on foil, skin-side up. Pour on remaining lemon juice. Wrap in foil; bake at 350 degrees for 1 hour and 30 minutes. Open foil 20 minutes before end of baking period to brown chicken. If desired, giblet gravy may be made by chopping giblets and neck and heating in liquid from chicken. Yield: 4 servings.

Mrs. Mary Belle Nutt, Cotulla H. S.
Cotulla, Texas

OVEN CHICKEN

1 2 to 3-lb. fryer
1 can cream of chicken soup
1 can chicken and rice soup
Chicken broth

Place chicken pieces in baking pan; do not stack. Add soups. Bake at 250 to 300 degrees for 3 hours, basting with broth. Serve hot with gravy, if desired. Yield: 4-5 servings.

May Lohmann, Miami H. S.
Miami, Oklahoma

PARTY PERFECT CHICKEN

6 tbsp. flour
1 ½ tsp. salt
1 tsp. ginger
2 fryers, quartered
6 to 8 tbsp. butter

Combine flour, salt and ginger in paper bag. Add chicken and coat well. Melt butter in pan. Dip chicken in butter and place, skin-side up, in baking pan. Bake, uncovered, at 400 degrees for 20 minutes.

CURRY GLAZE:

½ c. chopped onion
6 slices bacon, finely diced
2 tbsp. flour
1 tbsp. curry powder
1 tbsp. sugar
1 can condensed beef broth
2 tbsp. coconut
2 tbsp. applesauce
2 tbsp. catsup
2 tbsp. lemon juice

Mix ingredients in a saucepan; bring to a boil. Spoon one-half of glaze over chicken. Bake for 20 minutes. Add remaining glaze and cook for 20 minutes longer. Serve with cooked rice, if desired. Yield: 6-8 servings.

Mrs. Barbara Robinson, Glenn Voc. H. S.
Birmingham, Alabama
Jackie Kimberling, Bellevue H. S.
Bellevue, Washington

CHICKEN AND SPAGHETTI

1 5-lb. hen
1 lge. onion, chopped
1 bunch celery, chopped
1 lge. green pepper, chopped
3 garlic buttons, chopped
1 can mushrooms
Chicken fat
1 can cream of mushroom soup
1 can tomato soup
4 bay leaves
1 lb. spaghetti
1 to 1 ½ qt. chicken broth
¾ lb. Velveeta cheese

Cook, bone and cube chicken. Saute onion, celery, pepper, garlic and mushrooms in chicken fat. Add soups, bay leaves and chicken. Cook spaghetti for 6 minutes and drain; add to chicken mixture. Stir in broth. Cook in covered roaster at 250 degrees for 1 hour and 30 minutes. Stir in cheese; cook for 1 hour. Remove bay leaves; ganish with additional cheese. NOTE: May be frozen. Yield: 24 servings.

Mrs. Wana Miller, Seymour H. S.
Seymour, Texas

CHICKEN TETRAZZINI

1 2 ½ lb. chicken, quartered
Salt to taste
1 sm. can mushrooms, drained and thinly sliced
2 tbsp. butter
½ lb. Italian spaghetti, broken into small pieces
2 tbsp. flour
1 c. heavy cream
3 tbsp. Sherry wine
Grated Parmesan cheese

Simmer chicken in boiling salted water until tender. Cool in broth; shred chicken into fine pieces. Return skin and bones to broth. Cover and bring broth to boiling point. Simmer for 45 minutes. Uncover and boil vigorously for 10 to 15 minutes or until liquid is reduced to 2 cups. Strain broth. Saute mushrooms in butter over moderate heat until lightly browned. Cook spaghetti in large amount of boiling salted water for 15 minutes or until tender. Melt butter; stir in flour. Gradually add chicken broth, stirring until smooth and boiling point is reached. Stir in heavy cream and dry Sherry wine. Add shredded chicken to one-half the sauce; add spaghetti and mushrooms to remaining sauce. Place spaghetti mixture in baking dish; make a hole in center. Pour chicken mixture into center; sprinkle with cheese. Bake at 350 degrees for 10 minutes or until lightly browned. Yield: 6-8 servings.

Christine C. Risher, Noxubee Co. H. S.
Macon, Mississippi

QUICK CHICKEN STROGANOFF

2 ½ to 3 lb. thighs and legs
2 tbsp. butter
1 clove of garlic, minced
¼ c. minced onion
1 tsp. salt
⅛ tsp. pepper
1 8-oz. can tomato sauce
1 c. sour cream
1 4-oz. can mushrooms
1 8-oz. pkg. noodles

Brown chicken lightly in butter; push to one side. Add garlic and onion; cook until lightly browned and tender. Sprinkle with salt and pepper. Pour tomato sauce into bowl; add sour cream gradually, stirring to combine. Pour over chicken. Simmer, covered for 30 minutes or until tender, turning and basting once. Prepare noodles according to direction on package. Garnish chicken with drained and heated mushrooms; serve with hot noodles. Yield: 6 servings.

Mrs. Dalpha Boley, Splendora H. S.
Splendora, Texas

MAMIE'S CHICKEN PIE

1 lge. fryer or sm. hen
4 to 5 c. flour

(Continued on next page)

½ c. shortening
2 eggs
1 tsp. salt
1 c. cold water
1 pt. milk
Pepper to taste

Boil chicken until tender. Remove meat from bones; spread in 13 x 9 x 2-inch pan. Sift flour into large bowl. Make a well in center of flour; add shortening, eggs, salt and water. Mix until moistened. Roll out on well floured board. Cut part of dough into small pieces; drop into boiling chicken broth. Cook until done. Add milk; season with pepper. Pour dumpling mixture over chicken. Roll out remaining dough to fit pan; place over chicken mixture. Brush with butter; bake at 400 to 425 degrees until brown. Yield: 8-10 servings.

Beulah E. Grimes, Taylorsville H. S.
Taylorsville, Mississippi

CHICKEN IN FOIL

1 2½ to 3-lb. fryer, cut up
1 stick margarine
1 jar cocktail onions
1 can mushrooms
Dash of parsley
Dash of paprika
2 tbsp. light cream
1 tbsp. Sherry
3 c. cooked rice

Brown chicken in margarine; remove chicken. Brown onions and mushrooms in same skillet. Place chicken on heavy foil; add parsley, paprika, cream and Sherry. If too dry, add liquid from mushrooms. Add onions and mushrooms. Fold foil tightly. Bake at 425 degrees for 1 hour. Unfold foil; add rice. Yield: 6 servings.

Frances Stewart, Bowie H. S.
Bowie, Texas

CHICKEN AND RICE

1 c. uncooked rice
2 c. clear chicken broth
4 chicken pieces
½ pkg. dry onion soup mix
1 can cream of mushroom soup
Few grains paprika

Spread rice on bottom of buttered 9 1/2-inch square glass baking dish; add chicken broth. Place pieces of unseasoned chicken on top; sprinkle with onion soup mix. Spread with mushroom soup; sprinkle with paprika. Bake, uncovered, at 325 degrees for 1 hour and 30 minutes. Cover and bake for 30 minutes longer. Yield: 4 servings.

Mrs. June C. McIsaac
Hampton Twp. Jr.-Sr. H. S.
Allison Park, Pennsylvania

CHICKEN WITH RICE

1 chicken or 3 breasts and 3 thighs
1 can onion soup
1 can cream of mushroom soup
1 to 1 ½ soup cans water
1 c. rice
¼ tsp. salt
½ tsp. pepper

Brown chicken; add remaining ingredients. Bake, covered, at 350 degrees for 35 to 45 minutes. Uncover; bake for 35 to 45 minutes longer. Yield: 6 servings.

Sylvia Benson, Grant Union H, S.
John Day, Oregon

CHICKEN STUFFED WITH RICE

1 6-oz. can cream of mushroom soup
1 c. chicken broth
1 c. instant rice
1 tsp. salt or to taste
¼ c. butter or margarine
2 3-lb. broiler-fryers
2 tbsp. thinly slivered orange peel
¼ c. orange juice
½ c. light corn syrup
¼ tsp. ginger
½ tsp. monosodium glutamate

Combine mushroom soup, broth, rice, salt and margarine in covered saucepan; cook according to package directions for rice. Let stand for 15 minutes or until rice is fluffy. Fill cavities of fryers with rice mixture; place fryers, breast-side up, in an 8 x 11-inch baking dish or pan. Place remaining rice mixture around fryers. Bake at 375 degrees for 1 hour and 30 minutes. Combine remaining ingredients; brush chickens with glaze. Bake for 15 minutes longer. Let set for a few minutes before carving.

Mrs. Alice Hansberger, Canton H. S.
Canton, Illinois

STUART CHICKEN

3 chickens, cut up
2 tbsp. poultry seasoning
1 ½ tsp. salt
1 tsp. pepper
¼ lb. margarine, melted
2 ¼ c. water
2 tbsp. flour

Arrange chicken, skin-side up, in baking pan. Sprinkle poultry seasoning, salt and pepper over each piece. Pour melted margarine over skin of chicken. Cook, uncovered, at 450 degrees for 45 minutes or until skin is brown and brittle. Pour 2 cups of water in bottom of pan.

(Continued on next page)

Reduce heat to 300 degrees for 30 minutes or until chicken is tender. Remove chicken from pan. Pour flour diluted with 1/4 cup water into boiling juice of chicken for gravy. Yield: 15 servings.

Angela A. Lubert, Stuart Co. Day School
Princeton, New Jersey

EASY CHICKEN AND RICE

½ to 1 c. rice
1 can onion soup (opt.)
1 c. or soup can water
1 fryer, cut into quarters or pieces
Salt and pepper to taste (opt.)
1 can cream of celery or chicken soup

Sprinkle rice over bottom of baking pan; pour onion soup over rice. Add water. Wash and dry chicken; sprinkle with salt and pepper. Place over rice. Spread cream of celery soup over chicken. Bake, uncovered, at 325 to 350 degrees for 1 hour to 1 hour and 30 minutes. Add water as necessary to keep moist. NOTE: Curry powder may be added. Yield: 4 servings.

Mrs. Larry D. Schmidt, Velva H. S.
Velva, North Dakota
Mrs. J. B. Morris, Gooding H. S.
Gooding, Idaho
Mrs. Jeanne C. Hinton, Mainland Jr. H. S.
Daytona Beach, Florida

BAKED CHICKEN AND GRAVY

3 to 3 ½ lb. frying chicken pieces
¼ c. flour
¼ c. melted butter
1 1-lb. can whole onions, drained
¼ lb. sliced mushrooms
⅔ c. evaporated milk
1 10 ½-oz. can cream of mushroom soup
1 c. grated American cheese
½ tsp. salt
⅛ tsp. pepper
Dash of paprika

Coat chicken with flour. Arrange, skin-side down, in single layer in melted butter in 13 x 9 x 2-inch baking dish. Bake, uncovered, at 425 degrees for 30 minutes. Turn chicken; bake for 15 to 20 minutes or until brown and tender. Remove from oven; reduce temperature to 325 degrees. Pour off excess fat. Add onions and mushrooms to chicken. Combine undiluted milk, soup, cheese, salt and pepper. Pour over chicken; sprinkle with paprika. Cover with foil; return to oven. Bake for 15 to 30 minutes. Yield: 6 servings.

Mrs. Rebecca B. Johnson
North Chattanooga Jr. H. S.
Chattanooga, Tennessee
Mrs. Ernestine Scott, Eminence H. S.
Eminence, Kentucky

BURGUNDY CHICKEN

1 2 ½-lb. broiler-fryer, quartered
6 slices bacon
2 tbsp. butter
8 sm. white onions
1 8-oz. can whole mushrooms
⅔ c. sliced green onions
1 clove of garlic
2 tbsp. flour
1 tsp. salt
⅛ tsp. pepper
¼ tsp. dryed thyme leaves
2 c. Burgundy
1 c. canned chicken broth
8 sm. new potatoes
Chopped parsley

Wash and dry chicken. Saute bacon until crisp in a Dutch oven over medium heat. Add butter to bacon drippings; heat. Brown chicken well on all sides in hot fat; remove when browned. Set aside. Pour off all but 2 tablespoonfuls fat; add whole onions, mushrooms, green onions and garlic to Dutch oven. Cook, covered, over low heat for 10 minutes, stirring occasionally. Remove from heat; stir in flour, salt, pepper and thyme leaves. Gradually add Burgundy and chicken broth; bring mixture to a boil, stirring. Remove from heat. Add potatoes, chicken and bacon to Dutch oven; mix well. Cover; refrigerate overnight. Bake in preheated 400 degree oven for 1 hour and 50 minutes or until chicken and potatoes are tender. Sprinkle top with parsley before serving. Yield: 4 servings.

Mary Louise Alms, Meeteetse H. S.
Meeteetse, Wyoming

COUNTRY CAPTAIN

Flour
2 frying chickens
2 onions, finely chopped
2 green peppers, chopped
½ tsp. white pepper
1 tsp. salt
2 tsp. curry powder
2 cans tomatoes
½ tsp. chopped parsley
½ tsp. thyme
2 c. dry cooked rice
2 tbsp. currants
¼ lb. roasted almonds

Season chicken; roll in flour. Fry and remove to large roaster. Cook onions and peppers slowly in fat; stir constantly. Season with white pepper, salt, curry powder, tomatoes, parsley and thyme. Cover chicken with tomato mixture, adding water if needed. Cover roaster tightly. Bake at 350 degrees for 45 minutes or until chicken is tender. Place chicken in center of platter; surround with rice. Drop currants into tomato mixture; pour over rice and chicken. Scatter almonds over top of rice. Garnish with parsley and serve. Yield: 8-10 servings.

Mrs. Jean Morris, Central H. S.
Florence, Alabama

SPANISH-STYLE CHICKEN

1 chicken, cut up
1 lemon, sliced
1 c. sliced carrots
2 sm. cans tomato sauce
2 tbsp. brown sugar
Salt and pepper
4 tbsp. bacon drippings or lard

Salt and pepper chicken. Brown pieces in bacon drippings; place in shallow baking dish with ingredients. Bake at 350 degrees for 1 hour and 30 minutes or until tender, adding water if necessary. Yield: 4 servings.

Mrs. J. E. Simbeck, Mancos Schools
Mancos, Colorado

WORKING GIRL'S CHICKEN

4 whole chicken legs
4 whole chicken breasts
1 tsp. salt
½ tsp. pepper
⅛ tsp. garlic powder
1 can cream of mushroom soup
1 soup can milk

Season chicken with salt, pepper and a small amount of garlic powder. Dilute soup with milk. Place chicken in buttered casserole or baking dish; cover with diluted soup. Bake at 400 degrees for 1 hour or until tender.

Mrs. Mercer Clementson, East Ridge H. S.
Chattanooga, Tennessee

BROILED CHICKEN WITH RICE STUFFING

½ c. raw rice
1 egg, beaten
½ tsp. poultry seasoning
½ tsp. salt
Parsley
Marjoram
1 2 to 2 ½-lb. broiler
Oil
4 strips bacon

Cook rice according to package directions. Add egg, poultry seasoning, salt, parsley and marjoram. Brush skin of chicken with cooking oil. Place chicken, skin-side up, on broiler rack; broil 3 inches from heat for 10 minutes. Turn chicken; fill with rice stuffing and broil 5 inches from heat for 10 minutes longer. Place 2 strips of bacon on each chicken half; broil for 5 minutes or until bacon is brown and crisp. Yield: 2 servings.

Mrs. Lillian P. Dunbar, Abington H. S.
North Abington, Massachusetts

BROILED MARINATED CHICKEN

⅔ c. corn oil
⅓ c. vinegar
1 tsp. salt
¼ tsp. pepper
¼ tsp. thyme
¼ tsp. marjoram
1 clove of garlic, sliced
1 broiler-fryer, halved

Combine oil, vinegar, salt, pepper, thyme, marjoram and garlic in shallow dish. Add chicken; cover and refrigerate for at least 3 hours, turning frequently. Line inside of broiler pan with aluminum foil; grease rack lightly. Remove chicken from marinade; place, skin-side down, on rack in pan. Set pan under broiler so top of chicken is about 5 inches from heat. Broil chicken at 500 degrees for 55 minutes or until brown and tender, basting frequently with marinade and turning once. Yield: 2 servings.

Photograph for this recipe on page 135

CHICKEN CROQUETTE

1 4 ½-lb. hen, cooked
4 hard-cooked eggs
1 sm. can mushrooms, cut into small pieces
6 tbsp. butter or margarine
6 tbsp. flour
1 c. milk
1 c. chicken stock without fat
Salt
Red pepper
2 c. bread crumbs
2 eggs, beaten

Cool hen; cut into small pieces, discarding fat. Push eggs through sieve. Add mushrooms. Melt margarine; gradually stir in flour. Add milk, stock and 1 teaspoonful salt. Cook until thickened. Combine cream sauce with chicken, sieved eggs and mushroom mixture; season with salt and red pepper. Shape mixture into croquettes. Roll in bread crumbs, then beaten eggs; roll again in bread crumbs. Drop into deep fat; brown. Yield: 6-8 servings.

Mrs. Floy C. Poston, West Fannin H. S.
Blue Ridge, Georgia

CHICKEN CROQUETTES

½ c. margarine
½ c. flour
1 c. chicken broth
1 c. evaporated milk
1 tsp. dried parsley flakes
2 c. cooked chicken, chopped
Salt and pepper to taste
Fine dry bread crumbs
2 eggs, slightly beaten
2 tbsp. milk

(Continued on next page)

Melt margarine in heavy saucepan; stir in flour until smooth. Add chicken broth and milk; cook, stirring constantly, until very thick. Remove from heat; stir in parsley flakes and chicken. Season well with salt and pepper. Chill until easy to handle. Form into cone or cylinder shaped croquettes; roll in bread crumbs. Mix egg and milk; dip croquettes into milk mixture. Roll in crumbs again; allow to dry. Fry a few croquettes at a time in 375 degree deep fat for 2 to 3 minutes or until golden brown. Drain on absorbent paper. Keep warm in oven until serving time. Yield: 8 servings.

Mrs. Jean B. Walker, Whittle Springs Jr. H. S.
Knoxville, Tennessee

CHICKEN CROQUETTES

¾ c. chicken stock
¼ c. heavy cream
¼ tsp. curry
1 ¼ c. cooked chopped chicken
½ tsp. salt
¼ tsp. celery salt
Dash of cayenne pepper
1 tsp. lemon juice
Few drops of onion juice
1 tsp. chopped parsley
Beaten eggs
Crumbs

Mix chicken stock, heavy cream and curry. Combine remaining ingredients except eggs and crumbs. Add small amount of curry sauce. Shape croquettes; dip in eggs and crumbs. Fry in skillet or deep fat fry. Serve with sauce.

Gladys A. Brewer, Lynn View H. S.
Kingsport, Tennessee

CHICKEN CROQUETTES

1 ½ c. finely chopped cooked chicken
2 tbsp. finely chopped onion
¾ c. thick white sauce
⅛ tsp. pepper
1 tsp. salt
2 tbsp. water
1 egg, slightly beaten
½ c. finely chopped almonds
1 ¼ c. cracker crumbs

Combine chicken, onion, white sauce and seasonings. Shape into croquettes, using 1 rounded tablespoonful of mixture. Add water to egg. Combine nuts and cracker crumbs. Roll croquettes in crumb mixture; dip into egg, then roll again in crumb mixture. Set aside for 10 minutes to dry. Fry in 375 degree deep fat for 2 minutes. Yield: 4 servings.

Mrs. Thyra K. Davis, Manhattan H. S.
Manhattan, Kansas

CHICKEN CROQUETTES

3 tbsp. shortening
⅓ c. flour
1 tsp. salt
1 c. milk
2 c. cooked chopped chicken
1 tbsp. minced onion
2 tbsp. minced parsley
2 eggs
2 tbsp. lemon juice
⅓ c. fine dry bread crumbs

Melt shortening; blend in flour, salt and milk. Cook over low heat, stirring constantly, until smooth and thick. Add chicken, onion and parsley. Spread in greased shallow pan; chill thoroughly. Divide into 8 portions; shape into logs. With a fork, lightly beat eggs and lemon juice. Dip croquettes in egg mixture and then in crumbs. Fry until golden brown, 3 to 5 minutes, in deep fat heated to 365 degrees. Drain on absorbent paper. NOTE: Croquettes freeze well. Yield: 4 servings

Helen Perman, Emma Sanson H. S.
Gadsden, Alabama

CHICKEN FRITTERS

2 eggs, separated
2 c. chopped cooked chicken or turkey
½ c. minced celery and leaves
1 tsp. grated onion
¼ c. flour
½ tsp. salt
2 tbsp. oil
Chicken gravy

Mix egg yolks, chicken, celery, onion, flour and salt. Fold in beaten egg whites. Drop mixture from large spoon into heated oil; brown on both sides. Serve with chicken gravy. Yield: 6-8 servings.

Mrs. R. Gale Manley, Virginia H. S.
Bristol, Virginia

BUTTER-CRUSTED CHICKEN

3 tbsp. flour
1 tsp. salt
½ tsp. paprika
⅓ c. butter, melted
1 fryer, cut into pieces

Mix flour, salt and paprika; stir into melted butter. Brush each piece of chicken with mixture until coated. Place in foil-lined pan. Bake at 425 degrees for 20 minutes. Reduce heat to 350 degrees and continue baking for 1 hour longer. Yield: 4 servings.

Mrs. Josephine S. Loyd, Oneonta H. S.
Oneonta, Alabama

ALABAMA FRIED CHICKEN

1 lge. fryer
Salt and pepper to taste
1 tsp. garlic salt (opt.)
1 c. buttermilk
1 c. flour or 1 ½ c. self-rising flour
2 c. corn oil or 1 c. shortening

Cut chicken into serving pieces; wash and dry on paper towel. Sprinkle with salt, pepper and garlic salt; dip in buttermilk. Shake in flour in paper bag. Heat oil to 275 to 350 degrees. Add chicken. Cook until golden brown, turning once. Drain on paper towel. Arrange on platter. Garnish with parsley, if desired.

Mary Y. Thompson, Clay Co. H. S.
Ashland, Alabama
Mrs. Tressa Costley, Montebello Jr. H. S.
Natchez, Mississippi

CHICKEN KIEV

5 chicken breasts, boned and cut into halves
Salt and pepper
1 onion, finely chopped
10 pats butter or margarine
3 eggs
⅓ c. milk
Fine bread crumbs
2 c. cooking oil

Pound meat between two pieces of waxed paper until flat. Sprinkle each piece with salt and pepper. Spread each piece with finely chopped onion and 1 pat butter. Roll each into a log shape; fasten with picks. Beat eggs with milk. Roll each chicken log in bread crumbs, then dip in egg mixture. Roll again in crumbs; refrigerate for 6 to 8 hours or overnight. Heat oil to 350 degrees; fry logs for 8 minutes on each side or until a golden brown. Yield: 10 servings.

Amelie B. Sheffield, Manor H. S.
Eagle Springs, North Carolina

CHICKEN KIEV

4 chicken breasts
Salt and pepper
¼ lb. butter, chilled
¼ c. flour
¼ c. milk
1 c. fine fresh bread crumbs
1 qt. corn oil

Cut chicken breasts into halves; remove skin and peel bone. With point of knife, slit between meat and bones with small strokes. Pull meat away from bone. Be careful not to tear meat. Place each piece of breast between two sheets of waxed paper; pound with flat side of cleaver or wooden mallet until meat spreads out into a thin slice. Remove waxed paper; sprinkle with salt and pepper. Cut butter into eight equal crosswise pieces. Place a piece of butter off center toward narrow thick end of each piece of chicken; fold thick end over butter. Roll over tightly and press down edge; turn side edges under. Press down and fasten with toothpick. Dust rolls with flour; dip in milk. Roll in bread crumbs. Refrigerate for 1 hour or more. Heat corn oil in heavy 3-quart saucepan to 375 degrees. Add rolls slowly; turn with spoon to cook and brown on all sides, about 3 to 5 minutes. Drain on absorbent paper. Yield: 4-8 servings.

Catharine Ida Moyer, Wilson H. S.
West Lawn, Pennsylvania

CHICKEN RUSSE

2 c. sour cream
2 tbsp. lemon juice
2 tsp. salt
½ tsp. pepper
Garlic powder to taste
6 chicken breasts
Bread crumbs
½ c. butter or margarine

Combine sour cream, lemon juice and seasonings in a storage-size plastic bag; add chicken pieces. Seal bag and marinate in refrigerator overnight. Remove chicken; shake with crumbs in plastic bag. Fry chicken in melted butter for 25 to 30 minutes or until golden brown and tender. If gravy is desired, add water during cooking. Yield: 6 servings.

Mrs. Delores Weir, Comfrey H. S.
Comfrey, Minnesota

EASY CHICKEN

¼ c. flour
1 tsp. salt
Pepper to taste
1 chicken, cut up
¼ lb. margarine

Flour, salt and pepper chicken; place in greased baking dish, skin-side up. Cover with margarine. Bake at 300 degrees for 1 hour. Serve hot. Yield: 6 servings.

Bertha Harris, Mendenhall Attendance Center
Mendenhall, Mississippi

FRIED CHICKEN

1 1 to 2-lb. fryer, skinned
½ gal. cooking oil
1 c. flour
2 tsp. salt
1 tsp. paprika
½ tsp. celery salt
¼ tsp. pepper
1 egg, beaten
1 c. evaporated milk

(Continued on next page)

Mix all dry ingredients. Combine egg and milk; dip prepared chicken into egg-milk solution; coat thoroughly. Roll chicken into flour mixture, coating thoroughly; place in deep 375 degree oil. Fry for 16 minutes or until golden brown. Yield: 4-6 servings.

Mrs. Irene Allen, Wall School
Wall, Texas

FRIED CHICKEN SUPREME

Salt and pepper to taste
1 fryer, cut up
Flour or bread crumbs
1 egg
½ to 1 c. milk
Fat

Salt and pepper chicken pieces; roll in flour. Beat egg with milk; dip chicken into mixture. Dip into flour again; fry in deep fat. Place chicken one-layer deep in shallow pan; bursh with melted butter. Bake at 300 degrees for 40 minutes. Yield: 4 servings.

Mrs. Stacie O. Houser, Sun Valley H. S.
Monroe, North Carolina
Joy Criner, Avon Park H. S.
Avon Park, Florida

FRIED CHICKEN SUPREME

1 3 ½ to 4-lb. fryer, cut up
1 ¼ tsp. salt
⅛ tsp. pepper
¾ c. flour
½ lb. butter

Season chicken with salt and pepper; place chicken and flour in paper bag. Shake to coat chicken. Fry chicken in butter in electric skillet at 325 degrees, turning once, until brown. Add a few drops of water. Cover; bake at 375 degrees for a few minutes to tenderize. Uncover; continue to bake until crisp. Yield: 6 servings.

Frances Flint, Dimmitt Jr. H. S.
Seattle, Washington

MAMA'S GARLIC-FRIED CHICKEN

2 2 ½-lb. fryers, cut into pieces
1 c. sour cream
2 tbsp. lemon juice
¼ tsp. Worcestershire sauce
1 clove of garlic, grated
½ tsp. salt
¼ tsp. pepper
¼ tsp. celery salt
½ tsp. paprika
Flour

Wipe chicken with damp cloth. Place in refrigerator jar. Mix remaining ingredients except flour; pour over chicken, covering all pieces well. Refrigerate, tightly covered, overnight. Drain; dredge with flour. Fry until done. Yield: 6 servings.

Mrs. Jim Hudson, Celeste H. S.
Celeste, Texas

GARLIC-FRIED CHICKEN

1 fryer, cut up
Powdered garlic
Monosodium glutamate
Salt and pepper
Seasoned flour
Fat

Sprinkle chicken with powdered garlic and monosodium glutamate; sprinkle with salt and pepper. Drop one piece at a time into paper bag containing flour. Shake well. Fry in deep fat until well done and golden brown. Yield: 8 servings.

Bonnie O'Neal, New Summerfield H. S.
New Summerfield, Texas

MY BEST OVEN-FRIED CHICKEN

1 tsp. salt
½ tsp. pepper
½ c. melted butter or margarine
2 fryers, cut up
2 c. dry cereal, crushed

Add salt and pepper to butter. Dip chicken in seasoned butter; roll in cereal. Place chicken on foil-lined flat pan. Bake at 350 degrees for 1 hour. Yield: 8 servings.

Mrs. Josephine B. Lumpkin, Fairfield Jr. H. S.
Richmond, Virginia

OVEN CRISP CHICKEN

1 box cereal crumbs
2 fryers, cut up
¼ lb. butter, melted
1 tsp. paprika
Salt and pepper to taste

Place cereal crumbs in a shallow bowl. Dip pieces of chicken into melted butter; roll in crumbs. Place chicken, skin-side up, in an aluminum-lined baking pan. Season. Bake at 375 degrees for 1 hour. Yield: 6 servings.

Mrs. Mary Jean Jensen, Lemmon H. S.
Lemmon, South Dakota

OHIO OVEN-FRIED CHICKEN

Salt
1 fryer, cut up
3 eggs, well beaten
12 soda crackers, crushed

Salt chicken, dip in eggs; roll in cracker crumbs. Place in a buttered 8 x 8 x 2-inch baking pan. Bake at 350 degrees for 1 hour or until tender, turning chicken every 15 minutes. Yield: 6-7 servings.

Mrs. Charlene Dawson, Scipio-Republic
Republic, Ohio

OVEN-FRIED CHICKEN

4 c. bread crumbs
1 lb. butter or margarine, melted
Salt and pepper
6 chicken halves

Mix bread crumbs with small amount of melted butter. Salt and pepper chicken to taste. Brush pieces with melted butter; roll in buttered bread crumbs. Place chicken halves in buttered shallow baking pan. Bake at 325 degrees for 2 hours or until done. Serve while hot. NOTE: Some puree or garlic may be added to melted butter. Yield: 6 servings.

Nana E. James, Southeastern H. S.
Hammond, Louisiana

OVEN-FRIED CHICKEN

2 c. crushed potato chips
¼ tsp. garlic salt or seasoned salt
Dash of pepper
1 2½ to 3-lb. broiler-fryer, cut up
⅓ c. melted butter

Mix crushed potato chips, garlic salt and pepper. Dip chicken pieces in melted butter; roll in chip mixture. Place pieces, skin side-up, in greased baking dish. Sprinkle with remaining butter and crumbs. Bake, uncovered, at 375 degrees for about 1 hour or until done. Yield: 4-6 servings.

Mrs. Paul Ewing, Adena H. S.
Frankfort, Ohio
Mrs. Larry Anderson, Selby H. S.
Selby, South Dakota

OVEN-FRIED CHICKEN

1 fryer, cut up
Salt and pepper to taste
1 stick butter or margarine, melted
1 c. finely-rolled Ritz cracker crumbs or ½ c. cracker meal

Sprinkle chicken with salt and pepper. Dip in melted butter; roll in cracker crumbs. Place in baking dish. Bake at 300 to 325 degrees for 45 minutes. Turn chicken pieces; bake for 45 minutes longer. Yield: 4-6 servings.

Mrs. Linda Coombs, Centauri H. S.
LaJara, Colorado
Jean Brittingham, John M. Clayton School
Frankford-Dagsboro, Delaware

OVEN-FRIED CHICKEN

1 ½ c. margarine
4 tsp. salt
25 chicken pieces
Corn flake crumbs
Paprika

Line shallow pans with foil allowing enough to crimp ends together and fold under at the center top. Melt margarine; add salt. Dip chicken in margarine; roll in crumbs. Place in pan; shake paprika generously on top. Seal foil. Bake at 300 degrees for about 1 hour and 30 minutes. Increase temperature or open foil for browning. Yield: 25 servings.

Mrs. Eileen Skaggs, Alderson H. S.
Alderson, West Virginia

OVEN-FRIED PECAN CHICKEN

1 c. biscuit mix
1 ½ tsp. salt
2 tsp. paprika
2 tbsp. sesame seed (opt.)
½ tsp. poultry seasoning (opt.)
¼ to ½ c. finely chopped pecans
1 2½ to 4-lb. fryer, cut into serving pieces
½ c. evaporated milk or milk
¼ to ½ c. melted butter or margarine

Combine biscuit mix, seasonings and nuts. Dip chicken pieces into evaporated milk, then coat well with dry mixture. Place in 13 x 9 x 2-inch baking pan. Pour melted butter over chicken pieces, covering as completely as possible. Bake, uncovered, at 375 degrees for 1 hour or at 300 degrees for 2 hours or until tender. NOTE: Flour may be used instead of biscuit mix. Yield: 4-6 servings.

Betty Jo Hill, Carterville Jr. H. S.
Cartersville, Illinois
Mrs. G. T. Lilly, Murray H. S.
Murray, Kentucky

PAPRIKA CHICKEN

2 tsp. salt
1 2½-lb. chicken, cut up
½ to ¾ c. flour
¼ to ⅓ c. margarine or shortening
½ tsp. garlic powder (opt.)
1 to 3 tsp. parpika

(Continued on next page)

Dredge salted chicken in flour. Melt margarine in baking dish or iron skillet. Place chicken in dish; sprinkle with garlic powder and paprika. Bake at 400 degrees for 30 minutes. Turn chicken and continue cooking for 30 minutes. Yield: 5-6 servings.

Francis Sill, Camden Jr. H. S.
Camden, South Carolina
Mrs. Harvey Jacobs, Woodmere Jr. H. S.
Hewlett, New York

TEXAS OVEN-FRIED CHICKEN

1 3-lb. fryer, cut up
1 c. buttermilk
¾ c. flour
½ tsp. paprika
1 tsp. salt
½ tsp. pepper
½ tsp. thyme (opt.)
1 tbsp. instant minced onion
⅓ c. butter

Cover chicken pieces with buttermilk; set aside for 1 hout. Combine remaining ingredients except butter. Roll chicken pieces in flour mixture. Melt butter in shallow baking pan in 350 degree oven. Place chicken in pan; turn to coat with butter. Arrange in single layer with skin sides down. Bake for 1 hour or until tender, turning once. Make gravy from pan drippings, seasoned flour and additional buttermilk. Yield: 4 servings.

Anna Lee Davis, Schertz-Cibolo H. S.
Schertz, Texas

CHICKEN LIVER AND MUSHROOM GOURMET

2 tbsp. butter or margarine
½ lb. chicken livers
1 16-oz. can sliced mushrooms, drained
¼ c. chopped green onions
½ c. sour cream
1 ½ tsp. soy sauce
1 tbsp. chili sauce
Dash of pepper

Melt butter in skillet on medium heat; add chicken livers. Cover; cook for 5 minutes or until almost tender, turning occasionally. Add mushrooms and onions; continue to cook until onions and livers are tender. Combine remaining ingredients; add to livers. Heat and stir until sauce is hot. Serve on toast points, pancakes or with omelet, if desired. Yield: 4 servings.

Lula Smith, Sand Springs Jr. H. S.
Sand Springs, Oklahoma

CHICKEN LIVERS BAKED WITH RICE

¾ lb. chicken livers
Salt and pepper
Flour
4 tbsp. butter or margarine
3 tbsp. minced onion
3 tbsp. finely chopped celery
1 c. uncooked rice
2 c. chicken broth
1 tsp. minced parsley

Sprinkle chicken livers with salt and pepper; shake in small amount of flour in paper bag. Brown quickly in butter in hot skillet; place in 6-cup casserole. Saute onion, celery and rice in butter remaining in skillet until slightly browned. Add chicken broth; stir well. Add parsley; pour over chicken livers. Cover tightly; bake at 350 degrees for 30 minutes or until rice is tender and has absorbed the liquid. Add salt, if needed. Yield: 6 servings.

Imogene Brashear, Palatka H. S.
Palatka, Florida

CHICKEN LIVERS IN ONION GRAVY

12 chicken livers
2 tbsp. butter or margarine
1 ¾-oz. envelope brown gravy mix
1 ½ c. boiling water
½ envelope dry onion soup mix
4 c. hot cooked rice or noodles

Cook chicken livers in butter for 10 minutes. Prepare brown gravy mix with 1 cup boiling water. Add to livers with onion soup mix and remaining boiling water; mix well. Simmer for 15 minutes. Spoon over hot cooked noodles or rice. Yield: 4 servings.

Linda Chastain, Polk Central H. S.
Mill Spring, North Carolina

CHICKEN LIVERS PORTUGAL

5 tbsp. butter or margarine
1 clove of garlic, minced
2 tbsp. minced onion
6 tbsp. flour
1 c. condensed beef broth
½ tsp. salt
Dash of pepper
1 lb. fresh or frozen chicken livers, thawed
2 tbsp. sweet Madeira or Marsala

Melt 3 tablespoonfuls butter in a heavy saucepan or skillet. Add garlic and onion; cook until onion is tender but not brown. Blend in 2 tablespoonfuls flour. Add beef broth; cook and stir until sauce is smooth and thickened. Combine the remaining flour, salt and pepper; dredge livers in flour mixture. Brown livers quickly in remaining butter; gently stir into sauce. Add wine. Heat through; serve over wild rice, if desired. Yield: 4 servings.

Dickie Sue Felder, Tavares H. S.
Tavares, Florida

BIRD OF PARADISE

3 eggs
3 tbsp. milk
½ tsp. salt
4 boned fryer breasts
½ c. grated Parmesan cheese
½ c. butter
1 c. cooking Sherry

Beat eggs and milk. Sprinkle salt over chicken. Dip chicken into egg mixture; roll in grated cheese. Heat butter in electric skillet to 300 degrees; brown chicken on both sides. Add Sherry; cover and cook at 225 degrees for 45 minutes or until tender. Serve on a bed of wild rice. Yield: 4 servings.

Mrs. Sarah Perry, North Webster H. S.
North-Webster, Indiana

CHICKEN A LA KING

1 green pepper, chopped
8 tbsp. butter
6 tbsp. flour
3 c. milk
1 ½ tsp. salt
½ tsp. paprika
1 chicken, cooked and diced
1 can pimento
1 lge. can mushrooms
1 tsp. nutmeg

Fry green pepper in 3 tablespoonfuls butter. Combine remaining butter, flour and milk. Add all ingredients to sauce except nutmeg. Add nutmeg 1 hour before serving. Serve on toast or in timbales. Yield: 8 servings.

Antoinette Kelemen, Shelbyville H. S.
Shelbyville, Kentucky

CHICKEN ALMONDINE

¾ c. diced green pepper
4 tbsp. butter
⅓ c. flour
2 c. chicken broth
1 c. light cream
⅛ tsp. nutmeg
1 tsp. salt
Dash of pepper
3 ½ c. diced cooked chicken
1 lge. can mushrooms
3 tbsp. cooking Sherry
⅓ c. diced pimento
½ c. toasted almonds

Saute green pepper in butter; blend in flour until smooth. Stir in broth and cream. Add nutmeg, salt, pepper, chicken and mushrooms. Simmer. Add remaining ingredients just before serving. Serve in pattie shells or on toast points, if desired. Yield: 6-8 servings.

Mrs. J. L. Vance, Bowdon H. S.
Bowdon, Georgia

CHICKEN BREASTS HAWAIIAN

2 chicken breasts, split into halves
1 egg, slightly beaten
1 c. finely grated bread crumbs
1 tsp. salt
Fat
1 c. pineapple juice
2 tbsp. lemon juice
1 tbsp. cornstarch
¼ tsp. curry paste
1 tbsp. sugar
Slivered almonds

Remove bones from breasts, keeping meat in one piece; dip into egg. Roll in bread crumbs. Season with salt. Fry in 1/4-inch hot fat in a heavy skillet until brown. Remove fat from pan. Combine juices, cornstarch, curry and sugar; pour over chicken. Cover skillet; cook slowly for 20 to 25 minutes. Top with slivered almonds. Yield: 4 servings.

Jessie May Johnson, University H. S.
Waco, Texas

CHICKEN BREASTS WITH ORANGE GLAZE

3 lge. chicken breasts, split into halves
Salt and pepper
Butter
1 6-oz. can frozen orange juice
1 c. water
2 tbsp. butter
2 tbsp. flour
1 tbsp. grated orange rind and juice

Remove bones from breast with sharp knife; sprinkle with salt and pepper. Broil in butter on both sides until brown. Cover skillet; bake at 350 to 325 degrees until tender. Combine orange juice, water, butter and flour; add grated orange rind and juice. Pour sauce over chicken breasts; cook for a short while to form glaze. Serve on toast, if desired. Yield: 6 servings.

Mrs. Arthur F. Dean, Central H. S.
Nashville, Tennessee

CHICKEN, FARMER-STYLE

1 chicken, cut into serving pieces
Shortening
1 lge. onion, chopped

(Continued on next page)

3 sm. carrots, chopped
2 green peppers, chopped
1 sm. can or ¼ lb. fresh mushrooms
1 No. 2 can tomatoes
Cooked rice

Brown chicken pieces in shortening; remove from skillet. Pour off all but 1/4 cup fat. Saute onion, carrots, green pepper and mushrooms. Stir in tomatoes ; season to taste. Add chicken; cover. Cook for 1 hour and 30 minutes. Serve over cooked rice. Yield: 5-6 servings.

Mildred Mason, Cherokee Voc. H. S.
Cherokee Alabama

CHICKEN GUMBO

1 ¼ c. flour
½ c. shortening or cooking oil
2 qt. water
1 chicken, cut up
1 onion, minced
Chopped onion tops
Chopped parsley
¼ to ½ tsp. file

Brown flour in shortening, stirring constantly over medium heat. Add water, chicken and onion. Cook for about 1 hour or until tender. Add onion tops and parsley; season to taste. Serve over rice. File may be added after gumbo is on plate. Yield: 8-10 servings.

Mrs. Leo Thames, Robert E. Lee H. S.
Baton Rouge, Louisiana

CHICKEN PAPRIKA

3 med. onions, sliced
3 ½ tbsp. bacon drippings
1 tsp. paprika
1 ¼ tsp. salt
¼ tsp. pepper
½ c. water
1 3 to 4-lb. chicken, cut into serving pieces
3 tbsp. flour
1 ¼ c. sour cream

Cook onions in bacon drippings until light yellow. Add paprika, salt, pepper and water; mix well. Place chicken pieces on onions. Cover tightly and simmer for 2 to 3 hours or until tender. Remove chicken. Mix flour with sour cream; add to onions. Stir and cook until thick. Return chicken to skillet; simmer until hot. Yield: 6 servings.

Mrs. Beatrice Clark, Keller H. S.
Keller, Texas

CHICKEN RING

1 5-lb. hen
¼ lb. almonds
3 hard-cooked eggs, chopped
Cream sauce
Salt and pepper

Boil hen until tender. Grind meat with almonds in grinder. Add chopped eggs; mix with enough cream sauce to hold together. Turn into a buttered ring mold; steam for 1 hour. Unmold and fill center of ring with English peas and small onions, if desired. Serve hot. Yield: 8 servings.

Adele K. Lytle, Fort Mill H. S.
Fort Mill, South Carolina

CHICKEN SAUCE PIQUANT

1 hen, cut up
Salt and pepper to taste
3 tbsp. fat
4 or 5 lge. onions, chopped
1 or 2 green peppers, chopped
1 can tomato sauce
½ c. water
½ c. minced parsley and onion tops
1 tbsp. instant flour

Brown seasoned hen in fat. Add onions and green peppers; cook until soft. Add tomato sauce, water and parsley; simmer until thickened. Flour may be added if needed. Serve on rice. Yield: 6-8 servings.

Mrs. Guy Mitchell, Chataignier H. S.
Chataignier, Louisiana

CHICKEN TARRAGON

1 sm. fryer, cut up
Salt and pepper
Paprika
½ c. margarine
1 onion, sliced
1 can mushrooms
1 tbsp. tarragon or parsley

Dust fryer with salt, pepper and paprika. Brown lightly over low heat in margarine. Add onion and mushrooms to chicken. Steam slowly until tender, about 30 minutes. Add tarragon or parsley before serving. Yield: 4 servings.

Mrs. Donald C. Young, Greenwood H. S.
Greenwood, Arkansas

COMPANY CHICKEN BREASTS

Salt and pepper
4 chicken breasts
4 tbsp. butter
1 chicken bouillon cube
1 c. hot water
1 clove of garlic, pressed
1 onion, sliced

Salt and pepper chicken breasts; brown in butter until golden brown. Dissolve bouillon in hot

(Continued on next page)

water; add garlic. Slice onion over chicken. Pour liquid over top. Cover tightly; simmer for 1 hour. Thicken liquid and serve over chicken, if desired. Yield: 4 servings.

Mrs. Fred Liggitt, Azle H. S.
Azle, Texas

COZ AU VIN

Chicken pieces
½ stick margarine
2 cloves of garlic
1 tbsp. Kitchen Bouquet
2 c. dry red wine
½ tsp. salt
Dash of pepper
Monosodium glutamate

Brown chicken in butter in electric skillet. Add garlic, Kitchen Bouquet, wine, salt, pepper and monosodium glutamate. Simmer for 1 hour or until chicken is tender. Serve with rice. Yield: 4-8 servings.

Mrs. Patricia Bennett, West End H. S.
Nashville, Tennessee

CURRIED CHICKEN

1 3½-lb. fryer, cut into serving pieces
½ c. flour
1 tsp. salt
¼ tsp. pepper
½ c. corn oil
¼ c. curry powder
2 c. chicken stock or bouillon
1 tbsp. cornstarch
¼ c. water

Wash chicken; dry. Shake in paper bag with flour, salt and paper. Heat 6 tablespoonfuls corn oil in large heavy skillet. Brown chicken in hot oil, turning to brown both sides. Heat curry powder in saucepan; slowly stir in 2 tablespoonfuls oil. Thin stock with water. Bring to a boil, stirring constantly. Pour over chicken; cover skillet and simmer for 1 hour or until chicken is tender. Remove chicken; keep hot. Mix cornstarch with water; stir into skillet. Cook until gravy thickens, stirring constantly. Serve over chicken. Yield: 4 servings.

Jo Anna Littrel, Columbus Comm. H. S.
Columbus Jct., Iowa

CURRIED MINCED CAPON

1 4-lb. capon
1 sm. onion, chopped
2 tbsp. butter
4 tbsp. curry powder
2 tbsp. flour
Salt and pepper
Cayenne pepper

Simmer capon until tender; reserve 4 to 5 cups stock. Remove skin and bone. Cut meat into small pieces. Brown onion slightly in melted butter. Add curry powder and flour, stirring until smooth. Add stock; boil gently until mixture is the consistency of thick cream. Pour over rice mixed with chutney and buttered green peas, if desired. Yield: 8-10 servings.

Marie Denny, Cookville H. S.
Cookville, Tennessee

CHICKEN DUMPLINGS

1 2½ to 3-lb. chicken
1 sm. onion
2 c. flour
¼ c. shortening
1 egg
½ tsp. soda
½ tsp. salt
¾ to 1 c. buttermilk
1 can cream of chicken soup
1 to 1½ c. milk

Boil chicken with onion until tender. Bone chicken. Make dumpling dough using flour, shortening, egg, soda, salt and buttermilk. Add boned chicken and soup to chicken broth; bring to a rolling boil. Roll dough thin; drop into boiling broth and cook until tender. Add milk; bring to a boil. Serve immediately. Yield: 8 servings.

Jeanette Phillips, Bridgeport H. S.
Bridgeport, Texas

CHICKEN AND NOODLE DUMPLINGS

DUMPLINGS:

2 c. flour
2½ tsp. salt
4 eggs
¼ to ½ c. milk
2 qt. water

Mix flour and 1 1/2 teaspoonfuls salt; add eggs and mix well. Add milk if more liquid is needed to moisten dry ingredients. Boil the water with remaining salt. Dip small serving spoon into boiling salted water. Drop dough by 1 1/2 tablespoonfuls into water. Dip spoon into water so that following dumpling slips from spoon easily. Boil for 20 minutes. Drain when done.

CHICKEN:

1 2 to 3-lb. fryer, cut up
Salt and pepper
Monosodium glutamate
2 or 3 tbsp. fat
2 tbsp. flour
1 6-oz. can evaporated milk
¾ c. milk
1 can cream of chicken or mushroom soup
½ to 1 soup can water

(Continued on next page)

Season chicken; brown in fat in 10-inch skillet. Cover and bake at 350 degrees for 1 hour or until done. Remove chicken from pan, draining off all but 2 to 3 tablespoonfuls fat. Blend in flour. Cook for a few minutes over medium heat. Add evaporated milk, milk, soup and water; mix well. Add chicken and dumplings. Simmer for 15 to 20 minutes, stirring occasionally.

Grace Lamusga, Hosterman Jr. H. S.
Minneapolis, Minnesota

CHICKEN BREASTS SAUTE

⅓ c. flour
Salt and pepper to taste
8 sm. chicken breasts
¼ c. butter or margarine
¼ c. finely chopped onion
2 tbsp. chopped celery
⅔ c. chicken broth or bouillon
½ c. mushrooms (opt.)
1 c. seedless grapes
1 c. half and half

Season flour with salt and pepper. Dredge chicken in the flour; saute in butter until lightly browned. Add onion and celery; cook until vegetables are tender. Add broth and mushrooms. Cover; cook gently for 30 minutes or until chicken is tender. Add grapes; cook for 5 to 8 minutes longer. Before serving, remove breasts; stir in cream. Pour sauce over chicken. Garnish with parsley. Yield: 6-8 servings.

Isabelle Staley, Huron H. S.
Huron, South Dakota

CHICKEN IN ORANGE SAUCE

1 3-lb. fryer, cut into serving pieces
½ c. butter or margarine
¼ c. flour
2 tbsp. brown sugar
1 tsp. salt
½ tsp. ground ginger
⅛ tsp. pepper
1 ½ c. orange juice
½ c. water
2 oranges, pared and sectioned

Brown chicken pieces slowly in butter in large frying pan. Remove from pan and set aside. Blend flour, brown sugar and seasonings into drippings in pan. Cook, stirring constantly, until mixture bubbles. Stir in orange juice and water slowly. Cook and stir until sauce thickens and boils for 1 minute; remove from heat. Return chicken to pan, bring to boil. Cover and simmer for 30 minutes. Place orange sections around chicken and cook for 15 minutes longer or until chicken is tender. Serve with rice seasoned with chopped parsley, if desired. Yield: 4 servings.

Mrs. Katherine J. Wilshin
Stonewall Jackson H. S., Manassas, Virginia

GOLDEN ORANGE CHICKEN

6 to 8 drumsticks or thighs or 1 whole fryer, cut into serving pieces
¼ c. flour
¼ tsp. salt
¼ c. butter or margarine
2 tbsp. grated orange peel
½ c. fresh orange juice
1 tbsp. brown sugar
Orange slices

Coat chicken with flour seasoned with salt. Heat butter in large skillet. Saute chicken until golden on all sides. Blend orange peel, orange juice and brown sugar. Spoon over chicken pieces. Cover and cook over low heat for 30 minutes or until tender. Garnish with orange slices. Yield: 4-6 servings.

Mrs. George A. Montgomery
Central Union H. S.
Fresno, California

HAWAIIAN CHICKEN

1 chicken, cut into pieces and salted
Prepared pancake mix
Flour
1 sm. can pineapple chunks
1 tsp. Worcestershire sauce
¼ c. catsup
¼ c. barbecue sauce

Roll chicken pieces in prepared pancake mix, then in flour. Fry in deep hot fat until golden brown. Place pieces in heavy aluminum pan. Combine remaining ingredients and pour over chicken. Cover tightly and steam on lowest heat for 30 minutes. Yield: 6 servings.

Oleta Hayden, Milford H. S.
Milford, Texas

PINEAPPLE-SPICED CHICKEN

1 fryer, cut up
¼ c. oil
Salt and pepper to taste
1 13 ½-oz. can pineapple chunks with juice
1 onion, sliced
1 c. chicken broth
2 tbsp. lemon juice
3 tbsp. soy sauce
1 tbsp. cornstarch
½ tsp. dry mustard
1 sm. green pepper, sliced

Brown chicken in oil. Remove and sprinkle with salt and pepper. Drain pineapple, reserving juice. Cook onion for 3 minutes in drippings; add broth, pineapple juice and lemon juice. Mix soy sauce, cornstarch and mustard; add to hot liquid, stirring until clear and thickened. Add chicken. Cover and simmer for 20 minutes. Add green pepper and pineapple chunks. Cover and cook slowly for 5 minutes. Yield: 4 servings.

Mrs. Val C. Manley, Virginia H. S.
Bristol, Virginia

SAUTED BREAST OF CHICKEN

½ c. flour
Salt and pepper
12 sm. chicken breasts
½ c. butter
6 tbsp. finely chopped onion
1 c. dry white wine
2 c. chopped mushrooms
1 c. seedless grapes
1 ½ c. light cream
Chopped parlsey

Season flour with salt and pepper; dredge chicken breasts in flour. Saute in butter until lightly browned. Add onion; cook over low heat until onion is tender, but not brown. Add wine and mushrooms; cover and cook gently for 30 minutes or until breasts are done. Add grapes; cook from 3 to 5 minutes longer. Remove breasts to platter. Add cream to mushroom mixture; heat. Pour sauce over chicken breasts; sprinkle with chopped parsley. Yield: 12 servings.

Delois Alphin, Elaine H. S.
Elaine, Arkansas

WAIKIKI CHICKEN

1 broiler-fryer, cut up
Salt and pepper
Flour
Salad oil
1 c. undrained crushed pineapple
1 c. barbecue sauce
1 tbsp. cornstarch
½ tsp. ginger

Dredge chicken in seasoned flour; brown in oil. Drain off excess oil. Combine remaining ingredients; pour over chicken. Cover and simmer for 30 minutes. Yield: 4 servings.

Angeline Novak, Flatonia H. S.
Flatonia, Texas

NEW ORLEANS CHICKEN

½ c. chopped onion
½ c. chopped celery
1 stick margarine
1 lge. fryer, cut up
2 tbsp. parsley
½ tsp. thyme
2 sm. bay leaves
2 cloves of garlic
1 c. water

Cook onion and celery in margarine in a heavy skillet for 3 minutes or until transparent and golden. Add chicken; brown on each side. Add remaining ingredients. Bring to a quick boil. Cover and simmer for 1 hour or until meat can be detached easily from bone. Serve gravy from chicken over rice, if desired. Yield: 4 servings.

Mrs. Margaret Feild, Marshall H. S.
Marshall, Texas

CHICKEN NOODLES

2 tbsp. butter or margarine
1 c. chopped onions
1 c. chopped celery
1 clove of garlic, crushed
1 1-lb. 12-oz. can tomatoes
1 c. water
1 2-oz. can mushroom stems and pieces
1 chicken bouillon cube
½ tsp. salt
½ tsp. oregano
¼ tsp. pepper
¼ tsp. basil
3 c. chopped cooked chicken or turkey
8 oz. noodles

Melt butter in large saucepan. Add onions, celery and garlic; cook until onions are transparent. Stir in tomatoes, water, mushrooms and liquid, bouillon cube, salt, oregano, pepper and basil. Bring to a boil; reduce heat. Cover; simmer for 45 minutes, stirring occasionally. Stir in chicken and noodles; cover and simmer for 10 to 15 minutes longer or until noodles are tender, stirring occasionally. Serve immediately. Yield: 4-6 servings.

Requa K. Spears, Mullins H. S.
Pikeville, Kentucky

CHICKEN TETRAZZINI

1 5 to 5 ½-lb. hen
1 tbsp. salt
1 ½ qt. water
1 1-lb. pkg. macaroni or spaghetti, cooked
1 10-oz. pkg. frozen peas
1 4-oz. can mushrooms, undrained
1 4-oz. can pimento, chopped
4 tbsp. butter
4 tbsp. flour
¼ c. milk
½ lb. Velveeta cheese, sliced

Cook chicken; allow to cool in broth. Remove from broth; cut into bite-sized pieces. Bring broth to boil; add spaghetti. Cook, uncovered, until tender. Add more water if necessary, but most of liquid should be absorbed. Cook frozen peas in separate pan; add mushrooms and pimento. Combine butter, flour, milk and Velveeta; cook, stirring constantly, until cheese melts. Add chicken, peas, mushrooms and cheese sauce to macaroni. Stir until mixed. Cover; heat very slowly until serving temperature. Yield: 16 servings.

Mrs. Eunice Gordon, Shattuck H. S.
Shattuck, Oklahoma

CHICKEN TETRAZZINI

1 5-lb. hen, cooked
1 green pepper, chopped
Chopped onion
1 clove of garlic
Butter
1 lb. fine noodles
Chicken broth

(Continued on next page)

1 can pimento, diced
1 can cream of mushroom soup
1 sm. can ripe olives
Salt and pepper
1 lb. Velveeta cheese

Cut chicken into chunks. Saute green pepper, onion and garlic in butter. Cook noodles in chicken broth. Add remaining ingredients except cheese to small amount of broth. Chop cheese into lumps; stir into mixture until cheese melts. Yield: 10-12 servings.

Novella Mae Melton, Roswell H. S.
Roswell, New Mexico

CHICKEN IN ORANGE-ALMOND SAUCE

1 2-lb. fryer, cut up
½ tsp. salt
Butter
2 tbsp. flour
⅛ tsp. ginger
⅛ tsp. cinnamon
1 ½ c. orange juice
½ c. slivered blanched almonds
½ c. seedless raisins
1 c. fresh orange sections
3 c. cooked rice

Sprinkle fryer with 1/4 teaspoonful salt. Brown pieces lightly in butter in heavy skillet. Cool and remove meat from bones. Mix flour, remaining salt, ginger and cinnamon into drippings in pan to make a smooth paste, stirring constantly. Add orange juice. Cook and stir until sauce bubbles and thickens. Add chicken, almonds and raisins to sauce; stir well. Cover and cook over low heat for 45 minutes or until chicken is fork tender. Add orange sections and heat through just before serving. Serve on bed of cooked rice. Serve with any remaining sauce. Yield: 6 servings.

Mrs. Eleanor Hatch, Joseph H. S.
Joseph, Oregon

DAWN'S CHICKEN

1 fryer, skinned and cut up
2 tbsp. shortening
2 ½ stalks celery, chopped
½ green pepper, chopped
1 med. onion, chopped
2 tsp. chili powder
1 1-lb. can tomatoes
⅔ tomato can water
Salt and pepper
1 ¼ c. rice

Saute chicken in shortening. Add celery, green pepper, onion and chili powder. Pour tomatoes and water over chicken. Season. Cook until chicken is done. Add rice; cook over low heat until rice is done. Stir occasionally; add water as needed. Yield: 6 servings.

Lynn Lankford, Carrizo Springs H. S.
Carrizo Springs, Texas

MEXICAN RICE AND CHICKEN

1 fryer, cut up
¼ c. flour
2 ½ tsp. salt
1 ½ tsp. chili powder
⅓ c. salad oil
¾ c. raw rice
1 ½ c. water
¼ c. chopped onion
¼ c. chopped green pepper
¼ c. chopped celery
2 c. canned tomatoes

Separate chicken; pat dry between paper towels. Mix flour, 1/2 teaspoonful salt and 1/2 teaspoonful chili powder. Roll chicken in flour mixture. Saute chicken in oil until brown. Add remaining ingredients. Cover; simmer gently for 40 minutes or until chicken is tender and rice is done. Yield: 4-6 servings.

Elsie M. Sutton, Clinton H. S.
Clinton, Louisiana

YELLOW RICE AND CHICKEN

1 3 to 3 ½-lb. fryer, cut up
Chicken broth
1 5-oz. pkg. yellow rice mix

Boil chicken until well done. Remove meat from bones. Add water to broth to make 2 cups liquid. Place broth and meat in boiler. Bring to a boil; add yellow rice mix. Cook according to directions on package. Yield: 6 servings.

Mrs. Mary C. Patrick, Grand Ridge School
Grand Ridge, Florida

SHOYU CHICKEN

2 lb. chicken pieces
1 ¼ c. shoyu sauce
6 tbsp. sugar
2 cloves of garlic
3 1-in. slices fresh ginger or 2 tsp. powdered ginger

Place chicken in electric skillet. Pour shoyu sauce over chicken. Add remaining ingredients. Cover and cook slowly for 1 hour. Increase temperature; cook until sauce is thickened and chicken is well coated. Serve over rice. Yield: 6 servings.

Mrs. Claudine Meek, Midwest City H. S.
Midwest City, Oklahoma

ARTICHOKE CHICKEN

4 chicken breasts
¼ tsp. garlic salt
⅛ tsp. pepper
1 c. flour
Butter
¼ c. minced onion

(Continued on next page)

1 c. chicken broth
1 c. sliced mushrooms
1 jar marinated artichoke hearts
1 c. Sauterne

Dredge chicken in garlic salt, pepper and flour. Brown in butter. Add onion and brown. Add chicken broth; simmer for 20 minutes. Add mushrooms, artichokes and Sauterne; simmer for 10 minutes. Yield: 4 servings.

Sarah Elizabeth Cooper, Del Mar H. S.
San Jose, California

CHICKEN CACCIATORE

2 lb. chicken thighs or legs
2 tsp. seasoned salt
¼ c. salad oil
1 pkg. spaghetti sauce mix
1 1-lb. can tomatoes

Sprinkle chicken with seasoned salt. Brown in salad oil in large skillet. Remove chicken; drain off fat. Blend spaghetti sauce mix and tomatoes in skillet. Add chicken. Cover and simmer for 30 minutes or until chicken is tender. Serve with mostaccioli or other pasta. Yield: 4-6 servings.

Mrs. Evelyn Miller, Detroit H. S.
Detroit, Texas

CHICKEN CACCIATORE

1 3-lb. chicken, cut into serving pieces
Seasoned flour
Fat
2 med. onions, chopped
2 c. water
2 ½ c. canned tomatoes
1 8-oz. can tomato sauce
1 clove of garlic
1 sm. hot red pepper
1 bay leaf
½ tsp. celery seed
⅛ tsp. sage

Rub chicken with seasoned flour. Brown on all sides in hot fat. Remove chicken. Cook onions in the same fat until golden brown. Drain off excess fat; add remaining ingredients to skillet. Blend. Cover and simmer for 30 to 45 minutes. Add browned chicken. Simmer for 1 hour or until tender. Yield: 4 servings.

Sister Mary Roselina, B.V.M., Allenman H. S.
Rock Island, Illinois

CHICKEN CACCIATORE

1 2 ½ to 3-lb. broiler-fryer, cut up
¼ c. olive oil
2 med. onions, sliced
2 c. tomatoes
1 8-oz. can seasoned tomato sauce
1 tsp. salt
1 tsp. crushed oregano
¼ tsp. pepper
½ tsp. celery seed
2 bay leaves
¼ c. cooking Sauterne

Slowly brown chicken in hot olive oil; remove from skillet. Add onion slices; cook until tender, but not brown. Combine remaining ingredients except wine. Add chicken to skillet; pour sauce over. Cover; simmer for 45 minutes. Stir in wine. Cook for 20 minutes uncovered, turning occasionally, until chicken is tender and sauce is thick. Skim off excess fat and remove bay leaves. Yield: 4-6 servings.

Mrs. Bobbie K. Troutman
Rosiclare Comm. Unit Dist No. 1
Rosiclare, Illinois

CHICKEN CHOW MEIN

1 c. chopped onions
1 c. chopped celery
1 13 ¾-oz. can chicken broth
2 cans cream of mushroom soup
1 14-oz. can boned chicken, diced
½ tsp. salt
¼ tsp. pepper
2 tbsp. chopped pimento
1 pkg. frozen peas
2 No. 2 ½ cans chow mein noodles

Simmer onions and celery in chicken broth until tender. Add mushroom soup, diced chicken, salt, pepper and pimento. Cook slowly for 30 minutes. Add peas; cook until peas are tender. Serve over chow mein noodles. Yield: 10 servings.

Mrs. Thelma Terrell, Sullivan H. S.
Sullivan, Indiana

CHICKEN PROVENCALE

Salt and pepper
2 2-lb. broilers, cut up
⅓ c. olive oil
¼ c. Sauterne or dry white wine
1 clove of garlic, finely chopped
2 lge. onions, chopped
½ lb. sliced mushrooms
3 lge. tomatoes, peeled, seeded and diced
½ c. white wine
2 tbsp. chopped parsley

Salt and pepper chicken on both sides; brown well in oil. Reduce heat; add Sauterne. Cover and cook for 12 minutes. Add garlic and onions. Brown lightly; add mushrooms and tomatoes. Turn chicken; distribute vegetables evenly. Cook, covered, until chicken is tender. Remove chicken to hot platter. Add remaining wine to sauce in pan; blend well. Season; add parsley and pour over chicken. Serve with buttered rice. Yield: 4 servings.

Corinne Lipchitz, Dracut Jr., H. S.
Dracut, Massachusetts

CHICKEN SAUTE A LA RUSSE

Flour
Salt and pepper to taste
Breasts and thighs of 2 chickens
¼ lb. butter
8 scallions, sliced
3 med. tomatoes, peeled, seeded and chopped
1 c. dry white wine
3 tbsp. chopped parsley
1 c. sour cream
Cooked rice

Flour, salt and pepper chicken. Saute in butter until golden. Add scallions with some of tops. Cook for 2 to 3 minutes. Add tomatoes; cover and simmer for 30 minutes. Remove chicken to a warm platter. Add wine and parsley to juices in skillet; blend well. Stir in sour cream. Heat sauce slowly, but do not boil. Add salt and pepper to taste. Make ring of rice on platter around chicken; pour sauce over all. Yield: 6 servings.

Vada Nolen, Rainelle H. S.
Rainelle, West Virginia

CHOW MEIN

1 chicken
1 lge. onion, diced
1 c. chopped celery
Flour
1 tbsp. Kitchen Bouquet
1 can string beans, drained
2 cans chow mein noodles or 2 c. raw rice, cooked

Boil chicken; reserve 2 cups broth. Remove chicken from bones. Add onion and celery to broth; cook until tender. Thicken broth with flour to medium white sauce consistency; add Kitchen Bouquet, string beans and chicken to sauce. Heat. Serve over chow mein noodles or cooked rice. Yield: 6-8 servings.

Mrs. Eleanor Morford, Highmore H. S.
Highmore, South Dakota

COUNTRY CAPTAIN CHICKEN

1 tsp. salt
¼ tsp. pepper
1 broiler-fryer, cut into serving pieces
¼ c. butter
1 med. onion, chopped
1 clove of garlic, crushed
2 tsp. curry powder
½ tsp. thyme
1 1-lb. can seasoned stewed tomatoes
¼ c. currants or raisins
Rice
Toasted blanched almonds
Chutney

Salt and pepper chicken. Set dial of temperature controlled burner at 300 degrees. Brown chicken in melted butter in large skillet. Remove chicken from skillet; add onion, garlic, curry powder and thyme. Cook until onion is tender but not brown. Add stewed tomatoes, currants and chicken. Cover and cook for 30 minutes or until chicken is tender. Serve over rice with almonds and chutney. Yield: 2-4 servings.

Mrs. Joyce M. Mueller, Washington H. S.
Brainerd, Minnesota

BURGUNDY ROCK CORNISH HENS

1 stalk celery, chopped
¼ green pepper, chopped
¼ onion, chopped
6 tbsp. butter
1 c. cooked rice
¼ tsp. salt
¼ tsp. pepper
½ tsp. poultry seasoning
2 Rock cornish hens
¼ c. Burgundy wine

Saute celery, green pepper and onion in 2 tablespoonfuls butter. Stir in rice and seasonings. Stuff hens with mixture. Place hens in baking pan. Bake at 350 degrees for 1 hour and 30 minutes. Combine wine and remaining butter; baste hens with the wine sauce every 30 minutes during baking time. Yield: 4 servings.

Helena T. Martines, Gompers Jr. H. S.
Los Angeles, California

CORNISH GAME HEN IN SOUR CREAM

2 cornish game hens
½ c. flour
3 tbsp. butter
¾ c. sliced onions
1 ½ tsp. salt
1 tsp. paprika
¾ tsp. sweet basil leaves
½ tsp. pepper
1 3-oz. can sliced mushrooms, undrained
1 ½ c. sour cream

Rinse hens; drain and dry. Coat with flour. Saute in butter for 10 to 15 minutes or until golden brown. Add onions; cook, stirring, for5 minutes. Combine salt, paprika, basil, pepper and mushrooms; pour over hens. Bring to boil. Reduce heat; simmer, covered, for 30 to 45 minutes. Remove to a platter; keep warm. Gradually add sour cream to mixture, stirring constantly. Reheat; pour over hens. Garnish with parsley, if desired. Yield: 2 servings.

Louise A. Hall, Amador Co. H. S.
Sutter Creek, California

CORNISH GAME HENS SUPREME

4 cornish hens
Salt and pepper to taste
4 tsp. minced onion
3 tbsp. butter
1 c. chicken stock

(Continued on next page)

1 2 ½-oz. jar button mushrooms
Cornstarch
1 to 2 jiggers cooking Sherry

Clean hens; salt and pepper inside and out. Place, breast-side up, in shallow baking dish. Sprinkle onion over hens. Bake at 350 degrees for 45 minutes. Heat 2 tablespoonfuls butter and stock. Baste chicken four times during baking with butter mixture. Lightly brown mushrooms in remaining butter. Remove hens from dish. Measure drippings. Return hens to dish. Add 1 teaspoonful cornstarch for each cup of drippings to butter and mushrooms; mix thoroughly. Add drippings; stir and cook until clear. Stir in Sherry. Pour over hens. Bake for 10 minutes longer. Garnish with kumquats and parsley, if desired. Yield: 4 servings.

Mrs. Homer D. Shurbet, Katy H. S.
Katy, Texas

CORNISH HENS ON WILD RICE MINGLE

¼ c. butter
½ c. chopped celery
1 4-oz. can sliced mushrooms, drained
¾ c. rice
¾ c. wild rice
2 envelopes dry onion soup mix
3 ½ c. boiling water
4 1 ¼-lb. frozen Rock cornish hens, thawed
Salt

Heat 2 tablespoonfuls butter in medium skillet; saute celery and mushrooms until golden. Add white rice; saute until golden. Stir in wild rice. Spread on bottom of roasting pan. Combine soup mix with water; pour over rice mixture. Rub hens with 2 tablespoonfuls soft butter. Roast at 450 degrees for 50 minutes to 1 hour or until golden brown or tender, spooning liquid from pan occasionally over hens. Yield: 8 servings.

Marcia Swenson, Stoughton H. S.
Stoughton, Wisconsin

ROAST CORNISH HEN

2 Rock cornish hens
Garlic salt
Salt and pepper
4 tbsp. butter
1 onion, chopped
Celery tops

Season hens with garlic salt, salt and pepper. Rub 1 tablespoonful soft butter on outside of each hen. Stuff each hen with 1 tablespoonful butter, one-half of chopped onion and celery tops. Bake, uncovered, at 350 degrees until tender and golden brown. Cut each hen in half and serve. Yield: 4 servings.

Mrs. J. B. Rhodes, Mina H. S.
Bastrop, Texas

CORNISH HENS WITH WILD RICE DRESSING

½ c. wild rice
1 ½ c. boiling water
1 4-oz. can mushrooms, sliced
1 sm. onion, chopped
½ c. diced celery
½ c. butter
2 tbsp. chopped pimento
4 1-lb. cornish hens
2 tsp. salt

Add rice to boiling water; cover and cook for 40 minutes or until tender. Cook mushrooms, onion and celery in 1/4 cup butter until tender but not brown. Add with pimento to rice, tossing lightly to mix. Rub cavities of hens with salt; lightly fill with dressing. Close opening with skewers, wings in place. Place hens, breast-side up, on rack in roasting pan. Brush with remaining butter. Bake at 350 degrees for 1 hour to 1 hour and 30 minutes, basting frequently with drippings. Yield: 4 servings.

Mrs. Darlene Harms Hicks, Midland H. S.
Midland, Texas

ROAST CORNISH HEN

1 sm. cornish hen
Salt and pepper
Melted butter
1 ½ tbsp. honey

Split hen in half; wash and dry inside and out. Sprinkle both sides with small amount of salt and pepper. Brush with 3 tablespoonfuls butter; place, breast-side down, on rack in shallow pan. Bake at 325 degrees for 25 minutes. Turn and brush with melted butter. Cook for 25 minutes. Add honey in equal amounts with melted butter. Brush on hen; bake for 15 minutes. Turn hen again; brush with butter and honey mixture. Bake for 15 minutes longer. Do not add honey mixture until bird is tender or meat will burn. Serve with wild rice. Yield: 1 serving.

Mrs. Elizabeth C. Jackson, Hobbton H. S.
Newton Grove, North Carolina

ROAST CORNISH HENS

4 c. cooked rice
3 tbsp. salad oil
1 c. sauted sliced mushrooms
2 tbsp. minced green onion
1 tsp. chopped fresh ginger
2 eggs, slightly beaten
Soy sauce
Salt to taste
Slivered almonds (opt.)
8 to 10 cornish game hens
Sherry
Oil

Cook rice in salad oil for 5 minutes or until browned, stirring constantly. Add mushrooms, onion and ginger; cook for 3 minutes. Add eggs; cook and stir until eggs set. Season with 1 tablespoonful soy sauce and salt; add almonds. Stuff hens with mixture. Roast at 400 degrees for 40

(Continued on next page)

minutes, basting with equal parts of soy sauce, Sherry and oil. Yield: 8-10 servings.

Mrs. Jacquelyn Kappes, Great Valley H. S.
Malvern, Pennsylvania

ROAST ROCK CORNISH HENS

6 1 ¼-lb. frozen Rock cornish hens
¾ c. butter or margarine
¾ c. dry white wine
3 tbsp. dried tarragon
6 cloves of garlic, peeled
Salt and pepper
Garlic salt
1 bunch watercress

Thaw hens overnight in refrigerator. Melt butter in saucepan; add wine and 1 tablespoonful tarragon. Place 1 clove of garlic, 1 teaspoonful tarragon, 1/4 teaspoonful salt and 1/8 teaspoonful pepper in each hen. Sprinkle hens generously with garlic salt; refrigerate. Place hens in large shallow open pan without rack. Roast in preheated 400 to 450 degree oven for 1 hour or until browned and done, basting several times with sauce. Arrange on bed of watercress on serving platter; pour drippings over hens. If desired, serve with wild rice. Yield: 6 servings.

Ardis East, Ysleta H. S.
El Paso, Texas

ROCK CORNISH DELUXE

3 1-lb. Rock cornish hens, cut into halves
3 tbsp. butter
¼ c. minced onion
1 6-oz. can sliced broiled-in-butter mushrooms
¾ c. Muscatel or chicken broth
2 tbsp. cornstarch
¼ c. cold water
1 tsp. Kitchen Bouquet
1 c. sour cream

Place hens, skin-side down, and onion in melted butter in skillet. Saute for 10 minutes or until hens are brown and onion is tender. Drain mushrooms, reserving liquid. Add mushroom broth and wine to hens. Cover and simmer for 30 minutes. Remove hens; place on warm serving platter. Combine cornstarch, cold water and Kitchen Bouquet; stir into pan drippings. Cook, stirring constantly, until gravy thickens and is smooth. Stir in sour cream and mushroom. Heat gently until piping hot; do not boil. Serve in gravy boat or pour over hens on serving plates. Yield: 6 servings.

Mrs. Rex Todd Withers, Chief, Home Economics and Family Life Education Service, State Dept. of Public Instruction, Lansing, Michigan

ROCK CORNISH HENS WITH WILD RICE STUFFING

¾ c. wild rice
1 ½ c. chicken stock
3 tbsp. butter
1 ½ c. chopped celery
1 ½ c. chopped onions
2 tsp. seasoned salt
¼ c. Sherry
6 Rock cornish hens
¼ c. butter, melted

Wash rice well; place in a bowl. Add water to cover. Let rice soak for 2 hours. Drain; place in a 2-quart saucepan. Add chicken stock and 1 tablespoonful butter. Bring to a boil; reduce heat. Cover; simmer gently for 30 minutes or until rice is tender. Melt remaining butter. Add celery and onions to butter; saute until crisp-tender. Add vegetables, 1 teaspoonful seasoned salt and Sherry to cooked rice, mixing lightly to combine. Wash cornish hens; dry thoroughly. Stuff each hen lightly with 1/2 cup rice stuffing; truss. Blend melted butter and remaining seasoned salt. Brush each hen with seasoned butter. Roast at 350 degrees for 1 hour and 30 minutes. Yield: 6 servings.

Dorothy Maynard, Holston H. S.
Knoxville, Tennessee

GOOSE STUFFED WITH SAUERKRAUT

1 goose
1 lge. can sauerkraut
1 potato, grated
Salt and pepper

Place goose in 400 degree oven for 20 minutes. Boil sauerkraut with grated potato for 20 minutes. Salt and pepper inside of goose; stuff with sauerkraut. Bake at 300 degrees until done.

Mrs. Sadie Mundt, Owen-Withee H. S.
Owen, Wisconsin

ROASTED GOOSE

½ c. chopped onion
¼ c. butter
4 c. dry bread
Water
1 tsp. salt
½ tsp. pepper
2 eggs
1 lb. sausage
1 6 to 10-lb. goose

Saute onion in butter. Soak bread in water; squeeze out excess moisture. Mix sauted onions, moist bread, salt, pepper, eggs and sausage. Stuff goose with mixture. Place in roasting pan, breast-side down, in 3 inches of boiling water. Cover; bake at 350 degrees for 1 hour. Drain off water. Uncover; roast, back-side down for 2 hours, basting occasionally. Yield: 8 servings.

Sieglinde Regel, Kent-Meridian H. S.
Kent, Washington

AFRICAN GUINEA HEN

½ lb. butter
2 sm. guinea hens or 2 ½ lb. chicken, cut up
1 onion, chopped
1 clove of garlic, minced
1 tbsp. flour
¾ c. sweetened vinegar or apple juice
1 c. water
2 tsp. salt
½ tsp. pepper
1 bay leaf
3 tomatoes, chopped
3 sweet potatoes, peeled and cubed
5 bananas, sliced

Melt all but 3 tablespoonfuls butter in 10-inch saucepan or casserole. Add poultry, onion and garlic; saute until brown, stirring frequently. Sprinkle with flour; add juice, water, salt, pepper, bay leaf, tomatoes and potatoes. Mix well. Cover and cook over low heat for 35 minutes or until poultry and potatoes are tender. Add seasonings. Melt remaining butter in a skillet; saute bananas lightly. Arrange poultry in center of platter; place potato mixture around edges. Garnish with bananas. Serve with rice and gravy made from remaining liquid, if desired. Yield: 6-8 servings.

Mrs. Jacquelin Johnstone
Delta Secondary School
Ladner, British Columbia, Canada

BAKING A TURKEY

1 12 to 16-lb. turkey
Salt
Monosodium glutamate

Leave bird in original wrap. Place on a tray in refrigerator. When thawed, rinse bird with cold water; drain and pat dry. Rub skin and cavity lightly with salt and monosodium glutamate. Fold wings akimbo style; bring wing tips onto the back. Push drumsticks under band of skin at tail or tie with soft string. Line a shallow roasting pan with foil. Place bird on a rack in foil-lined pan. Brush entire bird with soft shortening. Bake at 350 degrees for 3 hours to 3 hours and 45 minutes. Cover with a loose tent of heavy aluminum wrap. NOTE: To make tent, tear off a sheet of heavy duty foil 5 to 10-inches longer than turkey. Crease lengthwise through center. Place over bird; press foil gently at drumsticks to anchor it. Giblet gravy may be made and served with turkey.

Mrs. Dorothy Sue T. Hill, Oberlin H. S.
Oberlin, Louisiana

POT ROAST OF TURKEY

¼ c. butter or margarine
1 6-lb. turkey
Salt and pepper
2 chicken bouillon cubes
1 c. boiling water
2 tbsp. paprika
Neck, gizzard and heart of turkey
⅓ c. flour
1 pt. sour cream

Place butter in Dutch oven; brown turkey for 20 to 30 minutes on all sides, sprinkling with salt and pepper. Place turkey on trivet in Dutch oven Dissolve bouillon cubes in boiling water; add paprika with neck, gizzard and heart. Simmer, covered, for 2 hours to 2 hours and 30 minutes, until tender, turning occasionally. Remove turkey to heated platter; keep warm. Chop heart and gizzard, discarding neck. Add enough water to liquid in Dutch oven to make 2 cups. Mix flour, 1 teaspoonful salt and a small amount liquid in small bowl; stir into remaining liquid. Cook, stirring until thickened. Add sour cream, heart and gizzard; heat. Serve on a bed of cooked rice, garnished with sauted mushrooms and parsley, if desired. Yield: 6 servings.

Mrs. Marian G. Craddock, Colorado City H. S.
Colorado City, Texas

ROAST TURKEY IN BROWN PAPER SACK

1 16 to 20-lb. turkey
Salt
Fat or shortening

Wash bird inside and out; dry well. Rub inside of bird with salt. Fill neck cavity with stuffing; fasten neck skin with skewer or pin. Fasten opening with skewers; lace shut. Tie leg ends to tail; bring cord crisscross over back and around base of wings. Tie. Lift wing tip up and over back for a natural brace when turned over. Brush entire bird with fat. Place in brown paper sack; seal. Place in shallow baking pan. Bake at 325 degrees for 5 hours and 30 minutes. Remove paper sack.

Frances Schneider, Menomonie H. S.
Menomonie, Wisconsin

SWEET-SOUR TURKEY

1 No. 2 can pineapple chunks
⅓ c. vinegar
¼ c. brown sugar
2 tbsp. cornstarch
1 tbsp. soy sauce
½ tsp. salt
2 ½ c. diced cooked turkey
¾ c. green peppers, cut into 1 ½-in. strips
¼ c. thinly sliced onion

Drain pineapple, reserving 1 cup juice. Combine pineapple juice, vinegar, brown sugar, cornstarch, soy sauce and salt. Cook over low heat until thickened and clear, stirring constantly. Remove from heat; add turkey. Let stand for 10 minutes. Place green peppers in boiling water to cover; let stand for 5 minutes. Drain well. Add green peppers, onion and pineapple chunks to turkey mixture; heat through. Serve over hot cooked rice. Yield: 4-6 servings.

Mrs . Anita Darnell, Greenville H. S.
Greenville, Texas

TURKEY-CRANBERRY SQUARES

2 tbsp. butter
½ c. sugar
1 tsp. grated orange peel
2 c. fresh cranberries
5 c. ground cooked turkey
1 c. turkey stock
1 c. milk
1 tsp. salt
¼ tsp. pepper
2 tbsp. finely chopped onion
2 c. soft bread crumbs or left-over stuffing
2 eggs, slightly beaten

Melt butter in 8-inch pan; blend in sugar and orange peel. Cover with cranberries. Combine remaining ingredients, mixing thoroughly. Pack firmly over cranberries. Bake at 400 degrees for 45 minutes. Turn, upside-down, on serving platter; cut into squares. Serve hot. Yield: 8 servings.

Mrs. M. Christiana Gates, Memorial H. S.
Middleboro, Massachusetts

TURKEY CROQUETTES

WHITE SAUCE:

3 tbsp. butter
4 tbsp. flour
1 c. milk
Salt
2 c. diced cooked turkey
⅛ tsp. paprika
⅛ tsp. celery salt
1 tsp. lemon juice
¼ tsp. grated onion
2 c. crushed corn flakes
1 egg, beaten
1 tbsp. cold water

Combine turkey, 1/2 teaspoonful salt, paprika, celery, salt, lemon juice, onion and 1 cup white sauce. Mix well; spread on a plate. Chill for 5 to 6 hours or overnight. Shape as desired. Dip into corn flake crumbs, then into egg with water and again into crumbs. Fry in deep fat until brown. Yield: 6 servings.

Emily J. Rickman, Area Supervisor
Home Economics Education, Danville, Virginia

TURKEY AND DRESSING

1 12-lb. turkey
1 can chicken consomme
1 lb. loose pork sausage
6 med. onions, chopped
3 c. chopped celery
½ c. chopped parsley
Butter
1 16 to 20-oz. pkg. seasoned bread stuffing mix
6 eggs
1 c. evaporated milk or cream
Flour
Paprika
Poultry seasoning
Salt and pepper

Clean turkey; drain and dry. Dilute consomme according to can directions. Boil neck with consomme. Saute sausage, onions, celery and parsley until tender. Add 1 cup butter, stuffing mix, eggs and milk. Stir gently. Fill turkey loosely with stuffing. Place folded cheese cloth over rear cavity. Secure with pins; gently fill neck cavity and stretch skin over cavity. Secure with pins. Place turkey on rack in foil-lined roasting pan. Baste generously with melted butter. Dredge with flour; carefully baste with enough butter to moisten flour. Sprinkle generously with paprika, poultry seasoning, salt and pepper. Fold foil and seal over turkey. Bake at 350 degrees for 20 minutes per pound, basting every hour with consomme. Open foil the last hour of baking to brown.

Mrs. Martz, Upland H. S.
Upland, California

TURKEY PUFF

½ c. finely chopped onion
½ c. diced celery
¼ c. diced green pepper
2 tbsp. butter
2 c. cooked turkey or chicken
1 can chicken-noodle soup
½ c. half and half
½ c. sliced mushrooms
2 tbsp. chopped pimento
½ c. toasted almonds
½ tsp. salt
¼ tsp. white pepper
4 eggs, separated
½ c. shredded cheese

Saute onion, celery and green pepper in butter in large pan. Add turkey, soup, half and half, mushrooms, pimento, almonds, salt and pepper. Blend well; cook over low heat just until hot. Pour into buttered 2-quart casserole. Beat egg yolks; add cheese. Fold in stiffly beaten egg whites. Pour egg-cheese mixture over casserole. Bake at 350 degrees for 30 minutes. Yield: 6 servings.

Jacqueline H. Howard, University H. S.
Los Angeles, California

Fish & Shellfish Favorites

BAKED BASS

1 3 to 4-lb. bass
Salt
1 tbsp. lemon juice
1 ½ c. bread cubes
¼ tsp. pepper
½ tsp. thyme
1 tsp. monosodium glutamate
Melted butter
1 egg, slightly beaten
½ c. finely chopped onion

Clean dressed fish; rub with 1 teaspoonful salt and lemon juice inside and out. Mix bread cubes, 1/2 teaspoonful salt, pepper, thyme, monosodium glutamate, 3 tablespoonfuls melted butter and onion. Stuff mixture into fish cavity. Fasten with skewers. Place in baking pan; brush with melted butter. Bake at 450 degrees for 15 minutes. Reduce heat to 400 degrees; bake for 45 minutes longer. Garnish with parsley and lemon wedges. Yield: 6 servings.

Ellen Beth Krumwiede, Reed Custer H. S.
Braidwood, Illinois

AL'S FAVORITE BLUEGILLS

¼ lb. salt pork, cubed
1 lge. onion, sliced
1 tsp. mixed spice
½ c. vinegar
½ c. sugar
1 tsp. salt
1 doz. bluegills

Fry salt pork until brown. Cook onion in small amount of water. Combine onion and pork; add spices, vinegar, sugar and salt. Cook fish in sauce for 10 minutes or until tender. Yield: 4 servings.

Edith Hansen, Mt. Pleasant Jr. H. S.
Mt. Pleasant, Michigan

BAKED CARP

Salt and pepper
Monosodium glutamate
1 3 to 4-lb. carp
¼ lb. butter
3 strips bacon
Watercress or parsley
2 lemons, sliced

Sprinkle seasonings generously over entire fish. Place butter inside and bacon on top of fish. Wrap tightly in heavy aluminum foil. Place in shallow pan. Bake at 350 degrees for 45 minutes. Serve on large platter on bed of watercress and lemon slices. Yield: 6 servings.

Mrs. Juanita Fryer, Bentonville H. S.
Bentonville, Arkansas

BATTERED CATFISH

1 can shortening
2 eggs, beaten
1 c. milk
Salt and pepper
12 lb. catfish, cut into steaks
Meal

Melt shortening in a deep thick kettle. Mix eggs and milk. Salt and pepper fish; dip into milk mixture. Roll fish in meal; drop into hot shortening. Fry until brown, turning once. Drain on absorbent paper. Serve hot with hush puppies, if desired. Yield: 12 servings.

Mrs. Mary Jo Gresham
Hickory Flat Attendance Center
Hickory Flat, Mississippi

CODFISH SUPPER QUICKIE

1 lb. frozen codfish or other fish
2 tbsp. dried green and red pepper flakes or
  4 tbsp. fresh green pepper
4 tbsp. shortening
1 sm. can chopped mushrooms
1 can cream of mushroom soup
½ tsp. salt
4 potatoes, cooked

Thaw frozen fish. Cut into 1-inch cubes. Cook peppers in shortening for 10 minutes. Add fish; cook for 10 minutes or until fish flakes easily when tested with fork. Add mushrooms, soup and salt. Heat; let stand for 5 minutes. Serve on potatoes. NOTE: May be served on toast or 2 cups cooked rice. Yield: 4 servings.

Mrs. Ella Adair, Bryce Valley H. S.
Tropic, Utah

BAKED FILLET OF FLOUNDER

1 lb. frozen fillet of flounder
½ tsp. salt
2 tbsp. lemon juice
3 tbsp. butter

Place frozen flounder in cold water; thaw only enough to separate pieces. Sprinkle with salt and lemon juice; dot with butter. Place on aluminum foil lined pan. Bake at 350 degrees for 20 minutes or until brown on top. Yield: 3 servings.

Mrs. Clarinda A. Britt, Maiden H. S.
Maiden, North Carolina

BAKED FLOUNDER FILLET SUPREME

6 lge. flounder fillets
Seasoned salt

(Continued on next page)

6 slices natural Swiss cheese
1 med. tomato, cut into 6 wedges
2 tbsp. butter
1 3 to 4-oz. can sliced mushrooms
2 sm. onions, chopped
1 ½ tbsp. flour
1 ½ tsp. salt
Snipped parsley
1 c. light cream
6 tbsp. Sherry
2 c. precooked rice

Sprinkle fish lightly on each side with seasoned salt; shape fish into a roll. Fold cheese slices in half, crosswise. Arrange fish rolls, seam-side down in baking dish. Place tomato and cheese slices down center of dish. Melt butter in large skillet. Drain mushrooms, reserving liquid. Saute mushrooms and onions in butter until golden; stir in flour, salt and 1/4 cup parsley. Add cream. Combine mushroom liquid with enough water to equal 1/2 cup; add liquid with Sherry to mixture, stirring. Bring mixture to a boil; pour over fish. Bake at 400 degrees until fish is golden brown. Prepare rice according to package directions. Stir in a small amount of parsley. Spoon rice along sides of fish. Yield: 4 servings.

Cheryle De Van, Rio Vista H. S.
Rio Vista, California

BATTER-FRIED FISH

1 1-lb. pkg. frozen haddock
Salt
1 egg
1 ¼ c. evaporated milk
1 c. flour
2 tsp. baking powder
¼ c. corn meal

Cut fish into serving pieces; sprinkle lightly with salt. Combine 1/4 teaspoonful salt with remaining ingredients. Dredge fish in batter. Fry in deep fat at 375 degrees for 5 minutes or until brown. Yield: 4-6 servings.

Mrs. Eleanor Ray, Elderton Jr. H. S.
Elderton, Pennsylvania

FILLETS EN CASSEROLE

1 lb. haddock, cod or flounder fillets
1 can cream of mushroom soup
½ pt. sour cream
Bread crumbs
Butter

Cut fillets into small pieces. Combine mushroom soup and sour cream. Place layer of fish on bottom of well greased casserole. Top with layer of soup mixture. Repeat layers. Cover with bread crumbs; pat with butter. Bake at 350 degrees for 30 minutes. Yield: 4-6 servings.

Sharon Anderson, Rochelle Twp. H. S.
Rochelle, Illinois

ROLLED STUFFED FILLETS

¼ c. chopped onion
¼ c. margarine
4 c. soft bread crumbs
¾ tsp. salt
Dash of pepper
1 tsp. poultry seasoning
1 c. mayonnaise
1 lb. frozen haddock fillets

Cook onion in butter until tender but not browned. Mix in crumbs and seasoning. Blend in 1/2 cup mayonnaise. Cut fillets into five strips 8-inches long. Spread each with stuffing; roll up in jelly roll fashion. Place in greased casserole or individual cooking cups. Place in a shallow pan. Bake at 350 degrees for 20 minutes. Spread with remaining mayonnaise. Bake for 20 minutes longer. Garnish with parsley. Yield: 5 servings.

Wilma Durbin Wood, Amanda Jr. H. S.
Middletown, Ohio

BROILED HALIBUT

1 egg, beaten
½ c. milk
6 slices halibut
1 c. flour
12 crackers, rolled
Salt and pepper
Paprika
Butter

Combine egg and milk; dip the fish into mixture. Roll in flour; dip in egg mixture and roll in flour again. Roll in cracker crumbs. Place fish on a greased cookie sheet. Sprinkle with salt and pepper and paprika. Dot with butter. Bake at 350 degrees for 20 minutes. Broil for 1 minute. Serve with parsley and lemon, if desired. Yield: 6 servings.

Virginia Stewart, Spanish Fork H. S.
Spanish Fork, Utah

CHINESE-STYLE FRIED HALIBUT

2 lb. halibut steaks or fillets
¼ c. flour
1 tsp. salt
Fat
½ c. vinegar
1 c. sugar
Water
3 chicken bouillon cubes
1 lge. green pepper, cut into strips
1 c. drained pineapple chunks
3 tbsp. cornstarch
1 ½ tsp. soy sauce

Cut steaks into serving pieces. Mix flour with salt; roll steaks in seasoned flour. Melt fat 1/8-inch deep in heavy frying pan. Brown fish in hot fat on each side, turning carefully. Drain on absorbent paper. Combine vinegar, sugar, 1 1/3

(Continued on next page)

cups water, bouillon cubes, green pepper and pineapple; simmer for 10 minutes. Mix cornstarch, 1 1/2 tablespoons water and soy sauce into a thin paste; add gradually to hot sauce. Cook until thick, stirring constantly. Serve sauce over fish. Yield: 6 servings.

Mrs. Esther Williams, Pocatello H. S.
Pocatello, Idaho

FISH PUDDING

1 qt. boiling water
½ lemon, sliced
1 onion, minced
Salt
Bay leaf
Whole allspice
1 ½ lb. halibut
6 tbsp. butter
6 tbsp. flour
2 c. milk
1 tsp. pepper
2 tsp. onion juice
4 eggs, separated

Combine water, lemon, onion, salt, bay leaf and allspice; simmer fish in liquid for 30 minutes. Reserve liquid. Remove skin and bones; flake. Make white sauce with butter, flour, milk and seasonings. Add egg yolks and fish. Beat egg whites stiff; fold into sauce. Pour into buttered ring mold; place in pan of hot water. Bake at 325 degrees for 45 minutes.

SAUCE:

3 egg yolks
1 tbsp. butter
1 tsp. lemon juice
Salt
Cayenne pepper
½ tsp. flour
¾ c. fish liquid
2 tbsp. capers (opt.)

Combine egg yolks, butter, lemon juice, salt to taste, cayenne and flour; add fish liquid and capers. Serve with pudding. Yield: 7-8 servings.

Mrs. Marion Morgan, La Grande H. S.
La Grande, Oregon

HOLLENDON HALIBUT

6 thin slices fat salt pork, cut into 2 ½-in. squares
1 sm. onion, thinly sliced
Piece of bay leaf
1 2-lb. piece chicken halibut
3 tbsp. butter
3 tbsp. flour
¾ c. buttered cracker crumbs
1 lemon, cut into fancy shapes
Finely chopped parsley
Paprika

Arrange pork in dripping pan. Cover with onion and a small piece bay leaf. Wipe halibut; place over pork and onion. Cream butter with flour; spread over halibut. Cover with buttered cracker crumbs; arrange thin strips of salt pork over crumbs. Cover with buttered paper. Bake at 350 degrees for 50 minutes. Remove paper during last 15 minutes of cooking to brown crumbs. Remove to hot serving dish; garnish with slices of lemon. Sprinkle with finely chopped parsley and paprika. Serve with any sauce desired. Yield: 6-8 servings.

Mrs. LeArta Hammond, West Side H. S.
Dayton, Idaho

GLORIFIED KING MACKEREL

½ c. cooking Sauterne
½ tsp. celery salt
½ tsp. onion salt
½ tsp. Worcestershire sauce
½ tsp. salt
1 1-lb. King mackerel fillet, cut into 1-in. squares
Self-rising flour
Bacon drippings
Cooking oil

Combine Sauterne, celery salt, onion salt, Worcestershire sauce and salt; marinate mackeral in mixture for 20 minutes. Lightly flour each piece; fry in deep fat of one-half bacon drippings and oil on medium heat until brown. Serve immediately. Yield: 6 servings.

Mrs. Nancye A. Laine, John Yeates H. S.
Suffolk, Virginia

NEW ENGLAND BAKED FISH

2 lb. mackerel fillets
¾ to 1 c. milk
Butter
Salt and pepper

Arrange fish in greased baking dish. Cover with milk; dot with butter. Sprinkle with salt and pepper. Bake at 350 degrees for 20 t0 25 minutes or until done. Serve with lemon butter or parsley, if desired.

Ellen F. Dow, Windsor H. S.
Windsor, Vermont

FRENCH-FRIED FISH

20 lb. frozen perch or sole, thawed and skinned
Salted water
1 doz. eggs
1 ⅔ c. evaporated milk
Cracker meal

Soak fish in salted water for 45 minutes. Drain: dry fish thoroughly. Beat eggs with milk: dip

(Continued on next page)

fish into milk mixture; drain slightly. Roll in cracker meal. Fry in deep fat at 375 degrees. Yield: 80 servings.

Pauline J. Harris, Pennsboro H. S.
Pennsboro, West Virginia

ROLL-UPS SUPREME

5 or 6 fillet of pike, sole or perch
1 No. 303 can long green beans or asparagus stalks
1 can cream of celery soup
1 tbsp. Worcestershire sauce
1 tbsp. lemon juice
¼ c. slivered almonds
¼ c. Parmesan cheese

Roll fillet around several stalks of beans or asparagus; place in an 8 x 10-inch baking dish. Mix soup with Worcestershire sauce and lemon juice; pour over roll-ups. Sprinkle with almonds and cheese. Bake at 350 degrees for 30 minutes. Yield: 5-6 servings.

Mrs. Louis Ivanish, Malta H. S.
Malta, Montana

GRANDMOTHER'S SALMON CAKES

1 1-lb. can pink salmon
2 eggs
Dash of salt
3 slices bread, crumbled
Fat or bacon drippings

Place salmon in mixing bowl; add eggs, salt and crumbled bread. Mix well. Shape into six cakes; let stand on paper towels for ten minutes. Panfry in small amount of fat or bacon drippings for about five minutes on each side or until slightly brown. Place in oven. Bake in preheated 375 degree oven for about 20 minutes.

Mrs. Virginia H. Brown, Soddy-Daisy Jr. H.S.
Daisy, Tennessee

SALMON CROQUETTES

1 can salmon
2 med. potatoes, cooked and mashed
Salt and pepper to taste
1 egg, beaten
Corn meal

Combine salmon and potatoes. Add salt and pepper; mix well. Shape into croquettes. Dip in beaten egg; coat with corn meal. Brown in hot fat in skillet. Yield: 6 servings.

Mrs. Lucile Horton, Del Rio H. S.
Del Rio, Texas

SALMON CROQUETTES

1 c. cracker crumbs, finely rolled
1 7 ¾-oz. can pink salmon
1 egg
Salt
Red or black pepper to taste
Juice of 1 lemon
2 tbsp. Worcestershire sauce
⅓ c. catsup
1 egg white, slightly beaten
1 c. cracker crumbs, finely rolled

Combine 1 cup cracker crumbs with all remaining ingredients except egg white. Shape salmon mixture into patties. Dip patties into egg white, then roll in cracker crumbs. Fry in deep fat. Yield: 12-15 servings.

Mrs. Sue Batchelor, Gordo H. S.
Gordo, Alabama

SALMON CROQUETTES

2 tbsp. margarine
4 tbsp. flour
½ tsp. salt
1 c. milk
1 tall can salmon
2 eggs, well beaten
1 c. cracker crumbs

Melt margarine in top of double boiler; stir in flour and salt. Mix well; add milk gradually. Cook until thick, stirring occasionally. Remove from heat; add salmon. Shape in cylinders about 2 inches long and roll in the beaten eggs and cracker crumbs. Cook in hot fat. Serve topped with mushroom sauce, if desired. Yield: 6 servings.

Mrs. John Hillhouse, Mathiston H. S.
Mathiston, Mississippi

SALMON CROQUETTES

1 1-lb. can salmon, partially drained
2 slices soft bread, finely crumbled or ½ c. cooked rice
¼ tsp. grated onion (opt.)
Dash of seasoned pepper
1 tsp. salt
½ can cream of mushroom soup
Corn meal

Flake salmon. Mix crumbs, onion, pepper and salt into soup, thinning with salmon liquid if necessary. Stir in salmon. Chill for 1 to 2 hours. Shape into croquettes. Roll in corn meal. Fry in deep fat until browned. Yield: 5-6 servings.

Martha Rast, Chester Co. H. S.
Henderson, Tennessee

SALMON CROQUETTES

1 1-lb. can salmon
Salt and pepper to taste
2 eggs, beaten
½ c. buttermilk
½ c. flour
¼ tsp. soda

Drain salmon; mash with fork. Add eggs, milk and combined flour and soda; mix well. Drop batter from a spoon into deep 375 degree fat. Fry until golden brown, turning once. Drain on absorbent paper. Yield: 6-8 servings.

Mrs. Max Parker, Gibson H. S.
Gibson, Tennessee

SALMON CROQUETTES

3 tbsp. butter
4 tbsp. flour
½ tsp. salt
⅛ tsp. pepper
1 c. milk
1 slice onion
2 c. flaked salmon
1 tsp. minced parsley
1 egg, beaten
2 tbsp. water
Fine bread or cracker crumbs

Melt butter in saucepan; blend in flour, salt and pepper. Remove from heat; add milk and onion. Return to heat; cook until thickened, stirring constantly. Cool; remove onion. Stir in salmon and parsley; chill for 2 to 3 hours. Shape into patties; dip in combined eggs and water. Roll in crumbs. Dry for 30 minutes; brown in deep fat. Yield: 6 servings.

Ellen Webb Massengill, Seminole H. S.
Seminole, Texas

SALMON PATTIES

4 tbsp. shortening
⅓ c. flour
½ tsp. salt
¼ tsp. celery salt
⅛ tsp. pepper
1 c. plus 3 tbsp. milk
1 1-lb. can salmon, drained
2 tbsp. lemon juice
2 tbsp. parsley
2 tsp. grated onion
1 egg, slightly beaten
1 c. finely ground cracker crumbs

Melt shortening in saucepan; blend in flour, salt, celery salt and pepper. Add 1 cup milk gradually; cook, stirring constantly, until thickened and smooth. Remove from heat. Remove skin and bones from salmon; flake fine. Add salmon to mixture. Blend in lemon juice, parsley and onion. Spread in greased shallow pan; chill. Flatten into balls. Mix egg and 3 tablespoonfuls milk. Dip balls into egg mixture and again in crumbs. Fry for 3 minutes in deep fat. Yield: 4 servings.

Mrs. Clyda Phillips, Star City H. S.
Star City, Arkansas

SALMON LOAF

1 1-lb. can salmon
¾ c. salad dressing
1 can cream of celery soup
1 egg, beaten
1 c. dry bread crumbs
½ c. chopped onion
¼ c. chopped green pepper
1 tbsp. lemon juice
1 tsp. salt
½ c. sour cream
¼ c. chopped cucumber

Combine all ingredients except 1/4 cup salad dressing, sour cream and cucumber. Pour into greased 8 1/2 x 4 1/2-inch loaf pan. Bake at 350 degrees for 1 hour. Mix remaining ingredients. Serve with loaf. Yield: 8 servings.

Sallie S. Dorroh, Whitmire H. S.
Whitmire, South Carolina

SALMON LOAF

1 1-lb. can salmon
Bread pieces
Milk
2 eggs, beaten
½ tsp. salt
¼ tsp. pepper
¼ c. minced celery or onion
2 tbsp. parsley
2 tbsp. butter

Empty salmon into large bowl. Using salmon can as measure, fill with bread and then milk. Add bread and milk to salmon. Add eggs, salt, pepper, celery and parsley. Melt butter in an 8 x 8-inch casserole; pour over salmon mixture. Mix quickly; pour into dish. Bake at 375 degrees for 1 hour or until inserted knife comes out clean. Yield: 4 servings.

Mrs. Eunice Cole Salomonson, Berthoud H. S.
Berthoud, Colorado

SALMON LOAF

1 1-lb. can salmon
1 egg, beaten
½ sm. onion, minced
1 tsp. salt
¼ tsp. pepper
½ c. evaporated milk
½ c. water
2 c. soft bread crumbs

Break salmon apart with fork; remove bones and skin. Add egg, onion, salt, pepper, milk and

(Continued on next page)

water; blend. Add bread crumbs; mix well. Place mixture in greased loaf pan. Bake at 375 degrees for 1 hour. Yield: 4 servings.

Irene E. Krause, Shawano H. S.
Shawano, Wisconsin

SALMON LOAF WITH SAUCE

2 c. salmon, flaked
1 c. soft bread crumbs
2 tsp. lemon juice
¼ tsp. salt
Few grains of cayenne pepper
2 eggs, slightly beaten
2 c. very thick white sauce
½ c. cooked green peas
2 tsp. chopped parsley
2 hard-cooked eggs, chopped
1 c. thick white sauce

Combine salmon, crumbs, lemon juice and seasonings. Add eggs to salmon mixture. Lightly blend in 2 cups very thick white sauce. Place salmon mixture in greased 8 1/2 to 9-inch loaf pan. Bake at 350 degrees for 25 minutes or until firm. Combine peas, parsley and eggs with 1 cup thick white sauce. Heat to serving temperature. Pour sauce over salmon loaf and serve.

Ruth W. Williams, Belmont H. S.
Belmont, North Carolina

SEAFOOD LOAF

1 1-lb. can salmon
1 10 ½-oz. can cream of celery soup
1 c. fine dry bread crumbs
2 eggs, slightly beaten
½ c. chopped onion
1 tbsp. lemon juice

Drain salmon, reserving 1/4 cup liquid. Remove skin and bones from salmon; flake. Thoroughly mix with salmon liquid and remaining ingredients. Pack into a well greased 9 x 5 x 3-inch loaf pan. Bake at 375 degrees for 1 hour or until browned. Cool loaf in pan for 10 minutes; loosen from sides of pan and turn out on platter. Yield: 4 servings.

Mrs. Ramona S. McPhail, Giddings H. S.
Giddings, Texas

SALMON BALLS

1 can salmon, drained
½ c. flour
1 c. corn meal
1 tsp. soda
2 eggs, beaten
1 c. buttermilk

Mash salmon; add flour, corn meal, soda, eggs and buttermilk. Shape teaspoonfuls of mixture into balls. Fry in 2 inches of hot fat; drain. Serve hot. Yield: 10 servings.

Mrs. Lila Wilkins, Smylie Wilson Jr. H. S.
Lubbock, Texas

SALMON CACHE

4 tbsp. margarine
4 tbsp. flour
2 c. milk
½ tsp. salt
Dash of pepper
Dash of paprika
1 tall can red salmon
1 sm. can mushrooms
½ c. sliced stuffed olives

Melt margarine over low heat; stir in flour. Gradually add milk, stirring constantly. Add salt, pepper and paprika. Add remaining ingredients; heat until blended and thoroughly heated.

CACHE:

1 tsp. lemon rind
2 c. sifted self-rising flour
3 tbsp. shortening
⅔ c. milk

Add lemon rind to flour; cut in shortening. Stir in milk until dry ingredients are moistened. Turn dough onto floured board; knead 20 strokes. Roll out 1/2-inch thick; cut with biscuit cutter. Place on baking sheet. Bake at 475 degrees for 12 minutes. Split biscuits; dot with butter. Pour hot salmon mixture over biscuits; serve. Yield: 6 servings.

Irene Cerlson, Clark Jr. H. S.
Mt. View, Alaska

SALMON-CHEESE PUFF

3 eggs, separated
¾ c. milk
1 c. soft bread crumbs
1 c. shredded Cheddar cheese
1 tsp. instant minced onion
½ tsp. salt
⅛ tsp. pepper
1 1-lb. can salmon, drained, boned and flaked
2 tsp. lemon juice

(Continued on next page)

Beat egg yolks with milk in mixing bowl. Add remaining ingredients except egg whites, mixing lightly but thoroughly. Beat egg whites until stiff but not dry; gently fold into salmon mixture. Turn mixture into shallow 1-quart baking dish. Bake in preheated 350 degree oven for 30 to 35 minutes or until knife inserted near center comes out clean.

PARSLEY SAUCE:

3 tbsp. butter
3 tbsp. flour
¾ tsp. salt
1 ½ c. milk
1 tbsp. lemon juice
1 ½ tbsp. chopped parsley

Melt butter in 1-quart saucepan; stir in flour and salt. Remove from heat; gradually stir in milk. Cook over medium heat, stirring constantly, until thickened. Cook for 2 minutes longer. Just before serving, stir in lemon juice and parsley. Serve over salmon. Yield: 6 servings.

Agnes Huffman, Thomas Downey H. S.
Modesto, California

SALMON CONFETTI

1 8-oz. pkg. elbow macaroni
1 c. chopped onions
1 c. chopped green peppers
½ c. chopped celery
¼ c. cooking oil
1 1-lb. can salmon
1 ½ c. milk
¼ c. flour
2 tbsp. chopped pimento
1 tsp. salt
⅛ tsp. pepper

Cook macaroni according to package directions; drain. Saute onions, green peppers and celery in oil until tender. Drain salmon; combine drained liquid with milk to make 2 cups Flake salmon. Stir flour into onion mixture; cook, stirring constantly, until blended. Stir in liquid; continue cooking and stirring until sauce thickens and bubbles. Stir in salmon, pimento, salt, pepper and macaroni. Heat through. Yield: 6-8 servings.

Hilda B. Cassell, Blackstone H. S.
Blackstone, Virginia

SALMON OMELET

5 eggs, slightly beaten
3 c. milk
1 c. evaporated milk
1 ½ tsp. salt
Dash of pepper
2 c. flaked salmon

Beat eggs; add milk, evaporated milk and seasoning; fold in salmon. Pour into well buttered casserole. Dot with butter. Bake at 350 degrees for 50 minutes. Yield: 8 servings.

Mrs. Renee Porter, American Fork H. S.
American Fork, Utah

SALMON POACHED IN COURT BOUILLON

8 c. water
1 lge. onion, sliced
4 carrots, sliced
2 stalks celery, sliced
2 bay leaves
1 bouquet garni
1 whole 6-lb. salmon
Lemon slices
Cucumber slices
Fresh watercress or parsley

Combine water with onion, carrots, celery, bay leaves and bouquet garni in a large kettle. Bring to a boil; skim. Reduce heat; simmer for 30 minutes. Cool slightly. Wrap salmon in thin muslin or cheesecloth; lower into bouillon. Add additional liquid, if needed. Simmer gently for 45 minutes to 1 hour or until fish flakes easily with a fork. Remove fish carefully from liquid; unwrap. Carefully remove skin. Arrange salmon on a hot platter; garnish with lemon slices, cucumber, watercress or parsley.

SAUCE:

1 c. mayonnaise
2 tbsp. finely chopped watercress or 4 tbsp. finely chopped parsley
2 tbsp. finely chopped tarragon leaves
2 tbsp. finely chopped onion
Lemon juice
Salt and freshly ground pepper

Combine all ingredients; mix well. Serve with salmon. Yield: 12 servings.

Velma L. Donald, Kenai Central H. S.
Kenai, Alaska

SALMON SOUFFLE

1 ½ c. canned pink salmon
1 tbsp. minced parsley
1 tsp. lemon juice
½ tsp. salt
⅛ tsp. pepper
⅛ tsp. paprika
1 ½ c. medium white sauce
3 eggs, separated

Shred salmon; combine with parsley, lemon juice, salt, pepper, paprika, white sauce and beaten egg yolks. Beat egg whites until stiff; fold into fish mixture. Turn into greased baking dish; set in a pan of hot water. Bake at 350 degrees until center is firm. Serve immediately. Yield: 6 servings.

Mrs. Berline Baldwin, Clarkton H. S.
Clarkton, North Carolina

SALMON SOUFFLE

1 7 ¾-oz. can salmon
1 can cream of mushroom soup
½ tsp. mustard
5 eggs, separated
1 tbsp. chopped parsley

Drain salmon, reserving liquid. Combine soup and mustard; stir in salmon liquid. Bring to a boil, stirring constantly. Beat egg yolks; blend in small amount of hot mixture. Return to remaining hot mixture. Cook, stirring, over low heat for 3 minutes. Cool for a few minutes. Mash salmon; add parsley and cooled sauce. Mix thoroughly. Beat egg whites until stiff, but not dry. Fold into salmon mixture. Pour into souffle dish. Bake at 375 degrees for 30 minutes. Serve immediately. Yield: 4 servings.

Ruby Townsley, Sulphur H. S.
Sulphur, Oklahoma

SALMON TREATS

4 tbsp. flour
1 tsp. salt
¼ tsp. pepper
4 tbsp. shortening, melted
1 c. milk
1 egg
1 ⅓ c. fine crumbs
1 ½ c. shredded salmon
½ tsp. onion juice
1 tbsp. lemon juice
1 egg, beaten
2 tbsp. water

Blend mixture of flour, salt and pepper into melted shortening. Add milk gradually. Cool slightly. Add egg, 1 cup crumbs, salmon, onion juice and lemon juice; mix. Pack into loaf pan and chill. Remove loaf and slice. Dip slices into remaining crumbs, then into mixture of egg and water. Dip into crumbs again; fry until browned on all sides. Yield: 4-6 servings.

Mrs. June Danell, Caprock H. S.
Amarillo, Texas

SIMPLE SALMON

1 1-lb. can salmon
Juice of ½ lemon
¼ tsp. salt
Dash of paprika
1 tsp. angostura
1 c. sour cream
3 slices onion, separated into rings

Drain salmon, reserving one-half the liquid. Place salmon in baking dish; remove bone and skin. Shape into oval; add reserved liquid. Pour lemon juice over top; sprinkle with salt and paprika. Add angostura to sour cream; pour over salmon. Place onion rings on top. Bake at 325 degrees for 40 minutes. Yield: 4 servings.

Lodi M. Pierce, Block H. S.
Jonesville, Louisiana

SWEET STUFFED SALMON OR STEAKS

2 salmon fillets or steaks
Salt and pepper
2 c. fine bread cubes
2 tbsp. chopped onion
1 tbsp. parsley
2 tbsp. chopped sweet pickle or relish
1 tbsp. lemon juice
4 tbsp. oil or melted shortening
3 slices bacon

Place fillet or steak in well greased baking dish; sprinkle each side with 1 teaspoonful salt and 1/3 teaspoonful pepper. Combine bread cubes with 1/2 teaspoonful salt, 1/8 teaspoonful pepper, onion, parsley, pickle, lemon juice and enough water to moisten mixture. Place stuffing on fish; cover with remaining fillet or steak. Fasten with toothpicks or skewers, brush top with melted shortening. Place bacon on top. Bake at 350 degrees for 30 to 40 minutes or until fish flakes easily when tested with fork. Remove fasteners; lift off bacon slices and peel skin back. Replace bacon; garnish as desired. Yield: 4-6 servings.

Mrs. Irene Knudsen, Del Norte Co. H. S.
Crescent City, California

BAKED FISH WITH SAUCE

½ c. cracker crumbs
½ c. bread crumbs
¼ c. hot water
1 tsp. chopped parsley
Butter
Salt
Few drops onion juice
1 tsp. chopped pickle
Pepper
1 5 to 6-lb. red snapper
Flour
Butter

Combine cracker crumbs, bread crumbs, water, parsley, 2 tablespoonfuls butter, 1/4 teaspoonful salt, onion juice, pickle and 1/8 teaspoonful pepper. Remove backbone of fish by running a knife down the back close to the bone. Fill fish with crumb mixture. Pin top of fish over stuffing to bottom half of fish with toothpicks, pressing firmly. Sprinkle fish with salt, pepper and flour. Dot with butter. Place two 1-inch wide strips of cloth in baking pan to remove fish from pan easily. Pour a small amount of water in pan. Place fish in pan. Bake at 350 to 375 degrees until brown and fish flakes. Garnish with parsley and lemon, if desired.

EGG SAUCE:

4 tbsp. butter
2 tbsp. flour
1 c. boiling water
¼ tsp. salt
Dash of pepper
2 hard-cooked eggs, sliced

Melt butter; blend in flour. Gradually add boiling water, salt and pepper. Cook, stirring, until smooth and thick. Add eggs. Serve hot with fish. Yield: 8 servings.

Mrs. Nell Pinkerton, East Nashville H. S.
Nashville, Tennessee

BAKED RED SNAPPER WITH CREOLE SAUCE

6 slices bacon
6 lb. red snapper
Salt and pepper
3 tbsp. flour
1 bunch celery, finely chopped
6 onions, finely chopped
2 green peppers, finely chopped
4 cloves of garlic, finely chopped
½ tsp. Tabasco sauce
3 cans or 8 tomatoes, diced
1 bunch green onions, diced
6 bay leaves
½ tsp. thyme
¼ tsp. oregano
1 bunch parsley
3 hard-cooked eggs, sliced
2 lemons, sliced
6 tbsp. cooking oil

Fry bacon. Grease snapper inside and out. Rub in salt and pepper; dust with flour. Bake at 350 degrees for 30 minutes. Saute remaining ingredients, except parsley, eggs and lemon slowly in oil and bacon grease. Pour over fish. Bake for 30 minutes longer. Garnish with eggs, lemon and parsley. Yield: 6 servings.

Mrs. R. C. Brock, Jr., Lee Jr. H. S.
Lee, Florida

DEEP FAT FRIED SMELT

Fresh or frozen smelt
1 egg, beaten
Cracker crumbs
Vegetable oil
Salt to taste

Dip smelt into beaten egg; coat with cracker crumbs. Fry in hot fat for 2 to 3 minutes or until golden brown. Drain on paper toweling. Salt to taste. Serve with a seafood sauce or tartar sauce, if desired.

Geraldine Bieniasz, Clear Lake H. S.
Clear Lake, Wisconsin

BAKED FILLET OF SOLE

1 ½ lb. frozen fillet of sole
1 sm. onion, sliced
Salt and pepper
Flour
1 can tomato soup

Place fillet in casserole. Place onion on fish. Season and sprinkle with flour. Add undiluted tomato soup. Bake at 350 degrees until heated through. Serve immediately.

Mrs. Maxiene Bodgener, Macleod Jr.-Sr. H. S.
Fort Macleod, Alberta, Canada

FILLET DE SOLE BONNE FEMME

2 tbsp. melted butter
2 to 3 tbsp. lemon juice
¼ c. finely chopped onion
1 lb. fillet of sole or flounder
½ c. cream of mushroom soup
1 1-oz. can small mushrooms

Combine butter, lemon juice and onion; pour into an 11 x 7-inch baking dish. Dip fish into mixture, turning to coat. Place, skin-side up, in dish. Bake at 350 degrees for 20 minutes. Add mushroom soup and mushrooms to fish; cook for 10 minutes longer. Yield: 4 servings.

Estelle Caffey, Friona School
Friona, Texas

FILLET OF SOLE SAN JOAQUIN

1 onion, chopped
¼ c. butter or margarine
½ c. chopped parsley
½ c. seasoned cooked rice
½ tsp. salt
⅛ tsp. pepper
2 eggs
¾ c. milk
8 fillets of sole
Fine dry bread crumbs
1 10 ½-oz. can cream of mushroom soup
1 c. white wine

Saute onion in butter; add parsley and cook until onion is soft and translucent. Add cooked rice; season mixture with salt and pepper. Beat eggs with milk; season lightly with a small amount additional salt. Spread rice mixture evenly over fillets; roll up and secure. Dip each fish roll into egg mixture; roll in bread crumbs. Refrigerate for 30 minutes or longer. Brown rolls lightly on all sides in melted butter. Remove rolls to flameproof platter. Heat soup with wine; simmer for 15 minutes, stirring frequently. Pour sauce around fish. Brown under broiler. Yield: 6-8 servings.

Mrs. Arvilla Griggs, Montpelier H. S.
Montpelier, Vermont

GOURMET FILLET OF SOLE

3 lb. fresh fillet of sole
1 can frozen shrimp soup
¼ c. Parmesan cheese

(Continued on next page)

Arrange fillet of sole in shallow 8 x 12-inch baking dish. Thaw soup and pour over fish. Top with Parmesan cheese. Bake at 325 degrees for 30 minutes. Serve immediately. Yield: 6 servings.

Mrs. Carol Hawkins, Turlock H. S.
Turlock, California

BROILED SWORDFISH FILLET

2 tbsp. garlic salt
2 tsp. pepper
2 swordfish fillets
2 tbsp. margarine

Sprinkle 1 tablespoonful garlic salt and 1 teaspoonful pepper on one side of fillet. Dot margarine evenly over surface of fillet to prevent drying out. Place on broiler pan; broil until golden brown. Turn fillet and repeat process with remaining ingredients. Cook until fork cuts easily into fillet. Sprinkle with lemon juice or tartar sauce. NOTE: More salt and pepper may be added, if desired. Yield: 2 servings.

Mrs. Helen Sherman Ellison
Santa Paula Union H. S.
Santa Paula, California

BAKED TROUT

2 12-oz. pkg. frozen trout, thawed
¼ c. butter or margarine
¼ c. finely chopped celery
1 tsp. salt
¼ tsp. pepper
1 tbsp. lemon juice
¼ c. chopped sweet mixed pickles

Arrange trout in greased 1 1/2-quart shallow baking dish. Melt butter over low heat. Add celery and cook until tender. Add remaining ingredients; mix. Pour over trout. Bake at 350 degrees for 20 to 25 minutes or until fish is tender. Garnish with lemon slices and parsley, if desired. Yield: 4 servings.

Photograph for this recipe on page 171 .

HERBED STUFFED TROUT

½ c. chopped onion
¼ c. plus 3 tbsp. butter
1 c. dry bread crumbs
1 tsp. summer savory
1 tsp. chervil
4 trout
Monosodium glutamate
1 tbsp. lemon juice

Saute onion in 3 tablespoonfuls butter until clear, but not brown. Remove from heat; add bread crumbs, savory and chervil. Sprinkle trout inside and out with monosodium glutamate. Fill with bread crumb mixture. Melt remaining butter; stir in lemon juice. Bake trout at 350 degrees for 35 minutes or until fish flakes easily with a fork, basting every 5 minutes with lemon butter. Yield: 4 servings.

LaDonna Snyder, South Central H. S.
Greenwich, Ohio

SOUTHERN BROILED TROUT

Salt and pepper
4 lge. fresh speckled trout
½ c. melted butter
⅓ c. lemon juice
5 tbsp. chopped parsley
½ c. grated onion
½ tsp. paprika
5 tbsp. Worcestershire sauce
Few grains cayenne pepper

Salt and pepper fish; place on foil. Combine remaining ingredients; pour over fish. Close foil. Broil in oven at 450 degrees until done. Yield: 6 servings.

Maggie Johnson, Varnado H. S.
Varnado, Louisiana

CREAMED TUNA

½ c. sliced celery
2 tbsp. chopped onion
1 tbsp. butter or margarine
1 11-oz. can Cheddar cheese soup
½ c. milk
1 7-oz. can tuna, drained and flaked
2 tbsp. chopped pimento
½ c. green peas
Chopped parsley
Hot cooked rice

Cook celery and onion in butter in saucepan until tender. Blend in soup and milk. Add tuna, pimento and green peas. Heat, stirring occasionally. Garnish with parsley; serve over rice. NOTE: Cream of vegetable soup or cream of celery soup may be substituted for Cheddar cheese soup. Yield: 4 servings.

Ilona M. Wooten, Tyner H. S.
Tyner, Tennessee

TUNA CROQUETTES

1 c. thick white sauce
1 tbsp. sweet pickle relish
1 tbsp. chopped onion
2 c. flaked tuna, salmon, crabmeat, cod or haddock
½ tsp. lemon juice
¼ tsp. salt
Finely sifted dried bread crumbs
1 egg
1 tbsp. water

(Continued on next page)

Combine white sauce, pickle relish, onion, fish, lemon juice and salt. Chill thoroughly. Shape into 3 x 1-inch croquettes; roll in bread crumbs. Mix egg with water; roll croquettes in egg. Roll again in bread crumbs. Chill again. Fry croquettes in 375 degree shortening 2 minutes or until golden brown. Drain on absorbent paper. Yield: 4 servings.

Mrs. Josephine W. McKee, North Duplin H. S.
Calypso, North Carolina

TUNA CROQUETTES

1 can tuna
1 egg, beaten
8 soda crackers, crushed

Flake tuna; add beaten egg. Add cracker crumbs. Divide mixture into four equal parts; shape into croquettes. Brown in hot skillet with fat. Yield: 4 servings.

Frances Watson, Lake H. S.
Millbury, Ohio

TUNA CROQUETTES

2 tbsp. butter or margarine
2 tbsp. flour
¼ tsp. salt
Dash of pepper
½ c. milk
3 tbsp. grated onion
1 can white flaked tuna, drained
2 c. soda cracker crumbs
4 eggs, slightly beaten

Slowly melt butter; remove from heat. Stir in flour, salt and pepper. Mix well; slowly add milk, stirring constantly. Return to heat; cook until very thick, stirring constantly. Set aside to cool. Add grated onion to tuna. Add cooled white sauce. Shape into oblong croquettes, using 1 tablespoonful tuna mixture for each croquette. Roll in cracker crumbs; dip into eggs, then roll again in crumbs. Place on tray or platter. Cover; chill thoroughly. Fry at 375 until brown. Drain on absorbent paper; serve immediately. Yield: 6 servings.

Donna L. Guckian, Prairie Valley, I. S. D.
Nacona, Texas

TUNA FRITTERS

2 c. biscuit mix
1 tsp. seasoned salt
1 egg
⅔ c. undiluted evaporated milk
2 tbsp. lemon juice
1 ½ c. tuna
2 tbsp. minced onion
2 tbsp. finely chopped green pepper
2 tbsp. chopped parsley
½ c. chopped celery
Fat

Blend biscuit mix, seasoned salt, egg, milk and lemon juice in bowl. Add all remaining ingredients except fat; blend well. Drop from teaspoon into deep 375 degree fat or into 1/2 inch hot fat in frying pan. Fry for 1 minute and 30 seconds to 2 minutes on each side.

CHEESE SAUCE:

1 ⅔ c. evaporated milk
½ tsp. salt
2 c. grated American cheese

Simmer milk and salt in saucepan over low heat for 2 minutes; add cheese. Stir until thickened and smooth. Serve over tuna. Yield: 5 servings.

Mrs. Kathleen F. Kerr, Shippensburg Area H. S.
Shippensburg, Pennsylvania

CURRIED TUNA WITH ALMOND RICE

4 tbsp. butter or margarine
4 tbsp. flour
1 ½ tsp. curry powder
2 c. milk
1 tsp. salt
½ tsp. pepper
1 7-oz. can tuna, drained and flaked

Melt butter or margarine over low heat; blend in the flour and curry powder. Add milk; cook until thickened, stirring constantly. Stir in salt, pepper and tuna. Cover; cook for 30 minutes over low heat.

ALMOND RICE:

1 c. chopped blanched almonds
4 tbsp. butter or margarine
3 c. hot cooked rice

Saute almonds and 2 tablespoonfuls butter or margarine. Stir in hot rice and remaining butter or margarine. Pour curried tuna over Almond Rice. Top with paprika. Yield: 4 servings.

Mrs. Bobbie K. Bland, Caprock H. S.
Amarillo, Texas

DEEP SEA DELIGHT

1 5-oz. pkg. noodles
1 10 ½-oz. can cream of mushroom soup
1 7-oz. can tuna, drained and flaked
1 No. 1 can cut green asparagus
1 sm. green pepper, chopped
½ tsp. salt
⅛ tsp. pepper
1 c. grated cheese

Cook noodles in salted boiling water. Drain, rinse and drain again. Add remaining ingredients, reserving a small amount of cheese for the top. Place in buttered baking dish; sprinkle

(Continued on next page)

with remaining cheese. Bake at 325 degrees for 30 minutes. Yield: 8-10 servings.

Mrs. Wilma A. Horton, Harrold H. S.
Harrold, Texas

GOURMET TUNA PIE

2 hard-cooked eggs, sliced
1 8-in. pastry shell, unbaked
2 cans tuna, drained and flaked
2 eggs, well beaten
¼ c. butter, melted
4 tsp. minced parsley
Salt
¼ tsp. sweet basil
⅔ c. shredded unpeeled cucumber
1 tsp. grated onion
¼ c. mayonnaise
2 tsp. vinegar
½ c. sour cream
Dash of pepper

Arrange sliced eggs in pastry shell. Combine tuna, beaten eggs, butter, 2 teaspoonfuls parlsey, 1/4 teaspoonful salt and basil; mix well. Pour over eggs. Bake at 425 degrees for 20 to 25 minutes or until golden brown. Press cucumber and onion in strainer to remove juice; combine with remaining ingredients and a dash of salt. Chill and serve. Yield: 6 servings.

Mrs. Shannon Norris, Riverside H. S.
Painesville, Ohio

QUICK TUNA SAUCE

1 c. sliced mushrooms
2 tbsp. butter
1 can cream of mushroom soup
¾ c. cream
1 tbsp. grated onion
1 tsp. Worcestershire sauce
Salt and pepper to taste
1 buffet can flaked tuna
Cooked ham slices
Buttered toast

Saute mushrooms in butter; add soup and cream. Add grated onion, Worcestershire sauce, salt and pepper; mix in tuna. Simmer for 5 to 10 minutes. Arrange thin slices of cooked ham on slices of buttered toast; cover with sauce. NOTE: May be served with rice, buttered noodles or spaghetti. Yield: 6 servings.

Clarabel Tepe, Fort Towson H. S.
Fort Towson, Oklahoma

SWEET-SOUR TUNA CHOW MEIN

2 tbsp. salad oil
1 c. sliced onions
1 ½ c. diced celery
⅛ tsp. pepper
1 4-oz. can sliced mushrooms
1 ½ c. vegetable or chicken stock
½ c. molasses
2 tbsp. vinegar
1 1-lb. can bean sprouts, drained
2 tbsp. cornstarch
3 tbsp. soy sauce
2 7-oz. cans tuna

Heat oil in large skillet; add onions, celery and pepper. Cook for 2 minutes, stirring occasionally. Drain mushrooms; add vegetable or chicken stock to mushroom liquid. Stir molasses and vinegar into liquid; add to skillet with mushrooms and bean sprouts. Cover; simmer for 10 minutes. Blend cornstarch with soy sauce; quickly stir into hot mixture. Add tuna; mix well. Cook, stirring constantly for 2 to 3 minutes longer or until mixture is thickened and heated through. Serve over hot cooked rice or fried noodles, if desired. Yield: 6 servings.

Sister Mary Rosario, S.C., Marian H. S.
Cincinnati, Ohio

TUNA CHOW MEIN

1 slice onion, chopped
4 tbsp. butter
4 tbsp. flour
¾ tbsp. salt
⅛ tsp. pepper
1 ¾ c. boiling water
2 chicken bouillon cubes, crushed
½ c. milk
1 12-oz. can tuna, cut into chunks
½ c. finely chopped celery
½ c. shredded carrot
1 ½ c. instant rice

Cook onion and butter for 2 minutes; add flour, salt and pepper, stirring until smooth. Add water, bouillon cubes and milk; stir until sauce boils. Add tuna, celery and carrot. Cook over medium heat for 10 to 20 minutes or until well heated. Cook rice according to package directions. Serve tuna mixture over rice. Yield: 4 servings.

Helen Pfaff, Fairview Jr. H. S.
Fairview, New Jersey

TUNA ROLL

1 c. biscuit dough
1 can grated tuna
1 egg
Salt and pepper to taste
Milk
1 can cream of chicken soup

Roll dough thin. Combine tuna with egg, salt, pepper and enough milk to make a spreading consistency. Spread mixture on dough; roll up like a jelly roll. Place roll in pan. Bake at 400 degrees for 15 to 20 minutes. Heat undiluted soup; pour over roll and serve. Yield: 3-4 servings.

Mrs. Judith Peavyhouse, Clarkrange H. S.
Clarkrange, Tennessee

TUNA PIZZA

¾ c. grated cheese
½ tsp. onion salt
½ c. evaporated milk
1 recipe baking powder biscuits or canned biscuits
½ c. catsup
¼ tsp. oregano
1 c. flaked tuna

Grate cheese finely into small bowl; add onion salt and evaporated milk. Let stand until thickened. Press biscuit dough on lightly greased pizza pan or cookie sheet. Bake at 450 degrees for 5 minutes. Loosen crust with spatula. Spread dough with cheese-milk mixture. Cover with catsup. Sprinkle oregano and tuna over catsup. Bake for 7 minutes or until crust is lightly browned. Yield: 4-6 servings.

Mrs. Shirley Gulbranson
Flandreau Indian H. S.
Flandreau, South Dakota

TUNA RING

3 or 4 lemon slices
2 6 ½ or 7-oz. cans tuna, drained and flaked
1 can cream of celery soup
3 eggs, separated
1 c. fine cracker crumbs
¼ c. chopped onion
2 tbsp. chopped pimento
2 tbsp. chopped parsley
1 tbsp. lemon juice
Dash of pepper

Place lemon slices in greased ring. Combine tuna, soup, slightly beaten egg yolks and remaining ingredients except egg whites. Fold in stiffly beaten egg whites. Spoon tuna over lemon slices. Bake at 350 degrees for 45 minutes or until center is firm. Invert onto platter and garnish. Yield: 6-8 servings.

Louise Curry, Richfield H. S.
Waco, Texas

SWEET 'N' SOUR TUNA

1 ¼ c. pineapple chunks and juice
½ c. coarsely chopped green pepper
½ c. sliced celery
½ c. coarsely chopped pimento
¼ c. vinegar
½ c. water
½ c. sugar
1 tbsp. soy sauce
Few drops of Tabasco sauce
3 tbsp. cornstarch
2 6 ½-oz. cans tuna
1 or 2 cans Chinese noodles

Combine all ingredients except cornstarch, tuna and noodles in a saucepan; bring to a boil. Add enough water to cornstarch to form a paste. Add part of cooked mixture to cornstarch; pour back into cooked mixture. Boil for 1 minute. Add tuna; heat. Serve over Chinese noodles. Yield: 4-6 servings.

Mrs. Mike Stone, Fannindel H. S.
Ladonia, Texas

BAKED FISH AU GRATIN

2 lb. white fish fillets
8 slices Cheddar cheese
1 tsp. thyme or oregano
¼ c. parsley
1 c. chopped onions
2 tbsp. vegetable oil
2 tbsp. flour
1 tsp. salt
⅛ tsp. pepper
1 c. milk

Place one-half of fillets in greased 9 x 9 x 3/4-inch baking dish. Cover with 4 slices of cheese. Repeat layers. Sprinkle with thyme and parsley. Saute onions in oil over medium heat until clear and lightly browned. Blend in flour, salt and pepper. Gradually stir in milk. Bring to a boil over low heat, stirring constantly, boil for 1 minute. Pour over fish. Bake at 400 degrees for 20 to 30 minutes. Yield: 6-8 servings.

Mrs. Mary Grant, Saranac Comm. Schools
Saranac, Michigan

ISLAND FRIED FISH

2 ½ to 3 lb. white fish fillets
½ c. soy sauce
½ c. flour
½ c. cornstarch
1 c. milk
1 egg
3 tsp. baking powder
1 tsp. salt
½ tsp. pepper
2 1-lb. 4 ½-oz. cans pineapple chunks
¾ c. sugar
Cooking oil
1 tbsp. cornstarch

Wash fish; pat dry. Cut into 1 1/2-inch square pieces. Marinate in soy sauce for 20 to 30 minutes, turning once or twice. Combine flour, cornstarch, milk, egg, baking powder and seasonings. Pour pineapple and syrup into saucepan; stir in sugar. Heat gently and thoroughly. Pour 1 1/2 inches oil into heavy skillet. Heat to 375 degrees. Drain fish of excess soy sauce; dip quickly into batter. Drain; drop into hot oil. Keep temperature of oil constant. Cook for 1 to 2 minutes or until crust is crisp. Remove to pan lined with paper towels; keep in warm oven until all fish is cooked. Mix cornstarch with 1/4 cup water; add to heated pineapple. Cook until syrup has thickened. Arrange pineapple in sauce on warm serving platter. Place fish carefully on top. Yield: 6 servings.

Virginia Malisheske, Jordan H. S.
Jordan, Minnesota

BAKED STUFFED WHITE FISH

1 4-lb. whole white fish
Salt and pepper
2 med. firm ripe tomatoes, diced
1 c. finely chopped onions
¼ c. finely chopped green pepper
2 tbsp. chopped parsley
Melted butter
1 tbsp. lemon juice

Wash and dry fish; season with salt and pepper. Combine 1/2 teaspoonful salt, dash of pepper, tomatoes, onions, green pepper and parsley. Loosely stuff fish. Close opening with poultry pins. Place on rack in baking pan. Generously pour on melted butter and sprinkle with lemon juice. Bake at 350 degrees for 10 minutes per pound or until lightly browned and tender. Yield: 4-6 servings.

Mrs. Adelaide Wolf, Harbor Creek H. S.
Harbor Creek, Pennsylvania

WHITE FISH AMANDINE

2 lb. white fish fillets
2 tbsp. lemon juice
2 tsp. salt
Dash of pepper
½ c. flour
½ c. melted fat or oil
½ c. blanched slivered almonds
2 tbsp. chopped parsley

Cut fillets into serving portions. Sprinkle fish with lemon juice, salt and pepper; roll in flour. Fry in hot fat over medium heat for 10 to 12 minutes or until browned, turning once. Remove fish to hot platter. Saute almonds until lightly browned; add parsley. Serve over fish. Yield: 6 servings.

Mrs. Irma B. Morley, Senior H. S.
Allegan, Michigan

BAKED FISH

3 to 4 lb. dressed fish
1 ½ tsp. salt
Dash of pepper
¼ c. butter or other fat, melted
3 slices bacon (opt.)

Sprinkle fish inside and out with salt and pepper. Place fish in well greased baking pan or dish. Brush with butter; lay bacon slices over top. Bake at 350 degrees for 40 to 50 minutes or until fish flakes easily, basting occasionally with drippings. Sprinkle with paprika before serving, if desired. Yield: 6 servings.

Virginia R. Garber, Grundy H. S.
Grundy, Virginia

BAKED FISH FILLETS

1 lb. fish fillets
1 egg, beaten
½ c. milk
1 c. cracker crumbs

Cut fish into serving pieces. Mix egg with milk; dip fish into egg mixture. Roll in cracker crumbs; place on greased cookie sheet. Bake at 350 degrees for 30 minutes or until golden brown. Yield: 3 servings.

Mrs. Wanda Newlin, Atwood-Hammond H. S.
Atwood, Illinois

BAKED FISH FILLETS

1 lb. fish fillets
½ tsp. salt
¼ tsp. pepper
1 carrot, grated
1 can tomato soup

Place fillets, skin-side up, in greased baking dish. Sprinkle with salt, pepper and grated carrot. Gently pour tomato soup over top. Add small amount of water, if desired. Bake at 350 degrees for 30 minutes or until fish is tender. Yield: 4 servings.

Mrs. Earline Baier Alsobrook, Brenham H. S.
Brenham, Texas

BAKED FISH WITH TOMATO SAUCE

2 pkg. frozen fish fillets, partially thawed
2 tbsp. minced onion
1 clove of garlic, minced
1 tbsp. butter
2 8-oz. cans tomato sauce
1 tsp. sugar
½ tsp. Worcestershire sauce
2 tbsp. lemon juice
Chopped parsley (opt.)

Cut fish into six portions. Arrange in greased shallow baking dish. Saute onion and garlic in butter until tender and transparent. Add tomato sauce, sugar, Worcestershire sauce and lemon juice. Simmer for 5 minutes. Pour over fish. Bake at 400 degrees for 20 t0 25 minutes. Sprinkle with chopped parsley, if desired. Yield: 6 servings.

Eva Jane Schwartz, Gettysburg Area H. S.
Gettysburg, Pennsylvania

BAKED FISH WITH VEGETABLES

1 tbsp. oil
1 lb. fish
1 12-oz. can mixed vegetables, drained
2 sm. onions, thinly sliced
2 sm. tomatoes, thinly sliced
1 tbsp. salt
1 tbsp. pepper
4 slices bacon

(Continued on next page)

Grease baking dish lightly with oil. Place fish, flesh-side up, in greased baking dish; sprinkle with salt and pepper. Spread mixed vegetables over fish. Place onion and tomato slices over vegetables; sprinkle lightly with salt and pepper. Top with bacon. Bake in preheated 400 degree oven for 30 to 45 minutes or until fish flakes easily. Yield: 4 servings.

Gladys S. Hendren, Central Jr. H. S.
Holly Hill, Florida

BROILED FISH FILLET

2 tsp. soy sauce
2 tbsp. salad oil
1 lb. fish fillets, cut into serving pieces
Fish drippings
2 tbsp. lemon juice

Combine soy sauce and salad oil. Season and arrange fish on oiled broiler rack. Broil for 8 minutes or until golden, basting frequently with soy sauce mixture. Turn and broil until done. Heat remaining oil and soy sauce with fish drippings; add lemon juice. Pour over fish. Garnish fish platter with lemon wedges, if desired. Yield: 3-4 servings.

Diane Builta, Grant Park H. S.
Grant Park, Illinois

FILLET STUFFED TOMATOES

6 lge. tomatoes
Salt and pepper
1 ½ lb. thin fish fillets
1 ½ c. soft bread crumbs
2 tbsp. chopped onion
6 tbsp. minced parsley
6 tbsp. butter, melted
2 tbsp. lemon juice
½ tsp. thyme
½ tsp. savory salt

Scoop out center of tomatoes; sprinkle with salt and pepper to taste. Cut fillets into six pieces. Combine 1 teaspoonful salt and 1/4 teaspoonful pepper with remaining ingredients; spread on fillets. Roll up; place one fillet in each tomato. Place in shallow baking dish. Bake in preheated 425 degrees oven for 30 minutes. Yield: 6 servings.

Mildred Snell, Austintown-Fitch H. S.
Youngstown, Ohio

FISH BALLS

2 tbsp. chopped onion
¼ c. butter
1 lb. fish fillets, chopped or ground
1 c. soft bread crumbs
½ c. milk
2 eggs, slightly beaten
1 tsp. salt
Dash of pepper
Buttered bread crumbs

Cook onion in 2 tablespoonfuls butter until tender; add fish. Soak bread crumbs in milk and 1 egg. Add salt and pepper; mix thoroughly. Add to fish mixture. Shape into 10 to 12 balls. Dip into remaining egg diluted with a small amount of water; roll in bread crumbs. Brown slowly in remaining butter for 15 minutes or until delicately brown. Garnish with parsley and serve with tomato sauce, if desired. Yield: 6 servings.

Mrs. Nadia Hamilton, Fort Le Boeuf H. S.
Waterford, Pannsylvania

FISH TURBANS

6 fresh or frozen fish fillets
¼ c. plus 3 tbsp. butter
¼ c. fresh mushrooms, chopped
¼ c. minced onion
1 ½ c. cooked rice
¼ c. chopped pecans
1 tsp. salt
Dash of pepper
1 tsp. crumbled rosemary

Thaw frozen fillets in refrigerator. Melt 3 tablespoonfuls butter in 9-inch skillet; add mushrooms and onion. Saute until tender and slightly brown; add to cooked rice with pecans, salt, pepper and rosemary. Spread each fillet with 3 tablespoonfuls rosemary-rice mixture. Roll up; fasten with toothpick. Place each turban in greased shallow dish, custard cup or ramekin. Fill hollow in each turban with 2 tablespoonfuls rosemary-rice mixture. Brush each top liberally with 2 tablespoonfuls melted butter. Bake at 350 degrees for 30 minutes or until fish flakes with a fork. Yield: 6 servings.

Mrs. Jean C. Vandergrift, Lee Jr. H. S.
Roanoke, Virginia

OVEN CRUSTY FISH

1 egg
1 tbsp. water
¾ tsp. Tabasco sauce
½ tsp. salt
1 ½ lb. fish fillets
1 c. corn flake crumbs
2 tsp. melted butter or vegetable oil
Lemon wedges
Finely chopped parsley

Combine egg, water, Tabasco sauce and salt; beat until well blended. Drain fish fillets, if necessary; dip into egg mixture. Coat generously with corn flake crumbs. Place on foil-lined baking sheet; drizzle with melted butter. Bake at 375 degrees for 20 to 30 minutes or until fish flakes easily. Serve with lemon wedges dipped into finely chopped parsley. Yield: 4 servings.

Julia J. Stegall, Sallisaw H. S.
Sallisaw, Oklahoma

OVEN-FRIED FISH WITH ALMOND BUTTER

1 tbsp. salt
1 c. milk
Fish fillets
1 c. fine dry bread crumbs
Melted butter (opt.)
Lemon juice (opt.)
½ c. chopped blanched almonds (opt.)

Combine salt and milk; dip fish in milk. Roll in bread crumbs; place in baking dish. Drizzle melted butter over fish. Bake at 500 degrees for 10 to 15 minutes, turning once. Sprinkle lemon juice over fish. Brown almonds in 6 tablespoonfuls butter. Serve with fish. NOTE: One-half cup evaporated milk and 1/2 cup water may be substituted for milk. Yield: 6 servings.

Annette R. Jacobson, South Jr. H. S.
Grants Pass, Oregon
Mary Alice Young, Clifton Forge H. S.
Clifton Forge, Virginia
Mardeen Christiansen, Newberg H. S.
Newberg, Oregon

PENNY PINCHING FISH DISH

2 c. white sauce
1 c. cooked diced celery
1 ½ c. flaked fish
Salt and pepper
1 ½ tbsp. catsup
Croutons

Make 2 cups creamed cooked celery in rich white sauce using celery water as base. Add fish, salt, pepper and catsup. Pour into baking dish; top with croutons. Bake at 300 degrees for 30 minutes. Yield: 4 servings.

Mrs. Ruth M. Allard, Lyndon Institute
Lyndon Center, Vermont

QUICK BAKED FILLETS

½ tsp. salt
¼ c. grated onion
¼ c. salad oil
⅓ c. lemon juice
2 tbsp. Worcestershire sauce
1 lb. fish fillets
4 c. corn flakes, finely crushed

Combine all ingredients except fish and corn flakes. Dip fish into lemon juice mixture; coat with corn flakes. Arrange fish fillets on well greased cookie sheet. Bake at 500 degrees for 15 minutes. Yield: 4-5 servings.

Mrs. Dorothy Samson, Clear Lake H. S.
Lakeport, California

SAUCE PIQUANTE

2 c. chopped onions
2 c. chopped green peppers
1 c. chopped celery
4 cloves of garlic, minced
2 No. 2 cans whole tomatoes
2 6-oz. cans tomato paste
2 8-oz. cans tomato sauce
1 c. mushrooms, chopped
¼ c. Worcestershire sauce
1 tbsp. oregano flakes
4 bay leaves
3 c. water
2 tsp. seasoned salt
¼ to 1 tsp. cayenne pepper
¼ c. chopped fresh or dried parsley
¼ c. chopped green onion tops
6 thin slices lemon
1 3 to 5-lb. boneless fried fish

Combine all ingredients except parsley, green onion tops, lemon slices and fried fish in 4-quart iron or aluminum pot. Cover and cook over very low heat for 2 hours or until done. Add parsley, green onion tops and lemon slices; simmer for 10 minutes longer. Pour over boneless fried fish. Yield: 10 servings.

Margaret A. McBride, Doyle H. S.
Livingston, Louisiana

SOUTHERN PAN-FRIED FISH

2 to 3 lb. fish
1 c. shortening
2 tbsp. salt
½ c. corn meal

Cut fish into serving pieces. Heat shortening to cover fish in a frying pan over medium heat. Mix salt and corn meal; roll fish in mixture. Drop into frying pan; fry for 3 minutes or until delicately browned. Yield: 4 servings.

Glendola Pinson, Hermitage H. S.
Hermitage, Arkansas

TENNESSEE DEEP FAT-FRIED FISH

Shortening
1 c. corn meal
1 c. flour
4 tbsp. salt
1 3 to 5-lb. dressed fish

Heat 3 to 4 inches shortening in deep fat fryer to 350 to 375 degrees. Measure meal, flour and salt into paper sack. Mix and place part of fish in sack. Shake until fish is well coated. Gently shake off loose meal; place fish in heated shortening. Do not crowd. Cook for 5 to 10 minutes or until fish floats. Remove with tongs; drain on paper towel. Serve hot with hush puppies, if desired. Yield: 6-8 servings.

Mrs. Steve Drone, College Grove H. S.
College Grove, Tennessee

DEVILED CLAMS

12 bull clams
½ green pepper
1 stalk celery
1 tbsp. onion
1 tbsp. parsley
3 slices soft bread, crumbled
Salt and pepper
1 c. thick white sauce
Buttered cracker crumbs

Steam clams; reserve liquid. Grind clams, pepper, celery, onion and parsley. Add bread crumbs; season with salt and pepper. Mix to a soft consistency with white sauce and clam liquid. Fill clam shells; allow to stand for 2 hours. Cover with buttered crumbs. Bake at 350 degrees for 20 minutes. Serve hot.

Mrs. Catherine R. Mordan, Millville Area H. S.
Millville, Pennsylvania

DEVILED CLAMS

1 doz. lge. clams
1 egg
2 med. potatoes, cooked and mashed
¼ c. chopped celery
1 med. onion, chopped
1 sprig parsley, chopped
½ tsp. dry mustard
⅛ tsp. pepper
1 tsp. salt
Fine dry bread crumbs

Scrub clams well. Steam in a small amount of boiling water until clams open. Remove from shells; put through food grinder, using medium blade. Break shells apart to separate. Mix remaining ingredients except bread crumbs. Add clams; mix well. Fill one-half of clam shells with mixture. Dip into bread crumbs; place on baking sheet. Bake at 350 degrees for 15 to 20 minutes or until lightly browned, but not dry. NOTE: Four slices bread soaked in water or milk may be subsituted for potatoes. Yield: 4-6 servings.

Mrs. Carol N. Hall, Columbia H. S.
Columbia, Pennsylvania

DEVILED QUAHOGS

1 qt. quahogs
¼ lb. lean salt pork
1 med. onion
1 pkg. unsalted Uneeda biscuits
¼ tsp. salt
Pinch of pepper

Grind all ingredients in a meat chopper; do not drain. Pack mixture into shells. Bake at 350 degrees for 50 minutes to 1 hour. NOTE: May be frozen; bake for 1 hour and 15 minutes to 1 hour and 20 minutes.

Mrs. Claire W. Anderson, Robert E. Fitch H. S.
Groton, Connecticut

BAKED CRAB YUMMY

½ c. butter
2 onions, finely chopped
2 tomatoes, chopped
2 green peppers, chopped
1 clove of garlic, minced
2 tbsp. chopped parsley
2 cans King crab meat
1 ½ tsp. salt
½ tsp. pepper
2 eggs, beaten
1 c. buttered crumbs
6 stuffed green olives, sliced

Heat butter in saucepan; add onions. Saute for 10 minutes, stirring occasionally. Add tomatoes, peppers, garlic and parsley; cook over low heat for 10 minutes. Add crab meat, salt and pepper; mix carefully. Cook over low heat for 5 minutes. Pour eggs over mixture; cook for 3 minutes, stirring constantly. Divide into individual ramekins; sprinkle with bread crumbs. Bake at 375 degrees for 15 minutes or until light brown on top. Place olives on top.

Dorothy Farst, Springfield H. S.
Akron, Ohio

CRAB CAKES

1 lb. crab meat
2 eggs, beaten
1 sm. onion, finely cut
2 tbsp. prepared mustard
1 tbsp. salad dressing
1 tsp. salt
Pepper to taste
1 c. mashed potatoes
½ c. cracker crumbs (opt.)

Drain and flake crab meat. Blend with remaining ingredients except crumbs. Shape into patties. If patties seem too moist, roll in cracker crumbs. Fry in deep fat until golden brown. Yield: 6 servings.

Mrs. Jane O. Shipway, Flintstone School
Flintstone, Maryland

CRAB IMPERIAL

2 tbsp. butter
2 tbsp. (heaping) flour
½ c. milk
½ tsp. salt
½ tsp. dry mustard
1 tsp. vinegar
½ tsp. Worcestershire sauce
2 tbsp. (heaping) mayonnaise
1 slice bread, broken
¼ c. milk
1 lb. crab meat

Melt butter; stir in flour. Add milk gradually. Add salt, mustard, vinegar and Worcestershire sauce; cook until thickened. Cool and add mayonnaise. Moisten bread crumbs with milk; add to crab meat. Mix crab meat mixture with sauce;

(Continued on next page)

place in eight ramkins. Bake at 350 degrees for 15 minutes. Yield: 8 servings.

Elizabeth L. Hudson, Fairfield Jr. H. S.
Richmond, Virginia

CRAB IMPERIAL

1 lb. crab meat
2 tsp. diced green pepper
1 tbsp. diced pimento
1 tsp. salt
¼ tsp. white pepper
¼ tsp. dry mustard
5 egg yolks
¼ c. plus 3 tbsp. mayonnaise

Combine crab meat, green pepper, pimento, salt, pepper and mustard. Beat 3 egg yolks slightly; add 1/4 cup mayonnaise. Stir into crab mixture. Place in crab shells, rounding center to a peak. Combine remaining egg yolks and mayonnaise; spread on shells. Bake at 350 degrees for 10 to 15 minutes. Yield: 4 servings.

Mrs. Marie J. Brown, Queen Anne's Co. H. S.
Centreville, Maryland

CRAB LOUIS

1 lb. crab meat
1 head lettuce, shredded
½ tsp. salt
1 cucumber, sliced
4 tomatoes, sliced
3 hard-cooked eggs, sliced
1 c. mayonnaise
3 tbsp. catsup
2 tbsp. chopped sweet pickle
1 tbsp. lemon juice

Remove any shells or cartilage from crab meat, being careful not to break meat into small pieces. Place lettuce in a large shallow salad bowl; sprinkle with salt. Arrange crab meat over lettuce. Place alternate slices of cucumber, tomato and hard-cooked egg around edge. Combine mayonnaise, catsup, pickle and lemon juice; spread over crab meat. Yield: 6 servings.

Mrs. Viola Gracey, Travis Jr. H. S.
Snyder, Texas

CRAB MEAT AU GRATIN

1 c. back fin crab meat
1 c. mayonnaise
2 tsp. horseradish
Dash of Tabasco sauce
1 c. grated Cheddar cheese

Combine crab meat, mayonnaise, horseradish and Tabasco; spread into greased shallow baking dish. Top with grated cheese. Broil for 8 minutes or until cheese is melted. Yield: 6 servings.

Virginia O. Savedge, Northampton H. S.
Eastville, Virginia

CRAB MEAT DELIGHT

2 tbsp. chopped green pepper
2 tbsp. butter
2 tbsp. flour
½ tsp. mustard
½ tsp. Worcestershire sauce
¼ tsp. salt
1 c. tomato juice
1 c. grated cheese
1 egg, beaten
¼ c. milk
1 c. flaked crab meat

Cook green pepper in butter for 3 minutes or until soft; blend in flour. Add mustard, Worcestershire sauce and salt. Stir in tomato juice; add cheese and egg. Cook for a few minutes over low heat until heated and cheese has melted. Heat milk to scalding. Add to cheese mixture. Stir in flaked crab meat; heat. May be served in pattie shells or on rounds of toast. Sprinkle with additional grated cheese, if desired. Yield: 6 servings.

Mrs. Ethel B. Miles, Westfield H. S.
Westfield, Massachusetts

CRAB MEAT IN SHELLS

¾ c. butter
6 tbsp. flour
¾ tsp. salt
1 ½ c. milk
3 tbsp. chopped parsley
6 tbsp. lemon juice
3 tsp. dry mustard
1 ½ tsp. horseradish
6 hard-cooked eggs, finely chopped
3 c. crab meat
1 ½ c. buttered bread crumbs

Melt butter; stir in flour and salt. Add milk gradually. Add parsley, lemon juice, dry mustard and horseradish; cook until thickened, stirring constantly. Add eggs and crab meat. Place mixture in shells; top with buttered bread crumbs. Bake at 400 degrees for 15 minutes. Yield: 12 servings.

Mrs. Mildred Perry, Shepherd H. S.
Shepherd, Michigan

CRAB PATTIES

2 c. back fin crab meat
1 tbsp. chopped parsley
¼ tsp. mace
1 tsp. (scant) salt
⅛ tsp. pepper
1 c. milk
1 tbsp. butter
2 tbsp. flour
2 egg yolks, beaten
1 egg, beaten
Bread crumbs

Flake crab meat with a silver knife; add parsley, mace, salt and pepper. Heat milk in a pan. Blend butter and flour; add to milk. Stir until smooth and thickened. Add egg yolks; cook for 1 minute longer. Remove from heat; stir in crab meat.

(Continued on next page)

Cool. Shape into patties; let stand until firm. Dip into beaten egg; roll in bread crumbs. Let stand. Fry a pattie at a time in deep, hot fat until golden brown. Drain on paper. Garnish with parsley; serve with tartar sauce, if desired.

Edna S. Ewing, Seventy First H. S.
Fayetteville, North Carolina

CREAMED MUSHROOMS AND CRAB MEAT

5 tbsp. butter
5 tbsp. flour
1 pt. sour cream
1 tbsp. instant onion flakes
1 tbsp. instant parsley flakes
¼ tsp. nutmeg
1 lb. crab meat, drained
2 4-oz. cans mushrooms, drained
3 tbsp. Sherry (opt.)

Melt butter in frying pan on low heat. Add flour; stir until smooth. Reduce heat; stir in sour cream and remaining ingredients. Cover; cook on warm heat for 25 to 30 minutes. Serve in rice ring, if desired. Yield: 6-8 servings.

Mrs. Mildred R. Buck, Linden H. S.
Linden, Alabama

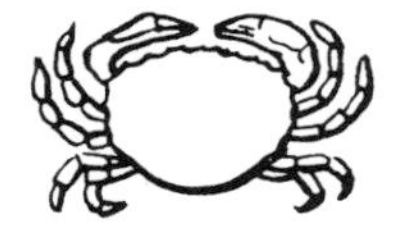

DEVILED CRAB

6 tbsp. margarine
3 tbsp. flour
¾ c. milk
3 c. crab meat
¾ tsp. salt
¾ tsp. paprika
Dash of pepper
¾ tsp. prepared mustard
3 tsp. chopped parsley
3 tsp. lemon juice
Yolks of 3 hard-cooked eggs, chopped
1 c. buttered crumbs

Melt margarine in a saucepan; blend in flour. Gradually add milk; cook over low heat, stirring constantly, until sauce boils and thickens. Fold in remaining ingredients except buttered crumbs. Turn into six cleaned crab shells. Sprinkle with buttered crumbs. Bake at 375 degrees for 10 minutes, or until crumbs are brown. Yield: 6 servings.

Mrs. Charla Mae Filla, Sterling H. S.
Sterling, Colorado

DEVILED CRAB MEAT

1 green pepper, chopped
1 sm. onion, grated
½ c. chopped celery
1 hard-cooked egg, chopped
1 6 ½-oz. can crab meat
½ tsp. dry mustard
2 crackers, crumbled
½ tsp. salt
½ tsp. Worcestershire sauce
½ tsp. Tabasco sauce
½ c. mayonnaise
1 egg, beaten
Buttered bread crumbs

Combine all ingredients except egg and bread crumbs; stir in egg. Place in casserole or individual baking dishes. Sprinkle bread crumbs on top. Bake at 350 degrees for 30 minutes. Yield: 4 servings.

Mrs. Mary E. Smith, Marlin H. S.
Marlin, Texas

DEVILED CRAB MEAT

1 ½ c. milk
1 ½ c. soft bread crumbs
2 c. flaked crab meat
5 hard-cooked eggs
1 ½ tsp. salt
⅓ tsp. dry mustard
⅛ tsp. cayenne pepper
½ c. butter, melted
Wheaties or buttered crumbs

Combine milk and bread crumbs; gently stir in crab meat and finely sliced egg whites. Blend in mashed egg yolks, seasonings and butter. Pour into a buttered 10 x 6 x 2-inch baking dish. Sprinkle with Wheaties or buttered crumbs. Bake at 450 degrees for 15 minutes. Serve hot.

Marian S. Russell, Northwestern H. S.
Hyattsville, Maryland

DEVILED CRABS

1 1-lb. can crab meat
1 c. diced soft bread
Juice of 1 lemon
1 green pepper, minced
1 sm. onion, minced
2 eggs, beaten
½ tsp. salt
3 dashes of cayenne pepper
½ c. milk
¼ c. melted butter

Flake crab meat; add bread, lemon juice, green pepper, onion, eggs, seasonings, milk and butter. Mix well; shape into cakes. Dip into corn flake crumbs. Fry in deep fat until golden brown. Yield: 6 servings.

Jean L. Hall, Frackville H. S.
Frackville, Pennsylvania

DEVILED CRABS

4 tbsp. butter or margarine
2 tbsp. flour
1 c. milk
1 tsp. salt
Parsley to taste
2 tsp. lemon juice
1 tsp. prepared mustard
½ tsp. horseradish
2 c. flaked crab meat
2 hard-cooked eggs, chopped
½ c. buttered bread crumbs

Melt butter; stir in flour to a smooth paste. Add milk gradually, stirring constantly, until mixture thickens. Simmer for 10 minutes. Add remaining ingredients except crumbs. Mix well; remove from heat. Fill scallop or crab shells or individual baking dishes with crab mixture. Top with bread crumbs. Bake at 375 to 400 degrees for 10 to 15 minutes or until crumbs brown. Yield: 6 servings.

Mrs. Bud Gaulke, Riddle Jr. H. S.
Riddle, Oregon

WHARF DEVILED CRAB

1 lb. crab meat, fresh or frozen
2 tbsp. chopped onion
3 tbsp. melted fat or oil
2 tbsp. flour
¾ c. milk
1 tbsp. lemon juice
1 ½ tsp. powdered mustard
1 tsp. Worcestershire sauce
½ tsp. salt
Dash of black pepper
Dash of cayenne pepper
3 drops of liquid hot pepper sauce
1 egg, beaten
1 tbsp. chopped parsley
¼ c. dry bread crumbs

Remove any remaining shell or cartilage from crab meat; cook onion in 2 tablespoonfuls fat until tender. Blend in flour. Add milk gradually; cook until thick, stirring constantly. Add lemon juice and seasonings. Stir a small amount of hot sauce mixture into egg; add to remaining sauce, stirring constantly. Add parsley and crab meat; blend well. Place in six well greased individual shells or 5-ounce custard cups. Combine 1 tablespoonful fat and crumbs; sprinkle over top of each shell. Bake at 350 degrees for 20 to 25 minutes or until brown. Yield: 6 servings.

Mrs. Zona Beth Cates, Tempe H. S.
Tempe, Arizona

EGG FOO YUNG WITH CRAB

½ c. chopped onion
Oil
½ c. chopped tomato
1 pkg. frozen crab meat
3 eggs, beaten
Salt and pepper
Monosodium glutamate
2 tbsp. soy sauce
1 c. soup stock
1 tbsp. cornstarch
1 tbsp. water

Saute onion in 1 tablespoonful oil; add tomatoes. Simmer for 2 minutes. Add crab meat and simmer until water has evaporated. Combine with mixture of eggs and seasonings. Form crab mixture into patties; fry in plenty of hot oil. Mix soy sauce and soup stock; bring to a boil. Thicken with mixture of cornstarch and water. Yield: 4 servings.

Mrs. Wilma C. Mitchell, Smithville H. S.
Smithville, Ohio

FRIED SOFT SHELL CRABS

12 fresh soft-shell crabs, dressed
2 eggs
¼ c. milk
2 tsp. salt
¾ c. flour
¾ c. dry bread crumbs

Rinse crabs in cold water; drain. Combine beaten eggs, milk and salt. Combine flour and crumbs. Dip crabs into egg mixture; roll in flour and crumb mixture. Panfry crabs in heavy pan in 1/8 inch of hot fat, browning on both sides. Drain on absorbent paper. Yield: 6 servings.

Margaret W. Cyrus
Herndon Intermediate School
Herndon, Virginia

IMPERIAL CRAB

1 lb. crab meat
2 slices day-old bread, crumbled
½ c. mayonnaise
1 tbsp. mustard
1 tbsp. Worcestershire sauce
1 tbsp. lemon juice
1 tbsp. capers
Dash of Tabasco sauce
1 ½ tbsp. minced pimento
1 ½ tbsp. green pepper

Pick over crab meat. Mix with bread crumbs, reserving a few crumbs for topping. Add remaining ingredients; mix. Place crab mixture in buttered baking dish. Cover with buttered bread crumbs. Bake at 350 degrees for 30 minutes. Yield: 4 servings.

Cora Anne Hollingsworth, Smithsburg H. S.
Smithsburg, Maryland

SEASHELL AU GRATIN

1 6-oz. can crab meat, shrimp or tuna
1 pt. white sauce
1 tsp. salt
½ tsp. pepper
6 oz. grated cheese
4 oz. butter

Mix crab meat into hot white sauce; add salt and pepper. Fill six buttered individual shells.

(Continued on next page)

Sprinkle with grated cheese. Dot with butter. Bake at 450 degrees for 5 to 10 minutes or until brown.

Mrs. John Griswold, Carrollton School
Carrollton, Illinois

SOUTHERN CRAB CAKES

3 c. flaked fresh or canned crab meat
1 ½ tsp. salt
1 tsp. dry mustard
½ tsp. pepper
1 egg yolk
2 tsp. Worcestershire sauce
1 tbsp. mayonnaise
2 tsp. snipped parsley
1 egg, slightly beaten
2 tbsp. water
Flour
Packaged dry bread crumbs
Butter or margarine

Mix crab meat, salt, mustard, pepper, egg yolk, Worcestershire sauce, mayonnaise and parsley; press mixture firmly into eight small cakes. Chill well. Combine egg and water. Dip cakes into flour; dip into egg mixture. Coat cakes with crumbs. Melt small amount of butter in skillet. Quickly saute cakes over high heat until golden. Yield: 4 servings.

Janice Ann Schuster, Grand Rapids H. S.
Grand Rapids, Ohio

CRAYFISH STEW

3 tbsp. fat
2 sm. onions, chopped
½ green pepper, chopped
2 stalks celery, chopped
½ clove of garlic, minced
2 tbsp. flour
½ c. tomato sauce
¼ tsp. pepper sauce
1 tbsp. Worcestershire sauce
Salt and pepper to taste
1 ½ c. water
2 lb. crayfish tails

Heat fat; add onions, green pepper, celery and garlic. Saute until clear; add flour, tomato sauce, seasonings, water and crayfish tails. Simmer on low heat for 30 minutes. Serve on hot rice, if desired. Yield: 8 servings.

Mrs. Elden Brunet, Oakdale H. S.
Oakdale, Louisiana

BAKED MAINE LOBSTER

4 live lobsters
16 crackers
¼ c. melted butter
¼ c. whole milk
Sherry
Dash of Worcestershire sauce
Garlic salt
Salt and pepper

Place lobsters on their backs; cross the large claws and hold firmly. Cut quickly through the entire length of the body and tail beginning at a point between the two large claws. Remove craw and veins. Leave tomalley in lobsters or mix with dressing. Roll crackers into fine crumbs; mix crumbs with butter and milk. Moisten to proper consistency with Sherry. Season with Worcestershire sauce, garlic salt, salt and pepper. Stuff lobsters with mixture. Pour additional butter over dressing. Sprinkle with Parmesan cheese, if desired. Bake at 450 to 500 degrees for 20 minutes. Yield: 4 servings.

Mrs. Karlene Mahaney, Boothbay Region H. S.
Boothbay Harbor, Maine

LOBSTER CASSEROLE SUPREME

½ c. butter
1 c. flour
1 ½ tsp. salt
8 c. milk
4 c. shredded Cheddar cheese
5 5 ½-oz. cans lobster, broken into pieces
⅔ c. chopped olives
1 8-oz. can sliced mushrooms, drained
8 hard-cooked eggs, sliced
3 c. prepared biscuit mix

Melt butter in large saucepan. Remove from heat; stir in flour and salt until smooth. Gradually add 7 cups milk, blending well. Cook and stir over low heat until mixture thickens; stir in 2 cups cheese. Cook until cheese is melted. Add lobster, olives, mushrooms and eggs. Spoon into two buttered 1-quart casseroles. Add remaining milk to biscuit mix. Roll dough 1/2-inch thick. Cover with remaining cheese. Roll dough as for jelly roll; cut into 1/2-inch slices. Cover lobster mixture with biscuits. Bake at 425 degrees for 15 minutes or until biscuits are browned. Yield: 16 servings.

Barbara E. Crockett, Potter Academy
Douglas Hill, Maine

LOBSTER DAINTIES

24 frozen miniature lobsters
¼ c. butter, melted
2 tbsp. paprika
1 c. corn meal
2 tbsp. Vermouth

Butterfly lobster tails; place in shallow baking pan. Add 1/4-inch water to pan to prevent drying during baking. Brush tails with melted butter. Mix paprika and corn meal; spread over lobster tails. Sprinkle with Vermouth. Bake at 450 degrees for 10 to 15 minutes or until tender. Place under broiler to brown. Yield: 4 servings.

Mrs. Sandra Weidling, Mauston H. S.
Mauston, Wisconsin

LUSCIOUS LOBSTER

4 tbsp. butter or margarine
2 7-oz. cans lobster meat, flaked
2 tbsp. chopped green onion
3 tbsp. flour
1 tsp. salt
Dash of cayenne pepper
1/8 tsp. nutmeg
1 1/2 c. milk or light cream
Chopped parsley

Melt butter in electric frying pan at 350 degrees. Saute lobster and onion in butter until lightly browned. Sift flour, salt, cayenne pepper and nutmeg; gradually blend into lobster mixture. Slowly add milk, stirring until smooth. Cook, stirring constantly, until thickened. Sprinkle with parsley; serve on hot buttered toast. NOTE: Chicken, turkey or crab meat may be used in place of lobster. Yield: 6 servings.

Mrs. Eleanor Puckett, North Mecklenburg
Huntersville, North Carolina

RICE AND LOBSTER

1 tsp. chopped onion
2 tbsp. butter
2/3 c. lobster or 1 can shrimp, broken into small pieces
1 1/3 c. hot cooked rice
2/3 c. light cream
1/4 tsp. celery salt
1/2 tsp. salt
Few grains of cayenne pepper
3 tbsp. tomato sauce

Cook onion in butter for 5 minutes; add lobster, rice and cream. Heat and add remaining ingredients. Yield: 5-6 servings.

Deanne Tufts, Valley Regional H. S.
Old Saybrook, Connecticutt

ROCK LOBSTER TAILS

6 4-oz. Rock lobster tails
1 3-oz. pkg. cream cheese
4 tbsp. heavy cream
4 tbsp. butter
3 tbsp. flour
1 1/2 c. milk
1 tsp. salt
1/4 tsp. curry powder
1/4 tsp. paprika

Drop frozen Rock lobster tails into boiling salted water. Boil for 1 minute. Drain and drench with cold water. Carefully remove meat from shells, reserving shells. Cut lobster into bite-sized pieces. Blend cream cheese with cream. Melt butter; stir in flour. Gradually add milk, stirring constantly. Cook until thickened. Add salt, curry powder, paprika and cream cheese mixture, stirring until sauce is smooth. Add lobster; simmer until heated through. Refill empty shells with mixture. Serve immediately granished with parsley, if desired. Yield: 6 servings.

Mrs. Frances Bode, Greenfield H. S.
Greenfield, Oklahoma

SEAFOOD NEWBURG

1/4 c. margarine
1 tbsp. cornstarch
1 tsp. salt
1 tsp. paprika
Dash of cayenne pepper
2 c. light cream
1/2 c. dry Sherry
2 egg yolks, slightly beaten
2 c. cut up cooked lobster, crab or shrimp
8 slices fresh bread

Melt margarine in saucepan; blend in cornstarch, salt, paprika and cayenne. Remove from heat; gradually blend in cream. Cook over medium heat, stirring constantly, until mixture comes to a boil; boil for 1 minute. Reduce heat; gradually stir in Sherry. Blend a small amount of hot mixture into eggs; stir back into saucepan with remaining hot mixture. Add seafood. Heat; do not boil. Trim crusts from bread. Brush on one side with additional margarine. Fit, buttered-side up, into medium-sized muffin cups, pressing down to form cup shape. Bake at 450 degrees for about 10 minutes or until edges are well browned. Fill with seafood mixture. Yield: 6-8 servings.

Isabel Howard Gist, Edmunds H. S.
Sumter, South Carolina

STUFFED LOBSTER TAILS

4 6-oz. frozen lobster tails
1/4 c. butter
2 onions, chopped
1 sm. clove of garlic, minced
1 sm. can mushrooms
1 tbsp. flour
3/4 c. Sherry or chicken bouillon
1 tsp. paprika
1 tsp. salt
1/4 tsp. pepper
1/2 c. grated Parmesan cheese

Cook lobster tails in boiling water; cool. Remove meat from shells, reserving shells. Cut meat into cubes. Melt 2 tablespoonfuls butter in a heavy skillet; add onions, garlic and mushrooms. Cook over low heat for 5 minutes. Sprinkle with flour. Gradually add Sherry or bouillon; cook for 5 minutes longer; stirring constantly. Add lobster meat, paprika, salt and pepper. Cover; cook over low heat for 10 minutes. Place lobster shells in shallow baking pan; spoon lobster mixture into shells. Sprinkle with cheese and remaining butter. Bake at 400 degrees for 10 minutes. Yield: 4 servings.

Joan Farley, Waldron Area School
Waldron, Michigan

FRIED OYSTERS

1 egg
1 egg yolk
1 tsp. baking powder
1 tbsp. oil
Milk
3 doz. oysters
Fat

Combine egg, 1 egg yolk, baking powder, oil and 4 tablespoonfuls milk. Beat until smooth. Add additional milk to make the consistency of thick cream. Chill for 30 minutes. Dip oysters into batter; fry in hot fat until golden brown.

BEARNAISE SAUCE:

2 egg yolks
1 tbsp. tarragon vinegar
2 tbsp. light cream
Salt
Cayenne pepper
2 tbsp. chopped fresh herbs
Garlic to taste

Combine remaining egg yolks, vinegar, cream, salt and cayenne pepper in double boiler over hot water; cook, beating constantly, until sauce begins to thicken; add 4 tablespoonfuls fat, herbs and garlic. Serve with oysters. Yield: 9-12 servings.

Elva Gloria Ruiz, Buckholts Rural H. S.
Buckholts, Texas

GOURMET OYSTER LOAF

1 long loaf sour dough French bread
¼ c. plus 2 tbsp. butter
1 tsp. garlic powder or 1 clove of garlic, mashed
6 tbsp. flour
½ tsp. salt
¼ tsp. pepper
2 jars small Pacific oysters, drained
4 tbsp. corn or olive oil

Cut a slice lengthwise off top of bread. Scoop out inside, leaving a shell. Mix 1/4 cup butter with garlic powder. Rub inside of lid and shell with the garlic butter. Combine flour, salt and pepper; dredge oysters in flour mixture. Fry in oil and remaining butter until golden brown. Place in buttered shell.

SAUCE:

½ stick butter
3 tbsp. flour
1 c. rich milk
½ tsp. salt
¼ tsp. pepper
1 tbsp. Worcestershire sauce
½ tsp. paprika
¼ tsp. thyme
¼ tsp. mace
Dash of Tabasco sauce
Dash or cayenne pepper
⅓ c. Sauterne wine
½ c. chopped ripe olives

Melt butter; blend in flour. Gradually add milk; cook until thick, stirring constantly. Stir in seasonings. Add Sauterne. Pour over oysters. Sprinkle with olives. Place lid on shell. Wrap in a damp cloth. Place on sheet cake pan. Bake at 300 degrees for 20 to 30 minutes. Cut into 2 to 3-inch slices. Garnish with parsley, if desired.

Bertha B. Boyd, University H. S.
Los Angeles, California

SCALLOPED OYSTERS

3 c. cracker crumbs
1 pt. cream
¼ c. butter
1 pt. oysters
¼ tsp. salt
Dash of pepper

Place layer of cracker crumbs in 8 x 11-inch shallow baking pan; sprinkle with 1/4 cup cream. Dot with some of the butter; add oysters in one thick layer. Sprinkle with salt and pepper. Top with remaining crumbs; dot with remaining butter. Add remaining cream. Bake at 350 degrees for 45 minutes. If using glass pan, reduce heat to 325 degrees. Yield: 4-6 servings.

Mrs. Alice Applegate, Knoxville H. S.
Knoxville, Ohio

BAKED SCALLOPS ON THE SHELL

1 lb. scallops
½ c. heavy cream
Salt and pepper
4 tbsp. bread crumbs
4 tbsp. butter

Place 4 or 5 scallops on each buttered scallop shell or individual casserole. Top each shell with 2 tablespoonfuls of cream. Sprinkle with salt and pepper and bread crumbs. Place 1 tablespoonful butter on top of each shell. Place on cookie sheet. Bake at 450 degrees for 20 minutes. Yield: 4 servings.

Ann C. Lowe, Forest Hills School
Saint John, New Brunswick, Canada

SAVORY SCALLOPS

½ c. chopped bacon
¼ c. minced onion
1 tsp. salt
¼ c. flour
⅛ tsp. Tabasco sauce
12 oz. frozen or fresh scallops
2 tbsp. Worcestershire sauce
¼ c. lemon juice
½ c. fresh minced parsley

Fry bacon slowly in a heavy skillet with a tight lid. Add onion and cook until golden. Sprinkle with salt, flour and Tabasco sauce. Do not stir;

(Continued on next page)

simmer until flour is absorbed in fat. If scallops are frozen, partially thaw to separate and drain any liquid into a cup. If fresh, rinse and dry on paper towel. Add scallops to skillet; stir just enough to mix. Cover and simmer for 15 minutes, stirring after 5 minutes or cooking. Add Worcestershire sauce and lemon juice to scallop juice; add with parsley to scallop mixture. Stir immediately; turn off heat. Continue stirring over warm burner until sauce covers each scallop. NOTE: If using fresh scallops, substitute 2 to 3 tablespoonfuls water for scallop liquid.

Christine Stage, New Lexington H. S.
New Lexington, Ohio

SCALLOPS EN CASSEROLE

½ tsp. salt
Dash of freshly ground white pepper
Dash of cayenne pepper
1 ½ c. fine fresh bread crumbs
2 eggs
4 tbsp. water
1 ½ lb. bay scallops
¼ c. butter, melted

Mix salt, white pepper, cayenne pepper and bread crumbs. Beat eggs with water. Dip scallops into egg mixture; roll in crumb mixture. Place closely in a shallow casserole; refrigerate for 30 minutes or until coating is firm. Pour melted butter over scallops. Bake at 450 degrees for 25 to 30 minutes or until scallops are brown and crisp. Serve with tartar sauce, if desired. Yield: 4 servings.

Mrs. Ruth K. Ockman, Maplewood Jr. H. S.
Maplewood, New Jersey

PEACHY SCALLOP

1 lb. fresh or frozen scallops
2 tbsp. melted butter or margarine
2 tbsp. lemon juice
½ tsp. salt
Dash of pepper
12 canned peach halves
¼ tsp. cinnamon
¼ tsp. cloves
¼ tsp. mace
3 slices bacon

Thaw frozen scallops. Rinse with cold water. Cut scallops into 1/2-inch pieces. Combine butter, lemon juice, 1/4 teaspoonful salt, pepper and scallops. Place peach halves in a 11 x 7 x 1-inch baking pan. Combine cinnamon, cloves, mace and remaining salt. Sprinkle over peaches. Place 2 tablespoonfuls scallop mixture in center of each peach. Cut bacon into fourths crosswise. Place bacon slice on each peach. Broil 4-inches from heat for 8 to 10 minutes or until bacon is crisp. Yield: 6 servings.

Lucille Reid Marker, Robertsdale H. S.
Robertsdale, Alabama

BAKED STUFFED JUMBO SHRIMP

¼ lb. butter or margarine
2 c. crushed Ritz crackers
½ c. milk
3 lb. jumbo shrimp

Melt butter in oven in a large pan with sides. Place cracker crumbs in a medium-sized bowl; place milk in separate bowl. Slice shrimp by cutting almost through the back; rinse. Dip shrimp into milk; drain slightly. Dip and turn in crumbs. Place in buttered pan. Bake in preheated 400 degree oven for 20 to 25 minutes or until fish flakes when tested with fork. Yield: 4 servings.

Brenda Diane Flint, Vilas H. S.
Alstead, New Hampshire

BAKED STUFFED SHRIMP

12 jumbo shrimp
¼ lb. saltine crackers, crushed
¾ c. melted butter or margarine
¼ c. lemon juice
1 bay leaf, crumbled
2 tbsp. parsley flakes
Milk or chicken broth
2 lemons, quartered

Split shrimp for stuffing. Combine cracker crumbs, 1/4 cup butter, lemon juice, bay leaf and parsley flakes; moisten with milk or chicken broth. Stuff shrimp with mixture. Arrange in 9 x 13-inch baking dish. Bake at 375 degrees for 25 minutes. Serve with lemon wedges sprinkled with parsley and remaining butter. Yield: 4 servings.

Mrs. Alice M. McLaughlin, North Quincy H. S.
Quincy, Massachusetts

BOILED SHRIMP

2 qt. water
3 c. diced celery
1 c. chopped onions
2 lemons, quartered
2 cloves of garlic, minced
6 bay leaves
3 tbsp. salt
1 tbsp. whole allspice
2 tsp. cayenne pepper
3 lb. headless shrimp

Bring water to boil in large kettle; add remaining ingredients except shrimp; simmer for 15 minutes or until shell turns pink and shrimp is tender. Remove from heat. Let stand for 20 minutes; drain. Peel off shells; remove black veins. Serve on platter of cracked ice with cocktail sauce, if desired.

Mrs. Thelma Valbracht, ROVA School
Oneida, Illinois

SHRIMP DE JONGHE

3 lb. shrimp
Salt and pepper
½ c. consomme
4 to 5 cloves of garlic
1 c. butter
2 c. dry bread crumbs
6 tbsp. minced parsley

Shell and remove black vein from shrimp; place 6 to 8 shrimp in six individual baking dishes. Season with salt and pepper. Pour consomme over shrimp. Cook garlic in butter until butter browns; remove garlic. Mix crumbs and parsley; sprinkle over shrimp. Bake in preheated 400 degree oven for 15 minutes. Do not overcook. Yield: 6 servings.

Mrs. Harold Bond, Scott H. S.
Madison, West Virginia

BOILED SHRIMP

2 qt. water
1 sprig parsley
1 stalk celery, chopped
½ tsp. salt
2 lb. raw shrimp, washed

Simmer water and seasoning for 5 minutes. Add shrimp. Cover; bring to a boil. Boil for 5 minutes. Drain shrimp in a colander; cool. Remove the shell by pulling it with fingers; remove the vein that runs on the outside of shrimp with the tip of a knife or toothpick. Yield: 4 servings.

Evelyn D. Wester, Geraldine H. S.
Geraldine, Alabama

FROZEN SHRIMP

2 tbsp. salt
1 bay leaf
5 lb. frozen shrimp
1 c. catsup
1 to 3 tsp. horseradish
¼ tsp. Tabasco sauce
½ tsp. Worcestershire sauce
¾ c. butter or margarine (opt.)

Fill 8-quart kettle with water; cover and bring to a boil. Add salt and bay leaf. Add shrimp. Cover; bring to a boil as rapidly as possible. Boil for 5 minutes; drain. Combine catsup, horseradish, Tabasco sauce and Worcestershire sauce. Serve sauce in custard cups with cold shrimp or serve hot shrimp with melted butter. Yield: 6-10 servings.

Ora Goodrich, Coudersport Area H. S.
Coudersport, Pennsylvania

SHRIMP COCKTAIL WITH ZIPPY COCKTAIL SAUCE

4 lb. shrimp in shells
9 qt. water
¼ c. salt
¼ c. vinegar
3 bay leaves
2 tsp. pickling spice
2 stalks celery or celery tops, chopped
4 lb. shrimp in shells

Bring water and all seasonings to a boil; add shrimp. Bring to a boil. Cover and simmer gently for 5 minutes. Rinse in cool water. Split shell and peel back. Remove dark vein with tip of knife. Chill.

ZIPPY COCKTAIL SAUCE:

1 c. salad dressing or mayonnaise
¼ c. catsup
¾ c. chili sauce
2 ½ tbsp. horseradish
¾ tsp. salt
1 tbsp. vinegar

Combine all ingredients, blending until smooth. Chill and serve over chilled shrimp in lettuce cup. Yield: 12 servings.

Mrs. Annetta Bailey, Agua Dulce H. S.
Agua Dulce, Texas

BROILED BUTTERFLY SHRIMP

1 lb. large shrimp
4 tbsp. butter
1 slice garlic, peeled
Salt and pepper
Paprika
Lemon slices

Prepare butterfly shrimp; leave tails on. Melt butter in saucepan with garlic slice. Add a small amount salt and grind of pepper; discard garlic. Spread shrimp in shallow pan; brush generously with garlic butter. Sprinkle with paprika. Broil under moderate heat for 3 to 5 minutes or until shrimp are heated through and barely done. Serve at once with lemon slices. Yield: 4 servings.

Mrs. Betty Rainwater, Lynn H. S.
Lynn, Arkansas

SHRIMP ERNIE

1 pt. oil
1 tbsp. salt
4 tbsp. catsup
1 tsp. paprika
1 sm. clove of garlic, minced
2 lb. shrimp, cleaned and deveined

Combine all ingredients except shrimp. Marinate shrimp in the sauce for 1 to 2 hours. Place shrimp on sides in shallow pan; pour part of sauce over shrimp. Do not cover. Broil at 350 degrees for 3 to 5 minutes on each side.

Mrs. J. M. Gay, Glen Oaks H. S.
Baton Rouge, Louisiana

CAJUN STEWED SHRIMP OR CRAYFISH

2 lb. shrimp or crayfish
2 tbsp. shortening
1 onion, chopped
2 tbsp. instant roux or flour
Salt and black pepper to taste
Red pepper to taste
1 6-oz. can tomato sauce
1 6-oz. can water
½ c. chopped green onion tops
½ c. chopped parsley

Brown seafood slightly in shortening. Add onion; brown slightly. Add roux, seasonings and tomato sauce. Stir well; add water, green onion tops and parsley. Simmer for 20 to 30 minutes or just until tender. Serve on hot rice. NOTE: One pound sausage, 1 pound tasso and chicken pieces may be substituted for seafood. Brown meat well; add remaining ingredients. Simmer for 1 hour and 30 minutes. Yield: 8 servings.

Mrs. Cherrie Y. Manuel, Mamou H. S.
Mamou, Louisiana

CREOLE SHRIMP

½ c. minced onion
2 tbsp. butter, melted
2 tbsp. flour
¼ c. diced celery
¼ tsp. pepper sauce
1 6 ¼-oz. can tomato paste
Dash of cayenne pepper
1 bay leaf, crushed
½ c. minced green pepper
½ tsp. salt
Sugar (opt.)
2 c. cooked shrimp

Saute onion in melted butter. Blend in remaining ingredients except shrimp. Cook slowly for 30 minutes or until thickened, stirring occasionally. Stir in shrimp. Serve over hot cooked rice. NOTE: Two 7-ounce cans shrimp may be used for 2 cups shrimp.

Dorothy Searcy, Lewisville H. S.
Lewisville, Arkansas

CREOLE SHRIMP IN RICE RING

1 lge. onion, chopped
1 clove of garlic, minced
4 stalks celery, chopped
2 tbsp. salad oil
1 No. 2 ½ can tomatoes
Salt and pepper
2 bay leaves
1 sprig thyme
Dash of Tabasco sauce
2 lb. fresh shrimp, washed and deveined
2 c. uncooked rice
¼ c. melted butter

Brown onion, garlic and celery in hot salad oil; add tomatoes, salt, pepper, bay leaves, thyme and Tabasco sauce. Cook for 40 minutes. Add shrimp; cook for 10 minutes. Cook rice in 4 quarts boiling salted water. Drain; rinse with hot water. Drain again. Add melted butter, salt and pepper; pack firmly into 10-inch greased ring mold. Let stand for 30 minutes in pan of hot water or in 350 degree oven. Unmold onto hot platter; fill with shrimp. Yield: 6-8 servings.

Mrs. Patricia Wilkinson, Sunnyslope H. S.
Pheonix, Arizona

EASY SHRIMP CREOLE

¼ c. finely chopped onion
¼ c. finely chopped green pepper
2 tbsp. butter
1 can tomato soup
½ c. water
1 tsp. vinegar
Dash of Tabasco sauce
⅛ tsp. pepper
1 1-lb. can large shrimp, drained

Saute onion and green pepper in butter. Add soup, water, vinegar, Tabasco sauce and pepper; simmer until thickened. Add shrimp and heat. Serve over cooked rice seasoned to taste, if desired. Yield: 6-8 servings.

Mrs. Marie Weir, Hardin H. S.
Hardin, Montana

MY BEST SHRIMP CREOLE

1 ½ c. uncooked rice
½ c. chopped onion
¼ clove of garlic, minced
½ c. chopped celery
⅓ c. chopped green pepper
2 tbsp. margarine
1 can tomato puree
2 c. canned tomatoes
2 c. water
½ tsp. Worcestershrie sauce
½ tsp. Tabasco sauce
½ tsp. salt
1 lb. shrimp, cooked and deveined

Cook rice as directed on package. Saute onion, garlic, celery and green pepper in margarine over moderate heat for 5 minutes. Add tomato puree, tomatoes and water; simmer for 10 minutes. Add sauces and salt; simmer for 50 minutes. Add shrimp; simmer for 10 minutes longer. Serve over rice. Yield: 4 servings.

Mrs. Peggy Tipton, Sugar Grove H. S.
Sugar Grove, Virginia

SHRIMP A LA CREOLE

1 tbsp. butter
1 tbsp. flour
1 c. milk
1 egg, slightly beaten
½ tsp. salt
¼ tsp. pepper
½ c. tomatoes

(Continued on next page)

2 canned pimentos
¼ c. chopped onion
1 7½-oz. can shrimp

Melt butter in double boiler. Add flour; blend. Add milk; stir until smooth. Add egg, salt and pepper; cook for 3 minutes. Add remaining ingredients. Reheat. Serve over chow mein noodles, toast or in timbale cases, garnished with parsley, if desired. Yield: 4 servings.

Mrs. Doris Schlumpf, Durand Unified Schools
Durand, Wisconsin

SHRIMP CREOLE

¼ lb. bacon
1 sm. onion, minced
1 sm. green pepper, minced
1 stalk celery, minced
1 tbsp. Worcestershire sauce
½ tsp. Tabasco sauce
¼ c. catsup
2 cans tomato soup
1 can cream of mushroom soup
Salt and pepper to taste
1 lb. small shrimp

Slightly brown bacon, onion, green pepper and celery in large saucepan. Add remaining ingredients except shrimp. Cook slowly for 1 hour. Add remaining ingredients except shrimp. Cook slowly for 1 hour. Add shrimp and cook for 10 minutes. Serve hot on rice, if desired. Yield: 8 servings.

Marthanne Limehouse, St. Paul's H. S.
Yonges Island, South Carolina

SHRIMP CREOLE

1 c. sliced peeled onions
1 c. sliced celery
¾ c. sliced green peppers
⅓ c. salad oil
1 tbsp. flour
¾ tsp. salt
1 tsp. bottled condiment sauce
¼ c. chili sauce
1 tsp. sugar
⅛ tsp. pepper
½ c. catsup
2 c. tomatoes
2 c. cooked shrimp

Saute onions, celery and green peppers in salad oil until tender but not brown. Blend in flour, salt, sauces, sugar, pepper and catsup. Add tomatoes; cook, stirring occasionally until mixture is slightly thickened. Add shrimp; heat thoroughly. Serve over hot rice. Yield: 6 servings.

Maude C. Pruett, Dadeville H. S.
Dadeville, Alabama

SHRIMP CREOLE

2 tbsp. butter or shortening
½ c. minced onion
¼ c. diced celery
½ c. diced green pepper
Cayenne pepper or hot sauce to taste
1 tsp. salt
2 c. cooked tomatoes
1 tbsp. lemon juice
1 tsp. sugar
2 c. cooked shrimp

Melt shortening; add onion, celery and green pepper. Fry until slightly soft. Combine remaining ingredients except shrimp. Simmer for 20 minutes; add shrimp. Heat thoroughly. Serve over hot fluffy rice. Yield: 6 servings.

Mrs. Marguerite Crews, Lewisburg Jr. H. S.
Lewisburg, Pennsylvania

SHRIMP CREOLE

1 3-lb. pkg. frozen shrimp
4 slices bacon
1 bunch celery, finely chopped
2 lge. onions, finely chopped
1 No. 2 can tomatoes
¼ tsp. salt
1 tbsp. vinegar
1 tbsp. sugar
1 lge. green pepper, finely chopped
1 tbsp. cornstarch

Prepare shrimp according to directions on package, reserving 3/4 cup shrimp broth. Fry bacon in large frying pan; remove when crisp. Fry celery and onions in bacon fat until wilted; add shrimp broth. Let simmer for 10 minutes, stirring occasionally. Add tomatoes, salt, vinegar and sugar. Let simmer for 10 minutes longer. Add green pepper to sauce; simmer for 10 minutes. Dissolve cornstarch in 1/4 cup cold water; stir into sauce. Boil for 2 to 3 minutes; add shrimp. Serve over rice, if desired. Yield: 6 servings.

Mrs. Joan Thuma, Genoa-Kingston H. S.
Genoa, Illinois

SHRIMP CREOLE DELUXE

3 tbsp. cooking oil
2 med. onions, finely chopped
2 green peppers, finely chopped
4 pieces celery, finely chopped
1 clove of garlic, minced
1 8-oz. can tomato sauce
1 tsp. chili powder
½ to ¾ tsp. red hot sauce
1 tbsp. Worcestershire sauce
Salt and pepper to taste
1 lb. shrimp

Heat oil in 10 or 12-inch heavy skillet; add onions, peppers, celery and garlic. Wilt ingredients; cook until clear. Add tomato sauce and seasonings; let simmer for 30 minutes. Add shrimp; cover tightly. Cook on low heat for 30 to 40 min-

(Continued on next page)

utes. Serve hot over hot rice, if desired. Yield: 4 servings.

Mrs. Ramona Hext, Newton H. S.
Newton, Texas

CURRIED SHRIMP

¼ c. melted butter
¼ c. flour
½ tsp. salt
Dash of paprika
¾ tsp. curry powder
1 ½ c. milk
3 tbsp. catsup
¼ c. cooking Sherry
1 ½ c. cleaned shrimp
2 c. cooked rice

Blend butter, flour and seasonings in saucepan; gradually stir in milk. Cook until thick and smooth, stirring constantly. Add catsup, Sherry and shrimp to mixture; heat through. Serve over mounds of fluffy hot rice. Sprinkle with chopped parsley, if desired. Yield: 2-4 servings.

Barbara A. Spears, Foothill H. S.
Bakersfield, California

CURRIED SHRIMP

⅓ c. shortening
3 tbsp. flour
2 tsp. curry powder
1 tsp. salt
¼ tsp. paprika
2 c. light cream or milk
1 lb. peeled, cooked and deveined shrimp
1 tbsp. lemon juice
¼ tsp. Worcestershire sauce
2 hard-cooked eggs, sliced
3 c. hot cooked rice

Melt shortening; add flour, curry powder, salt and paprika. Gradually add cream; cook until thickened. Add shrimp, lemon juice, Worcestershire sauce and eggs; heat thoroughly. Serve over hot rice. Yield: 5-6 servings.

Mrs. Etta Gentry Champagne, Pettus H. S.
Pettus, Texas

FRENCH-FRIED SHRIMP AND SAUCE

Frozen unshelled shrimp
Prepared pancake mix
Fat
Chili sauce
Mayonnaise

Thaw shrimp. Remove tails and shells. Devein; wash and drain on absorbent paper. Add enough water to pancake mix to make consistency of batter. Dip shrimp into batter. Drop into hot 375 degree deep fat; fry until golden brown, turning once. Drain on absorbent paper; serve with sauce made by mixing two parts chili sauce to one part mayonnaise.

Mrs. Laurie Williams, Stromsburg H. S.
Stromsburg, Nebraska

SOUTHERN-FRIED SHRIMP

3 c. deviened shrimp
2 ¼ tsp. salt
¼ tsp. pepper
1 egg, well beaten
½ c. light cream or milk
½ c. yellow corn meal
½ c. flour
½ tsp. baking powder

Season shrimp with 2 teaspoonfuls salt and pepper; let stand at room temperature for 15 minutes. Combine beaten egg, milk, corn meal, flour, baking powder and remaining salt in a small mixing bowl. Mix until well blended and smooth. Add batter mixture to shrimp; stir until all shrimp are well coated with batter. Drop shrimp in hot fat in clusters of 2 or 3 shrimp. Cover; fry until light brown. Yield: 6-8 servings.

Mrs. Valerie S. Trahan, Abbeville H. S.
Abbeville, Louisiana

STUFFED FRIED SHRIMP

1 c. minced onions
1 c. finely chopped celery
1 green pepper, finely chopped
3 tbsp. butter
1 c. crab meat
½ tsp. salt
1 clove of garlic, crushed
½ tsp. poultry seasoning
½ c. thick white sauce
2 egg yolks, beaten
1 ½ c. bread crumbs
Chopped parsley
12 jumbo shrimp

Saute onions, celery and green pepper in butter until golden brown; add crab meat, salt, garlic and poultry seasoning. Heat thoroughly. Remove from heat; blend in white sauce and egg yolks. Toss with bread crumbs and parsley. Clean shrimp; devein and split backs. Fill shrimp with crab meat mixture; refrigerate for 2 hours.

BATTER:

1 c. flour
½ tsp. salt
1 ¼ tsp. baking powder
⅔ c. milk
1 tbsp. salad oil
2 egg whites, stiffly beaten

Combine dry ingredients; stir in milk and oil. Fold in egg whites. Dip shrimp into batter; fry until golden brown. Yield: 4 servings.

Mrs. C.L. Hillis, Pine Tree H. S.
Longview, Texas

INDIA CURRY

1 lge. onion, chopped
Butter or margarine
2 tbsp. flour
1 ½ tsp. curry powder
1 tbsp. sugar
1 tsp. salt
1 ½ lb. shrimp
1 lge. can tomatoes
1 can whole green beans
Rice
Coconut
Chopped egg yolk
Chopped egg white
Chopped sweet pickle
Chopped cashews
Chutney

Brown onion in butter or margarine in a saucepan. Mix flour, curry powder, sugar and salt; add shrimp and stir to coat. Place shrimp in pan with onion; add tomatoes and green beans. Simmer for 1 hour over very low heat, stirring frequently. Serve on a platter in the center of a rice ring. Surround the platter with six small dishes containing coconut, egg yolk, egg white, pickle, nuts and chutney. Yield: 4-6 servings.

Mrs. Marilyn Bushnell, Avonworth School
Pittsburgh, Pennsylvania

LOUISIANA-STYLE SHRIMP

2 tbsp. butter
1 tsp. chopped onion
⅔ c. cooked or canned shrimp, broken into pieces
⅔ c. hot boiled rice
⅔ c. heavy cream
½ tsp. salt
¼ tsp. celery salt
Dash of cayenne
3 tbsp. catsup (opt.)

Cook butter with onion for 5 minutes, stirring constantly. Add shrimp, rice and cream. Heat well; add salt, celery salt, cayenne and catsup. Yield: 4-6 servings.

Mrs. Billie Nowlin, Rising Star H. S.
Rising Star, Texas

MANDARIN SHRIMP

½ c. salad oil
2 lb. shrimp
2 onions, sliced
6 stalks celery, sliced
1 6-oz. can mushrooms, drained
1 5-oz. can water chestnuts, drained and sliced
1 lge. can Mandarin orange sections, drained
3 tbsp. soy sauce
1 ½ tbsp. sugar
1 tsp. salt

Place oil in kettle. Layer shrimp, onions, celery, mushrooms, chestnuts and oranges in kettle. Sprinkle with soy sauce, sugar and salt. Cover; cook over low heat until tender. Serve with rice, if desired. Yield: 6 servings.

Mrs. Mary Sullivan Debevec, Chisholm H. S.
Chisholm, Minnesota

MARINATED SHRIMP

1 12-oz. bottle cocktail sauce
1 ½ c. mayonnaise
1 tbsp. Worcestershire sauce
¼ tsp. Tabasco sauce
2 tsp. celery seed
¼ tsp. garlic salt
1 onion, thinly, sliced
Salt and pepper to taste
2 lb. boiled and peeled shrimp

Mix all ingredients except shrimp. Add shrimp. Store in a covered dish in refrigerator for 6 to 8 hours. Yield: 4 servings.

Mrs. Johnnie Broome, Blackshear H. S.
Blackshear, Georgia

PICKLED SHRIMP

2 2 ½-lb. pkg. shrimp
½ c. celery tops
¼ c. mixed pickling spice
1 tbsp. salt
2 c. sliced onions
7 bay leaves
1 ½ c. salad oil
¾ c. white vinegar
3 tbsp. capers and juice
2 ½ tsp. celery seed
1 ½ tsp. salt
3 drops of Tabasco sauce

Cover shrimp with boiling water; add celery, spice and salt. Cover and simmer for 5 minutes. Drain; peel and devein shrimp. Alternate shrimp, onions and bay leaves in shallow baking dish. Combine remaining ingredients; pour over shrimp. Cover and chill for at least 24 hours, spooning marinade over shrimp occasionally. Yield: 8 servings.

Lou Ann Restad, Columbia Heights H. S.
Minneapolis, Minnesota

SCALLOPED SHRIMP

2 tbsp. minced onion
1 tbsp. minced green pepper
4 tbsp. butter, melted
4 tbsp. flour
¼ tsp. dry mustard
2 c. milk
2 c. cooked shrimp
1 c. buttered crumbs

Cook onion and green pepper in butter until tender. Blend in flour and mustard. Add milk; cook until thickened, stirring constantly. Add shrimp.

(Continued on next page)

Pour into greased casserole; cover with buttered crumbs. Bake at 350 degrees for 20 minutes. Yield: 6 servings.

Mrs. Lana Giehl, Groveport-Madison H. S.
Groveport, Ohio

SCAMPI A LA MARINARA

2 cloves of garlic, minced
5 tbsp. olive or salad oil
1 No. 2 ½ can Italian tomatoes
2 tbsp. snipped parsley
½ tsp. dried basil
2 ½ tsp. salt
½ tsp. pepper
1 tsp. dried oregano
⅔ c. canned tomato paste
½ tsp. garlic salt
2 lb. cooked, shelled and deveined shrimp
Grated Parmesan cheese
Hot cooked spaghetti or rice (opt.)

Brown garlic in hot oil in skillet. Add undrained tomatoes, parsley, basil, salt and pepper. Simmer, uncovered, for 30 minutes. Stir in oregano and tomato paste. Cook, uncovered, for 15 minutes. Stir in garlic salt and shrimp. Heat. Top with grated cheese; serve over spaghetti. Yield: 4 servings.

Mrs. Marvel Wax, Bel Air H. S.
El Paso, Texas

SHRIMP WITH CHEESE AND ONION SAUCE

½ c. butter
¾ c. minced onions
1 clove of garlic, minced
½ tsp. dry mustard
½ tsp. salt
½ c. dried grated American cheese
½ c. dry Sherry
1 lb. cooked shrimp

Melt butter; add onions and garlic. Simmer for 3 minutes. Stir in mustard, salt and cheese. Cook and stir over very low heat until cheese is melted. Add Sherry and shrimp; simmer for a few minutes or until shrimp are heated. Place in baking dish; brown lightly under broiler. Serve over rice. Yield: 3-4 servings.

Eleanor Mathews, Edison H. S.
Edison, New Jersey

SHRIMP ELEGANTE

2 tbsp. minced shallots
2 tbsp. butter
1 lb. deveined cleaned shrimp
¼ lb. sliced mushrooms
1 tsp. salt
⅛ tsp. pepper
3 tbsp. chili sauce
1 ⅔ c. water
1 ⅓ c. instant rice
1 c. sour cream
1 tbsp. flour
1 tbsp. chopped chives

Saute shallots in butter until golden; add shrimp and mushrooms. Saute, stirring, until shrimp are pink. Combine salt, pepper, chili sauce and water; add to shrimp mixture. Bring to a boil; stir in rice. Cover and simmer for 5 minutes. Combine sour cream and flour; add to rice mixture. Sprinkle with chives. Yield: 4 servings.

Mrs. Gail S. McDougall, Marshall H. S.
Marshall, Michigan

SHRIMP JAMBALAYA

3 tbsp. butter or margarine
½ c. chopped onion
½ c. chopped green onions
½ c. chopped green pepper
½ c. chopped celery
¼ lb. cooked ham, diced
2 cloves of garlic, minced
2 c. chicken broth
3 lge. tomatoes, chopped
¼ c. chopped parsley (opt.)
½ tsp. salt
⅛ tsp. pepper
¼ tsp. thyme
1 bay leaf
⅛ tsp. cayenne pepper
1 c. uncooked rice
3 4 ½-oz. can shrimp

Heat butter in large heavy skillet over low heat. Stir in onions, 1/2 cup green pepper, celery, ham and garlic; cook over medium heat for 5 minutes or until onions are tender. Stir in broth, tomatoes, parsley, salt, pepper, thyme, bay leaf and cayenne; cover and bring to a boil. Add rice gradually, stirring with a fork. Simmer, covered, for 20 minutes or until rice is tender. Mix in shrimp and 1/4 cup green pepper; simmer, covered, for 5 minutes longer. Yield: 6-8 servings.

Mrs. Jewell T. Johnson, Albany H. S.
Albany, Georgia

SHRIMP AND ONION CURRY

2 c. sliced onions
¼ lb. margarine
1 c. cooked shrimp
1 tsp. salt
1 tsp. curry
1 c. raw rice, cooked

Cook onions in small amount of water or saute in butter until almost tender. Add margarine, onions, shrimp, salt and curry to rice. Yield: 4-6 servings.

Virginia Moses, Northwood H. S.
Silver Springs, Maryland

SHRIMP LUNCHEON DISH

3 tbsp. butter
¼ c. grated onion or 1 onion, minced
1 green pepper, minced
Garlic
¼ c. minced pimento
1 c. rice
½ c. mushrooms
1 ½ c. shrimp, cleaned
1 tsp. salt
1 bay leaf
2 to 3 c. water

Melt butter in pan. Add onion, green pepper, garlic, pimento and rice. Add mushrooms and shrimp. Add salt, bay leaf and water. Cover; heat until steaming. Reduce heat; simmer for 30 to 45 minutes. NOTE: Cooked shrimp may be used. Add shrimp 10 minutes before serving. Yield: 4-6 servings.

Louise Wilcox, Fairview H. S.
Ashland, Kentucky
Mrs. Pansy Gaskill, Rich Land Jr. H. S.
Fort Worth, Texas

SHRIMP WITH RICE

2 lb. shrimp
5 cloves of garlic, mashed
2 sticks margarine
3 lge. onions, cut into large chunks
3 green peppers, cut into large chunks
2 No. 2 cans tomatoes
1 can tomato sauce
Salt and pepper to taste
1 bottle clam juice
2 ½ c. rice

Cook shrimp in boiling salted water until done. Drain shrimp, reserving water. Place garlic and margarine in roasting pan; add shrimp. Bake in preheated 375 degree oven for 45 minutes, tossing occasionally. Add onions and green peppers to mixture of tomatoes and tomato sauce; cook until tender. Season sauce with salt and pepper. Cook rice in reserved liquid and clam juice. Mix rice, tomato mixture and shrimp lightly and serve. Yield: 12 servings.

Mrs. Glenellen Woodward, Glenwood H. S.
Chatham, Illinois

SHRIMP VICTORIA

1 ½ lb. fresh or frozen shrimp
½ c. chopped onion
½ c. butter or margarine
1 c. sliced fresh or canned mushrooms
2 tbsp. lemon juice
1 tbsp. Worcestershire sauce
2 tbsp. flour
1 ½ tsp. seasoned salt
Dash of pepper
1 ½ c. sour cream
1 tbsp. chopped parsley

Cook shrimp and onion in hot butter in large skillet or electric frypan, stirring occasionally, for 5 minutes or until shrimp are almost tender. Add mushrooms, lemon juice and Worcestershire sauce; cook, stirring occasionally for 5 minutes longer. Remove from heat or turn off heat on frypan. Stir in flour, seasoned salt and pepper; stir in sour cream. Cook over low heat, stirring occasionally, until hot but not boiling. Sprinkle with parsley; serve immediately over rice or buttered toast. Yield: 6 servings.

Frances M. Hallett, Southington H. S.
Southington, Connecticut

SPICED SHRIMP

1 ½ lb. shrimp
1 bunch celery tops
1 bunch parsley
1 ½ tsp. crushed bay leaves
1 ½ tsp. whole allspice
1 ½ tsp. whole red peppers
1 ½ tsp. peppercorns
¾ tsp. whole cloves
1 c. vinegar
¼ c. salt
2 qt. boiling water

Wash shrimp, but do not remove shells. Tie celery, parsley and spices in piece of cheesecloth. Add vinegar, salt and bag of seasonings to the water. Cover and simmer for 45 minutes. Add shrimp; cover and return to boiling. Simmer for 5 minutes. Drain and clean. Serve with cocktail sauce, if desired. Yield: 6 servings.

Elsie H. Strode, Swansboro H. S.
Swansboro, North Carolina

ZIPPY SHRIMP SAUCE WITH SPAGHETTI

2 cloves of garlic, finely chopped
¼ c. cooking oil
1 14-oz. can tomatoes
2 ½ tsp. salt
½ tsp. dried basil
1 6-oz. can tomato paste
1 tsp. dried oregano
½ lb. cooked, shelled and deveined shrimp
½ tsp. garlic salt
1 tsp. prepared horseradish
8 oz. spaghetti, cooked
Grated Parmesan cheese

Brown garlic in oil; add tomatoes, salt and basil. Simmer, uncovered, for 30 minutes. Stir in tomato paste and oregano; simmer for 15 minutes longer. Stir in shrimp, garlic salt and horseradish; heat. Serve over hot spaghetti. Sprinkle with cheese. Yield: 4 servings.

Elizabeth Miller, Itawamba Jr. College
Fulton, Mississippi

BAKED CRAB MEAT AND SHRIMP

1 med. green pepper, chopped
1 med. onion, chopped
1 c. chopped celery
1 6 ½-oz. can crab meat, flaked

(Continued on next page)

1 can shrimp, cleaned
½ tsp. salt
⅛ tsp. pepper
1 tsp. Worcestershire sauce
1 c. mayonnaise
1 c. buttered crumbs

Combine all ingredients except crumbs. Place in individual sea shells. Sprinkle with buttered crumbs. Bake at 350 degrees for 30 minutes. NOTE: Fresh shrimp may be used; use 1 cup baked shrimp to 1 cup crab meat. Yield: 8-12 servings.

Sue McDowell, Lederle Jr. H. S.
Southfield, Michigan
Mrs. Lillian J. Rhodes, Neshoba Central H. S.
Philadelphia, Mississippi

DEVILED SEAFOOD SPECIAL

1 6 ½-oz. can tuna, flaked
1 can shrimp
½ c. chopped green pepper
1 c. finely chopped celery
1 tsp. finely chopped onion
1 tsp. dry mustard
1 tsp. Worcestershire sauce
½ tsp. salt
⅛ tsp. pepper
1 c. salad dressing
2 c. soft bread crumbs
2 tbsp. margarine

Combine all ingredients except bread crumbs and margarine; toss until well blended. Place in four ramkins or sea shells. Mix bread crumbs with margarine; sprinkle over top. Bake at 350 degrees for 30 minutes. Yield: 4 servings.

Janice Vanderbeck, M. S. D. Oregon Davis
Hamlet, Indiana

NEW ORLEANS BAKED FISH

2 c. milk
2 tbsp. flour
2 tbsp. butter
Salt and pepper to taste
6 fish fillets
Dried parsley
1 lb. cooked shrimp, cut into small pieces
½ lb. canned crab meat, cut into small pieces

Make a white sauce with milk, flour, butter and seasonings. Prepare six squares of heavy paper or aluminum foil, making a French fold in centers. Place a fillet on each piece of paper or foil. Add shrimp and crab meat to white sauce; spread over fillets. Wrap each fillet; seal ends tightly. Place on cookie sheet. Bake at 450 degrees for 15 minutes. Unfold paper; tuck under fish. Serve in paper. Yield: 6 servings.

Mrs. Hobert Keller, Rabun Co. H. S.
Clayton, Georgia

SEAFOOD BISQUE

½ c. butter
¼ c. flour
½ tsp. salt
¼ tsp. monosodium glutamate
4 c. milk
Few grains of nutmeg
1 10-oz. pkg. frozen scallops, chopped
2 6-oz. cans tuna
1 10-oz. pkg. frozen shrimp

Melt butter; stir in flour, salt and monosodium glutamate. Mix well; add milk. Simmer, stirring constantly, for 15 minutes. Add nutmeg and mix well. Add scallops, tuna and shrimp. Simmer for 20 minutes. Serve over biscuits or timbale cases. Yield: 24 servings.

Mrs. Neva Porath, Black River Falls H. S.
Black River Falls, Wisconsin

SEAFOOD IN SHELLS

4 tbsp. butter or margarine
4 tbsp. flour
1 c. milk
¼ c. cooking Sherry
2 c. cooked diced shrimp
1 c. cooked diced lobster
Parmesan cheese
Paprika

Melt butter; blend in flour. Gradually add milk; stir until thick. Add Sherry, shrimp and lobster; place in six seafood casserole shells. Sprinkle generously with Parmesan cheese and paprika. Broil until lightly browned. Yield: 6 servings.

Mrs. William Oberg, Huguenot H. S.
Richmond, Virginia

SEAFOOD SALAD

1 10-oz. can frozen condensed cream of shrimp soup
1 7-oz. can tuna
¼ c. cream or whole milk
¼ lb. Longhorn cheese, grated
1 c. finely diced celery
¼ c. chopped onion
¼ c. chopped green pepper
Boiled rice

Heat shrimp soup with remaining ingredients to boiling or just long enough to wilt vegetables. Serve over rice. Yield: 6 servings.

Mrs. Janis Thomas, Port Washington H. S.
Port Washington, Ohio

SEAFOOD STILLIMEADOW

1 1 ½-oz. can crab meat
2 cans cream of mushroom soup
2 cans shrimp, drained or 1 ½ lb. fresh shrimp
1 10 ½-oz. can minced clams, undrained
1 4-oz. can sliced mushrooms, undrained
¼ tsp. Worcestershire sauce

(Continued on next page)

Remove any pieces of bone from crab meat. Pour mushroom soup into saucepan; add crab, shrimp, clams, mushrooms and Worcestershire sauce. If mixture is too thick, add a small amount of cream. Bring to boil; serve hot on curry rice, if desired. Yield: 4-6 servings.

Mrs. Howard Pierce, Trimble H. S.
Trimble, Tennessee

SEAFOOD SUPREME

½ c. margarine
2 sm. onions, chopped
3 green peppers, chopped
2 cans sliced mushrooms
⅔ c. flour
2 tsp. salt
½ tsp. pepper
4 c. milk
1 ½ c. grated sharp Cheddar cheese
1 tbsp. lemon juice
1 tsp. dry mustard
1 tsp. Worcestershire sauce
1 12-oz. pkg. frozen lobster, cooked
1 12-oz. pkg. frozen King crab, cooked
1 12-oz. pkg. frozen shrimp, cooked

Melt margarine; add onions, green pepper and mushrooms. Cook until limp. Remove from heat; blend in flour, salt and pepper. Stir in milk; cook until thick. Add cheese, lemon juice, mustard and Worcestershire sauce. Add seafood. Serve over rice. Yield: 8 servings.

Mrs. Nelle M. Dotson, West Henderson H. S.
Hendersonville, North Carolina

SHRIMP AND CRAB GUMBO

3 tbsp. flour
½ c. cooking oil
½ c. chopped celery
2 med. onions, chopped
1 clove of garlic, finely chopped
2 c. tomatoes
1 ½ c. fresh chopped okra
1 lb. cleaned shrimp
1 can crab meat
1 bay leaf
1 tbsp. parsley
Salt and pepper to taste

Brown flour in cooking oil; add celery, onions and garlic. Cook for 5 minutes. Add tomatoes and okra; cook for 5 minutes longer. Add remaining ingredients; pour in 3 pints hot water. Let simmer for 1 hour and 30 minutes to 2 hours. Serve on rice, if desired.

Jewell Westbrook, Central H. S.
Baton Rouge, Louisiana

SHRIMP AND HALIBUT

1 lb. cooked shrimp, cleaned
1 lb. sliced halibut
1 clove of garlic
3 tbsp. butter or oil
6 green onions, chopped
1 fresh tomato, peeled or chopped
1 c. beef bouillon
½ c. dry white wine
Juice of ½ lemon
1 tbsp. Worcestershire sauce
1 tsp. salt
Dash of pepper
Dash of Tabasco sauce

Steam halibut until tender; break into coarse chunks. Mash clove of garlic slightly; saute in butter for 2 to 3 minutes. Remove and add onions. Cook until soft; add tomato, bouillon, wine, lemon juice and seasonings. Simmer until sauce is cooked down. Add fish; heat through. Serve on hot fluffy rice, if desired. Yield: 4 servings.

Mrs. Phyllis Greene McAfee
Old Rochester Regional H. S.
Mattapoisett, Massachusetts

SIMPLIFIED SEAFOOD A LA KING

1 can tuna, flaked
1 can small shrimp, drained
1 bottle olives, sliced
1 can peas
1 qt. white sauce
Pattie shells, baking powder biscuits or rice

Add tuna, shrimp, olives and peas to white sauce in top of double boiler. Blend with fork. Cook until heated through. Pour over pattie shells; garnish with deviled eggs, if desired. Yield: 12 servings.

Mrs. Barbara C. Sleeper, Dover H. S.
Dover, New Hampshire

STUFFED FLOUNDER

2 tbsp. flour
Salt
1 tbsp. mustard
½ tsp. Worcestershire sauce
3 ½ tsp. lemon juice
Dash of pepper
Dash of Tabasco sauce
6 tbsp. melted butter or margarine
⅔ c. milk
2 c. crab meat
8 fillets of flounder or sole

Stir flour, salt, mustard, Worcestershire sauce, 1/2 teaspoonful lemon juice, pepper and Tabasco sauce into melted butter. Gradually add milk; cook over low heat, stirring constantly, until thickened. Add crab meat and mix. Arrange 4 flounder fillets in greased shallow pan; spread each with one-fourth crab meat mixture. Top with remaining fillets; brush with butter and 1 tablespoonful lemon juice. Bake at 350 degrees for 25 minutes. Serve stuffed fillets in halves. Yield: 8 servings.

Cora E. Fairbanks, Rockport H. S.
Rockport, Massachusetts

Wild Game Favorites

BARBECUED BEAR

1 2 to 3-lb. bear roast
Salt and pepper
1 clove of garlic
2 tbsp. brown sugar
1 tbsp. paprika
1 tsp. dry mustard
¼ tsp. chili powder
⅛ tsp. cayenne pepper
2 tbsp. Worcestershire sauce
¼ c. vinegar
1 c. tomato juice
¼ c. catsup
½ c. water

Place roast in small roaster. Season with salt, pepper and garlic. Roast at 350 degrees for 1 hour or until well done. Slice into thin slices. Mix 1 teaspoonful salt with remaining ingredients in heavy skillet. Simmer for 15 minutes. Add meat; simmer for 1 hour or until meat is tender. Yield: 6-8 servings.

Patricia P. Jermyn, St. Regis H. S.
St. Regis, Montana

DOVES

14 to 16 doves
Salt and pepper
Flour
½ c. salad oil
½ c. chopped green onions
1 ½ c. water
1 c. Sherry
¼ c. chopped parsley

Season doves with salt and pepper. Roll in flour. Place in oil in a heavy roaster. Bake at 400 degrees until brown. Add onions, water and Sherry; cover. Bake until tender, basting with Sherry occasionally. Add parsley to gravy just before serving. Yield: 6-8 servings.

Mrs. Ovida Hicks, Sidney Lanier H. S.
Montgomery, Alabama

DOVE PIE

6 doves
1 qt. water
1 onion, chopped
1 sm. bunch parsley, chopped
3 whole cloves
2 tbsp. flour
2 tbsp. butter
Salt and pepper to taste
Pastry

Clean and split the doves; cover with water. Add onion, parsley and cloves; cook until tender. Remove the doves. Skim liquid; thicken with flour and butter. Season with salt and pepper. Remove from heat. Line a baking dish with one-half pastry. Place cooked birds in dish. Cover with gravy; top with remaining pastry. Bake at 350 degrees for 1 hour. Yield: 4-6 servings.

Mrs. Jane Horner, Prosper H. S.
Denton, Texas

SMOTHERED DOVES

Salt and pepper
8 dove breasts
½ c. flour
8 tbsp. fat
4 tsp. Worcestershire sauce
4 tsp. lemon juice
1 c. water

Salt and pepper doves. Put flour in paper bag. Drop breasts into flour. Close bag; shake well. Melt fat in skillet. Fry doves in fat until golden brown. Put 1/2 teaspoonful Worcestershire sauce and 1/2 teaspoonful lemon juice on top of each dove. Add 1 cup water; cover skillet. Simmer for 1 hour or until tender. Add water if necessary. Serve with rice. Yield: 4 servings.

Mrs. Louie E. Kemp, Louisville H. S.
Louisville, Mississippi

BARBECUED MALLARDS

4 Mallard ducks, dressed
1 c. orange marmalade
½ c. orange juice
1 tbsp. soy sauce
1 tsp. basil
1 tsp. salt
¼ tsp. fresh ground pepper
Cornstarch

Broil ducks on rotisserie for 50 minutes to 1 hour. Combine remaining ingredients except cornstarch in a saucepan; bring to a boil. Make a thin paste of cornstarch and water. Gradually add to orange mixture, stirring continuously. Cook until mixture coats a spoon. Baste duck with sauce three times during the last 30 minutes of cooking time. Yield: 4 servings.

Ann Moore, Bliss H. S.
Bliss, Idaho

BROILED WILD DUCK

1 1 ½-lb. wild Mallard duck, halved
Baking soda (opt.)
¼ c. butter or margarine, melted
1 tsp. salt
¼ c. melted currant jelly

Rinse duck thoroughly; pat dry with paper towels. If desired, rub entire surface of duck with 1 tablespoonful baking soda; rinse thoroughly. Place duck, skin-side down, on broiler rack. Combine butter and salt with 2 tablespoonfuls water; brush duck with part of mixture. Broil 6 inches from heat for 5 to 15 minutes, depending on desired doneness. Brush occasionally with butter mixture. Turn duck; broil for 5 to 15 minutes longer, brushing occasionally with butter mixture. Remove; brush with currant jelly. Yield: 2 servings.

Rebecca L. Thomas, Wilton Jr. H. S.
Wilton, Connecticut

DUCKLING

1 5-lb. duckling
1 ½ tsp. salt
2 tsp. fat
1 ¼ c. orange juice
½ tsp. Tabasco sauce
½ tsp. allspice
2 oranges

Split duck down the back; sprinkle with 1 teaspoonful salt. Heat fat in large skillet; add duck. Cook at 300 degrees until browned. Combine orange juice, Tabasco sauce, allspice and remaining salt. Pour over duck. Cover and cook over low heat, turning several times, for 1 hour or until duck is tender. Slice oranges 1/4-inch thick. Add last 15 minutes of cooking. Yield: 4 servings.

Mrs. Harold E. Parker, North Davidson School
Lexington, North Carolina

MALLARD A LA LACASSINE REFUGE

1 ½ tsp. salt
1 tsp. white pepper
½ tsp. poultry seasoning
3 Mallards
3 whole apples
1 to 1 ½ c. Rose wine

Rub mixture of salt, pepper and poultry seasoning on outside of ducks; place any remaining into cavities. Place whole unpeeled apple in each cavity. Brown in a large Dutch oven over medium heat. Lower heat and cover. Continue roasting until tender. Add wine, 2 tablespoonfuls at a time, as moisture is needed. Baste occasionally. Drippings may be used for gravy. NOTE: The amount of the wine may vary depending on the age and size of the ducks. Yield: 4-6 servings.

Mrs. Jack E. Perkins, Lake Arthur H. S.
Lake Arthur, Louisiana

PLANTATION WILD DUCK

1 duck
1 onion, sliced
1 stick butter
Salt and pepper
2 c. water
1 bay leaf
1 c. sliced mushrooms
⅛ tsp. thyme
2 tbsp. flour

Prepare duck for roasting. Disjoint; brown with onion and butter. Salt and pepper. Add water and bay leaf. Bake at 250 degrees for 1 hour and 30 minutes. Saute mushrooms; add thyme and flour. Spoon mixture over ducks; cook for 30 minutes longer. Serve with wild rice, if desired. Yield: 4 servings.

Mrs. Carrie M. Ward, Lambert H. S.
Lambert, Mississippi

MALLARD DUCK

Salt and pepper
1 lge. duck
3 oranges, peeled
4 strips bacon

Salt and pepper duck thoroughly. Place oranges inside duck. Place bacon strips over top of duck. Bake at 250 to 300 degrees for 3 to 4 hours, basting frequently with pan drippings. Yield: 4-6 servings.

Mrs. Eric Turner
Mississippi School for The Blind
Jackson, Mississippi

DUCK AND POTATOES

1 wild duck, cleaned
1 unpeeled apple, cut into halves
Salt and pepper to taste
4 to 5 lge. potatoes, diced
1 lge. onion
2 to 3 tbsp. dry leaf sage

Place whole duck and apple in a 5-quart kettle with 3 to 4 cups water; cover. Boil for 30 minutes. Discard water and apple. Add 3 to 4 cups water to parboiled duck; salt and pepper to season. Cover. Bake at 350 degrees for 45 minutes. Add potatoes, onion, sage and seasonings. Bake for 45 minutes to 1 hour or until duck and potatoes are tender. If necessary, add water as there should be sufficient liquid on duck and potatoes. Yield: 6 servings.

May Schlechtemier Koch, Converse Co. H. S.
Douglas, Wyoming

ROAST DUCK WITH APPLE STUFFING

2 lge. Mallards
½ c. chopped celery
½ c. chopped onion
2 med. apples, cut up
¼ c. brown sugar
¼ c. chopped walnuts
2 to 4 slices bread, cubed
¼ c. raisins
Dash of pepper
⅛ tsp. marjoram
Dash of sage
½ tsp. salt
1 bouillon cube
1 c. warm water

Soak ducks overnight in salt and water brine. Drain ducks; place in roasting pan. Mix celery, onion, apples, brown sugar, walnuts, bread crumbs, raisins and seasonings. Dissolve bouillon cube in 1 cup warm water; add 1/2 cup bouillon to dressing mixture to moisten. Place dressing around ducks. Pour remaining bouillon over ducks. Bake at 325 degrees for 1 hour and 30 minutes or until done. Yield: 4 servings.

Mrs. Joan Liljenberg, Blaine Jr.-Sr. H. S.
Blaine, Washington

ROAST DUCKLING

1 3 ½ to 5-lb. duckling
Salt
3 c. bread cubes
2 c. finely diced celery
1 tbsp. grated orange peel
⅔ c. diced orange sections
½ tsp. poultry seasoning
Dash of pepper
1 egg, beaten
¼ c. melted butter or margarine
2 tbsp. honey
1 tsp. Kitchen Bouquet

Cut wing tips and first joints from duckling, leaving meaty second joints. Rub inside with salt. Toss bread cubes with celery, orange peel, orange sections, poultry seasoning, 3/4 teaspoonful salt and a dash of pepper. Combine egg and butter; add to bread mixture, tossing lightly. Stuff duckling with mixture. Do not prick skin or truss. Skewer opining and lace. Place duckling, breast-up in shallow pan. Do not add water. Roast, uncovered, at 350 degrees for 1 hour and 30 minutes to 2 hours for medium doneness or 2 hours to 2 hours and 30 minutes for well doneness. Mix honey with Kitchen Bouquet and brush duckling 30 minutes before end of baking. Yield: 4 servings.

Sue Aebie, Allensville H. S.
Allensville, Ohio

WILD DUCK

2 ducks
2 slices stale bread
1 tbsp. butter
2 tbsp. chopped onion
2 apples, peeled and cored
½ tsp. celery salt
1 tsp. nutmeg
¼ tsp. pepper
¼ tsp. paprika
Flour
Salt

Parboil ducks for 5 to 10 minutes; drain. Soak bread in water; squeeze out excess water. Add remaining ingredients except flour and salt; cook for a few minutes. Stuff ducks with dressing; dredge lightly with flour and salt. Bake at 450 degrees for 30 minutes. Reduce heat to 350 degrees; cook for 20 minutes per pound or until done.

ORANGE SAUCE:

3 tbsp. butter
3 tbsp. flour
1 c. water
½ tsp. salt
Dash of cayenne
½ c. orange juice

Melt butter; blend in flour. Cook until mixture begins to brown. Add water gradually; stir until smooth. Add salt and cayenne. Just before serving, add orange juice.

Avanell Conner, Central Jr. H. S.
West Helena, Arkansas

WILD DUCK

Dressed wild ducks
Sliced apples, onions, or carrots
Sliced salt pork
Pepper
1 wine glass water

Stuff ducks with a few slices of apples, onions or carrots. Place in a deep covered pan. Place 2 or 3 slices of salt pork over breasts and in bottom of pan. Sprinkle well with pepper. Pour water in dish. Cover; bake at 350 degrees for 30 minutes. Uncover; bake until brown.

Patricia Chaffee, New London H. S.
New London, New Hampshire

WILD DUCK WITH APPLE-RAISIN STUFFING

6 c. dry bread cubes
1 c. chopped apple
½ c. raisins
¾ c. butter, melted
2 tsp. salt
½ tsp. pepper
¼ tsp. cinnamon
⅛ tsp. ginger
3 ducks

Combine all ingredients except ducks in a large bowl. Stuff cavity of each duck with mixture. Close opening of birds with skewers or string. Place ducks breast-side up in roasting pan. Roast, uncovered, at 450 degrees for 15 minutes; reduce temperature to 325 degrees. Cover ducks. Bake for 2 hours until tender. Yield: 6 servings.

Helen Myers, Mountain Home H. S.
Mountain Home, Idaho

WILD DUCK, FLORIDA STYLE

2 2 to 2 ½-lb. wild ducks
6 slices bacon
1 6-oz. can frozen Florida orange juice concentrate, thawed
1 clove of garlic
¾ tsp. dry mustard
½ tsp. ground ginger
½ tsp. salt
1 tbsp. cornstarch
1 c. water

Clean ducks; tie legs and wings close to body. Place in shallow pan, breast-side up. Lay strips of bacon over ducks. Roast in 450 degree oven for 20 to 25 minutes. Combine undiluted orange juice concentrate, garlic, mustard, ginger and salt in small saucepan. Heat to boiling. During last 10 minutes of roasting, remove bacon and brush sauce generously over birds. Mix cornstarch with a small amount of water; stir into remaining orange sauce. Add remaining water. Stir over low heat until thickened. Yield: 4 servings.

Photograph for this recipe on page 205

WINE-SPICED WILD DUCK

1 c. white wine or broth
1 clove of garlic, crushed
1 tsp. thyme
1 tsp. oregano
1 tsp. seasoned salt
1 tsp. pepper
¼ c. oil or melted butter
2 duck breasts
Bacon strips

Combine all ingredients except breasts and bacon. Cover duck breasts with mixture; place in refrigerator for two to three days. Place marinade and breasts in saucepan; cover. Simmer for 2 hours or until tender. Add water if necessary. Place breasts on broiler rack; top with bacon. Broil for 3 to 5 minutes.

Mrs. Carol Frazee, Burlington Jr. H. S.
Burlington, New Jersey

ROASTED PHEASANT

1 pheasant
Salt
Pepper
1 c. wild rice
1 c. apricot juice

Place pheasant on aluminum foil; place in roaster. Rub interior with salt and pepper; cover with uncooked rice. Pour fruit juice over all. Wrap tight with foil. Bake at 325 degrees for 1 hour or until breast is easily pierced with fork. NOTE: Other juices may be substituted for apricot. Yield: 4 servings.

Mrs. Floyd King, Malden H. S.
Malden, Illinois

PHEASANT SOUP

Pheasant bones, skin and left-over meat
Parsley
Thyme
1 bay leaf
1 sm. onion, chopped
2 carrots, chopped
1 to 2 whole cloves
Celery leaves, chopped
Salt to taste
2 to 3 peppercorns, crushed
Chicken stock (opt.)
¼ c. Sherry wine

Combine left-over pheasant with a few sprigs of parsley and thyme; add bay leaf, onion, carrots, cloves, celery leaves, salt and peppercorns. Barely cover with water or one-half water and one-half chicken broth; simmer for 2 hours. Strain broth; add Sherry. Serve with melba toast, if desired. Yield: 4 servings.

Jean Passino, Keewatin-Nashwauk Jr. H. S.
Keewatin, Minnesota

VIRGINIA PHEASANT WITH SAUCE

½ c. flour
1 tsp. salt
1 tsp. paprika
⅛ tsp. pepper
2 pheasants, cut into pieces
¼ c. butter
1 clove of garlic, crushed
¼ c. chopped ripe olives
½ c. water
½ tsp. Worcestershire sauce
½ c. white cooking wine

Combine flour, salt, paprika and pepper; coat pheasant with seasoned flour. Brown on all sides in butter in skillet. Add garlic, olives, water and Worcestershire sauce; cover tightly. Simmer for 45 minutes. Turn pheasant; add wine. Cover; simmer for 45 minutes longer or until tender. Serve hot in skillet with sauce. Yield: 6 servings.

Frances W. Banner, Castlewood H. S.
Castlewood, Virginia

ROAST PHEASANT

Salt
1 whole young pheasant
1 bay leaf
3 to 4 celery leaves
4 slices bacon
⅓ c. salad oil
½ c. mushroom pieces
1 lge. onion, sliced

Thoroughly salt pheasant inside and out; fill cavity with bay leaf and celery leaves. Wrap pheasant breast with bacon; secure in place with string. Place pheasant in roaster. Pour salad oil over pheasant. Add mushrooms and onion slices. Bake at 350 degrees for 1 hour and 30 minutes. Turn pheasant at 30 minute intervals, basting with drippings from pan. Place on platter; remove string, celery leaves and bay leaf. Garnish with spiced apples and parsley.

Mrs. Lonnie Disterhaupt, Lyons Public School
Lyons, Nebraska

FRENCH-FRIED PHEASANT

2 pheasant, cleaned and cut up
Flour
1 recipe batter

Boil pheasant in salted water for 30 minutes. Roll in flour; dip in batter. Fry in deep fat at 375 degrees until golden brown. Yield: 4-6 servings.

Mrs. Rosalie Millar, Edgemont H. S.
Edgemont, South Dakota

GOURMET PHEASANT

3 sm. pheasant, dressed
½ c. milk
Salt and pepper
2 apples, pared, cored and sliced
2 thin slices onion
3 tbsp. butter
3 c. sour cream
4 slices toast
Watercress

Brush birds inside and out with milk. Season with salt and pepper. Stuff cavity with apple slices. Saute onion lightly in butter in deep flame-proof casserole. Brown birds in onion flavored butter. Pour sour cream over birds. Season lightly with salt and pepper. Cover; bake at 375 degrees for 1 hour, basting birds every 15 minutes. Serve hot on toast, if desired. Garnish with watercress. Yield: 3-6 servings.

Mrs. Lorraine Nugent
Cimarron Consolidated School
Cimarron, Kansas

KANSAS ROAST PHEASANT

2 pheasant
Salt to season
Freshly ground black pepper
2 sm. bay leaves
1 clove of garlic
2 whole cloves
2 slices onion
2 slices lemon
4 tbsp. chopped celery leaves
2 tbsp. parsley
4 bacon slices or larding fat
8 sm. onions
2 c. chicken stock
2 tbsp. lemon juice
Flour
1 c. spiced cranberries and juice (opt.)
⅓ c. red currant jelly (opt.)
12 sauted mushroom caps (opt.)

Rub pheasants inside and out with salt and freshly ground pepper. Inside each bird place 1 small bay leaf, 1/2 clove of garlic, 1 whole clove, 1 slice onion, 1 slice lemon, 2 tablespoonfuls chopped celery leaves and 1 tablespoonful parsley. Cover breast of each bird with thick slices of bacon. Truss birds; place in roasting pan. Around birds place 8 small onions. Pour chicken stock and lemon juice over birds; sprinkle with pepper and salt. Cover and roast at 350 degrees for 1 hour. Uncover and remove larding fat. Continue baking for 15 minutes longer or until well browned and tender. Thicken stock with taste of flour and water. Add cranberries and juice and jelly. Pour over birds. Garnish with mushroom caps. Yield: 8-10 servings.

Mrs. Larry Clark
Cowley Co. Comm. Jr. College
Arkansas City, Knasas

PHEASANT IN MILK

Pheasant
Salt
Pepper
Flour
Fat
Milk

Cut pheasant into serving pieces. Season with salt and pepper; roll in flour. Brown in fat, turning continually. Place in covered roaster. Cover with milk; roast at 350 degrees until tender.

Mrs. Ethel F. Johnson, New Brockton H. S.
New Brockton, Alabama

WILD PHEASANT ON RICE

1 pheasant, cut up
Salt and pepper
1 c. flour
1 c. shortening
1 pkg. brown gravy mix
1 pkg. onion gravy mix
1 c. rice
2 c. water

Season pheasant with salt and pepper; roll in flour. Brown in shortening in skillet; place in baking dish. Prepare brown gravy mix and onion gravy mix as directed on package. Pour over pheasant; cover. Bake at 300 degrees for 2 hours. Pheasant may be cooked in pressure saucepan for 45 minutes at 15 pounds pressure. Place rice, 1 teaspoonful salt and water in saucepan; cover. Bring to a boil; reduce heat and simmer for 14 minutes. Serve with pheasant. Yield: 4 servings.

Joanne Snider, Dimmitt H. S.
Dimmitt, Texas

QUAIL BAKED IN WINE

2 shallots, chopped
2 cloves of garlic, finely chopped
½ bay leaf
1 tsp. peppercorn
2 cloves
½ c. plus 4 tbsp. butter
6 quail
4 tbsp. flour
1 pt. white wine
½ tsp. salt
⅛ tsp. pepper
1 tsp. finely cut chives

Slowly cook shallots, garlic, bay leaf, peppercorn and cloves in 1/2 cup butter for 8 minutes, stirring constantly. Saute quail until well browned. Add white wine; simmer for 30 minutes. Remove quail; strain and reserve sauce. Melt remaining butter in a saucepan; blend in flour. Slowly stir in reserved sauce; cooking until thick. Add remaining ingredients and quail. Cover and heat to boiling. Serve. Yield: 8 servings.

Mrs. Mary P. Light, King H. S.
Kingsville, Texas

QUAIL WITH MUSHROOMS

6 slices bacon
6 quail, dressed
Salt and pepper
½ lb. mushroom caps
1 bunch green onions, chopped
3 tbsp. melted butter
2 tbsp. prepared mustard
½ tsp. dry ginger
1 c. orange marmalade

Wrap a slice of bacon around each quail; arrange in rows on a large sheet of heavy-duty aluminum foil. Season with salt and pepper. Saute mushroom caps and green onions in butter. Pour all over quail; seal with a double wrap. Bake at 325 degrees for 1 hour. Combine remaining ingredients; serve with quail. Yield: 6 servings.

Mrs. Elizabeth W. Knape, Douglas H. S.
Douglas, Arizona

CHERYL'S BARBECUED RABBIT

1 American domestic rabbit, cut up
Melted butter
Finely crushed corn flakes
2 tsp. vinegar (opt.)
⅛ c. Worcestershire sauce
½ clove of garlic, finely minced
½ c. water
1 tbsp. lemon juice
1 ½ tsp. dry mustard
¼ c. catsup
1 tsp. sugar
⅓ c. grated onion
⅓ tsp. Tabasco sauce

Soak rabbit in salted water for 20 minutes. Drain and pat dry. Roll meat in melted butter, making sure all joints and folds are covered. Roll rabbit pieces in corn flakes. Brown in hot oil. Combine remaining ingredients; simmer for 15 minutes. Pour over rabbit. Reduce heat and cook slowly for 1 hour and 15 minutes.

Mrs. Lucy Roths, McLoughlin H. S.
Milton-Freewater, Oregon

EASY RABBIT BAKE

1 2 ½ to 3-lb. rabbit
2 tsp. salt
½ tsp. pepper
Milk
1 tbsp. flour

Rub rabbit with salt and pepper; wrap securely in foil. Place in shallow baking pan. Bake at 350 degrees for 1 hour. Unwrap rabbit; drain broth into measuring cup. Add enough milk to make 1 cup liquid. Blend in flour. Pour into baking pan; stir over medium heat until gravy is smooth and thick.

Dorothy Lewis, Llano H. S.
Llano, Texas

BARBECUED WILD RABBIT

1 lge. onion, minced
1 clove of garlic, minced
2 green peppers, minced
1 can tomato juice
1 c. water
1 c. vinegar
½ c. catsup
½ c. Worcestershire sauce
¼ c. butter
1 tsp. salt
½ tsp. cayenne or red pepper pods
2 or 3 rabbits, cut up

Combine all ingredients except rabbits; boil for 5 to 10 minutes. Place rabbit pieces in pan in single layer. Pour sauce over rabbit, covering completely. Bake at 250 degrees for 3 hours or until tender, turning occasionally. Yield: 6-8 servings.

Mrs. Maurine E. Patton, Cookeville Jr. H. S.
Cookeville, Tennessee

FRIED RABBIT OR SQUIRREL

1 rabbit or squirrel, cut up
Seasoned flour
2 slices bacon

Dip rabbit into seasoned flour. Place rabbit in frying pan. Top with bacon. Brown and reduce heat. Add small amount of hot water. Cover; cook until tender.

Mrs. Lula S. Patrick, Monticello H. S.
Monticello, Kentucky

RABBIT SMOTHERED WITH ONIONS

3 lge. onions, sliced
3 tbsp. shortening
1 3-lb. rabbit, cut up
Flour
1 c. sour cream
Salt and pepper to taste

Fry onions in shortening in a skillet; remove from skillet. Dredge rabbit in flour. Saute rabbit in remaining shortening in skillet until brown on both sides. Cover with onions; pour sour cream over the top. Cover; cook slowly for 1 hour on top of stove or bake at 350 degrees for 35 to 45 minutes. Uncover; bake for 15 minutes longer. Season with salt and pepper.

Mrs. Walter Wigger, Anamosa Comm. School
Anamosa, Iowa

SMOTHERED RABBIT

1 rabbit, cut up
Seasoned flour
1 onion, chopped
1 c. water

(Continued on next page)

Roll rabbit in seasoned flour; brown in hot fat. Add onion and water. Cover; simmer until meat simmer for 1 hour or until meat is tender.

Mrs. Phyllis C. Cockrell, Hollywood School
Saluda, South Carolina

SQUIRREL AND GRAVY

1 squirrel, cut up
Water
2 tbsp. flour
⅛ tsp. salt
Dash of pepper

Place squirrel in a 1 1/2-quart cooker. Cover with water; cook over low heat for 1 hour and 30 minutes or until tender. Remove squirrel; drain off all but 2 tablespoonfuls drippings.Stir in flour, salt and pepper. Add 1 cup water or milk; place squirrel in gravy and heat. Yield: 8 servings.

Alice Faye Noble, Hazard H. S.
Hazard, Kentucky

SQUIRREL MULLIGAN

½ gal. shortening
12 to 15 squirrels
1 clove of garlic
1 gal. onions
1 gal. boiling water
1 gal. potatoes, cooked and creamed
1 lge. loaf bread, broken into small pieces
Black pepper
Red pepper
Salt to taste

Heat shortening piping hot in large container; add squirrels and garlic to hot grease. Cook until water cooks out; add onions and boiling water. Cook until meat comes off bone. Add more water if necessary. Add creamed potatoes, bread and seasonings to mixture. Yield: 50 servings.

Sandra Kay Methvin, Oak Hill H. S.
Elmer, Louisiana

SQUIRREL JAMBALAYA

1 med. squirrel
Salt and red pepper to taste
2 lge. onions, chopped
3 ribs celery, chopped
1 clove of garlic, chopped (opt.)
¼ green pepper, chopped
4 tbsp. parsley, chopped
3 tbsp. cooking oil
2 c. uncooked rice, washed
1 ½ c. water
2 tsp. salt

Cut squirrel into serving pieces; season well with salt and red pepper. Fry squirrel until brown; remove from skillet. Saute onions, celery, garlic, green pepper and parsley in oil until wilted. Put squirrel back into skillet; cover. Cook slowly for about 30 minutes or until squirrel is tender. Add rice and water. Stir thoroughly for 2 to 3 minutes. Add salt; cook slowly for about 30 minutes or until rice is cooked. Yield: 6 servings.

Mrs. Annie R. Gonzales, Prescott Jr. H. S.
Baton Rouge, Louisiana

BRAISED MOOSE

4 lb. ripened moose
4 strips salt pork
Salt and pepper
⅛ tsp. cinnamon
⅛ tsp. cloves
⅔ c. claret or weak vinegar
½ c. water
½ bay leaf
1 onion, sliced
1 c. cranberry juice or claret
1 c. milk

Trim any musty parts of moose; lard with salt pork. Sprinkle with salt, pepper, cinnamon and cloves. Marinate in claret for two to three days in refrigerator. Drain; place in baking pan. Add water. Cover and cook at 300 degrees for 1 hour. Add bay leaf, onion and cranberry juice; cover and cook for 1 hour or until tender. Remove meat; add milk to drippings. Heat to boiling; serve with moose. Yield: 6-8 servings.

Shirley Ann Thompson, Candor Central School
Candor, New York

BRAISED VENISON

2 c. flour
1 tsp. salt
½ tsp. pepper
8 venison steak
2 tbsp. fat
¾ c. onion rings
Garlic salt
2 c. water

Sift dry ingredients except garlic salt. Coat venison with dry ingredients. Brown in fat. Top with onion rings; sprinkle with garlic salt. Add water; simmer for 1 hour over medium heat. Yield: 8 servings.

Mrs. Brooksie Rentz, Brookland-Cayce H. S.
Cayce, South Carolinia

VENISON BROILED FILET MIGNON

1 lb. venison tenderloin
8 bacon strips
Salt and pepper to taste

Cut venison tenderloin into 1-inch thick slices. Wrap each piece of venison in strip of bacon, fastening ends together with a toothpick. Salt and pepper to taste. Broil until done. Yield: 4 servings.

Dorene Nehr, Three Rivers H. S.
Three Rivers, Texas

CHICKEN-FRIED VENISON

Salt and pepper
Flour
2 venison rounds
1 egg, beaten
2 tbsp. water
4 tbsp. margarine

Add salt and pepper to flour. Dip venison into seasoned flour and into mixture of egg and water. Dip into flour again; brown on both sides in margarine. Cover and cook slowly for 20 to 30 minutes. Yield: 4 servings.

Mrs. Fern Ruck, Rangely H. S.
Rangely, Colorado

MOOSE STEAK

½ c. chopped onions
2 tbsp. butter
1 moose steak
1 c. mushrooms, chopped
2 tbsp. flour

Fry onions brown in butter; sear steak on both sides in butter and onion. Cover and simmer for 30 minutes. When almost tender, add mushrooms and flour, stirring into mixture. Cover and simmer for 20 minutes.

Mary C. Wood, Pickens H. S.
Pickens, South Carolinia

MOOSE STROGANOFF

2 lb. moose round steak, cut into small pieces
2 cans cream of mushroom soup
1 soup can milk
¼ c. chopped onions

Brown meat in fat in fry pan. Season to taste. Combine meat, soup, milk and onions in casserole. Bake at 350 degrees for 1 hour. Serve over rice, if desired. Yield: 4 servings.

Mrs. David Olerud, Haines Public School
Haines, Alaska

PANFRIED VENISON

6 tbsp. butter or margarine
6 thin venison steaks
⅔ c. flour
Salt and pepper

Place butter in medium skillet; heat slowly. Roll steaks in flour, salt and pepper; place in skillet. Cook over medium heat for 30 minutes or until brown and tender. Yield: 6 servings.

Carol Noffsinger, Pinconning Area H. S.
Pinconning, Michigan

SMOTHERED VENISON

1 1-lb. venison steak, cut ½-in. thick
1 c. plus 3 tbsp. flour
¼ c. cooking oil
3 tbsp. flour
2 c. milk
Salt and pepper to taste
Garlic salt
1 lge. onion, sliced

Tenderize venison; cut into serving pieces. Dip meat into flour; brown in hot oil in cast iron skillet. Remove meat when browned. Stir 3 tablespoonfuls flour into oil; gradually add 2 cups milk. Cook until thick. Add all seasonings and browned steak. Place onion slices on top of steak. Gravy should cover steak and onions. Cover and bake at 250 to 300 degrees for 2 hours. Yield: 4 servings.

Rosanne Looney, Westlawn Jr. H. S.
Texarkana, Texas

SMOTHERED VENISON STEAK

Flour
Seasoning salt to taste
Pepper to taste
4 venison steaks or 2 venison rounds
Fat
1 pkg. dry onion soup mix
1 ½ c. water
1 tbsp. Worcestershire sauce

Mix flour with seasoning salt and pepper. Hack steaks; roll in flour mixture. Brown steaks in small amount of fat; add dry onion soup mix, water and Worcestershire sauce. Simmer for 1 hour or until tender. Serve over rice, if desired. Yield: 4-6 servings.

Mrs. Martha Jo Bredemeyer, Lancaster H. S.
Lancaster, Texas

SPECIAL BURGERS

2 lb. ground venison
1 c. grated American cheese
¾ c. finely chopped onion
1 c. chopped pickles or pickle relish
1 tsp. salt
½ tsp. pepper

(Continued on next page)

Roll venison meat out on a sheet of aluminium foil as for pie crust. Cover one-half of the meat with cheese, onion and pickle mixture; season with salt and pepper. Fold over uncovered meat; seal edges. Wrap in aluminium foil; broil on grill. Serve plain or on a bun, if desired. Yield: 6 servings.

Mrs. Betty Rogers, Atkinson Public H. S.
Atkinson, Nebraska

SWEET-SOUR WILD MEAT

Venison steaks or roast
6 tbsp. olive oil
1 ½ tsp. salt
½ c. brown sugar
2 tsp. mustard
2 tbsp. vinegar

Brown steak in oil; place in Dutch oven or covered roaster. Combine remaining ingredients. Layer steak with sauce. If a roast, use the sauce to cover the roast and then use the remaining to baste frequently while cooking. Bake at 400 degrees for 20 mintues per pound.

Mrs. Fern Eardley, Mt. View H. S.
Mt. View, Wyoming

VENISON MEAT BALLS

2 c. grated raw potatoes
1 ½ lb. ground venison
1 tbsp. chopped onion
1 ½ tsp. salt
⅛ tsp. pepper
1 egg
¼ c. milk
¼ c. butter
3 c. water
2 to 3 tbsp. flour
2 c. sour cream
1 tsp. dill seed

Combine potatoes, venison, onion, salt, pepper, egg and milk; shape into 1 1/2-inch balls. Brown balls slowly in butter in large skillet. Add 1/2 cup water; cover. Simmer for 20 minutes or until done. Remove meat balls. Stir in flour and remaining water; simmer until thick. Reduce heat; stir in cream and dill. Add meat balls; heat but do not boil. NOTE: May be cooked by alternate method. Brown meat balls; remove to casserole. Make gravy; add sour cream and dill. Pour gravy over meat balls and finish in oven. Yield: 8 servings.

Mrs. Elizabeth A. Harris, West Fargo H. S.
West Fargo, North Dakota

VENISON MINCEMEAT

3 lb. venison, cooked and ground
1 lemon, ground
3 lb. seedless raisins
1 lb. seeded raisins
½ lb. currants
1 lb. ground suet
6 lb. pared chopped apples
1 pt. grape juice
1 qt. cider or apple juice
2 tsp. cinnamon
1 tsp. ground cloves
1 tsp. allspice
1 tsp. salt
3 c. sugar

Combine all ingredients. Cook in large pan on low heat for 3 hours or until apples are tender. Cool; store in refrigerator or freezer until serving time. Yield: 8 quarts.

Mrs. Linda Lewis, Kendrick H. S.
Kendrick, Idaho

VENISON MINCEMEAT

1 qt. raisins
4 qt. sugar
1 ½ qt. meat broth
2 lb. currants
¼ lb. ground suet
2 tbsp. cinnamon
2 tbsp. allspice
2 tbsp. cloves
1 tbsp. pepper
1 tbsp. salt
1 qt. sorghum
3 qt. ground cooked venison
5 lb. apples, chopped
1 qt. cidar vinegar
Juice of 3 lemons

Combine all ingredients. Store in freezer. Yield: 6 quarts.

Mrs. Jean Gilleece, Lamar H. S.
Lamar, Colorado

VENISON ROAST

1 3 to 4-lb. venison roast
1 tsp. salt (opt.)
Pepper to taste
1 pkg. dry onion soup mix
1 envelope hamburger seasoning (opt.)
1 clove of garlic or garlic salt to taste (opt.)
1 can cream of mushroom or celery soup
½ to 2 c. water

Season roast with pepper to taste. Sprinkle soup mixture over meat; add hamburger seasoning. Sprinkle garlic over seasoning. Spread celery soup over roast; add water. Cover; bake at 250 to 350 degrees for 2 hours and 30 minutes to 3 hours. Add more water, if necessary. Yield: 8-10 servings.

Mrs. Bonnie B. Wren, Nicholls H. S.
Nicholls, Georgia
Mrs. V. G. Thigpen, Waycross H. S.
Waycross, Georgia

Variety Meat Favorites

CORNED BEEF AND CABBAGE

½ c. chopped parsley
1 c. chopped celery
1 lge. green pepper, chopped
1 lge. onion, chopped
1 tsp. garlic powder or 4 cloves of garlic, chopped
2 tbsp. cooking oil
1 can corned beef, crumbled
1 2-lb. cabbage, cut into eighths
1 lge. can tomatoes
¼ c. Worcestershire sauce
Salt and pepper to taste
Water

Saute parsley, celery, green pepper, onion and garlic in cooking oil in large deep pot for about 5 minutes. Turn heat to low; add corned beef. Separate cabbage leaves; place in the pot. Add tomatoes, Worcestershire sauce, salt and pepper. Add enough water to cover cabbage. Increase heat; bring to a boil. Reduce heat to medium; cover. Cook for 2 hours and 30 minutes to 3 hours. Serve with corn bread, if desired.

Lynda Dean, Vidor H. S.
Vidor, Texas

CORNED BEEF HASH

1 can corned beef
1 c. cooked tomatoes
¼ c. chopped celery
¼ c. chopped green peppers
¼ c. chopped onion
1 tbsp. shortening

Combine all ingredients; pour into shallow greased baking dish. Bake at 350 degrees for 30 to 40 minutes. Yield: 6 servings.

Janie O. Sutton, Hardin-Jefferson School
Sour Lake, Texas

GRANDMOTHER'S CORNED BEEF HASH

1 12-oz. can corned beef, ground
2 med. onions, ground
8 med. potatoes, ground
¼ c. shortening
1 tsp. salt
Pepper to taste
1 c. water

Combine corned beef, onions and potatoes; place in melted shortening on low heat. Season with salt and pepper; add water. Cover; cook for 45 minutes or until potatoes are tender. Uncover; brown slightly. Yield: 6 servings.

Mrs. Carolyn Fillmore Fredrick, Brighton H. S.
Brighton, Michigan

DRIED BEEF ROLLS

6 slices dried beef
2 to 3 tbsp. minced dried beef
2 tbsp. minced green pepper
1 ½ c. mashed potatoes
1 tbsp. butter

Spread out slices of dried beef. Add minced beef and green pepper to potatoes; spread mixture on slices of beef. Roll up; fasten with toothpicks. Place rolls in baking dish. Dot with butter; cover. Bake at 325 degrees for 20 minutes. Yield: 4-6 servings.

Mrs. Dorothy Zimmerman, Canby Public H. S.
Canby, Minnesota

GOLDEN GOODIES

Brains
Flour
Butter
Salt and pepper

Roll brains in flour. Fry in heavy skillet with butter, salt and pepper until golden brown. Serve with toast, if desired. Yield: 4 servings.

Mrs. Margaret Swigart, Culbertson H. S.
Culbertson, Montana

BARBECUED FRANKFURTERS

1 onion, chopped
3 tbsp. fat
1 tbsp. sugar
1 tsp. dry mustard
1 tsp. salt
½ tsp. pepper
1 tsp. paprika
½ c. catsup
½ c. water
¼ c. vinegar
1 tbsp. Worcestershire sauce
¼ tsp. Tabasco sauce
12 frankfurters

Lightly brown onion in fat. Combine all remaining ingredients except frankfurters; add to onions and fat. Simmer for 15 minutes. Split frankfurters lengthwise; place in an 8 1/2 x 11-inch baking dish. Pour barbecue sauce over frankfurters. Bake at 350 degrees for 30 minutes, basting several times. Yield: 6 servings.

Mary Kay Pearson, Waupaca H. S.
Waupaca, Wisconsin

BARBECUED FRANKFURTERS

1 med. onion
2 tbsp. vinegar
1 tbsp. flour
1 ½ tbsp. Worcestershire sauce
1 tsp. paprika
¼ tsp. pepper
1 tsp. chili powder or mustard
½ c. catsup
2 tsp. brown sugar
2 tbsp. hot water
1 lb. frankfurters

(Continued on next page)

Put onion through food chopper, using fine knives. Blend vinegar and flour; add to onion. Add remaining ingredients except frankfurters; mix well. Pierce each frankfurter with a fork; dip into sauce. Arrange frankfurters and sauce in a greased baking dish. Bake at 350 degrees for 1 hour. Yield: 8 servings.

Mrs. Carolyn R. Stone, Whitingham H. S.
Jacksonville, Vermont

CAROLINA CORN DOGS

¾ c. self-rising flour
¼ c. self-rising corn meal
1 tbsp. sugar
1 tsp. dry mustard
2 tbsp. onion
1 egg, beaten
½ c. milk
1 lb. frankfurters

Mix flour, meal, sugar, mustard and onion. Combine egg and milk. Mix with dry ingredients; roll frankfurters in dough mixture. Fry in deep fat. Yield: 6 servings.

Mrs. Elizabeth M. Culbreth, Chapman H. S.
Inman, South Carolina

CHEESE PUPPIES

6 frankfurters
6 4 x ½ x ¼-in. cheese strips
3 bacon slices, cut into halves

Slit frankfurters lengthwise to within 1/2 inch of each end. Put cheese strip in each frankfurter. Place bacon over cheese. Hold bacon in place at each end with a toothpick. Arrange frankfurters in a shallow baking pan. Broil under direct heat until bacon is crisp and cheese is melted. Yield: 6 servings.

Mrs. Evia C. Arnold, Rio Vista School
Rio Vista, Texas

CORN DOGS

¾ to 1 c. corn meal
1 c. flour
2 tbsp. sugar
1 ½ to 2 tsp. baking powder
½ to 1 tsp. salt
1 egg, slightly beaten
¾ to 1 c. milk
2 tbsp. melted fat
1 lb. wieners

Sift corn meal and flour with sugar, baking powder and salt; add egg and milk to dry ingredients. Blend in fat. Mix well. Dip wieners into batter, holding with a fork or skewer. Drain excess batter over bowl. Fry in a wire basket in 375 degree fat until golden brown. Drain on asborbent paper. Serve hot with mustard or catsup. Yield: 6-8 servings.

Jewell West, Crowder H. S.
Crowder, Oklahoma
Mrs. Velma Grizzle, Meeker H. S.
Meeker, Oklahoma

COWBOY SUPPER

2 tbsp. butter or margarine
½ c. chopped onion
½ c. chopped green pepper
1 doz. frankfurters, quartered
2 c. chopped fresh tomatoes
½ tsp. caraway seed
½ tsp. salt
1 bay leaf
¼ tsp. paprika
4 hard-cooked eggs, quartered

Heat butter or margarine in skillet. Add onion and green pepper; cook until onion is yellow. Add remaining ingredients except eggs; simmer for 15 minutes. Top with eggs; simmer for 10 minutes longer. Serve on thin slices of corn bread or crisp toast. Yield: 8-10 servings.

Marble Henderson, Tahlequah H. S.
Tahlequah, Oklahoma

FRANKFURTERS WITH TWO-BEAN SUCCOTASH

1 lb. frankfurters
Fat
1 12-oz. can whole kernel corn
1 box cut green beans
1 box frozen Fordhook lima beans
Salt and pepper
2 tbsp. butter or margarine
Chopped green onion

Score frankfurters diagonally several times with sharp knife; brown lightly in small amount of fat in skillet. Remove from heat; keep hot. Drain liquid from corn into skillet; add green beans and limas. Season with salt and pepper to taste. Cook for 10 minutes, breaking up blocks with fork. Add a small amount water, if needed. Add corn and heat. Mix vegetables well; season with butter or margarine. Top with frankfurters; sprinkle with onion. Serve from skillet. Yield: 4 servings.

Mrs. Elizabeth H. Kneesha, New Hope H. S.
Goldsboro, North Carolina

GOURMET HOT DOGS

1 pkg. fresh mushrooms, sliced or 1 lge. can sliced mushrooms
3 tbsp. flour
4 tbsp. butter or margarine
½ tsp. salt
2 tbsp. water
Wieners

(Continued on next page)

Roll mushrooms in flour. Brown butter in an 8-inch frying pan; add mushrooms. Saute until brown; season with salt. Add water; cook until tender. Place weiners on top of mushrooms. Cover; steam for 7 to 10 minutes or until weiners are puffed. Garnish with parsley, if desired. Yield: 4-5 servings.

Mrs. Marjorie P. Vickery, Holland H. S.
Holland, Texas

FRILLY FRANKFURTERS

8 frankfurters, split
2 tbsp. prepared mustard
2 c. heated seasoned mashed potatoes
¼ c. chopped parsley
¼ c. minced onion
1 tbsp. chopped pimento
⅛ tsp. pepper
¼ c. grated American cheese
4 tsp. melted butter

Spread frankfurters with mustard. Combine potatoes, parsley, onion, pimento, pepper and cheese. Spoon potato mixture on frankfurters; brush with melted butter. Place on broiler rack; broil 4 inches from heat at 350 degrees for 8 minutes or until lightly browned. Yield: 6-8 servings.

Joan McCready, Missouri Valley H. S.
Missouri Valley, Iowa

HAWAIIAN FRANKFURTERS

4 frankfurters
Margarine
1 sm. can crushed pineapple, drained
4 tbsp. mustard
4 slices bread

Warm frankfurters in skillet with small amount of margarine. Mix pineapple with mustard. Split franks lengthwise; place across slices of bread. Spread with pineapple mixture. Fold sides of bread over franks; place in skillet with a small amount of margarine. Heat over low heat for 15 minutes. Yield: 4 servings.

Mrs. Angela Gish, Bazine Rural H. S.
Bazine, Kansas

HOT DOG DAINTIES

2 c. flour
½ tsp. salt
2 tsp. baking powder
2 tbsp. shortening
⅔ c. milk
12 thin slices cheese
Mustard
12 wieners

Sift flour with salt and baking powder; cut in shortening. Stir in milk to make a soft dough. Roll out to 1/4-inch thick. Cut into twelve 4-inch squares. Place a slice of cheese on each square. Brush wieners with mustard; place a wiener diagonally across each square of dough. Fasten with toothpicks. Place in a greased pan. Bake at 450 degrees for 12 to 15 minutes. Yield: 12 servings.

Mrs. Jack O'Neill, Belmont Comm. School
Belmont, Wisconsin

MACARONI AND FRANKFURTER SKILLET DISH

4 oz. elbow macaroni
¼ c. sliced onion
1 sm. clove of garlic, minced
2 tbsp. margarine
1 can cream of celery soup
1 c. water
1 c. shredded cheese
1 tsp. prepared mustard
8 frankfurters

Cook macaroni in boiling salted water until tender; drain. Saute onion and garlic in butter; add soup, water, cheese and mustard. Blend well. Cut frankfurters into halves lengthwise and crosswise in the center. Add frankfurters and macaroni to soup mixture. Yield: 4 servings.

Linda Medlen, Lake Co. H. S.
Tiptonville, Tennessee

POTATO-TOPPED FRANKFURTERS

6 frankfurters, cooked
1 ½ to 2 c. hot mashed potatoes
6 strips Cheddar cheese
Paprika

Split frankfurters; stuff generously with mashed potatoes. Lay cheese strips down the middle of potato filling; sprinkle lightly with paprika. Broil until cheese melts and potatoes are slightly brown. Yield: 6 servings.

Mrs. Carolyn Saxe, Edwards H. S.
Albion, Illinois

STUFFED WIENERS

6 wieners
1 c. grated American cheese
¼ c. chopped onion
2 tbsp. chopped green pepper

Slit wieners on one side three-fourths through. Mix remaining ingredients; stuff each wiener with mixture. Place on broiler rack. Broil for 8 minutes or until brown. Serve hot. Yield: 6 servings.

Helen Sergent, Rye Cove H. S.
Clinchport, Virginia

FRICASSEE CHICKEN GIZZARDS

2 lb. chicken gizzards
1 lge. onion, diced
2 cloves of garlic, finely diced
Water
3 chicken consomme cubes
Salt and pepper to taste
3 tbsp. cornstarch

Saute gizzards with natural fat until rendered; add onion and garlic. Saute until golden brown. Add enough water to halfway cover gizzards; simmer for 1 hour. Add consomme cubes, salt and pepper. Simmer for 1 hour or until tender. Thicken with cornstarch paste before serving. Serve on noodles, rice, mashed potatoes or toast, if desired. Yield: 5 servings.

Ruth C. Reese, Technical H. S. No. 67
Jacksonville, Florida

BRAISED STUFFED HEART

1 3-lb. beef heart
Sour milk, buttermilk or vinegar
1 tsp. salt
2 c. coarse soft bread crumbs
½ tsp. poultry seasoning (opt.)
Pepper to taste
1 egg, beaten
¾ c. milk
¼ c. chopped celery
1 tsp. chopped onion
2 tbsp. melted butter
½ c. water

Split heart open halfway down on one side. Cut away arteries and veins at the top and the stringy fibers and dividing membranes on the inside. Wash thoroughly. Soak in sour milk for 3 to 4 hours to tenderize. Drain; sprinkle inside with one-half of the salt. Combine bread crumbs with remaining salt and seasonings; add egg and milk. Add remaining ingredients except water; stuff into heart. Tie or sew up heart. Place in buttered casserole or Dutch over; add water. Cover; bake at 350 degrees for 3 hours to 3 hours and 30 minutes or until tender. Add additional water if necessary. Thicken liquid for gravy, if desired. Yield: 6 servings.

Mrs. Gladyce Davis, Poteau H. S.
Poteau, Oklahoma
Mrs. Gary Cramer, DeSmet H. S.
DeSmet, South Dakota

HEART ITALIENNE

1 2-lb. beef or veal heart
½ c. chopped onion
1 clove of garlic, minced (opt.)
3 tbsp. lard or drippings
1 ½ tsp. salt
⅛ tsp. pepper
2 tbsp. chopped pimento or green pepper
1 6-oz. can tomato paste
1 No. 2 ½ can tomatoes
1 8-oz. pkg. spaghetti, cooked
½ c. grated Cheddar cheese

Wash beef heart thoroughly; remove veins and hard parts. Cut meat into 1-inch cubes. Brown meat, onion and garlic in lard or drippings; add salt, pepper, pimento, tomato paste and tomatoes. Simmer for 2 hours or until meat is tender and mixture is thick. Serve over spaghetti; top with grated cheese. Yield: 6-8 servings.

Barbara Leistikow, Williamsburg H. S.
Williamsburg, Iowa

HEART STROGANOFF

½ beef heart
¼ c. flour
¼ c. fat, melted
½ tsp. salt
Dash of pepper
1 c. broth
3 tbsp. tomato juice
1 tbsp. prepared mustard
1 tbsp. Worcestershire sauce
¾ c. sour cream

Cut beef heart into 3-inch strips, 1/2 inch wide; cook in pressure cooker for 30 minutes at 10 pounds pressure. Combine all remaining ingredients; bring to a boil. Add beef heart. Simmer for 20 to 25 minutes or until tender. Serve over rice or potatoes. Yield: 8-10 servings.

Mrs. Sheryl Beckmann, Coleman H. S.
Coleman, South Dakota

STUFFED BEEF HEART

1 beef heart
Water
3 c. cubed dry bread
1 tsp. salt
⅛ tsp. pepper
½ c. chopped celery
⅛ c. chopped onion
⅛ tsp. ground sage
⅛ c. melted margarine
Flour
Fat

Simmer heart in water for 2 hours and 30 minutes or until tender. Cool slightly; remove excess fat and connective tissue. Combine bread, salt, pepper, celery, onion, sage and margarine; add enough water or broth to moisten. Fill cavity of heart; lace with cord and skewers to close. Roll in flour; brown in fat in a Dutch oven. Add 1 cup water. Cover; simmer for 35 to 40 minutes. Yield: 6-8 servings.

Audrey A. Oleson, Byron H. S.
Byron, Illinois

STUFFED BEEF HEART

1 beef heart
1 tsp. salt
1 sm. onion, quartered
1 pkg. seasoned poultry stuffing

(Continued on next page)

Trim off coarse fiber at top and inside of heart; wash well. Place in pan; cover with water. Add salt and onion. Cover; simmer for 1 hour and 30 minutes. Remove from broth. Reserve broth. Moisten stuffing with part of broth. Stuff heart with the mixture. Place in shallow pan. Pour 1 to 2 cups broth around heart. Bake at 350 degrees for 1 hour. Serve hot with gravy made by thickening remaining broth, if desired. Yield: 8-10 servings.

Mrs. Nancy R. Cumbow, Abingdon H. S.
Abingdon, Virginia

BRAISED KIDNEY ON TOAST

1 kidney
1 to 2 tbsp. shortening
Flour
Salt and pepper to taste
Water
Toast

Wash, trim and cut kidney into cubes. Roll in flour and season to taste. Brown in shortening. Cover; cook until tender. Add water and thicken for gravy. Serve over toast. Yield: 2 servings.

Mrs. Margaret Swigart, Bainville H. S.
Bainville, Montana

STUFFED HEART

4 c. dry bread, cubed
Milk or hot water
1 tsp. salt
¼ tsp. pepper
¼ tsp. poultry seasoning
1 egg, slightly beaten
3 tbsp. chopped onion
3 tbsp. butter
1 beef heart
2 tbsp. fat
1 onion
½ c. cold water

Moisten bread cubes with milk or hot water. Add salt, pepper, poultry seasoning and egg. Simmer chopped onion in butter slightly; add to dressing. Mix gently. Cut pocket in heart; remove skin and soak in cold salted water for 15 minutes. Wipe dry. Stuff heart with dressing. Fasten with toothpicks or skewer. Heat pressure cooker; add fat and heart. Season with salt and pepper. Add onion and water. Cover; cook according to cooker directions for 15 minutes. Let steam return to normal. Remove from cooker; slice and serve hot.

Lynette Teer, Hallettsville H. S.
Hallettsville, Texas

SAUTED KIDNEY, VINTNER'S-STYLE

1 beef kidney
3 tbsp. vinegar
1 qt. water
1 c. flour
3 tbsp. butter or margarine
1 med. onion, chopped
¼ lb. mushrooms, sliced
1 bouillon cube
1 ½ c. boiling water
½ tsp. salt
⅛ tsp. pepper
½ tbsp. Worcestershire sauce
2 tbsp. pimento
¼ c. red cooking wine
2 tbsp. chopped parsley

Soak kidney in vinegar and water for 2 hours. Rinse; remove fat and tubes with sharp knife. Slice kidney thinly. Coat thoroughly with flour. Melt butter in skillet; saute onion and mushrooms. Remove and set aside. Add kidney to remaining fat in skillet; brown quickly on both sides. Add bouillon cube to boiling water; pour over kidney. Add salt, pepper, Worcestershire sauce, pimento, onion, mushrooms and wine. Cover skillet; reduce heat. Simmer 10 minutes. Sprinkle with parsley just before serving. Yield: 4 servings.

Mrs. Mari Hurley, Central Union H. S.
El Centro, California

VIRGINIA SCRAPPLE

1 hog head, cleaned
2 c. sifted corn meal
Salt to taste
Sage to taste
Sausage seasoning to taste

Cover hog head with water; cook until meat can easily be removed from bone. Remove meat and chop; cook broth until reduced to 1/2 gallon; add corn meal. Cook until thickened. Add finely chopped meat and seasonings to taste. Pour into four 5 x 10-inch loaf pans until 3-inches thick. Chill; cut into 1/4 to 1/2-inch thick slices. Fry quickly in small amount of hot fat until browned. Serve with sausage and eggs, if desired.

Mrs. Martha G. Akers, Auburn H. S.
Riner, Virginia

BARBECUED BREAST OF LAMB

2 lb. boned breast of lamb, quartered
1 tsp. salt
⅛ tsp. pepper
1 med. onion, peeled and sliced
½ c. chili sauce
¼ tsp. paprika
1 tbsp. vinegar
1 c. water

Sprinkle lamb with salt and pepper. Arrange lamb pieces in skillet with remaining ingredients. Cover and simmer for 1 hour and 30 minutes. Uncover; skim off fat. Simmer for 20 minutes or until sauce is almost absorbed. Yield: 4 servings.

Swanie Smoot, Scott H. S.
Madison, West Virginia

BROILED LAMB WITH VEGETABLES

2 tbsp. chopped onion
1 tbsp. lard
2 c. boiled rice
1 c. tomato juice
Dash of salt
Dash of pepper
1 No. 2 can string beans
6 shoulder lamb chops

Brown onion in lard. Add rice, tomato juice and seasonings to skillet; heat. Place rice mixture in middle of bottom broiler pan. Place beans around edge. Place lamb chops on rack. Broil for 10 minutes on each side. Yield: 4-6 servings.

Shirley Humphrey, Albin Consolidated School
Albin, Wyoming

JULET LAMB CHOPS

2 tsp. diced mint
4 double loin lamb chops
Salt and pepper to taste
2 tsp. butter
4 canned pineapple slices
⅓ c. bourbon

Press mint into surface of chops. Season with salt and pepper. Broil 3 to 4 inches from heat for 8 minutes on each side or until done. Heat butter in electric skillet or large chafing dish. Add pineapple slices; brown lightly on each side. Arrange chops on pineapple slices. Sprinkle with bourbon. Ignite and serve. Yield: 4 servings.

Juanita Patton, Inola School
Kingston, Oklahoma

LAMB CHOP BROIL

¼ c. vinegar
1 c. chili sauce
¼ c. sugar
2 tsp. salt
Dash of pepper
1 tsp. oregano
6 thick lamb chops

Combine all ingredients except lamb chops. Brush lamb chops with sauce. Broil for 5 minutes on each side. Yield: 6 servings.

Mrs. Rosamond Fuller, Danube H. S.
Danube, Minnesota

LAMB CHOPS

4 lge. loin lamb chops, cut 1-in. thick
1 tsp. salt
1 tsp. pepper, freshly ground
1 tsp. garlic salt
1 lemon, sliced ¼-in. thick
4 tsp. Worcestershire sauce
4 tsp. catsup

Place lamb chops in flat baking dish. Sprinkle 1/4 teaspoonful salt, pepper and garlic salt over each chop. Place 1 lemon slice in center of each chop. Cover each lemon slice with 1 teaspoonful Worcestershire sauce and 1 teaspoonful catsup. Bake at 350 degrees for 35 to 40 minutes. Yield: 4 servings.

Mrs. Dorothy W. Stone, Regional Supervisor
Bureau of Homemaking Education
State Department of Education
Los Angeles, California

LAMB CHOPS DELUXE

6 arm or blade lamb chops, cut ¾-in. thick
3 tbsp. shortening
1 ½ tsp. salt
¼ tsp. pepper
1 tsp. garlic salt
1 tsp. paprika
½ tsp. nutmeg

Brown chops on both sides in shortening. Combine seasonings and sprinkle on both sides of chops. Pour off drippings. Cover and cook slowly for 40 to 45 minutes. Yield: 6 servings.

Mrs. Sally A. Kmon, Memorial H. S.
Manchester, New Hampshire

LAMB CHOPS IN WINE

6 rib, loin or shoulder lamb chops
1 lge. clove of garlic
Salt and pepper
2 tbsp. butter
2 tbsp. olive oil
6 or 8 scallions, chopped
1 tbsp. chopped parsley
2 tbsp. flour
1 ½ c. dry white wine

Rub chops with garlic, salt and pepper. Heat butter and olive oil in large skillet; add chops. Brown on both sides; remove to baking dish. Add remaining butter to skillet; saute scallions and parsley until scallions are soft. Stir in flour, blending well; gradually add wine. Cook, stirring constantly, until mixture begins to thicken. Pour over lamb chops. Cover and bake in preheated 350 degree oven for 20 to 25 minutes. Remove cover and continue baking for 10 minutes longer. Yield: 3 servings.

Mrs. Estelle G. Albert, Oak St. Jr. H. S.
Basking Ridge, New Jersey

ORIENTAL LAMB CHOP GRILL

½ c. soy sauce
½ c. water
4 lge. lamb loin chops
1 No. 303 can asparagus
4 bacon slices, cut into halves
8 pineapple spears
4 cooked potatoes, cut into halves
4 tbsp. grated American cheese

(Continued on next page)

Combine soy sauce and water. Marinate chops in this mixture in refrigerator for 1 hour. Pour asparagus into broiler pan; place broiler grid over broiler pan. Arrange marinated chops on broiler grid. Broil 3 inches from heat source for 10 minutes. Wrap bacon strips around pineapple spears. Turn chops; place pineapple spears and cooked potatoes on grid. Broil for 10 minutes longer. Turn pineapple spears once. Just before removing from broiler, sprinkle cheese on potatoes; broil until cheese is melted. Yield: 4 servings.

Mary Elizabeth Kloos, Helix H. S.
La Mesa, California

LAMB FARCI AUX HERBS

½ c. minced parsley
½ to 1 clove of garlic, crushed
½ tsp. basil
1 tsp. salt
¼ tsp. pepper
⅛ tsp. ground ginger
1 tbsp. olive oil or pure vegetable oil
1 6-lb. leg of lamb, boned and flattened
Softened butter or margarine
Dash of salt

Combine parsley, garlic, basil, salt, pepper and ginger with oil; mix well. Spread evenly over meat; roll as for jelly roll, tucking in ends. Tie with clean white cord into an even roll. Rub outside of meat with softened butter; sprinkle with salt. Bake at 400 degrees for 1 hour and 30 minutes or until done. Remove to heated platter; cut cord and remove before serving. Yield: 8-10 servings.

Mrs. Eileen H. MacDonald, Jenifer Jr. H. S.
Lewiston, Idaho

LAMB ROAST WITH TERIYAKI SAUCE

⅔ c. soy sauce
½ c. honey
1 ½ c. water
⅓ c. vinegar
2 cloves or garlic, minced
1 tsp. ground ginger
½ tsp. basil
½ tsp. salt
1 6-lb. leg of lamb
2 tbsp. cornstarch

Combine soy sauce, honey, 1/2 cup water, vinegar, garlic, ginger, basil and salt; mix well. Place roast in pan; pour on soy mixture. Marinate in refrigerator for 4 hours, or overnight, turning occasionally. Drain meat, reserving marinade. Place lamb on rack in shallow roasting pan. Roast at 325 degrees for 2 hours to 2 hours and 30 minutes or until done. During last hour of roasting, baste with part of marinade, reserving 1 cup marinade. Blend cornstarch with remaining water in pan; add reserved marinade and pan drippings. Cook, stirring until thickened. Serve with rice. Yield: 8 servings.

Anne Mackie, Dallas H. S.
Dallas, Oregon

LEG OF LAMB

Salt and pepper
1 5 ½-lb. leg of lamb
Flour
Powdered ginger

Salt and pepper leg of lamb; roll in flour. Cut down to the bone about 2 inches apart. Sprinkle ginger between slices. Place in roaster. Bake at 325 degrees for 20 to 25 minutes per pound. Serve with mint jelly, if desired. Yield: 7 servings.

Mrs. Vivian Harwood
Harbor Beach Comm. School
Harbor Beach, Michigan

ROAST LAMB WITH CAPER SAUCE

1 6 to 7-lb. leg of lamb
¼ lb. butter
2 cloves of garlic, crushed
1 tsp. salt
Dash of cayenne
Pinch of saffron
1 c. heavy cream
1 tbsp. cornstarch
½ 2 ¼-oz. bottle capers, drained

Have butcher bone the lamb; reserve bones. Roll meat and tie up securely. Work butter with garlic, salt and cayenne. Rub over entire surface of lamb. Wrap lamb with bones securely in heavy-duty foil; refrigerate overnight. Bring meat to room temperature; place in roasting pan without removing foil. Roast in preheated 325 degree oven for 25 to 30 minutes per pound or until done. Remove foil; add saffron and cream. Stir cornstarch and capers into pan drippings. Yield: 6-8 servings.

Mrs. Almeda B. Thomas, Maynard H. S.
Maynard, Arkansas

ROAST LEG OF LAMB WITH MARINADE

3 c. pineapple-grapefruit juice
1 tsp. crushed Rosemary
½ tsp. oregano
1 bay leaf
¼ c. chopped parsley
½ c. wine vinegar
¼ c. chopped green onions
1 clove of garlic, quartered
1 tsp. salt
1 6-lb. leg of lamb
2 tbsp. butter or margarine
2 tbsp. flour
Beef bouillon cube

Mix juice, herbs, parsley, vinegar, onions and seasonings. Pour over lamb in deep container.

(Continued on next page)

Refrigerate for 6 to 8 hours or overnight. Turn twice. Remove lamb from marinade. Place in shallow pan. Roast, uncovered, at 325 degrees for 3 hours or until done. Remove from roasting pan. Melt butter in pan; add flour. Dissolve bouillon cube in 2 cups marinade. Heat; add flour mixture slowly. Bring to a boil, stirring constantly. Slice lamb; serve with hot sauce. Yield: 8-10 servings.

Mrs. Florence B. Fisackerly, Inverness H. S.
Inverness, Mississippi

WINE LEG OF LAMB

1 5-lb. leg of lamb
¾ c. dry red wine
½ tsp. salt
6 cloves of garlic, peeled and halved
1 med. can pitted ripe olives

Remove fell from lamb. Place lamb in roasting pan; pour wine over lamb. Add garlic and salt to wine. Let stand for 2 hours, basting every 15 minutes. Bake at 350 degrees for 30 minutes per pound or until meat thermometer registers 175 to 180 degrees, basting every 30 minutes. Cut each olive into 5 or 6 slices. Add olives to liquid in pan. Yield: 8 servings.

Priscilla Barss, Culver H. S.
Culver, Oregon

GOURMET LAMB SHANKS

2 tbsp. salad oil
4 1-lb. lamb shanks
1 tsp. paprika
1 lge. onion, sliced
1 c. sliced fresh mushrooms
1 c. water
1 tbsp. horseradish
¾ tsp. rosemary
1 tsp. salt
¼ tsp. pepper
1 c. sour cream

Heat oil; add lamb. Sprinkle with paprika; add onion and mushrooms. Cook until lamb is slightly browned on all sides. Add mixture of water, horseradish, rosemary, salt and pepper. Cover and cook over low heat until lamb shanks are tender. Remove shanks; add sour cream to mixture in skillet. Heat to serving temperature over low heat, stirring constantly. Serve cream mixture over lamb shanks. Yield: 4 servings.

Louetta Greeno, Highlands H. S.
Fort Thomas, Kentucky

LAMB SHANKS FRENCHETTE

4 sm. lamb shanks
Salt
¼ tsp. pepper
2 onions, peeled and cut up
2 cloves of garlic, peeled and minced
½ c. dry red wine
½ tsp. thyme
½ tsp. oregano

Crack lamb shanks; remove all visible fat. Rub skillet with oil; heat. Rub shanks with 2 teaspoonfuls salt and pepper; brown on all sides. Add onions, garlic, wine, salt, thyme and oregano. Cover and simmer over very low heat for 3 hours or until tender. Strain gravy; quick freeze to remove congealed fat. Heat and serve with meat. Yield: 4 servings.

Mrs. Jeanne Damhof, Manton Consolidated H. S.
McBain, Michigan

POLYNESIAN LAMB

3 lb. lamb shanks
1 onion, chopped
¾ c. water
1 tsp. salt
1 tsp. allspice
½ tsp. garlic salt
½ tsp. powdered ginger
¼ c. lemon juice
1 tbsp. Worcestershire sauce
1 8-oz. baby food jar prunes
1 8-oz. baby food jar orangesauce and apricots
4 c. steamed rice

Brown shanks slowly in heavy fryer. Remove and set aside. Brown onion; add 1 tablespoonful water. Stir in salt, allspice, garlic salt, ginger, remaining water, lemon juice and Worcestershire sauce. Pour over browned lamb shanks. Heat to boiling; stir in fruits. Cover and simmer, stirring occasionally, for 2 hours to 2 hours and 30 minutes or until meat is tender. Arrange shanks in center of platter; spoon rice around meat. Garnish with parsley. Yield: 6-8 servings.

Mrs. Mildred Pirgan, Ciega H. S.
St. Petersburg, Florida

LAMB EMILY

3 onions, thinly sliced
½ stick butter
3 lb. shoulder lamb, cut into stewing pieces
4 eggs, beaten
3 tbsp. lemon juice
4 tbsp. chopped fresh parsley
½ c. grated Romano or Parmesan cheese
1 tsp. salt
¼ tsp. pepper

Saute onions in butter; add meat and brown. Cover meat with water; simmer until one-half the water evaporates. Combine remaining ingredients; add to meat. Cook until thickened. Serve hot. Yield: 6 servings.

Emily E. Demeo, Bloomfield H. S.
Bloomfield, New Jersey

LAMB A LA L MADEIRA

1 tsp. salt
¼ tsp. pepper
½ tsp. crushed basil
1 5-lb. boned lamb shoulder, rolled and tied
1 1-lb. can purple plums, sliced
1 lge. can sliced pineapple
2 tbsp. cornstarch
Red food coloring (opt.)
½ c. Madeira wine or orange juice

Mix salt, pepper and basil; rub over lamb. Place lamb on rack in shallow roasting pan. Bake at 325 degrees for 2 hours. Drain syrup from plums and pineapple; stir syrup into cornstarch in saucepan. Cook, stirring, until glaze is thickened and clear. Add a few drops of food coloring, if desired. Drain off lamb drippings; pour 1 cup glaze over lamb, reserving remaining glaze for sauce. Bake lamb for 30 minutes to 1 hour longer; baste occasionally with glaze from bottom of pan. Garnish lamb with pineapple and plums; Stir wine and 2 tablespoonfuls of pan glaze into reserved glaze; heat. Serve with lamb. Yield: 6-8 servings.

Mary E. Mason, James Monroe H. S.
Fredericksburg, Virginia

SHOULDER ROAST OF LAMB

1 4 to 5-lb. square shoulder of lamb
Garlic salt
½ c. orange juice
½ c. pineapple juice
¼ tsp. cinnamon

Have butcher slice and tie lamb. Sprinkle lamb with garlic salt. Arrange on rack in shallow roasting pan. Bake at 325 degrees for 1 hour and 30 minutes. Combine remaining ingredients; mix well. Pour over lamb. Bake for 30 minutes to 1 hour or until meat thermometer registers 175 to 180 degrees. Baste lamb with orange-pineapple mixture frequently during roasting period. Garnish with pear halves and mint jelly or peach halves, cottage cheese and red cherries, if desired. Yield: 6 servings.

Mrs. Irene Kathy Lee, Washington H. S.
El Dorado, Arkansas

LAMB SPARERIBS, GREEK-STYLE

3 lb. lamb spareribs
1 tsp. curry powder
1 tsp. salt
¼ tsp. pepper
⅓ c. finely chopped celery
¼ c. chopped parsley
1 tsp. grated lemon rind
1 c. orange juice
1 med. orange, sliced
1 med. lemon, sliced
1 med. pineapple, pared, cored and sliced

Place spareribs on rack in shallow roasting pan. Roast at 325 degrees for 1 hour and 30 minutes. Drain off drippings. Combine curry powder, salt, pepper, celery, parsley, lemon rind and orange juice; mix well. Pour over spareribs. Top with orange, lemon and pineapple slices. Roast for 45 minutes longer, basting lamb frequently. NOTE: Four slices drained, canned pineapple may be substituted for fresh pineapple. Yield: 4 servings.

Mrs. Hazel C. Tassis, Imperial H. S.
Imperial, California

BAKED LAMB STEW WITH CORN MEAL BISCUITS

1 ½ lb. cubed lamb shoulder
1 c. sliced onions
1 ½ c. sliced beets
1 ½ c. cut green beans
2 c. diced tomatoes
1 c. sliced mushrooms
3 c. stock or bouillon
Salt and pepper to taste
1 ½ c. biscuit mix
½ c. yellow corn meal
½ c. milk

Combine lamb and onions; cook over low heat until lamb is browned on all sides. Add beets, green beans, tomatoes, mushrooms, stock and seasonings. Mix well; turn into 3-quart casserole. Cover and bake at 350 degrees for 1 hour. Combine biscuit mix and corn meal. Add milk; mix lightly. Turn onto lightly floured surface; knead gently ten times. Roll out 1/2-inch thick. Cut into 2 1/2-inch rounds, using floured cutter. Arrange biscuits over stew. Bake at 400 degrees for 15 minutes or until browned. Yield: 6 servings.

Mrs. Lou Massey, Laneburg Central H. S.
Camden, Arkansas

BARBECUED LAMB HASH

1 onion, chopped
Fat
¾ c. catsup
2 tbsp. vinegar
2 tbsp. brown sugar
4 tbsp. lemon juice
3 tbsp. Worcestershire sauce
½ c. water
Salt to taste
3 c. diced cooked lamb
¼ c. grated onion
4 potatoes, cooked and diced

Brown chopped onion in 2 tablespoonfuls fat. Add remaining ingredients except lamb, onion and potatoes. Simmer for 30 minutes. Brown lamb and onion lightly in fat. Add sauce and simmer for 5 minutes. Add potatoes and heat thoroughly. Yield: 6 servings.

Mrs. Sally K. Karbowski, Fanning Trade H. S.
Worcester, Massachusetts

BRUSSELS SPROUTS AND LAMB IN NOODLE RING

⅔ c. flour
4 tsp. salt
¼ tsp. pepper
½ tsp. allspice
1 ½ lb. diced lamb shoulder
¼ c. butter or margarine
3 c. stock or bouillon
1 tbsp. brown sugar
3 10-oz. pkg. frozen California Brussels sprouts
3 med. onions, chopped
¾ c. dried apricots
½ c. dried prunes, pitted
4 slices fresh lemon, cut into quarters

Blend flour and seasonings; coat lamb with some of seasoned flour. Melt butter in soup kettle or Dutch oven; add lamb and brown on all sides. Drain off drippings, if necessary. Add 2 1/2 cups stock, brown sugar, Brussels sprouts, onions, apricots, prunes and lemon to lamb. Cover and cook for 15 to 20 minutes or until tender. Stir remaining stock into remaining seasoned flour, forming a smooth paste; slowly stir into stew. Stir over low heat until thickened.

NOODLE RING:

2 tbsp. salt
4 to 6 qt. boiling water
1 lb. medium egg noodles

Add salt to rapidly boiling water. Gradually add noodles so that water continues to boil. Cook, uncovered, stirring occasionally, until tender. Drain in colander. Turn into greased 9-inch ring mold. Let stand for 5 minutes. Unmold onto serving platter. Serve with Brussels sprouts and lamb. Yield: 6 servings.

INDIAN LAMB CURRY

1 tsp. salt
1 tsp. curry powder
3 tbsp. cornstarch
1 pt. lamb stock, skimmed of fat
2 c. boiled or stewed lamb, cut into 1-in. pieces
2 c. hot cooked rice
Chopped green pepper
Fruit chutney
½ c. coconut, finely cut
½ c. chopped walnuts

Combine seasonings and cornstarch with 1/4 cup water. Add to boiling stock. Stir until mixture is thickened and smooth. Add meat and heat through. Serve in individual rice rings. Sprinkle with green pepper, chutney, coconut and walnuts. Serve immeidately. Yield: 3-4 servings.

Mrs. Marion Blackburn, Middleton H. S.
Middleton, Idaho

JACOB'S STEW

Olive oil
2 ½ lb. shoulder or leg or lamb, cubed
1 lge. clove of garlic, minced
1 med. yellow onion, chopped
1 ½ tsp. salt
⅛ tsp. pepper
1 lge. bay leaf
1 whole clove
3 tbsp. chopped fresh parsley or 1 ½ tbsp. dried parsley
3 tbsp. celery, chopped
½ tsp. powdered ginger
2 lge. ripe tomatoes, chopped or 2 c. canned tomatoes
2 med. yellow onions, cut into 8 wedges
1 c. raisins or chopped dates or combination
⅓ c. fresh almonds
2 c. chopped Chinese cabbage, Swiss chard

Heat 1/4 cup oil in Dutch oven. Brown lamb, garlic and 1 chopped onion. Add salt, pepper, bay leaf, whole clove, parsley, celery, ginger and tomatoes. If using fresh tomatoes, add 1/2 cup water. Cover; simmer 1 hour or until lamb is tender, stirring occasionally. Slowly saute remaining onions in shallow olive oil until golden. Add to stew with raisins and whole almonds. Add vegetable; simmer for 15 minutes longer. Yield: 6-10 servings.

Mrs. Gwen Bayer, Summerville Union H. S.
Tuolumne, California

LAMB AND CELERY WITH LEMON SAUCE

2 lb. boneless lamb shoulder, cubed
1 med. onion, finely chopped
2 tbsp. butter
Salt and pepper to taste
¼ tsp. dill weed
1 lge. bunch celery
2 eggs, slightly beaten
3 tbsp. lemon juice
1 c. boiling broth or stock

Saute meat and onion in the butter in casserole until meat is browned. Season with salt, pepper and dill weed. Add 1 cup water; cook for a few minutes, scraping up glaze. Cover and simmer for 1 hour and 30 minutes or until meat is almost tender. Peel strings from celery stalks using vegetable peeler. Cut each stalk lengthwise, then crosswise into 2-inch pieces. Add celery; simmer for 15 minutes or until tender. Add dash of salt to eggs; beat in lemon juice. Gradually beat in broth, beating constantly. Add sauce to lamb; heat slowly until thickened, stirring constantly. Do not boil. Yield: 6 servings.

Mrs. Hal J. Puett, North Cobb H. S.
Acworth, Georgia

LAMB BARBECUED

¾ c. diced celery
2 tbsp. margarine
¾ tsp. dry mustard
2 tbsp. brown sugar
1 ½ tsp. salt
¾ tbsp. chili powder
3 tbsp. vinegar
1 ½ c. tomato juice
½ c. water
2 c. lamb, cut into narrow strips

Saute celery in margarine. Add remaining ingredients except lamb. Simmer for 20 minutes. Add lamb and simmer for 30 minutes longer or until sauce has thickened. Serve over rice, if desired. Yield: 4 servings.

Mrs. Carol Dawes, Morena Valley H. S.
Sunnymead, California

LAMB CURRY

3 tbsp. flour
1 tbsp. curry powder
1 tsp. sugar
½ tsp. salt
Dash of monosodium glutamate
⅛ tsp. pepper
2 c. chicken broth
1 tbsp. lemon juice
½ c. chopped peeled apple
3 tbsp. butter
½ c. onion
½ c. seedless raisins
3 c. diced cooked lamb

Saute onion and apple in hot butter until onion is tender. Blend in flour, curry powder, sugar, salt, monosodium glutamate and pepper. Stir in broth and juice; add raisins. Simmer, stirring constantly, until sauce is smooth and thickened. Add lamb; simmer until flavors are blended. Serve over rice. Serve with mango chutney and other condiments. Yield: 4 servings.

Dorothy M. Hardin, Lebanon Comm. H. S.
Lebanon, Illinois

LAMB STEW

1 tsp. salt
½ tsp. pepper
1 lb. lamb stew meat
9 lge. prunes
2 lge. onions
¼ tsp. saffron

Brown seasoned meat in small amount of fat in large saucepan. Add enough water to cover bottom of pan. Cover and simmer until meat is almost tender. Add prunes, onions and saffron. Continue to cook over low heat until all ingredients are done. Serve hot. Yield: 3 servings.

Arva McCarty Knight, Bellevue H. S.
Bellevue, Texas

LAMB STROGANOFF

1 lb. lamb, thinly sliced
Seasoned flour
1 clove of garlic, chopped
½ c. chopped onion
¼ c. butter or margarine
1 lb. mushrooms, sliced
1 10 ½-oz. can cream of celery soup
Salt and pepper to taste
1 c. sour cream

Cut lamb into 1/4-inch strips; coat with seasoned flour. Cook lamb, garlic and onion in melted butter until lamb is lightly browned on all sides. Add mushrooms, soup, salt and pepper. Cover and cook over low heat for 20 minutes, stirring occasionally. Add sour cream and mix well. Serve over cooked rice, if desired. Yield: 4 servings.

Mrs. Jean Harris, Highland H. S.
Cowiche, Washington
Nancy Anderson, East Jordan H. S.
East Jordan, Michigan

SHASHLIK

2 c. low calorie Italian salad dressing
4 bay leaves
4 lb. boneless leg of lamb, cut into 1-in. cubes
16 lge. mushroom caps
4 green peppers, cut into squares
2 c. catsup
4 tsp. Worcestershire sauce
4 lge. firm tomatoes, quartered

Combine salad dressing and bay leaves in glass bowl; add lamb. Cover and refrigerate overnight, turning lamb occasionally. Drain lamb, reserving marinade. On each of sixteen 10-inch skewers, thread lamb alternately with mushroom cap and green pepper squares. Brush with marinade. Broil shashlik for 15 minutes 4 inches from heat, turning and brushing occasionally with marinade. Combine catsup and Worcestershire sauce. Place a tomato quarter on end of each skewer; brush shashlik all over with catsup and Worcestershire sauce mixture. Broil for 5 to 10 minutes or until lamb is tender. Yield: 16 servings.

Mrs. Pauline Curry Hubbard, Dos Palos H. S.
Dos Palos, California

SHERHERDS PIE

2 c. diced cooked lamb
½ c. chopped onion
3 tbsp. flour
1 c. cooked peas
1 3-oz. can sliced mushrooms
¾ c. stock or bouillon
½ tsp. oregano
1 tsp. salt
½ tsp. pepper
1 tsp. Worcestershire sauce
Seasoned mashed potatoes
Evaporated milk

Combine lamb and onion. Cook over medium heat for 10 minutes. Add remaining ingredients except mashed potatoes and evaporated milk; mix well.

(Continued on next page)

Turn into 2-quart casserole. Top with mashed potatoes; brush with evaporated milk. Bake at 325 degrees for 40 minutes. Yield: 4 servings.

Judith Adams, Stillwater H. S.
Stillwater, Minnesota

SHISH KABOBS

1 leg of lamb, boned
1 lge. onion
1 tbsp. basil, crushed
Salt and pepper
¼ c. vegetable oil
¼ c. red wine

Cut lamb into 1 1/2-inch cubes. Slice onion over cubes. Add remaining ingredients; mix thoroughly. Marinate for several hours. Thread meat on metal or wooden skewers. Broil or grill to desired doneness. Yield: 6 servings.

Agnes Dervishian, Caruthers Union H. S.
Caruthers, California

SHISH KABOBS

2 lb. boneless leg or shoulder lamb, cut into 1 ¼-in. cubes
1 c. garlic salad dressing
2 med. green peppers, cubed
1 1 ½-lb. can small onions

Place meat in shallow dish; cover with dressing. Marinate at room temperature for 2 hours, turning occasionally, or overnight in refrigerator. String kabobs with lamb, green pepper, lamb and onions in that order. Broil over coals or 4 inches from heat for 10 to 15 minutes on each side, brushing occasionally with dressing. Yield: 4 servings.

Mrs. Laura C. Webb, Imperial Jr. H. S.
Ontario, California

SHISH KABOBS

½ leg of lamb, cut into 1-in. cubes
1 jar 1890 salad dressing
4 lge. sweet pickles
4 lge. cherry tomatoes
12 sm. onions or 1 lge. onion, cut into wedges
1 13 ½-oz. can pineapple chunks

Wipe meat clean with wet paper towel. Marinate meat in salad dressing for several hours or overnight. Cover a large pan or cookie sheet with aluminum foil. Place lamb cubes, sweet pickles, tomatoes, onions and pineapple chunks on skewers. Brush kabobs with any remaining dressing; broil for 10 minutes. Turn and brush with dressing. Broil for 10 minutes longer. Serve immediately. Yield: 4 servings.

Mrs. Susan Richman, J. W. Dodd Jr. H. S.
Freeport, New York

TABASCO KABOBS

½ tsp. Tabasco sauce
½ c. salad oil
¼ c. lime or lemon juice
¼ c. red wine (opt.)
1 tbsp. onion juice
1 tsp. dry mustard
½ tsp. salt
⅛ tsp. basil
2 lb. boneless lamb shoulder or beef chuck, cut into 1 ½-in. cubes
1 green pepper, cut into 1-in. pieces
3 tomatoes, quartered
12 sm. whole onions

Blend Tabasco sauce, salad oil, lime juice, wine and onion juice in bowl; add dry mustard, salt and basil. Add meat cubes. Let stand for 5 hours or overnight. Alternate meat and vegetables on skewers. Place in preheated broiler or on grill about 4 inches from heat. Broil for about 10 minutes on each side. NOTE: If chuck is used, sprinkle with unseasoned meat tenderizer according to label directions before marinating. Yield: 6 servings.

Photograph for this recipe on page 215.

BARBECUED BAKED LIVER

1 lb. beef liver
½ c. flour
1 sm. onion, sliced
4 slices bacon
1 c. barbecue sauce

Wash liver; coat with flour. Place in non-stick roaster. Place onion over liver. Lay bacon slices on top of liver. Pour one-half of barbecue sauce over liver. Bake at 300 degrees for 20 minutes. Turn liver; pour remaining sauce over liver. Bake for 15 minutes longer. Yield: 4 servings.

Mrs. Gertrude Swartz, Avondale H. S.
Auburn Heights, Michigan

BARBECUED LIVER

12 oz. beef liver, sliced
Seasoned flour
4 tbsp. bacon drippings
½ c. catsup
2 tbsp. sugar
¾ c. water
¼ c. lemon juice
1 tbsp. Worcestershire sauce
½ tsp. salt
⅛ tsp. pepper
1 tsp. paprika
½ med. onion, finely chopped

Thoroughly cover liver with seasoned flour; brown in hot bacon drippings. Combine remaining ingredients; pour over browned liver. Cover; cook slowly for about 1 hour or until sauce is thick and liver tender. Yield: 6 servings.

Mrs. Betty Dillard, Marion Jr. H. S.
Marion, Virginia

BRAISED LIVER

1 lb. sliced beef or lamb liver
½ c. flour
¾ tsp. salt
¼ tsp. pepper
2 ½ tbsp. bacon fat
¾ c. boiling water

Wipe liver with damp cloth. Remove any tubes; cut edge in several places to prevent curling. Mix flour, salt and pepper on waxed paper; coat liver on both sides. Heat bacon fat in skillet; brown liver on both sides. Add boiling water. Cover and simmer for 15 to 20 minutes or until liver is tender. Yield: 6 servings.

Kathryn Woods, Woodrow Wilson H. S.
Beckley, West Virginia

BEEF CREOLE LIVER

1 ½ lb. beef liver
Flour
3 tbsp. hot butter
1 ¾ c. sliced onions
2 c. heated canned tomatoes
¾ c. diced celery
1 ½ c. thinly sliced green pepper
¾ tsp. salt
Dash of cayenne

Cut liver into thin slices; dust with flour. Brown liver in butter; add onions, tomatoes, celery, green pepper, salt and cayenne. Simmer, covered, for 20 minutes. Drain. Add 2 tablespoonfuls flour to a small amount of liquid; add to pan drippings. Add liver and vegetables. Simmer for 2 minutes longer. Yield: 6 servings.

Mrs. Patsy Steagald, Bradford Jr. H. S.
Starke, Florida

FRIED LIVER

1 lb. beef liver, sliced ¼ to ½-in. thick
½ c. flour or fine dry bread crumbs
½ tsp. salt
⅛ tsp. pepper
1 c. oil

Cut liver into serving pieces. Combine flour, salt and pepper. Dip liver into flour mixture. Fry in oil in heavy pan for 25 minutes or until done. Yield: 4 servings.

Lessie Oaks, Treadwell H. S.
Memphis, Tennessee

FRIED LIVER PATTIES

1 lb. beef or lamb liver
½ c. onion, chopped
½ c. fine bread crumbs
1 tsp. salt
⅛ tsp. pepper
2 tbsp. milk
1 egg, slightly beaten
3 tbsp. vegetable shortening

Remove membrane from liver and grind coarsely. Mix ground liver with onion, crumbs, salt, pepper, milk and egg. Melt shortening in skillet until hot. Drop liver mixture by tablespoonfuls into skillet. Fry for 2 minutes or until nicely browned on both sides. Yield: 18 patties.

Betty Lou Stomm, Auburn H. S.
Auburn, Indiana

ITALIAN LIVER

1 lb. liver
½ c. red wine
½ c. vinegar
1 c. bread crumbs
1 tsp. Italian herbs
¼ c. grated Parmesan cheese
¼ c. olive oil
1 clove of garlic

Marinate liver in wine and vinegar. Mix bread crumbs, Italian herbs and Parmesan cheese. Dip liver into the crumbs; cook in olive oil and garlic until brown. Remove liver; add remaining bread crumb mixture and the wine-vinegar mixture. Cook to a thick sauce. Return liver to sauce and heat. Yield: 4 servings.

Helen M. McKinley, Oxnard H. S.
Oxnard, California

LIVER CAKES

1 lb. liver
2 slices bacon
1 tbsp. chopped onion
1 tbsp. flour
1 egg, beaten
Salt and pepper to taste

Grind liver and bacon. Mix thoroughly with remaining ingredients. Form into cakes; fry in hot fat. Yield: 6 servings.

Hilda Rohlf, Tallmadge H. S.
Tallmadge, Ohio

LIVER CREOLE

4 slices bacon, finely chopped
1 lb. beef or pork liver
4 tbsp. flour
1 tsp. salt
¼ tsp. pepper
1 sm. green pepper, cut into strips
1 sm. onion, sliced into rings
1 ½ c. tomato juice

Fry bacon for 2 minutes. Sprinkle liver with flour, salt and pepper. Brown quickly with bacon. Continue heating; add green pepper and onion. Add tomato juice. Simmer slowly for 20 minutes. NOTE: Tomato paste and water may be substituted for tomato juice. Yield: 4 servings.

Judith G. Collins, Stilwell H. S.
Stilwell, Oklahoma

LIVER CREOLE

6 slices bacon
1 lb. beef liver
⅓ c. flour
1 lge. onion, diced
1 14-oz. can V-8 juice
Dash of garlic powder
Salt and pepper

Brown bacon in skillet until crisp. Remove from skillet; crumble. Coat liver with flour; brown in bacon grease. Add onion, V-8 juice, garlic powder and salt and pepper to taste. Simmer for 15 to 20 minutes or until liver is tender. Serve piping hot garnished with crumbled bacon. Yield: 6 servings.

Mrs. Maureen F. Jensen
Mormon Trails Comm. Schools
Humeston, Iowa

LIVER CROQUETTES

2 tsp. shortening or bacon fat
4 tbsp. flour
1 c. milk
1 lb. liver, cubed
1 tsp. salt
¼ tsp. cayenne pepper
¼ tsp. black pepper
2 slices fried bacon, chopped
1 tbsp. horseradish
1 egg, beaten
1 c. bread crumbs

Melt shortening; blend in flour. Gradually stir in milk; cook until thick. Combine all ingredients except egg and crumbs; shape into patties. Dip into egg and bread crumbs. Chill well. Fry in hot fat until brown. Yield: 8 servings.

Sister Mary Madeleine, C.H.M.
Great Falls Central H. S.
Great Falls, Montana

LIVER DUMPLINGS

Liver
1 c. bread crumbs
1 or 2 eggs
Cream
Pinch of cloves
Sage
Salt and pepper
Sugar
Allspice
Flour
Broth

Finely chop the liver. Add bread crumbs, eggs, enough cream to moisten, cloves, sage, salt, pepper, a small amount of sugar, allspice and flour. Stir well. Form into 1 1/2-inch balls. Bring broth to a boil; drop in dumplings. Cook slowly for 10 to 15 minutes. Remove the dumplings from broth; serve with roast fowl, if desired. Yield: 8 servings.

Mildred M. Meier, Sterling H. S.
Sterling, Nebraska

LIVER LOAF

1 lb. liver
1 med. onion
½ c. celery
3 hard-cooked eggs, diced
Salt and pepper
Mayonnaise

Fry or boil liver until tender. Put all ingredients except eggs, seasonings and mayonnaise through food chopper. Season to taste. Add diced eggs. Mix with mayonnaise. Mold into a loaf; chill. NOTE: May be used as a sandwich filling.

Jessie Musgrove, Ragley H. S.
Ragley, Louisiana

LIVER LOAF

1 ½ lb. liver
Bacon slices
2 wheat biscuits, crumbled
3 eggs, well beaten
1 c. milk
¾ c. corn meal
2 tsp. salt
½ tsp. pepper
1 tsp. powdered sage
½ c. catsup

Scald liver; put liver and 4 slices bacon through food grinder. Add wheat biscuits, eggs, milk, corn meal, salt, pepper, sage and catsup; mix thoroughly. Line loaf pan with bacon slices; place liver mixture in pan. Cover with bacon slices. Bake at 350 degrees for 1 hour. Yield: 4 servings.

Mrs. Ruth Lathrope, Wonewoc-Center H. S.
Wonewoc, Wisconsin

LIVER AND MUSHROOMS

2 tbsp. flour
½ tsp. salt
⅛ tsp. pepper
1 lb. beef or pork liver, sliced ½-in. thick
2 tbsp. lard or drippings
1 4-oz. can mushroom stems and pieces
1 tbsp. soy sauce
¼ tsp. ground coriander
½ tsp. parsley flakes
¼ c. water

Combine flour, salt and pepper. Dredge liver in seasoned flour. Brown in lard or drippings. Pour off drippings; add mushrooms and liquid, soy sauce, coriander, parsley flakes and water. Cover tightly; simmer for 20 minutes. Yield: 4 servings.

Jean C. Boychuk, Motley Public Schools
Motley, Minnesota

LIVER AND ONIONS

Bacon drippings
1 lge. onion, thinly sliced

(Continued on next page)

1 lb. beef liver
Flour
Salt and pepper

Pour enough bacon drippings into skillet to cover bottom of pan. Cook onion in drippings until golden brown. Remove from pan. Remove all membrane and veins from liver; dip into seasoned flour. Brown on both sides over medium heat. Brown 2 tablespoonfuls flour in skillet with liver. Place onions on top of liver. Add enough water to make gravy. Reduce heat; cover and simmer until tender. Yield: 4 servings.

Mrs. William E. Holt, Lawrence Co. H. S.
Lawrenceburg, Tennessee

LIVER PUFFS

1 ½ lb. liver
1 c. hot water
3 onions
1 egg, beaten
1 c. cracker crumbs
1 tsp. salt
Bacon fat

Simmer liver in water until firm; grind with onions. Add remaining ingredients except fat; blend. Shape into six patties. Panfry in hot bacon fat until brown on both sides. Yield: 6 servings.

Mary De Lorme, Wheelerville Union Free School
Caroga Lake, New York

LIVER SAUTE

¾ c. V-8 juice
1 lb. beef liver, thinly sliced
1 clove of garlic, cut
Salt and pepper
Flour

Pour V-8 juice over liver in bowl. Add garlic. Let stand for 30 minutes. Shake off excess juice; add salt and pepper. Dust with flour. Saute in 1/8 inch hot fat for 1 to 2 minutes on each side or until brown. Yield: 6-8 servings.

Avis Leach, Weatherford H. S.
Weatherford, Oklahoma

LIVER IN SOUR CREAM

1 ½ lb. liver, sliced ¾-in. thick
⅓ c. butter
2 tbsp. flour
1 ¼ tsp. salt
Dash of pepper
1 ½ c. sour cream

Trim skin and tough fibers from liver. Brown liver on both sides in butter; remove liver. Add flour, salt and pepper to butter; blend until smooth. Add cream. Cook for 1 minutes, stirring constantly. Return liver to skillet. Cover and bake at 300 degrees for 1 hour or until liver is tender. Yield: 5-6 servings.

Mrs. Alice V. McKelvie, Edgar School
Edgar, Nebraska

LIVER WITH SOUR CREAM SAUCE

1 lb. beef liver
Flour
3 tbsp. bacon fat
2 tbsp. chopped onion
2 4-oz. cans mushrooms
1 beef bouillon cube
Salt and pepper to taste
½ c. sour cream

Cut liver into 1/2-inch cubes. Dredge liver in flour; brown in bacon fat with onion. Cook for 8 minutes. Do not overcook. Add mushrooms and bouillon cube dissolved in water. Simmer. Season with salt and pepper. Add sour cream before serving. Yield: 4 servings.

Mrs. Rosetta Bartels, Inman H. S.
Inman, Kansas

LIVER IN WHITE WINE

1 lb. liver, sliced
Flour
4 tbsp. olive oil
2 cloves of garlic, split into halves
1 sm. onion, minced
Salt and pepper
1 tsp. basil
½ c. white wine

Dredge liver with flour; brown slowly in hot oil. Remove from oil; keep warm. Brown garlic in pan drippings; add onion. Stir well; cook for 5 minutes. Return liver to pan; spoon garlic and onion over top of liver. Season with salt and pepper and basil. Pour wine over top. Cover; cook slowly for 30 minutes, basting every 10 minutes. Discard garlic before serving. Yield: 4 servings. ings.

Leila Steckelberg, Mount Vernon Union H. S.
Mount Vernon, Washington

PANBROILED LIVER AND BACON

4 strips bacon
1 ¼ lb. liver, sliced ¼-in. thick
1 ½ tbsp. flour
Salt and pepper

Partially cook bacon in a heavy skillet; drain on absorbent paper. Roll liver in flour. Broil liver in bacon fat until brown on one side; season with salt and pepper. Turn and brown the other side. Finish cooking bacon; arrange liver on warm platter and top with bacon. Yield: 4 servings.

Mrs. Neila B. Swann, Centerville H. S.
Centerville, Louisiana

PANBROILED LIVER

1 lb. sliced calves liver
1 c. milk
4 tbsp. butter or margarine
Salt and pepper

Remove veins and skin around liver; soak for 2 to 3 hours in milk. Heat skillet; melt butter. Add liver; cook slowly on one side for 6 minutes. Turn; season with salt and pepper to taste. Continue cooking for 5 minutes. Drain on paper towels. Serve at once on warm platter, garnished with crisply fried bacon, if desired. Yield: 4 servings.

Mrs. Margaret Carter Thornton
Crystal City H. S.
Crystal City, Texas

PANFRIED LIVER

1 ½ lb. calves liver
½ c. flour
Dash of pepper
¼ c. bacon drippings
1 med. onion, sliced ¼-in. thick and separated into rings

Remove veins and membranes from liver; cut edges at several points to 3/8-inch. Mix flour and pepper. Dip liver into flour mixture, coating each piece. Heat bacon drippings in frying pan over medium heat; add liver and cook until golden brown or until slices are just tender, turning once. Drain liver on absorbent paper. Place slices back in pan; add onion rings. Cook slowly until onion rings wilt. Remove and place on platter; garnish with onion rings. Yield: 4-6 servings.

Delores Stone Barber, Laurel Hill H. S.
Laurel Hill, North Carolina

SAVORY LIVER

1 lb. beef or pork liver
Garlic or onion salt
Flour

Pour boiling water over liver; drain. Slice into 1/2 x 3-inch strips. Sprinkle with salt; roll in flour. Let stand for 5 minutes. Fry in deep fat at 350 degrees for 3 to 5 minutes. Yield: 4 servings.

Mrs. June Patchett, Young America H. S.
Metcalf, Illinois

SAVORY LIVER

1 lb. baby beef liver, sliced
1 tsp. salt
⅛ tsp. pepper
¼ c. butter
¼ c. catsup
1 tsp. lemon juice
1 tbsp. vinegar
1 tbsp. water

Sprinkle liver with salt and pepper; saute in butter for 3 minutes on each side. Remove to a heated platter; keep warm. Add remaining ingredients to pan drippings; heat to a boil. Pour over liver. Serve hot. Yield: 4-5 servings.

Mrs. Jeanne Bunch, Van Buren School
Van Buren, Ohio

SAVORY LIVER

2 thin slices young beef liver
2 tbsp. flour
½ tsp. dry mustard
⅛ tsp. chili powder

Wipe liver with a damp cloth. Combine flour, mustard and chili powder; coat liver with the mixture. Fry in a small amount of hot fat for 4 to 5 minutes on each side. Yield: 2 servings.

Mrs. Ann Hunt, Nampa H. S.
Nampa, Idaho

SPANISH LIVER

1 lb. sliced liver
½ c. flour
2 tbsp. fat, melted
1 tsp. salt
½ tsp. pepper
1 tsp. chili powder
1 med. onion, sliced
½ c. catsup or tomato sauce

Cut liver into serving sized pieces; remove outer membrane. Dredge in flour; brown quickly on both sides in melted fat. Season with salt, pepper and chili powder. Cover liver with onion slices and catsup. Reduce heat and continue cooking slowly until liver is tender. Serve at once. Yield: 4 servings.

Julie Gorman, Mound City H. S.
Mound City, Kansas

SWISS LIVER

3 tbsp. flour
½ tsp. salt
Dash of pepper
1 lb. liver, sliced
2 tbsp. bacon drippings
1 c. catsup
1 onion, sliced
1 green pepper, sliced

Combine flour, salt and pepper. Roll liver in seasoned flour. Saute lightly in the bacon drippings. Cover with catsup, onion and green pepper. Cover; simmer until tender. Yield: 4 servings.

Fernette Honaker, Menaul Presbyterian H. S.
Albuquerque, New Mexico

GLAZED LUNCHEON BAKE

2 cans luncheon meat
2 cans sweet potatoes, sliced
3 tbsp. melted butter
1 12-oz. glass orange marmalade

Cut each loaf of meat into fourths about three-fourths through. Place loaves in a buttered 13 x 9 x 2 1/2-inch baking pan. Place potatoes between slices of meat and around loaves. Brush meat and potatoes well with melted butter. Spread orange marmalade over top. Bake at 400 degrees for 20 minutes.

Mrs. Louise Simpson, New Site H. S.
Alexander City, Alabama

HAM 'N' PEACHES

⅓ c. brown sugar
½ tsp. vinegar
1 tsp. prepared mustard
1 tsp. water
1 can luncheon meat
½ c. canned sliced peaches, drained

Combine brown sugar, vinegar, mustard and water. Cut lengthwise slits in loaf of meat. Fill slits with sliced peaches. Bake at 350 degrees for 15 minutes. Baste with brown sugar mixture. Bake for 5 minutes. Yield: 4 servings.

Donna F. Crews, Westwood Jr. H. S.
Winter Haven, Florida

OVEN BARBECUE

1 can luncheon meat
1 sm. can tomato sauce
¼ c. water
2 tbsp. brown sugar
1 tbsp. finely grated onion
¼ tsp. Worcestershire sauce

Slice meat lengthwise. Place in greased shallow baking dish. Combine remaining ingredients; pour over meat. Bake at 400 degrees for 30 minutes, basting occasionally. Yield: 4 servings.

Mrs. Elizabeth L. Bateman, Alice Drive Jr. H. S.
Sumter, South Carolina

SPEEDY KABOBS

1 12-oz. can luncheon meat, cut into 12 cubes
1 green pepper, cut into 12 squares
1 sm. can ripe olives
12 canned pineapple chunks
1 8-oz. can tomato sauce
½ c. pineapple syrup
¼ c. chopped green onions
¼ c. butter
1 tsp. Worcestershire sauce
1 tsp. monosodium glutamate
½ tsp. salt
2 med. tomatoes, quartered

Alternate meat, green pepper, ripe olives and pineapple chunks on four skewers. Combine remaining ingredients except tomatoes; simmer for 15 minutes. Brush ingredients on skewers with mixture. Broil 5 to 6 inches from heat for 8 to 9 minutes or until lightly browned. Turn and place tomatoes on each end of skewers. Brush with tomato sauce mixture. Broil for 4 to 5 minutes longer. Serve immediately with remaining sauce. Yield: 4 servings.

Mary Ann Fugate, Reddick H. S.
Reddick, Illinois

SWEET AND SOUR LUNCHEON MEAT

1 12-oz. can luncheon meat, ground
¼ lb. cheese, ground
½ c. oats
1 egg, beaten
1 tbsp. fat
1 tbsp. brown sugar
1 tbsp. cornstarch
1 c. water
1 c. undrained pineapple chunks
1 tbsp. vinegar
¼ tsp. ginger

Combine meat, cheese, oats and egg in medium bowl. Form into eight large balls; place in shallow baking pan. Bake at 400 degrees for 20 minutes. Heat fat in a saucepan; blend in brown sugar and cornstarch. Stir in water, pineapple, vinegar and ginger; cook, stirring constantly, until thick. Drain off fat. Bake for 10 minutes longer. Yield: 6-8 servings.

Mrs. Ruth Eleazer, E. L. Wright Jr. H. S.
Columbia, South Carolina

WAGON WHEEL PIE

½ c. chopped onion (opt.)
2 tbsp. butter
1 12-oz. can luncheon meat
1 ½ pkg. frozen mixed vegetables or 1 1-lb. can Veg-All, drained
½ c. grated Cheddar cheese
1 c. evaporated milk
2 eggs, beaten
2 tbsp. flour
½ tsp. salt
¼ tsp. paprika
1 pastry shell, unbaked

Steam onion in butter in covered saucepan over low heat for 10 minutes. Cut meat lengthwise into 1/4-inch slices. Reserve 5 slices. Cut remaining slices into bite-sized pieces. Partially cook frozen vegetables; drain. Combine vegetables, cheese, eggs, flour, salt and paprika. Pour into pastry shell. Cut reserved meat into halves diagonally. Arrange on top of filling. Bake at 400 degrees for 35 to 40 minutes. Cool for 10 minutes before serving. Yield: 6 servings.

Mrs. Gretta E. Litchfield, Taunton H. S.
Taunton, Massachusetts

SWEET BREADS A LA KING

½ lb. sweetbread
1 c. chopped celery
½ c. chopped green pepper
½ c. chopped red sweet pepper
4 tbsp. butter or margarine
4 tbsp. flour
2 c. milk
4 hard-cooked eggs, sliced
Salt and pepper

Boil sweetbread slowly in salted water until tender. Cool; remove fibers. Chop into small pieces. Boil celery and green pepper in salted water until tender; drain. Melt butter; blend in flour. Gradually add milk, stirring until thick. Add sweetbreads, celery, peppers and hard-cooked egg. Season with salt and pepper. Serve hot on toast or in patty shells, if desired.

Kathryn Davis, Comm. H. S.
Pinckneyville, Illinois

BARBECUED TONGUE

1 beef tongue
1 can tomato soup
1 onion, chopped
1 c. vinegar
1 c. liquid from tongue
¼ c. sugar
¼ c. butter
1 tbsp. whole cloves
Cinnamon to taste
Allspice to taste
Salt to taste

Boil tongue in salted water until tender. Cool; remove skin. Place tongue in baking dish. Combine remaining ingredients; pour over tongue. Bake at 300 degrees for 1 hour and 30 minutes, basting often. Yield: 6-8 servings.

Mrs. Eloise Peterson, University H. S.
Spokane, Washington

PICKLED TONGUE

1 beef tongue
1 ½ tsp. salt
1 c. vinegar
¾ c. water
¼ c. sugar
Dash of marjoram
Dash of thyme
Dash of cloves

Wash tongue; cover with salted water, using 1/2 teaspoonful salt. Cook until tender. Cool; open and clean. Slice. Combine remaining ingredients; bring to a boil. Pour sauce over sliced tongue while sauce is hot. Yield: 8 servings.

Mrs. Vanora Fry, Little River H. S.
Little River, Kansas

BOILED TONGUE WITH CHILI SAUCE

1 2 to 3-lb. beef tongue
¼ tsp. oregano
½ tsp. salt
¼ tsp. marjoram
¼ tsp. summer savory

Cover tongue with water; add spices. Boil until tender. Peel and slice.

SAUCE:

¼ c. chopped onion
¼ c. butter
¼ tsp. red chili powder
Salt and pepper to taste
1 can tomato soup

Fry onion in butter until clear; add seasonings and soup. Simmer for 5 minutes. Serve with sliced tongue over rice, if desired. Yield: 8 servings.

Mrs. Ruth L. Auge, Belen Jr. H. S.
Belen, New Mexico

CUMBERLUND TONGUES

1 beef tongue
1 c. currant jelly
2 tbsp. prepared mustard
1 tbsp. lemon juice
1 tbsp. grated orange rind

Cook tongue in pressure saucepan for 1 hour at 10 pounds pressure. Cut into thin slices. Heat jelly with mustard and lemon juice; add orange rind. Cover tongue with mixture. Cover; cook slowly for 10 to 20 minutes. Yield: 6 servings.

Jean Collins, Sauk Rapids Jr. H. S.
Sauk Rapids, Minnesota

PICKLED TONGUE

1 beef tongue
2 c. vinegar
¼ c. sugar
1 tsp. salt
1 tbsp. pickling spice

Cover tongue with cold water; simmer for 1 hour or until tender. Drain and reserve 2 cups broth. Combine reserved broth with remaining ingredients. Place tongue in bowl or jar. Cover with vinegar mixture. Cover; chill for 48 hours.

Mrs. Bettie Brown, Shelton H. S.
Shelton, Nebraska

PICKLED TONGUE

1 2 to 2 ½-lb. beef tongue
1 c. vinegar
1 c. water
1 c. sugar
1 med. or lge. onion, sliced

Simmer tongue in salted water until tender or pressure cook at 15 pounds pressure for 1 hour.

(Continued on next page)

Cool; remove skin and trim. Cut into slices about 1/4-inch thick. Heat vinegar, water and sugar to boiling. Alternate layers of tongue and onion in a bowl. Pour vinegar over layers. Allow to set overnight or several hours before serving. Yield: 6-8 servings.

Mrs. Frances Roberts, Pomeroy H. S.
Pomeroy, Ohio

SPICED TONGUE

1 beef tongue
Hot water
5 whole cloves
1 tsp. salt
2 bay leaves
2 tsp. vinegar

Cover tongue with hot water; simmer for 1 hour. Add remaining ingredients; cover. Simmer for 1 hour or until tender. Cool; remove skin and trim roots. Slice crosswise. Serve cold. Yield: 10 servings.

Mrs. Shirley Stewart, Prince Andrew H. S.
Dartmouth, Nova Scotia, Canada

SWEET-SOUR TONGUE

1 beef tongue
½ c. brown sugar
1 tsp. dry mustard
1 tbsp. flour
2 tbsp. vinegar
2 tbsp. lemon juice
1 ½ c. water
⅓ c. raisins

Cook tongue in salted water until tender. Place in baking dish. Combine brown sugar, dry mustard and flour; mix in vinegar, lemon juice and water. Add raisins. Cook until thickened. Pour over tongue. Bake at 350 degrees for 30 minutes. Slice and spread sauce over slices. Serve hot. Yield: 6 servings.

Mrs. Margaret C. Hoffman, Victory School
Harrisville, Pennsylvania

TONGUE IN SWEET TOMATO SAUCE

1 3-lb. beef tongue
1 c. diced celery
1 onion, diced
1 10-oz. can mushrooms
1 10-oz. can tomato soup
½ soup can water
1 tbsp. brown sugar
1 15-oz. can green peas

Boil tongue until tender; slice very thin. Saute very thin. Saute celery, onion and mushrooms in a small amount of oil. Add tomato soup, water and brown sugar; simmer for 10 minutes. Add green peas and tongue; simmer for 30 minutes longer. Yield: 6 servings.

Mrs. A. Blatt, Edmund Partridge School
Winnipeg, Manitoba, Canada

VEAL-TONGUE ESPANOLE

1 veal tongue
1 qt. boiling water
2 tbsp. cooking oil
1 ½ tbsp. flour
2 tbsp. diced onion
2 tbsp. diced green pepper
1 med. can whole tomatoes
¼ tsp. cumin seed, mashed
2 cloves of garlic, mashed
Pinch of pepper

Simmer tongue in boiling water for 1 hour and 30 minutes or until tender. Cool; peel off thick skin and dice. Reserve 2 cups stock for gravy. Heat oil; blend in flour. Add vegetables and seasonings. Add reserved stock, stirring constantly, until thick. Add tongue. Yield: 8 servings.

Mrs. Jilma Vidaurri, King H. S.
Kingsville, Texas

VIRGINIA BEEF TONGUE

1 beef tongue
1 c. brown sugar
1 c. stewed cranberries
¼ c. butter
1 tbsp. whole cloves
½ lemon, sliced

Cover tongue with water; simmer until tender. Remove skin and trim off the root end. Combine 1 cup of tongue liquid to brown sugar, cranberries, butter, cloves and lemon. Simmer tongue in the mixture for 15 minutes. Garnish with slices of lemon and sprigs parsley, if desired. Yield: 6 servings.

Lillian S. Ealy, Gadsden H. S.
Anthony, New Mexico

BAKED BARBECUED HEART AND/OR TONGUE

5 lb. tongues and hearts
½ tsp. sage
½ tsp. allspice
½ tsp. cloves
½ tsp. cinnamon
2 c. tomatoes
2 c. tomato juice or 4 c. tomato puree
½ c. chopped onion
3 tbsp. vinegar
2 c. tomato hot sauce
¼ c. sugar
2 tbsp. salt
2 tbsp. pepper

Simmer tongues and hearts in salted water for 4 to 5 hours or until tender, Trim and remove skin and connective tissues. Place spices in cheesecloth bag. Place in saucepan with remaining ingredients and heat. Place hearts and tongues in a casserole or small roaster pan. Pour sauce over top; add enough juice from cooking hearts and tongues to cover. Bake at 350 degrees for 2 hours. Slice and serve with sauce. Yield: 12-18 servings.

Princess L. Egbert, Grants Pass H. S.
Grants Pass, Oregon

Combination Meat Favorites

ALLIE'S MEAT BALLS

1 lb. ground beef
1 4 ½-oz. can deviled ham
1 envelope mushroom soup mix
2 eggs, beaten
½ c. milk
½ c. water

Combine beef, ham, soup mix and eggs. Form into 12 balls; brown in small amount of fat. Add milk and water; simmer for 30 minutes. Yield: 6 servings.

Ada Millett, Central H. S.
Memphis, Tennessee

MEAT BALLS AND NOODLES MONTE CARLO

1 lb. mixed ground beef, lamb and veal
¼ c. fine dry bread crumbs
⅓ c. chopped onion
1 tsp. salt
⅛ tsp. pepper
⅔ c. evaporated milk
¼ c. butter or margarine
2 5 ½-oz. cans tomato juice
1 envelope spaghetti sauce mix
1 c. water
1 8-oz. pkg. noodles
½ c. sliced pitted ripe olives

Combine ground meat, bread crumbs, onion, salt, pepper and evaporated milk, mixing lightly but thoroughly. Shape mixture into 12 meat balls. Melt butter on margarine in a large skillet over medium heat; add meat balls and brown evenly on all sides. Push meat balls to one side of skillet; add tomato juice. Stir in spaghetti sauce mix and water, blending well. Bring mixture to a boil; stir in noodles and olives. Cover skillet. Reduce heat and simmer for 15 minutes, stirring occasionally until noodles are tender. Serve hot. Yield: 4-6 servings.

Mrs. Grace Koller, Queen City H. S.
Queen City, Texas

SMOTHERED MEAT BALLS

¼ lb. ground pork
2 lb ground beef
1 egg
1 tbsp. grated onion
¼ tsp. mace
2 slices stale bread, trimmed
Sliced onion (opt.)
Butter
4 tbsp. flour
Salt and pepper to taste

Combine beef, pork, egg, grated onion and mace. Moisten bread with hot water; add to meat. Knead for 5 to 10 minutes. Wet hands with cold water; roll meat mixture into small balls. Fry meat balls and sliced onion in butter until brown. Spoon meat balls into casserole. Remove onion from skillet. Brown flour in meat juice in pan; thin to desired consistency with hot water. Add salt and pepper to taste. Scrape all browned particles from pan into gravy. Boil for 3 minutes. Pour gravy over meat balls. Bake at 350 degrees for 30 minutes. Remove from oven. Place meat balls and gravy in pan. Cover and simmer for 30 minutes. Serve hot with noodles, rice or mashed potatoes, if desired. Yield: 6 servings.

Barbara A. West, Cradock H. S.
Portsmouth, Virginia

MEAT BALLS IN SOUR CREAM

1 lb. ground beef
¾ lb. ground pork
1 c. cracker crumbs
2 tsp. salt
Dash of pepper
Dash of thyme
Dash of oregano
½ c. milk
2 eggs
2 tbsp. fat
2 c. sour cream
1 6-oz. can broiled sliced mushrooms, drained

Combine meats, crumbs, seasonings, milk and eggs; mix well. Form into 1 1/2-inch balls; brown in hot fat. Drain off excess fat. Add 1 1/2 cups sour cream. Cover; simmer for 1 hour. Remove meat balls to warm serving dish. Stir remaining sour cream into mixture in skillet; add mushrooms and heat to boiling point. Pour mixture over the meat balls. Yield: 6 servings.

Faye Quinley, Corsicana H. S.
Corsicana, Texas

SPAGHETTI AND MEAT BALLS

¾ lb. ground beef
¼ lb. ground pork
1 c. bread crumbs
½ c. Parmesan cheese
1 sprig parsley, chopped
1 clove of garlic, minced
½ c. milk
2 eggs, beaten
Salt and pepper
Olive oil
1 onion, chopped
3 tbsp. fat
2 ½ c. canned tomatoes
2 6-oz. cans tomato paste
2 c. water
1 tsp. salt
1 bay leaf
Cooked spaghetti

Combine meats, crumbs, cheese, parsley, garlic, milk and eggs; season with salt and pepper. Shape into balls; brown in olive oil. Saute onion in fat; add remaining ingredients except spaghetti. Season with salt and pepper. Pour over meat balls. Simmer for 15 minutes. Serve over spaghetti.

Mrs. Ruth F. Raynor, Grand Gorge Central H. S.
Grand Gorge, New York

SPECIAL MEAT BALLS

1 ½ lb. ground beef
½ lb. bulk sausage
1 tsp. salt
½ tsp. pepper
1 tsp. oregano
1 tbsp. Worcestershire sauce
1 tbsp. parsley flakes
2 tbsp. very finely chopped onion
Fat

Combine all ingredients; form in balls. Brown in hot fat, turning frequently. Cool slowly for 30 minutes.

SAUCE:

½ c. catsup
½ c. brown sugar
½ c. seasoned vinegar
1 tbsp. prepared mustard

Combine all ingredients; cover meat balls with sauce. Cook over low heat until done. Yield: 6 servings.

Mrs. Emery Coates, Union City Area H. S.
Union City, Pennsylvania

SURPRISE MEAT BALLS

1 lb. ground beef
½ lb. ground pork
Salt and pepper
¼ c. cream
2 c. sm. toasted bread cubes
1 sm. onion, finely chopped
1 tbsp. chopped parsley
3 tbsp. salad oil
1 tsp. poultry seasoning
1 10 ½-oz. can cream of mushroom soup
½ can water

Combine meats, seasonings and cream; mix thoroughly. Form into 16 patties. Combine bread cubes, onion, parsley, salad oil, salt, pepper and poultry seasoning; place stuffing on 8 patties. Cover with remaining patties; press into ball. Brown in hot fat; add mushroom soup diluted with water. Cover and bake at 350 degrees for 1 hour. Yield: 8 servings.

Mrs. Gladys Meier, Grant Jr. H. S.
Detroit, Michigan

SWEDISH MEAT BALLS

¾ lb. ground pork
¾ lb. ground veal
3 boiled potatoes, mashed
1 egg
1 sm. onion, chopped
¼ tsp. allspice
¾ c. milk

Combine all ingredients; shape into 1-inch balls. Brown in small amount hot fat. Place in a casserole. Bake at 350 degrees for 20 minutes. Yield: 6 servings.

Antoinette L. Bryan, Southwestern H. S.
Detroit, Michigan

SWEDISH MEAT BALLS

1 lb. ground beef
½ lb. ground pork
½ lb. ground veal
1 c. soft bread crumbs
1 c. applesauce
2 eggs, slightly beaten
1 med. onion, grated
½ tsp. allspice
½ tsp. mace
1 tsp. salt
Flour
Fat
1 can beef consomme or ½ can beef consomme and ½ can beef broth

Combine meats, bread crumbs, applesauce, eggs, onion, allspice, mace and salt; shape into 1-inch balls. Roll balls in flour; brown in a small amount of hot fat. Remove from pan. Add enough fat to pan drippings to make 4 tablespoonfuls fat. Stir in 4 tablespoonfuls flour and brown. Gradually stir in consomme. Return meat balls to gravy. Cover; simmer for 30 to 45 minutes. Yield: 6-8 servings.

Jane Sullivan, Schenley H. S.
Pittsburgh, Pennsylvania

SWEDISH MEAT BALLS

½ lb. ground beef
½ lb. ground sausage
½ c. fine graham cracker crumbs
1 egg
⅛ tsp. pepper
1 tsp. nutmeg
1 tsp. allspice
1 tsp. ginger
½ c. cream
¼ c. dry bread crumbs
1 ½ tsp. salt
½ c. water

Combine all ingredients, except water; form into balls. Brown slightly in a small amount of butter. Add water. Cover; simmer for 30 minutes. Pour into casserole. Bake at 300 degrees for 1 hour. Yield: 6-8 servings.

Clara E. Ander, Pipestone H. S.
Pipestone, Minnesota

SWEDISH MEAT BALLS

1 lb. ground beef
¾ lb. ground pork
½ lb. ground veal
1 sm. onion, chopped
1 tbsp. salt
Pepper to taste
2 eggs
1 ½ c. bread crumbs
2 tsp. caraway seeds
1 to 1 ½ c. water

Mix all ingredients thoroughly; shape into 1 1/2-inch meat balls. Fry, turning frequently to brown evenly on all sides. Yield: 6 servings.

Sandra Brown, Stowe H. S.
Stowe, Vermont

SWEDISH MEAT BALLS

½ c. fine, dry bread crumbs
½ c. warm cream
½ lb. beef
¼ lb. veal
¼ lb. pork
½ c. milk
2 egg yolks, slightly beaten
2 tbsp. minced onion
3 tbsp. salt
⅓ tsp. pepper
⅛ tsp. allspice
4 tbsp. fat

Soak crumbs in cream. Grind meats three times, using fine blade of food chopper. Combine crumbs and meat; mix thoroughly. Add milk, egg yolks, onion and seasonings. Form into medium or very small balls; brown on all sides in hot fat. Keep warm over hot water. Yield: 8 servings.

Mrs. R. M. Field, White Station H. S.
Memphis, Tennessee

SWEDISH MEAT BALLS

2 c. soft bread crumbs
¾ c. milk
½ c. minced onion
¼ c. butter or margarine
¾ lb. finely ground beef
¼ lb. finely ground pork
1 egg, beaten
2 tsp. salt
¼ tsp. paprika
¼ tsp. nutmeg
½ c. flour
2 c. light cream

Soak bread crumbs in milk for 10 minutes. Brown the onion in 2 tablespoonfuls butter. Add onion, meat, egg, 1 1/2 teaspoonfuls salt, paprika and nutmeg to the bread mixture. Blend thoroughly; form into 1 1/2-inch balls. Roll in flour; brown in remaining butter. Sprinkle with remaining flour. Dissolve remaining salt in cream; pour over meat balls. Cover; simmer for 15 minutes. Yield: 8 servings.

Hazel Edberg, Modesto H. S.
Modesto, California

BREAST OF CHICKEN SUPREME

6 chicken breasts
Salt and pepper
1 c. heavy cream
1 c. flour
⅓ c. butter
6 thin slices boiled ham
6 slices crisp buttered toast

Remove skin from chicken breast. Sprinkle lightly with salt and pepper; dip in heavy cream. Roll in flour. Saute chicken in butter until lightly browned and tender. Arrange ham on buttered toast. Place a chicken breast on top of a ham slice. Keep hot.

SAUCE SUPREME:

2 tbsp. butter
2 tbsp. flour
1 c. chicken stock
½ c. light cream
½ tsp. salt
Dash of nutmeg
1 egg yolk, slightly beaten
1 c. sauted mushroom caps

Melt butter in double boiler; add flour and stir until well blended. Add chicken stock and cream gradually; bring to the boiling point, stirring constantly. Season with salt and nutmeg. Cook over hot water for 10 minutes. Mix one-third of hot sauce with egg yolk; return to remaining hot sauce. Cook for 1 to 2 minutes longer. Do not allow the sauce to boil again. Serve over chicken. Garnish with mushrooms. Yield: 6 servings.

Joyce Gandy Garrison, Chesnee H. S.
Chesnee, South Carolina

CHICKEN TIPPIRARY

4 whole chicken breasts, halved
8 slices Canadian bacon, ham or pressed ham
4 tbsp. butter
2 eggs, slightly beaten
2 tbsp. water
1 tsp. water
1 tsp. onion salt
¼ tsp. pepper
1 c. instant potato flakes or bread crumbs
Oil

Remove skin from breasts; flatten each, using a meat mallet, until large enough to cover bacon slice. To prevent breasts from tearing when pounding, cover with several layers of waxed paper. Place one slice bacon or ham, 1 tablespoonful butter and second bacon slice on each half of chicken breast. Top with second breast half. Secure with wooden picks or strings. Repeat. Combine egg, water, onion salt and pepper in bowl; dip chicken breasts into egg mixture. Roll in potato flakes or crumbs. Brown in oil for 15 minutes in large skillet over medium heat. Turn, brown second side for 15 minutes. Yield: 4 servings.

Mrs. Miriam Toth, Castro Valley H. S.
Castro Valley, California

CITY CHICKEN LEGS

1 to 1 ½ lb. pork, cubed
1 to 1 ½ lb. veal, cubed
1 egg, beaten
Cracker or bread crumbs
Salt and pepper to taste

Alternate pork and veal on skewers. Dip in egg. Coat with cracker crumbs. Brown in frying pan.

(Continued on next page)

Season to taste. Cover; cook slowly or until done. Yield: 8 servings.

Mrs. Virginia Carlson
Port Allegany Area School
Port Allegany, Pennsylvania
Kathleen P. Burton, Star Valley H. S.
Afton, Wyoming

HOOSIER COUNTRY SCRAPPLE

4 c. ground cooked pork, beef and liver
4 c. meat broth
1 ½ c. corn meal
2 tsp. salt
½ tsp. sage (opt.)

Combine meat and meat broth; bring almost to a boil. Dampen corn meal with a little water; stir into meat mixture. Add salt and sage. Boil, stirring constantly, until thick. Pour into two loaf pans. Chill for 12 hours. Slice and fry in slightly greased skillet. Yield: 20 servings.

Mrs. Hilda Mae Kuhlman, Jefferson H. S.
New Paris, Ohio

MRS. WIER'S CITY-FRIED CHICKEN

8 lean pork chops, boned
2 round steaks
2 eggs, well beaten
Cracker meal
Salt and pepper to taste

Cut chops and steak into strips of 1/2-inch in width. Alternate pork and beef on skewers to size of chicken drum stick. Roll in egg and then cracker meat. Season with salt and pepper. Fry in deep fat. Yield: 4-6 servings.

Mrs. Lillian King Wier, Odem H. S.
Odem, Texas

CARAMEL-HAM LOAF

⅓ c. dark brown sugar
½ tsp. powdered cloves
½ lb. cooked ground ham
1 lb. beef ground chuck
¼ tsp. salt
⅛ tsp. pepper
1 tsp. prepared mustard
1 tsp. grated onion
1 egg, slightly beaten
⅔ c. bread crumbs
1 tbsp. parsley, finely chopped
1 c. milk

Combine sugar and cloves; sprinkle on bottom of loaf pan. Combine remaining ingredients; press firmly into loaf pan. Bake at 350 degrees for 1 hour and 30 minutes. Let stand in pan for 5 minutes before inverting onto platter. Yield: 6 servings.

Mrs. Jerry Barton, Matthews Jr. H. S.
Lubbock, Texas

EASY HAM LOAF

3 lb. cured ham, ground
½ lb. beef or veal, ground
3 eggs, beaten
2 c. bread crumbs
3 tsp. baking powder
Salt and pepper (opt.)
Sliced pineapple
3 tbsp. brown sugar

Combine meat, eggs, bread crumbs, baking powder, salt and pepper; mix well. Line a greased baking dish with pineapple slices; cover with brown sugar. Pat meat mixture over sugar. Bake at 350 degrees for 1 hour and 30 minutes. Drain off juice. Yield: 12-15 servings.

Mrs. Lewis Frazier, Drakesboro H. S.
Drakesboro, Kentucky

GLAZED INDIVIDUAL HAM LOAVES

½ lb. fresh beef
½ lb. smoked ham
½ lb. fresh pork
⅓ c. cracker crumbs
1 sm. onion chopped
1 egg, beaten
¾ c. milk
Salt and pepper

Grind the meats twice. Combine meats with remaining ingredients; pack lightly in large muffin tins. Shape the meat so it rounds up well but does not come to the top of the pan. Bake at 350 degrees for 20 minutes.

SAUCE:

1 c. brown sugar
3 tbsp. vinegar
1 tbsp. dry mustard

Blend all ingredients; boil for 1 minute. Pour part of the sauce over each meat loaf. Bake for 20 minutes longer. Yield: 10 servings.

Mrs. Astrid Ahrens, Delavan H. S.
Delavan, Minnesota

HAM AND BEEF LOAF

1 lb. ground beef
1 c. bread crumbs
1 c. milk
1 lb. ground ham
1 egg, beaten
2 tbsp. brown sugar
1 tsp. ground mustard
Vinegar or sweet pickle juice
Whole cloves

Combine ground beef, bread crumbs, milk, ham and egg. Press into a loaf pan. Make a paste of brown sugar, ground mustard and vinegar or sweet pickle juice. Spread over loaf; stick cloves in top. Bake at 350 degrees for 45 minutes. Yield: 6 servings.

Mrs. Ella Furr Long, Terry H. S.
Terry, Mississippi

HAM LOAF

½ c. milk
1 ½ c. bread crumbs
2 eggs, beaten
2 tsp. mustard
2 tbsp. brown sugar
½ tsp. pepper
1 green pepper, shredded
2 carrots, grated
1 ½ lb. ham, ground
½ lb. hamburger
½ c. cold water

Pour milk over bread crumbs. Add beaten eggs, seasoning, shredded pepper and grated carrots. Mix ham and hamburger thoroughly; add to bread mixture. Mix well. Pack into loaf pan. Pour cold water over loaf. Bake at 350 degrees for 45 minutes. Yield: 8 servings.

Helen J. Morgan, Burley H. S.
Burley, Idaho

HAM LOAF

1 ¼ lb. ground ham
½ lb. sausage
1 ¼ lb. ground veal
4 eggs, beaten
1 c. milk
1 c. cracker crumbs
¾ c. brown sugar
½ tsp. dry mustard
⅛ c. vinegar
⅛ c. water
¼ tsp. paprika

Combine ham, sausage, veal, eggs, milk and cracker crumbs. Pack into loaf pan. Combine brown sugar, mustard, vinegar, water and paprika. Bake ham loaf at 350 degrees for 1 hour and 30 minutes, basting every 15 minutes with brown sugar mixture.

HORSERADISH SAUCE:

¼ c. horseradish
Dash of salt
1 tbsp. salad dressing
½ c. whipped cream

Combine horseradish, salt and salad dressing; fold in whipped cream. Serve with ham loaf. Yield: 6 servings.

Mrs. Donna Wetter, La Creole Jr. H. S.
Dallas, Oregon

HAM LOAVES

2 lb. ground beef
1 lb. ground ham
2 c. oats
1 c. bread crumbs
3 eggs
1 c. milk
1 sm. ground onion
2 tsp. salt
¼ tsp. pepper
1 qt. plus 2 pt. tomato juice

Combine all ingredients except 1 quart tomato juice; form into loaves. Place in deep baking dish. Add tomato juice. Bake at 325 degrees for 2 hours. Yield: 20 servings.

Mrs. Frances Detmer, Weeping Water H. S.
Weeping Water, Nebraska

HAM LOAF DELUXE

1 lb. ground cured ham
2 lb. hamburger
2 eggs
1 c. bread crumbs
½ tsp. pepper
1 tbsp. salt
½ c. milk

Combine all ingredients; shape into loaf. Place in a greased baking dish. Bake at 325 degrees for 1 hour. Yield: 10-12 servings.

Mrs. Maxine King, Unity H. S.
Mendon, Illinois

HAM MEAT LOAF

2 eggs
1 c. milk
1 c. bread crumbs
2 c. ground beef
2 c. ground ham
½ c. brown sugar
1 tsp. dry mustard
2 tbsp. vinegar
1 can pineapple chunks, drained

Beat eggs slightly with a fork; add milk, crumbs, ground ham and ground beef. Mix thoroughly. Mix the sugar, mustard and vinegar in shallow casserole; arrange pineapple on sugar mixture. Place the meat mixture over the pineapple. Bake at 350 degrees for 1 hour and 30 minutes. Invert to serve. Yield: 8-10 servings.

Mrs. Jean Ehrke, Fort Atkinson H. S.
Fort Atkinson, Wisconsin

HAM RING WITH CHERRY SAUCE

1 lb. ground uncooked smoked ham
1 lb. ground beef
2 eggs, beaten
1 ½ c. wheat flakes
½ c. milk
⅛ c. chopped green pepper
¼ c. brown sugar
1 tsp. prepared mustard
¼ tsp. cloves

Combine meats, eggs, wheat flakes, milk and green pepper; place in 1 1/2-quart ring mold. Mix brown sugar, mustard and cloves. Spread over meat. Bake at 350 degrees for 1 hour.

CHERRY SAUCE:

½ c. sugar
2 tbsp. cornstarch

(Continued on next page)

¼ tsp. cloves
1 can pie cherries
Red food coloring

Combine sugar, cornstarch and cloves. Drain cherries, reserving liquid. Stir cornstarch mixture into cherry liquid. Boil until thick. Add food coloring and cherries. Serve over ham ring. Yield: 8 servings.

Mrs. Rea B. Judd, Medina H. S.
Medina, North Dakota

JUICY HAM LOAF

½ lb. ground smoked ham
½ lb. ground steak
½ ground pork steak
½ c. cracker crumbs
¾ c. milk
½ c. tomato soup
½ tsp. salt
1 egg, slightly beaten
⅓ c. brown sugar

Combine all ingredients except brown sugar. Sprinkle in ungreased 5 x 8-inch pan with brown sugar. Pack meat mixture into pan. Bake at 350 degrees for 1 hour and 30 minutes.

Mrs. Clara O'Neal, North Jr. H. S.
Rapid City, South Dakota

MRS. HOLMES' HAM LOAF

1 lb. ground smoked ham
½ lb. ground beef
½ lb. ground fresh pork
½ c. cracker crumbs
½ c. milk

Combine all ingredients; blend well. Form into a loaf. Wrap in a cheesecloth. Steam in large steamer for 2 hours. Yield: 6 servings.

Emma K. Manghan, Weber H. S.
Odgen, Utah

MY BEST HAM LOAF

1 lb. ground smoked ham
½ lb. ground beef
½ lb. ground pork
2 eggs
½ c. bread crumbs
⅓ c. milk
Salt to taste
1 c. water or tomatoes

Combine all ingredients except water or tomatoes. Shape into a loaf; place in 9-inch pan. Pour water or tomatoes over loaf. Cover; bake at 350 degrees for 1 hour and 15 minutes. Yield: 8 servings.

Mrs. Margaret B. Snook, Ford H. S.
Ford, Kansas

LIVER LOAF

1 lb. beef liver
½ lb. pork sausage
1 med. onion, chopped
1 c. dry bread crumbs
1 tsp. Worcestershire sauce
1 tbsp. lemon juice
1 tsp. salt
1 tsp. celery salt
Dash of pepper
2 eggs, beaten
4 slices bacon

Cover liver with hot water; simmer for 5 minutes; drain and reserve 1/2 cup stock. Put liver and onion through food chopper, using medium blade. Add liver stock and remaining ingredients except bacon. Form mixture to fit a 10 x 5 x 3-inch loaf pan. Top with bacon slices. Bake at 350 degrees for 45 minutes. Yield: 6-8 servings.

Mrs. Reva Bishop, North Hardin H. S.
Vine Grove, Kentucky

RED-CAPPED LIVER LOAF

1 lb. liver
1 c. boiling water
½ lb. pork sausage
1 lge. onion
1 c. bread crumbs
2 eggs, slightly beaten
¼ c. chopped green pepper
1 tsp. salt
1 tsp. paprika
¼ c. chili sauce
¼ tsp. dry mustard
1 tsp. Worcestershire sauce

Cook liver in boiling water for 10 minutes; drain, reserving liquid. Put liver, sausage and onion through a meat grinder. Mix bread crumbs, reserved lqiuid, eggs, green pepper, salt and paprika with meat mixture. Pack into a 9-inch loaf pan. Bake at 350 degrees for 45 minutes. Combine chili sauce, mustard and Worcestershire sauce. Spread over loaf. Bake for 15 minutes longer. Yield: 6 servings.

Mrs. Gail Patton, Hollywood Jr. H. S.
Memphis, Tennessee

LIVERWURST LOAF

½ lb. liverwurst
1 lb. ground beef
1 ¼ c. fine bread crumbs
1 egg, slightly beaten
1 tsp. salt
Dash of pepper

Mash liverwurst; add remaining ingredients. Place in greased 9 x 5-inch loaf pan. Bake at 350 degrees for 45 minutes. Yield: 6-8 servings.

Mrs. Mary Bray, Clinton H. S.
Clinton, New York

BARBECUED MEAT LOAVES

3 strips bacon
½ c. dry bread crumbs
½ c. evaporated milk
1 egg
2 tsp. salt
2 tbsp. chopped onion
1 ½ lb. ground chuck
½ lb. lean ground pork
½ c. catsup
½ c. vinegar
1 tbsp. Worcestershire sauce
1 tsp. chili powder
2 tbsp. chopped onion

Mix bacon with crumbs, milk, egg and salt; add onion, beef and pork. Shape into eight small individual meat rolls; place on shallow oiled baking pan. Combine catsup, vinegar, Worcestershire sauce, chili powder and onion. Heat and pour over meat rolls. Bake at 350 degrees for 45 minutes. Baste with sauce occasionally. NOTE: One-half strip bacon may be placed on top each roll before baking.

Mrs. Berivice Peterson
Anthon-Oto Comm. School, Anthon, Iowa

COVERED WAGON

8 strips bacon
1 egg, beaten
1 lb. minced round steak
1 lb. minced lean pork
3 tbsp. chopped onion
½ tsp. salt
½ c. tomato soup

Line loaf pan with bacon slices. Combine remaining ingredients.

BREAD STUFFING:

2 ½ c. crumbs
1 tsp. salt
½ tsp. sage
½ tsp. parsley
2 tbsp. butter, melted
1 sm. onion, chopped

Combine all ingredients; mix well. Press one-half of meat mixture into pan; cover with stuffing mixture. Add remaining meat mixture. Bake at 425 degrees for 45 minutes. Yield: 8 servings.

Mrs. M. H. McPherson, Branton School
Calgary, Alberta, Canada

FLUFFY MEAT LOAF

1 lb. ground veal
½ lb. ground lean pork
3 med. slices soft bread, torn into small pieces
1 c. milk
1 egg, beaten
¼ c. minced onion
1 ¼ tsp. salt
¼ tsp. pepper
¼ dry mustard
¼ tsp. celery salt
¼ tsp. garlic salt
1 tbsp. Worcestershire sauce

Combine all ingredients; shape into loaf on shallow baking pan. Bake at 350 degrees for 1 hour and 30 minutes. Yield: 8 servings.

Frances Rodriguez, Espanola H. S.
Espanola, New Mexico

HORSERADISH MEAT LOAF

1 ½ lb. ground beef
½ lb. ground pork
¼ c. grated or ¾ c. chopped onion
2 eggs
1 c. ground dry bread crumbs or 2 c. soft bread crumbs
2 tbsp. to ⅓ c. horseradish
1 tsp. mustard
1 tsp. salt
⅛ tsp. pepper
¼ to ⅓ c. catsup or tomato soup
¼ to ⅓ c. milk

Thoroughly mix all ingredients; shape into loaf. Score top in diagonal lines. Bake at 350 degrees for 1 hour or until done. Yield: 6-8 servings.

Mrs. Theda Moser, Meridian Jr. H. S.
Meridian, Ohio
Mrs. Helen Mason, Cascade H. S.
Clayton, Indiana

INDIAN MEAT LOAF

1 lb. ground chuck
½ lb. ground pork or sausage
2 tsp. salt
¼ tsp. pepper
1 egg
½ c. corn meal
2 tsp. sage
½ c. cream-style corn
1 ¼ c. canned tomatoes
¼ c. chopped green pepper (opt.)
¼ c. chopped onion
Tomato juice

Combine meats; brown slowly in skillet. Pour off grease. Combine meats, salt, pepper, egg, corn meal, sage, corn, tomatoes, green pepper and onion. Pack into loaf pan. Cover with tomato juice. Bake at 350 degrees for 35 to 45 minutes. Yield: 6-8 servings.

Mrs. Willa Didway, Post H. S.
Post, Texas

MEAT LOAF

1 lb. ground beef
½ lb. sausage
1 onion, finely chopped
1 egg, beaten
1 cup canned tomatoes
1 c. fine bread crumbs
1 tsp. salt
⅛ tsp. pepper

Mix all ingredients well; shape into loaf. Place in pan. Bake in preheated 350 degree oven for 1 hour to 1 hour and 30 minutes. Yield: 4 servings.

Mary Lynch Chesnutt, Fulton H. S.
Knoxville, Tennessee

MEAT LOAF

1 lb. minced beef
½ lb. minced veal
1 c. quick cooking cereal
2 tsp. salt
½ tsp. garlic salt
¼ tsp. pepper
1 med. onion, finely chopped
2 stalks celery with leaves, chopped
3 tbsp. diced green pepper
1 egg, slightly beaten
1 c. tomato soup
1 tbsp. mustard
1 tsp. vinegar
1 tsp. water

Combine meats, cereal, salt, garlic salt, pepper, onion, celery, green pepper, egg and tomato soup. Press into a well greased loaf pan. Mix mustard, vinegar and water; spread over top of the meat loaf. Bake at 350 degrees for 1 hour and 30 minutes. Yield: 6 servings.

Mrs. Barbara Goedicke
Lindsay Thurber Composite H. S.
Red Deer, Alberta, Canada

MEAT LOAF

1 lb. ground beef or veal
½ lb. lean ground pork
2 c. soft bread crumbs
1 egg, beaten
1 ½ c. milk
4 tbsp. minced onion
2 tbsp. minced mango (opt.)
2 tsp. salt
¼ tsp. pepper
1 tbsp. catsup (opt.)
¼ tsp. dry mustard (opt.)
⅛ tsp. sage (opt.)
2 tbsp. Worcestershire sauce (opt.)

Combine all ingredients; pack into greased 9 x 5 x 3-inch loaf pan. Bake at 350 degrees for 1 hour and 30 minutes. Yield: 8 servings.

Mrs. Dorothy J. Campbell, Riverside H. S.
Milan, Washington
Elaine Buerkel, Buckeye Valley H. S.
Columbus, Ohio

MEAT LOAF WITH SPICED PEACHES

1 ½ c. fine dry bread crumbs
1 c. milk
1 c. catsup
4 tsp. salt
¼ tsp. pepper
4 tsp. Worcestershire sauce
2 tsp. prepared mustard
4 eggs
6 tbsp. chopped onion
½ lb. ground pork
3 ½ lb. ground chuck

Combine bread crumbs, milk, catsup, salt, pepper, Worcestershire sauce and mustard in a 4-quart bowl. Add eggs; beat well with spoon. Add onion, pork and chuck; mix thoroughly. Divide mixture in half; shape into 10 x 5-inch loaves on greased shallow baking pan. Bake at 350 degrees for 1 hour. Turn out onto platter.

SPICED PEACHES:

2 No. 2 ½ cans peach halves, drained
2 whole cloves
¼ c. brown sugar
2 tbsp. butter

Cut peaches into halves; stud with cloves. Arrange in shallow baking pan. Sprinkle with brown sugar; dot with butter. Bake at 350 degrees for about 15 minutes. Arrange Spiced Peaches around meat loaf. Yield: 16-20 servings.

Mrs. Lucille King, Nazareth, H. S.
Nazareth, Texas

PECAN MEAT LOAF

1 ½ lb. ground beef
¼ lb. ground pork
3 wieners, ground
1 can tomato soup
1 can pecans, chopped
3 slices bread, soaked
Salt and pepper

Combine meats, 1/2 can soup, pecans, bread, salt and pepper. Shape into loaf. Place loaf in greased pan. Add 4 to 6 tablespoonfuls water. Bake at 350 degrees for 45 minutes. Slice. Add remaining soup to juices in pan. Serve with sauce. Yield: 6-8 servings.

Mrs. Hazelle P. Wright, Wilkinson Co. H. S.
Irwinton, Georgia

PERFECT MEAT LOAF

1 ½ lb. ground beef
½ lb. ground pork
¼ c. finely chopped onion
2 tbsp. finely chopped celery
½ tsp. salt
½ tsp. poultry seasoning
¼ tsp. dry mustard
4 slices soft bread, cubed
½ c. milk
2 eggs
1 tbsp. Worcestershire sauce

(Continued on next page)

Mix meats thoroughly; add onion, celery and seasonings. Soak bread in milk; add eggs and Worcestershire sauce. Beat with rotary beater. Combine meats and egg mixture; form into a loaf. Bake at 350 degrees for 1 hour. Yield: 8-10 servings.

Alberta Ball Bickerdike, East Pike School
Milton, Illinois

SAVORY MEAT LOAF

½ lb. ground beef
½ lb. ground veal
½ lb. ground pork
6 slices bread
1 c. milk
1 c. buttermilk
¼ c. grated onion
½ c. grated raw potato
2 tsp. salt
½ tsp. pepper
2 tsp. sugar

Grind meats together three times. Remove crusts from bread; soak in milk for 1 hour. Thoroughly mix all ingredients. Pack into 5 x 9-inch loaf pan. Bake at 350 degrees for 1 hour and 30 minutes. Yield: 6 servings.

Mrs. Irene Wells, Ulysses, H. S.
Ulysses, Kansas

STUFFED MEAT LOAF SUPREME

1 lb. ground round beef
½ lb. ground pork
¾ c. quick cooking oats
1 egg, slightly beaten
¼ c. chopped onion
1 tsp. seasoned salt
¼ tsp. pepper
1 8-oz. can tomato sauce

Combine all ingredients except 1/2 can tomato sauce. Pack into 9 x 5 x 3-inch pan, reserving 2 cups of mixture.

STUFFING:

2 tbsp. chopped onion
1 ½ c. chopped carrots
⅔ c. chopped green pepper
⅓ c. margarine
½ tsp. dried thyme
½ tsp. salt
⅛ tsp. pepper
1 ½ c. white toast cubes
1 egg, slightly beaten

Saute onion, carrots and green pepper in margarine. Combine with remaining ingredients. Spread over meat mixture in pan. Top with remaining meat. Bake at 350 degrees for 1 hour and 15 minutes. Pour remaining tomato sauce over top. Bake for 15 minutes longer.

Mrs. Irene Alexander, Du Pont H. S.
Belle, West Virginia

VENISON MEAT LOAF

1 lb. ground venison
¾ lb. sausage
1 lge. onion, chopped
¼ c. green pepper, chopped
2 tbsp. fat
1 c. milk
1 ½ c. bread or cracker crumbs
2 eggs, well beaten
1 No. 2 can tomatoes
1 tsp. monosodium glutamate
1 tsp. salt
½ tsp. pepper

Combine venison and sausage. Brown onion and green pepper in fat. Combine milk, bread crumbs, eggs, tomatoes, monosodium glutamate, salt and pepper; add onion and meat. Mix well; form into two loaves. Bake at 350 degrees for 45 minutes to 1 hour. Yield: 8-10 servings.

Mrs. Barbara McClanahan, Central H. S.
Columbia, Tennessee

HUM-DINGERS

2 eggs
1 c. catsup
1 ½ lb. ground pork
1 ½ lb. ground beef
1 onion, chopped
1 green pepper, chopped
1 ½ c. oats
1 ½ tsp. salt
½ tsp. pepper
10 strips bacon

Combine all ingredients except bacon; shape into 10 balls. Flatten to 1 inch thickness. Wrap each pattie with a bacon strip. Place on foil-lined cookie sheet. Bake at 350 degrees for 20 minutes. Turn patties. Bake at 15 minutes longer or until done.

Carolyn Wayman, Mooreland H. S.
Mooreland, Oklahoma

PATTIES WITH MUSHROOM SOUP

1 lb. ground beef
½ lb. ground pork
Salt and pepper
¼ c. cream
2 c. toasted bread cubes
1 sm. onion, finely chopped
1 tbsp. chopped parsley
3 tbsp. salad oil
1 tbsp. poultry seasoniong
1 10 ½-oz. can cream of mushroom soup
½ soup can water

Combine meats, seasonings and cream; mix thoroughly. Form into 16 patties. Combine bread cubes, onion, parsley, salad oil, additional salt, pepper and remaining seasonings. Place stuffing on eight patties; cover with remaining patties. Press into balls. Brown in hot fat. Add mushroom soup mixed with water. Cover

(Continued on next page)

and bake at 350 degrees for 1 hour. Yield: 8 servings.

Mrs. Palm, Kathleen H. S.
Kathleen, Florida

PARTY-STYLE CROQUETTES

1 8-oz. pkg. link pork sausage, diced
1 c. finely chopped onions
2 c. diced cooked turkey or chicken
1 can cream of chicken soup
2 tbsp. snipped parsley
1 egg, lightly beaten
50 potato snack crackers, finely rolled
¾ c. cracker meal

Brown sausage pieces in frying pan. Remove sausage. Saute onions in drippings until tender. Add sausage and remaining ingredients except cracker meal. Mix well. Shape into 10 or 12 croquettes. Roll in cracker meat. Store in refrigerator until serving time. Brush with salad oil. Bake at 350 degrees for 20 minutes.

SHERRY CHEESE SAUCE:

¼ c. Sherry
¼ c. grated Parmesan cheese
1 can cream of chicken soup

Add Sherry and cheese to soup. Heat slowly until cheese melts. Spoon over croquettes.

Photograph for this recipe on page 235.

HAMBURGER, SAUSAGE AND CORN PIE

1 lb. sausage
2 lge. onions, chopped
1 green pepper, chopped
1 lb. hamburger, chopped
1 recipe corn bread

Fry sausage, onions and green pepper until almost done; add hamburger. Cook until hamburger is nearly done. Place in 13 x 11-inch baking pan. Pour corn bread batter over top. Bake at 375 degrees for 20 minutes or until done. Yield: 12 servings.

Mrs. Dorothy Bent, Whitcomb H. S.
Bethel, Vermont

MEAT OR PORK PIE

1 ½ lb. fresh ground pork
¾ lb. fresh ground beef
1 sm. onion, finely chopped
¾ tsp. salt
¼ tsp. pepper
½ tsp. ground cloves
1 ¼ c. mashed cooked potatoes
Pastry for two-crust pie

Mix pork, beef, onion, salt, pepper and cloves in large skillet; brown over medium heat. Add mashed potatoes; mix thoroughly. Remove from heat. Spoon mixture into pastry-lined pie pan; cover with top crust. Bake at 375 degrees for 25 to 30 minutes. Serve hot. Yield: 12 servings.

Sister Mary Constance, Holy Family H. S.
Fitchburg, Massachusetts

NATCHITOCHES MEAT PIES

½ c. plus 1 tbsp. shortening
Flour
½ lb. ground beef
1 ½ lb. ground pork
2 lge. dry onions, chopped
6 green onions, chopped
3 tbsp. parsley, chopped
Salt and pepper to taste
2 tsp. baking powder
2 eggs
Milk

Make a roux of 1 tablespoonful shortening and 2 tablespoonfuls flour; add meats, onions, parsley, salt and pepper. Cook thoroughly; cool. Sift 4 cups flour and baking powder; add 1/2 cup melted shortening and eggs. Add enough milk to make stiff dough. Roll very thin. Cut circles of dough, using saucer. Fill one-half full with meat mixture. Fold dough over; dampen edges with water. Crimp edges with fork. Fry in deep fat until golden brown. Pies may be baked. Yield: 18 pies.

Mrs. Mary S. Parsons, Roanoke H. S.
Roanoke, Louisiana

BEST EVER BEEF ROLL UPS

1 round steak, cut ½-in. thick
½ lb. ground beef
¼ lb. fresh pork sausage
1 c. soft bread crumbs
2 tbsp. chopped onion
2 tbsp. chopped parsley
¼ tsp. curry powder
¼ tsp. garlic salt
¼ c. flour
3 tbsp. fat
1 10 ½-oz. can consomme
2 tbsp. catsup

Cut steak into six pieces; pound to 1/4-inch thickness. Mix ground beef with sausage, bread crumbs, onion, parsley, curry powder and garlic salt. Place about 1/4 cup meat-crumb mixture on each piece of steak; roll as for a jelly roll. Fasten with toothpicks or skewers. Dredge beef rolls in flour; brown slowly in fat or drippings. Pour off drippings. Combine consomme and catsup; add to meat. Cover tightly. Cook slowly for 1 hour and 30 minutes or until meat is tender. Thicken cooking liquid with additional flour for gravy, if desired. Yield: 6 servings.

Mrs. June G. Walker, Eastern Jr. H. S.
Silver Springs, Maryland

CHICKEN-HAM ROLLS

2 c. sifted flour
2 ½ tsp. baking powder
¾ tsp. salt
4 to 6 tbsp. shortening
⅔ to ¾ c. milk
⅓ c. finely chopped onions
2 tbsp. butter
1 ½ c. around cooked ham
3 c. ground cooked chicken
1 ¼ c. cold chicken-milk gravy

Sift flour with baking powder and salt; cut in shortening. Stir in milk to form a soft dough. Roll out on floured board to 1/4-inch thick. Brown onion in butter; combine onion, ham, chicken and gravy. Spread on dough. Roll dough as for jelly roll. Cut in 1-inch slices. Place in a greased shallow pan; brush with additional melted butter. Bake at 450 degrees for 15 minutes. Serve with cheese sauce, if desired. Yield: 10 servings.

Betsy Mynette Wright
Stephen F. Austin Jr. H. S.
Galveston, Texas

HAM SWIRLS

2 c. prepared biscuit mix
⅔ c. milk
Melted butter
1 tsp. brown sugar
1 tsp. salad mustard
1 tsp. catsup
Salt to taste
⅓ lb. ground pork
⅓ lb. ground veal
⅓ lb. ground ham

Combine biscuit mix and milk; roll into 8 x 12-inch rectangle. Brush with melted butter. Combine remaining ingredients; spread on dough. Roll as for jelly roll. Cut into seven slices. Place on greased sheet. Bake at 400 degrees for 30 minutes. Serve with cheese or mushroom sauce, if desired.

Mrs. Mary Ann Block, Neponset H. S.
Neponset, Illinois

THREE TASTES ROAST

1 ½ lb. round steak, ¼-in. thick
1 ½ lb. fresh ham steak, ¼-in. thick
1 ½ lb. veal steak, ¼-in. thick
Salt and pepper
½ c. snipped parsley
2 tbsp. shortening
1 10 ½-oz. can consomme
½ c. sliced celery
1 med. onion, sliced
4 whole cloves
¼ c. flour
¼ c. water

Sprinkle steaks with salt, pepper and parsley. Stack steaks, starting with round and ending with veal. Roll steaks as for jelly roll; tie with a cord. Brown meat roll on all sides in shortening in Dutch oven at medium heat. Pour into consomme; add celery, onions and cloves. Cover; roast at 325 degrees for 2 hours and 30 minutes or until tender. Remove meat; untie cord. Strain gravy; blend flour with water. Stir into gravy; cook over medium heat, stirring until thickened. Slice meat; serve with gravy. Yield: 8-10 servings.

Mrs. Paula E. Compton, Custer Co. H. S.
Miles City, Montana

VEAL AMANDINE

1 onion, chopped
¼ c. plus 2 tbsp. butter
½ lb. chicken livers
2 cloves or garlic, crushed
2 tbsp. chopped parsley
2 tbsp. Bouquet Garni
2 tbsp. thyme
Salt and pepper
1 egg, slightly beaten
16 slices veal
1 can chicken broth
1 c. sour cream

Saute onion in 2 tablespoonfuls butter until tender; add chicken livers and garlic. Cook for 10 minutes. Mash livers; add parsley, Bouquet Garni, thyme, 1 teaspoonful salt, 1/8 teaspoonful pepper and egg. Tenderize veal; sprinkle lightly with salt and pepper. Spread stuffing on veal slices; roll tightly and tie with two pieces of string. Saute veal rolls until golden brown in remaining butter. Place in 3-quart casserole. Pour chicken broth on top. Cover; bake at 350 degrees for 45 minutes. Spread sour cream on top. Bake for 15 minutes. Serve with noodles or rice, if desired. Yield: 6-8 servings.

Aldine M. Bullard, North Bethesda Jr. H. S.
Bethesda, Maryland

BARBECUED SAUSAGE AND CHICKEN

1 ½ c. catsup
1 c. water
Juice of 1 lemon
1 lemon, sliced
4 tbsp. brown sugar
3 tbsp. Worcestershire sauce
1 tbsp. prepared mustard
1 c. finely chopped celery
1 tbsp. onion salt
1 tsp. garlic salt
1 pkg. Polish sausage, cut into serving pieces
1 2 to 3 ½-lb. chicken, cut up

Combine all ingredients except sausage and chicken; heat to boiling point. Brown sausage in heavy skillet. Add sausage and chicken to the sauce. Simmer for 1 hour and 30 minutes. Serve hot. Yield: 6-8 servings.

Mrs. Nerine Kinsey, Gatesville H. S.
Gatesville, Texas

CAJUN SPAGHETTI SAUCE

1 2 to 3-lb. chicken
2 to 3 lb. onions

(Continued on next page)

2 cloves of garlic
1 lb. hot link sausage, cut up
1 tbsp. brown sugar
3 tbsp. chili powder
Salt and pepper to taste
1 tbsp. Worcestershire sauce
2 lge. cans tomato paste
1 can cream of mushroom soup

Cook chicken in water until tender; remove from broth and remove bones. Cook onions and garlic in broth until tender. Add chicken, sausage, seasonings and tomato paste to onions. Simmer for 1 to 2 hours on low heat. Add soup; serve over spaghetti or rice, if desired.

Sandra King, Assistant Supervisor
Southwest Dist. State Department of Education
Montevallo, Alabama

CHICKEN AND OYSTER GUMBO

1 c. flour
1 ½ c. cooking oil
2 onions, minced
1 c. minced celery
1 green pepper, minced
Seasonings to taste
1 4 to 5-lb. chicken, cut up
3 c. cold water
2 qt. boiling water
1 pt. oysters
½ c. minced parsley
½ c. minced onion tops
1 tbsp. file

Cook flour in hot oil until dark brown, stirring rapidly. Add onions, celery and green pepper; saute for 3 minutes. Season chicken. Add chicken to onion mixture; cook for 15 minutes. Turn heat to low. Gradually add cold water, stirring constantly. Add boiling water; cook until meat is tender. Season to taste. Add oysters, parsley and onion tops; cook for 15 minutes. Remove from heat; add file. Stir well. Serve with cooked rice, if desired. Yield: 10 servings.

Mrs. Evelyn B. Fontenot, Church Point H. S.
Church Point, Louisiana

CUBAN CHICKEN

1 c. converted rice
¼ c. salad oil
¼ tsp. pepper
4 tbsp. minced onion
1 clove of garlic, minced
2 c. chicken stock
2 tsp. salt
1 tsp. paprika
1 chicken, boiled and cut into pieces
1 c. cooked slivered ham
½ c. stuffed olives, sliced
Asparagus tips
Peas
Pimento, cut into strips

Wash rice. Heat salad oil and pepper in large frying pan; add onion, garlic and rice. Cook over low heat until rice is yellow. Add stock, salt and paprika. Cover tightly; cook over low heat until rice is cooked. Add chicken, ham and olives. Heat thoroughly; place in center of large platter. Surround with cooked asparagus tips and peas; garnish with strips of pimento. Yield: 6 servings.

Mrs. Janelle Farrell, Cleburne H. S.
Cleburn, Texas

RASOITT

1 to 6 chicken giblets
1 lge. hamburger pattie
¼ med. onion, chopped
1 clove of garlic
1 tsp. parsley
1 tsp. Italian seasoning
Salt and pepper to taste
Mushrooms (opt.)
2 tbsp. table wine
2 tbsp. tomato sauce
2 c. instant rice
2 qt. chicken broth
½ c. grated cheese

Brown giblets, hamburger, onion and seasonings. Add wine and tomato sauce, then rice and 4 cups chicken broth. Cook for 20 minutes adding remaining chicken broth as necessary. Before serving, add grated cheese.

Mrs. Nancy E. Perotti, Quincy Jr.-Sr. H. S.
Quincy, California

SOUTHSEAS CHICKEN

1 6-lb. roasting chicken
2 tbsp. peanut oil
1 6-oz. can water chestnuts, sliced
1 6-oz. can bamboo shoots, cut into 1-in. squares
9 stalks celery, sliced
6 oz. ham, diced
1 ½ c. chicken broth
1 tsp. salt
¼ tsp. monosodium glutamate
1 tbsp. cornstarch
1 tbsp. flour
1 tbsp. soy sauce
1 6-oz. can small mushrooms

Remove skin from chicken; slice meat off bone against grain into small pieces. Heat oil in a large skillet; saute chicken for 10 minutes or until brown. Mix chestnuts, bamboo shoots, celery, ham and 1 cup chicken broth; cover. Bring to a boil; cook over low heat for 10 minutes. Mix salt with monosodium glutamate, cornstarch, flour and soy sauce; add remaining chicken broth. Add to ham mixture, stirring constantly; add mushrooms. Cover; cook over low heat for 5 to 10 minutes. Serve over wild rice, if desired.

Jane Poole, Asheboro Jr. H. S.
Asheboro, North Carolina

STUFFED CABBAGE

1 green cabbage
1 lb. ground beef
½ lb. ground pork
2 eggs, beaten
1 med. onion, chopped
½ c. cooked rice
2 tsp. salt
¼ tsp. pepper
⅓ c. milk
1 c. tomato juice
1 c. beef broth
¼ c. cider vinegar
2 tbsp. sugar
1 bay leaf
¼ tsp. pepper

Leave cabbage whole but ream out some of the solid core. Cover with boiling water; cook for 10 minutes. Drain cabbage carefully; pull off 16 to 18 of the large outer leaves. Trim off part of the thick center ribs. Combine beef, pork, eggs, onion, rice, salt, pepper and enough milk to make a soft mixture. Place a heaping tablespoonful of filling in the center of each cabbage leaf; roll up and tuck in the ends, making a neat package. Place side by side in a shallow baking dish. Combine remaining ingredients; pour over cabbage rolls. Cover; bake in preheated 350 degree oven for 1 hour. Yield: 6 servings.

Esther Darst Minton, Nogales H. S.
Nogales, Arizona

CITY CHICKEN

2 lb. veal steak
2 lb. pork tenderloin
1 egg, beaten
1 c. cracker crumbs or 1 c. cracker meal
4 tbsp. butter
Salt and pepper to taste
2 c. water
1 c. milk

Cut meat into 1 1/2-inch squares; place three veal and three pork pieces alternately on skewers. Roll in egg and cracker crumbs. Brown in butter on all sides; season with salt and pepper. Place in roaster, Dutch oven or electric skillet. Add water. Cover; bake at 350 degrees for 2 hours or until tender. Remove chicken; add milk to broth left in pan. Serve with meat. Yield: 12 servings.

Mrs. Deloris C. Boggess, Lumberport H. S.
Lumberport, West Virginia

EXTRA SPECIAL BAKED CHICKEN

1 3-oz. pkg. sliced dried beef
3 lge. chicken breasts, boned, skinned and halved
6 slices bacon
1 can cream of mushroom soup
1 c. sour cream

Run cold water over dried beef; drain. Arrange in bottom of 12 x 8 x 2-inch baking dish. Place halved chicken breasts over beef; top each half with a slice of bacon. Bake, uncovered, at 350 degrees for 30 minutes. Combine soup and sour cream; pour over chicken. Bake for 25 minutes longer. Bake for 25 minutes longer. Yield: 6 servings.

Nancy Simonton, Wade Hampton H. S.
Greenville, South Carolina
Mrs. Darrell Bare, Graham H. S.
Graham, North Carolina

PETTI DI POLLO LOMBARDY

12 chicken breast halves, boned
Salt and pepper
4 cloves of garlic, crushed
Flour
3 tbsp. butter
3 tbsp. oil
½ tsp. dried tarragon
1 ½ c. chicken broth
½ c. dry white wine (opt.)
12 slices boiled ham
12 thin slices Mozzarella cheese

Sprinkle both sides of chicken with salt, pepper and garlic; dredge lightly with flour. Heat butter and oil in heavy skillet; saute chicken until golden brown. Remove chicken to shallow casserole; sprinkle with tarragon. Add broth to pan drippings and heat while scraping up the brown particles. Add wine; bring to a boil and pour over chicken. Cover; bake at 350 degrees for 30 minutes. Top each breast with 1 slice of ham. Bake 20 minutes longer. Top ham with cheese. Bake, uncovered, for about 5 minutes or until cheese is melted.

Sister Romaine, C. D. P., Marycrest H. S.
Allison Park, Pennsylvania

VEAL-HAM DINNER

1 thin slice veal
Flour
Butter
1 slice Swiss cheese
1 slice ham
Salt and pepper to taste
Cream of mushroom soup
Dash of cooking Sherry

Dredge veal in flour; brown in butter. Place veal in oiled casserole. Place slice of cheese on top of veal; place ham slice on top of cheese. Season with salt and pepper to taste. Pour on mushrooms soup and Sherry. Bake at 350 degrees for 35 minutes. Yield: 1 serving.

May M. Rorick, The Dalles H. S.
The Dalles, Oregon

Appetizer Favorites

APPETIZER MEAT BALLS

1 lb. lean beef, ground
1 tsp. salt
½ c. corn flake crumbs
¼ tsp. pepper
¼ c. catsup or chili sauce
1 tbsp. Worcestershire sauce
¼ c. finely chopped onion
½ c. evaporated milk

Mix all ingredients in a 2-quart bowl. Shape mixture into 3 dozen tiny meat balls, using a teaspoonful of mixture for each. Place in a 13 x 9-inch pan. Bake at 400 degrees for 12 to 15 minutes or until brown. It is not necessary to turn meat balls as they bake. Insert a toothpick in each. Serve with hot barbecue sauce, if desired. NOTE: May be frozen after baking. Just before serving, reheat in barbecue sauce. Insert toothpicks to serve, Yield: 18 servings.

Mrs. Evelyn Rosenbaum, East Bernard H. S.
East Bernard, Texas

APPETIZER SWEDISH MEAT BALLS

1 lb. ground chuck
1 lge. can deviled ham
⅛ tsp. garlic juice
Salt and pepper to taste
Margarine
1 pt. sour cream
1 tbsp. horseradish

Mix ground chuck, deviled ham, garlic juice, salt and pepper; shape into small balls. Brown balls in a small amount of margarine; shake balls while browning to retain shape. Heat sour cream and horseradish over low heat; add meat balls. Serve on toothpicks. Yield: 40 meat balls.

Shannon Fewell, Jacksonville H. S.
Jacksonville, Arkansas

BITS-O-BEEF EN BROCHETTE

2 lb. beef round, cut into ¼-in. slices
¾ c. soy sauce
1 tbsp. Worcestershire sauce
1 clove of garlic, mashed
¼ c. Sherry
1 tsp. sugar
½ tsp. minced onion

Cut beef slices into 1 1/2 to 2-inch squares. Combine all remaining ingredients; blend well. Pour mixture over meat; stir well to coat. Marinate beef for several hours or overnight. Place beef on small metal skewers; broil for 5 minutes or until brown, turning occasionally. May be served with a sweet-sour sauce, if desired. Yield: 6 servings.

Mrs. Gail Henderson, Spencerville H. S.
Spencerville, Ohio

CHINESE MEAT BALLS

1 lb. ground steak
Milk
Bread crumbs
1 egg
2 tbsp. flour
Salt and pepper to taste
½ c. peanut oil
1 can pineapple chunks
1 c. chicken broth or bouillon
2 lge. green peppers, cut into 1-in. pieces
3 tbsp. cornstarch
1 tbsp. soy sauce
½ tsp. monosodium glutamate
½ c. brown sugar

Mix meat with a small amount of milk and bread crumbs; shape into 20 to 30 small balls. Combine egg, flour, salt and pepper; mix until smooth. Heat peanut oil in large skillet. Dip meat balls into batter; fry until brown on all sides. Remove meat balls; keep warm. Drain pineapple, reserving 1/2 cup juice. Drain all but 1 teaspoonful fat from skillet; add broth, green peppers and pineapple chunks. Cover; cook over medium heat for 10 minutes. Blend reserved pineapple juice with all remaining ingredients; add to skillet. Cook, stirring constantly, until thick. Return meat balls to sauce; heat. Yield: 6-8 servings.

Patsy Trapini, Memorial Jr. H. S.
Valley Stream, Long Island, New York

INDIVIDUAL ITALIAN PIZZAS

1 can tomato sauce
¼ tsp. garlic salt
½ tsp. oregano
½ tsp. pepper
¼ tsp. dry mustard
1 tsp. chili powder
¼ c. minced onion
1 can biscuits
Cooked ground beef
Olives
Mushrooms
Grated or sliced cheese

Combine tomato sauce, garlic salt, oregano, pepper, mustard, chili powder and onion in saucepan. Bring to a boil. Roll out individual pizzas from biscuits. Spread with ground beef, olives, mushrooms and cheese. Cover mixture with sauce. Bake at 400 degrees for 15 to 20 minutes or until edges are brown. NOTE: Tuna, bologna or pepperoni sausage may be used instead of or with ground beef. Yield: 10 servings.

Mrs. Barbara H. Thompson, Tom Bean H. S.
Tom Bean, Texas

MINIATURE MEAT BALLS FOR APPETIZER

1 ½ lb. ground beef
1 egg
¾ c. oats
½ tsp. salt
½ tsp. garlic salt (opt.)

(Continued on next page)

¼ tsp. pepper
¼ tsp. sage
¼ c. finely minced onion
2 tbsp. milk
1 8-oz. can tomato sauce
1 tbsp. vinegar
3 tbsp. brown sugar
1 tbsp. Worcestershire sauce

Combine ground beef with egg, oats, salt, garlic salt, pepper, sage, onion and milk; mix well. Shape into 1-inch balls. Fry in shortening in a large skillet until done. Pour off excess fat. Insert a toothpick into each ball; place in chafing dish. Combine remaining ingredients in a saucepan; heat. Pour sauce into a small bowl; place bowl beside chafing dish. Dip meat balls into sauce. NOTE: Meat balls may be simmered in sauce and served from chafing dish. Yield: 6 dozen meat balls.

Mrs. Ramona Norstedt, Hemet Union H. S.
Hemet, California

PARTY MEAT BALLS

1 lb. ground beef
1 egg, beaten
½ clove of garlic, minced
½ tsp. salt
2 oz. Bleu cheese, cubed
½ c. flour
¼ c. shortening
½ c. beef bouillon

Combine beef and egg; add garlic and salt. Mix well. Shape 1 tablespoonful meat mixture around 1 cube of cheese. Roll in flour; brown in hot shortening. Add bouillon; cover. Simmer for 10 minutes. Insert colored picks in each meat ball; serve hot. Yield: 8 servings.

Mrs. Wade H. Harris, Seagrove H. S.
Seagrove, North Carolina

PUFFS WITH BEEF

1 c. water
½ c. butter
1 c. flour
1 pkg. dry onion soup mix
4 eggs
Ground cooked or dried beef
Chopped pickles
Catsup or Tabasco sauce

Heat water and butter to boiling; stir in flour. Stir constantly until mixture leaves sides of pan and forms a ball. Remove from heat. Shake soup mix through a sieve over flour mixture. Beat in an egg at a time; beat until smooth. Drop mixture by 1/2 teaspoonfuls onto ungreased baking sheet. Bake at 400 degrees for 12 to 15 minutes or until dry. Cool. Combine all remaining ingredients; add enough salad dressing to moisten. Cut open puffs; fill with beef mixture. Yield: 24 servings.

Ethel G. Burns, Chinook H. S.
Chinook, Montana

SWEET AND SOUR MEAT BALLS

1 lb. ground beef
½ tsp. salt
½ tsp. black pepper
¼ c. sliced water chestnuts
4 tbsp. oil
½ c. cold water
2 tbsp. flour
2 tbsp. cornstarch
½ c. sugar
½ c. vinegar
1 tbsp. soy sauce
1 green pepper, chopped
1 red pepper, chopped
1 can pineapple chunks, undrained

Mix beef, salt, black pepper and water chestnuts. Add cold water; mix thoroughly. Form into small balls; roll lightly in flour. Heat oil; brown meat balls. Combine all remaining ingredients; heat. Pour mixture over meat balls; serve with toothpicks. Yield: 6 servings.

Mrs. June Plant, Mesa H. S.
Mesa, Arizona

SWEDISH MEAT BALLS

1 lb. ground beef
¼ lb. ground pork
1 egg
½ c. milk
1 ½ c. bread crumbs
4 tbsp. butter
2 tbsp. minced onion
1 tsp. salt
⅛ tsp. pepper
¼ tsp. nutmeg
¼ tsp. allspice

Combine meats. Mix egg, milk and bread crumbs. Let stand for 15 minutes. Saute onion in 1 tablespoonful butter. Add onion, meat and seasonings to bread crumb mixture; mix thoroughly. Shape into 1-inch balls. Chill until firm. Melt remaining butter in skillet; brown meat balls. Place browned meat balls in baking pan. Bake at 350 degrees for 1 hour. Keep warm until serving. Yield: 10-15 servings.

Mrs. Ann Kretsinger, Central H. S.
Cheyenne, Wyoming

TEENIE HAMBURGER APPETIZERS

1 lb. ground beef
½ c. oats
3 tbsp. chopped onion
1 ½ tsp. salt
¼ tsp. pepper
⅔ c. tomato juice
2 10 ½-oz. cans tomato soup
½ c. sweet pickle relish
½ c. chopped onion
2 tbsp. brown sugar
2 tbsp. vinegar
2 tbsp. Worcestershire sauce

(Continued on next page)

Combine beef, oats, onion, salt, pepper and tomato juice; mix thoroughly. Shape tablespoonfuls of mixture into balls; flatten. Panfry to desired doneness. Combine all remaining ingredients in a saucepan; cover. Simmer until onion is tender. Insert toothpick into each ball; dip into sauce mixture. Yield: 15 to 20 servings.

Sister M. Tabitha, O.S.F., Archbishop Ryan H. S.
Omaha, Nebraska

CHICKEN-ALMOND CANAPE SPREAD

¾ c. cooked or canned chicken
2 tbsp. canned diced roasted almonds
2 tbsp. chopped parsley
¼ tsp. salt
⅛ tsp. cayenne pepper
1 tsp. lemon juice
2 tbsp. mayonnaise

Cut chicken into small pieces; add almonds, parsley, salt, cayenne and lemon juice. Mix well. Moisten with mayonnaise. Spread on crackers or bread. Garnish with an almond and sprig of parsley. Yield: 15 servings.

Sister Mary Ignatius, O.S.F., Madonna H. S.
Chicago, Illinois

CHICKEN-CHEESE TEASER

1 can chicken spread
1 3-oz. pkg. cream cheese, softened
2 tbsp. finely chopped onion
2 tbsp. finely chopped celery
¼ tsp. curry powder

Mix all ingredients; chill. Thin to desired consistency with milk. Serve as dip or spread on crackers. Yield: 1 1/4 cups.

Mrs. Miriam Bobo Templeton
Hickory Tavern H. S.
Gray Court, South Carolina

CHICKEN DELICIOUS SPREAD

1 c. minced chicken
2 crisp bacon slices, crumbled
2 tbsp. diced pared apple
¼ tsp. salt
Dash of pepper
¼ c. mayonnaise
¼ c. cream cheese

Combine all ingredients in blender; blend well. Place in bowl or green pepper half. Surround with bread squares, triangles, toast and crisp crackers, if desired. Yield: 10 servings.

Mrs. M. Jean Henk
Cannon McMillian Jr., H. S.
Canonsburg, Pennsylvania

SNAPPY CHICKEN SPREAD

1 can chicken spread
2 tbsp. mayonnaise
½ tsp. prepared horseradish
¼ tsp. Worcestershire sauce
⅛ tsp. dry mustard
Milk
Crackers

Combine chicken spread, mayonnaise, horseradish, Worcestershire sauce and mustard; chill. Thin to desired consistency with milk. Spread on crackers. Garnish with parsley or crisp bacon, if desired.

Mrs. Mary Weyant, Memorial Jr.-Sr. H. S.
East Paterson, New Jersey

APPETIZER HAM BALL

2 4 ½-oz. cans deviled ham
3 tbsp. chopped stuffed green olives
1 tbsp. prepared mustard
Tabasco sauce to taste
1 3-oz. pkg. cream cheese, softened
2 tsp. milk
Parsley (opt.)

Blend deviled ham with olives, mustard and Tabasco sauce. Form into a ball or place in serving dish. Chill. Combine cream cheese and milk; frost ball with mixture. Keep refrigerated. Remove 15 minutes before serving. Trim with parsley. Yield: 8 servings.

Mrs. Audrey Buhl, Gaylord H. S.
Gaylord, Minnesota
Mrs. Revia C. Munch, Branford H. S.
Branford, Florida
Betty Phillips, Scurry-Rosser School
Scurry, Texas

DEVILED HAM-CHEESE DIP

1 4 ½-oz. can deviled ham
¼ c. grated Swiss cheese
2 tsp. pickle relish
¼ tsp. Tabasco sauce
4 tsp. mayonnaise

Combine deviled ham and cheese; stir in pickle relish, Tabasco sauce and mayonnaise. Serve with potato chips, pretzels or crisp crackers. Yield: 2/3 cup.

Elizabeth Chenoweth, Area Consultant
Home and Family Life Education
Texas Education Agency
Corpus Christi, Texas

DEVILED HAM DIP

1 4 ½-oz. can deviled ham
1 8-oz. pkg. cream cheese, softened
1 tbsp. catsup
1 to 2 tbsp. finely chopped onion
2 tbsp. finely chopped stuffed green olives

Combine all ingredients; blend well. If dip is too stiff, a small amount of salad dressing may be added. Yield: 1 2/3 cups.

Mrs. Joel Ferrell, Brinkley H. S.
Brinkley, Arkansas

FRANKFURTER DIP

1 sm. jar yellow mustard
1 sm. jar currant jelly
1 lb. frankfurters

Place mustard and jelly in saucepan; heat over very low heat. Cut frankfurters into diagonal 1/2 to 1-inch slices. Add frankfurters to mustard-jelly mixture. Heat through over low heat. Just before serving, transfer mixture to a chafing dish. Spear frankfurters pieces with toothpicks. Yield: 20-25 servings.

Mrs. Amy Martzke, Oak Creek H. S.
Oak Creek, Wisconsin
Mrs. E. H. Price, Washington H. S.
South Bend, Indiana

PASTRY COCKTAIL DOGS

1 pkg. refrigerated crescent rolls
24 cocktail wieners
8 tbsp. hot mustard

Cut each crescent roll into three triangles; wrap around weiners. Deep fat fry wrapped weiners for 3 to 5 minutes or until golden brown. Serve on toothpicks or with cocktail forks on tray with hot mustard dish in center of tray; dip weiners into hot mustard. Yield: 24 cocktail dogs.

Mrs. Walter A. Kipps, III
Ridgefield Memorial H. S.
Ridgefield, New Jersey

SPICY FRANKS

1 ½ lb. frankfurters, cut into 1-in. pieces
1 tbsp. butter
1 tbsp. prepared mustard
1 10 ¾-oz. can tomato soup
1 tbsp. Worcestershire sauce
2 tsp. lemon juice

Brown frankfurters in butter; stir in all remaining ingredients. Cook over low heat for 5 minutes, stirring occasionally. Serve on toothpicks. Yield: 10-15 servings.

Mrs. Sandra Sue Riedel, Morland H. S.
Morland, Kansas

LAMB AND CHEESE PINWHEELS

2 c. sifted flour
1 ½ tsp. salt
⅔ c. shortening
½ c. grated Cheddar cheese
⅓ c. cold water
½ c. mayonnaise
1 lb. ground lamb
½ tsp. rosemary
⅛ tsp. pepper

Combine flour and 1 teaspoonful salt; cut in shortening until mixture is like corn meal. Stir in cheese. Add water; mix lightly. Press into ball. Roll out on lightly floured surface into 12 x 18-inch rectangle; spread with mayonnaise. Combine remaining ingredients; mix well. Sprinkle over mayonnaise. Roll up like a jelly roll. Starting at the longest side, cut into 1/2-inch slices. Place on ungreased baking sheets. Bake at 425 degrees for 15 minutes or until pastry is lightly browned. Yield: 36 servings.

Mrs. Gloria J. Love, Cumberland Valley H. S.
Mechanicsburg, Pennsylvania

CHICKEN LIVER PATE

2 or 3 chicken livers
1 med. onion, finely chopped
1 tbsp. margarine
Salt and pepper
1 hard-cooked egg

Saute livers and onion in margarine; add salt and pepper to taste. Chop livers with egg until fine; add onion and margarine. If mixture is too dry, an additional tablespoonful of melted margarine may be added. Serve on salted crackers or onion wafers. Yield: 4-6 servings.

Mrs. B. Steinberg, Edison Jr. H. S.
West Orange, New Jersey

CHICKEN LIVER PATE

1 lb. chicken livers
1 ½ c. boiling water
¼ c. butter, melted
1 c. chopped pared apples
⅓ c. chopped onion
1 clove of garlic, crushed
Dash of thyme
Dash of marjoram
¼ c. cooking Sherry
¼ tsp. salt
Dash of pepper

Simmer chicken livers in water for 2 to 3 minutes. Drain; reserve 3/4 to 1 cup of liquid. Saute livers in butter until brown; add apples, onion, garlic, thyme and marjoram. Add Sherry and reserved liquid. Simmer for 15 minutes or until liquid is absorbed; grind in food chopper or blender until fine. Add salt and pepper; chill. Yield: 2 cups.

Marleen Hendershot, Attica Local
Attica, Ohio

CHICKEN LIVER SPREAD

1 med. onion, chopped
1 stick butter
1 lb. chicken livers

Saute onion in butter; add livers and brown. Cover. Refrigerate for 2 hours. Blend in blender. Serve with small crackers or toast rounds, if desired.

Mrs. Annette Blomquist Tramm
Bradley-Bourbonnais Comm. H. S.
Bradley, Illinois

CHOPPED LIVER

½ lb. calves liver or chicken livers
1 onion, finely chopped
2 hard-cooked eggs, finely chopped
Salt and pepper to taste
4 tbsp. dissolved chicken fat

Broil liver; cool. Finely chop liver; mix with onion, eggs, salt, pepper and chicken fat. Spread on crackers. Yield: 6-8 servings.

Agnes D. Ingram, West Montgomery H. S.
Mt. Gilead, North Carolina

LIVER SPREAD

½ lb. cooked liver sausage or chicken livers
3 hard-cooked eggs, chopped
Salt and pepper to taste
1 3-oz. pkg. cream cheese, softened
3 tbsp. salad dressing

Cut liver into small pieces; cream along side of bowl. Add chopped egg, salt and pepper; cream again. Add cream cheese and salad dressing. Serve with crackers, if desired. NOTE: May be combined in blender for a more uniform spread.

Mrs. Barbara Miles, Rogers H. S.
Wyoming, Michigan

MELT-IN-YOUR-MOUTH

1 8-oz. pkg. frozen chicken livers
Chopped walnuts
12 slices bacon, cut into halves

Broil chicken livers as directed on package until just thawed. Remove. Roll in walnuts. Wrap bacon around each piece of liver. Fasten with a toothpick. Broil about 10 minutes or until bacon is done; turn occasionally. Yield: 24 servings.

Mrs. Mildred L. Callahan
Thomas Jefferson Jr. H. S.
Miami, Florida

BRUNSCHWEIGER CHIP DIP

½ lb. brunschweiger
3 oz. cream cheese
1 tsp. onion juice
1 tbsp. caraway seed
½ pt. sour cream

Combine all ingredients except sour cream in a bowl; mix with electric mixer. When smooth and well mixed, stir in sour cream. Chill for 2 hours. Serve with chips or snack crackers, if desired. Yield: 25-35 servings.

Mrs. Ella Mae Korthals, Huron Jr. H. S.
Huron, South Dakota

MUSHROOM-LIVER PATE

½ lb. mushrooms, sliced
1 tbsp. butter
1 lb. liverwurst
1 tbsp. chopped scallions
1 tsp. soy sauce
1 c. sour cream
4 tbsp. Cognac or brandy
Dash of cayenne
1 tsp. sharp prepared mustard

Saute mushrooms in butter. Have liverwurst at room temperature; mash and blend with mushrooms and remaining ingredients. Place in dish; garnish with parsley. Chill. Serve with melba rounds.

Mrs. Ruth L. Smith, Hillman Comm. School
Hillman, Michigan

SPICED CELERY PIECES

4 stalks celery
¼ lb. liverwurst or brunschweiger, softened
Watercress

Wash celery stalks; fill with brunschweiger. Cut into 1-inch pieces. Garnish with watercress. Yield: 4 servings.

Mrs. Mary L. Weaver
Schwenksville Union School
Schwenksville, Pennsylvania

CHEESE -BACON ROLLS

12 slices bread
1 5-oz. jar sharp Cheddar cheese spread
½ lb. bacon, sliced and cut into thirds

Remove crusts from bread slices. Roll bread paper thin with rolling pin; spread with cheese. Cut bread slices into halves lengthwise; roll up as for jelly roll with strip of bacon on outside of bread. Secure with toothpick. Bake at 350 degrees for 30 minutes. Serve hot or cold. Yield: 6 servings.

Mrs. Gertrude G. Wilson, Nahant Jr., H. S.
Nahant, Massachusetts

BACON 'N' CHEESE PARTY TIDBITS

¼ c. mayonnaise
3 tsp. finely chopped onion
2 tsp. prepared mustard
⅓ c. shredded sharp cheese
6 slices white bread
8 slices bacon, cooked

Combine mayonnaise, onion, mustard and cheese; blend. Remove crusts from bread; cut each slice into four triangular pieces. Place bread on baking sheet; toast in broiler on one side. Turn toast points; spread with 1 teaspoonful of cheese mixture. Cut each slice of cooked bacon; place over cheese mixture. Place appetizers under broiler for about 1 minute to melt cheese and blend flavors. Serve immediately. Yield: 24 servings.

Gwen Morgenstern, Hamden H. S.
Hamden, Ohio

COCKTAIL HAM NUGGETS

½ lb. ground ham
½ lb. ground fresh pork
¼ c. chopped green onions and tops
1 can water chestnuts, drained and chopped
1 egg, beaten
1 tbsp. milk
1 sm. clove of garlic, finely chopped

Combine all ingredients; mix well. Shape into small balls, using about 1 teaspoonful of mixture for each ball. Brown balls slowly on all sides. Serve hot.

Mrs. Rush Valentine, Starkville H. S.
Starkville, Mississippi

COCKTAIL SAUSAGE BALLS

5 lb. sausage
2 onions, finely diced
2 garlic buttons, finely diced
4 eggs
2 cans peach nectar

Blend sausage, onions, garlic and eggs until well mixed; mold into balls the size of a quarter. Quickly brown balls in heavy skillet. Heat peach nectar; add browned sausage balls. Simmer slowly for 2 hours, turning occasionally. Yield: 30 servings.

Mrs. Londaline Gibbs, Bel Air H. S.
El Paso, Texas

SAUSAGE BALLS

1 lb. sausage
1 can refrigerated biscuits

Roll sausage into small bite-sized balls. Pull biscuit apart by sections or layers. Roll biscuit around sausage ball until sausage is covered. Place on broiler pan. Bake at 350 degrees for 20 minutes. Yield: 8-12 servings.

Mrs. Jamie H. White, Signal Mountain Jr. H. S.
Signal Mountain, Tennessee

SAUSAGE PINWHEELS

2 c. flour
3 tsp. baking powder
½ tsp. soda
⅓ c. shortening
½ c. buttermilk
1 lb. bulk hot sausage

Sift dry ingredients; cut in shortening. Add buttermilk. Place dough on floured board; knead flour into dough until smooth. Roll out paper thin; pat sausage onto dough. Roll up; freeze. Slice very thin. Bake at 400 to 450 degrees until done. Serve immediately. Yield: 25 servings.

Mrs. Glenda Ballinger, Kirkman Technical H. S.
Chattanooga, Tennessee

MOLDED CHEESE SPREAD

2 cans anchovy fillets
1 tsp. capers
1 8-oz. pkg. cream cheese
½ c. butter
3 tbsp. sour cream
½ tsp. salt
1 tbsp. chopped onion
1 tbsp. mustard
1 ½ tsp. paprika
1 tsp. caraway seed

Mash 1 can anchovy fillets and capers with a fork. Mix cream cheese with butter and sour cream. Add salt, onion, mustard, paprika and caraway seed to cheese; mix well. Place on waxed paper; form into a round ball. Chill. Ridge up and down ball with fork. Sprinkle with additional paprika; place remaining anchovy fillets on toothpicks and decorate. Serve with crackers, if desired. Yield: 12 servings.

Mrs. Blanche Weaver, Herrin H. S.
Herrin, Illinois

CLAM-CHEESE DIP

1 7 ½-oz. can clams
2 3-oz. pkg. cream cheese
1 tsp. lemon juice
1 tsp. Worcestershire sauce
½ tsp. salt
Corn chips

Drain clams, reserving 2 tablespoonfuls liquid. Mix cheese and lemon juice; add Worcestershire sauce, salt and reserved clam liquid. Add clams. Serve as a dip with corn chips.

Suzanne Pruitt, Drane Jr. H. S.
Corsicana, Texas

CLAM PUFFS

1 8-oz. pkg. cream cheese, softened
1 7-oz. can minced clams, drained
¼ tsp. salt
2 tsp. fresh, frozen or canned lemon juice
1 tbsp. grated onion
1 tbsp. Worcestershire sauce
1 egg white, stiffly beaten

(Continued on next page)

Beat cream cheese until smooth. Combine all ingredients. Mound on toasted round. Bake at 450 degrees for 3 minutes. Yield: 36 puffs.

Jo Ann Crow, Newnan H. S.
Newnan, Georgia

HOT CLAM DIP

3 tbsp. butter
1 sm. onion, finely chopped
½ green pepper, finely chopped
1 10 ½-oz. can minced clams, drained
¼ lb. New York State cheese, cubed
4 tbsp. catsup
1 tbsp. Worcestershire sauce
1 tbsp. Sherry wine
¼ tsp. red pepper

Melt butter in top of a double boiler; add onion and green pepper. Saute for 3 minutes; add clams, cheese, catsup, Worcestershire sauce, Sherry and red pepper. Cook until cheese melts, stirring often. Serve in chafing dish with melba toast or party rye, if desired. Yield: 30 servings.

Mrs. Ruth H. Hughes, Abbeville H. S.
Abbeville, South Carolina

TOASTED WALNUT-CLAM ROLL

2 8-oz. pkg. cream cheese, softened
1 7 ½-oz. can minced clams, well drained
2 tbsp. finely chopped onion
2 tbsp. lemon juice
Garlic salt to taste
1 ¼ c. chopped toasted walnuts

Beat cream cheese with clams until smooth; beat in onion, lemon juice and garlic salt. Stir in 1/2 cup walnuts. Turn mixture out onto foil or waxed paper; shape into one or two logs, 1 3/4 inches in diameter by rolling back and forth. Roll in remaining walnuts until surface is well coated. Wrap in foil; chill for several hours until firm. Cut into slices; serve with cracker. Yield: 36 slices.

Sister M. Carolita, F.S.P.A.
Hayes Catholic H. S.
Muscatine, Iowa

CRAB MEAT DIPPIES

1 6-oz. can crab meat, flaked
2 tsp. mayonnaise
1 tsp. grated onion
24 sm. crispy crackers
½ c. grated Cheddar cheese

Toss crab meat with mayonnaise and onion. Spoon onto crackers. Sprinkle generously with cheese. Broil 3 inches from source of heat for 1 to 2 minutes or until cheese is melted and slightly browned. Serve hot. Yield: 20-24 canapes.

Jean Abrahamson, Luverne Jr.-Sr. H. S.
Luverne, Minnesota

CRAB MEAT-CHEESE APPETIZERS

1 8-oz. pkg. Velveeta cheese
2 tbsp. butter or margarine
1 8-oz. can crab meat
1 tsp. lemon juice
½ tsp. salt
2 tsp. Worcestershire sauce
Dash of paprika
Dash of onion salt
8 to 10 slices bread, toasted

Melt cheese and butter over low heat. Combine crab meat with all remaining ingredients except bread. Combine crab meat with cheese mixture. Cut toast into various shapes. Place a small amount of mixture on each piece of bread. Place under broiler until lightly browned and bubbly. Serve hot. Yield: 12-15 servings.

Mrs. Ruth Ragsdale, Douglas S. Freeman H. S.
Richmond, Virginia

CRAB SPREAD

1 c. (packed) crab meat
1 4 ½-oz. can chopped ripe olives
2 hard-cooked eggs, chopped
¼ c. mayonnaise
1 tbsp. Worcestershire sauce
2 tbsp. lemon juice
2 tsp. prepared horseradish
2 tsp. catsup
1 tsp. minced chives

Combine all ingredients except chives in a bowl; mix until well blended. Spoon mixture into serving bowl; sprinkle with minced chives. Serve with crisp whole wheat or rye crackers. Yield: 1 1/2 cups.

Mrs. Jeanne P. Dabney, Valley H. S.
Albuquerque, New Mexico

CREAMY CRAB MEAT CANAPES

1 8-oz. pkg. cream cheese, softened
1 tbsp. cream-style horseradish
½ tsp. lemon juice
¼ tsp. onion salt
Dash of pepper
Dash of garlic salt
1 ½ c. crab meat
1 c. chopped peeled cucumbers
4 loaves French bread
Margarine
Chopped parsley

Combine cream cheese, horseradish, lemon juice and seasonings; mix until well blended. Stir in crab meat and cucumbers. Split French bread loaves; spread each half with margarine. Top with crab meat mixture; sprinkle with parsley. Cut loaves diagonally into fourths. Yield: 32 appetizers.

Mrs. Lane B. Kennedy, Savannah H. S.
Savannah, Georgia

CURRIED CRAB MEAT CANAPES

½ tsp. minced onion
2 tbsp. butter or margarine
1 ½ tsp. flour
½ tsp. curry powder
⅛ tsp. salt
¼ c. light cream
½ c. flaked crab meat
4 thin slices toasted bread
3 tbsp. grated Parmesan cheese

Saute onion in butter until lightly browned. Combine flour, curry powder and salt; stir into onion. Slowly pour in cream, stirring constantly. Mix in crab meat. Remove crust and quarter toast. Spread crab meat mixture on toast squares; sprinkle with cheese. Place on a cookie sheet; broil until cheese melts. Serve hot. Yield: 16 canapes.

Mrs. Mary N. Davis, North Shore H. S.
Houston, Texas

DEVILED CRAB

1 med. onion, chopped
2 tbsp. butter
2 tbsp. flour
1 tbsp. lemon juice
Dash of cayenne pepper
1 tbsp. Worcestershire sauce
1 sm. can evaporated milk
1 egg, beaten
1 can crab meat
Fine bread crumbs
5 crab shells
1 c. buttered bread crumbs

Cook onion in butter; add flour. Blend well. Add lemon juice, cayenne, Worcestershire sauce and milk. Cook, stirring until thick. Add egg, crab meat, and small amount of fine crumbs. Fill crab shells with mixture; sprinkle with buttered crumbs. Pat smooth with hands. Bake at 350 degrees until brown. Serve with lemon slices and tartar sauce. Yield: 5 servings.

Mrs. Russell Hart, Madison Co. H. S.
Danielsville, Georgia

DELICIOUS SHRIMP HORS D'OEUVRE

1 c. catsup
⅓ c. soy sauce
⅛ tsp. salt
Dash of ginger
1 c. sugar
1 10-oz. pkg. frozen shrimp, cleaned
8 slices bacon

Combine catsup, soy sauce, salt, ginger and sugar; marinate shrimp in sauce. Place shrimp on a cookie sheet. Bake at 325 degrees for 15 minutes. Fry bacon until transparent; cut into thirds. Wrap bacon around shrimp; hold with toothpick. Keep hot in chafing dish. Yield: 8 servings.

Mrs. Naomi Stone, Staples H. S.
Staples, Minnesota

FRESH SHRIMP DIP

1 8-oz. pkg. cream cheese
3 tbsp. lemon juice
10 green onions, minced
¼ tsp. hot sauce
¼ tsp. Worcestershire sauce
¼ tsp. pepper
½ tsp. salt
2 lb. finely ground boiled shrimp
Mayonnaise

Combine cream cheese and lemon juice; add onions, hot sauce, Worcestershire sauce, pepper and salt. Blend in shrimp. Add enough mayonnaise to make desired dipping consistency. Let stand for 6 to 8 hours before serving. Serve with chips or crackers. Yield: 10-14 servings.

Mrs. Renee Nowlin, Aldine Jr. H. S.
Houston, Texas

MARINATED SHRIMP

3 cloves of garlic, chopped
1 med. onion, chopped
1 tsp. chopped basil
1 tsp. dry mustard
1 tsp. salt
¼ c. chopped parsley
Juice of 1 lemon
½ c. salad oil
2 lb. uncooked shrimp

Combine all ingredients except shrimp. Shell and clean shrimp. Add shrimp to marinade mixture. Refrigerate; marinate overnight. Broil for a few minutes. Serve hot.

Yvonne Lindrum, Montebello Jr. H. S.
Montebello, California

MINIATURE SHRIMP PIZZAS

¼ pkg. dry yeast
¾ c. plus 2 tbsp. warm water
3 to 3 ¼ c. flour
2 c. tomatoes, sieved
½ tsp. oregano
½ tsp. rosemary
½ tsp. salt
¼ tsp. pepper
½ c. grated Parmesan cheese
1 6 ½-oz. can whole shrimp

Dissolve yeast in water. Blend in flour; knead lightly on floured surface. Place in greased bowl;

(Continued on next page)

turn to grease top. Cover and let rise in warm place until doubled. Combine all remaining ingredients except cheese and shrimp. Roll dough 1/8-inch thick; cut into circles 1 1/2-inches in diameter. Press identation in center; fill with sauce. Sprinkle with Parmesan cheese; top with shrimp. Bake at 425 degrees for 8 to 10 minutes. Yield: 3 dozen.

Mrs. Arlene Voecks, Wells-Easton H. S.
Wells, Minnesota

NEW ORLEANS SHRIMP

3 qt. water
1 bay leaf
3 sprigs parsley
1 tbsp. salt
3 stalks celery, chopped
¼ c. pepper
5 lb. unpeeled shrimp
1 bottle catsup
½ bottle Worcestershire sauce
¼ lb. butter
Juice of 1 lemon

Combine water, bay leaf, parsley, salt and celery; boil for 5 minutes. Add pepper and shrimp; cook for 10 minutes. Drain. Mix catsup, Worcestershire sauce, butter and lemon juice in saucepan; cook for 2 minutes. Dip shrimp in sauce to serve. NOTE: The 1/4 cup black pepper adds flavor to shrimp.

Margaret Molitor, Goodrich H. S.
Goodrich, Michigan

PICKLED SHRIMP

¾ c. olive oil
3 cloves of garlic, minced
2 onions, chopped
2 lb. cooked cleaned shrimp
2 onions, thinly sliced
½ c. vinegar
1 ½ tsp. salt
¼ tsp. dry mustard
½ tsp. pepper
¼ tsp. ground chili
2 pickled chili peppers

Heat 1/4 cup oil in pan; add garlic and onions. Brown thoroughly. Add shrimp; saute for 5 minutes. Remove from heat; cool. Add remaining ingredients. Refrigerate for 24 hours. Place in large bowl. Serve cold, speared with toothpicks.

Florence Hughes, Toaz Jr., H. S.
Huntington, New York

SHRIMP BALLS

1 lb. frozen prawns
16 canned or fresh water chestnuts, minced
1 tsp. salt
1 tsp. crushed red pepper
1 tbsp. minced green onion
½ tbsp. minced parsley
Seasoned flour

Thaw, shell and devein prawns. Chop prawns very fine. Add water chestnuts, salt, red pepper onion and parsley to prawns. Roll mixture into small balls the size of walnuts. Dip into seasoned flour; fry in deep fat until golden. Drain on absorbent paper. Serve on toothpicks with chili sauce or catsup with a few dashes Tabasco sauce, if desired. Yield: 20 servings.

Joyce Jeffers, Arroyo H. S.
San Lorenzo, California

SHRIMP DIP

1 10-oz. can shrimp, drained
1 8-oz. pkg. cream cheese
¼ c. Dr. Pepper
3 tbsp. mayonnaise
2 tsp. fresh lemon juice
⅛ tsp. onion salt
Dash of garlic powder
1 tsp. Worcestershire sauce
3 to 4 drops of Tabasco sauce

Place 1/2 can shrimp and remaining ingredients in blender or electric mixer; blend until fluffy and smooth. Coarsely chop remaining shrimp; fold into mixture. Keep refrigerated until ready to serve.

Mrs. Emaline Miller, Dixie School
Lake City, Arkansas

SHRIMP DIP

1 can frozen cream of shrimp soup, thawed
½ c. sour cream
1 tbsp. horseradish
¼ tsp. Worcestershire sauce

Combine all ingredients; mix well. Serve with an assortment of crackers and wafers, if desired. Yield: 20 servings.

Mrs. Joseph S. Klimczak, Jr., Bogalusa H. S.
Bogalusa, Louisiana

SHRIMP DIP

1 8-oz. pkg. cream cheese
4 tbsp. mayonnaise
2 tsp. lemon juice
2 tbsp. grated onion
1 5-oz. can shrimp
Worcestershire sauce to taste
Salt and pepper

Mix cream cheese, mayonnaise and lemon juice until smooth; add onion. Devein and mash shrimp; add to mixture. Add remaining ingredients to taste.

Mrs. Patricia H. Fuller, Rosedale H. S.
Rosedale, Mississippi

SHRIMP HORS D'OEUVRES

1 lb. fresh shrimp, cleaned and cooked or 2 5-oz. cans shrimp
1 tbsp. minced onion
1 tsp. minced celery
1 tsp. finely chopped green pepper
2 tsp. lemon juice
½ tsp. grated lemon rind
¼ tsp. salt
4 to 5 drops of Tabasco sauce
¾ c. mayonnaise
1 tsp. horseradish
Dash of pepper
Bread

Combine all ingredients except bread; chill. Cut bread into shapes; spread with mix. Use on 1 slice of bread or between 2 slices. Spread on cocktail crackers, if desired. Yield: 24 servings.

Mrs. Marcella K. Hromy
Our Lady of Providence H. S.
Clarksville, Indiana

SHRIMP PARTY DIP

1 c. mayonnaise
½ c. sour cream
¼ c. catsup
1 tbsp. lemon juice
Salt to taste
Chives (opt.)
Curry powder (opt.)
Chopped celery (opt.)
Diced pepper (opt.)
Avocado (opt.)
1 lb. boiled shrimp

Combine mayonnaise with sour cream, catsup, lemon juice and salt; add chives, curry, celery, pepper or avacoda to taste. Heap shrimp on serving platter with dip in a center bowl. Yield: 6 servings.

Mrs. Bill Hester, Webster Jr. H. S.
Collinsville, Illinois

SHRIMP TOAST

1 lge. can shrimp, drained
½ tsp. salt
Dash of pepper
½ tsp. shoyu sauce
2 stalks green onions, finely chopped
1 egg
1 tbsp. cornstarch
1 loaf bread, sliced
Oil

Place shrimp and seasonings in a bowl. Add onions with egg and cornstarch to shrimp. Mix well. Trim crust off bread; cut each slice into four squares. Spread 1 teaspoonful shrimp mixture on bread squares. Heat oil in deep pan to 350 degrees; place bread squares in hot oil, filling-side down. Brown on each side. Drain on paper towels; serve immediately. Yield: 12 servings.

Mrs. Kikuye S. Kohashi, Hilo H. S.
Hilo, Hawaii

CURRIED TUNA TOASTIES

2 7-oz. cans chunk-style tuna
1 c. mayonnaise
1 tbsp. instant minced onion
1 tsp. curry powder
2 loaves fresh, unsliced white bread
Soft butter
Paprika

Combine tuna, mayonnaise, onion and curry powder until creamy. Carefully trim all crust from each loaf of bread with sharp knife. Lay each loaf on the side. Starting at the bottom, slice off five 1/2-inch slices lengthwise. Lightly spread slices with butter. Spread each slice with 2 rounded tablespoonfuls tuna mixture; sprinkle with paprika. Starting at narrow end, roll up each slice; wrap tightly in waxed paper. Refrigerate overnight or freeze. Just before serving, cut each roll crosswise into 6 or 7 slices. Lay on a cookie sheet; toast under broiler, turning once. Serve hot. Yield: 60 servings.

Mrs. Syble Griffin, Pulaski H. S.
New Britain, Connecticut

TUNA APPETIZER TRAY

2 6 ½-oz. cans tuna in vegetable oil
½ c. mayonnaise or sour cream
2 tbsp. chili sauce or catsup
2 tsp. horseradish
1 tbsp. lemon juice
½ tsp. Worcestershire sauce

Drain oil from tuna; add oil to mayonnaise and beat until blended. Stir in remaining ingredients. Add half the dressing to drained tuna; turn into center of serving dish. Serve with cucumber slices, diagonally cut celery, tomato wedges, cauliflower and other desired vegetables. Pass remaining dressing. Yield: 6 servings.

Photograph for this recipe on page 249.

TUNA-CHEESE ROLL

1 8-oz. pkg. cream cheese
1 sm. onion, minced
Salt and pepper to taste
¼ tsp. Tabasco sauce
½ c. chopped Brazil nuts
1 can tuna
½ c. finely chopped parsley

Combine cream cheese, onion, seasonings, nuts and tuna; add 2 tablespoonfuls chopped parsley. Beat until thick and smooth. Form mixture into roll 1 1/2 inches in diameter. Spread remaining parsley on waxed paper. Roll tuna-cheese roll in parsley. Chill well; slice. Yield: 50 servings.

Bertha Hundley, Red Bank H. S.
Chattanooga, Tennessee

TUNA MARBLES

1 8-oz. can tuna, drained
1 tbsp. minced onion
1 egg
1 tsp. lemon juice
½ tsp. mustard
½ c. oatmeal
Cracker or bread crumbs

Combine all ingredients except crumbs; mix well. Roll into 1-inch balls; roll in crumbs. Fry in deep fat until golden brown. May be served with toothpicks or on a tray. Yield: 20 servings.

Mrs. Elizabeth Scaggs, Cerro Gordo H. S.
Cerro Gordo, Illinois

TUNA PINWHEELS

20 slices bread
Butter
1 6 ½-oz. can tuna, drained and flaked
½ c. mayonnaise
½ c. finely chopped celery
4 tbsp. chopped sweet pickle
1 tsp. prepared mustard
Paprika

Remove crusts from bread; butter each slice. Toast if desired. Combine all remaining ingredients except paprika. Spread thinly over buttered bread. Roll bread as for a jelly roll; cut each roll into three pinwheels. Fasten with toothpicks. Brush pinwheels lightly with paprika; broil until lightly toasted. Yield: 60 servings.

Linda H. Wagers, Walhalla Jr. H. S.
Walhalla, South Carolina
Mrs. Mary June Sheets, Ashe Central H. S.
Jefferson, North Carolina

CHEESE MOON CRESCENTS

16 Vienna sausages or wieners
1 slice American cheese
1 pkg. refrigerated crescent roll dough

Split sausage lengthwise three-fourths through. Cut cheese slice into 16 even portions. Insert one piece into sausage. Remove rolls from can and separate as directed. Cut each triangle through the center, making a long triangle. Place a cheese stuffed sausage on wide side of each triangle. Roll dough as directed on package. Place rolls on baking sheet, cheese-side up. Bake at 375 degrees for 18 to 20 minutes or until golden brown. Serve hot. Yield: 8 servings.

Mrs. Jean Haynes, Whittle Springs Jr. H. S.
Knoxville, Tennessee

MEAT KREPLACH

1 tsp. salt
1 ½ c. flour
4 eggs, beaten
1 lb. lean cooked meat
1 sm. onion
2 tbsp. melted margarine
4 qt. boiling water

Add 1/2 teaspoonful salt and flour to 3 eggs in bowl; mix. If too sticky, add more flour. Roll thin on floured board; cut into 2-inch squares. Grind meat on onion; add 1 egg, 1/2 teaspoonful salt and melted margarine. Mix well. Place 1 teaspoonful meat mixture in center of dough square; fold dough to form a triangle. Press edges firmly. Boil for 20 minutes in boiling water. Drain; let dry. Fry in oil until brown and crisp. Yield: 12 servings.

Mrs. Frances Baratz, Clark Lane Jr. H. S.
Waterford, Connecticut

Salad Favorites

MAIN DISH SALAD

2 c. julienne cooked beef or pork
1 No. 2 can red kidney beans, drained
1 c. chopped celery
¼ c. chopped onion
2 hard-cooked eggs, chopped
2 tbsp. sliced sweet pickle
¼ c. mayonnaise
1 tbsp. chili sauce
1 tsp. salt
1 head lettuce

Chill all ingredients. Combine meat, beans, celery, onion, eggs, pickle, mayonnaise, chili saucc and salt. Toss lightly; chill in covered bowl for 30 minutes. Serve in lettuce cups. Yield: 4-6 servings.

Mrs. Aline Wilson, Ringgold H. S.
Ringgold, Louisiana

MOLDED CORNED BEEF SALAD

1 pkg. unflavored gelatin
½ c. cold water
¼ tsp. salt
Juice of ½ lemon
1 c. boiling water
1 med. onion, finely chopped
2 stalks celery, chopped
1 12-oz. can corned beef
¾ c. mayonnaise
½ c. chopped sweet pickles

Sprinkle gelatin onto cold water to soften. Add salt, lemon juice and boiling water; stir until thoroughly dissolved. Chill until partially set. Add onion, celery, corned beef, mayonnaise and chopped pickles. Place in 3-cup ring mold. When ready to serve, unmold onto lettuce. Yield: 8 servings.

Mrs. Marjorie Grout, Glens Fall H. S.
Glen Falls, New York

ROAST BEEF SALAD

1 c. diced cooked beef
2 hard-cooked eggs, sliced
2 tomatoes, quartered
1 sm. head lettuce
French dressing or mayonnaise

Toss beef with eggs and tomatoes. Serve on lettuce with French dressing or mayonnaise. NOTE: Diced cooked ham, tongue or corned beef may be substituted for beef if desired. Yield: 6 servings.

Mrs. Johnnie Mae Proctor, Dilley H. S.
Dilley, Texas

TACO SALAD

1 lb. hamburger
½ head lettuce, shredded
1 tomato, diced
½ c. grated cheese
1 med. onion, chopped
1 tbsp. mayonnaise
1 29-cent pkg. corn chips

Brown hamburger; drain off grease and cool. Add lettuce, tomato, cheese, onion and mayonnaise; toss lightly. Add corn chips; toss well. Yield: 6 servings.

Mrs. Raymond McCullough, Avalon H. S.
Waxahachie, Texas

HAM AND CUCUMBER

2 3-oz. pkg. lemon-lime gelatin
1 tsp. salt
2 c. boiling water
1 ½ c. cold water
¼ c. vinegar
1 c. slivered cooked ham
1 c. sliced celery
1 9-oz. can drained pineapple chunks
½ c. thinly sliced quartered cucumber
¾ tsp. grated onion
3 tbsp. prepared horseradish

Dissolve gelatin and salt in boiling water. Add cold water and vinegar. Chill until thick. Fold in remaining ingredients. Pour into 1-quart ring mold. Chill until firm. Yield: 8 servings.

Mrs. H. M. Callaway, Oglethorpe Co. H. S.
Lexington, Georgia

HAM SALAD MOLD

3 c. finely chopped cooked ham
¾ c. diced celery
¼ c. diced green pepper
¼ c. chopped ripe olives
½ tsp. salt
2 tbsp. unflavored gelatin
½ c. cold water
1 c. pineapple juice, heated
1 tsp. mustard
1 tsp. horseradish
Juice of 1 lemon
1 c. evaporated milk, chilled

Mix ham, celery, green pepper, olives and salt. Soak gelatin in cold water for about 5 minutes; combine with hot pineapple juice. Stir in mustard, horseradish and lemon juice. Cool. Beat chilled milk until peaks form; slowly add cooled gelatin mixture, beating continuously. Fold in ham mixture. Pour into greased 9 x 5-inch pan. Chill until firm. Unmold and slice. Yield: 6-8 servings.

Mrs. Betty Lou James, Western H. S.
Russiaville, Indiana

CHICKEN-ALMOND SALAD

3 c. cubed cooked chicken
1 ½ c. diced celery
3 tbsp. lemon juice
1 c. seedless grapes
1 c. toasted almonds
1 tsp. dry mustard
1 ½ tsp. salt
⅛ tsp. pepper
1 tbsp. capers
¼ c. light cream
1 c. mayonnaise
2 hard-cooked eggs, sliced

(Continued on next page)

Combine chicken, celery and lemon juice; chill for 1 hour. Add grapes and almonds. Combine remaining ingredients; add to chicken. Toss. Garnish with additional slices of hard-cooked eggs. Yield: 8-10 servings.

Dorothy Adcock, Fulton H. S.
Knoxville, Tennessee

Dissolve gelatin in hot chicken stock; combine all remaining ingredients. Place in an oblong glass dish. Place in refrigerator until congealed. Serve on lettuce leaf with a small amount of mayonnaise and a stuffed olive on top if desired. Yield: 8-10 servings.

Euna Anderson, Paris H. S.
Paris, Texas

CHICKEN-COTTAGE CHEESE SALAD

1 pkg. lime gelatin
1 c. hot water
½ c. cold water
2 tbsp. lemon juice
½ tsp. salt
½ c. mayonnaise
1 c. creamed cottage cheese
½ c. diced celery
1 c. diced cooked chicken
½ c. finely chopped pickles

Dissolve gelatin in hot water; add cold water, lemon juice, salt and mayonnaise. Blend well; chill until partially set. Whip with beater until light and fluffy. Fold in remaining ingredients. Chill until firm. Unmold. Serve on lettuce leaves if desired. Yield: 6-8 servings.

Elizabeth Heard, Central H. S.
Jackson, Mississippi

CHICKEN MAYONNAISE

1 3 ½ to 4-lb. hen or 2 fryers
1 c. almonds, toasted and chopped
1 ½ c. chopped celery
1 lge. can small peas
4 hard-cooked eggs, finely chopped
½ pt. mayonnaise
5 tbsp. relish
1 envelope unflavored gelatin
¼ c. cold water
1 c. hot chicken stock

Stew chicken; chop finely. Mix with almonds, celery, peas and liquid, eggs, mayonnaise and relish. Soften gelatin in cold water; dissolve in hot stock. Pour over remaining ingredients; pour into serving dish or mold. Chill until firm. Serve on lettuce leaves. Yield: 10-12 servings.

Mrs. Orrissa P. Simpson, Regional Supervisor
Home Economics Education
State Department of Education
Knoxville, Tennessee

CHICKEN MAYONNAISE

2 tbsp. unflavored gelatin
1 ½ c. chicken stock
2 c. chopped cooked chicken
1 c. diced celery
1 c. small English peas, drained
½ c. chopped pecans
3 hard-cooked eggs, diced
1 tbsp. sweet relish
1 sm. can pimento, diced
1 tsp. salt

CHICKEN MOUSSE

½ pkg. lemon gelatin
1 c. hot chicken broth
2 c. diced cooked chicken
1 c. finely chopped celery
1 pimento, finely mashed
1 tbsp. vinegar
½ tsp. salt
Dash of cayenne pepper
½ c. heavy cream, whipped
Crisp lettuce
6 to 8 olives

Dissolve gelatin in hot broth. Chill until slightly thickened. Beat with rotary beater until consistency of whipped cream. Combine chicken, celery, pimento, vinegar, salt and cayenne. Fold into gelatin. Fold in whipped cream. Turn into individual molds. Chill until firm. Unmold onto lettuce and garnish with stuffed olives. Yield: 6 servings.

Mrs. Sophia Cook, Ruston H. S.
Ruston, Louisiana

CHICKEN MOUSSE

1 tbsp. unflavored gelatin
2 tbsp. cold water
3 egg yolks, slightly beaten
1 ½ c. chicken broth
1 tsp. salt
2 c. chopped chicken
½ c. blanched almonds
2 tbsp. pimento
½ c. heavy cream, whipped

Soak gelatin in cold water. Add egg yolks to chicken broth; cook in double boiler until spoon is coated. Add gelatin and salt. When partially set, add remaining ingredients. Mold in attractive container in refrigerator. Yield: 8 servings.

Mrs. Sue Rogers, Krum H. S.
Krum, Texas

CHICKEN MOUSSE

2 envelopes unflavored gelatin
¼ c. cold water
½ can cream of mushroom soup
1 ½ c. chicken broth
1 tsp. salt
Dash of pepper
½ c. mayonnaise
3 c. finely diced chicken
¾ c. finely diced celery
1 tbsp. finely diced pimento

(Continued on next page)

1 tbsp. finely diced ripe olives
¼ c. finely diced green pepper
2 tsp. finely minced onion
1 tbsp. finely minced parsley
¼ c. chopped mushrooms
½ tsp. Worcestershire sauce
1 tbsp. lemon juice
1 c. heavy cream, whipped

Sprinkle gelatin onto cold water to soften. Combine soup, broth, salt and pepper in saucepan; cook until blended and hot. Dissolve gelatin in hot mixture; cool. Blend in mayonnaise. Add chicken, vegetables, Worcestershire sauce and lemon juice; fold in whipped cream. Spoon into a lightly oiled 3-quart copper mold. Cover; chill until set. Unmold onto crisp lettuce. Garnish and serve. Yield: 8 servings.

Mrs. Jane Tyler, Oneonta H. S.
Oneonta, New York

CHICKEN AND RICE SALAD

1 ½ c. diced cooked chicken
1 c. cold cooked rice
¾ c. chopped celery
2 tbsp. chopped green pepper
1 tbsp. chopped sour pickle
6 stuffed olives, chopped
12 pecan halves, chopped
½ tbsp. chopped parsley
⅔ c. mayonnaise
⅔ c. whipped cream
1 tbsp. unflavored gelatin
2 c. cold water
½ tsp. salt
Dash of black pepper
Dash of red pepper
Dash of paprika

Combine chicken, rice, celery, green pepper, sour pickle, olives, pecans, parsley, mayonnaise and whipped cream. Soften gelatin in cold water for 5 minutes; dissolve over hot water. Stir into chicken mixture. Cool. Add salt, pepper and paprika. Pour into mold; chill until firm. Yield: 8 servings.

Arlene Lenort, Pine Island H. S.
Pine Island, Minnesota

CHICKEN SALAD

4 c. cooked cubed chicken
1 c. chopped celery
1 c. grated carrots
1 tbsp. chopped onion
1 c. heavy cream, whipped
1 c. salad dressing
1 6 or 8-oz. can shoestring potatoes

Combine all ingredients except potatoes in a bowl; just before serving, add potatoes. If added too soon, potatoes will loose crispness. Yield: 8 servings.

Corinne Anderson, Morgan Park H. S.
Duluth, Minnesota

CHICKEN SALAD

2 qt. chopped cooked chicken
6 hard-cooked eggs, chopped
6 c. diced celery
1 ½ tbsp. salt
½ tsp. pepper
1 ¼ c. salad dressing or mayonnaise
½ to 1 c. chopped pickles

Combine chicken with remaining ingredients; toss lightly. Chill and serve. Yield: 25 servings.

Mrs. Clara Grace Spence, Pitkin H. S.
Pitkin, Louisiana

CHICKEN SALAD

1 chicken
White wine
Salad dressing or mayonnaise
Chopped pecans or almonds
Chopped white grapes

Cook chicken until tender; remove bones. Soak overnight in refrigerator in wine. Chop chicken. Mix any remaining wine with salad dressing. Combine chicken, nuts and grapes with salad dressing. Refrigerate; serve on lettuce leaf.

Flora Fry, Coleman H. S.
Coleman, Texas

CHICKEN SALAD

2 c. chopped cooked chicken
1 c. cubed celery
1 c. seedless white grapes, sliced
½ tsp. monosodium glutamate
1 tsp. salt
¼ c. sour cream (opt.)
½ c. mayonnaise
1 head lettuce, shredded
¼ to ½ c. toasted almonds, sliced

Combine chicken, celery and grapes. Add seasonings to cream and mayonnaise. Toss mayonnaise mixture with chicken mixture. Serve on shredded lettuce; sprinkle with almonds. Yield: 6 servings.

Mrs. Margaret C. Weeks, Highland Jr. H. S.
Highland, California
Mrs. R. Watson Durham, Patrick Henry H. S.
Ashland, Virginia

CHICKEN SALAD

1 5-lb. hen, cooked and cubed
1 sm. jar olives, chopped
1 c. chopped celery
½ c. toasted pecans, chopped
½ c. sweet pickles, chopped
6 hard-cooked eggs, chopped
1 ½ tbsp. sugar
¾ tsp. salt
½ tsp. dry mustard
Few grains of cayenne pepper
3 tbsp. flour
2 tbsp. melted fat
3 egg yolks
¾ c. milk
¼ c. vinegar

Combine cubed chicken, olives, celery, pecans, sweet pickles and hard-cooked eggs. Mix sugar, seasonings and flour in saucepan; add fat. Blend. Beat egg yolks until thick; add milk, stirring. Add to sugar mixture. Cook, stirring, until mixture begins to thicken; cool. Add vinegar; cook, stirring, until thickened. Add to chicken mixture. Yield: 8 servings.

Mrs. Mark Thomas, East Limestone School
Athens, Alabama

CHICKEN SALAD MOLD

2 ½ c. cubed chicken
1 c. white grapes, halved
1 c. diced celery
½ c. chopped nuts
1 c. chicken broth
1 tsp. salt
2 tbsp. unflavored gelatin
8 tbsp. cold water
½ c. heavy cream, whipped
1 c. salad dressing

Combine chicken, grapes, celery, nuts, broth and salt. Mix and chill for 2 hours. Combine gelatin and cold water; let stand for 5 minutes. Dissolve gelatin and water over hot water. Blend whipped cream and salad dressing; add dissolved gelatin. Chill until mixture begins to thicken; combine with chicken mixture. Pour into tube mold or individual molds. Chill and serve. Yield: 10 servings.

Mrs. Louise Shanahan, Harlingen H. S.
Harlingen, Texas

CHICKEN SALAD SUPREME

2 c. cubed cooked chicken
2 tbsp. chopped green olives
¾ c. chopped celery
½ c. toasted almonds
2 tbsp. chopped ripe olives
2 tbsp. chopped mixed pickles or sweet pickles
2 hard-cooked eggs, sliced
¾ c. mayonnaise

Combine all ingredients; toss lightly. Serve on lettuce with watercress garnish. Yield: 6 servings.

Mrs. Martha Wilson, Ogden H. S.
Ogden, Illinois

CHICKEN SALAD WITH CURRY

2 chicken breasts, cooked
2 c. chopped celery
½ c. mayonnaise
3 tbsp. lemon juice
1 tbsp. sugar
1 tsp. curry powder
Dash of salt

Cut chicken into large chunks; combine with chopped celery. Mix all remaining ingredients; add to celery and chicken. Toss lightly. Chill. Serve on lettuce or in cream puffs. Yield: 6 servings.

Mrs. Ruth D. Jordan, Benjamin Russell H. S.
Alexander City, Alabama

CONGEALED CHICKEN SALAD

2 tbsp. lemon juice
2 c. diced cooked chicken
2 tbsp. unflavored gelatin
½ c. cold water
1 ½ c. hot stock
2 tbsp. chopped pickles
1 c. diced celery
3 hard-cooked eggs, chopped
1 tbsp. Worcestershire sauce
1 tsp. salt
3 tbsp. chopped pimento
1 c. mayonnaise

Pour lemon juice over chicken. Soak gelatin in cold water; dissolve in stock. Chill. Mix chicken with remaining ingredients except mayonnaise; add gelatin mixture. Add mayonnaise. Chill until mixture begins to congeal. Pack into waxed paper-lined loaf pan. Chill until set. Remove from pan and slice. Yield: 10-12 servings.

Mrs. Shirley Ann Boddie, Calvin H. S.
Calvin, Louisiana

CONGEALED CHICKEN SALAD

2 envelopes unflavored gelatin
½ c. cold water
2 c. hot chicken broth
1 5-lb. chicken, cooked and cubed
1 can green peas
2 c. chopped celery
¼ c. diced green pepper
2 tbsp. diced red pimento
4 hard-cooked eggs, diced
Salt to taste
2 tbsp. chopped olives (opt.)
1 c. dressing or mayonnaise

Soften gelatin in cold water; dissolve in hot broth. Cool; add remaining ingredients. Turn into pan, ice cream cartons or individual molds. Chill until firm. Yield: 18 servings.

Mrs. Ora Avant, Tabor City H. S.
Tabor City, North Carolina

CRANBERRY-CHICKEN LOAF

2 tbsp. unflavored gelatin
¾ c. cold water
1 can cranberry sauce
½ c. orange juice
½ c. finely chopped celery
½ c. chopped pecans
1 c. hot chicken broth
½ c. evaporated milk
½ tsp. salt
⅔ c. mayonnaise or salad dressing
2 c. sliced chicken

Soften 1 tablespoonful gelatin in 1/2 cup cold water. Mash cranberry sauce. Add orange juice. Heat, stirring until melted. Stir in softened gelatin; chill until thickened. Add celery and nuts. Pour into 9 x 9-inch pan. Chill until firm. Soften remaining gelatin in remaining cold water. Stir in broth; chill until partially set. Blend in remaining ingredients. Spoon over cranberry layer; chill. Yield: 9-12 servings.

Sue English, Stephen F. Austin State College
Nacogdoches, Texas

DREAM LOAF

1 envelope unflavored gelatin
¼ c. cold stock
3 c. boiling stock
1 lge. hen, boiled and diced
1 c. chopped nuts
6 hard-cooked eggs, sliced
2 c. diced celery
2 c. English peas, seasoned and cooked
1 c. mayonnaise
Juice of 1 lemon

Soak gelatin in cold stock; add hot stock. Combine with remaining ingredients. Pour into mold. Refrigerate until set. Unmold; garnish and serve. Yield: 20 servings.

Mrs. Willie Mae Cornwell, Midway H. S.
Waco, Texas

FROSTY CHICKEN SALAD

1 ½ tsp. unflavored gelatin
2 tbsp. water
1 c. heavy cream, whipped
2 c. diced cooked chicken
½ c. chopped English walnuts
½ c. chopped ripe olives
¼ c. chopped pimento
½ tsp. salt
¼ tsp. pepper
½ tsp. monosodium glutamate
1 tbsp. minced onion
½ c. mayonnaise

Soften gelatin in water; dissolve over hot water. Add to whipped cream. Combine all ingredients. Pour into foil-lined pans. Freeze. Thaw salad for 30 minutes before serving. Cut into squares. Place on slice of tomato or pineapple ring and arrange on salad greens; garnish with stuffed olive or sliced hard-cooked egg, if desired. Yield: 6 servings.

Mrs. Maurice R. Silk, Cooper H. S.
Abilene, Texas

EVELYN'S KELAGUIN UHANG

1 green pepper, chopped
1 sm. onion, chopped
⅛ tsp. Tabasco sauce
Juice of 1 lemon
1 coconut, grated
1 chicken, boiled and chopped

Place pepper and onion in bowl; add Tabasco sauce. Add lemon juice, coconut and chicken. Mix well; refrigerate for 3 hours before serving. Garnish with lettuce or other salad greens. NOTE: Shrimp may be substituted for chicken. Yield: 6 servings.

Ruth C. Moss, Robert E. Lee Jr. H. S.
Danville, Virginia

MOLDED CHICKEN SALAD

1 pkg. lemon gelatin
1 c. boiling water
1 tbsp. vinegar
Pinch of salt
1 c. salad dressing
¾ c. chopped cooked or canned chicken
2 c. chopped celery
½ c. green pepper
½ c. chopped olives
½ c. chopped nuts

Dissolve gelatin in boiling water; add vinegar and salt. Let stand until mixture begins to thicken slightly. Fold in salad dressing, chicken, celery, green pepper, olives and nuts. Refrigerate until gelatin is set. Serve over lettuce. Yield: 6-8 servings.

Eileen Loken, Wolsey H. S.
Wolsey, South Dakota

PARTY CHICKEN SALAD

2 c. coarsely chopped cold cooked chicken
1 c. chopped celery
1 tbsp. lemon juice
Salt and pepper to taste
½ c. mayonnaise
1 c. green grape halves
6 leaves lettuce

Toss chicken, celery, lemon juice, salt and pepper lightly. Mix in mayonnaise. Fold in grapes; arrange mounds of salad in lettuce cups. Yield: 6 servings.

Mrs. Betty Eggland, Stanhope Jr. H. S.
Stanhope, Iowa

PRESSED CHICKEN

1 envelope unflavored gelatin
½ c. cold water
2 c. hot broth
Juice of 1 lemon
1 c. relish
1 c. mayonnaise
1 ½ c. finely chopped celery
4 hard-cooked eggs, finely chopped
4 to 5 c. finely chopped chicken
1 tsp. salt

(Continued on next page)

Soak gelatin in water. Add hot broth and lemon juice. Add relish and mayonnaise to celery, eggs and chicken. Season; mix with gelatin. Pour into mold; refrigerate. Yield: 14 servings.

Mrs. Margaret Hollingsworth, Tuscaloosa H. S.
Tuscaloosa, Alabama

PRESSED CHICKEN

2 envelopes unflavored gelatin
1 c. hot skimmed chicken stock
1 lge. hen, cooked, boned and ground
2 c. chopped celery
4 hard-cooked eggs, chopped
2 c. peas (opt.)
1 to 2 c. mayonnaise
4 tbsp. chowchow or ground sweet pickle (opt.)
2 c. chopped almonds or pecans (opt.)

Soften gelatin in cold water according to directions on package; dissolve in hot chicken stock. Add remaining ingredients; mold in square pans. Chill until firm. Cut into squares. Serve on lettuce with dressing if desired. Yield: 20 servings.

Mrs. Elizabeth R. Whisnant
East Rutherford H. S.
Forest City, North Carolina
Myrtle Little, Hattiesburg H. S.
Hattiesburg, Mississippi

PRESSED CHICKEN

1 lge. hen
⅔ c. sliced celery
3 hard-cooked eggs
2 pimentos
6 tbsp. chopped pickle
5 crackers, finely crumbled
5 tbsp. lemon juice
1 c. mayonnaise
1 tbsp. unflavored gelatin
½ c. cold water
1 c. chicken broth

Cook hen until tender; remove from bones. Finely chop chicken; mix with celery, eggs, pimentos, pickle, crackers, lemon juice and mayonnaise. Dissolve gelatin in cold water; add with chicken broth to mixture. Place in mold; chill for 8 hours. Yield: 12 servings.

Mrs. M. L. McCarty, Beaumont H. S.
Beaumont, Mississippi

PRESSED CHICKEN LOAF

1 lge. hen
6 hard-cooked eggs
1 can pimento
1 envelope unflavored gelatin
2 tbsp. cold water
2 c. boiling chicken broth
2 tbsp. chopped parsley

Cook hen until tender; grind in food chopper. Grind eggs and pimento. Soften gelatin in cold water; dissolve in boiling broth. Mix all ingredients; place in glass loaf pan to congeal. Slice when firm; serve.

Mrs. Rebecca L. Yarbrough, St. Clair Co. H. S.
Odenville, Alabama

SHOESTRING SALAD

½ c. salad dressing
Cream
Vinegar (opt.)
Sugar (opt.)
1 c. shredded carrots
¼ c. minced onion
1 c. diced chicken or tuna
1 c. diced celery
1 can shoestring potatoes

Thin salad dressing with cream; add a small amount of vinegar and sugar. Combine all ingredients except potatoes; chill. Add potatoes just before serving. Serve on lettuce leaves if desired. NOTE: If tuna is used, pour hot water over tuna, then drain. Yield: 5-6 servings.

Eileen Brenden, Independent District No. 432
Mahnomen, Minnesota

SPANISH CHICKEN SALAD

3 ½ c. diced cooked chicken
1 lge. onion, thinly sliced
1 sm. head crisp lettuce, shredded
3 tomatoes, cut into wedges
½ c. olive oil
¼ c. red wine vinegar
1 tsp. salt
½ tsp. pepper

Combine chicken with onion, lettuce and tomato wedges in a bowl. Mix oil, vinegar, salt and pepper; add to chicken mixture. Toss lightly. Serve with additional greens, if desired. Yield: 6 servings.

Flora Moyer, Somerset Area H. S.
Somerset, Pennsylvania

SPICED PRESSED CHICKEN

1 envelope unflavored gelatin
2 ½ c. cold chicken stock
4 hard-cooked eggs
3 c. diced cooked chicken
1 c. diced celery
¼ c. diced green pepper
1 ¾ tsp. salt
⅛ tsp. pepper
¼ tsp. ground allspice
1 tbsp. lemon juice
1 tsp. onion salt
½ tsp. garlic powder

Soften gelatin in 1/4 cup chicken stock. Place over hot water to melt. Add to remaining stock. Slice an egg; arrange lengthwise down center of 9 x 5 x 3-inch loaf pan. Pour in 1/2 cup stock.

(Continued on next page)

Chill until firm. Dice remaining eggs; mix lightly with chicken, celery and green pepper. Turn into loaf pan. Combine gelatin mixture and remaining ingredients; pour over chicken mixture. Cover and chill until firm. Unmold; slice to serve. Serve with salad dressing and lemon wedges. Yield: 8 servings.

Elizabeth McClure, Greencastle H. S.
Greencastle, Indiana

SUPREME CHICKEN SALAD LOAF

4 envelopes unflavored gelatin
½ c. cold chicken broth
2 c. boiling chicken broth
2 c. diced chicken
1 c. diced celery
¼ c. finely cut green pepper
1 7-oz. can pimento
3 to 4 tbsp. lemon juice
Nuts (opt.)
¼ c. sweet pickle relish
Onion juice (opt.)
1 c. mayonnaise
Salt and pepper to taste
1 c. heavy cream, whipped

Soften gelatin in cold broth; dissolve in boiling broth. Cool; when mixture begins to congeal, addall remaining ingredients except cream. Mix well; fold in whipped cream. Chill until firm. Yield: 8-12 servings.

Mrs. Frances Baker Bishop, Denton H. S.
Denton, Texas

CRANBERRY-TURKEY MOLD

2 tbsp. unflavored gelatin
4 tbsp. cold water
2 c. hot turkey broth
1 tsp. grated onion
Salt and pepper to taste
1 c. finely diced celery
2 c. diced cold turkey
2 pimentos, chopped
1 ½ c. sugar
¾ c. hot water
4 c. cranberries
1 stick cinnamon
6 cloves
Grated rind of 1 orange
½ c. finely diced apple
½ c. chopped nuts

Soften 1 tablespoonful gelatin in 2 tablespoonfuls cold water; dissolve in hot turkey broth. Add onion and seasoning to taste. Cool until slightly thickened. Fold in celery, turkey and pimentos. Pour into a fancy mold; chill until almost firm. Boil sugar and water; add cranberries, spices and orange rind. Cook until cranberry skins pop. Put through fine sieve. Soften remaining gelatin in remaining cold water; dissolve in hot cranberry mixture. Cool until thickened; add apple and nuts. Pour over firm gelatin in mold. Chill until firm. Unmold onto lettuce and garnish with mayonnaise if desired. Yield: 6-8 servings.

Mrs. Ethel S. Nash, Ridgefield H. S.
Ridgefield, Connecticut

CRANBERRY-TURKEY SALAD LOAF

2 envelopes unflavored gelatin
2 ¼ c. turkey or chicken bouillon or broth
1 tsp. salt
1 tsp. onion juice
2 c. diced turkey
1 c. chopped celery
2 tbsp. chopped green pepper
2 c. cranberries
1 ¼ c. water
¾ c. sugar
1 tbsp. lemon juice
½ tsp. salt
½ c. chopped apple
¼ c. chopped nuts

Soften 1 envelope gelatin in 1/4 cup cold broth. Heat remaining broth; add 1/2 teaspoonful salt, onion juice and softened gelatin. Remove from heat; stir until dissolved. Cool. Chill until mixture begins to thicken; add turkey, 1/2 cup celery and green pepper. Turn into loaf pan; chill until firm. Cook cranberries in 1 cup water until skins pop, about 7 minutes; strain through fine sieve. Add sugar; simmer for 5 minutes. Soften remaining gelatin in remaining water; dissolve in hot cranberry juice. Add lemon juice and remaining salt. Cool. Chill until mixture begins to thicken. Fold in remaining celery, apple and nuts. Pour on top of firm turkey layer; chill. Unmold onto crisp greens and serve with mayonnaise, if desired. Yield: 8-10 servings.

Mrs. Esther Sigmund, Christen Jr. H. S.
Laredo, Texas

TURKEY SALAD DELUXE

1 10-oz. pkg. frozen green peas
1 10-oz. pkg. frozen asparagus
1 c. diced cooked turkey
¾ c. mayonnaise
½ tsp. salt
⅛ tsp. pepper
6 lge. tomatoes

Cook peas and asparagus separately as directed on packages; drain. Mix vegetables; chill. Add turkey, mayonnaise and seasonings; blend. Remove stem ends from tomatoes. Divide each tomato into four parts, cutting through to within 1 inch of bottom; spread petals apart. Fill tomatoes with salad mixture. Serve on crisp lettuce with additional mayonnaise, if desired. Yield: 6 servings.

Mrs. Marvin L. Henning, Glasco H. S.
Glasco, Kansas

ALMOND-CRAB SALAD

1 6 ½-oz. can crab meat, flaked
1 hard-cooked egg, diced
1 c. sliced celery
2 tbsp. diced pimento
½ c. toasted, blanched and slivered almonds
⅓ c. mayonnaise
1 tbsp. lemon juice
½ tsp. salt
Dash of Tabasco sauce
Lettuce

(Continued on next page)

Combine crab meat, egg, celery, pimento and almonds. Mix mayonnaise with lemon juice, salt and Tabasco sauce. Toss with crab mixture. Serve at once on crisp lettuce. Yield: 3-4 servings.

Mrs. Don Senger, Sumner Jr. H. S.
Sumner, Washington

CAPERS-CRAB MEAT SALAD

6 med. tomatoes
⅓ c. French dressing
2 c. flaked crab meat
½ c. diced celery
6 tbsp. mayonnaise
¼ c. capers
Paprika
Watercress

Scald, peel and chill tomatoes; scoop out centers to form cups. Marinate inside of tomatoes with French dressing for 30 minutes. Mix crab meat, celery and French dressing gently so crab meat will not be broken. Stuff tomatoes; garnish with mayonnaise, capers and paprika. Place on salad plates on a bed of watercress. Yield: 6 servings.

Patricia A. Glass, Dill City H. S.
Dill City, Oklahoma

CHINESE CRAB-RICE SALAD

2 bundles Chinese long rice
1 egg, slightly beaten
1 sm. cucumber, halved lengthwise
2 slices boiled ham
2 leaves cabbage
1 green scallion
1 7 ¾-oz. can crab meat, flaked
⅓ c. vinegar
½ c. sugar
2 tbsp. soy sauce
1 tsp. ginger juice
2 tsp. sesame oil

Cut long rice into 3-inch lengths; soak in water for 15 minutes. Drain. Cook rice in salted boiling water for 15 minutes or until transparent. Remove from heat; drain and rinse with cold water. Set aside. Fry beaten egg; set aside. Remove seed from cucumber. Cut cucumber, egg, ham, cabbage and scallion into thin strips; add to rice. Add crab meat to rice mixture. Combine remaining ingredients; pour over long rice mixture, tossing gently. Refrigerate until ready to serve. Serve on a bed of leaf lettuce. Yield: 6 servings.

Mrs. Asahi T. Oshima
Highlands Intermediate School
Pearl City, Hawaii

CRAB AND DEVILED EGG SALAD

1 c. crab meat
1 tsp. lemon juice
1 tsp. grated onion
¼ tsp. celery
½ c. sliced radishes or celery
2 tbsp. mayonnaise
2 deviled eggs

Toss crab with remaining ingredients except eggs. Serve salad in lettuce cups garnished with deviled eggs.

Marilyn K. Jenkins, Oxford Comm. School
Oxford, Nebraska

CRAB LOUIS

3 6 ½-oz. cans cooked crab meat, flaked
6 c. shredded lettuce
2 hard-cooked eggs, diced
2 tbsp. chopped onion or chives
1 ⅓ c. mayonnaise
⅓ c. heavy cream
½ c. chili sauce
2 tbsp. horseradish
4 tsp. lemon juice
1 tsp. salt
¼ tsp. pepper
¾ tsp. Worcestershire sauce
Tomato wedges

Combine crab meat, lettuce, eggs and onion in a large salad bowl. Combine mayonnaise with cream, chili sauce, horseradish, lemon juice, salt, pepper and Worcestershire sauce; mix well. Pour mayonnaise mixture over crab meat mixture; toss lightly. Garnish with tomato wedges. Serve on individual salad plates. Yield: 6 servings.

Mrs. Stenson Terry, San Perlita H. S.
San Perlita, Texas
Mrs. May Round, R. H. Watkins H. S.
Laurel, Mississippi

CRAB LOUIS

1 lb. crab meat
1 head lettuce, shredded
½ tsp. salt
4 tomatoes, sliced
1 cucumber, sliced
3 hard-cooked eggs, sliced
1 c. mayonnaise
3 tbsp. catsup
2 tbsp. chopped sweet pickle
1 tbsp. lemon juice

Remove any shell or cartilage from crab meat. Place lettuce in a large shallow bowl; sprinkle with salt. Arrange crab meat over lettuce. Place alternate slices of tomatoes, cucumbers and eggs around edge of bowl. Combine remaining ingredients; chill. Spread over crab mixture. Yield: 6 servings.

Mrs. Nancy Frizzell, Cleburne H. S.
Cleburne, Texas

CRAB MEAT SALAD

2 envelopes unflavored gelatin
1 ¼ c. cold water
1 c. boiling bouillon
2 tbsp. lemon juice
1 tsp. salt
3 hard-cooked eggs, sliced
6 olives, sliced
½ c. finely chopped celery
¼ c. finely chopped olives
1 6 ½-oz. can crab meat
¾ c. salad dressing

Soak gelatin in 1/4 cup cold water; dissolve in boiling bouillon. Add 1/2 cup cold water, lemon juice and salt. Place egg slices with sliced olives between each in ring mold. Pour a small amount of gelatin mixture into mold. Chill until firm. Chill remaining gelatin mixture until partially thickened; add remaining ingredients. Pour into mold. Chill until firm. Unmold. Yield: 6 servings.

Marjory Ramage, Portland Jr. H. S.
Portland, Connecticut

CRAB MEAT SALAD

1 3-oz. pkg. lemon gelatin
¼ tsp. salt
1 c. boiling water
½ c. cold water
Dash of pepper
1 tbsp. lemon juice
¼ c. mayonnaise
1 c. whipped cream
½ c. cottage cheese
1 ¼ c. crab meat
½ c. diced celery

Dissolve gelatin and salt in boiling water. Add cold water, pepper and lemon juice. Chill until thick. Combine mayonnaise and whipped cream. Fold cottage cheese, crab meat, celery and mayonnaise-whipped cream mixture into gelatin mixture. Pour into 1-quart mold. Chill until firm. Unmold onto salad greens. Yield: 8 servings.

Mrs. Charmiane W. Freeman, Halls H. S.
Halls, Tennessee

CRAB SALAD

1 pkg. lemon gelatin
1 c. hot water
1 can crab meat
1 c. heavy cream
½ c. chili sauce
1 c. cottage cheese
1 c. mayonnaise

Dissolve gelatin in hot water; cool slightly. Combine remaining ingredients; fold into gelatin. Chill until firm. Yield: 8 servings.

Barbara Edwards, Tulid H. S.
Tulid, Texas

CRAB SALAD

1 c. diced celery
3 tbsp. lemon juice
½ c. diced green pepper
½ tsp. salt
½ tsp. monosodium glutamate
2 hard-cooked eggs, chopped
1 6 ½-oz. can crab meat
½ c. mayonnaise
1 head lettuce
2 med. tomatoes, sliced

Combine celery, lemon juice, green pepper, salt, monosodium glutamate and eggs in mixing bowl. Add crab and mayonnaise; mix well. Place on lettuce leaves; arrange tomatoes around salad. Yield: 6 servings.

Mrs. Kathleen K. Horne, Powell Valley H. S.
Big Stone Gap, Virginia

WEST INDIES CRAB SALAD

1 med. onion, finely chopped
1 lb. crab meat
Salt and pepper to taste
4 oz. cooking oil
3 oz. cider vinegar
4 oz. ice water

Spread one-half the onion in large bowl. Place crab meat on onion. Top with remaining onion. Salt and pepper to taste. Pour oil, vinegar and ice water over crab-onion mixture. Cover; refrigerate for 2 to 12 hours. Toss lightly, but do not stir. Yield: 6 servings.

Earline S. Phillips, Weogufka H. S.
Weogufka, Alabama

LOBSTER IN CUCUMBER

½ sm. onion
Juice of 1 lime
2 ¼ c. mayonnaise
¾ c. chili sauce
Salt and black pepper to taste
Cayenne pepper
10 7 to 8-in. cucumbers
1 ½ lb. lobster, cooked and diced
¾ c. minced celery
3 tbsp. minced parsley
3 tbsp. minced dill

Mince the onion in a bowl until it is almost pureed; turn into a cloth dampened with cold water. Press out all the juice into a larger bowl. Add lime juice, mayonnaise and chili sauce; mix well. Season to taste with salt, pepper and cayenne pepper. Peel the cucumbers; cut into halves. Hollow out cucumbers to make 20 shallow boats. Mix lobster, minced celery and 2 cups of the dressing. Fill the cucumber boats with lobster mixture. Sprinkle each boat with mixed parsley and dill. Chill. Serve on lettuce, if desired. Serve with remaining dressing. Yield: 10 servings.

Anne C. Chiungos, Dracut H. S.
Dracut, Massachusetts

MOCK LOBSTER AND CELERY SALAD

1 lb. fillet of haddock
1 c. boiling water
2 ¼ tsp. salt
1 stalk celery
2 tbsp. fresh lemon juice
1 ½ c. diced celery
¼ c. chopped green pepper
⅛ tsp. pepper
½ tsp. crumbled thyme leaves
¼ c. mayonnaise
Head lettuce
Fresh parsley
Radish roses
Paprika

Tie fish in cheesecloth bag; place in boiling water with 1 teaspoonful salt and celery stalk. Cook for 10 to 15 minutes or until fish is flaky. Remove from water; sprinkle with lemon juice. Chill. Flake fish; toss lightly with diced celery, green pepper, pepper, thyme, mayonnaise and remaining salt. Serve on lettuce; garnish with parsley, radishes and paprika. Yield: 6 servings.

Photograph for this recipe on page 261.

SALMON CAESAR SALAD

1 1-lb. can salmon
1 clove of garlic, peeled and quartered
½ c. olive oil or salad oil
1 ½ c. toasted bread cubes, cut into ½-in. pieces
8 c. mixed torn salad greens
1 sm. onion, thinly sliced
½ tsp. salt
Dash of finely ground pepper
1 egg
2 tbsp. lemon juice
⅓ c. grated Parmesan cheese

Drain salmon; break into large pieces. Add garlic to oil; let stand for at least 1 hour. Remove garlic from oil. Gradually pour 1/4 cup of garlic oil over bread cubes, mixing lightly until all oil is absorbed. Place salad greens in a large salad bowl. Separate onion slices into rings; add to salad greens. Sprinkle with salt and pepper. Pour remaining garlic oil over greens, tossing lightly. Cook egg for 1 minute; break into salad. Add lemon juice; mix thoroughly. Add cheese, bread cubes and salmon; toss lightly. Serve immediately. Yield: 6 servings.

Mrs. Mildred H. Beck, Fairhope H. S.
Fairhope, Alabama

SALMON MOUSSE

2 tbsp. unflavored gelatin
½ c. cold water
1 c. boiling water
2 tbsp. lemon juice
2 tbsp. vinegar
1 c. mayonnaise
1 c. heavy cream, whipped
½ tsp. salt
2 c. flaked red salmon
1 onion, grated
1 c. chopped celery
1 c. chopped cucumbers

Soak gelatin in cold water; dissolve in boiling water. Add lemon juice and vinegar; cool. When mixture begins to thicken, add mayonnaise and whipped cream. Add remaining ingredients; pour into a large oiled fish mold. Chill until firm. Turn out onto platter; surround with lettuce. Garnish with lemon and pickles. Yield: 12 servings.

Mrs. Ruth L. DeFriese, Young H. S.
Knoxville, Tennessee

SALMON SALAD

2 c. salmon
3 hard-cooked eggs, chopped
1 ½ c. cooked macaroni
¼ c. diced pickles
½ c. diced celery
1 sm. onion, diced
¼ c. salad dressing
½ tsp. salt
¼ tsp. pepper

Combine all ingredients in mixing bowl; mix lightly. Pile onto crisp salad greens and garnish with paprika, if desired. Yield: 6 servings.

Louise O. Gurley, Sun Valley H. S.
Monroe, North Carolina

COLD RICE AND SEAFOOD SALAD

1 c. shrimp, crab meat or lobster
1 c. drained canned peas
¼ c. diced pimento
¼ c. chopped ripe olives
1 ½ c. cooked rice
2 tsp. grated onion
1 tsp. salt
Dash of pepper
2 tsp. lemon or lime juice
⅔ c. mayonnaise
1 lge. head lettuce
Green pepper strips

Combine all ingredients except lettuce and green pepper strips. Chill. Wash lettuce; cut out core to make a cavity large enough for stuffing. Pack cold salad into lettuce cavity. Chill; cut into wedges. Garnish with green pepper strips. Yield: 4 servings.

Jane Johnston, Southwest Dekalb H. S.
Decatur, Georgia

JELLIED SHRIMP SALAD

3 c. canned tomatoes
1 ½ c. water
1 ½ tsp. salt
3 cloves
1 bay leaf
1 tsp. mustard
1 onion, grated
1 tbsp. sugar
2 tbsp. unflavored gelatin
½ c. cold water
2 c. shrimp
1 c. diced celery
1 green pepper, diced
4 hard-cooked eggs, sliced

(Continued on next page)

Cook tomatoes, water, salt, cloves, bay leaf, mustard, onion and sugar until soft; strain. Add gelatin soaked in water; chill until thick. Add shrimp, celery and pepper; alternate layers of gelatin mixture with sliced eggs in ring mold. Chill until firm. Yield: 8-10 servings.

Mrs. Reba Wilson, Brainerd H. S.
Chattanooga, Tennessee

MOLDED SHRIMP SALAD

2 tbsp. unflavored gelatin
½ c. cold water
2 c. tomato juice
3 3-oz. pkg. cream cheese
1 c. salad dressing
1 ½ c. diced celery
1 green pepper, chopped
1 6 ½-oz. can shrimp, broken

Dissolve gelatin in cold water. Heat tomato juice; pour over cheese. Add gelatin mixture with cheese mixture and remaining ingredients. Pour into a 13 x 7 x 1 1/2-inch pan or individual molds. Refrigerate until firm. Serve on lettuce leaves. NOTE: Two tablespoonfuls onion juice may be add to salad mixture. Yield: 8 servings.

Mrs. Frances Barrett, Concord H. S.
Concord, Arkansas

MACARONI-SHRIMP SALAD

3 c. cooked drained shell macaroni
1 6-oz. can cocktail shrimp, drained
1 tsp. salt
¼ tsp. pepper
1 tbsp. instant onion or ¼ c. fresh chopped onion
¾ c. mayonnaise
Lettuce leaves

Combine all ingredients except lettuce; toss lightly. Refrigerate for 2 hours before serving to blend flavors. Serve in bowl lined with lettuce leaves. Yield: 6 servings.

Mrs. Lucy Jo Tormey, Butte Co. H. S.
Arco, Idaho

SHRIMP REMOULADE

6 tbsp. salad oil
3 tbsp. lemon juice
1 tbsp. chili sauce
3 tbsp. catsup
1 tbsp. horseradish
1 tbsp. prepared mustard
½ tsp. paprika
Dash of cayenne pepper
1 clove of garlic, minced
1 head lettuce
1 lb. boiled shrimp, chilled

Combine salad oil, lemon juice, chili sauce, catsup, horseradish, prepared mustard, paprika, pepper and garlic in a mixing bowl. Tear lettuce into pieces; line individual bowls with lettuce. Place chilled shrimp on lettuce. Pour sauce over shrimp. Yield: 4-6 servings.

Margaret G. Williamson, Northside H. S.
Warner Robins, Georgia

SHRIMP SALAD

2 7-oz. cans shrimp
5 stalks celery, diced
1 No. 303 can pineapple chunks, drained
1 c. pecans
Mayonnaise

Chill all ingredients. Mix all ingredients lightly. Serve in lettuce cup. Yield: 4-6 servings.

Mrs. Gary Wiltse, Powder River H. S.
Broadus, Montana

SHRIMP SALAD

3 c. cold cooked or canned shrimp, cut into small pieces
3 hard-cooked eggs, diced
6 ripe olives, cut up
Salt and pepper to taste
1 tsp. chopped onion
3 tbsp. chopped celery
French dressing
Lettuce leaves
Mayonnaise

Combine all ingredients except French dressing, lettuce and mayonnaise; marinate in a small amount of French dressing. Serve in lettuce cups; garnish with additional olives. Serve with mayonnaise. Yield: 6-8 servings.

Helen M. Pyburn
Southeastern Louisiana College
Hammond, Louisiana

SHRIMP SALAD

2 c. cooked macaroni or 1 ½ boxes juniorette macaroni, cooked
1 c. chopped celery
1 sm. or med. onion, chopped
¼ c. chopped green pepper
¼ c. chopped pimento
¼ c. French dressing
3 c. cooked or 2 4-oz. cans shrimp
2 to 5 hard-cooked eggs, sliced
½ tsp. salt
Pepper to taste (opt.)
¼ tsp. paprika (opt.)
1 c. salad dressing or mayonnaise

Chill macaroni; add remaining ingredients. Mix well. Yield: 4-6 servings.

Mrs. Ruth Stoffel, Hazel Green H. S.
Hazel Green, Wisconsin
Karen Mae Lindstrom, Anaheim H. S.
Anaheim, California

QUICK TUNA SALAD

1 can white chunk tuna
2 hard-cooked eggs, chopped
1 ½ c. diced celery
1 apple, diced
2 pickles, chopped or 3 tbsp. pickle relish
2 tsp. mustard
½ c. salad dressing
½ tsp. paprika
1 tbsp. finely crushed dry onion soup mix

Combine tuna, eggs, celery and apple in a large bowl. Combine pickles, mustard and salad dressing; pour over tuna mixture. Toss lightly. Chill for 2 hours. Sprinkle with paprika and onion soup. Serve on lettuce leaf with corn chips, if desired. Yield: 4-5 servings.

Mrs. Sevola Fulgham, Safford H. S.
Safford, Arizona

SEA BREEZE MOLD

2 tbsp. unflavored gelatin
¾ c. water
⅓ c. lemon juice
2 6-oz. cans chunk-style tuna or 1 1-lb. can salmon
1 c. mayonnaise
1 c. celery
¼ c. chopped green pepper or 2 tbsp. chopped olives
½ tsp. salt

Soften gelatin in water; dissolve over hot water. Add remaining ingredients. Pour into oiled mold; chill until firm. Decorate with lemon, olives or parsley, if desired. Yield: 4-6 servings.

Mrs. Regina R. Duncan, West Fannin H. S.
Blue Ridge, Georgia

TUNA CRUNCH LOAF

2 envelopes unflavored gelatin
½ c. cold water
1 can cream of celery soup
¼ c. lemon juice
1 tbsp. prepared mustard
1 tsp. salt
Dash of pepper
1 c. mayonnaise
2 6 ½-oz. cans tuna, flaked
1 c. chopped celery
½ c. grated or chopped cucumber
½ c. chopped green pepper

Soften gelatin in cold water. Heat soup just to boiling; add gelatin, stirring to dissolve gelatin. Stir in lemon juice, mustard, salt and pepper. Chill until partially set. Add mayonnaise, tuna, celery, cucumber and green pepper. Pour into 8 1/2 x 4 1/2 x 2 1/2-inch loaf pan. Chill until firm. Yield: 6 servings.

Nan Lindsey, Wade Hampton H. S.
Greenville, South Carolina
Mrs. Priscilla Watkins, Evans H. S.
Evans, Georgia

TUNA-MACARONI SALAD

1 c. uncooked macaroni
1 can tuna
½ to ¾ c. sandwich spread
½ c. chopped celery (opt.)
2 hard-cooked eggs

Cook macaroni as directed on package; drain. Cool quickly under cold running water; drain again. Drain tuna; add to macaroni. Add sandwich spread and celery; mix lightly. Garnish with slices of hard-cooked eggs. Yield: 4 servings.

Mrs. Marjorie Petefish, Holbrook Public School
Holbrook, Nebraska

TUNA SALAD

1 6 ½-oz. can tuna, flaked
1 tbsp. lemon juice
1 c. sliced celery
1 tsp. finely chopped onion
¼ green pepper, chopped
10 stuffed green olives, sliced
¼ c. salad dressing
1 hard-cooked egg, cut into wedges
Dash of paprika

Sprinkle tuna with lemon juice. Add celery, onion, green pepper and olives; toss lightly with salad dressing. Chill. Serve on lettuce, garnished with egg and paprika. Yield: 4 servings.

Katherine W. Rebbe, Wakefield Comm. H. S.
Wakefield, Nebraska

TUNA SALAD

2 cans tuna
2 apples, chopped
1 celery heart, chopped
3 hard-cooked eggs, chopped
1 lemon
Pepper
Mayonnaise

Place tuna in a sieve; rinse slightly under running water. Drain. Mix apples, celery and eggs with tuna chunks. Squeeze lemon juice over mixture. Sprinkle with pepper. Mix in mayonnaise. Serve on a crisp lettuce leaf. Yield: 6 servings.

Mrs. Charles Moore, C.C. Snell Jr. H. S.
Bayard, New Mexico

TUNA SOUFFLE SALAD

1 pkg. lemon gelatin
1 c. hot water
½ c. cold water
2 tbsp. lemon juice
½ c. mayonnaise
¼ tsp. salt
1 No. ½ can tuna
¾ c. chopped celery
¼ c. sliced stuffed olives
2 tbsp. chopped pimento
½ tsp. grated onion

(Continued on next page)

Dissolve gelatin in hot water; add cold water, lemon juice, mayonnaise and salt. Blend well with rotary beater. Pour into refrigerator tray; quick chill in freezing unit for 15 to 20 minutes or until firm about 1-inch from edge, but soft in center. Turn mixture into bowl; whip with rotary beater until fluffy. Fold in remaining ingredients. Pour into 1-quart mold. Chill until firm. Unmold and garnish. Yield: 4-6 servings,

Mrs. Ruth Nolte, Buda H. S.
Buda, Texas

MOLDED FISH SALAD

2 c. cooked fish
1 ½ tbsp. unflavored gelatin
¼ c. water
1 tbsp. lemon juice
½ c. unpeeled diced apple
1 c. diced celery
1 c. drained canned pineapple, diced
¼ c. stuffed olives, chopped
1 tsp. salt
1 c. mayonnaise

Flake fish. Soak gelatin in cold water for 5 minutes; place over boiling water to dissolve. Add lemon juice to diced apple; combine with fish, celery, pineapple, olives and salt. Add mayonnaise and dissolved gelatin; mix thoroughly. Pour into molds. Chill until firm. Serve on lettuce, if desired. Yield: 6 servings.

Lyvonne Johnson, Trafalgar Jr. Sec. H. S.
Nelson, British Columbia, Canada

ASPARAGUS-MEAT MOLD

2 tsp. unflavored gelatin
¼ c. cold water
1 c. hot meat broth
2 c. chopped cooked meat
1 c. asparagus tips
¼ c. chopped green pepper
½ c. chopped celery
½ tsp. salt
Mayonnaise
Stuffed olives

Soften gelatin in cold water; add hot meat broth. Stir until dissolved. Chill until partially set. Arrange meat, asparagus, pepper and celery in a mold; season with salt. Add gelatin. Chill until firm. Turn out on a bed of crisp lettuce. Garnish with mayonnaise and olives. Yield: 6 servings.

Mrs. C. R. Ledbetter, Black Rock H. S.
Black Rock, Arkansas

CHEF MEAT SALAD BOWL

2 c. diced meat
2 hard-cooked eggs, diced
1 c. diced sharp Cheddar cheese
4 c. chopped mixed greens
2 tbsp. grated onion
1 c. finely diced celery
2 tomatoes, cut into wedges
½ tsp. salt
¼ clove of garlic, crushed
Pepper to taste
Salad dressing

Place all ingredients except dressing in mixing bowl in order given. Toss lightly with dressing just before serving; serve cold. Garnish with watercress or parsley. Yield: 4-6 servings.

Mrs. Buena B. Hedden, Hayesville H. S.
Hayesville, North Carolina

MACARONI-FRANK SALAD BOWL

4 oz. macaroni
1 sm. clove of garlic
1 sm. onion
1 c. thick sour cream
¼ c. French dressing
½ tsp. salt
2 med. tomatoes
2 c. torn curly endive
1 c. diced celery
¼ c. thinly sliced radishes
¼ c. sliced green onions
4 frankfurters, sliced

Cook macaroni in boiling, salted water with garlic and onion until tender; drain. Remove and discard garlic and onion. Blend hot macaroni, sour cream, French dressing and salt. Chill thoroughly. Peel and cut tomatoes into wedges; chill. Place endive, celery, radishes, green onions and frankfurters in large salad bowl; add macaroni mixture and tomato wedges. Toss lightly to mix thoroughly. Yield: 6 servings.

Carolyn Kinard, Norphlet H. S.
Norphlet, Arkansas

MEAL-IN-ONE SALAD

6 slivered slices tongue, corned beef or luncheon meat
¼ lb. slivered Swiss cheese
2 hard-cooked eggs
1 cucumber, chopped
1 green pepper, chopped
1 carrot, chopped
2 tomatoes, chopped
1 tsp. minced onion
1 tsp. vinegar
4 tbsp. mayonnaise
3 tbsp. milk or cream
Sharp cream dressing

Combine all ingredients except cream dressing. Serve with sharp cream dressing. Yield: 6 servings.

Pearle Peterson, Perth Amboy H. S.
Perth Amboy, New Jersey

Sandwich Favorites

BARBECUED BEEF IN BUNS

1 ¼ lb. beef, cut into 1-in. cubes
Lard
1 c. water
1 c. thinly sliced onions
1 clove of garlic, minced (opt.)
1 tbsp. Worcestershire sauce
½ c. catsup
1 ½ tsp. salt
¼ tsp. pepper
12 hamburger buns

Brown beef cubes in hot lard. Add water; cover. Simmer for 1 hour and 30 minutes or until tender. Brown onions and garlic in hot lard; add to cooked meat with Worcestershire sauce, catsup, salt and pepper. Heat. Fill buns with mixture. Yield: 12 servings.

Mary Ann DeVore, Fort Recovery H. S.
Fort Recovery, Ohio

ITALIAN ROAST BEEF SANDWICHES

2 lb. chuck roast
Margarine
1 onion, finely chopped
2 stalks celery, finely chopped
½ tsp. oregano
2 tsp. rosemary
Dry parsley leaves
½ tsp. garlic salt
2 bay leaves
1 8-oz. can tomato sauce
1 ½ c. water
Salt and pepper
Round buns

Trim fat from roast; sear in margarine in pan. Add onion, celery, oregano, rosemary, parsley, garlic salt, bay leaves, tomato sauce and water; add salt and pepper to taste. Bake at 350 degrees for 1 hour. When done, pull meat apart with fork until meat has a shredded appearance. Remove bay leaves. Pile meat mixture onto hard buns. Yield: 8 servings.

Mrs. Patricia T. Stealey
Mapletown Jr.-Sr. H. S.
Greensboro, Pennsylvania

ITALIAN STEAK SANDWICHES

Butter or margarine
1 Bermuda onion, sliced
1 8-oz. can tomato sauce
⅛ tsp. salt
⅛ tsp. instant minced onion
½ tsp. oregano
Dash of pepper
Dash of garlic salt
½ tsp. Worcestershire sauce
1 ¼ lb. sandwich steak, thinly sliced
4 hard or soft Italian rolls
Olive oil
2 med. dill pickles, sliced

Melt 2 tablespoonfuls butter in frying pan. Brown onion slices in butter slowly until tender. Combine tomato sauce and seasonings; bring to a boil. Stir in 1 teaspoonful butter and Worcestershire sauce. Cover and simmer for 10 minutes. Quickly brown steak in pan with onion. Slice rolls; sprinkle with olive oil. Place 2 tablespoonfuls of sauce in each roll; add steak and onions. Top with remaining sauce. Garnish with pickle slices and additional oregano. Serve immediately. Yield: 4 servings.

Mrs. Marjorie Richards Leinbach
Bald Eagle H. S.
Wingate, Pennsylvania

ARROYO GRANDE EAGLEBURGERS

1 lb. ground meat
½ med. onion, grated
¼ c. water
⅓ c. instant dry milk
1 tbsp. catsup
1 tsp. salt
¼ tsp. pepper
1 egg, slightly beaten
6 slices bread
2 tbsp. butter or margarine

Place ground meat and onion in mixing bowl. Place water in 1-cup liquid measuring cup; add dry milk solids, catsup, salt, pepper and slightly beaten egg. Stir with fork until mixture is smooth. Add to meat and onion; mix again until all ingredients are well blended. Divide into six equal portions. Toast bread on one side only. Spread untoasted side with butter or margarine. Spread buttered, untoasted side with meat mixture, being sure to cover bread crusts completely. Broil 6 inches from heat for 6 minutes or to desired doneness.

Ann Bauer, Arroyo Grande H. S.
Arroyo Grande, California

BARBECUES

1 lb. hamburger
1 med. onion, finely cut
1 c. finely cut celery (opt.)
½ c. catsup
2 to 3 tbsp. brown sugar
1 tbsp. chopped mango (opt.)
Dash of cinnamon (opt.)
1 to 2 tbsp. Worcestershire sauce
1 to 2 tbsp. vinegar
½ tsp. salt
Chili powder (opt.)
Sandwich buns or bread

Brown meat. Simmer onion and celery in a small amount of water for 15 minutes; drain. Add meat and remaining ingredients except buns. Simmer until meat is done. Serve on sandwich buns or bread.

Hazel E. Schaad, Fulton Comm. H. S.
Fulton, Illinois
Mrs. Janice Furnish, Henryville H. S.
Henryville, Indiana

BARBECUES

10 lb. ground meat
4 bottles catsup
1 bottle steak sauce
1 bottle Worcestershire sauce
1 bottle barbecue sauce
1 sm. jar mustard
Hot sauce to taste
Hamburger buns

Sear meat in a small amount of shortening; add remaining ingredients except buns. Simmer for 4 to 6 hours. Serve on hamburger buns. Yield: 40 servings.

Mrs. Patsy Harris Stemple, Gillham H. S.
Gillham, Arkansas

BARBECUED HAMBURGER

2 lb. ground beef
Salt to taste
1 sm. onion, chopped
½ c. catsup
1 tbsp. prepared mustard
1 tbsp. chili powder
Buns

Brown meat with salt and onion; add catsup, mustard and chili powder. Cook in double boiler for 1 hour. Serve on hot buns. Yield: 12 servings.

Glenda Cochran, Vidor H. S.
Vidor, Texas

BARBECUED HAMBURGER

1 onion, chopped
1 tbsp. fat
2 lb. hamburger
½ c. catsup
2 tbsp. brown sugar
2 tbsp. vinegar
2 tsp. mustard
1 tsp. Worcestershire sauce
Buns

Fry onion in fat until golden brown. Add hamburger and brown. Pour off excess fat. Combine remaining ingredients except buns. Add to meat mixture; simmer until hot. Serve in buns. Yield: 8 servings.

Janice M. Mountz
Brandywine Heights Area School
Topton, Pennsylvania

BARBECUED HAMBURGER

1 ½ c. catsup
4 tbsp. vinegar
4 tbsp. Worcestershire sauce
Dash of salt
2 tsp. sugar
4 tbsp. prepared mustard
2 tsp. celery seed
2 lb. hamburger
2 tbsp. lard
16 hamburger buns
1 ½ c. shredded cabbage

Boil catsup, vinegar, Worcestershire sauce, salt, sugar and mustard for 15 minutes. Add celery seed. Fry hamburger in lard until well done. Pour sauce into hamburger. Cook for 5 minutes. Serve on hamburger buns with shredded cabbage. Yield: 8 servings.

Barbara Smith, Washington Jr. H. S.
New Britain, Connecticut

BEAN BURGERS

1 med. onion, finely chopped
⅓ c. chopped green pepper
2 tbsp. shortening
1 lb. ground beef
1 6-oz. can tomato paste
½ c. water
1 ½ tsp. salt
1 to 2 tsp. chili powder
1 No. 303 can pork and beans
6 hamburger buns

Saute onion and green pepper in shortening until tender; add ground beef. Cook until tender and brown; add tomato paste, water, salt, chili powder and beans. Mix well. Bring to a boil; reduce heat and simmer for 10 minutes. Serve on buns. Yield: 6 servings.

Mrs. Mary W. Hall, John L. McClellan H. S.
Little Rock, Arkansas

BEEFBURGER SURPRISE

2 lb. ground beef
Salt and pepper to taste
Left-over beans
6 slices bacon
6 buns, toasted

Form ground beef into 12 patties; sprinkle with salt and pepper. Round out six patties with bottom of spoon; place 2 teaspoonfuls of beans on each of the six patties. Place remaining beef patties over the beans. Seal the edges of the patties. Wrap bacon slice around patties; secure with toothpicks. Broil on grill for 5 minutes on each side. Serve on buns. Yield: 6 servings.

Blanche Burns, Union H. S.
Strathmore, California

BLEU CHEESE BURGERS IN BARBECUE SAUCE

1 ½ lb. ground beef
¾ c. quick cooking oats
½ tsp. salt
½ c. milk
½ c. crumbled Bleu cheese

(Continued on next page)

Combine beef, oats, salt and milk. Shape into 12 patties. Sprinkle Bleu cheese on six patties. Top with remaining patties and press together. Pan-fry burgers until brown. Pour off excess fat.

BARBECUE SAUCE:

1 8-oz. can tomato sauce
¼ c. molasses
1 tbsp. mustard
1 tbsp. vinegar
1 tsp. chopped onion
¼ tsp. garlic salt
1 tbsp. Worcestershire sauce
¼ tsp. salt
¼ tsp. pepper
Buns

Combine all ingredients except buns; bring to a boil. Boil for 1 minutes. Pour over patties. Heat for 15 minutes. Serve on buns. Yield: 6 servings.

Vivian L. Reagan, Millvale H. S.
Pittsburgh, Pennsylvania

BUN BURGERS

1 lb. ground beef
½ tsp. Worcestershire sauce
1 tsp. steak sauce (opt.)
Dash of sage
Dash of chili powder
Dash of onion salt
½ c. catsup
1 recipe biscuit dough or 6 to 8 hamburger bun halves

Combine all ingredients except biscuit dough or buns. Roll biscuit dough 1/8 to 1/4-inch thick. Cut into indivudual rounds with a large biscuit cutter; slightly round dough on sides. Place on cookie sheet. Fill with hamburger mixture. Bake at 375 degrees for 25 to 30 minutes. Yield: 6-8 servings.

Mrs. Glennie E. Bogue, South Edgecombe School
Pinetops, North Carolina

CHEESEBURGER TURNOVERS

½ lb. hamburger
1 tbsp. chopped onion
¼ tsp. salt
⅛ tsp. pepper
1 can refrigerated biscuits
5 slices American cheese, cut into halves

Fry hamburger until it loses its red color; add onion, salt and pepper. Place 2 biscuits slightly overlapping on well floured surface. Roll each biscuit to an oval about 5 inches long. Place about 3 tablespoonfuls of meat mixture on 1 rolled biscuit; top with 2 halves of sliced cheese. Moisten edges with water; fold the second biscuit over the meat and cheese. Seal with fork. Prick top. Repeat until all ingredients are used. Bake at 425 degrees for 8 to 10 minutes or until golden brown. Serve hot. Yield: 10 servings.

Lucille Cook, Wilmer-Hutchins H. S.
Hutchins, Texas

CHILI-STUFFED ROLLS

1 lb. ground beef
1 tbsp. shortening
1 med. onion, finely chopped
2 tsp. chili powder
1 tsp. salt
⅛ tsp. garlic powder
⅛ tsp. pepper
4 slices American cheese
10 frankfurter buns

Brown meat in shortening; add onion, chili powder, salt, garlic powder and pepper. Cook for 5 minutes, stirring constantly. Cut cheese into 1/2-inch squares; stir into mixture. Heat just enough to half melt cheese. Heat buns and fill each with mixture. Yield: 10 servings.

Mrs. Ted Trotter, Independence H. S.
Independence, Louisiana

CHUCKWAGON BARBECUES

1 lb. ground beef
½ c. chopped onion
⅓ c. chopped green pepper
1 tsp. salt
¼ tsp. chili powder
¼ tsp. pepper
3 tbsp. flour
⅔ c. catsup
2 tsp. Worcestershire sauce
1 7-oz. bottle or 1 c. 7-Up
10 hamburger buns

Cook meat, onion and green pepper in heavy skillet until lightly browned. Stir in salt, chili powder, pepper and flour. Add catsup, Worcestershire sauce and 7-Up, stirring until smooth. Cook, stirring occasionally, for 15 minutes. Spoon onto buns. NOTE: Buns may be toasted before spreading with meat mixture. Yield: 10 servings.

Janice Sapp, Bartlett Jr. H. S.
Savannah, Georgia

HAMBURGER SNACKS

1 ¼ lb. hamburger
¾ tsp. salt
¼ tsp. pepper
3 drops of Worcestershire sauce
½ c. minced onion
½ c. catsup
½ tsp. prepared mustard
Hamburger buns

Combine all ingredients except buns; spread 1/2-inch thick on hamburger buns. Spread to edge to keep from burning. Broil for 8 minutes or to desired doneness. NOTE: May be served as open-faced or with top. A slice of tomato may be added if top is used.

Mrs. Pauline I. Kuydendall
Kernersville Jr. H. S.
Kernersville, North Carolina

GIRL SCOUT SLOPPY JOES

1 onion, chopped
Fat
1 lb. ground beef
1 can red kidney beans
1 can vegetable soup
1 can tomato soup
Hamburger buns

Brown onion in a small amount of fat; add ground beef. Cook, stirring, until brown. Pour kidney beans, vegetable soup and tomato soup over meat. Let simmer until hot. Serve over hamburger buns. Yield: 6 servings.

Malta O. Ledford, Jupiter H. S.
Jupiter, Florida

HOGGIE POGGIES

1 lb. hamburger
1 med. onion, diced
½ sm. can evaporated milk
3 tbsp. catsup or barbecue sauce
3 tbsp. mustard (opt.)
1 tbsp. Worcestershire sauce (opt.)
Salt and pepper to taste
Hamburger buns

Combine all ingredients except buns. Cut buns into halves. Spread hamburger mixture on each half. Broil until done.

Mrs. Barbara Irwin, Fremont H. S.
Fremont, Michigan
Mrs. J. H. Claypool, Marshall H. S.
Marshall, Illinois

JUMBO PIZZA SANDWICH

1 1-lb. loaf French or Vienna bread
¼ c. sliced or chopped ripe olives
⅛ tsp. pepper
¼ tsp. ground oregano
½ to ¾ tsp. salt
⅛ tsp. garlic salt (opt.)
2 tbsp. finely chopped green onion or chives
½ to 1 lb. ground beef
¼ c. finely grated Parmesan cheese
1 6-oz. can tomato paste
½ paste can water (opt.)
1 8-oz. pkg. sliced process cheese

Cut French bread in half, lengthwise. Combine olives, pepper, oregano, salts, green onion, beef, Parmesan cheese and tomato paste. Divide meat mixture equally; spread over cut sides of bread. Place on a cookie sheet, spread-side up. Bake at 375 to 400 degrees for 15 minutes. Cut cheese slices into halves diagonally; cover mixture with eight overlapping triangular slices. Return to oven for 5 to 10 minutes. Serve hot. Yield: 8-12 servings.

Beatrice P. Grace, Dardanelle H. S.
Dardanelle, Arkansas
Mrs. Merry Emme, Chamberlain H. S.
Chamberlain, South Dakota
Goldie Tranbarger, Greenfield H. S.
Greenfield, Illinois

LONGBOY CHEESEBURGERS

½ lb. ground meat
½ tsp. salt
¼ tsp. pepper
½ sm. onion, finely chopped
1 tbsp. (heaping) catsup
1 tbsp. (heaping) chili sauce or powder
1 ½ tsp. Worcestershire sauce
Dash of hot sauce
½ sm. can evaporated milk
1 c. crushed corn flakes
Buns
Grated cheese

Mix all ingredients except buns and cheese thoroughly. Pat mixture onto buns. Place buns under broiler for 10 minutes; remove. Sprinkle with grated cheese. Place under broiler until cheese is melted. NOTE: Cheeseburgers may be wrapped in foil and frozen. Yield: 4 servings.

Mrs. Ann Edwards, Corsicana H. S.
Corsicana, Texas

OPEN-FACED HAMBURGERS

1 lb. ground beef
1 tsp. salt
1 tsp. Worcestershire sauce
¼ c. evaporated milk
8 to 10 slices bread

Combine all ingredients except bread; spread on slices of bread. Broil 3 inches from heat until done.

Mrs. Robert L. Abney, Jr., Bay Springs H. S.
Bay Springs, Mississippi

PICKLEBURGERS

1 ¼ lb. ground beef
1 tbsp. horseradish
1 med. onion, chopped
1 tsp. Worcestershire sauce
1 tsp. salt
½ tsp. pepper
½ tsp. celery salt
1 egg
3 dill pickles
Frankfurter buns, toasted

Mix all ingredients except dill pickles. Cut pickles into quarters, lengthwise. Shape hamburgers mixture around each strip. Broil for 6 minutes on each side. Serve on buns. Yield: 6 servings.

Mrs. Rama Steen, Caldwell H. S.
Caldwell, Ohio

PIZZABURGERS

4 hamburger buns
¾ c. chili sauce
1 lb. ground beef
1 tbsp. minced onion or 1 tsp. onion juice
1 tbsp. chopped parsley or 1 tsp. parsley flakes (opt.)

(Continued on next page)

1 tsp. salt
½ tsp. oregano
4 slices cheese, cut into 16 strips

Split buns. Spread with about 1/2 cup of chili sauce. Combine beef, remaining chili sauce, onion, parsley, salt and oregano. Spread on bun halves. Place on rack of broiler pan. Broil 3 inches from heat for 10 minutes. Place 2 strips of cheese on top of each burger. Broil until cheese melts. Yield: 8 servings.

Mrs. Ola W. Hendren, Jonesville H. S.
Jonesville, North Carolina
Mrs. Nelle B. Underwood, Flomaton H. S.
Flomaton, Alabama

PIZZA LOAF

1 loaf French bread
1 ½ lb. ground beef
⅔ c. grated Parmesan cheese
½ c. chopped onion
½ c. chopped ripe olives
2 tsp. salt
1 ½ tsp. oregano
⅛ tsp. cayenne pepper
2 6-oz. cans tomato paste
1 8-oz. pkg. sharp cheese slices
3 tomatoes, thinly sliced

Cut bread into thirds lengthwise. Combine remaining ingredients except cheese slices and tomatoes. Spread mixture evenly on each third of bread. Broil 5 inches from heat for 12 to 15 minutes. Cut cheese slices into halves diagonally; place on top of sandwiches alternately with tomato slices. Broil until cheese melts. Yield: 12-15 servings.

Mary Nan Fitch, Electra H. S.
Electra, Texas

PLATE-SIZED PIZZA BURGERS

1 loaf round white bread
1 lb. ground chuck
⅓ c. grated Parmesan cheese
¼ c. finely chopped onion
¼ c. chopped pitted ripe olives
1 tsp. salt
1 tsp. crushed oregano
Dash of pepper
1 6-oz. can tomato paste
3 to 6 oz. sliced Mozzarella cheese
Cherry tomatoes

Cut three 3/4-inch slices horizontally from center of loaf; toast. Combine remaining ingredients except Mozzarella cheese and tomatoes; spread one-third meat mixture on each round. Broil 5 inches from heat for 9 minutes or until meat is done. Add Mozzarella cheese and halved cherry tomatoes. Broil until cheese begins to melt. Top with additional cherry tomatoes and ripe olives. NOTE: If beef is lean, have 2 ounces suet ground with meat. Yield: 3-6 servings.

Janice Bell, Perris H. S.
Perris, California

QUICKIE BARBECUES

1 lb. ground beef
½ tsp. onion salt
¼ to ½ tsp. garlic salt
1 tsp. salt
1 10½-oz. can tomato soup
1 tsp. prepared mustard
1 ½ tbsp. brown sugar
Buns

Brown beef in frying pan; stir continuously with a fork to separate into fine pieces. Add onion salt, garlic salt and salt. Add tomato soup, mustard and brown sugar. Stir well. Simmer for 10 to 15 minutes. Serve on large buns. Yield: 4-6 servings.

Mrs. Maureen Nelson, Paynesville H. S.
Paynesville, Minnesota

RANCH BURGERS

½ lb. hamburger
½ c. milk
1 egg, beaten
Salt and pepper to taste
6 hamburger buns

Combine hamburger, milk, egg, salt and pepper. Spread mixture thinly on both sides of opened hamburger buns. Place on cookie sheet. Broil 7 inches from heat until done. Serve with sliced tomatoes or dill pickles, if desired. Yield: 6 servings.

Mrs. Phoebe S. Stout, Stephen Decatur H. S.
Berlin, Maryland

READI-BURGERS

1 lb. hamburger
1 egg
2 tbsp. horseradish mustard
1 tsp. salt
1 tsp. pepper
1 onion, minced
8 slices bread or 5 hamburger buns, toasted

Combine hamburger, egg, horseradish mustard, salt, pepper and onion together in a bowl. Lightly toast bread or buns. Spread hamburger mixture well over edges of bread or buns. Broil 3 to 4 inches from heat for 5 minutes. Yield: 4-5 servings.

Mrs. Eileen Roberts, Royall H. S.
Elroy, Wisconsin

RHINE BURGER STACKS

1 lb. ground beef
1 tsp. salt
¼ tsp. caraway seed
⅛ tsp. pepper
½ c. well drained sauerkraut
8 slices bacon
Butter
8 slices square pumpernickel bread

(Continued on next page)

Mix ground beef lightly with salt, caraway seed and pepper; shape into eight patties, about 1/2-inch thick. Place 2 tablespoonfuls sauerkraut on each of four patties; top with remaining patties. Wrap 2 slices bacon around each; fasten with moistened wooden picks. Broil 4 inches from heat for 6 minutes on each side for medium doneness or until bacon is crisp. Serve each between 2 slices pumpernickle. Yield: 4 servings.

Mrs. Martha Zimmerman, Taylorville H. S.
Taylorville, Illinois

ROAST BEEF BARBECUES

1 c. ground left-over roast beef
½ c. catsup
1 ½ tsp. Worcestershire sauce
1 tbsp. vinegar
½ tsp. prepared mustard
1 tbsp. brown sugar
½ tsp. salt
⅛ tsp. allspice
½ c. water
Buns

Place ground roast beef in saucepan or frypan. Combine remaining ingredients except buns. Pour over meat. Cover pan tightly. Simmer for 30 minutes. Serve on toasted buns. Yield: 6 servings.

Mrs. June C. Powell, Atkinson Comm. H. S.
Atkinson, Illinois

RUBINOFF'S HAMBURGER

2 med. onions
2 lb. ground beef
Salt
½ c. cracker meal
Ice water

Finely grate onions so they are almost liquid. Mix meat, salt, onions and cracker meal; add enough ice water to soften and shape. Sprinkle additional cracker meal on waxed paper. Dip hands into ice water; shape patties and roll lightly in cracker meal. Broil patties on rack 2 inches from heat. Serve on buns or as hamburger steak, if desired. Yield: 8-10 servings.

Helen E. Bortz, Norton Comm. Schools
Norton, Kansas

SKILLETBURGERS

1 lb. ground beef
1 ½ c. chopped onions
1 ½ c. chopped celery
1 8-oz. can seasoned tomato sauce
1 can tomato soup
Few drops of Tabasco sauce
1 tsp. salt
½ tsp. monosodium glutamate
¼ tsp. chili powder
Toasted buns

Brown meat in a small amount of hot fat; add onion and celery. Cook until tender but not brown. Add tomato sauce, tomato soup, Tabasco sauce, salt, monosodium glutamate and chili powder. Simmer, uncovered, for 20 minutes. Spoon onto split toasted buns. Yield: 5-6 servings.

Iona Ross, Freer H. S.
Freer, Texas

SLOPPY JOES

1 lb. lean ground round
1 tbsp. fat
1 c. chopped onions
1 c. chopped green peppers
½ tsp. sugar (opt.)
2 tbsp. prepared mustard
1 tbsp. vinegar
1 tsp. salt
¼ tsp. powdered cloves
1 c. catsup
6 to 8 hamburger buns

Brown beef in fat; add remaining ingredients except buns. Cover; simmer for 30 minutes. Spoon onto hamburger buns. Yield: 6-8 servings.

Mrs. Dub Stewart, Haltom H. S.
Fort Worth, Texas
Mrs. H. M. Thomas, Breckenridge H. S.
Breckenridge, Texas

SLOPPY JOES

1 lb. ground beef
½ c. chopped onion
1 tbsp. shortening
1 can chicken gumbo soup
2 to 4 tbsp. catsup
1 tbsp. prepared mustard
Dash of pepper
6 buns

Brown beef and onion in shortening; separate meat particles. Add soup and seasonings. Simmer for 5 to 10 minutes, stirring often. Serve on toasted buns. Yield: 6 servings.

Doreen Nielson, Murray H. S.
Murray, Utah
Katherine McIlquham, Chippewa Falls H. S.
Chippewa Falls, Wisconsin
Mrs. Marlin Kell, Elberfeld Elem. School
Elberfeld, Indiana

SLOPPY JOES

1 lb. ground beef or chuck
1 tsp. monosodium glutamate
2 tbsp. minced onion
¼ c. diced green pepper
1 can tomato soup
Few grains of salt
Few grains of pepper
8 hamburger buns

(Continued on next page)

Mix meat and monosodium glutamate; fry on low heat until meat is browned. Add onion, green pepper, tomato soup, salt and pepper; mix well. Cover; cook slowly for 20 minutes. Heat hamburger buns in warm oven; add a generous amount of hamburger mixture to buns. Serve. Yield: 8 servings.

Mrs. J. Balish, Colonia Jr. H. S.
Colonia, New Jersey

SLOPPY JOES

2 lb. ground beef
1 med. onion, chopped
2 tsp. salt
1 8-oz. can barbecue sauce
½ c. catsup
½ c. water
3 tbsp. vinegar
1 tbsp. brown sugar
Hamburger buns

Brown meat and onion; pour off excess fat. Add salt, barbecue sauce, catsup, water, vinegar and brown sugar. Simmer for 45 minutes. Serve on hamburger buns. Yield: 12 servings.

Mrs. Nita De Grand, Nacogdoches H. S.
Nacogdoches, Texas

SLOPPY JOES WITH DEVIL SAUCE

1 lb. ground beef
1 green pepper, chopped
1 med. onion, chopped
Oil or butter
3 tbsp. catsup
1 tbsp. dry mustard
2 tsp. Worcestershire sauce
1 can cream of chicken or cream of mushroom soup
1 tsp. sugar
1 tbsp. chili powder
Dash of garlic powder (opt.)

Cook beef, green pepper and onion in a small amount of oil until onion is golden brown and beef loses red color. Stir in remaining ingredients. Simmer for 10 minutes, stirring occasionally.

DEVIL SAUCE:

1 tbsp. minced onion
3 tbsp. tarragon vinegar
½ c. canned tomatoes
1 tbsp. butter
1 tbsp. flour
½ tsp. chopped parsley
½ tsp. chopped tarragon
½ tsp. chopped chervil
Dash of Tabasco sauce or cayenne pepper
Salt and black pepper to taste
¼ tsp. chili powder (opt.)

Simmer onion and vinegar in saucepan until vinegar is reduced by one-half. Stir in tomatoes; bring to a boil. Blend butter and flour; stir into sauce. Bring to a boil, stirring constantly. Stir in remaining ingredients. Season to taste. Serve over sloppy joes. Serve on hamburger buns, if desired. Yield: 10-12 servings.

Bertha Hale, North H. S.
Phoenix, Arizona

SLOPPY JOE HAMBURGERS

1 lb. hamburger
1 ½ tsp. onion salt
¼ c. finely chopped stuffed green olives
1 6-oz. can tomato paste, sauce or soup
1 tsp. Worcestershire sauce
1 to 4 tbsp. chopped onion (opt.)
2 to 4 tbsp. chopped green pepper (opt.)
⅛ tsp. pepper
1 c. chopped pickles (opt.)
Hamburger buns

Cook hamburger over low heat until browned, stirring occasionally. Blend in remaining ingredients, mashing well with fork. Heat thoroughly. Serve hot on hamburger buns. Yield: 4 servings.

Mrs. Ann Hoit, Ousley Jr. H. S.
Arlington, Texas
Mary B. Mills, Vina H. S.
Vina, Alabama
Sheela Worsfold, Pleasantville H. S.
Pleasantville, New Jersey

SPECIAL HAMBURGERS

1 lb. ground beef
2 tbsp. finely chopped green pepper
¼ c. chopped onion
3 tbsp. catsup
1 tbsp. horseradish
1 tsp. salt
½ tsp. dry mustard
Buttered buns

Combine all ingredients except buns; mix well. Form into four to six patties. Broil until done. Place in greased shallow baking dish. Bake at 375 degrees for 30 minutes. Serve on warm buttered buns. Yield: 4-6 servings.

Linda J. McCraw, Gaffney H. S.
Gaffney, South Carolina

SPREAD-A-BURGERS

1 ½ lb. ground beef
1 10 ½-oz. can tomato or cream of mushroom soup
⅓ c. finely chopped onion
1 tbsp. prepared mustard
1 tbsp. Worcestershire sauce
1 tsp. horseradish
1 tsp. salt
Dash of pepper
6 frankfurter buns, split and toasted

(Continued on next page)

Thoroughly mix beef, soup, onion and seasonings; spread mixture ovenly over bun halves, covering edges completely. Broil about 4 inches from heat for 12 to 15 minutes. Yield: 6 servings.

Mrs. Willie Vee Hill, Neshoba Central H. S.
Philadelphia, Mississippi

SUPPER ON A BREAD SLICE

⅔ c. evaporated milk
1 ½ lb. ground beef
½ c. cracker meal
1 egg
½ c. chopped onion
1 tbsp. mustard
1 ½ tsp. salt
⅛ tsp. pepper
1 loaf French bread
2 c. grated process cheese

Combine all ingredients except bread and cheese. Cut French bread in half lengthwise. Spread meat mixture evenly over top surface of bread. Wrap heavy aluminum foil around crust-side of each half, leaving top uncovered. Place on cookie sheet. Bake at 350 degrees for 25 minutes. Garnish with grated cheese. Bake for 5 minutes longer. Cut across or diagonally. Yield: 8 servings.

Mrs. Sue Bush, Northside Jr. H. S.
Columbus, Indiana

TASTY BARBECUE

2 lb. ground beef
1 onion, minced
2 tbsp. brown sugar
1 tbsp. vinegar
1 tbsp. Worcestershire sauce
2 tbsp. pickle relish
1 tbsp. parsley flakes
½ c. catsup
1 can tomato soup
Salt and pepper
Hamburger buns

Brown ground beef and onions; add brown sugar, vinegar, Worcestershire sauce, pickle relish, parsley flakes, catsup and tomato soup. Mix well. Add salt and pepper to taste. Simmer for 20 minutes. Serve on hot hamburger buns. Yield: 12-15 servings.

Marilyn Oelschlager, Flanagan H. S.
Flanagan, Illinois

THE THINGS

2 med. onions, chopped
1 lb. cheese, grated
2 sm. cans sliced black olives
4 sm. cans tomato sauce
2 lb. ground beef
Buns

Combine onions, cheese, olives and tomato sauce. Fry ground beef, stirring often, until browned. Add to cheese mixture; stir thoroughly. Spoon onto buns. Broil until browned.

Mrs. D. G. Headley, Glendora H. S.
Glendora, California

WINEBURGERS

1 med. onion, minced
1 tbsp. butter
1 lb. ground beef
2 tbsp. flour
1 can tomato soup
⅓ c. Burgundy wine
Salt and pepper
1 tsp. chili powder
6 hamburger buns

Cook onion in butter until soft. Add meat; cook until all pinkness disappears. Sprinkle flour over meat; blend. Add soup and wine. Cook, stirring constantly, until thick. Add seasonings; simmer, uncovered, for 10 minutes. Serve over buns. Yield: 6 servings.

Pat Jaggers, Moore Jr. H. S.
Tyler, Texas

CHEESY CORNED BEEF BARBECUE SANDWICHES

1 12-oz. can corned beef
6 slices bread, toasted
½ c. catsup
2 tsp. horseradish
2 tsp. mustard
2 tsp. vinegar
2 tsp. finely chopped onion
6 slices Cheddar cheese

Chill corned beef; cut lengthwise into six slices. Place a slice of corned beef on each slice of toast. Combine catsup, horseradish, mustard, vinegar and onion. Spread one-half of sauce over corned beef. Top each sandwich with slice of cheese. Broil 6 inches from heat until cheese melts. Serve remaining sauce with sandwiches. Yield: 6 servings.

Mrs. Retha George, Biloxi H. S.
Biloxi, Mississippi

COLD CORNED BEEF SANDWICHES

Rye bread
Mustard or horseradish dressing
Sauerkraut
Cold corned beef

Spread rye bread with mustard; add a layer of sauerkraut and a slice of cold corned beef. Yield: 1 serving.

Mrs. Dorothy Marie Jarrett, Keota H. S.
Keota, Oklahoma

HASH AND CHILI BURGERS

2 15 ½-oz. cans corned beef hash
½ c. chili sauce
2 tbsp. instant minced onion
8 hamburger buns, split
6 hard-cooked eggs, sliced

Mix hash, chili sauce and onion. Spread on bun halves; top with egg slices and remaining bun halves. Wrap in aluminum foil. Bake at 300 degrees for 10 minutes or over grill, turning occasionally. Yield: 8 servings.

Mrs. Eugene S. Turner, Lexington H. S.
Lexington, Tennessee

CHIPPED BEEF SUPREME

1 3 ½-oz. pkg. chipped dried beef
2 slices American cheese, cut into small pieces
½ c. crushed pineapple, drained
⅓ c. salad dressing
Hamburger buns

Tear beef into a 2-quart mixing bowl; add remaining ingredients. Spread on open hamburger buns. Place a triangular slice of cheese on top. Broil for 5 to 7 minutes. NOTE: French bread cut lengthwise of loaf may be substituted for hamburger buns. Yield: 6 servings.

Mrs. Richard Chambers
Mason Co. Central H. S.
Scottville, Michigan

BARBECUED BOLOGNA CROWN

½ c. minced onion
¼ c. butter
1 c. chili sauce
¼ c. vinegar
1 tbsp. Worcestershire sauce
4 tsp. brown sugar
1 tsp. celery salt
½ tsp. prepared mustard
1 1-lb. loaf Italian bread
12 slices bologna, ¼-in. thick
1 c. grated Cheddar cheese

Cook onion in butter in saucepan until tender; add chili sauce, vinegar, Worcestershire sauce, brown sugar, celery salt and mustard. Cook, uncovered, on thermostatic top burner set at 210 degrees until thick. Cut bread into 13 crosswise slices, almost through to bottom crust; place on large piece of aluminum foil on cookie sheet. Spread 1 tablespoonful chili sauce mixture in each cut. Turn loaf of bread on the side. Insert 1 folded slice of bologna into each cut, folded edge to the outside. Loaf bends into crown shape as it is filled. Spread remaining chili sauce mixture over loaf; sprinkle with grated cheese. Cup foil around lower part of loaf to form container. Bake at 375 degrees for 15 minutes. Lift crown to serving plate. Snip slices apart with scissors to serve. Yield: 6 servings.

Mrs. Sandra Miller, Lakewood H. S.
Hebron, Ohio

BOLOGNA-CHEESE TRIANGLES

2 lb. bologna
4 dill pickles
½ c. salad dressing
2 ½ lb. sharp cheese
1 sm. can pimento
1 ½ tbsp. lemon juice
½ c. coleslaw dressing
White bread
Whole wheat bread

Grind bologna and dill pickles; add salad dressing. Grind the cheese; add pimento, lemon juice and coleslaw dressing. Beat with electric mixer until fluffy. Use a slice of dark and white bread for each sandwich. Place meat spread and cheese spread in alternate layers on bread. Cut into quarters; hold together with colored toothpicks. Yield: 24 servings.

Marel Lee Bolger, Bentley H. S.
Flint, Michigan

BROILED DEVILED HAMBURGERS

1 3-oz. pkg. cream cheese
1 4 ½-oz. can deviled ham
3 tbsp. catsup
⅛ tsp. grated onion
¼ tsp. baking powder
1 pkg. hamburger buns

Soften the cream cheese; add deviled ham, catsup and onion. Mix thoroughly. Add baking powder just before broiling. Spread on each half of buns. Place open-faced burgers on cookie sheet. Broil until they begin to brown. Serve warm. Yield: 4-6 servings.

Mrs. Constance Ackerson, Grand Ledge H. S.
Grand Ledge, Michigan

BAKED HOT DOGS IN A BUN

¾ c. hot water
½ c. sugar
1 tbsp. salt
3 tbsp. shortening
1 c. warm water
2 pkg. active dry yeast
1 egg, beaten
5 ¼ c. unsifted flour
2 doz. wieners
Butter

Mix hot water, sugar, salt and shortening; cool to lukewarm. Measure warm water into large warm bowl; sprinkle in yeast. Stir until dissolved. Stir in lukewarm sugar mixture, egg and one-half of flour; beat until smooth. Stir in enough remaining flour to make a soft dough. Turn out onto lightly floured board; knead until smooth and elastic, about 10 minutes. Let dough rise until doubled in bulk, about 1 hour. Punch down. Cut dough into twenty-four 2-inch balls. Using one ball for each wiener, wrap each wiener entirely in dough. Let rise again until doubled in bulk on greased cookie sheet. Bake at 400 de-

(Continued on next page)

grees for 20 to 25 minutes. Brush with butter. Yield: 24 servings.

Margaret Seaton, Fertile H. S.
Fertile, Minnesota

BARBECUED HOT DOGS

½ c. diced onion
1 tbsp. butter
1 tsp. paprika
½ tsp. pepper
4 tsp. sugar
1 tsp. mustard
4 tsp. Worcestershire sauce
¼ tsp. Tabasco sauce
¼ c. catsup
3 tbsp. vinegar
1 lb. wieners
Wiener buns

Brown onion in butter; add seasonings. Simmer for a few minutes. Slash each wiener diagonally; place in baking dish. Cover with sauce. Bake at 350 degrees for 20 to 30 minutes, basting frequently. Serve on wiener buns with remaining sauce. Yield: 5-6 servings.

Mrs. Lois Beeson, Northridge H. S.
Johnstown, Ohio

KRAUT ROUND DOGS WITH BACON STRIPS

2 c. sauerkraut, drained
⅓ c. chili sauce
6 frankfurters
6 slices bacon
6 hamburger buns, split

Combine sauerkraut and chili sauce; mix well. Cook over low heat for 10 minutes, stirring occasionally. Cut 10 deep slits in each frankfurter without cutting all the way through. Wrap bacon slice around each frankfurter. Broil frankfurters 5 to 7 inches from heat for 3 to 5 minutes. Turn. Arrange buns on broiler pan with frankfurters. Broil 3 minutes or until hamburger buns are lightly browned and bacon is crisp. Arrange kraut mixture and frankfruters on bun bottoms. Top with bun tops. Yield: 6 servings.

Photograph for this recipe on page 275.

PEEL DEALS

10 frankfurter buns
¼ c. melted butter or margarine
Mustard or catsup
10 sm. strips cheese
10 frankfurters
Baked beans, pickle relish or chopped olives

Split frankfurters buns; brush inside and out with melted butter. Spread cut-sides with mustard; cover with strip of cheese. Place frankfurter in center; top with drained baked beans. Wrap each filled bun in foil. Bake in preheated 375 degree oven until heated, about 12 to 15 minutes. Yield: 10 servings.

Mrs. Maurice E. Eskridge, Tryon H. S.
Bessemer City, North Carolina

HAM AND CHEESE BUNS

12 hamburger buns
½ lb. ham, finely diced
¼ lb. Velveeta cheese, diced
¼ lb. Old English cheese, diced
1 tbsp. chopped onion (opt.)
2 hard-cooked eggs
¼ c. pickle relish
3 tbsp. mayonnaise
¼ tsp. mustard
1 tbsp. catsup or barbecue sauce

Hollow out centers of bun halves, forming a well. Mix all remaining ingredients. Fill centers of buns; wrap individually in foil. Bake at 400 degrees for 15 minutes. Yield: 12 servings.

Mrs. Verna J. Erickson, Elgin Local H. S.
Marion, Ohio

SUNDAY EVENING SUPPER SANDWICHES

1 lb. cooked ham, diced
½ lb. American cheese, diced
1 med. onion, chopped
½ c. sliced olives
1 to 2 tbsp. barbecue sauce
2 ½ c. mayonnaise
18 hot dog buns, sliced

Combine all ingredients except hot dog buns; place mixture in buns. Wrap in foil; freeze. When ready to use, remove from freezer. Bake at 375 degrees for 20 to 25 minutes. Yield: 18 sandwiches.

Mrs. Shirley Moore, Western H. S.
Russiaville, Indiana

HAM SURPRISES

1 can luncheon meat or chopped ham, ground
¼ lb. cheese, ground
2 tbsp. catsup
2 tbsp. milk
1 tsp. grated onion (opt.)
Buns

Combine meat, cheese, catsup, milk and onion. Spread on buns and broil until hot. Yield: 6-8 servings.

Mrs. Dorothy Soderlund, Milaca H. S.
Milaca, Minnesota

PICNIC SPECIAL

1 12-oz. can luncheon meat, coarsely shredded
¼ lb. Cheddar cheese, shredded
2 tbsp. pickle relish
2 tbsp. grated onion
2 tbsp. prepared mustard
8 frankfurter buns

(Continued on next page)

Combine all ingredients except buns; mix well. Cut frankfurter rolls lengthwise almost through; fill with meat mixture. Wrap each roll in aluminum foil; seal ends. Bake at 350 degrees for 20 minutes. Yield: 8 servings.

Mrs. Barbara Hiller, Winnebago Comm. School
Winnebago, Minnesota

POW-WOW BUNS

½ can luncheon meat, ground
1 ½ tbsp. finely chopped onion
2 tbsp. chopped sweet pickle
½ c. grated cheese
1 tbsp. catsup
2 hard-cooked eggs, chopped
2 tbsp. melted butter
6 to 8 lge. buns

Combine all ingredients except buns and butter. Slice buns into halves; spread lightly with butter. Fill with meat mixture. Wrap each bun in foil; place on cookie sheet. Bake at 375 degrees for 15 minutes. Serve hot in the wrapper. Yield: 6-8 servings.

Mrs. Kathryn Byram, Mapleton H. S.
Mapleton, Minnesota

SANDWICH FILLING

1 can luncheon meat, ground
1 sm. onion, ground
1 8-oz. pkg. cream cheese
½ green pepper, chopped (opt.)
5 to 6 stuffed olives, chopped
⅔ can tomato paste
6 tbsp. melted butter
Buns

Combine all ingredients except buns. Spread on buns. Wrap in foil. Place under broiler until heated.

Mrs. Nancy Moland, Clearbrook H. S.
Clearbrook, Minnesota

AMERICAN PIZZA

5 slices bacon, ground
2 hard-cooked eggs, ground
½ lb. Velveeta cheese, ground
1 sm. onion, ground
1 c. chili sauce
8 sandwich buns, split

Combine bacon, eggs, cheese, onion and chili sauce. Spread the mixture on bun halves; toast in broiler until desired browness. Yield: 16 servings.

Mrs. Janet P. Berkebile, Penn Manor H. S.
Millersville, Pennsylvania

BAKED SANDWICH

12 slices bread
6 slices sharp cheese
Prepared mustard
½ lb. ground ham
4 eggs, slightly beaten
3 c. milk
½ tsp. salt
1 can cream of mushroom soup
1 c. chicken broth

Cut crust off bread; place 6 slices in greased 9 x 3-inch pan. Cover with slices of cheese; brush with mustard. Cover with ground ham. Butter remaining bread; place, buttered-side up, on top of ham. Mix eggs with milk and salt; pour over sandwiches. Refrigerate overnight. Remove 1 hour before baking. Bake at 300 degrees for 1 hour. Serve with sauce made with mushroom soup and chicken broth. Yield: 6 servings.

Judy Kalbfleisch, Clarkston H. S.
Clarkston, Michigan

HAM SALAD SPREAD

2 c. cubed boiled ham, beef, pork or chicken
2 c. diced celery or apples
½ c. salad dressing
Salt to taste
¼ c. finely chopped green pepper
¼ c. chopped pecans
¼ c. chopped onion (opt.)

Combine meat, celery and salad dressing; chill thoroughly. Just before spreading, add remaining ingredients. Yield: 6-8 servings.

Freda Ferguson, Dale H. S.
Dale, Oklahoma

LUNCHEON SANDWICH

⅔ c. mayonnaise
⅓ c. catsup
6 slices toast
6 slices baked ham
3 hard-cooked eggs, sliced
2 tomatoes, sliced

Combine mayonnaise and catsup. On each slice of toast, place a slice of ham, several slices of egg and 2 or 3 slices of tomato. Spread with dressing. Yield: 6 servings.

Mrs. Edith B. Gill, Butler H. S.
Butler, New Jersey

NUTTY HAM AND CHEESE GRILLS

4 slices bread
Butter or margarine
Prepared mustard or horseradish mustard
4 slices cooked ham
4 slices process cheese
Coarsely chopped walnuts or pecans

(Continued on next page)

Spread one side of bread with butter. Place on cookie sheet; broil 6 to 7 inches from heat until golden brown. Remove from oven and brush unbuttered side with mustard. Place a slice of ham and a square of cheese on each slice of bread; top with a single layer of nuts. Press nuts gently into cheese. Broil for 2 to 3 minutes or until cheese is bubbly. Serve immediately. Yield: 4 servings.

Mary Ann Eltife, Windthorst H. S.
Windthorst, Texas

CHICKEN ON A BUN

2 7-oz. cans boned chicken
¼ c. chopped stuffed olives
¾ c. diced celery
¾ c. chopped sweet pickles
2 tbsp. chopped onion
½ c. mayonnaise
8 hamburger buns
Butter
16 slices American cheese

Combine chicken, olives, celery, pickles and onion; add mayonnaise. Slice buns into halves; spread with butter. Spread chicken mixture on buns; top with 1 slice cheese. Place buns on cookie sheet. Bake at 350 degrees for 10 to 15 minutes or until cheese is melted. Yield: 16 sandwiches.

Mrs. Shirley Keenlance, Manawa H. S.
Manawa, Wisconsin

CHICKEN BURGERS

2 c. finely chopped cooked chicken
¼ c. chopped almonds, walnuts or pecans
½ tsp. grated onion
¼ c. dry bread crumbs
2 tsp. chopped parsley
1 tsp. lemon juice
¼ c. milk
Salt and pepper to taste
2 to 4 tbsp. melted butter
8 hamburger buns, toasted

Mix all ingredients except butter and buns; shape into eight patties. Place on broiler tray; brush with melted butter. Broil on both sides until browned. Serve on toasted hamburger buns. Yield: 8 servings.

Ida Mae Gray, Belzoni H. S.
Belzoni, Mississippi

CHICKEN RAREBIT SANDWICH

2 tbsp. butter
2 tbsp. flour
1 c. milk
2 c. shredded American cheese
½ tsp. mustard
1 tsp. Worcestershire sauce
Salt to taste
6 slices crisp toast
Sliced cooked chicken
Paprika

Melt butter in saucepan over low heat; blend in flour. Add milk, stirring constantly. Cook and stir until sauce is smooth and thickened. Add cheese, mustard, Worcestershire sauce and salt. Stir over low heat only until cheese is melted. Arrange toast in individual custard cups or one shallow baking pan; top with thick slices of chicken. Cover with cheese sauce; sprinkle lightly with paprika. Heat under broiler until cheese sauce is lightly browned. Yield: 6 servings.

Nancy Hinkemeyer, Big Piney H. S.
Big Piney, Wyoming

CLUB SANDWICHES

8 slices bread, toasted
Salad dressing
8 slices cooked turkey
4 lge. slices tomato
16 slices bacon, fried
8 leaves lettuce

Spread toast with salad dressing. Place 2 slices turkey, 1 slice tomato, 2 slices bacon and 2 lettuce leaves on each of 4 slices toast. Cover with remaining toast. Cut diagonally into fourths. Yield: 4 servings.

Mrs. Virginia Kendrick Craun, Nelagoney H. S.
Pawhuska, Oklahoma

HOT BACK YARD SUPPER BUNS

¾ c. chopped cooked chicken
¼ c. mayonnaise
⅓ c. chopped celery
¼ tsp. salt
½ c. grated cheese
1 tbsp. minced onion
6 hot dog buns

Combine all ingredients except buns. Spread on buns. Wrap individually or together in aluminum foil. Heat in 350 degree oven for 15 minutes. Serve at once. NOTE: Sandwiches may be made the night before and stored in the refrigerator for quick use next day. Yield: 6 servings.

Marguerite Holloway, Petersburg Harris H. S.
Petersburg, Illinois

HOT CHICKEN SALAD ON A BUN

2 c. diced cooked chicken
½ c. finely diced celery
4 tbsp. chopped green pepper
3 sm. green onions, chopped
¼ c. mayonnaise
Salt and pepper to taste
6 hamburger buns
1 ½ c. grated Cheddar cheese or cheese spread
Butter

Combine all ingredients except buns, cheese and butter; mix well. Split buns; spread with cheese. Top each half bun with chicken mixture; dot with butter. Wrap each half in foil; seal tightly. Refrigerate. Bake in preheated 450 degree oven for 10 minutes. Yield: 12 servings.

Mrs. John Leischner, DeLand-Weldon H. S.
DeLand, Illinois

POLYNESIAN CHICKEN SALAD SANDWICHES

½ c. drained crushed pineapple
¼ c. mayonnaise
1 tsp. soy sauce
¼ tsp. salt
¼ tsp. ground ginger
⅛ tsp. garlic powder
1 c. chopped cooked chicken

Combine all ingredients; chill. May be used as sandwich filling for hors d'oeuvres, open-faced, closed sandwiches or spread on toasted English muffin halves and broiled or baked until heated through.

Mrs. Verda E. McConnell, Adams City H. S.
Commerce City, Colorado

SANDWICHES

1 can cream of chicken soup
⅓ c. milk
⅓ c. shredded sharp Cheddar cheese
1 5 to 6-oz. can or ⅔ c. cooked cubed chicken
1 14 ½-oz. can cut asparagus, drained
6 slices toast

Blend soup and milk in saucepan; add cheese, chicken and asparagus. Heat until cheese is melted, stirring occasionally. Serve over toast. NOTE: One-fourth cup sliced pimento stuffed green olives may be added. Yield: 6 servings.

Katherine C. Donahue, Uxbridge H. S.
Uxbridge, Massachusetts

BARBECUED CRAB MEAT SANDWICHES

4 oz. cream cheese
½ c. catsup
1 6-oz. can crab meat
1 tsp. horseradish
½ tsp. Worcestershire sauce
2 tbsp. finely chopped celery
2 tbsp. chopped green pepper
2 tbsp. sweet pickle relish
1 tbsp. finely chopped onion
2 tsp. vinegar
Butter
1 doz. small buns
½ c. grated sharp cheese

Soften cream cheese with mixer; add catsup and blend until smooth. Remove mixer. Stir in remaining ingredients except butter, buns and cheese. Split and butter buns; spread generously with crab meat mixture. Sprinkle with cheese. Broil for 5 to 6 minutes. Serve hot. Yield: 24 servings.

Mrs. Marie Peterson
Mary Jane Shannon, Jr. Secondary School
North Surrey, British Columbia, Canada

BROILED CRAB MEAT-CHEESE SANDWICHES

½ c. cubed Cheddar or process cheese
½ c. butter
⅛ tsp. garlic salt (opt.)
1 6 ¼-oz. can crab meat, flaked
4 to 6 hamburger buns, halved

Place cheese, butter and garlic salt in saucepan; place over low heat. Heat until cheese is melted. Add crab meat and blend. Toast bun halves lightly, about 4 inches from heat. Spread with cheese mixture. Place on grill about 3 inches from heat; broil for 2 minutes or until mixture bubbles and begins to brown. Yield: 6 servings.

Sister Alice Veronica
The Academy of the Holy Angels
Richfield, Minnesota
Mrs. Roselynn A. Cobb, Mosinee H. S.
Mosinee, Wisconsin

CRAB-BUN DELIGHT

1 6 ½-oz. can crab
2 2-oz. pkg. cream cheese, softened
¼ c. grated Cheddar cheese
1 tsp. horseradish
¼ tsp. Tabasco sauce
1 tsp. prepared mustard
¼ tsp. garlic salt
Mayonnaise
Hamburger buns
Paprika

Combine crab, cream cheese, cheese, horseradish, Tabasco sauce, mustard and garlic salt. Add enough mayonnaise to moisten. Spread on halves of toasted hamburger buns. Sprinkle with paprika. Broil until bubbly.

Sandra Warjone, Raymond Jr.-Sr. H. S.
Raymond, Washington

CRAB-FILLED BUNS

1 sm. can crab meat, flaked
1 c. chopped ripe or green olives
1 ¼ c. diced Swiss cheese
1 tbsp. minced green onion

(Continued on next page)

¼ c. mayonnaise
1 tbsp. lemon juice
Salt and pepper to taste
Butter
8 hamburger buns

Combine crab meat, olives, cheese and onion; add mixture of mayonnaise and lemon juice, then seasonings. Fill buttered buns with mixture; wrap each in foil. Bake at 350 degrees for 25 to 30 minutes. Yield: 8 servings.

Mrs. Carole Christofferson
Northwest Jr. Academic Vocational School
Calgary, Alberta, Canada

CRAB MEAT SANDWICHES

1 c. crab meat
2 hard-cooked eggs, chopped
¼ c. French dressing
¼ c. pickle relish
12 slices bread
Salad dressing
Tomato slices
4 slices process cheese

Combine crab meat, hard-cooked eggs, French dressing and pickle relish. Toast bread; spread each slice with salad dressing. Place tomato slice on slice of toast; top with slice of toast. Place crab meat mixture on second slice; cover with a third slice of toast. Repeat until all ingredients are used. Cut each sandwich into half diagonally. Place a triangle of process cheese on each sandwich half. Bake at 400 degrees for 4 to 7 minutes or until cheese melts. Garnish with radish rose and avocado slice, if desired.

Mrs. Jessie Clausen, Central H. S.
Independence, Oregon

FRIDAY NIGHT CRAB SANDWICH

1 can crab meat
2 stalks celery, chopped
4 green onions, chopped
1 sm. can mushrooms
1 tsp. caraway seed
½ c. mayonnaise or sour cream
8 slices bacon
4 slices bread
4 slices Cheddar cheese

Mix crab meat, celery, onions, mushrooms, caraway seed and mayonnaise. Fry bacon. Toast bread on one side only; spread crab meat mixture on untoasted side. Cover with bacon; top with slice of cheese. Heat under broiler until cheese melts. Yield: 4 servings.

Marilyn Cerny, Lederle Jr. H. S.
Southfield, Michigan

BROILED TUNA SANDWICH

1 7-oz. can light tuna, rinsed, drained and flaked
¼ c. salad dressing
¼ c. chili sauce
12 stuffed olives, sliced
½ tsp. Worcestershire sauce
6 slices bread
½ c. grated cheese

Combine tuna, salad dressing, chili sauce, olives and Worcestershire sauce. Toast bread on one side. Spread mixture on untoasted sides of bread; sprinkle with cheese. Broil sandwiches 3 inches from preheated broiler until brown as desired. Yield: 6 servings.

Mrs. D. E. Slay, Gibsland H. S.
Gibsland, Louisiana

BUMSTEADS

¼ lb. American, Cheddar or Velveeta cheese, chopped
2 tbsp. chopped green pepper
2 tbsp. chopped olives (opt.)
2 tbsp. chopped sweet pickle
1 to 2 tbsp. chopped onion (opt.)
½ c. mayonnaise
3 hard-cooked eggs, diced
1 can tuna
6 to 8 hot dog buns

Combine all ingredients except buns; spread filling in buns. Wrap in aluminum foil or place in paper bag. Bake at 325 degrees for 25 minutes. Yield: 6-8 servings.

Margaret Lauderdale, Waterloo H. S.
Waterloo, Wisconsin
Mrs. Barry Hoffman, McComb Local School
McComb, Ohio
Sister Mary Lelia, S.S.N.D., Lourdes H. S.
Oshkosh, Wisconsin
Mrs. Evelyn Van Vleet, Garden City H. S.
Garden City, Kansas
Mrs. Jean McOmber, Spring Lake H. S.
Spring Lake, Michigan
Gertrude Quinby Brubaker
Portage Area Schools
Portage, Pennsylvania
Mrs. Josephine Kelm, Morgan Public School
Morgan, Minnesota

BUNSTARDS

3 hard-cooked eggs, chopped
2 tbsp. chopped green pepper
2 tbsp. chopped onion
2 tbsp. chopped stuffed olives
1 7-oz. can tuna, flaked
½ c. mayonnaise
Buns

Mix all ingredients except buns. Split oblong buns; fill with mixture. Wrap each bun in foil. Bake at 300 degrees for 30 minutes or until heated through. Yield: 8 servings.

Mrs. Jane C. Richardson, Toccoa H. S.
Toccoa, Georgia

SEA BURGERS

1 can tuna, salmon or crab, drained and flaked
½ lb. cheese, cut into cubes
¼ c. mayonnaise
¼ c. chopped onion
¼ c. chopped pickle
½ c. catsup
1 c. diced celery
2 tsp. salt
½ tsp. pepper
2 tsp. cut pimento
12 hamburger buns

Combine fish and cheese; add remaining ingredients. Split buns almost through; fill with mixture. Stand in baking pan with cut-side up. Cover with aluminum foil. Bake at 350 degrees for 20 minutes. Yield: 12 servings.

Sister M. Casimir, S.C.C., St. Paul's Jr. H. S.
Kensington, Connecticut

SUNDAY SUPPER SANDWICHES

1 6-oz. can tuna, flaked
2 tbsp. chopped onion
2 tbsp. chopped pickle (opt.)
1 to 2 tbsp. salad dressing or mayonnaise
4 to 6 round flat buns
Butter
4 to 6 slices American cheese

Combine tuna, onion, pickle and salad dressing. Split buns; spread with butter and tuna mixture. Top with a slice of cheese. Broil for 3minutes. or until cheese melts. Yield: 6 servings.

Mrs. Marilyn B. Packard
Troy Comm. Joint Schools
Troy, Pennsylvania
Mrs. Madra Fischer, Mendota H. S.
Mendota, Illinois

TUNA BURGERS

4 slices white bread
⅔ c. evaportaed milk
1 8-oz. can tuna
1 tsp. prepared mustard
1 tsp. catsup
1 tsp. pickle relish
6 hot dog or hamburger buns, split

Soften the bread in milk; add tuna, mustard, catsup and relish. Heat mixture on bun halves; place on cookie sheet. Broil at 500 degrees for 10 minutes or until slightly brown. Yield: 12 servings.

Flora Harmon, Spring Hill School
Hope, Arkansas

TUNA BURGERS

1 can tuna
1 can cream of mushroom soup
1 to 4 tbsp. finely chopped onion
1 to 4 tbsp. finely chopped green pepper
6 to 8 hamburger buns
Butter

Mix tuna, cream of mushroom soup, onion and pepper; spread on open hamburger buns. Close buns; lightly brush top of buns with butter. Arrange buns on baking sheet. Bake at 425 degrees for 15 minutes. Serve hot. Yield: 8 servings.

Hilda Harman, Smithville H. S.
Smithville, Mississippi
Mary B. McGlone, St. Rose Academy
Vincennes, Indiana
Sister M. Del Rey, St. Mary H. S.
Dell Rapids, South Dakota

TUNA BURGERS

6 slices bread
Butter
1 10 ½-oz. can cream of mushroom soup
1 6 ½-oz. can tuna or 1 c. diced cooked chicken
¼ c. thinly sliced celery
¼ c. chopped cashew nuts
1 tbsp. minced instant onion
1 tsp. soy sauce
1 c. grated cheese

Place bread on cookie sheet; toast one side under the broiler. Spread butter on untoasted side. Combine soup, tuna, celery, nuts, onion and soy sauce. Spread on buttered side of bread, covering edges completely. Sprinkle with grated cheese. Broil until the cheese is hot and bubbly. Serve hot. Yield: 6 servings.

Claudia M. Thomsen, North Fremont H. S.
Ashton, Idaho

MEAT KABOBS

1 lb. ground beef
¾ c. soft bread crumbs
¼ c. milk
2 tbsp. chopped onion
1 egg, slightly beaten
½ tsp. salt
Dash of pepper
6 frankfurters
1 c. catsup
¼ c. butter or margarine, melted
¼ c. molasses
2 tbsp. vinegar
6 slices bacon
Toasted wiener buns

Combine ground beef, crumbs, milk, onion, egg, salt and pepper; mix lightly. Divide mixture into six portions. Shape meat around frankfurters, covering completely; roll between waxed paper to make uniform. Chill. Insert skewers lengthwise through frankfurters. Combine catsup, butter, molasses and vinegar; brush over kabobs. Wrap each kabob spiral-fashion with slice of bacon; secure with toothpicks. Broil about 6 inches from heat for about 15 minutes, turning as needed to cook bacon. Brush kabobs with sauce again before removing from heat. Serve on toasted buns. Yield: 6 servings.

Genevieve Miller, Tyrone Jr. H. S.
St. Pettersburg, Florida
Mrs. Mary E. Jones, Jefferson Jr. H. S.
Detroit, Michigan

Casserole Favorites

HAMBURGER PIE

2 lb. hamburger
Salt and pepper to taste
2 tsp. chopped onion
2 pkg. frozen French fries
1 can cream of chicken soup
1 can cream of mushroom soup

Pat hamburger into bottom of cake pan; add salt, pepper and onion. Arrange frozen French fries in layer over meat; spread soups over French fries. Bake at 350 degrees for 1 hour. Cut into squares to serve. Yield: 8 servings.

Mary H. Sargent, North H. S.
Minneapolis, Minnesota

HOMINY PIE

1 to 1 ½ lb. hamburger
1 med. onion, chopped
1 tsp. salt
½ tsp. pepper
1 tsp. chili powder
1 tbsp. (heaping) flour
2 c. canned tomatoes
2 ½ c. hominy
¼ lb. grated American cheese

Sear meat until brown; add onion and brown lightly. Add salt, pepper and chili powder; blend well. Add flour and tomatoes. Cook for a few minutes, stirring constantly. Add hominy. Place mixture in a shallow baking dish; sprinkle cheese on top. Bake at 325 degrees until bubbling hot. Yield: 6-8 servings.

Frances Jones, Littlefield H. S.
Littlefield, Texas

QUICK TAMALE PIE

½ c. chopped onion
2 tbsp. fat
½ lb. ground beef
1 tsp. salt
1 can whole kernel corn
1 can tomatoes
½ tbsp. chili powder
½ c. meal
½ c. flour
1 tbsp. sugar
1 tsp. baking powder
1 c. milk
1 egg

Brown onion in hot fat; add beef. Brown well. Add 1/2 teaspoonful salt, corn, tomatoes and chili powder. Cook for 15 minutes. Pour into a baking dish. Combine meal, flour, sugar, baking powder, 1/2 teaspoonful salt, milk and egg; mix well. Pour over beef mixture. Bake at 425 degrees for 25 to 30 minutes. Yield: 6 servings.

Mrs. Mildred Bridi, Trap Hill H. S.
Surveyor, West Virginia

TAMALE PIE

1 c. chopped onions
1 c. chopped green peppers
¾ lb. ground beef
2 8-oz. cans seasoned tomato sauce
1 12-oz. can whole kernel corn, drained
1 c. chopped ripe olives
1 clove of garlic, minced
1 tbsp. sugar
1 tsp. salt
2 to 3 tsp. chili powder
Dash of pepper
1 ½ c. shredded sharp process American cheese

Cook onion and green pepper in a small amount of hot fat until just tender. Add meat; brown lightly. Add remaining ingredients except cheese; simmer for 20 to 25 minutes or until thick. Add cheese; stir until melted. Pour into greased 10 x 6 x 1 1/2-inch baking dish.

CORN MEAL TOPPING:

¾ c. yellow corn meal
½ tsp. salt
2 c. cold water
1 tbsp. butter

Stir corn meal and salt into cold water; cook, stirring until thick. Add butter; mix well. Spoon over hot meat mixture in three lengthwise strips. Bake at 375 degrees for 40 minutes. Yield: 6 servings.

Mrs. Elodee McCormick, Pasco H. S.
Dade City, Florida

TAMALE PIE

Corn meal
4 c. water
1 tsp. salt
Seasoning to taste
1 ½ lb. ground beef
1 lge. onion, diced
1 can pitted olives
2 c. tomatoes, cooked
1 No. 2 can cream-style corn

Mix 1 cup corn meal, water, 1 teaspoonful salt and seasoning in saucepan; cook until thick. Brown ground beef and onion. Add olives, tomatoes, corn and corn meal; cook until thickened. Line greased 9 x 12-inch casserole with corn meal. Place ground beef mixture on top. Cover with foil. Bake at 350 degrees for 30 minutes. NOTE: May be frozen; cook for 1 hour. Yield: 8 servings.

Mrs. Margaret J. Wahl
Schneider Vocational School
Stockton, California

BEAN-MACARONI CASSEROLE

1 7-oz. pkg. elbow macaroni, cooked
1 lb. ground beef
¼ c. minced onion
2 tsp. salt

(Continued on next page)

1 No. 2 can kidney beans
1 No. 2 can tomatoes
4 slices fried bacon, crumbled
½ lb. American cheese, grated

Place one-half the macaroni in greased 2-quart casserole. Brown ground beef, onion and salt in skillet. Cook until onion is clear. Add beans and tomatoes; mix well. Add one-half the beef mixture to macaroni in casserole. Repeat layers. Sprinkle with bacon. Cover with cheese. Bake at 350 degrees for 30 to 40 minutes or until cheese melts and begins to brown. Yield: 8-10 servings.

Mrs. Madge D. Tapp, Webster Co. H. S.
Dixon, Kentucky

CASSEROLE FOR A CROWD

1 ½ lb. ground beef
1 c. chopped onions
1 12-oz. can whole kernel corn, drained
1 can cream of mushroom soup
1 can cream of chicken soup
1 c. sour cream
¼ c. chopped pimento
¾ tsp. salt
½ tsp. monosodium glutamate
¼ tsp. pepper
3 c. cooked medium macaroni or noodles
1 c. bread crumbs, toasted
1 stick margarine, melted

Brown meat over medium heat. Add onions; cook until tender but not brown. Add corn, soups, sour cream, pimento and seasonings. Stir in noodles. Pour into two buttered 2-quart casseroles. Combine crumbs and butter; sprinkle over top of casserole. Bake at 350 degrees for 20 minutes. May be frozen, if desired. Yield: 12 servings.

Mrs. Imogene D. Crawford
East Henderson H. S.
Flat Rock, North Carolina

CHOP SUEY

1 c. uncooked macaroni, spaghetti or noodles
2 tbsp. chopped onion
2 tbsp. butter
1 lb. round steak, ground
1 can tomato soup

Cook macaroni in boiling salted water until tender; drain. Fry onion in butter in large frying pan until tender; add ground steak. Fry until done. Blend macaroni and meat mixture; add tomato soup. Mix well. Place in buttered casserole; top with cheese slices, if desired. Bake at 350 degrees for 1 hour. Yield: 6 servings.

Mrs. Gertrude I. Young
Lawrencetown Consolidated School
Lawrencetown, Novia Scotia, Canada

HAMBURGER MEAL-IN-ONE

1 med. onion, chopped
1 lb. ground hamburger
2 tbsp. shortening
1 7-oz. box quick cooking macaroni
2 cans tomato soup
¾ c. catsup
1 tbsp. Worcestershire sauce
1 tsp. salt
¼ tsp. pepper
½ lb. American cheese, grated
1 c. finely crushed potato chips

Brown onion and hamburger in hot shortening; add macaroni and brown slightly. Add soup, catsup, Worcestershire sauce, salt, pepper and cheese. Pour into a well greased casserole. Bake at 350 degrees for 45 minutes. Top with potato chips. Bake for 15 minutes longer. Yield: 6 servings.

Mrs. Loretta Schrowang, Hennepin H. S.
Hennepin, Illinois

MACARONI AND MEAT CASSEROLE

1 lb. ground beef
1 med. onion, chopped
1 stalk celery, chopped
2 tsp. salt
Dash of monosodium glutamate
¼ tsp. pepper
1 20-oz. can tomatoes
1 ½ c. raw macaroni, cooked
½ c. bread crumbs (opt.)

Fry ground beef for a few minutes until the fat has been rendered. Tilt pan slightly; push meat to one side and spoon out excess fat. Add onion and celery; continue to fry for 5 minutes longer. Add seasonings and tomatoes. Simmer for a few minutes. Combine sauce and macaroni; serve topped with bread crumbs. Yield: 5 servings.

Mrs. S. MacDonald
Maple Ridge Secondary School
British Columbia, Canada

QUICK MACARONI CASSEROLE

½ lb. cooked elbow macaroni
1 to 1 ½ lb. cooked ground beef
1 tsp. salt
1 tsp. Worcestershire sauce
3 tsp. minced dried onion
½ tsp. pepper
2 cans tomato soup
1 med. can tomatoes
Sliced cheese

Combine all ingredients except cheese in a casserole. Arrange cheese slices on top. Bake at 350 degrees for 20 to 30 minutes. Yield: 8 servings.

Doris Gilson, Torrington H. S.
Torrington, Connecticut

POLLY'S GOULASH

2 lb. ground beef
Margarine
1 8-oz. pkg. small shell macaroni, cooked
3 onions, chopped
1 green pepper, chopped
3 cloves of garlic
1 8-oz. can tomato paste
1 12-oz. can whole grain yellow corn
1 3-oz. can mushrooms
1 c. grated sharp cheese
1 tbsp. brown sugar
1 tbsp. Worcestershire sauce
1 tbsp. chili powder
2 tsp. salt
¼ tsp. pepper
1 c. Sherry

Cook meat in margarine; add all remaining ingredients. Pour into two 1 1/2-quart casseroles. Refrigerate overnight. Bake, covered, at 350 degrees for 1 hour. Yield: 10 servings.

Mrs. Pauline S. Slate, Greensville Co. H. S.
Emporia, Virginia

SPANISH MACARONI

1 c. macaroni
1 med. onion, chopped
½ green pepper, chopped
1 tbsp. margarine
¼ to ½ lb. ground beef
½ tsp. salt
Few grains of pepper
1 10½-oz. can tomato soup
¼ lb. cheese, cut into pieces
Bread crumbs

Cook macaroni in baking salted water; drain. Saute onion and green pepper in margarine; add ground beef, salt and pepper. Cook until meat loses the pink color. Add tomato soup and cheese. Combine meat mixture with macaroni. Place in 1-quart baking dish. Top with bread crumbs. Bake at 350 degrees for 25 to 30 minutes. Yield: 4 servings.

Mrs. Margaret K. Gorman, Pine H. S.
Ansonia, Connecticut

BEEF-NOODLE BAKE

1 lb. ground beef
2 tbsp. butter
1 clove of garlic, minced
1 tsp. salt
Dash of pepper
1 tsp. sugar
2 8-oz. cans tomato sauce
1 8-oz. can flat noodles
6 scallions and tops, chopped
1 lge. pkg. cream cheese
1 c. sour cream
½ c. grated cheese

Cook beef in butter until crumbly; add garlic, salt, pepper, sugar and tomato sauce. Cover; cook slowly for 15 to 20 minutes. Cook noodles according to directions; drain. Mix scallions with cream cheese and sour cream. Layer in a 9 x 14-inch casserole, beginning with noodles and ending with meat. Repeat layers; top with grated cheese. Bake in preheated 250 degree oven for 20 to 30 minutes or until bubbly. Yield: 4-6 servings.

Karen Bryant, Moore Academy
Pineapple, Alabama

BEEF-NOODLE BAKE

1 lge. onion, sliced
2 tbsp. fat
1 lb. ground beef
1 tsp. salt
¼ tsp. pepper
1 can tomato soup
1 sm. can sliced mushrooms, drained
½ lb. process American cheese, diced
1 pkg. wide noodles, cooked and drained

Saute onion in fat; add ground beef. Cook until done. Add all remaining ingredients except noodles. Simmer until cheese is well blended. Add noodles; mix thoroughly. Place in a 2-quart casserole. Bake, uncovered, at 350 degrees until light brown on top.

Mrs. Helen Roberts, Alvin H. S.
Alvin, Texas

CASHEW-BEEF BAKE

1 lb. ground chuck or round
1 c. chopped onions
1 c. diced celery
3 tbsp. butter
1 6 or 8-oz. pkg. noodles, cooked and drained
1 can cream of chicken soup
1 can cream of mushroom soup
1 c. milk or half and half
1 tsp. salt
¼ tsp. pepper
1 c. salted cashews

Brown beef, onions and celery in butter. Arrange beef mixture and noodles in layers in greased 2-quart casserole. Combine soups, milk and seasonings; pour over beef and noodles. Cover and bake at 325 degrees for 1 hour. Uncover; sprinkle with cashews. Bake for 10 minutes longer. Yield: 8 servings.

Mrs. Mary Kaye Hancock
Sesser Comm. Unit School
Sesser, Illinois

HAMBURGER CASSEROLE

1 lb. ground beef
Salt
2 med. potatoes, sliced
Uncooked or left-over peas or other vegetables
½ c. uncooked noodles
1 can onion soup

(Continued on next page)

Crumble 1/2 pound ground beef in 2 1/2-quart casserole; add salt to taste. Add one-half of sliced potatoes, then a layer of peas; spread noodles over peas. Add remaining potatoes; salt to taste. Cover with remaining ground beef. Pour onion soup over all. Bake at 350 degrees for 1 hour. Yield: 6 servings.

Mrs. Faith Cornelius
Rockwell City Comm. H. S.
Rockwell City, Iowa

HAMBURGER CORN CASSEROLE

1 onion, chopped
1 green pepper, chopped
2 tbsp. butter
1 lb. ground beef
1 pkg. frozen corn
Salt and pepper to taste
6 oz. fine egg noodles, uncooked
1 lge. can tomato juice
Grated American cheese

Cook onion and green pepper in butter until soft; add ground meat. Cook until well browned. Add corn; season to taste. Butter a 1 1/2-quart casserole. Place a layer of meat mixture in casserole; add layer of uncooked noodles. Alternate layers of meat mixture and noodles until all are used, ending with meat layer. Pour tomato juice over layers; cover with grated cheese. Bake at 350 degrees for 30 minutes or until noodles are cooked and cheese is melted. Yield: 6 servings.

Ruth R. Harberleu, Greensburg Salem H. S.
Greensburg, Pennsylvania

HAMBURGER HEAVEN

1 lb. ground beef
1 c. fine noodles
1 No. 2 can tomatoes
1 c. finely chopped onions
1 c. diced green peppers
1 c. chopped celery
1 3 to 4-oz. can mushroom stems and pieces
1 c. ripe olives, sliced
¼ tsp. garlic salt
¼ lb. American or Cheddar cheese, cubed

Brown ground beef in a large, heavy skillet; layer beef with remaining ingredients, except cheese, in order given, using vegetable liquids. Cover skillet with a tight fitting lid. Cook on low heat or 350 degrees on automatic burner. Cook, covered, for 25 minutes. At end of cooking period, sprinkle cheese over casserole. Replace lid; turn off burner. Allow 5 to 8 minutes for cheese to melt. NOTE: Three-fourths cup instant rice may be substituted for noodles. Yield: 6 servings.

Mrs. Margaret McIntosh, Lostant H. S.
Lostant, Illinois

HAMBURGER-NOODLE DISH

⅔ 8-oz. pkg. noodles
1 lge. onion
2 lb. ground beef
⅓ c. melted butter
3 10 ½-oz. cans tomato soup
1 ½ oz. Parmesan cheese

Boil noodles in 2 quarts boiling water for 7 minutes. Brown onion and ground beef in butter. Place beef, onions and tomato soup in casserole. Spread noodles over top of mixture; sprinkle with cheese. Pour on melted butter. Bake at 350 degrees for 1 hour. Yield: 8 servings.

Betty V. Rentschler, Wilson Jr. H. S.
West Lawn, Pennsylvania

EASY LASAGNA

1 lb. ground beef
2 cloves of garlic, minced
1 6-oz. can tomato paste
1 1-lb. 4-oz. can tomatoes
1 tsp. salt
¾ tsp. pepper
½ tsp. oregano
1 8-oz. pkg. lasagna noodles
1 ½ c. diced Swiss cheese
1 12-oz. carton cottage cheese

Brown ground beef and garlic in small amount of fat; add tomato paste, tomatoes, salt, pepper and oregano. Cover and simmer for 20 minutes. Cook noodles as directed on package. Alternate layers of meat sauce, noodles and cheeses in 11 1/2 x 7 1/2 x 1 1/2-inch baking dish, beginning and ending with meat sauce. Bake in preheated 350 degree oven for 20 to 30 minutes. Sprinkle with grated Parmesan cheese, if desired. Yield: 6-8 servings.

Carmen Chavira, San Felipe H. S.
Del Rio, Texas
Mrs. Harriet Willard, Conkling School
Utica, New York

LASAGNA

1 lb. ground beef
1 med. onion, chopped
1 clove of garlic, minced
2 tbsp. olive oil
2 ½ c. tomatoes
1 6-oz. can tomato paste
1 tbsp. parsley
1 tsp. oregano
Salt and pepper to taste
⅓ c. water
9 lasagna noodles
⅔ lb. Mozzarella cheese, thinly sliced
6 tbsp. Parmesan cheese
⅔ lb. Velveeta cheese, sliced

Brown ground beef, onion and garlic in olive oil in a large saucepan; add tomatoes, tomato paste, parsley, oregano, salt, pepper and water. Simmer for 30 minutes. Cook lasagna noodles in a large amount of boiling salted water for 15 minutes. Drain and lay in single layers until

(Continued on next page)

dry. Arrange one-half of noodles, one-third of the sauce, one-half Mozzarella cheese, 2 tablespoonfuls Parmesan cheese and one-half Velveeta cheese in 9 x 13-inch pan. Repeat the layers. Cover with remaining sauce and Parmesan cheese. Bake at 350 degrees for 30 to 35 minutes. Yield: 8-10 servings.

Sara Dinsmore, Crestview H. S.
Ashland, Ohio

LASAGNA

½ lb. lasagna noodles
Olive oil
1 lb. ground beef
2 cloves of garlic, crushed or garlic powder
Salt to taste
½ to 1 tsp. oregano
1 8-oz. can tomato paste
1 No. 2 can tomatoes, well drained
½ lb. dry small curd cottage cheese
1 pkg. sliced Swiss cheese
½ c. Parmesan cheese

Boil noodles in salted water with 1 tablespoonful olive oil. Brown meat in 2 tablespoonfuls olive oil with garlic. Season. Add tomato paste and well drained tomatoes to meat mixture. Place noodles in bottom of greased dish. Add meat mixture. Spread cottage cheese over meat. Top with Swiss cheese. Sprinkle with Parmesan cheese. Bake at 350 degrees for 45 minutes or until brown and bubbly. Remove from oven; cool for 10 minutes. Slice into squares. Yield: 4 servings.

Mrs. Josephine Rummler, Belding Area Schools
Belding, Michigan

LASAGNA CASSEROLE

1 lb. hamburger
2 cloves of garlic, crushed or 1 tsp. garlic powder
2 tbsp. salad oil
1 8-oz. can tomato sauce
1 No. 2 can tomatoes
1 ½ tsp. salt
¼ tsp. oregano
8 oz. lasagna noodles, cooked
½ lb. Mozzarella cheese
¾ lb. cottage cheese
½ c. Parmesan cheese

Saute hamburger and garlic in oil; add tomato sauce, tomatoes, salt and oregano. Simmer for 20 minutes. Cook noodles. Alternate layers of noodles, Mozzarello cheese, cottage cheese, meat sauce and Parmesan cheese, ending with sauce and Parmesan cheese. Bake at 375 degrees for 1 hour. Yield: 5 servings.

Arlene C. McBride, Laurel Jr. H. S.
Laurel, Montana

MOSTACCIOLI CASSEROLE

½ c. chopped green pepper
½ c. chopped onion
2 tbsp. oil
1 lb. ground beef
1 1-lb. can tomatoes
1 6-oz. can tomato paste
1 8-oz. can tomato sauce
½ c. water
¾ tsp. salt
¼ tsp. pepper
⅓ tsp. basil
1 bay leaf
½ lb. box mostaccioli noodles, cooked
½ lb. process cheese, sliced

Saute green pepper and onion in oil. Add ground beef; cook until brown. Stir in tomatoes, tomato paste, tomato sauce, water, salt, pepper, basil and bay leaf. Simmer for 15 minutes. Arrange alternate layers of noodles, cheese slices and meat mixture in 3-quart casserole. Bake at 350 degrees for 30 minutes. Yield: 6-8 servings.

Mrs. Betrice J. Birchard, Hackettstown H. S.
Hackettstown, New Jersey

NED'S GOOP

1 ½ lb. ground chuck
Salt and pepper
1 tbsp. chili powder
1 lge. onion, chopped
1 green pepper, chopped
1 sm. can chopped mushrooms
Dash of monosodium glutamate
1 c. grated cheese
1 sm. bottle sliced olives
1 No. 303 can whole kernel corn
1 pkg. small noodles, cooked and drained
2 cans cream of tomato soup
Toasted almonds

Brown meat; add seasonings, onion, green pepper and mushrooms. Cook over low heat, stirring frequently, for 30 to 40 minutes. Pour into large mixing bowl. Stir in monosodium glutamate, cheese, olives, corn and liquid noodles and soup. Pour into casserole. Bake at 300 to 350 degrees until thoroughly heated and bubbly. Top with toasted almonds and additional grated cheese, just before serving. Yield: 8-12 servings.

Mrs. Janiece Crisp Byrd, Banquete H. S.
Banquete, Texas

NUTTY NOODLES

1 8-oz. pkg. egg noodles
2 lb. ground beef
1 c. cubed process cheese
¼ c. chopped green olives
1 10 ½-oz. can cream of mushroom soup
1 can chow mein noodles

Cook noodles according to package directions; drain. Brown ground beef in small amount of fat; drain. Combine beef, noodles, cheese olives and soup in large casserole or 13 x 9 x 2-inch cake pan. Cover; bake at 350 degrees for

(Continued on next page)

30 minutes. Uncover; add chow mein noodles. Bake for 30 minutes longer. Yield: 12 servings.

Joyce Miles, Paxon H. S.
Jacksonville, Florida

RUSSIAN FLUFF

1 ½ lb. ground round steak
1 onion, chopped
1 stalk celery, chopped
1 green pepper, chopped
1 can tomato soup
1 can peas
1 pkg. medium noodles, cooked

Brown ground beef with onion, celery and green pepper. Add soup, peas and noodles. Place in casserole. Bake at 350 degrees for 30 to 45 minutes. Yield: 6 servings.

Rose Chandler, Calhoun City H. S.
Calhoun City, Mississippi

CUBAN SPAGHETTI

2 lb. hamburger
3 lge. onions, chopped
1 lge. green pepper, chopped
½ lge. bunch celery, chopped
2 cans tomato soup
Red pepper
Black pepper
Salt
Tabasco sauce
1 can mushrooms
1 can peas
1 pkg. spaghetti, partially cooked
1 lb. sharp cheese, grated
1 bottle stuffed olives

Fry hamburger with onions; add green pepper, celery, tomato soup and seasonings to taste. Cook until tender. Place in baking dish in layers with mushrooms, peas, spaghetti, cheese and olives. Bake at 325 degrees for 1 hour. Yield: 12 servings.

Sara M. Gantt, Wagener H. S.
Wagener, South Carolina

GROUND ROUND CASSEROLE

1 sm. onion, chopped
1 lb. ground beef
Salt
Pepper
Paprika
1 tbsp. margarine
½ c. grated cheese
1 can tomato soup
½ c. water
1 No. 2 can mixed vegetables
1 c. spaghetti

Brown onion, ground beef, a dash of salt, pepper and paprika in margarine. Combine mixture with remaining ingredients in greased casserole. Bake at 350 degrees for 20 to 25 minutes. Top with grated cheese; cook until cheese melts.

Mrs. Elizabeth S. Richardson, Orangeburg H. S.
Orangeburg, South Carolina

SAVORY SPAGHETTI CASSEROLE

1 lb. ground beef
½ c. chopped onion
¼ c. chopped green pepper
2 tbsp. butter
1 10 ½-oz. can cream of mushroom soup
1 10 ½-oz. can tomato soup
1 soup can water
1 clove of garlic, minced
1 c. shredded sharp process cheese
½ lb. spaghetti, cooked and drained

Cook beef, onion and green pepper in butter until meat is lightly browned and vegetables are tender; stir to separate meat particles. Add soups, water and garlic; heat. Blend with 1/2 cup cheese and spaghetti in 3-quart casserole; top with remaining cheese. Bake at 350 degrees for 30 minutes or until bubbling and hot. Yield: 4-6 servings.

Mrs. Patricia Larson, Milaca H. S.
Milaca, Minnesota

SPAGHETTI CASSEROLE

1 lb. hamburger
1 tbsp. shortening
Salt
½ tsp. black pepper
¼ c. chopped green pepper
2 c. uncooked spaghetti
1 can tomato sauce
1 can tomato soup
½ c. cheese cubes

Brown hamburger with shortening; add 1 teaspoonful salt, black pepper and green pepper. Cook spaghetti in 5 cups water with 2 teaspoonfuls salt. When spaghetti is tender, drain and combine with hamburger mixture, tomato sauce and soup in a casserole. Add cheese, reserving a small amount to sprinkle on top. Bake at 350 degrees for 45 minutes to 1 hour. Yield: 6 servings.

Elaine Peters, Mohall H. S.
Mohall, North Dakota

SPAGHETTI AND GROUND MEAT CASSEROLE

1 ½ lb. hamburger
1 med. onion, chopped
2 tsp. salt
¼ tsp. pepper
2 tbsp. chili powder
1 c. catsup
2 7-oz. pkg. spaghetti
1 ½ tsp. sugar
1 clove of garlic
1 can cream of mushroom soup
½ lb. grated cheese

(Continued on next page)

Brown meat and onion in skillet. Add salt, pepper and chili powder; cook until browned. Add catsup. Cook spaghetti according to package directions; add sugar and garlic. Drain; toss with meat mixture. Place in large casserole; top with undiluted soup and cheese. Bake at 375 degrees until heated through. Yield: 10 servings.

Mrs. Ruth Phellips, Garrison H. S.
Garrison, Texas

SPAGHETTI CASSEROLE

8 c. water
2 tsp. salt
1 c. spaghetti
½ to 1 lb. hamburger
1 sm. onion, chopped
1 ½ c. tomatoes
1 tbsp. Worcestershire sauce
½ c. grated cheese
Dash of paprika

Bring water to a boil; add salt and spaghetti. Cook until tender. Brown hamburger and onion in skillet; add tomatoes and Worcestershire sauce. Simmer for 20 minutes. Add spaghetti to meat mixture; mix well. Pour into a 2-quart casserole; top with cheese and paprika. Bake at 350 degrees for 20 minutes. Yield: 4-6 servings.

Mrs. Carol Pino, O. Henry Jr. H. S.
Austin, Texas

BEEF AND RICE CASSEROLE

1 lb. ground beef
2 tbsp. oil
½ c. chopped onion
1 c. chopped celery
¼ c. chopped green pepper
1 c. uncooked rice
1 lge. can tomatoes
2 tsp. salt
1 tbsp. chili powder
¼ tsp. pepper
½ tsp. Worcestershire sauce
1 c. chopped ripe olives

Brown beef in oil. Remove meat. Add onion, celery, green pepper and rice to fat. Cook, stirring until browned. Add tomatoes, seasonings, meat and olives. Bring to a boil; pour into 2-quart casserole. Cover and bake at 325 degrees for 1 hour. Yield: 6-8 servings.

Mrs. Marjorie W. Browning, Pensacola H. S.
Pensacola, Florida

HAWAIIAN HAMBURGER CASSEROLE

1 lb. hamburger
1 c. chopped onions
1 c. chopped celery
1 can cream of mushroom soup
1 can cream of chicken soup
1 ½ soup cans water
¾ c. uncooked rice
1 sm. can chow mein noodles

Brown hamburger, onions and celery; combine soups and water. Mix rice, hamburger mixture and soups in casserole. Bake at 350 degrees for 45 minutes. Cover with noodles; bake for 15 minutes longer. Yield: 6-8 servings.

Mrs. Lucile H. Proctor, Panguitch H. S.
Panguitch, Utah

MOCK CHOW MEIN

1 lb. hamburger
1 onion, chopped
2 tbsp. oil
1 can cream of mushroom soup
3 cans (scant) water
1 ½ c. diced celery
½ c. uncooked rice
4 tbsp. soy sauce
1 can broken mushroom pieces (opt.)

Brown hamburger and onion in oil; add remaining ingredients. Place in greased casserole. Bake at 350 degrees for 1 hour and 30 minutes, stirring often. Skim off excess grease. Serve with additional soy sauce. Yield: 8 servings.

Kathleen Berg, Mingus Union H. S.
Jerome, Arizona

SEVEN-LAYER CASSEROLE

1 c. rice
1 c. canned whole kernel corn
Salt and pepper
2 cans tomato sauce
1 ½ sauce cans water
½ c. finely chopped onion
¼ c. finely chopped green pepper
¾ lb. ground beef
4 slices bacon, cut into halves

Combine rice and corn in casserole; sprinkle with salt and pepper. Mix 1 can tomato sauce with 1 can water; pour over rice mixture. Add onion and green pepper to ground beef; sprinkle with salt and pepper. Pour 1 can tomato sauce mixed with 1/2 can water over casserole. Place bacon slices over top. Cover. Bake at 350 degrees for 1 hour. Uncover; bake for 30 minutes longer until bacon is crisp. Yield: 6 servings.

Myra D. Sorensen, Ritchfield H. S.
Ritchfield, Utah

BEEF GARDEN CASSEROLE

1 med. onion, chopped
Fat
1 lb. ground beef
¾ tsp. salt
½ tsp. pepper
1 1-lb. can cut green beans, drained
1 c. undrained whole kernel corn
1 10-oz. can tomato soup

Cook onion in a small amount of fat until tender but not brown. Add ground beef and seasoning;

(Continued on next page)

brown lightly. Add green beans, corn and tomato soup. Pour into 1 1/2-quart casserole.

CHEESE SPINS:

2 tbsp. shortening
1 c. sifted self-rising flour
⅓ c. milk
½ c. grated sharp Cheddar cheese

Cut shortening into flour; stir in milk. Turn out onto floured board. Knead lightly; roll out to a rectangle. Spread cheese over biscuit dough; roll up like jelly roll. Cut into 1-inch slices; place on casserole. Bake in preheated 425 degree oven for 15 to 20 minutes. Yield: 6-8 servings.

Nadine H. Shipp, Fyffe H. S.
Fyffe, Alabama

BEEF PATTIE CASSEROLE

2 lb. ground beef
Freshly ground pepper
1 c. soft bread crumbs
½ c. tomato juice
1 egg
½ tsp. curry powder
¼ c. butter
2 lge. onions, thinly sliced
2 lb. potatoes, peeled and thinly sliced
3 c. beef stock

Mix beef, pepper, bread crumbs, juice, egg and curry powder; form into patties about 1/4-inch thick. Brown patties in butter; remove meat from pan. Brown onion slices in same butter. Layer potatoes, onions and beef patties in a 3 to 4-quart casserole, beginning and ending with potatoes. Pour in beef stock. Bake at 350 degrees for 45 to 50 minutes or until potatoes are tender. Yield: 6-8 servings.

Mrs. Evelyn Fuller, Albert G. Parrish H. S.
Selma, Alabama

BEST HOT DISH

1 ½ to 2 lb. ground round
1 onion, diced
2 c. diced celery
2 cans cream of mushroom soup
1 can cream
1 can mixed vegetables, undrained
1 can mushrooms, undrained
4 tbsp. soy sauce
2 lge. cans chow mein noodles

Brown ground round and onion; add all remaining ingredients. Place in casserole dish; top with additional noodles at 325 degrees for 1 hour or longer. Yield: 6 servings.

Mrs. Betty Lund, Nashwauk-Keewatin H. S.
Nashwauk, Minnesota

BUSY DAY MEAT

1 lb. hamburger
1 tsp. salt
½ tsp. pepper
2 c. sliced potatoes
1 c. sliced onions
1 can cream of mushroom soup
1 soup can water

Season meat with salt and pepper; press into a casserole. Place potatoes and onions in layers on top. Dilute soup with water; pour over top of casserole. Bake at 375 degrees for 2 hours or until potatoes are tender. Yield: 12 servings.

Maude Haynes, Lawhon School
Tupelo, Mississippi

CHEESEBURGER CASSEROLE

1 lb. ground beef
1 med. onion, shredded
1 tsp. salt
⅛ tsp. pepper
1 tbsp. Worcestershire sauce
1 12-oz. can whole kernel corn, drained
1 c. shredded cheese
¾ c. catsup
½ c. potato chip crumbs

Brown meat and onion in ungreased skillet; add all remaining ingredients except crumbs to meat. Mix well. Pour into casserole; top with crumbs. Bake in preheated 350 degree oven for 30 minutes. Yield: 5-6 servings.

Mrs. George Wooton, West Hopkins H. S.
Nebo, Kentucky

FIVE- LAYER MEAL

1 lb. ground beef
⅔ c. chopped onions
1 tbsp. shortening
1 ½ tsp. salt
2 tsp. chili powder
Pepper to taste
2 tbsp. fat
2 lge. white potatoes, thinly sliced
⅓ c. uncooked long grain rice, washed
⅔ c. chopped green peppers
1 No. 2 can tomatoes
⅓ c. catsup
⅓ c. water

Place ground beef and onions in skillet with shortening; brown, stirring frequently. Add salt, chili powder and pepper. Cover bottom of greased baking dish with potatoes; sprinkle rice evenly over potatoes. Spread browned beef and onions on top of rice. Sprinkle green peppers over beef mixture; add tomatoes. Pour catsup and water over mixture. Cover dish with foil. Bake at 350 degrees for 1 hour. Yield: 6-8 servings.

Mrs. Ann B. Jones, Mountainburg H. S.
Mountainburg, Arkansas

HAMBURGER-CORN BAKE

1 onion, chopped
Oil
2 lb. hamburger
1 c. cream-style corn
¼ c. chopped celery
½ c. sour cream
2 tsp. salt
1 c. flour
1 c. corn meal
2 tbsp. sugar
4 tsp. baking powder
1 egg
1 c. milk

Saute onion in 2 tabelspoonfuls oil; add meat and brown. Add corn, celery, sour cream and 1 teaspoonful salt; simmer for 5 minutes. Sift flour with corn meal, sugar, baking powder and 1 teaspoonful salt; add egg, milk and 1/4 cup oil. Stir until smooth. Spread meat mixture over bottom of a greased 2-quart casserole. Drop corn bread topping by tablespoonfuls on top. Bake at 425 degrees for 20 to 25 minutes or until brown. Yield: 6 servings.

Carole Oates, Tulia Schools
Tulia, Texas

RUSSIAN FLUFF

1 lge. onion, minced
Butter
1 ½ lb. ground beef
½ green pepper, chopped
1 can whole kernel corn
¼ c. uncooked rice
1 c. mushroom pieces
1 c. tomato soup
⅛ tsp. pepper
½ tsp. salt

Cook onion in butter until golden. Add meat and cook until brown. Add remaining ingredients; place in casserole. Bake at 350 degrees for 1 hour and 30 minutes. Yield: 8 servings.

Mrs. Merle Twesme, Arcadia H. S.
Arcadia, Wisconsin

SHIPWRECK STEW

3 or 4 med. potatoes, diced
2 onions, diced
1 lb. hamburger
1 No. 2 ½ can chili
⅓ c. uncooked rice
1 can tomato soup
1 ½ c. water
1 beef bouillon cube
1 tsp. salt
¼ tsp. pepper
¼ tsp. Worcestershire sauce

Place potatoes and onions in a large casserole or baking pan. Crumble hamburger over onions and potatoes. Spread chili over hamburger and sprinkle with rice. Mix tomato soup, water, bouillon cube, salt, pepper and Worcestershire sauce; pour over ingredients in casserole. Cover and bake at 325 degrees for 1 hour and 30 minutes. Yield: 12 servings.

Mrs. Marvel Hughes, Nooksack Valley H. S.
Nooksack, Washington

TAMALE BAKE

½ c. diced onion
¼ c. diced green pepper
½ c. diced celery
1 lb. ground beef
1 tbsp. fat
½ c. corn meal
1 No. 2 can tomatoes
1 No. 2 can whole kernel corn
½ c. chopped olives
2 ½ tsp. salt
1 ½ tsp. chili powder
1 ½ tsp. Worcestershire sauce
½ c. grated American-cheese

Brown onion, green pepper, celery and beef in hot fat. Cook corn meal in tomatoes for 5 to 10 minutes; add to meat mixture. Stir in corn, olives and seasonings. Pour into greased casserole; top with grated cheese. Bake at 325 degrees for 45 minutes.

Mrs. Kathrine Elrod, Mackenzie Jr. H. S.
Lubbock, Texas

TATER TOT DISH

1 lb. ground beef
1 sm. onion, chopped
1 can french-style green beans
1 pkg. tater-tots
1 can cream of chicken soup
1 can milk

Lightly brown ground beef and onion; place in flat baking dish. Add a layer of green beans and tater-tots. Beat chicken soup and milk with egg beater; pour over mixture. Bake at 350 degrees for 1 hour and 15 minutes. NOTE: Cream of vegetable or mushroom soup may be substituted for chicken.

Janet Ruhsam, Elkhorn H. S.
Elkhorn, Wisconsin

VEGETABLE-HAMBURGER SPECIALTY

2 lb. ground beef
1 lge. onion
1 c. diced celery
4 to 5 c. raw diced potatoes
2 tsp. salt
½ tsp. pepper
1 can tomato soup
1 can cream of mushroom soup

Brown beef and onion; alternate layers of celery, potatoes and seasonings in buttered casserole. Mix tomato and mushroom soups; pour over ingredients in casserole. Cover.

(Continued on next page)

Bake at 350 degrees for 1 hour and 30 minutes, removing cover the last 15 minutes of baking. Yield: 10 servings.

Fern A. Soderholm, Willmar Jr. H. S.
Willmar, Minnesota

BEEF CASSEROLE

1 ½ lb. ground beef
1 c. chopped onions
¼ c. milk
1 10 ½-oz. can cream of mushroom soup
1 8-oz. pkg. cream cheese, softened
1 tsp. salt
¼ c. catsup
1 can biscuits

Brown beef and onions. Drain. Combine milk, soup and cream cheese; add salt, catsup and meat. Pour into 2-quart casserole. Bake, uncovered, at 375 degrees for 10 minutes. Place biscuits on top. Bake at 375 degrees for 15 to 20 minutes or until biscuits are golden brown. Yield: 5-6 servings.

Nancy A. Menninger, Miamisburg H. S.
Miamisburg, Ohio

CHILI POT

2 bunches green onions, chopped
1 clove of garlic
1 lb. hamburger
Salt and pepper to taste
2 c. cooked pinto beans
1 can enchilada sauce
1 c. grated cheese
2 15-cent pkg. corn chips

Saute onions and garlic in small amount of fat. Add hamburger; season with salt and pepper. Cook until brown. Add beans and enchilada sauce. Simmer for 5 to 10 minutes. Pour one-half of meat mixture into casserole. Sprinkle with 1/2 cup grated cheese and 1 package corn chips. Repeat. Bake at 350 degrees for 20 minutes. Yield: 6-8 servings.

Mrs. Betty Hall, Fort Cobb School
Fort Cobb, Oklahoma

CREAMED TACOS

1 ½ lb. ground beef
1 lge. onion, diced
1 lge. green pepper, diced
Salt and pepper to taste
1 6-oz. can hot sauce
1 6-oz. can enchilada sauce
1 pkg. tortillas
½ lb. cheese, grated
1 lge. can evaporated milk

Saute ground beef, onion and green pepper; salt and pepper to taste. Add sauces to mixture. Place in a greased casserole a layer of tortillas, a layer of sauce and a layer of cheese; repeat until all ingredients are used. Pour milk over mixture. Bake at 350 degrees for 45 minutes or until milk thickens. Yield: 8 servings.

Mrs. Rachel M. Pearce, Castleberry H. S.
Fort Worth, Texas

ENCHILADA CASSEROLE

1 10-oz. can Mexican-style tomato sauce
1 10-oz. can water
1 8-oz. can tomato sauce
1 lb. ground beef
1 lge. onion, chopped
2 cloves of garlic, chopped
1 hard-cooked egg, chopped (opt.)
1 4 ½-oz. can chopped ripe olives
½ tsp. salt
6 tortillas
½ lb. dry Monterey Jack cheese, grated

Heat hot sauce, water and tomato sauce. Brown meat with onion and garlic; add egg, olives, salt and 1/2 cup sauce. Dip tortillas into sauce; layer in casserole with meat mixture and cheese. Pour on remaining sauce; top with cheese. Bake at 350 degrees for 25 minutes. Yield: 6 servings.

Maxine Barber, Allcombia H. S.
Martinez, California

HOT SPANISH PRONTO LOAF

1 lb. lean ground beef
1 med. onion, diced
1 c. grated Cheddar cheese
1 c. tostados or corn chips
2 sm. jalapeno pickled peppers, thinly sliced
½ tsp. powdered garlic
1 tsp. salt
½ tsp. pepper
¼ c. evaporated milk

Brown hamburger and onion in skillet. Alternate layers of cheese, tostados, meat, peppers and seasonings in 5 x 8 1/2-inch casserole. Pour milk over top. Bake in preheated 375 degree oven for 30 minutes. Serve hot. Yield: 4 servings.

Betty Sadberry, Amherst H. S.
Amherst, Texas

JIFFY CHILI-HOMINY BAKE

1 lb. ground meat
½ c. chopped onion
1 1-lb. can chili with beans
1 tbsp. chili powder
1 can cream of chicken soup
1 1-lb. 4-oz. can yellow hominy, drained
2 tbsp. sliced ripe olives
½ c. shredded American cheese

Cook ground beef and onion until meat is browned; stir in remaining ingredients, except cheese.

(Continued on next page)

Spoon into 2-quart casserole. Cover; bake at 350 degrees for 25 minutes. Sprinkle with cheese; continue baking, uncovered, for 5 minutes. Yield: 6 servings.

Mrs. J. C. Embry, Forestburg H. S.
Forestburg, Texas

MEAT BALL CASSEROLE

1 lb. hamburger
3 eggs
1 c. milk
1 tbsp. minced onion
1 tsp. salt
1 tsp. monosodium glutamate
½ tsp. pepper
20 saltine crackers, crushed
Flour
1 can cream of mushroom soup
1 soup can milk or water

Combine all ingredients except flour, soup and milk; shape into balls. Roll in flour. Brown in skillet. Place in large casserole. Dilute soup with milk; pour over meat balls. Bake at 350 degrees for 1 hour. Yield: 5 servings.

Claudia Tharpe, Bunker Hill H. S.
Clarmont, North Carolina

MEAT BALL CASSEROLE

1 lb. ground beef
½ c. pork sausage
½ c. dry bread crumbs
1 ⅓ c. evaporated milk
2 tbsp. chopped onion
1 tsp. chili powder
⅛ tsp. pepper
1 can cream of mushroom soup
1 can cream of celery or cream of vegetable soup
½ c. water

Combine beef, sausage, crumbs, 1/3 cup evaporated milk, onion, chili powder and pepper; shape into balls. Brown in hot fat. Cover; cook for 10 minutes. Place in 2 1/2-quart casserole. Heat soups, remaining milk and water. Pour over meat balls.

CHILI-CHEESE BISCUITS:

1 ⅓ c. sifted flour
3 tsp. baking powder
½ tsp. chili powder
¼ tsp. salt
⅓ c. shortening
1 egg
⅓ c. evaporated milk
1 ½ c. grated American cheese

Sift dry ingredients; cut in shortening until particles are very fine. Combine egg and milk; add to dry ingredients, stirring until dough clings together. Knead lightly on floured surface. Roll out to a 12-inch square. Sprinkle with cheese; roll up as for jelly roll. Cut into eight slices. Place on top of casserole. Bake at 400 degrees for 20 to 30 minutes. Yield: 8 servings.

Genia Thames, Townsend H. S.
Townsend, Tennessee

MEAT LOAF WITH SAUCE

3 slices stale bread
½ lge. onion, chopped
2 stalks celery, chopped
1 ½ lb. ground beef
1 egg
Catsup
1 ½ tsp. salt
Dash of pepper
2 tbsp. brown sugar
1 tsp. dry mustard

Soak bread in water. Combine onion, celery, meat and egg. Squeeze water from bread; add to meat mixture. Add 1/3 cup catsup, salt and pepper; mix until well blended. Place mixture in casserole. Combine 1/2 cup catsup, brown sugar and mustard; spread over meat mixture. Bake at 350 degrees for 1 hour and 15 minutes. Yield: 6 servings.

Mrs. Irma M. Barbour, Exeter H. S.
Exeter, New Hampshire

MOCK TURKEY CASSEROLE

2 lb. hamburger
1 tbsp. butter
2 cans cream of chicken soup
1 can cream of celery soup
3 soup cans milk
1 pkg. unseasoned stuffing mix
Salt and pepper to taste

Brown hamburger in butter; stir to keep loose. Combine all remaining ingredients; add to meat. Pack mixture into a large casserole. Bake at 350 degrees for 1 hour. Yield: 8 servings.

Mrs. Mary M. Radford, Waverly H. S.
Waverly, Ohio

LASAGNA

1 onion, chopped
1 clove of garlic, chopped
2 oz. olive oil
1 lb. chopped chuck
1 can tomato paste
1 No. 2 ½ can Italian tomatoes
1 c. water
1 tsp. salt
½ tsp. mace
¼ tsp. pepper
1 tsp. (scant) oregano
10 strips lasagna noodles
1 pkg. Ricotta cheese
½ lb. Mozzarella cheese
Parmesan cheese

(Continued on next page)

Saute onion and garlic lightly in olive oil; remove from pan. Fry meat in remaining oil. Place tomato paste, tomatoes, water, sauted onions and garlic in a large pan; cook until meat is done. Add meat to sauce mixture; add seasonings. Simmer, uncovered, for about 1 to 2 hours or until thickened. Cook lasagna noodles according to package directions; drain. Place a small amount of sauce in greased flat oblong baking dish. Lay strips of lasagna noodles in dish; spread with layers of Ricotta, Mozzarella and sauce until all are used. Sprinkle heavily with Parmesan cheese. Bake at 375 degrees for 20 to 30 minutes. Yield: 6-8 servings.

Susan Wright, Clovis H. S.
Clovis, New Mexico

MEAT PIE

2 c. diced cooked beef or chicken
2 c. white sauce
1 c. cooked mixed vegetables
1 onion, minced
1 tsp. Worcestershire sauce
Salt and pepper to taste
1 recipe pastry

Combine meat, white sauce, vegetables and seasonings; pour into greased casserole. Roll pastry dough; place on top of casserole. Bake at 425 degrees for 25 to 30 minutes. NOTE: Do not use potatoes in vegetables. A two-crust pie may also be used. Yield: 4 servings.

Mrs. J. E. Robertson, Friendship H. S.
Friendship, Tennessee

BEEF STEW CASSEROLE

2 lb. stew beef
1 tbsp. flour
1 tbsp. fat
1 tbsp. vinegar
1 tbsp. brown sugar
1 tsp. salt
½ tsp. pepper
1 sm. can tomato sauce
2 med. onions, sliced
4 med. carrots, sliced
1 12-oz. can. frozen peas

Trim excess fat from beef; cut into 1-inch cubes. Flour well. Brown in fat in large skillet. Remove to bowl. Add vinegar, brown sugar, salt, pepper and tomato sauce to drippings. Simmer for 1 minute. Layer meat, onions, carrots and peas in 2-quart casserole. Repeat layers. Pour liquid from skillet over casserole; add water to top of mixture. Cover and bake at 325 degrees for 2 hours. Yield: 6-8 servings.

Mrs. Mary Reid, Lord Byng Secondary School
Vancouver, British Columbia, Canada

MOTHER'S STEW BEEF CASSEROLE

2 lb. stew beef
1 sm. onion, chopped
1 bay leaf
1 tsp. salt
Dash of pepper
4 med. carrots, sliced
3 stalks celery, chopped
1 can tomato soup
½ c. water

Mix all ingredients in buttered 2-quart casserole. Bake at 325 to 350 degrees for 4 to 5 hours, stirring occasionally. Reduce heat if casserole gets too brown. Yield: 8-10 servings.

Jill Fox, Falmouth H. S.
Falmouth, Maine

STAY ABED STEW

1 10-oz. can tomato soup
½ soup can water
2 lb. stew beef, cubed
1 can peas
1 c. sliced carrots
2 onions, chopped
1 tsp. salt
Dash of pepper
1 lge. potato, sliced

Dilute soup with water. Combine all ingredients in casserole. Cover and bake at 275 degrees for 5 hours. Yield: 8 servings.

Marilyn Kay Clark
University of Nebraska School of Agriculture
Curtis, Nebraska

ALENE'S VEAL CASSEROLE

⅓ c. flour
1 tsp. paprika
2 lb. veal round steak, cubed
¼ c. shortening
1 ¾ c. cooked onions
2 cans cream of chicken soup
1 ½ soup cans water or onion liquid

Mix flour and paprika; pound into meat. Brown in shortening; transfer to casserole. Add onions. Heat 1 1/2 cans of soup; add water. Bring to a boil; pour over meat. Bake at 350 degrees for 45 minutes.

(Continued on next page)

DUMPLINGS:

2 c. flour
2 tsp. baking powder
½ tsp. salt
1 tsp. poultry seasoning
1 tsp. poppy seed
1 tsp. onion flakes
¼ c. salad oil
1 c. milk
¼ c. melted butter
1 c. bread crumbs
1 c. sour cream

Sift dry ingredients; add seasonings. Blend oil and milk; lightly stir into dry ingredients. Combine butter and crumbs; drop dumplings into crumb mixture. Drop dumplings on top of casserole. Bake at 425 degrees for 20 to 25 minutes. Heat remaining soup and sour cream; serve with casserole. Yield: 8 servings.

Mrs. Jean Cummings, Kingsford H. S.
Kingsford, Michigan

CHINESE VEAL

1 lb. cubed veal, round or chuck steak
Fat
1 c. finely cut celery
2 sm. onions, finely cut
1 can chicken-noodle soup
1 can cream of mushroom soup
2 soup cans water
½ c. uncooked rice
4 tsp. soya sauce

Cut fat from meat. Brown meat in a small amount of fat; place in casserole. Cook celery and onions slowly in fat; add soups, water, rice and soya sauce. Heat thoroughly. Mix with meat. Place in casserole. Bake at 325 degrees for 2 hours. Yield: 6 servings.

Rosalie Wentzell
William E. Hay Composite H. S.
Stettler, Alberta, Canada

BAKED PORK CHOPS WITH RICE

½ c. uncooked rice or 1 c. instant rice
4 pork chops
1 10 ½-oz. can beef bouillon
2 tbsp. minced onion

Place all ingredients in casserole. Bake at 350 degrees for 1 hour or until pork chops are tender. Yield: 4 servings.

Vades Koonst, Sherman H. S.
Moro, Oregon

PORK CHOPS WITH APRICOT DRESSING

8 pork chops
½ c. uncooked rice
¼ c. minced onion
⅓ lb. dried apricots
5 tsp. dried parsley
¼ tsp. salt
Dash of pepper
⅓ c. sugar
1 tsp. grated lemon rind
2 ⅔ c. chicken stock or 3 bouillon cubes

Brown chops in pan. Remove chops; brown rice and onion in drippings. Mix apricots, parsley, salt, pepper, sugar and lemon rind. In a large casserole dish, place a layer of chops, layer of rice mixture and another layer of chops; top with remaining rice mixture. Pour chicken stock over all. Bake at 350 degrees for 1 hour or until all is absorbed. Yield: 8 servings.

Mrs. Edgar Barber, Wall School
Wall, South Dakota

PORK CHOP CASSEROLE

4 center-cut pork chops
4 med. potatoes, thinly sliced
½ tsp. salt
Dash of pepper
1 can cream of mushroom soup
½ soup can milk

Lightly brown pork chops. Alternate layers of potatoes and pork chops in greased casserole; season with salt and pepper. Mix soup and milk; pour over all. Bake at 350 degrees for 40 to 50 minutes or until tender. Yield: 4 servings.

Mrs. Irene Brown, Wilmington H. S.
Wilmington, Illinois

PORK CHOPS FLORENTINE

6 loin pork chops, ¾ to 1-in. thick
Seasoned salt
2 pkg. frozen spinach
3 tbsp. margarine
3 tbsp. flour
1 c. milk
1 tsp. salt
⅛ tsp. pepper
½ c. grated Cheddar cheese
Bottled mustard sauce

Trim fat from chops; brown until golden. Sprinkle with seasoned salt. Cook spinach as directed on package. Drain. Melt margarine; stir in flour. Add milk, salt, pepper and cheese. Cook until smooth. Combine spinach and cheese sauce; turn into oiled -quart casserole. Arrange chops over top. Cover. Bake in preheated 350 degree oven for 30 minutes. Remove cover; bake for 15 minutes longer or until chops are done. Serve with sauce. Yield: 6 servings.

Alma R. Frerichs, Grants Pass H. S.
Grants Pass, Oregon

PORK CHOP-POTATO SCALLOP

4 pork chops
1 can cream of mushroom soup
½ c. sour cream

(Continued on next page)

¼ c. water
4 c. thinly sliced uncooked potatoes
2 tbsp. chopped parsley
1 med. onion, sliced (opt.)
1 tsp. salt
¼ tsp. pepper

Brown pork chops. Combine soup, sour cream and water. Place potatoes, parsley, onion, soup mixture and chops in layers in 2-quart casserole; sprinkle potatoes and chops with salt and pepper. Cover; bake at 375 degrees for 1 hour and 15 minutes. Yield: 4 servings.

Mrs. Sadie M. Jacques, Newfound Memorial H. S.
Bristol, New Hampshire
Bernadine Herring, Cobre H. S.
Bayard, New Mexico

PORK AND RICE CASSEROLE

1 ½ c. brown rice
3 c. boiling water
2 tsp. salt
½ to 1 c. chopped almonds
1 c. chopped celery
6 pork chops
¼ tsp. pepper

Cook rice in boiling water with 1 1/2 teaspoonfuls salt until tender; drain. Add nuts and celery. Place mixture in a 9 x 13 x 2-inch baking pan; arrange chops on top. Season chops with remaining salt and pepper. Bake at 350 degrees for 1 hour. Yield: 6 servings.

Mrs. Laura Anderson, Sutherlin H. S.
Sutherlin, Oregon

PORK CHOPS-RICE CASSEROLE

Salt and pepper
6 pork chops
1 med. onion, sliced
Sliced fresh tomato (opt.)
1 c. uncooked rice
1 can beef consomme
1 soup can water

Salt and pepper pork chops; place on bottom of casserole. Lay a slice of onion and tomato on each chop. Cover with rice. Add consomme and water. Bake at 350 degrees for 1 hour or until meat is tender. Add more water, if necessary. Yield: 6 servings.

Mrs. Bernice Britt, West Hardin H. S.
Saratoga, Texas

PORK CHOPS ON SCALLOPED POTATOES

Peeled potatoes
¼ c. margarine or butter
4 tbsp. flour
¼ c. grated Velveeta cheese
Salt and pepper to taste
2 c. milk
Pork chops

Arrange alternate layers of potatoes, margarine, flour, cheese, salt and pepper in 1 1/2 or 2-quart casserole. Pour milk over layers. Arrange pork chops on top of potatoes. Bake, uncovered, at 350 degrees for 1 hour and 30 minutes.

Mrs. Jane Davis, South Park Jr. H. S.
Corpus Christi, Texas

CHOP-TOP CASSEROLE

1 ½ c. dried white beans
1 lge. onion
1 med. bay leaf
1 ½ tsp. salt
4 thick lean pork chops
Garlic salt
Coarsely ground black pepper
1 1-lb. can stewed tomatoes

Cook beans as package directs, adding whole onion and bay leaf. Stir in salt when beans are nearly tender. Cook until tender; remove onion and bay leaf. Drain beans lightly. Brown pork chops, sprinkling generously with garlic salt and pepper. Remove chops from skillet; pour in stewed tomatoes, stirring to blend in meat juices. Add beans; pour mixture into a 2-quart casserole. Arrange chops on top. Bake at 350 degrees for 1 hour or until chops are fork tender. Yield: 4 servings.

Mrs. Jean S. McHargue, Beltsville Jr. H. S.
Beltsville, Maryland

PORK CHOPS AND WILD RICE

3 to 4 pork chops
Salt and pepper to taste
1 10 ½-oz. can wild rice
1 can cream of mushroom soup
1 c. water
1 c. diced celery
Mushrooms (opt.)

Brown pork chops in skillet; salt and pepper. Drain on paper towels. Mix remaining ingredients in baking dish or casserole; lay pork chops on top. Cover and bake at 350 degrees for 30 minutes. Yield: 3-4 servings.

Sara Lu Greeley, Preston H. S.
Preston, Minnesota

ITALIAN PORK AND RICE CASSEROLE

5 or 6 med. onions, sliced
1 clove of garlic
4 tbsp. salad oil
1 10 ¾-oz. can beef broth
3 8-oz. cans tomato sauce
1 3-oz. can whole mushrooms, undrained
2 tbsp. minced parsley
1 3-lb. pork loin, cut into ¼-in. slices
1 ¼ tsp. salt
¼ tsp. pepper
2 c. uncooked rice
3 seeded green peppers, cut into ⅛-in. pieces

(Continued on next page)

Saute 2 onions and garlic in 2 tablespoonfuls oil until golden; discard garlic. Add broth, tomato sauce, mushrooms and parsley. Simmer, uncovered, for 1 hour. Sprinkle pork with 3/4 teaspoonful salt and 1/4 teaspoonful pepper. Saute in skillet in remaining oil until brown. Remove pork; add a small amount of tomato sauce to drippings, stirring to dissolve meat particles. Add to remaining sauce. Arrange one-half the pork in 3-quart casserole. Top with mixture of rice and one-half the remaining sauce. Add one-half the remaining onions and remaining pork. Cover with remaining onions, then peppers. Sprinkle with remaining salt; pour on remaining sauce. Refrigerate. Cook, covered, at 350 degrees for 1 hour and 15 minutes. Yield: 12 servings.

Mrs. Jewel Mayfield, University H. S.
Waco, Texas

PORK-NOODLE TREAT

3 c. uncooked noodles
1 ½ lb. pork shoulder or round steak
1 ¼ tsp. salt
Pepper to taste
Margarine
3 tbsp. flour
1 c. milk
3 oz. Bleu cheese, crumbled
3 tbsp. chopped green pepper
3 tbsp. chopped pimento

Cook noodles in boiling salted water until tender; rinse and drain. Cut pork or steak into 1-inch cubes; brown and season with 1/2 teaspoonful salt and dash of pepper. Add enough margarine to pan drippings to make 3 tablespoonfuls fat; blend in flour, remaining salt and pepper to taste. Stir in milk. Cook and stir until thick. Add cheese; stir until cheese melts. Combine noodles, green pepper, pimento, pork cubes and cheese sauce. Place in ungreased 10 x 6 x 1 1/2-inch baking dish. Bake at 350 degrees for 30 minutes or until done. Yield: 6 servings.

Mary Jane Bertrand, Blackfoot H. S.
Blackfoot, Idaho

PORK AND SPAGHETTI CASSEROLE

2 ½ lb. pork, cubed
Fat
¾ c. chopped onions
½ c. chopped celery
2 4-oz. cans mushrooms, drained
2 c. lima or butter beans, drained
7 oz. spaghetti, cooked and drained
2 c. canned tomatoes
Salt and pepper to taste

Brown pork in a small amount of fat; remove meat. Add onions and celery to skillet; cook until tender. Combine all ingredients in large casserole. Bake at 325 degrees for 1 hour. Yield: 10 servings.

Vivian Delene, Baraga H. S.
Baraga, Michigan

PORK STEAK HOT DISH

1 lb. lean pork steak, cubed
1 10 ½-oz. can chicken soup
1 soup can water
1 lb. noodles, cooked
1 1-lb. can whole kernel corn
½ lb. diced American cheese
1 c. diced celery
¼ c. chopped pimento
Salt and pepper to taste
½ c. dry bread crumbs

Fry meat; add soup and water. Simmer for 30 minutes. Combine all ingredients except crumbs; place in casserole. Sprinkle with crumbs. Bake at 350 degrees for 1 hour. Yield: 10 servings.

Mrs. Curtis Hardevidt, Jackson H. S.
Jackson, Minnesota

HAM CASSEROLE

4 med. potatoes, peeled and thinly sliced
1 med. onion, diced
Salt and pepper to taste (opt.)
2 c. cooked string beans
1 slice cooked ham
⅓ c. bean liquid (opt.)

Place potatoes in buttered heavy baking dish or cast iron skillet; cover with onion. Season lightly, if desired. Cover with beans; place ham over beans. Pour bean liquid over ham. Cover and bake at 350 degrees for 1 hour. Yield: 3-4 servings.

Mrs. Corene Herbster, Lincoln H. S.
Lincoln, Nebraska

BAKED LASAGNA

1 lb. Italian sausage, bulk pork sausage or ground beef
1 clove of garlic, minced
3 tbsp. parsley flakes
1 tbsp. basil
3 ½ tsp. salt
1 1-lb. can tomatoes
2 6-oz. cans tomato paste
10 oz. lasagna or wide noodles
3 c. cream-style cottage cheese
2 eggs, beaten
½ tsp. pepper
½ c. grated Parmesan cheese
1 lb. Mozzarella cheese, sliced

Brown meat slowly; spoon off excess fat. Add garlic, 1 tablespoonful parsley, basil, 1 1/2 teaspoonfuls salt, tomatoes and tomato paste. Simmer for 30 minutes to blend flavors, stirring occasionally. Cook noodles in boiling salted water until tender; drain and rinse in cold water. Combine cottage cheese with eggs, remaining seasonings and Parmesan cheese. Place one-half the noodles in 13 x 9 x 2-inch baking dish; spread one-half the cottage cheese mixture over noodles. Top with one-half the Mozzarella cheese and one-half the meat sauce. Repeat layers. Bake at 375 degrees for 30 minutes. Garnish with triangles of Mozze-

(Continued on next page)

rella cheese. Let stand for 10 to 15 minutes before cutting into squares. Yield: 12 servings.

Mrs. Laura Van De Mark
McLouth Rural H. S., McLouth, Kansas
Mrs. F. L. Reinhardt, Southeast H. S.
Samoset, Florida

BAKED SAUSAGE AND CORN

1 lb. sausage links
1 No. 303 can cream-style corn
½ tsp. dry mustard
¼ c. milk
2 eggs, beaten
¼ c. chopped green pepper
1 sm. onion, chopped

Parboil sausage in water for 10 minutes; drain. Mix corn, mustard, milk, eggs, pepper and onion; place mixture in greased 1 1/2-quart casserole. Arrange sausage links on corn mixture. Bake at 350 degrees for 1 hour. Yield: 4 servings.

Mrs. Edward Swift, H. B. Burkland Jr. H. S.
Middleboro, Massachusetts

SAUSAGE CASSEROLE

1 ½ lb. mild pork sausage
4 or 5 green onions, chopped
1 lge. green pepper, chopped
1 med. stalk celery and leaves, chopped
2 pkg. chicken noodle soup mix
4 ½ c. water
1 c. cooked rice
1 sm. can water chestnuts, sliced

Fry sausage, stirring to crumble; drain off most of grease. Cook onions, green pepper and celery until tender in pan drippings; add soup mix, water, rice and chestnuts. Simmer for 15 minutes. Turn into casserole. Cover; bake at 350 degrees for 1 hour and 30 minutes. NOTE: Casserole may be frozen and reheated to serve. Yield: 6 servings.

Mrs. Audra Carolyn Smallwood, Estill Co. H. S.
Irvine, Kentucky

SAUSAGE AND RICE

1 lb. bulk sausage
1 c. chopped onions
1 c. chopped celery
1 green pepper, chopped
1 clove of garlic, minced
1 c. uncooked rice
1 can cream of mushroom soup
2 cans cream of chicken soup
½ c. grated cheese

Brown sausage; pour off fat. Add onions, celery, green pepper and garlic. Simmer until tender. Add remaining ingredients except cheese. Pour into baking dish. Sprinkle cheese on top. Bake at 350 degrees for 1 hour and 30 minutes. Yield: 6 servings.

Mrs. C. D. Huston, Greenwood Jr. H. S.
Greenwood, Mississippi

CHICKEN BREAST CASSEROLE

4 chicken breasts
1 3-oz. can mushrooms, drained
1 can cream of mushroom soup
1 c. sour cream
½ soup can Sherry wine
Paprika

Arrange chicken pieces in a 1-quart baking dish; do not overlap chicken. Top with mushrooms. Mix mushroom soup with sour cream and Sherry until smooth; pour over chicken, entirely covering. Sprinkle with paprika. Bake at 350 degrees for 1 hour and 30 minutes. Yield: 4 servings.

Mrs. Bennie Jones, Union Grove School
Gladewater, Texas

CHICKEN CASSEROLE

4 c. diced cooked chicken
4 c. diced celery
1 c. toasted slivered almonds
1 tsp. salt
4 tbsp. grated onion
4 tbsp. lemon juice
2 c. mayonnaise
1 c. grated American cheese
2 c. crushed potato chips

Mix chicken, celery, almonds, salt, onion, lemon juice and mayonnaise; turn into casserole. Cover top with grated cheese, then with potato chips. Bake at 350 degrees for 10 minutes or until cheese is melted and casserole hot throughout. Yield: 8 servings.

Margaret Tisdale, Treadwell H. S.
Memphis, Tennessee

CHICKEN CASSEROLE

2 c. chopped cooked chicken
½ c. chopped celery
2 hard-cooked eggs, sliced
1 tbsp. minced onion
1 c. cream of mushroom soup
¼ c. mayonnaise
2 tbsp. lemon juice
¼ c. chopped peanuts
Crushed potato chips

Mix all ingredients except potato chips; place in casserole. Top with crushed potato chips. Bake at 350 degrees for 30 minutes. Yield: 4-6 servings.

Mrs. Gershon Kuster, Fort Defiance H. S.
Fort Defiance, Virginia

CHICKEN CASSEROLE

6 whole chicken breasts
½ c. chopped celery
1 c. mayonnaise
1 10-oz. can cream of chicken soup
1 10-oz. can cream of celery soup
1 can chow mein noodles

Cook chicken breasts until tender; remove bones and skin. Cut into bite-sized pieces. Mix chicken, celery and mayonnaise; place on bottom of a 9-inch square baking dish. Spread top with chicken and celery soup. Top with chow mein noodles. Bake at 350 degrees until bubbling hot. Yield: 12 servings.

Mrs. Nancye H. Shannon, Greenbrier H. S.
Greenbrier, Tennessee

CHICKEN CASSEROLE

3 slices white bread
1 can button mushrooms
1 egg, slightly beaten
1 can chicken noodle soup
1 can cream of mushroom soup
3 chicken legs, cooked and boned

Cut bread slices into cubes; place in greased casserole. Combine remaining ingredients; pour over bread cubes. Bake at 350 degrees for 35 to 40 minutes. NOTE: Left-over chicken may be used. Yield: 6 servings.

Glenna A. Starbird, Oxford Hills H. S.
South Paris, Maine

CHICKEN-CHILI CASSEROLE

1 med. onion, chopped
1 clove of garlic, minced
Hot fat
3 c. white sauce
1 or 2 cans green chili
1 doz. corn tortillas, torn into strips
1 stewing hen, cooked
¾ lb. Cheddar cheese, grated

Cook onion and garlic in hot fat until golden brown; add to white sauce with green chili. Alternate layers of corn tortillas, chicken, sauce and cheese in buttered casserole; repeat until all ingredients are used. Bake at 350 degrees for 35 minutes or until bubbling hot. Yield: 10 servings.

Linda Carol Gillum, Mineral Wells H. S.
Mineral Wells, Texas

CHICKEN CHOW MEIN CASSEROLE

1 onion, chopped
1 stick margarine, melted
2 sm. cans chicken
2 cans cream of mushroom soup
2 cans cream of chicken soup
1 sm. jar sliced pimento
1 lge. can chow mein noodles

Saute onion in margarine in 1-quart casserole; add all remaining ingredients in order given except one-half of noodles. Top with remaining noodles. Bake at 350 degrees for 20 minutes or until brown and bubbly.

Mrs. Cecile Poling, North Shore Jr. H. S.
Houston, Texas

CHICKEN ON EGG BREAD

1 pt. meal
1 tsp. soda
2 eggs, beaten
1 c. buttermilk
6 tbsp. shortening
1 tsp. baking powder
1 hen, baked, boned and diced
3 tbsp. minced onion
3 tbsp. minced celery
½ c. butter
4 tbsp. flour
1 ½ pt. chicken broth
¼ c. milk
Salt and pepper to taste

Combine meal, soda, eggs, buttermilk, shortening and baking powder. Bake at 425 degrees until done. Slice bread into layers. Alternate layers of bread and chicken twice in casserole. Brown onion and celery in butter. Add remaining ingredients; cool until thick. Pour over layers in casserole; serve hot. Yield: 6-8 servings.

Mrs. Jesse Safley, Bellevue H. S.
Bellevue, Tennessee

CHICKEN-NOODLE CASSEROLE

2 c. cooked chicken, cut into bite-sized pieces
½ c. chopped celery
½ c. mayonnaise
¼ c. slivered almonds
3 hard-cooked eggs, chopped
1 tbsp. lemon juice
2 c. chicken gravy or 1 can chicken soup
1 sm. can Chinese noodles

Mix all ingredients except noodles in casserole; top with noodles. Bake at 375 degrees until mixture is bubbly. Yield: 4-6 servings.

Virginia Coltrane, North Surry H. S.
Mount Airy, North Carolina

CHICKEN PIE

1 4 to 5-lb. hen, stewed and boned
2 c. rich white sauce
1 can cream of mushroom soup
1 can mushrooms
1 sm. can pimento
1 c. almonds
6 hard-cooked eggs, diced
½ c. diced celery
½ c. diced onion
Salt to taste
Pie pastry

(Continued on next page)

Remove chicken from bones; cut into small pieces. Mix white sauce with chicken and all remaining ingredients except pastry in saucepan. Cook for 10 minutes. Line a baking dish with pastry; place mixture over pastry. Cover with crust. Bake at 300 to 350 degrees until crust is golden brown. NOTE: Pie freezes well. Yield: 20 servings.

Mrs. Sara C. Faulkner, Clover H. S.
Clover, South Carolina

CHICKEN SOUFFLE

4 slices bread, cut into cubes
3 ½ c. chopped cooked chicken
4 to 6 whole slices of bread, crusts removed
½ c. salad dressing or mayonnaise
3 tbsp. diced green pepper (opt.)
½ c. celery, diced
¼ to ½ c. diced onion
2 to 4 eggs, well beaten
½ to 3 c. milk
1 can cream of mushroom soup
1 c. grated cheese

Sprinkle bread cubes in buttered 9 x 13-inch pan; top with chicken. Cover chicken with bread slices. Combine salad dressing, green pepper, celery, onion, eggs and milk; pour over bread slices. Refrigerate overnight. Bake at 325 degrees for 15 minutes. Spread with soup and sprinkle with cheese. Bake for 1 hour to 1 hour and 30 minutes longer. Yield: 15 servings.

Kathleen L. Zehr, Carthage Jr.-Sr. H. S.
Carthage, New York

CHICKEN TACO PIE

1 2 to 3-lb. chicken, cut up
1 lge. can enchilada sauce
1 can cream of mushroom soup
1 lge. onion, chopped
½ tsp. garlic salt
Dash of pepper
1 lge. pkg. corn chips
1 c. grated cheese

Boil pieces of chicken until tender; reserve 1 cup broth. Remove bones; cut chicken into bite-sized pieces. Combine chicken, enchilada sauce, mushroom soup, onion, garlic salt and pepper. Line a greased baking dish with part of corn chips. Add chicken mixture; sprinkle with grated cheese, cover with remaining corn chips. Add reserved chicken broth. Bake at 350 degrees for 30 minutes. Yield: 6 servings.

Mrs. Emma Frances McCluskey
Cotton Center H. S.
Cotton Center, Texas

CRUNCHY CHICKEN

2 c. chopped cooked chicken
1 c. chopped celery
½ c. slivered almonds
2 hard-cooked eggs, sliced
2 tbsp. Worcestershire sauce
¼ c. mayonnaise
1 can cream of chicken soup
1 c. crushed potato chips

Combine all ingredients except potato chips; place in 1 1/2-quart casserole. Top with crushed potato chips. Bake at 350 degrees for 30 minutes. Yield: 8 servings.

Mrs. Virginia C. Taylor, Springville H. S.
Springville, Alabama

GOOD NEIGHBOR CASSEROLE

8 slices bread, without crusts
4 c. diced cooked chicken
1 can mushroom pieces, sauted
1 can pimento, diced
½ c. mayonnaise
8 slices sharp cheese
4 eggs, beaten
2 c. milk
1 tsp. salt
2 cans cream of celery soup
2 c. buttered bread crumbs

Place bread in greased 13 x 9-inch pan. Top with cheese. Add chicken, mushrooms, pimento and mayonnaise. Mix eggs, milk and salt. Pour over casserole. Spread undiluted soup on top. Refrigerate for several hours or overnight. Bake at 350 degrees for 1 hour and 30 minutes. Add bread crumbs the last 15 minutes.

Ruth Royer, Warrior Run Area H. S.
Turbotville, Pennsylvania

HOT CHICKEN CASSEROLE

2 c. chopped cooked chicken
2 c. chopped celery
½ c. chopped pecans or blanched salted almonds
⅓ c. chopped green pepper (opt.)
2 tbsp. chopped pimento (opt.)
2 tbsp. minced onion or 1 tbsp. grated onion
½ to 1 tsp. salt
2 to 6 tsp. lemon juice
½ tsp. monosodium glutamate
½ to 1 c. mayonnaise
⅓ to 1 c. grated Swiss or other cheese
1 to 3 c. crushed potato chips

Blend all ingredients except cheese and potato chips; turn into buttered 1 1/2-quart casserole. Top with cheese and potato chips. Bake at 350 to 375 degrees for 15 to 25 minutes or until cheese is melted and ingredients are hot throughout. Yield: 4-6 servings.

Dorothy C. Daggert, Warsaw H. S.
Warsaw, Illinois
Mrs. Frankie Skeels, Bolton H. S.
Alexandria, Louisiana
Bertha Williams, Blair Jr. H. S.
Norfolk, Virginia
Ruth Blomgren, Eastern Jr. H. S.
Silver Springs, Maryland
Mrs. LaVerne Stokes, Westwood H. S.
Palestine, Texas

HOT CHICKEN CASSEROLE

2 c. cubed chicken
2 c. chopped celery
½ c. blanched slivered almonds
1 c. water chestnuts, quartered
½ c. grated Cheddar cheese
2 tbsp. minced green onion without tops
½ tsp. seasoned salt
⅛ tsp. white pepper
2 tbsp. lemon juice
Mayonnaise
½ tsp. Worcestershire sauce
1 jar small button mushrooms
2 hard-cooked eggs, quartered
½ c. finely rolled dry bread crumbs
2 tbsp. melted butter
¼ c. grated Parmesan cheese

Combine chicken, celery, almonds, chestnuts, cheese, onion, salt and pepper. Toss lightly, moisten with lemon juice, mayonnaise and Worcestershire sauce. Spoon into buttered 9-inch square or 8 x 13-inch baking dish. Place mushrooms and eggs on chicken mixture. Mix crumbs into butter; add Parmesan cheese. Sprinkle over chicken salad. Heat at 450 degrees for 10 minutes; reduce temperature to 350 degrees. Heat for 15 to 20 minutes or until bubbly. Serve hot. Yield: 6-8 servings.

Mrs. Ruth Cooper, Culver City H. S.
Culver City, California

HOT CHICKEN SALAD

3 c. cubed cooked chicken
1 ½ c. diced celery
½ c. chopped almonds
1 tbsp. minced onion
1 ½ tbsp. lemon juice
Dash of pepper
1 c. mayonnaise
1 ½ c. grated Cheddar cheese
1 ½ c. crushed potato chips

Combine chicken, celery, almonds, onion, lemon juice and pepper in large mixing bowl; add mayonnaise and toss. Place in 2-quart baking dish. Cover top with grated cheese and potato chips. Bake at 350 degrees for 25 minutes. Yield: 8 servings.

Mrs. Mary A. Moore, Socorro H. S.
El Paso, Texas

HOT CHICKEN SALAD CASSEROLE

2 c. chopped chicken
2 c. chopped celery
¼ c. minced green pepper
2 tbsp. pimento
1 tbsp. minced onion
2 tbsp. Worcestershire sauce
2 tbsp. lemon juice
½ c. mayonnaise
1 can cream of chicken soup
Potato chips
Grated cheese
Almonds

Combine all ingredients except potato chips, cheese and almonds. Top with potato chips, cheese and almonds. Bake at 350 degrees for 25 minutes. NOTE: May be served in individual pastry cups. Yield: 4-6 servings.

Mrs. Joan M. Miller, Jefferson H. S.
Jefferson, South Carolina

JIFFY ITALIAN CHICKEN

Seasoning to taste
1 2-lb. fryer, cut up
1 envelope spaghetti sauce mix
3 c. tomato juice
½ med. onion, chopped
½ med. green pepper, chopped

Season chicken; place in a 1 1/2 to 2-quart flat casserole dish. Mix spaghetti sauce, tomato juice, onion and green pepper; heat until blended. Pour sauce mixture over chicken. Bake at 350 degrees for 1 hour. Yield: 4 servings.

Mrs. Linnda H. Graham, Mason H. S.
Mason, Texas

KING RANCH CASSEROLE

2 c. cooked diced chicken
½ can tomatoes with green chili peppers
1 can cream of chicken soup
1 can cream of mushroom soup
½ soup can chicken broth or bouillon
1 pkg. soft tortillas, cut into small pieces
1 lge. onion, chopped
1 c. grated sharp Cheddar cheese

Layer chicken, tomatoes, soups, broth and tortillas in a greased 2-quart casserole; add a layer of onion. Repeat layers. Top with grated cheese. Bake at 350 degrees for 1 hour. Yield: 8 servings.

Mrs. Ronnie Watson, Johnston Jr. H. S.
Houston, Texas

MONTEQUMA PIE

12 tortillas, cut into fourths
1 lge. onion, chopped
2 cans peppers, chopped
2 c. tomato juice
Salt to taste
1 pt. half and half
2 c. diced Velveeta cheese
1 5 to 6-lb. hen, cooked and chopped

Brown tortillas in very hot oil; drain. Saute onion in small amount of butter. Add peppers, tomato juice and salt; simmer for 30 minutes. Blend half and half with cheese; heat until cheese is melted. Add chicken. Alternate layers of chicken and tortillas in casserole. Bake at 350 degrees until hot. Yield: 10 servings.

Mrs. Lucille Jordan, Cleburne H. S.
Cleburne, Texas

OVEN CHICKEN SALAD

2 c. cubed cooked chicken
2 c. thinly sliced celery
1 c. toasted bread cubes
1 c. mayonnaise
½ c. toasted chopped or slivered almonds
2 tbsp. lemon juice
2 tsp. grated onion
½ tsp. salt
½ c. grated cheese
1 c. toasted bread cubes or crushed potato chips

Combine all ingredients except cheese and 1 cup bread cubes; pile lightly into individual baking dishes. Sprinkle with cheese and reserved bread cubes. Bake in preheated 450 degree oven for 10 to 15 minutes or until bubbly. Yield: 6 servings.

Mrs. Naomi L. Himes, Rochelle Twp. H. S.
Rochelle, Illinois

SALAD CASSEROLE

6 oz. chicken, tuna or ham
1 can cream of mushroom soup
1 c. diced celery
2 tsp. minced onion
½ c. almonds or pecans
½ tsp. salt
¼ tsp. pepper
¾ c. salad dressing
3 hard-cooked eggs, chopped
2 c. crushed potato chips

Combine all ingredients except potato chips; pour into casserole. Top mixture with potato chips. Bake at 425 degrees for 15 to 20 minutes. NOTE: Green pepper or peas may be added, if desired. Yield: 4-6 servings.

Marilyn C. Anderson, Hoffman Public School
Hoffman, Minnesota

WARM CHICKEN SALAD

2 c. cubed cooked chicken or turkey
2 c. thinly sliced celery
½ c. cashews (opt.)
½ tsp. salt
2 tsp. grated onion
2 tsp. lemon juice
1 c. mayonnaise
1 sm. can mushrooms, strained (opt.)
½ c. grated American cheese
1 c. lightly crushed potato chips

Toss chicken with remaining ingredients except cheese and potato chips. Place in ungreased casserole. Sprinkle cheese and potato chips on top. Bake at 450 degrees for 10 to 20 minutes. Serve at once. Yield: 6 servings.

Mrs. M. Judelle Jones, Turlock H. S.
Turlock, California
Mrs. Lois P. Norred, Hillcrest H. S.
Dallas, Texas
Mrs. Nell K. Green, Oxford H. S.
Oxford, Mississippi

BAKED CHICKEN AND CORN BREAD DRESSING

3 eggs, slightly beaten
2 c. crumbled corn bread
1 ½ c. dry bread crumbs
3 ½ to 4 c. chicken stock
½ c. butter, melted
⅓ c. finely diced onion
⅛ tsp. pepper
1 tsp. salt
2 tbsp. chopped celery (opt.)
1 ½ tsp. sage (opt.)
1 3 ½ to 4-lb. hen, cooked

Combine all ingredients except chicken; mix well. Pour one-half of dressing into a greased baking dish. Remove chicken from bone; place chicken in baking dish. Add remaining dressing. Bake at 450 degrees for 30 minutes. Yield: 8-10 servings.

Mrs. Leon Davis, Lumpkin Co. H. S.
Dahloega, Georgia

CHICKEN AND DRESSING

1 4 to 5-lb. chicken
2 tsp. minced onion
6 tsp. butter
½ tsp. celery salt
1 tsp. salt
1 tsp. sage
Pepper to taste
3 or 4 c. soft bread
⅓ c. shortening
⅓ c. flour
6 eggs, well beaten
Dried bread crumbs

Place chicken in a deep kettle; cover with boiling water. Simmer, covered, until tender, allowing 20 to 30 minutes per pound. Cool; reserve broth. Remove meat from bones in large pieces. Saute onions in butter with celery salt, salt, sage, pepper and crumbs. Toss lightly to mix. Pack lightly into well greased baking pan. Arrange layer of chicken on top. Melt shortening; blend in flour. Gradually stir in 6 cups cooled chicken broth. Cook for 5 minutes, stirring constantly. Cool slightly; add eggs. Cook slowly for 3 minutes longer, stirring constantly. Pour over chicken. Sprinkle with dry bread crumbs. Bake at 350 degrees for 45 minutes to 1 hour or until mixture is heated through and crumbs are browned. Yield: 12 servings.

Mrs. Eleanor Howard, Kent-Meridian H. S.
Kent, Washington

CHICKEN AND DRESSING

1 3 to 4-lb. chicken, cut up
1 stalk celery, chopped
1 onion, sliced
Salt
1 ½ qt. dry bread cubes
½ tsp. sage
¼ tsp. pepper
¼ c. minced onion
⅓ c. butter or drippings
½ c. chicken fat

(Continued on next page)

¾ c. flour
4 c. chicken broth
4 egg yolks, well beaten

Simmer chicken, celery, sliced onion and salt in water to almost cover. Cook for 2 hours or until chicken is tender. Remove bones; cut meat into large pieces. Arrange in 2-quart casserole. Combine bread cubes, sage, 1/8 teaspoonful pepper and 1/2 teaspoonful salt. Brown minced onion in butter; add to bread mixture. Spread over chicken. Melt fat in heavy skillet. Add flour with 1 1/2 teaspoonfuls salt and remaining pepper; stir until smooth. Blend in chicken broth; cook until thick and smooth, stirring constantly. Mix a small amount of gravy with yolks; pour into remaining gravy. Cook over medium heat for 3 minutes, stirring constantly. Pour over chicken and dressing. Bake at 375 degrees for 35 minutes or until golden brown and gravy is set. Yield: 8 servings.

Mrs. Dorothy Pomraning, Big Springs H. S.
Newville, Pennsylvania

CHICKEN AND DRESSING BAKE

1 c. diced celery
⅔ c. minced onions
3 tbsp. butter or margarine
2 eggs, slightly beaten
3 c. milk or chicken broth
½ tsp. salt
¼ tsp. pepper
5 c. coarse bread crumbs
1 2-lb. pkg. chicken breasts or lge. fryer
Seasoned flour

Cook celery and onions in butter or margarine in large skillet for 5 minutes; add to egg, milk, seasonings and bread crumbs. Spoon lightly in a 2-quart baking dish. Roll chicken in seasoned flour and brown. Arrange chicken on top of dressing. Bake in 350 degree oven for 30 minutes. Cover with foil. Bake at 350 degrees for 20 minutes. Uncover; bake for 10 minutes longer. Yield: 6 servings.

Catherine H. Maeder, Alva H. S.
Alva, Florida

SCALLOPED CHICKEN

1 4-lb. hen, cooked and boned
1 ½ c. chopped celery
1 onion, finely chopped
1 ½ c. cubed cheese
½ tsp. pepper
1 tbsp. salt
1 can cream of mushroom soup
2 eggs, beaten
6 c. chicken broth
4 c. Ritz crackers, crushed

Mix all ingredients except cracker crumbs; pour into large baking dish. Sprinkle with cracker crumbs. Bake at 350 degrees for 1 hour.

Mrs. Mary Westman, Alameda H. S.
Denver, Colorado

SCALLOPED CHICKEN

1 5-lb. hen
2 qt. boiling water
Salt
1 ½ c. butter or margarine
6 sprigs parsley, chopped
6 green onions and tops, thinly sliced
1 ½ loaves bread, trimmed and crumbled
Dash of pepper
1 tsp. poultry seasoning
1 c. flour
1 c. milk
4 eggs, beaten

Cook hen in boiling water with 2 teaspoonfuls salt until tender. Cook giblets separately. Cool chicken; remove bones. Shred; remove all skin and put through food chopper. Set skin aside. Put giblets through food chopper; set aside. Melt butter over low heat; add parsley and green onions. Cook slowly for 5 minutes. Mix with bread crumbs. Add salt, pepper and poultry seasoning. Add 6 tablespoonfuls broth and chopped skin. Skim fat from broth; melt 1 cup fat in saucepan. Add flour, 4 cups heated broth and heated milk. Add 2 teaspoonfuls salt. Boil until thick. Add a small amount of sauce to eggs; stir back into sauce. Add giblets. Cover bottom of greased casserole with layer of dressing; cover with layer of sauce, then layer of chicken. Top with sauce and dressing. Bake at 375 degrees for 20 to 30 minutes. Yield: 15-18 servings.

Mrs. Ruth J. Reisdorfer, Seligman H. S.
Seligman, Arizona

SCALLOPED CHICKEN

1 chicken
1 c. cracker crumbs
½ c. cream
Dash of pepper
½ tsp. salt
1 egg
2 tbsp. butter
½ c. chicken broth

Boil chicken until tender in salted water; remove meat from bones. Combine chicken, cracker crumbs and cream, pepper and salt. Beat in egg. Place in casserole; dot with butter. Add enough broth to moisten. Bake at 350 degrees for 30 to 40 minutes. Yield: 8 servings.

Mary Beth Stine, Flora Twp. H. S.
Flora, Illinois

CHICKEN CASSEROLE

Salt and pepper
1 5-lb. hen
3 ½ c. chicken stock
1 c. half and half
1 can cream of mushroom soup
3 c. cooked elbow macaroni, cooled
1 can pimento, drained and finely chopped
2 c. rolled cracker crumbs
¼ lb. butter
1 tbsp. paprika

(Continued on next page)

Salt and pepper hen; place in pot. Cover with water; cook until tender. Cool; remove bone, skin and fat, Cut chicken into small pieces. Mix chicken into small pieces. Add macaroni and pimento. Add chicken; mix well. Pour mixture into buttered 15 x 10 x 2-inch baking pan. Cover with a thick layer of cracker crumbs. Dot with butter; sprinkle with paprika. Bake at 350 degrees for 2 hours. Remove from oven; let stand for 30 minutes before cutting into squares to serve. Yield: 18-20 servings.

Mrs. Frances T. Hudson, Spearman H. S.
Spearman, Texas

CHICKEN DELICIOUS

3 tbsp. butter
3 tbsp. flour
1 tsp. salt
3 c. chicken broth
4 c. cooked chopped chicken
8 hard-cooked eggs, chopped
1 pkg. frozen peas, cooked
1 4-oz. can mushroom pieces
3 c. macaroni, cooked
½ c. buttered bread crumbs or potato chips

Melt butter; add flour and salt. Add chicken broth slowly, stirring constantly. Cook over low heat until thickened. Remove from heat; stir in chicken, eggs, peas, mushrooms and macaroni. Pour mixture into a shallow greased 2-quart casserole or baking dish. Top with bread crumbs or potato chips. Bake at 350 degrees for 30 minutes. Yield: 10 servings.

Ghlee Kershner, Montpelier Comm. Corp.
Montpelier, Indiana

SCALLOPED CHICKEN

1 4-lb. stewing hen
8 tbsp. flour
9 oz. cream cheese
2 c. raw shell macaroni, cooked
4 c. bread crumbs
Butter
1 c. heavy cream

Stew hen in water until tender; cool in broth. Remove bones and dice chicken. Measure 4 cups of broth; thicken broth with flour. Add to chicken. Add cream cheese and macaroni. Pour into large pan. Brown bread crumbs in butter and cream. Spread on top of chicken mixture. Bake at 350 degrees for 30 minutes or until golden brown. Yield: 20 servings.

Edna Mae Van Tuyl, Holyrood Rural H. S.
Holyrood, Kansas

CHICKEN CASSEROLE

1 stewing chicken
1 lge. pkg. egg noodles
2 cans cream of mushroom soup
2 tbsp. pimento
½ c. pecans or water chestnuts
2 c. chicken broth
Buttered bread crumbs

Stew chicken until tender; remove meat from bones and dice. Cook egg noodles until almost tender. Mix diced chicken, mushroom soup, pimento, pecans, chicken broth and noodles. place in casserole; cover with bread crumbs. Bake at 350 degrees for 30 minutes. Yield: 8 servings.

Mrs. Billye D. Freeland, Eastwood H. S.
El Paso, Texas

CHICKEN AND STUFFING SCALLOP

1 ¾ c. herb-seasoned stuffing
1 ½ c. cubed cooked chicken
¼ c. butter
¼ c. flour
Salt and pepper to taste
2 c. chicken broth
3 eggs, slightly beaten

Prepare stuffing according to package directions; spread in a 10 x 6 x 1 1/2-inch baking dish. Top with chicken. Melt butter in a saucepan; blend in flour, salt and pepper. Add chicken broth; cook and stir until mixture thickens. Stir a small amount of hot mixture into slightly beaten eggs; return to hot mixture. Pour over chicken. Bake at 325 degrees for 35 to 40 minutes or until knife inserted off center comes out clean. Let stand for 5 minutes to set. Yield: 6 servings.

Mrs. Mary S. Sodergren
E. A. Poe Intermediate School
Annandale, Virginia

CHICKEN FINALE

2 c. medium noodles
¼ c. chopped green pepper
¼ c. minced onion
2 tbsp. butter
1 10 ½-oz. can cream of chicken soup
1 c. sour cream
¼ c. milk
¼ c. sliced ripe olives
½ tsp. salt
¼ tsp. pepper
1 ½ c. diced cooked chicken
¼ c. blanched quartered almonds
1 tbsp. minced parsley

Cook noodles according to directions on package. Saute green pepper and onion in butter until tender; add soup, sour cream, milk, olives, salt, pepper and chicken. Stir in noodles. Turn into greased 1 1/2-quart casserole; sprinkle with almonds and parsley. Bake in preheated 350 degree oven for 35 to 40 minutes. Yield: 6 servings.

Mrs. Gail Kelly, Clearfield H. S.
Clearfield, Pennsylvania
Mrs. Margaret Jones, United H. S.
New Florence, Pennsylvania

PERFECT CHICKEN CASSEROLE

1 can chicken soup
½ c. milk
1 can boned chicken
2 c. cooked noodles
2 tbsp. diced pimento
1 tbsp. chopped parsley
2 tbsp. buttered bread crumbs

Blend soup and milk in 1 1/2-quart casserole; add chicken, noodles, pimento and parsley. Sprinkle crumbs on top. Bake at 375 degrees for 25 minutes. Yield: 4 servings.

Mrs. Francis Reeves, Wilmer-Hutchins H. S.
Hutchins, Texas

QUICK CHICKEN TETRAZZINI

1 sm. onion, chopped
2 tbsp. chopped green pepper
2 tbsp. chopped celery
1 tbps. margarine
1 8-oz. can boned chicken
1 can cream of mushroom soup
1 box chicken and noodles dinner, cooked

Saute onion, green pepper and célery in margarine; add chicken, soup and chicken and noodles dinner. Turn into casserole. Bake at 325 degrees for 25 minutes. Yield: 6 servings.

Mrs. Helen L. Scott, Haynesville H. S.
Haynesville, Louisiana

CHICKEN AND SPAGHETTI

1 ¼ c. broken spaghetti
1 tsp. salt
1 ½ c. chopped boiled chicken
¼ c. pimento, finely chopped
1 lge. green pepper, finely chopped
1 onion, finely chopped
1 sm. can mushrooms
1 c. chicken broth
1 ¾ c. shredded cheese

Cook spaghetti in salted water until tender; drain. Add chicken, pimento, pepper, onion, mushrooms and chicken broth; mix well. Pour into greased baking dish. Sprinkle with cheese. Bake at 350 degrees for 1 hour. When cheese melts, stir lightly into mixture. Yield: 8-10 servings.

Mrs. Inez P. Curvin, Benjamin Russell H. S.
Alexander City, Alabama

CHICKEN SPAGHETTI

1 4 to 5-lb. hen
1 lge. onion, chopped
3 cloves of garlic, minced
1 c. chopped celery
1 lge. green pepper, chopped
1 can mushrooms, chopped
1 lge. can tomatoes
1 tsp. cumin powder
Salt and pepper to taste
1 lb. spaghetti
3 to 4 c. chicken broth

Cook hen until done; reserve broth. Remove meat from bone; chop into small pieces. Skim 4 tablespoonfuls chicken fat; place in skillet. Saute onion, garlic, celery and green pepper in fat until tender. Add mushrooms, tomatoes, cumin powder, salt and pepper; simmer. Cook spaghetti in chicken broth until almost tender. Do not drain. Mix spaghetti with chicken and sauce. Cook slowly in a 325 dgeree oven until spaghetti is tender and flavors are blended. Yield: 10-12 servings.

Doris Strauss, Atlanta H. S.
Atlanta, Texas

CHICKEN SPAGHETTI

1 4-lb. hen, cooked
Seasoning
1 med. onion, chopped
1 green pepper, chopped
1 No. 2 can tomatoes
1 tsp. garlic powder
1 sm. can tomato sauce
1 box spaghetti,cooked
2 c. chicken broth
1 can mushrooms
½ lb. grated cheese

Cook hen in seasoned water until tender; remove from bone and chop. Set aside. Saute onion; combine with chicken and green pepper. Add tomatoes, garlic powder, tomato sauce, spaghetti, chicken broth and mushrooms. Cook for 1 hour. Remove any grease. Store, covered, overnight. Cover casserole with grated cheese. Bake at 350 degrees for 45 minutes. Yield: 12 servings.

Mrs. R. N. McEachern, Chireno H. S.
Chireno, Texas

CHICKEN SPAGHETTI

½ can tomato paste
½ c. chopped celery
½ c. chopped onion
½ can pimento, chopped
½ can cream of mushroom soup
1 5-oz. can boned chicken
1 c. spaghetti, cooked and drained
Salt and pepper to taste
1 ½ c. grated cheese

Combine tomato paste, celery, onion, pimento and soup; cook for 30 minutes. Add chicken, spaghetti, salt and pepper. Place in 9 x 9-inch baking dish. Cover top with grated cheese. Bake at 350 degrees until cheese is melted. Yield: 4-6 servings.

Mrs. Rowena Ballew, Richland H. S.
Fort Worth, Texas

CHICKEN TETRAZZINI

1 7-oz. pkg. spaghetti
Chicken broth
1 stalk celery, chopped
1 med. green pepper, minced
2 med. onions, minced
1 5 to 6-lb. chicken, cooked and diced
¾ lb. margarine
1 c. flour
4 c. milk
1 lb. American cheese, grated
1 can cream of mushroom soup
Salt and pepper to taste
Garlic salt (opt.)
Paprika
1 box Ritz cracker crumbs

Cook spaghetti in chicken broth according to package directions. Cook celery; drain. Add green pepper, onions, chicken and celery to spaghetti. Combine 1/2 pound margarine, flour and milk; cook, stirring until thickened. Add cheese and soup. Season to taste. Combine with spagehtti mixture. Pour into large oblong baking dish. Top with mixture of remaining melted margarine and cracker crumbs. Bake at 350 degrees for 30 minutes. Yield: 15-20 servings.

Mrs. Susie Tucker, Savoy H. S.
Savoy, Texas

BAKED CHICKEN SUPREME

1 can cream of celery soup
1 can cream of mushroom soup
1 ½ c. instant rice
1 c. milk
1 or 2 chickens, cut up
½ box dry onion soup mix

Mix soups, rice and milk; place in oblong baking dish. Place chicken pieces on top of rice mixture. Sprinkle onion soup mix over all. Cover with aluminum foil. Bake at 275 to 300 degrees for 1 hour or until tender.

Mrs. Alvenia Nimmo, Burns Flat School
Burns Flat, Oklahoma
Mrs. Evelyn Suomi, Washington H. S.
New London, Wisconsin

CHICKEN CASSEROLE

2 c. cooked rice
½ c. milk
2 c. chopped cooked chicken
1 c. mushrooms, drained
1 pimento, sliced
½ c. grated cheese

Combine all ingredients except cheese; place in buttered glass baking dish. Bake at 350 degrees for 30 minutes. Sprinkle with grated cheese about 3 minutes before removing from oven. NOTE: Cook rice in chicken broth. Yield: 6 servings.

Mrs. Mary Pinkston Whaley
Tuscaloosa Co. H. S.
Northport, Alabama

CHICKEN CASSEROLE

1 qt. diced cooked chicken
2 c. (scant) soft bread crumbs
1 c. raw rice, cooked
½ c. diced pimento
4 eggs, beaten
1 tbsp. salt
¼ c. melted butter
3 c. chicken stock

Combine all ingredients; place in casserole. Bake at 325 degrees for 2 hours. Yield: 8 servings.

Mrs. Lewis Vance
Jefferson-Morgan Jr. Sr. H. S.
Jefferson, Pennsylvania

CHICKEN CHARTREUSE

4 4 to 5-lb. chickens
8 c. uncooked rice
8 cans cream of mushroom soup
½ c. chopped onion
8 c. bread crumbs

Cook chickens. Cut meat into bite-sized pieces. Skim fat from stock; reserve fat. Cook rice according to package directions. Heat soup add onion. Pack one-half the rice in greased baking dishes; add layer of chicken. Add a layer of rice. Pour soup mixture over casserole. Moisten bread crumbs in chicken fat; sprinkle over casseroles. Bake at 350 degrees until bubbly on top. Yield: 50 servings.

Mrs. Carol Barry, Waynedale H. S.
Apple Creek, Ohio

CHICKEN CONTINENTAL

1 chicken, cut up
1 c. uncooked rice or 1 ¼ c. instant rice
1 can cream of chicken soup
2 ½ tbsp. grated onion
1 tsp. salt
Dash of pepper
1 tbsp. minced parsley
½ tbsp. celery flakes
1 ⅓ c. water

Fry chicken. Cook rice according to package directions. Place chicken in casserole; place rice over chicken. Combine remaining ingredients in pan; bring to a boil. Pour over chicken and rice. Bake at 375 degrees for 20 minutes. Sprinkle with paprika, if desired. Serve hot. Yield: 4-6 servings.

Lillian A. Newell, Wren H. S.
Peedmon, South Carolina
Mrs. L. R. Boyter, St. Bernard H. S.
St. Bernard, Louisiana

CHICKEN FAVORITE

2 3-lb. whole broiler-fryers
1 c. water
1 c. dry Sherry
1 ½ tsp. salt
½ tsp. curry powder
1 med. onion, sliced
½ c. sliced celery
1 lb. fresh mushrooms or 1 can mushrooms
¼ c. butter or margarine
2 6-oz. pkg. long grain and wild rice with seasonings
1 c. sour cream
1 10 ½-oz. can cream of mushroom soup

Place chicken in deep kettle. Add water, Sherry, salt, curry powder, onion and celery. Bring to boil; cover tightly. Reduce heat; simmer for 1 hour. Remove from heat; strain broth. Refrigerate chicken and broth at once. Remove meat from bones; discard skin. Cut into bit-sized pieces. Wash mushrooms and pat dry; saute in butter until golden brown, reserving enough for top of casserole. Measure chicken broth; use as part of liquid for cooking rice, following package directions for firm rice. Combine chicken, rice and mushrooms. Blend sour cream and mushroom soup; toss with chicken mixture. Arrange reserved mushrooms in circle on top of casserole. Cover and refrigerate. Bake at 350 degrees for 1 hour. Yield: 8-10 servings.

Mrs. Violet Moseley, Avon Park H. S.
Avon Park, Florida

CHICKEN AND RICE

1 can chicken stock
1 can cream of mushroom soup
1 can cream of celery soup
1 tsp. salt
1 sm. onion, minced
¼ c. butter
1 c. uncooked rice
1 fryer, cut up

Combine chicken stock, soups, salt and onion. Grease 9 x 13-inch pan with the butter; sprinkle rice in pan. Pour liquid ingredients over rice. Place chicken, skin-side up, on top. Bake at 275 degrees for 2 hours. Yield: 6-8 servings.

Elvira Benne, Columbus H. S.
Columbus, Nebraska

CHICKEN AND RICE AU GRATIN

¾ c. chicken fat
¾ c. flour
1 ½ qt. chicken stock
1 5-lb. chicken, cooked and cubed or 1 qt. cooked cubed chicken
1 c. light cream
1 tbsp. salt
¼ tsp. pepper
1 tsp. Worcestershire sauce
2 ½ lb. rice
1 gal. boiling salted water
2 c. grated cheese
3 c. buttered bread crumbs

Melt chicken fat; blend in flour. Gradually stir in chicken stock; cook until thick, stirring constantly. Add chicken, cream, seasonings and Worcestershire sauce. Cook rice in boiling salted water until tender; drain. Alternate layers of rice and chicken mixture in a 14 x 9 x 2-inch pan. Sprinkle with cheese and buttered bread crumbs. Bake at 450 degrees for 20 minutes. Yield: 50 servings.

Mrs. Zelota M. Yates, Needham Broughton H. S.
Raleigh, North Carolina

CHICKEN-RICE CASSEROLE

3 c. cooked rice
1 4-oz. can pimento, chopped
1 ½ c. diced cooked chicken
¼ to ½ c. canned mushrooms
½ c. blanched almonds
1 ¾ c. chicken broth
1 ½ tbsp. flour
Salt and pepper to taste

Combine rice and pimento; place one-third of rice mixture in greased casserole. Alternate layers of remaining rice, chicken, mushrooms and nuts over rice in casserole. Pour mixture of broth, flour and seasonings over all. Bake at 350 degrees for 1 hour. Yield: 6-8 servings.

Mrs. Eileen Randel, McCook H. S.
McCook, Nebraska

CHICKEN-RICE CASSEROLE

2 c. chopped cooked chicken
1 can chicken soup
½ c. mayonnaise
1 c. chopped celery
½ c. chopped onion
1 tbsp. lemon juice
1 c. cooked rice
½ c. slivered almonds
Salt and pepper to taste
Cereal

Mix all ingredients except cereal; place in greased casserole. Cover with crisp cereal. Bake at 350 degrees for 30 minutes. Yield: 6 servings.

Mrs. Wilma Tucker, Marion H. S.
Marion, Louisiana

CLUB CHICKEN CASSEROLE

¼ c. flour
¼ c. butter or margarine, melted
1 c. chicken broth
1 14 ½-oz. can evaporated milk
½ c. water
1 ½ tsp. salt
3 c. cooked rice
2 ½ c. diced cooked chicken
1 3-oz. can broiled sliced mushrooms, drained
¼ c. chopped pimento
⅓ c. chopped green pepper
½ c. blanched toasted almonds, slivered

(Continued on next page)

Blend flour into butter; add broth, milk and water. Cook over low heat until thick, stirring constantly. Stir in salt, rice, chicken and vegetables. Pour into a greased 11 1/2 x 7 1/2 x 1 1/2-inch baking dish. Bake at 350 degrees for 30 minutes. Top with almonds. Yield: 8 servings.

Mrs. Patricia T. Edwards, Rock Ridge School
Wilson, North Carolina

CHICKEN SUNDAY DINNER

1 c. uncooked rice
1 fryer, cut up or breasts
Salt and pepper to taste
1 pkg. dry onion soup mix
1 can cream of mushroom soup
1 to 1 ½ soup cans water

Spread rice in greased glass dish. Layer fryer over rice; sprinkle with salt, pepper and onion soup mix. Top with mushroom soup and water. Cover and bake at 325 degrees for 2 hours.

Belva Jean Norwood, Greeleyville H. S.
Greeleyville, South Carolina
Mrs. Beverly Waugh
Sunbury West Regional H. S.
Fredericton Junction, New Brunswick, Canada

SUNDAY CHICKEN

1 can cream of mushroom soup
1 can cream of celery soup
½ c. milk
1 ¼ c. uncooked instant rice
1 fryer, cut up
Salt and pepper to taste

Heat soups and milk. Place rice in greased roaster; place chicken on top of rice, skin-side up. Salt and pepper to taste; pour soup mixture over all. Bake at 300 degrees for 2 to 3 hours. Yield: 4-6 servings.

Mrs. Jeanette Peters, Lewiston H. S.
Lewiston, Nebraska

CHICKEN DIVAN

5 lb. chicken breasts or 1 whole chicken
1 tbsp. salt
1 c. water
1 lge. bunch broccoli
1 c. Parmesan cheese, grated
2 c. medium white sauce
¼ tsp. nutmeg
½ c. Hollandaise sauce or mayonnaise
½ c. heavy cream, whipped
1 tsp. Worcestershire sauce

Sprinkle chicken with salt; add water. Cover and simmer for 45 minutes or until tender. Remove meat from bone and cut in thin slices. Cook and drain broccoli; place broccoli in shallow buttered baking dish. Place chicken on broccoli; sprinkle with one-half of the cheese. Combine white sauce with remaining ingredients except cheese; pour over chicken. Sprinkle with remaining cheese. Bake at 300 degrees for 30 minutes. Broil a few minutes to brown. Yield: 8 servings.

Dorothy Yoder, Maquoketa Comm. H. S.
Maquoketa, Iowa

POTATOES BOSPHORUS

3 lge. potatoes, cooked
Butter
Salt and pepper
1 sm. onion, chopped
1 c. cold chopped chicken, ham or beef
1 c. tomato paste
2 paste cans water
1 c. mushrooms
5 hard-cooked eggs, sliced
½ c. almonds, chopped
Grated cheese

Mash potatoes; add butter, salt and pepper. Brown onion in small amount of butter in skillet; add chicken. Brown. Add tomato paste and water. Saute mushrooms in 2 tablespoonfuls butter. Place a layer of mashed potatoes in a greased deep baking dish; top with a layer of tomato sauce. Sprinkle with mushrooms. Add another layer of potatoes; top with eggs and nuts. Repeat layers. Top last layer with grated cheese. Bake, uncovered, at 450 degrees for 15 minutes. Yield: 8 servings.

Mrs. Mary Roberson, Lawrence Co. H. S.
Moulton, Alabama

PHEASANT AND DRESSING

2 pheasant, cut up
4 med. carrots, cut up
4 stalks celery, cut up
1 med. onion, chopped
Dry bread, without crusts
⅔ tsp. sage
2 eggs
2 tbsp. butter
Flour

Cook pheasant, carrots, celery and onion in enough salted water to cover until tender. Remove meat from bones; cut into medium-sized pieces. Place a layer of dry bread in a 10 x 14-inch greased cake pan; sprinkle with additional chopped onion and sage. Remove carrots and celery from broth; place over dressing with pheasant pieces. Make gravy of broth, eggs, butter and enough flour to thicken. Pour over pheasant; sprinkle with crushed potato chips. Bake at 375 degrees for 1 hour. Yield: 12 servings.

Mrs. Beverly Sampson, Redfield H. S.
Redfield, South Dakota

TURKEY DIVAN

1 bunch broccoli
1 tsp. salt
¼ tsp. pepper

(Continued on next page)

Sliced left-over turkey
½ c. grated Parmesan cheese
3 c. medium cream sauce

Cut broccoli into lengthwise slices; cook until tender. Drain; arrange in a layer in a greased shallow casserole. Season with salt and pepper. Cover with turkey. Add 1/4 cup Parmesan cheese to cream sauce; pour over turkey. Sprinkle with remaining cheese. Broil until brown and bubbly. Yield: 6 servings.

Helen Phillips, Metamora H. S.
Metamora, Ohio

CURRIED SALMON CASSEROLE WITH CHEESE PINWHEELS

1 10-oz. pkg. frozen mixed vegetables
1 1-lb. can salmon, drained
1 10-oz. can cream of mushroom soup
Milk
¼ tsp. salt
¼ tsp. curry powder
¼ tsp. ground black pepper
2 c. prepared biscuit mix
½ c. shredded sharp American or Cheddar cheese

Cook frozen mixed vegetables according to package directions. Drain. Mix salmon, vegetables, soup, 1/4 cup milk and seasonings. Turn into 6 x 12 x 2-inch baking dish. Combine biscuit mix and 2/3 cup milk according to package directions. Roll out 1/8-inch thick. Sprinkle with shredded cheese. Roll up as for jelly roll. Cut into 1-inch pieces. Arrange over salmon mixture. Bake in preheated 375 degree oven for 30 minutes or until biscuits are golden brown. Yield: 6 servings.

Photograph for this recipe on page 291.

CHOW MEIN CASSEROLE

1 can tuna
1 can cream of mushroom soup
1 soup can water
1 c. diced onions
1 c. diced celery
1 ½ lb. pkg. cashew nuts, broken
1 No. 2 ½ can Chinese noodles

Combine all ingredients except noodles; mix well. Pour mixture into a casserole dish. Bake at 375 degrees for 40 minutes. Remove from oven; sprinkle noodles over top of casserole. Bake at 425 degrees for 10 minutes longer. Yield: 4-6 servings.

Jeanne C. Jackson, Lehi H. S.
Lehi, Utah

SCALLOPED TUNA

1 ½ c. milk
1 c. bread crumbs
½ tsp. salt
4 tbsp. butter
1 onion, finely chopped
2 tbsp. minced green pepper
1 7-oz. can tuna, flaked
2 eggs, well beaten

Scald milk in double boiler; add bread crumbs, salt, butter, onion and green pepper. Add tuna. Add tuna mixture to eggs. Mix well. Bake at 350 degrees for 50 minutes to 1 hour. Yield: 4 servings.

Mrs. Charlotte R. Card, Deering H. S.
Portland, Maine

SALMON TURBOT

3 tbsp. butter
3 tbsp. flour
2 c. milk
3 eggs, beaten
2 tbsp. lemon juice
Seasonings to taste
1 1-lb. can salmon, flaked
½ c. buttered crumbs

Melt butter; blend in flour. Gradually add milk. Cook and stir until thickened. Slowly add eggs and lemon juice. Season to taste. Layer sauce and salmon in alternate layers in a greased casserole. Cover with buttered crumbs. Bake at 350 degrees for 45 minutes or until a knife inserted in center comes out clean. Yield: 6 servings.

Mrs. Cynthia Ebert, Ripon H. S.
Ripon, Wisconsin

SCALLOPED TUNA

1 c. medium white sauce
1 tbsp. pimento
1 tbsp. chopped green pepper
2 tbsp. butter
1 c. bread crumbs
1 c. tuna, flaked

Combine white sauce with pimento and pepper. Mix butter with crumbs. Place alternate layers of fish and crumbs in greased pan. Pour white sauce over top; spread top with crumbs. Bake at 375 degrees for 20 to 30 minutes. Yield: 6 servings.

Delores Hickenbottom, Bloomfield H. S.
Bloomfield, Nebraska

TUNA CASSEROLE

1 c. macaroni
1 can cream of mushroom soup
1 family-sized can tuna
4 oz. sharp cheese
1 c. peas
1 c. crushed potato chips

Cook macaroni in salted water; drain and blanch. Mix in soup. Layer with tuna, cheese

(Continued on next page)

and peas in buttered casserole. Top with potato chips. Bake at 350 degrees until heated through.

Doris R. Hahn, Saydel H. S.
Des Moines, Iowa

PERFECT TUNA

1 10 ½-oz. can cream of vegetable or chicken soup
⅓ to ½ c. milk
1 7-oz. can tuna, drained and flaked
2 hard-cooked eggs, sliced (opt.)
1 c. cooked peas
1 c. crushed potato chips

Blend soup and milk in 1-quart casserole; stir in tuna, eggs and peas. Top with potato chips. Bake at 350 degrees for 30 minutes. NOTE: Cream of celery or mushroom soup may be used instead of vegetable or chicken soup. Yield: 6 servings.

Bettie Lou Horton, Tanner H. S.
Tanner, Alabama
Mrs. Janet Urbanz, Bear Creek H. S.
Bear Creek, Wisconsin

TUNA-BROCCOLI CASSEROLE

1 10-oz. pkg. frozen broccoli
1 7-oz. can tuna
1 10 ½-oz. can cream of mushroom soup
½ soup can milk
½ c. crushed potato chips

Split stalks from broccoli; cook for 3 minutes. Drain. Place in 1 1/2-quart baking dish. Cover with flaked tuna. Mix cream of mushroom soup and milk; pour over tuna. Sprinkle crushed potato chips over top. Bake at 450 degrees for 15 minutes. Yield: 4 servings.

Jessie D. Lombard, Windsor H. S.
Windsor, Vermont

TUNA-VEGETABLE SUPPER

1 med. cauliflower
1 c. sliced carrots
2 tbsp. chopped onion
1 tbsp. butter or margarine
1 10 ½-oz. can cream of mushroom or celery soup
2 tbsp. milk
1 7-oz. can tuna, drained and flaked
Dash of nutmeg
½ c. crumbled crackers

Separate cauliflower into flowerets. Cook with carrots in boiling salted water until tender-crisp. Drain. Saute onion in butter until tender. Combine onion, soup, milk, tuna and nutmeg; mix well. Turn carrots and cauliflower into 1 1/2-quart casserole. Pour soup mixture over vegetables. Sprinkle with cracker crumbs. Bake at 350 degrees for 40 minutes or until slightly browned. Yield: 4 servings.

Mrs. Ruth Park, Bend H. S.
Bend, Oregon

CRAB MEAT CASSEROLE

2 tbsp. butter
2 tbsp. flour
1 c. milk
½ c. grated Cheddar cheese
½ tsp. salt
Few grains of pepper
1 lb. crab meat
1 can cream of mushroom soup

Melt butter in saucepan; add flour and mix to make a smooth paste. Add milk slowly, stirring constantly, until blended. Cook over low heat until sauce thickens; add grated cheese and continue cooking until cheese is melted. Season with salt and pepper. Place crab meat in buttered 1-quart casserole. Cover with mushroom soup and cheese sauce. Sprinkle buttered crumbs over top. Bake at 350 degrees for 45 minutes. Yield: 4 servings.

Elizabeth W. Miner, Stonington H. S.
Pawcatuck, Connecticut

CRAB MEAT CASSEROLE

½ c. cooking Sherry
2 c. medium white sauce
1 lb. crab meat
Grated sharp cheese

Add Sherry to white sauce. Remove any small shells from crab meat. Place crab meat and white sauce in alternate layers in casserole, ending with white sauce. Top with grated cheese. Bake at 350 degrees until cheese browns and mixture bubbles. Yield: 4 servings.

Mrs. Patricia M. Baldy
Margaret Mace Public School
North Wildwood, New Jersey

SEAFOOD CASSEROLE

1 6-oz. pkg. wide noodles
⅓ c. butter or margarine
3 tbsp. flour
1 tsp. salt
Dash of pepper
2 c. milk
½ c. shredded cheese
¼ c. sliced onion
1 c. sour cream
1 c. large curd cottage cheese
1 can crab meat, tuna or shrimp
¼ c. corn flake crumbs

Cook noodles according to package directions; drain. Melt 3 tablespoonfuls butter; add flour, salt and pepper. Add milk, stirring constantly. Cook until smooth and thickened. Blend in 1/4 cup cheese, onion, sour cream, cottage cheese and noodles. Arrange in layers with seafood in 2-quart casserole. Melt remaining butter; add corn flake crumbs and remaining cheese. Mix; spoon around edge of casserole. Bake at 350 degrees for 40 to 50 minutes or until thoroughly heated. Yield: 10 servings.

Gertrude Wagner, Concord H. S.
Concord, Vermont

LOBSTER SUPREME

12 oz. lobster
1 10 ½-oz. can cream of celery soup, heated
1 10 ½-oz. can tomato soup, heated
2 tbsp. Sherry
1 tbsp. lemon juice
Salt and pepper to taste
¼ c. bread crumbs
2 tbsp. butter

Combine lobster, soups, Sherry, lemon juice and seasonings. Pour into well buttered casserole. Top with bread crumbs; dot with butter. Bake at 400 degrees until browned. Yield: 4 servings.

Martha Dawson, Dover H. S.
Dover, Delaware

NEW ENGLAND LOBSTER SCALLOP

8 oz. medium fine noodles
2 qt. water
1 3-lb. lobster, boiled
3 c. milk
½ c. plus 1 tbsp. butter
1 egg
½ c. plus 1 tbsp. flour
1 8-oz. can mushroom stems and pieces
½ c. finely chopped green pepper
½ c. buttered bread crumbs

Cook noodles in 2 quarts boiling salted water for 15 minutes; drain. Pour boiling water over noodles; drain again. Cut lobster meat into large pieces; reserve tamale from lobster for cream sauce. Make cream sauce of milk, butter, egg, tamale and flour. Place a layer of lobster in a 2-quart casserole; sprinkle with mushrooms and green pepper. Add a layer of noodles, then cream sauce. Repeat layers, ending with cream sauce; sprinkle with buttered crumbs. Bake at 350 degrees for 30 minutes or until crumbs are brown and casserole is thoroughly heated. Yield: 8-10 servings.

Mrs. Sarah M. Gleason, East Walpole Jr. H. S.
East Walpole, Massachusetts

CHINESE CASSEROLE

1 lge. can chow mein noodles
1 can cream of mushroom soup
½ c. water
1 c. finely cut celery
1 lge. can shrimp

Combine all ingredients; mix well. Place in flat casserole. Bake at 350 degrees for 30 minutes. Yield: 4 servings.

Madeline Johnson, Pinehurst Jr. H. S.
Pinehurst, Idaho

SEAFOOD CASSEROLE

1 sm. onion, minced
¼ c. butter
3 tbsp. flour
1 ½ tsp. salt
½ tsp. mustard
¼ tsp. pepper
3 c. milk
4 c. sharp grated cheese
½ c. Sherry or milk
6 c. cooked chopped shrimp, crab or halibut
¼ c. lemon juice
1 lb. macaroni shells, cooked
1 c. crushed saltine crackers

Saute onion in butter. Blend in flour, salt, mustard and pepper. Add milk; cook and stir until thick. Add 3 cups cheese, stirring until cheese is melted. Add Sherry. Sprinkle shrimp with lemon juice. Alternate layers of macaroni, shrimp and cheese sauce in buttered casserole, ending with cheese sauce. Sprinkle with remaining cheese and cracker crumbs. Bake at 400 degrees for 35 minutes. Yield: 15 servings.

Florence D. Tolli, Plainville Jr. H. S.
Plainville, Connecticut

BAKED CRAB AND SHRIMP CASSEROLE

¾ c. chopped green peppers
½ to ¾ c. chopped onions
1 c. chopped celery
1 6 ½-oz. can crab meat, flaked
1 6 ½-oz. can shrimp
½ tsp. salt
⅛ tsp. white pepper
1 tsp. Worcestershire sauce
1 c. mayonnaise
1 c. buttered crumbs

Combine all ingredients except buttered crumbs in greased casserole. Sprinkle top with buttered crumbs. Bake at 350 degrees for 30 to 40 minutes. May be served in individual baked pastry cups. Yield: 6-8 servings.

Mrs. Louise A. Petty, Dallas H. S.
Dallas, Georgia
Mrs. Lois R. Cook, Cazenovia Central School
Cazenovia, New York

CHILI PIE

1 No. 2 can chili, heated
½ c. chopped onion
2 tbsp. chili powder (opt.)
1 c. grated cheese

Combine all ingredients except cheese in greased casserole in order given. Top with cheese. Bake at 350 to 400 degrees for 20 to 30 minutes. Serve hot. NOTE: One pound hamburger may be added. Brown hamburger. Casserole may be layered, if desired. Yield: 6 servings.

Emma Joe Thomas, Burkeville H. S.
Burkeville, Texas
Mrs. Nancy Jones, J. C. Ferguson Jr. H. S.
Arlington, Texas
Mary Corinne Brooke, Opheim H. S.
Opheim, Montana

Sauce & Dressing Favorites

BARBECUE SAUCE

2 tsp. paprika
1 tsp. sugar
1 tsp. salt
½ tsp. pepper
¼ tsp. dry mustard
1 tsp. monosodium glutamate
¾ c. butter or oil, melted
½ c. fresh lemon juice
½ c. hot water
2 tbsp. grated onion (opt.)

Stir paprika, sugar, salt, pepper, mustard and monosodium glutamate into melted butter. Blend in lemon juice, hot water and grated onion thoroughly. Marinate meat in sauce for several hours before cooking.

Mrs. Emily J. Rickman
Area Supervisor, Home Economics Education
Danville, Virginia

BARBECUE SAUCE

1 tsp. salt
½ tsp. pepper
1 tsp. sugar
1 med. onion, finely chopped
1 c. tomato puree or catsup
¼ c. butter
½ c. hot water
⅓ c. lemon juice
1 tbsp. Worcestershire sauce
1 tbsp. paprika

Mix all ingredients in saucepan; heat to a boil. Remove from heat.

Mrs. Nancy Monsen, Thornton Twp. H. S.
Harvey, Illinois

BARBECUE SAUCE

½ c. vinegar
2 tbsp. sugar
½ c. catsup
2 tbsp. Worcestershire sauce
1 tsp. mustard
⅛ tsp. pepper
1 clove of garlic, minced

Combine all ingredients, mixing well. Use on hamburgers, spareribs, chicken or pork chops.

Dixie B. Williams, Pinedale H. S.
Pinedale, Wyoming

BARBECUE SAUCE

1 14-oz. bottle catsup
½ c. undiluted consomme
¼ c. wine vinegar
2 tbsp. soy sauce
1 tbsp. brown sugar
⅛ tsp. garlic powder
½ tsp. salt
⅓ c. salad oil

Place all ingredients in blender; cover. Blend well. Heat sauce on grill. Use to baste chicken, steak or chops during barbecuing. Yield: 2 1/2 cups.

Mrs. Aussie A. Miller, Newton H. S.
Newton, Texas

BARBECUE SAUCE FOR CHICKEN

½ c. Worcestershire sauce
¼ lb. margarine
½ c. salad oil
⅔ c. garlic wine vinegar
1 tsp. salt
½ tsp. black pepper
¼ tsp. red pepper

Combine Worcestershire sauce, margarine, salad oil, vinegar and spices; heat until margarine is melted. Baste chicken with sauce frequently during cooking. Yield: 1 pint.

Mrs. Mildred Hickman, La Marque Jr. H. S.
La Marque, Texas

CHICK-N-QUE SAUCE

½ c. corn oil
¾ c. lemon juice
¼ c. water
2 tbsp. salt
2 tbsp. sugar
1 tbsp. Tabasco sauce

Combine all ingredients in order listed; stir well. Bring mixture to a boil. Yield: Sauce for 3 chickens.

Mrs. Mary Leathers, Tupelo H. S.
Tupelo, Mississippi

LOUIE'S BARBECUE SAUCE FOR CHICKEN OR RIBS

1 qt. vinegar
1 ½ tbsp. sugar
½ tsp. salt
1 tsp. black pepper
1 tsp. red pepper
1 tbsp. Worcestershire sauce
½ c. catsup
Juice of ½ lemon
½ c. butter
3 slices onion

Combine all ingredients; heat to a simmer. Do not boil. Keep hot. Baste chicken or ribs while cooking over charcoal.

Mrs. Margaret B. Sanders, Dale Co. H. S.
Midland City, Alabama

MILD BARBECUE SAUCE

1 6-oz. can frozen lemon juice
2 juice cans water
2 tbsp. sugar
1 c. catsup
½ oz. ground red pepper
1 oz. salt
1 pt. vinegar
2 tsp. Worcestershire sauce
½ lb. margarine

Combine all ingredients; mix well. Serve over chicken.

Mrs. Lucille Jordan, Cary H. S.
Cary, North Carolina

QUICK BARBECUE SAUCE

1 c. catsup
¾ c. water
⅓ c. Worcestershire sauce
1 tbsp. chili powder
1 tsp. salt
¼ tsp. pepper
2 tbsp. brown sugar (opt.)
1 tbsp. prepared mustard (opt.)
1 sm. onion, chopped or instant onion flakes

Combine all ingredients; mix thoroughly. Pour over meat. NOTE: If cooking meat on the grill, marinate meat in sauce and baste with remaining sauce.

Mrs. Dora R. Wray, Henrico H. S.
Richmond, Virginia

REUBEN'S BARBECUE SAUCE

1 lb. butter or margarine
1 bottle Worcestershire sauce
1 sm. jar prepared mustard
Juice of 6 lemons
½ c. sugar
1 tsp. salt
Red pepper to taste
Black pepper to taste

Melt butter; add Worcestershire sauce, mustard, lemon juice, sugar, salt and peppers. Boil for 5 minutes.

Mrs. Katherine B. Floyd, Newberry H. S.
Newberry, South Carolina

SASSER SASS

1 c. vinegar
1 tbsp. prepared mustard
2 tbsp. paprika
1 tbsp. black pepper
1 tbsp. salt
1 tbsp. cayenne pepper
1 bottle catsup
1 bottle Heinz 57 sauce
1 bottle chili sauce
½ bottle A-1 sauce
½ bottle Worcestershire sauce
1 c. salad oil

Combine vinegar, mustard, paprika, black pepper, salt and cayenne pepper in a large 2-quart mixing bowl or glass container. Add the remaining ingredients in order given, beating after each addition. Stir until well mixed. Yield: 1 1/2 quarts.

Mrs. Barbara Knowlton, Florence H. S.
Florence, Colorado

TEXAS BARBECUE SAUCE

½ c. finely chopped onion (opt.)
2 tbsp. brown sugar
1 to 3 tsp. paprika
1 tsp. salt
1 tsp. dry mustard or 2 tbsp. prepared mustard
¼ tsp. chili powder
⅛ tsp. red or cayenne pepper
2 tbsp. Worcestershire sauce
¼ c. vinegar
1 c. tomato juice
¼ c. catsup (opt.)
½ c. water (opt.)

Combine all ingredients in saucepan; simmer for 15 minutes. NOTE: One 4-ounce can tomato sauce may be substituted for tomato juice. Yield: 1 pint.

Mrs. Frances D. Daniel
Central Gwinnett-Lawrenceville School
Lawrenceville, Georgia
Madeline M. Thomas, Appomattox H. S.
Appomattox, Virginia
Mrs. Virginia A. York, Groveland H. S.
Groveland, Florida
Nancy J. Ross, Del Rio H. S.
Del Rio, Texas

ZESTY BARBECUE SAUCE

⅔ c. chopped onions
¼ c. chopped green pepper
1 c. catsup
2 tbsp. brown sugar
2 tbsp. vinegar
¼ c. lemon juice
⅔ c. water
2 tbsp. Worcestershire sauce

Combine ingredients; simmer, stirring occasionally, for 15 minutes. Serve over or with cooked meat. Yield: 2 cups sauce.

Mrs. Norma Drothy, Dawson H. S.
Welch, Texas

BEST HOT DOG CHILI

1 lb. ground beef
1 c. chopped onions
1 c. tomato catsup
1 tbsp. sugar
1 tbsp. vinegar
1 tsp. chili powder
1 tsp. Worcestershire sauce

(Continued on next page)

Brown beef and onions lightly in a large skillet; add remaining ingredients. Simmer for 20 minutes.

Gracie Rexrode, Rupert H. S.
Rupert, West Virginia

CHERRY SAUCE

1 can cherry pie filling
1 tsp. cinnamon
⅛ tsp. cloves
1 ½ tsp. grated lemon rind
2 to 4 tbsp. vinegar

Combine all ingredients. Bring to a boil. Lower heat; simmer for about 5 minutes, stirring constantly. Serve hot over ham.

Mrs. Doris Neill, Palco Rural H. S.
Palco, Kansas

COCKTAIL SAUCE

½ to ¾ c. chili sauce
⅓ c. catsup (opt.)
2 to 4 tbsp. lemon juice
2 to 6 tsp. horseradish
1 to 2 tsp. Worcestershire sauce
1 tsp. grated onion (opt.)
Few drops of Tabasco sauce
Salt to taste
Dash of pepper (opt.)

Combine all ingredients; chill. Serve with seafood cocktails.

Jo Anne Tuttle, Spencer H. S.
Spencer, Iowa
Jane H. Osborne, Goodlettsville H. S.
Goodlettsville, Tennessee

COLD SEAFOOD SAUCE

1 c. sour cream
2 tbsp. prepared horseradish
1 can skinless and boneless sardines, mashed
1 sm. cucumber, diced
1 tsp. lemon juice

Combine all ingredients; serve cold. Serve with cold boiled fish.

Martha M. McDaniel, Gray Court-Owings H. S.
Gray Court, South Carolina

COME BACK SAUCE

1 clove of garlic
Juice of 1 lemon
1 tsp. salt
½ tsp. pepper
1 onion, chopped
1 tbsp. Worcestershire sauce
¼ tsp. hot sauce
1 tsp. horseradish
½ bottle chili sauce
½ c. salad oil
1 tbsp. sugar
1 tbsp. water
1 c. mayonnaise
½ c. catsup
1 tbsp. mustard

Place all ingredients in a quart jar; shake vigorously. Serve as sauce for fish, shrimp or as a salad dressing.

Mrs. J. F. Green, Jr.
Leakesville Attendance Center
Leakesville, Mississippi

CREOLE SAUCE

2 c. chopped onions
2 c. chopped green peppers
1 qt. stewed or canned tomatoes
⅛ tsp. paprika
1 clove of garlic
Salt and pepper

Melt butter; add paprika. Blend. Add onions, green peppers and garlic; saute until tender. Simmer for 15 minutes. NOTE: May be added to fish during final cooking.

Mrs. Fran Caldwell, Garland H. S.
Garland, Texas

DELUXE STEAK BUTTER

¼ lb. butter
¼ tsp. garlic powder
1 tsp. shredded green onion
1 tsp. dill weed
1 tsp. lemon juice
¼ tsp. cracked peppercorns
1 tsp. paprika

Soften butter at room temperature; blend in garlic powder, green onion, dill weed, lemon juice, pepper and paprika. Spread on broiled steak, hamburgers or chops.

Sr. M. Dorinda, C.S.A.
St. Mary's Springs Academy
Fond du Lac, Wisconsin

FISH SAUCE

½ c. mayonnaise
1 tsp. chili sauce
1 tsp. sweet pickle vinegar
1 tsp. chopped red or green pepper
1 tsp. chopped pickle
1 tsp. chopped parsley or watercress

Mix all ingredients. Serve with fish.

Mrs. Gladys Fletcher, Everett H. S.
Maryville, Tennessee

MARINADE FOR SHISH KABOBS

½ c. vinegar
Juice of ½ lemon
1 c. oil
1 c. tomato paste
¼ c. soy sauce
2 tsp. salt
½ tsp. pepper
1 tsp. oregano
1 tsp. parsley flakes
½ tsp. thyme

Combine all ingredients; marinate meat cubes in sauce for 3 hours or overnight. Baste kabobs with sauce while broiling or barbecuing.

Beatrice F. Gulnac, Phillipsburg H. S.
Phillipsburg, New Jersey

MELBA SAUCE

1 sm. glass currant jelly
½ c. sugar
1 c. sieved fresh raspberry pulp and juice
½ tbsp. cornstarch
1 tbsp. cold water
⅛ tsp. salt
¼ tsp. lemon juice

Combine jelly, sugar and raspberry pulp and juice. Bring to a boil. Combine cornstarch and cold water; add with salt and lemon juice to raspberry sauce. Cook, stirring constantly, until mixture thickens and becomes clear. Strain through double cheesecloth. Cool; serve with any meat.

Rebecca Puryear, Loap Independent School
Loap, Texas

MINT SAUCE

3 tbsp. water
1 ½ tbsp. confectioners sugar
⅓ c. finely chopped mint leaves
½ c. strong vinegar

Heat water; dissolve sugar in water. Cool syrup; add remaining ingredients. Serve on roast lamb. Yield: 1 cup.

Mable Elrod Allen, Joppa Comm. H. S.
Joppa, Illinois

ORANGE SAUCE

½ c. fresh orange juice
2 tbsp. lemon juice
1 tbsp. vinegar
½ tsp. salt
Dash of white pepper
Dash of paprika
¼ c. sugar
1 tsp. cornstarch
1 tsp. cold water
1 can Mandarin oranges, drained
2 tbsp. butter

Combine juices, vinegar, salt, pepper, paprika and sugar in top of double boiler; heat. Blend cornstarch with cold water; mix with small amount of heated sauce. Blend cornstarch mixture into sauce; stir until thickened. Add orange sections when mixture is heated through; mix in butter. Serve with ham, turkey or desired meat. Yield: 2 1/2 cups sauce.

Mrs. William Cooke, West Bainbridge H. S.
Bainbridge, Georgia

PICKLE TOMATO SAUCE

1 12-oz. can tomato juice
½ c. dill pickle liquid
1 ½ tsp. curry powder
1 tbsp. sugar

Combine all ingredients; mix well. Heat to serving temperature, stirring occasionally. Serve with hamburgers, if desired. Chill and serve cold, if desired. Yield: 2 cups.

Photograph for this recipe on page 321.

RAISIN SAUCE

5 boxes raisins
2 c. brown sugar
2 c. white sugar
1 tbsp. cinnamon
1 tbsp. allspice
5 No. 2 cans pineapple chunks
⅓ box cornstarch
2 sticks margarine

Place raisins in large container; cover with water and bring to boil. Add sugars to raisins, stirring. Add cinnamon and allspice. Drain pineapple, reserving liquid. Add pineapple liquid to raisin mixture. Dissolve cornstarch in enough cold water to make proper consistency; add to mixture. Fold in pineapple chunks and margarine. Remove from heat.

Mrs. Laura C. Clenney, Bakerhill H. S.
Bakerhill, Alabama

RAISIN SAUCE FOR HAM

½ c. brown sugar
1 to 1 ½ tsp. dry mustard
½ tbsp. flour or 2 tbsp. cornstarch
½ tbsp. salt (opt.)
⅛ tsp. pepper (opt.)
¼ tsp. grated lemon rind (opt.)
¼ tsp. cloves (opt.)
Few grains of mace (opt.)
Few grains of nutmeg (opt.)
Few grains of cinnamon (opt.)
¼ to ½ c. raisins
¼ c. vinegar
1 ½ c. water

Mix dry ingredients; add raisins, vinegar and water. Cook to a syrup; serve hot. May be reheated, if desired. NOTE: Two tablespoonfuls lemon juice may be substituted for 2 tablespoonfuls vinegar.

Deanna Brosten, McFarland H. S.
McFarland, California
Mrs. Betty Garey, Arapahoe H. S.
Arapahoe, Nebraska

REMOULADE SAUCE

Sieved yolks of 4 hard-cooked eggs
4 cloves of garlic, finely chopped
3 tbsp. prepared mustard
3 c. mayonnaise
2 tbsp. paprika
2 tbsp. Worcestershire sauce
Dash of Tabasco sauce
4 tbsp. vinegar
4 tbsp. (heaping) chopped parsley
Salt and pepper to taste

Combine all ingredients; blend well. Refrigerate for 12 hours before serving. Yield: 6 servings.

Mabel Moorhouse, Belen H. S.
Belen, New Mexico

SAUCE FOR HAM LOAF

¼ c. canned tomato soup
¼ c. prepared mustard
¼ c. vinegar
½ c. (scant) sugar
¼ c. horseradish
1 egg yolk, beaten
1 tsp. butter

Combine all ingredients; cook, stirring, until thickened. If sauce is too thick, add a small amount water or vinegar to desired consistency. Use on ham loaf.

Mrs. Dorothy Brown, Iowa Falls H. S.
Iowa Falls, Iowa

SEAFOOD COCKTAIL SAUCE

½ c. salad oil
2 tbsp. lemon juice
1 tbsp. Worcestershire sauce
1 tbsp. horseradish
Salt and pepper
½ c. tomato catsup
½ tsp. Tabasco sauce

Combine salad oil with lemon juice; add remaining ingredients. Serve cold with seafood.

Mrs. Fay Foster
Brownsboro Independent School Dist.
Brownsboro, Texas

SHRIMP COCKTAIL SAUCE

¾ c. catsup
2 tbsp. (heaping) horseradish
Juice of 1 lemon

Mix all ingredients. Serve with chilled shrimp.

Mrs. Derrell Martin, Sallisaw H. S.
Sallisaw, Oklahoma

SOUR CREAM AND RELISH SAUCE

1 c. sour cream
⅓ c. sweet pickle relish
½ tsp. celery salt
⅛ tsp. pepper

Combine all ingredients; mix well. Serve with hamburgers, as desired. Yield: 1 1/3 cups.

Photograph for this recipe on page 321.

FREEZER MEAT SAUCE

3 cloves of garlic, minced
3 green peppers, chopped
3 lge. onions, chopped
⅓ c. salad oil
3 lb. lean ground beef
2 c. boiling water
4 8-oz. cans tomato sauce
3 6-oz. cans tomato paste
1 tbsp. salt
1 tbsp. paprika
1 tbsp. celery salt
1 tsp. chili powder
2 tbsp. Worcestershire sauce
3 tbsp. bottled thick meat sauce
3 tbsp. chili sauce

Cook garlic, peppers and onions in hot oil for 5 minutes. Add meat; cook over high heat until red color disappears. Add water and remaining ingredients. Simmer, uncovered, for 2 hours. Cool quickly. Freeze in 1-pint freezer containers. Yield: 7 pints.

Mrs. Oleta M. Smith, O' Donnell H. S.
O'Donnell, Texas

ITALIAN MEAT SAUCE

⅓ c. oil or cooking fat
1 clove of garlic, crushed
1 green pepper, chopped

(Continued on next page)

1 lge. onion, finely sliced
1 lb. ground beef
1 can tomato paste
1 can tomato sauce
1 c. boiling water
1 tsp. salt
1 tsp. paprika
⅓ tsp. celery salt
⅓ tsp. garlic salt
⅓ tsp. chili powder
2 tsp. Worcestershire sauce
1 tbsp. steak sauce
1 tbsp. chili sauce

Heat oil in heavy kettle; add garlic, green pepper and onion. Cook over low heat for 5 minutes. Add meat; mix well. Cook on high heat until lightly browned. Add tomato paste, tomato sauce and water. Cook over low heat for 2 hours; add seasonings. Use immediately. NOTE: May be cooled, packaged and frozen.

Mrs. Elizabeth Trennepohl, Angola H. S.
Angola, Indiana

ITALIAN MEAT SAUCE

½ c. chopped onion
2 tbsp. salad oil
1 lb. hamburger
2 cloves of garlic, minced or 1 tsp. garlic salt
2 1-lb. cans tomatoes
1 3-oz. can sliced mushrooms
1 tsp. salt
½ tsp. red pepper
1 tsp. chili powder

Cook onion in oil in large fry pan until tender. Add meat and garlic; brown. Add remaining ingredients. Simmer, uncovered, for 2 hours to 2 hours and 30 minutes or until sauce is thick, stirring occasionally. Serve over hot spaghetti. Yield: 6 servings.

Lenda Edwards, Bennettsville H. S.
Bennettsville, South Carolina

ITALIAN SPAGHETTI SAUCE

2 lb. ground beef
1 med. onion, chopped
3 cloves of garlic, chopped
3 cans tomato sauce
1 tsp. cinnamon
1 tsp. allspice
1 tsp. chili powder
1 tsp. nutmeg
1 tsp. salt

Brown ground beef; add onion and garlic and brown. Add tomato sauce with a small amount water, cinnamon, allspice, chili powder, nutmeg and salt. Simmer for 2 hours.

Reynola Pakusich, Sedro-Woolley H. S.
Sedro-Woolley, Washington

ITALIAN SPAGHETTI SAUCE

1 tbsp. olive oil
1 med. onion, diced
1 sm. clove of garlic, minced
1 ½ lb. ground beef
1 tbsp. oregano
1 tsp. salt
1 tsp. poultry seasoning
1 tbsp. parsley flakes
1 tsp. pepper
1 lge. can tomatoes or stewed tomatoes
2 6-oz. cans tomato paste
2 6-oz. paste cans water

Combine oil, onion and garlic in a large heavy skillet or saucepan. Cook until tender but not brown. Add beef and seasonings, breaking up meat with a fork. Do not brown. Add remaining ingredients. Break up large pieces of tomato. Cover and let simmer for 6 to 8 hours. Yield: 6-8 servings.

Marie Evanoff, Glenrock H. S.
Glenrock, Wyoming

MEAT SAUCE

1 green pepper, diced
1 lge. onion, diced
1 tsp. minced garlic
Margarine or shortening
1 lb. hamburger
Salt and pepper
1 sm. can tomato paste
2 c. canned tomatoes
½ tsp. chili powder

Brown green pepper, onion and garlic in margarine or shortening; add meat with salt and pepper to taste. Brown. Place in heavy pot; add tomato paste, tomatoes, chili powder, salt and pepper. Simmer slowly for 2 hours. Serve with spaghetti, if desired.

Euzelia M. Vollbracht, Burns-at-Fallston H. S.
Fallston, North Carolina

MEAT SAUCE FOR SPAGHETTI

1 med. onion, chopped
2 or 3 cloves of garlic, chopped
2 tbsp. chopped fresh parsley
1 lb. lean ground beef
2 tbsp. olive oil
1 tsp. salt
¼ tsp. oregano
¼ tsp. basil
1 tsp. Worcestershire sauce
2 No. 2 cans tomato juice
2 cans tomato paste
3 whole cloves
2 to 3 tbsp. sugar

Saute onion, garlic, parsley and ground beef in olive oil until beef is done but not brown. Add remaining ingredients; simmer for 1 hour or until sauce is thickened. Stir occasionally during cooking. Remove cloves before serving.

Mary Osborne, Washington H. S.
Massillon, Ohio

QUICK SPAGHETTI SAUCE

1 ½ lb. hamburger
Margarine
1 tsp. seasoned salt
1 lge. can tomato sauce or 2 cans tomato paste
Water
1 pkg. spaghetti sauce mix
1 can mushrooms

Fry hamburger in margarine; sprinkle with seasoned salt. Add tomato sauce or paste and an equal amount of water. Add spaghetti sauce mix and mushrooms. Simmer for 30 minutes.

Lillian McKinney, Fulton Schools
Middleton, Michigan

SPAGHETTI MEAT SAUCE

1 lb. ground steak
Pimento oil
1 sm. can pimento
1 med. onion, chopped
1 green pepper, chopped (opt.)
1 lge. can tomatoes
1 can tomato soup
Salt and pepper to taste
¼ c. catsup
½ tsp. Worcestershire sauce

Fry meat in pimento oil until done; add pimento, onion and green pepper. Cook for 5 minutes. Place in large boiler or pan. Add tomatoes and tomato soup. Cook slowly for 2 hours. Add seasonings, catsup and Worcestershire sauce. NOTE: Sauce may be frozen.

Elizabeth A. Cantrell, Fairforest Jr. H. S.
Fairforest, South Carolina

SPAGHETTI SAUCE

1 ½ lb. ground beef
1 onion, chopped
1 green pepper, chopped
1 tsp. salt
⅛ tsp. pepper
1 sm. can tomato paste
1 tbsp. Worcestershire sauce
½ tbsp. steak sauce
1 tsp. lemon juice
1 bay leaf
1 tsp. chili powder
1 qt. tomatoes
Pinch of oregano
½ tsp. sugar
½ c. catsup

Brown meat in a large skillet with onion, green pepper, salt and pepper. When brown, add remaining ingredients. Cook on low heat for 3 to 4 hours. Serve over cooked spaghetti. Yield: 6 servings.

Mrs. Gerald Head, Hinson Jr. H. S.
Attalla, Alabama

SPAGHETTI SAUCE

¾ c. chopped onions
1 clove of garlic, minced
3 tbsp. olive oil
2 1-lb. cans tomatoes
2 6-oz. cans tomato paste
1 c. water
1 tbsp. sugar
1 ½ tsp. salt
½ tsp. pepper
1 ½ tsp. crushed oregano
1 bay leaf
Italian meat balls

Cook onions and garlic in hot oil until tender but not brown; stir in remaining ingredients. Simmer for 30 to 40 minutes. Remove bay leaf. Add meat balls; simmer for 30 to 40 minutes longer. NOTE: Sauce may be frozen.

Mrs. Edna Earl Jesse, Rossville H. S.
Rossville, Georgia

SPAGHETTI SAUCE

6 med. onions, chopped
Oil
2 lb. ground chuck
2 lb. ground pork shoulder
2 tbsp. Worcestershire sauce
4 cans tomato sauce
1 bottle catsup
1 can chopped mushrooms
4 bay leaves
Pinch of basil leaves
4 to 6 drops of Tabasco sauce
1 tbsp. sugar
2 cloves of garlic

Saute onions in oil. Brown meats with Worcestershire sauce. Combine meats, onions and remaining ingredients. Cook slowly for 4 to 6 hours. Yield: 16 servings.

Jeanne S. Stokes, Northwest Jr. H. S.
Winston-Salem, North Carolina

SPAGHETTI SUPREME

1 lb. ground beef
1 tbsp. oregano
1 tbsp. sugar
1 tsp. salt
1 tsp. garlic salt
⅛ tsp. red pepper (opt.)
½ c. diced onion
⅓ c. grated Parmesan cheese
1 sm. can tomato paste
1 can tomato soup

Brown ground beef; add remaining ingredients. Simmer for 3 hours. Yield: 4 servings.

Maralyn A. Braford, Sparta Jr. H. S.
Sparta, Michigan

SPANISH SAUCE

2 tbsp. minced onion
1 tbsp. minced green pepper
2 tbsp. butter
1 whole clove
1 clove of garlic, split
½ tsp. salt
⅛ to ¼ tsp. cayenne pepper
1 tbsp. sugar
2 c. tomatoes

Cook onion and green pepper in butter over low heat until clear; add remaining ingredients. Simmer until thickened. Remove garlic and clove. Serve with meat, fish or omelets. Yield: 6-8 servings.

Judy Christensen, Radway School
Radway, Alberta, Canada

STEAK GOULASH

Trimmed fat from loin or rib steaks or ¼ c. cooking oil
2 med. green or firm tomatoes, diced
2 med. onions, diced
2 med. green peppers, diced
1 4-oz. can mushroom stems and pieces
1 ½ c. water
Salt and pepper to taste

Cut fat into small cubes. Brown in electric frypan until all grease is cooked out; remove fat cubes. Combine vegetables in large bowl; add mushrooms. Pour vegetable mixture into hot fat. Add water; season to taste. Stir; bring to a boil. Cover; reduce heat. Simmer for 1 hour, stirring occasionally. Add more water during cooking if needed. Serve with broiled steak. Yield: 6 servings.

Mrs. Norma Womble, Broadway H. S.
Broadway, North Carolina

SWEET PICKLE AND EGG SAUCE

1 c. mayonnaise
¼ c. prepared mustard
½ tsp. garlic salt or powder
½ c. sweet fresh cucumber pickles, diced
1 hard-cooked egg, diced

Combine all ingredients and mix well. Garnish with pickles, as desired. Serve with hamburgers, as desired. Yield: 1 1/2 cups.

Photograph for this recipe on page 321.

TARTAR SAUCE

1 ⅔ c. mayonnaise
3 tbsp. chopped pickle relish
3 tbsp. chopped stuffed olives
1 to 1 ½ tbsp. minced onion
1 tbsp. minced parsley
2 tsp. vinegar

Combine all ingredients; chill. Serve with fish or seafood. Yield: 2 cups.

Mrs. Judy Mulkey Waite, Molino Jr. H. S.
Cantonment, Florida

TEXAS WIENER SAUCE

1 lb. hamburger
1 can tomato paste
5 tomato paste cans water
½ sm. can chili powder
Dash of sugar
½ tsp. salt
¾ c. finely chopped onions

Combine all ingredients in a large skillet; simmer over low heat for 3 hours or until thick. Serve as a sauce on wieners or grilled hamburgers.

Eileen B. Gillern, West Jr. H. S.
Binghamton, New York

CHESTNUT DRESSING

1 c. yellow corn meal
1 c. buttermilk
1 egg
2 tsp. baking powder
1 tsp. soda
Salt
1 tbsp. sugar
10 slices bread
15 crackers
6 hard-cooked eggs, chopped
5 c. broth
1 5-oz. can water chestnuts, chopped
1 tsp. rubbed sage
Pepper to taste

Combine meal, buttermilk, egg, baking powder, soda, 1 teaspoonful salt and sugar. Pour into well greased pan. Bake at 450 degrees until done. Brown bread slices and crackers; crumble with corn bread. Add eggs, 5 cups or more broth, water chestnuts and seasonings. Bake at 400 degrees for 20 minutes. Yield: 12 servings.

Mrs. Helen Ellis, New Summerfield H. S.
New Summerfield, Texas

CORN BREAD DRESSING

¼ c. shortening
¼ c. chopped onion
2 c. diced celery
2 c. small bread cubes
4 c. crumbled corn bread
1 tsp. salt
½ tsp. pepper
1 tsp. poultry seasoning or 1 tsp. sage
1 ½ to 2 c. poultry broth

Melt shortening in skillet; cook onion and celery in shortening over low heat until onion is soft but not browned. Stir occasionally. Blend bread cubes and corn bread with seasonings. Add onion,

(Continued on next page)

celery and shortening. Blend. Gradually pour broth over surface, stirring lightly. Add additional seasonings, if desired. Spread in a 9-inch square casserole. Bake at 350 degrees for 30 to 45 minutes. Yield: 8 servings.

Mrs. Colleen Stevenson, Alexander H. S.
Nekoosa, Wisconsin

RICE DRESSING

1 lb. ground meat
2 tbsp. cooking oil
1 c. chopped onions
½ c. chopped green pepper
1 c. chopped celery
½ clove of garlic, finely chopped
1 c. water
1 tsp. salt
⅛ tsp. red pepper
2 to 3 c. cooked rice

Brown meat in hot cooking oil in Dutch oven; add onions, green pepper, celery and garlic. Fry until wilted. Add water; cook until tender. When most of water has evaporated, add salt and pepper. Mix. Add rice; mix lightly. Yield: 8 servings.

Hilda Harmon, Crowley H. S.
Crowley, Louisiana

WILD RICE DRESSING

1 8-oz. pkg. wild rice
1 lb. white rice
1 stalk celery, chopped
2 med. onions, chopped
2 sticks margarine
1 sm. can pimento

Cook wild and white rices separately according to directions on box. Saute celery and onions in margarine just until tender; toss with rice and pimento. Heat in casserole.

Mrs. Bernice Bagwell, Connally H. S.
Waco, Texas

APPLE-RAISIN STUFFING

6 apples, pared and diced
1 c. raisins
1 tsp. cinnamon
⅛ tsp. nutmeg
1 tsp. salt
12 slices dry bread, cubed
½ c. sugar
1 tsp. seasoning salt

Combine apples, raisins, cinnamon, nutmeg, salt, bread cubes, sugar and seasoning salt. Blend in enough hot water to moisten well. Use dressing with poultry, pork, pork rib roast, pork chops, turkey or chicken.

Zona Kay Bunger, Woodland H. S.
Woodland, Washington

CHEESE STUFFING

1 c. finely chopped onions
¼ c. butter or fat
2 c. soft bread crumbs
½ c. grated cheese
2 tbsp. chopped parsley
2 tsp. dry mustard
1 tsp. salt
⅛ tsp. pepper

Cook onions in butter until soft; add remaining ingredients. Toss lightly. Yield: Stuffing for 3 to 4-pound dressed fish.

Adelle Vallaster, Brooks Jr. Secondary School
Powell River, British Columbia, Canada

CORN BREAD STUFFING

1 c. corn meal
1 c. sifted flour
2 ½ tsp. salt
4 tsp. baking powder
3 eggs
1 c. milk
¼ c. vegetable oil
½ c. margarine
6 c. soft bread crumbs
1 c. chopped celery
½ c. chopped onion
½ c. chopped green pepper
1 tsp. sage
1 ½ tsp. poultry seasoning
4 c. broth or water

Sift corn meal with flour, 1/2 teaspoonful salt and baking powder; add 1 egg, milk and oil. Beat with a rotary beater until smooth. Pour into a greased 8-inch square pan. Bake at 425 degrees for 20 to 25 minutes. Crumble corn bread. Cut margarine into small pieces; mix with corn bread and bread crumbs. Lightly brown celery, onion and green pepper in a small amount of fat. Add remaining salt and seasonings to corn bread mixture; mix thoroughly. Beat remaining eggs; add to mixture. Gradually sprinkle broth over surface, stirring lightly until dressing is of desired moistness. Stuff dressing lightly into body cavity of bird or bake in separate pan in oven with turkey for about 45 minutes.

Mrs. Gladys Ashlock, Lamar Jr. H. S.
Bryan, Texas

CORN BREAD STUFFING

5 c. fine dry bread crumbs
¾ to 1 c. milk
3 eggs, slightly beaten
3 c. crumbled corn bread
2 tsp. salt
¼ c. chopped parsley
1 tsp. sage
1 c. chopped onions
1 ½ c. finely chopped celery
1 c. margarine, melted

Moisten bread crumbs with milk; add eggs. Add corn bread; mix well. Add salt, parsley and sage.

(Continued on next page)

Saute onions and celery; add to mixture. Add margarine; mix well. NOTE: If desired, add onion and celery without sauteing to add crispness to stuffing. Yield: Stuffing for 15-pound turkey.

Mrs. Pat De Jong, Valsetz H. S.
Valsetz, Oregon

GIBLET STUFFING

Giblets and neck of turkey, chopped
2/3 c. diced apples
1 c. chopped celery
10 c. soft bread crumbs
1/4 c. chopped parsley
1/3 c. chopped onion
1/4 tsp. pepper
1/3 c. butter or margarine, melted
3/4 tsp. salt
1 egg, beaten
Sage to taste
1/4 tsp. poultry seasoning (opt.)

Combine ingredients with 1/2 cup broth. Stuff turkey or shape into balls; place on greased baking sheet. Bake at 350 degrees for 20 minutes or until lightly browned. Yield: Stuffing for 10-pound turkey.

Mrs. Mary Ann Wolcott, Odell H. S.
Odell, Nebraska

OLD-FASHIONED BREAD

1 1/2 c. finely chopped onions
1 1/2 c. finely chopped celery
1/3 c. butter
8 c. dry bread cubes
1 1/2 tsp. salt
1/8 tsp. pepper
1/2 tsp. poultry seasoning
1/2 tsp. sage
1/4 c. water
1 egg, well beaten

Cook onions and celery in butter in skillet until tender. Add to bread cubes in large bowl or pan. Sprinkle with mixed seasonings. Combine; add water and egg. Toss with forks. Yield: Stuffing for 12-pound bird.

Mrs. Burma Williams, Coeur D' Alene Jr. H. S.
Coeur D' Alene, Idaho

OYSTER STUFFING FOR TURKEY

1/2 c. chopped celery
1/2 c. chopped onion
1 bay leaf
1/4 c. butter or margarine
6 c. dry bread crumbs
1 tbsp. chopped parsley
3 c. chopped oysters
1 tsp. poultry seasoning
Salt and pepper to taste
2 eggs, beaten

Cook celery, onion and bay leaf in butter until tender, but not brown. Remove bay leaf. Add crumbs and parsley to butter mixture. Mix thoroughly. Drain oysters; reserve liquid. Add enough milk to oyster liquid to make 1 3/4 cups. Add oysters, seasonings and eggs to mixture. Add enough of liquid mixture to moisten. Yield: Stuffing for 10 to 12-pound turkey.

Sister Mary Calasanctius, O.S.F.
St. Francis H. S.
Little Falls, Minnesota

MUSHROOM AND WILD RICE STUFFING

1 4-oz. can sliced mushrooms
1/4 c. butter
1/4 c. minced onion
1 tbsp. minced parsley
1/2 c. diced celery
2 c. cooked wild rice
3/4 tsp. salt
Dash of pepper

Saute mushrooms in butter for 5 minutes. Remove mushrooms; add onion, parsley and celery. Cook until onion is yellow. Add rice, salt, pepper and mushrooms; mix well. Stuff 4 to 5-pound chicken or 4 to 5 cornish game hens with stuffing. Yield: 4-5 servings.

Arlene Olson, Southview Jr. H. S.
Edina, Minnesota

RICE AND ORANGE STUFFING

1 c. uncooked rice
1 sm. onion, minced
2 tbsp. shortening or chicken fat
1 lge. orange
2 tbsp. seedless raisins
1/2 tsp. salt
1/8 tsp. pepper
1/2 tsp. celery salt

Cook rice in boiling lightly salted water until barely tender; drain thoroughly. Saute onion in shortening until golden. Grate rind of orange. Remove membrane and seed; chop orange pulp coarsely. Place rind, chopped orange, rice, onion and raisins in bowl. Combine seasonings; add to orange mixture. Mix well. Yield: Stuffing for one 5 to 6-pound bird.

Mrs. Imogene Simpson, Bristow H. S.
Bristow, Oklahoma

RICE STUFFING

2 lb. rice
1 gal. boiling broth
2 2/3 tsp. salt
1 1/3 c. finely chopped celery
1 1/3 c. finely chopped onions
2/3 lb. butter
2 qt. corn bread crumbs
8 eggs, well beaten
12 hard-cooked eggs, chopped
2 2/3 tbsp. sage
1 1/3 tbsp. pepper
1 1/3 qt. broth
1 1/3 qt. milk

(Continued on next page)

Spread rice in pan; place in 400 degree oven. Stir well as rice begins to toast; continue cooking for 15 minutes or until light brown. Remove rice from oven; add to boiling broth. Add salt; cover. Cook for 15 minutes or until rice is tender. Cook celery and onions in butter until tender. Combine celery and onion mixture with cooked rice. Add bread crumbs, beaten eggs, hard-cooked eggs, sage, pepper, broth and milk. Mix well. Use as stuffing for fowl or bake at 350 degrees for 35 to 45 minutes. Yield: 100 servings.

Mrs. Theresa J. King, Wellman H. S.
Wellman, Texas

WILD RICE AND MUSHROOM STUFFING

⅓ c. chopped onion
¼ c. butter
1 c. chopped mushrooms
¼ lb. sausage
3 c. boiled wild rice
1 tsp. salt

Saute onion in 2 tablespoonfuls butter for 5 minutes or until lightly browned. Remove from pan; add remaining butter and mushrooms. Cook for 5 minutes; remove from pan. Fry sausage until lightly browned, stirring constantly; remove from heat and stir in onion and mushrooms. Add rice and salt, mixing lightly. Yield: 5 cups.

Mrs. Sandra Faber, North Chicago H. S.
North Chicago, Illinois

SCOTCH STUFFING

2 ½ c. oats
½ lb. butter, softened
1 med. onion, diced
Salt and pepper to taste

Combine all ingredients. Fill bird cavity lightly with stuffing. Roast. NOTE: May be used for chicken or turkey. Yield: 4 cups.

Mrs. Frances Paul Farnham, Fridley H. S.
Minneapolis, Minnesota

STUFFING

1 ½ c. dry bread crumbs
Milk
1 sm. onion, chopped
2 tbsp. butter
2 eggs
3 sm. potatoes, cooked and mashed
1 lb. hamburger or ground giblets and livers
¼ c. finely chopped celery
1 tbsp. finely chopped parsley
1 tbsp. salt
½ tsp. pepper

Moisten bread crumbs with enough milk to cover crumbs; let stand for 30 minutes to soften. Brown onion in butter; add with crumb mixture to remaining ingredients. Mix well. Stuff bird and bake.

Sister M. Daniel, Andrean H. S.
Gary, Indiana

SWEET POTATO AND SAUSAGE STUFFING FOR TURKEY

½ lb. sausage
3 tbsp. chopped onion
1 c. chopped celery
4 c. canned sweet potatoes, mashed
2 c. dry bread crumbs
2 tsp. salt
¼ tsp. paprika
3 tbsp. chopped parsley

Saute sausage until light brown: break up with a fork. Remove from pan. Add onion and celery to pan; saute for 3 minutes. Add sausage, sweet potatoes, dry crumbs, salt, paprika and parsley; mix well. Stuff turkey.

June Kreutzkampf, Jefferson H. S.
Jefferson, Iowa

TOASTED BREAD DRESSING

1 c. diced celery
½ c. minced onion
¾ c. butter, melted
2 ½ qt. toasted bread crumbs or cubes
1 tsp. sage or poultry seasoning
Salt and pepper to taste
1 ½ c. hot meat broth
1 ½ c. milk, heated

Saute celery and onion in part of butter. Place bread in large bowl; pour remaining melted butter over bread. Add seasonings, celery and onion; mix. Pour hot broth over bread; mix. Add enough milk to make a soft mixture. Use to stuff fowl or place in pan and bake. NOTE: Two packages croutettes may be substituted for toasted bread; omit seasoning.

Mrs. Dorothy Anderson, Montrose H. S.
Montrose, South Dakota

Soup Favorites

BEST EVER BEEF STEW

1 ½ lb. ground beef
2 tbsp. butter
3 or 4 med. potatoes, diced
6 carrots, sliced ¼-in. thick
10 to 12 sm. onions, sliced
1 8-oz. can kidney beans
1 8-oz. can peas
1 8-oz. can corn
1 sm. rutabaga, sliced
2 tbsp. (heaping) brown sugar
1 tsp. salt
½ tsp. pepper
1 tbsp. vitalox
1 tbsp. butter

Cook meat in 2 tablespoonfuls butter until meat is no longer red; add vegetables on top of meat. Mix brown sugar, salt, pepper and vitalox; add to vegetables and meat. Add butter. Cover with hot water. Simmer for 3 hours, adding more water as needed. NOTE: Meat may be made into patties and rolled in flour and browned lightly. Yield: 12 servings.

Mrs. Vera Troyer, Bennett Co. H. S.
Martin, South Dakota

CHILI

2 tbsp. fat
2 sm. onions, chopped
1 lb. hamburger
1 tsp. salt
2 tbsp. chili powder
2 ½ c. canned tomatoes
2 ½ c. kidney beans

Heat fat; add onions, hamburger, salt and chili powder. Cook slowly until browned. Place tomatoes and beans in kettle; add enough water to make approximately 8 cups. Add meat mixture. Cook slowly for 1 hour. Yield: 8 servings.

Mrs. Flo W. Johnson, Gordon H. S.
Decatur, Georgia

CHILI

2 tbsp. fat
1 ½ c. diced onions
1 sm. clove of garlic (opt.)
1 lb. ground beef
1 to 2 tbsp. chili powder
2 tbsp. cold water
2 c. canned tomatoes
2 tsp. salt
1 tsp. sugar
4 c. red kidney beans, cooked
Cooked spaghetti (opt.)

Melt fat; add onion and garlic. Cook until partially tender, stirring frequently. Add beef; fry, uncovered, until slightly browned. Mix chili powder with cold water; add with tomatoes, salt and sugar to ground beef. Bring to boil; cover and simmer for 1 hour. Add beans; heat well. Add spaghetti, if desired. Serve hot. Yield: 8 servings.

Mrs. Peggy Hendrickson, Lone Jack H. S.
Fourmile, Kentucky

CHILI CON CARNE

1 onion, diced
2 tbsp. fat (opt.)
2 c. canned tomatoes
1 lb. ground beef
2 c. cooked kidney beans
Chili powder to taste
¾ to 1 tsp. salt

Saute onion in fat until golden brown; add tomatoes, meat, beans and seasonings. Cover; cook slowly for about 1 hour. Add water if mixture becomes too dry. NOTE: Meat may be browned with onion, if desired. Yield: 6 servings.

Iona Ross, Freer H. S.
Freer, Texas
Bernadine J. Bash, Hempfield Area H. S.
Greensburg, Pennsylvania

CHILI MAC

3 tbsp. fat
1 lb. ground beef
5 onions, peeled and chopped
3 med. green peppers, seeded and diced
2 1-lb. cans tomatoes
1 8-oz. pkg. spaghetti
1 to 2 cans tomato soup
1 tsp. chili powder
Pepper (opt.)
2 tsp. salt

Melt fat in electric frying pan; add ground beef and fry until lightly browned. Add onions and peppers; cook until wilted and medium brown. Add tomatoes; cook slowly with lid on for 1 hour. Add spaghetti 20 to 30 minutes before serving. Add 1 can tomato soup and chili powder; add remaining soup if mixture is too thick. Season to taste. Yield: 12 servings.

Alya Ray Taylor, Winterville H. S.
Winterville, North Carolina

TEXAS CHILI

2 lge. dried black peppers
4 lb. ground chuck
1 ½ oz. chili powder
5 sm. whole dried chili peppers
5 cloves of garlic, chopped
1 tsp. ground cumin seed
3 tsp. salt
9 c. water
2 cans pinto beans, drained and rinsed
¼ to ½ c. flour

Cut off stems and remove seed from black peppers; boil in water for 15 minutes. Remove from water; slit peppers open and scrape out inside. Combine peppers with remaining ingredients except beans and flour. Bring to boil quickly; cook slowly for 1 hour and 15 minutes. Add pinto beans 20 minutes before serving time. Thicken with flour, as desired. Yield: 12 servings.

Mary G. Beckham, Lake Air Jr. H. S.
Waco, Texas

EASY CHILI

1 lb. ground beef
2 tbsp. cooking oil
3 tbsp. flour
4 tbsp. chopped onion
1 ½ tbsp. chili powder
1 sm. can tomato paste
2 c. water
1 can chili beans

Brown ground beef in oil. Add remaining ingredients; cook slowly for 1 hour. Serve with crisp corn sticks, if desired. Yield: 6 servings.

Mrs. W. B. Thompson, Solomon Jr. H. S.
Greenville, Mississippi

GROUND BEEF AND VEGETABLE SOUP

1 lb. ground beef
2 c. cold water
1 med. onion, chopped
3 med. carrots, diced
2 med. potatoes, cubed
2 c. tomatoes or tomato juice
½ c. uncooked noodles
Salt and pepper to taste

Simmer ground beef and water for 15 minutes. Add remaining ingredients. Simmer until vegetables are tender. Yield: 6 servings.

Mrs. Jolene Hartman, Lancaster H. S.
Lancaster, Texas

HAMBURGER SOUP

3 tbsp. margarine
1 ¼ lb. ground beef
4 carrots
4 sm. potatoes
1 green pepper, cut into small pieces
1 1-lb. 12-oz. can tomatoes
1 can beef consomme
1 can onion soup
¼ c. chopped celery tops
¼ c. chopped parsley
1 bay leaf
½ tsp. Italian seasoning
1 c. water

Melt margarine in a large kettle; add ground beef. Cook over medium heat, stirring, until browned. Peel and cut carrots into bite-sized pieces. Add potatoes, carrots and green pepper to meat. Add all remaining ingredients. Bring mixture to a boil. Reduce heat; simmer, covered, for 45 minutes or until vegetables are tender, stirring occasionally. Yield: 8-10 servings.

Mrs. Robert A. Gruber, Gypsum H. S.
Gypsum, Kansas

HAMBURGER-VEGETABLE CHOWDER

2 tbsp. fat
½ lb. ground beef
1 c. canned tomatoes
½ c. diced carrot
½ c. diced celery
1 onion, chopped
2 tsp. salt
¼ c. barley or rice
½ tsp. pepper
1 ½ c. water
1 c. cubed potatoes

Heat 4-quart pressure saucepan; add fat. Brown meat in fat; add remaining ingredients. Cover and cook at 15 pounds pressure for 15 minutes. Serve hot with crackers or croutons, if desired. Yield: 6 servings.

Mrs. Zora S. Brasher, Martin H. S.
Martin, Tennessee

HAMBURGER-VEGETABLE SOUP

1 lb. hamburger
2 c. frozen mixed vegetables
2 c. wide soup noodles
1 tsp. salt
¼ tsp. pepper
1 bay leaf
1 beef bouillon cube

Brown hamburger. Cook mixed vegetables according to package directions; drain reserving liquid. Combine vegetables, liquid, noodles, meat, salt, pepper, bay leaf and bouillon cube in large pot. Simmer for 50 minutes, adding water if needed. Remove bay leaf; serve. Yield: 6-10 servings.

Mrs. Judith Miller, Fisher Jr. H. S.
Trenton, New Jersey

HAMBURGER-VEGETABLE SOUP

1 lb. ground beef
1 lge. onion, chopped
1 1-lb. can tomatoes
1 lb. canned mixed vegetables

Brown ground beef and onion in skillet; pour off excess fat. Add tomatoes and mixed vegetables. Bring to a boil; reduce heat and simmer for 15 minutes. Yield: 12 servings.

Virginia Boxley, Berryville H. S.
Berryville, Arkansas

HEARTY CHUCK SOUP

3 tbsp. butter
1 onion, coarsely chopped
1 ½ lb. ground chuck
1 1-lb. 12-oz. can tomatoes
3 10 ½-oz. cans consomme
2 consomme cans water
4 carrots, peeled and quartered
1 bay leaf
4 celery tops, chopped
6 sprigs parlsey
½ tsp. thyme
10 peppercorns
1 tbsp. salt

(Continued on next page)

Melt butter in soup kettle; add onion. Cook until onion is limp, but not brown. Add meat; cook and stir until meat is no longer red. Add remaining ingredients. Cover and simmer for 45 minutes. Yield: 8 servings.

Mrs. Louise Barton, Herrin H. S.
Herrin, Illinois

THICK CREAM OF HAMBURGER SOUP

2 c. sliced onions
3 tbsp. bacon fat
½ lb. hamburger
4 c. water
2 tsp. salt
⅛ tsp. pepper
1 c. shredded carrots
1 tbsp. chopped parsley
½ c. uncooked elbow macaroni
½ c. tomato juice
2 tbsp. margarine
2 tbsp. flour
1 c. milk

Saute onions in bacon fat in heavy kettle for 5 minutes; add hamburger and brown lightly. Add water, salt, pepper, carrots and parsley. Cover and bring to a boil; reduce heat and simmer for 10 minutes. Add macaroni and tomato juice; simmer for 15 minutes or until macaroni is tender. Melt margarine; blend in flour. Gradually add milk. Cook until thick, stirring constantly. Add to soup; simmer for 5 minutes, adding more seasonings, if desired. Yield: 4-6 servings.

Mrs. Russell Ruby, East Side H. S.
Nappanee, Indiana

BEEF STEW

2 lb. beef, cut into 1 ½ to 2-in. cubes
Flour
2 tbsp. fat
2 c. water
1 bay leaf
2 whole cloves
2 tsp. salt
1 lge. onion, sliced
6 carrots, sliced
1 c. sliced celery
4 med. potatoes, quartered

Dredge meat in 1/3 cup flour; brown meat in fat in 10-inch skillet. Add water, bay leaf, cloves and salt. Cover and simmer for 1 hour and 30 minutes. Remove cloves and bay leaf. Add onion, carrots, celery and potatoes. Cook for 30 minutes or until tender. Mix 3 tablespoonfuls flour with 1/2 cup cold water; add to stew. Simmer until thickened. Yield: 6 servings.

Mrs. Mary F. Dunn, Byers H. S.
Byers, Texas

BEEF STEW

1 ½ c. beef, cut into 1-in. cubes
Salt and pepper
Flour
Drippings
1 ½ c. water
3 potatoes, diced
2 onions, sliced
3 carrots, diced
1 c. green beans

Sprinkle meat with salt and pepper; roll in flour. Brown in drippings. Add water. Cover and simmer until almost tender, 2 to 3 hours. Add vegetables; season with salt and pepper. Simmer, covered, until vegetables are done, stirring occasionally. Yield: 4 servings.

Mrs. Betty Porter, Oilton H. S.
Oilton, Oklahoma

BEEF STEW

2 lb. lean beef, cut up
2 tbsp. flour
2 tbsp. fat
2 c. water
1 can tomato sauce
2 tsp. salt
¼ tsp. pepper
6 onions, chopped
6 carrots, chopped
6 potatoes, chopped
1 c. green peas

Wipe beef with damp cloth. Roll meat in flour; brown in fat in heavy saucepan. Add water, tomato sauce and seasonings. Cover tightly and cook over low heat until almost tender, about 1 hour and 30 minutes. Add onions, carrots and potatoes. Cook for 30 to 45 minutes longer. Add peas just before vegetables are tender. Yield: 6 servings.

Les V. Edmonds, Franklin H. S.
Franklin, Louisiana

BEEF STEW

⅓ c. flour
1 ¾ lb. chuck, cut into 1-in. cubes
Salt
4 tbsp. shortening
2 c. water or stock
¼ tsp. pepper
1 tsp. Worcestershire sauce
12 sm. onions
6 med. carrots, cut up
4 med. potatoes, cut up

Place flour in bowl. Sprinkle beef cubes with salt; dredge in flour. Heat shortening in skillet over medium heat; brown meat. Remove from pan. Continue until all pieces are browned. Mix remaining flour and 1 cup water or stock. Stir until smooth; pour into skillet. Add 1/2 teaspoonful salt, pepper and Worcestershire sauce; stir until blended. Gradually add remaining water; stir until smooth. Add meat to gravy; cover. Simmer until done. Add vegetables; simmer until done. Yield: 6 servings.

Mrs. Margaret W. Lyles, Westminster H. S.
Westminster, South Carolina

BEEF STEW BOURBONNAIS

1 ½ lb. chuck, cut into 1-in. pieces
1 tbsp. fat
1 clove of garlic, minced
1 med. onion, chopped
½ tsp. salt
½ tsp. pepper
1 can tomato soup
¾ c. red wine
¼ c. water
½ tsp. basil
¼ tsp. thyme
½ c. catsup
4 med. carrots, cut into 1-in. pieces
1 ½ c. celery, cut into 1-in. pieces
5 med. potatoes, peeled and quartered

Brown meat lightly in fat. Add garlic and onion. Cook until onion is transparent; add salt and pepper. Stir in soup, wine and water. Cover and simmer for 30 minutes. Add herbs and catsup. Arrange vegetables on meat and gravy. Cover; simmer for 1 hour and 30 minutes or until all ingredients are blended. Add more water, if necessary. Yield: 6 servings.

Mrs. Alice Blakeney, Runge Independent School
Runge, Texas

BEEF STEW WITH GRAVY

1 lb. boneless beef, cut into small cubes
1 tsp. salt
2 beef bouillon cubes
2 tbsp. flour
1 to 2 c. cold water

Place beef cubes in Dutch oven; brown thoroughly over high heat. Reduce heat and add enough water to cover. Cook for 2 to 3 hours or until beef is tender. Add bouillon cubes, desired seasonings and flour dissolved in cold water; cook until desired thickness is obtained. Serve hot with crackers or toast. Yield: 4 servings.

Clara Mae Chatham, Smithville H. S.
Smithville, Oklahoma

BEEF-VEGETABLE SOUP

1 lb. boneless stew meat
Salt and pepper
2 onions or 1 lge. onion and 2 or 3 green onions, chopped
2 or 3 carrots, peeled and chopped
1 or 2 potatoes, peeled and chopped
½ c. chopped celery
4 or 5 pods of okra, chopped
¼ green pepper, chopped
1 No. 2 ½ can tomato juice or tomatoes

Cut meat into small pieces; sprinkle with salt and pepper. Cover with water; cook until tender. Salt and pepper fresh vegetables; add with tomatoes to stew. Cover and cook until vegetables are tender. Add more water, if needed. Yield: 12 servings.

Mrs. L. A. Boyd, Vernon H. S.
Vernon, Texas

EASY BEEF STEW

2 beef bouillon cubes
2 c. boiling water
1 tsp. salt
½ tsp. pepper
½ tsp. monosodium glutamate
½ tsp. thyme
3 med. Irish potatoes, peeled and cut up
1 lge. onion, cut into chunks
3 med. carrots, cut into chunks
1 No. 2 ½ can beef or left-over roast
1 No. 2 ½ can tomatoes, cut up

Add bouillon to boiling water; dissolve completely. Add seasonings; stir and add fresh vegetables. Simmer until tender. Add beef and tomatoes. Simmer until very hot. Yield: 4 servings.

Rudene Wilbanks, McEachern Schools
Powder Springs, Georgia

MINUTE STEAK STEW

4 minute or cubed steaks
2 tbsp. flour
Salt and pepper to taste
2 tbsp. butter
1 tbsp. finely chopped onion
1 c. cooked English peas and carrots, mixed
½ c. vegetable liquid
6 to 8 med. potatoes, cooked
1 8-oz. can tomato sauce

Cut steaks into 1-inch strips; dredge in flour mixed with salt and pepper. Heat butter in skillet until bubbling. Add meat; brown well on all sides. Stir in all remaining ingredients. Cover skillet; simmer for 10 to 12 minutes. Yield: 4 servings.

Mrs. Fannye M. Franks, Caldwell Jr. H. S.
Columbus, Mississippi

OCTOBER BEEF STEW

2 tsp. salt
½ tsp. pepper
¼ tsp. ginger
¼ c. flour
3 lb. beef cubes
½ c. hot oil
1 c. chopped onions
1 clove of garlic
1 46-oz. can V-8 juice
2 sticks cinnamon
4 lge. carrots, cut up
8 stalks celery, cut up
8 sm. potatoes, cut up
1 zucchini squash, cut up
8 prunes
16 dried apricots

Combine salt, pepper, ginger and flour; dredge beef cubes in mixture. Brown in oil; add onions, garlic, V-8 juice, cinnamon and carrots. Simmer for 1 hour; add celery, potatoes, zucchini, prunes and apricots. Simmer for 1 hour longer. Yield: 8 servings.

Marjory Nielsen, Billings H. S.
Billings, Montana

VEAL STEW WITH DUMPLINGS

2 lb. veal shoulder, cut into 1-in. cubes
1 onion, sliced
Water
2 ¾ tsp. salt
¼ tsp. pepper
½ tsp. Worcestershire sauce
2 c. diced potatoes
6 carrots, diced
1 ½ c. plus 4 tbsp. flour
3 tsp. baking powder
2 tbsp. shortening
¾ c. milk

Simmer veal and onion in 1 quart water for 1 hour. Add 2 teaspoonfuls salt, pepper, Worcestershire sauce, potatoes and carrots; cook until vegetables are tender. Thicken mixture with 4 tablespoonfuls flour and 1/4 cup cold water; stir until smooth. Sift remaining flour with baking powder and remaining salt; cut in shortening. Add milk; mix lightly. Drop dumplings by teaspoonfuls into hot veal; cover tightly. Steam for 12 minutes. Garnish with parsley, if desired. Yield: 6-8 servings.

Anita Smith, Edinburg H. S.
Edinburg, Texas

VEAL-VEGETABLE SOUP

1 lb. veal
1 tsp. salt
3 med. carrots, sliced
1 can peas, drained
1 tbsp. butter
1 tbsp. flour
1 sm. onion, minced

Cut veal into 1-inch cubes; place in 2 quarts water. Add salt. Add carrots; cook until carrots are well done. Add peas; cook slowly for 15 minutes. Melt butter; blend in flour. Brown slightly. Add onion and 1/2 cup water. Bring to a boil. Add sauce to soup; bring to a boil. Yield: 6 servings.

Mrs. Mary Louise Klingensmith
Washington Twp. H. S., Apollo, Pennsylvania

BROWN LAMB STEW

4 tbsp. butter
2 lb. lamb shoulder cubes, well trimmed
1 tsp. salt
½ tsp. pepper
¼ tsp. mace
2 cans beef bouillon
1 tbsp. pickling spices
8 sm. onions, halved
1 c. sliced carrots
1 c. diced celery
8 sm. potatoes, cubed
1 8-oz. pkg. frozen peas

Melt butter in Dutch oven. Add cubed meat; brown on all sides. Season with salt, pepper and mace. Add enough water to bouillon to make 1 quart liquid; add with pickling spices tied in cheesecloth bag to meat. Bring to a boil. Cover and simmer for 1 hour to 1 hour and 30 minutes. Add onions, carrots, celery and potatoes; simmer for 45 minutes. Add more broth as needed. Add peas; cook for 15 minutes longer. To thicken stew, blend 3 tablespoonfuls of flour in 1/3 cup water; stir into mixture. Continue cooking until stew thickens. Yield: 4-6 servings.

Mrs. Leila Blajeski, Kaukauna H. S.
Kaukauna, Wisconsin

IRISH STEW

2 lb. stewing lamb, cubed
½ c. cubed carrots
½ c. cubed turnip
1 onion, sliced
1 potato, cubed
2 c. sliced potatoes
Salt and pepper to taste

Cover meat with boiling water. Cover and simmer for 1 hour. Add carrots, turnip, onion and cubed potato; cook for 30 minutes. Add sliced potatoes; cook for 30 minutes longer. Season. Serve with dumplings, if desired. Yield: 6 servings.

Mrs. Rebecca B. Sish, Brentwood Jr. H. S.
Pensacola, Florida

LAMB STEW

1 ½ lb. lean lamb or mutton
1 ½ tsp. salt
⅛ tsp. pepper
2 tbsp. flour
2 tbsp. shortening
¼ c. chopped onion
3 potatoes, diced
1 turnip, diced
2 tbsp. chopped parsley

Cut lamb into 1-inch cubes. Add seasonings; sprinkle with flour. Cook lamb in hot shortening until light brown, stirring occasionally. Add onion; cook until golden, stirring occasionally. Add water to cover lamb; simmer for 1 hour and 30 minutes to 2 hours and 30 minutes or until tender. Add vegetables to stew; cook for 20 minutes or until tender. Garnish with parsley. NOTE: For thicker mixture, brown 2 tablespoonfuls flour in 400 degree oven or in heavy skillet. Mix flour and 1 tablespoonful cold water; add 2 to 3 tablespoonfuls liquid from stew, stirring. Add paste to stew when vegetables are tender, stirring. Cook until thickened. Yield: 6 servings.

Mrs. Marguerite Craig, Fulton H. S.
Swanton, Ohio

SPRINGTIME LAMB STEW

1 ½ lb. boneless lamb, cubed
¼ tsp. salt
¼ tsp. pepper
2 tbsp. butter or margarine
2 10 ½-oz. cans mushroom gravy
1 c. water
½ tsp. dried mint flakes, crushed
4 carrots, cut into 2-in. pieces
12 small white onions
¼ c. dry white wine
1 10-oz. pkg. frozen lima beans

(Continued on next page)

Season lamb with salt and pepper. Brown in butter in Dutch oven. Add gravy, water and mint. Cover; cook over low heat for 1 hour. Add carrots and whole onions. Cover; simmer for 45 minutes or until vegetables are tender. Add wine and lima beans; cook for 15 minutes longer. Yield: 4 servings.

Mrs. Phyllis L. Barton, Fort Hunt H. S.
Alexandria, Virginia

THICK LAMB STEW WITH PARSLEY NOODLES

1 ½ lb. cubed lamb shoulder
1 c. chopped onions
3 tbsp. flour
Salt
½ tsp. pepper
¼ tsp. mace
1 c. stock or bouillon
1 c. diced carrots
½ c. chopped green pepper
1 c. lima beans
3 qt. boiling water
8 oz. wide egg noodles
½ c. melted butter
¼ c. chopped parsley

Combine lamb and onions. Cook over low heat until lamb is browned on all sides. Add flour, 1 1/2 teaspoonfuls salt, pepper and mace; blend. Gradually add stock or bouillon; cook, stirring constantly, until thickened. Add carrots, green pepper and beans. Cover; cook over low heat, stirring occasionally, for 1 hour and 30 minutes. Add 1 tablespoonful salt to rapidly boiling water. Gradually add noodles so that water continues to boil. Cook, uncovered, stirring occasionally until tender. Drain in colander. Combine noodles, butter and parsley. Serve with stew. Yield: 4 servings.

Carolyn Nordlund, Mayville H. S.
Mayville, Wisconsin

FLEMISH PEASANTS FEAST

1 tbsp. butter or margarine
2 lb. diced pork shoulder
2 c. beer
½ c. boiling water
½ tsp. rosemary
4 med. onions, halved
2 c. vegetable stock
3 10-oz. pkg. frozen California Brussels sprouts
2 c. diced cooked potatoes
1 ¾ c. cooked whole carrots
¼ c. flour
Liquid smoke to taste (opt.)

Melt butter in large kettle or Dutch oven; add pork and brown on all sides. Add beer, water and rosemary. Cover and cook over low heat for 45 minutes. Add onions; cook for 30 minutes. Stir in 1 1/2 cups stock and Brussels sprouts. Cover and cook for 10 minutes longer or until Brussels sprouts are tender. Add potatoes and carrots. Stir remaining stock into flour to form a smooth paste. Slowly stir into stew. Add liquid smoke. Cook until stock is thickened. Yield: 6-8 servings.

Photograph for this recipe on page 383.

HAM-BEAN SOUP

1 ½ c. dried navy beans
1 med. onion, chopped
1 ham bone or left-over ham
Salt and pepper

Thoroughly wash beans; cover with cold water. Let soak for several hours or overnight. Let drain. Add onion, ham bone and water to cover. Heat to boiling; reduce heat. Cover and simmer for 1 hour and 30 minutes to 2 hours or until beans are tender. Remove bone; cut off meat and return to soup. Season to taste. Yield: 4 servings.

Lois E. Clarchick, Plum H. S.
Pittsburgh, Pennsylvania

HAM AND PEA SOUP

1 lge. ham bone
1 c. split peas
½ to 1 c. chopped onions
1 c. chopped celery
1 c. diced carrots
2 tbsp. parsley, finely cut
Salt and pepper to taste

Place ham bone in covered 4-quart pan; cover with 2 quarts of water. Bring to boil; simmer for 1 to 2 hours. Remove bone and excess pieces of fat; add split peas. Cook over low heat for 20 minutes. Add all remaining ingredients; boil at low heat until vegetables are tender. Season to taste; serve. NOTE: For a thinner or thicker soup, vary amount of peas and liquid. For a smooth soup, place soup in blender; blend according to blender directions. Reheat to serving temperature. Yield: 12 servings.

Mrs. Marguerite S. Drechsel Darnall
Mt. Empire Jr. H. S., Campo, California

KOREAN EGG BROTH

⅓ c. diced celery
2 qt. water
2 chicken broth cubes
½ lb. pork, thinly sliced
½ tsp. salt
½ tsp. monosodium glutamate
Dash of pepper
2 eggs, beaten

Place celery in water; bring water to a boil. Add chicken broth cubes; dissolve completely. Add pork; cook until done. Add seasonings; simmer for 30 minutes. Bring quickly to a boil; add eggs. Remove from heat immediately. Yield: 8 servings.

Leanne Luke, Sacred Hearts Academy
Honolulu, Hawaii

SOUP KETTLE SUPPER

8 strips bacon
1 c. diced cooked ham or beef
1 1/3 c. beef broth
2 c. water
1 1/3 c. sweet whole kernel corn
1 2/3 c. drained French-style green beans
2 c. canned tomatoes
1 to 2 tsp. salt
1/8 tsp. pepper
1 4 1/2-oz. pkg. instant rice
1 tbsp. finely chopped parsley

Fry bacon in large heavy saucepan until crisp. Pour off all fat except 2 tablespoonfuls. Crumble bacon and ham. Saute in drippings until slightly browned. Add remaining ingredients except rice and parsley. Bring to a boil. Add rice. Cover; let stand for 10 minutes. Add parsley, just before serving. If chowder becomes too thick, add a small amount of water. Yield: 8-10 servings.

Mrs. Ina Hooper, Elizabeth H. S.
Elizabeth, Louisiana

BRUNSWICK STEW

1 5-lb. stewing hen
4 slices bacon, chopped
2 c. diced raw potatoes
1 10-oz. pkg. frozen lima beans
1 1-lb. can tomatoes
1 med. onion, chopped
2 tsp. salt
1/4 tsp. pepper
1 1/2 tsp. Worcestershire sauce
1 10-oz. pkg. frozen whole kernel corn

Cook chicken in large kettle until tender in water to cover; cool. Remove skin and bones; chop meat. Fry bacon until crisp; reserve drippings. Measure chicken broth; add water to make 1 quart, if necessary. Combine all ingredients except corn in large kettle. Simmer for 1 hour. Add corn; simmer for 30 minutes longer. Yield: 8 servings.

Mrs. Helen Godwin, Northwest H. S.
Greensboro, North Carolina

BRUNSWICK STEW

1 chicken, cut up
4 tbsp. flour
1/2 c. vegetable oil
1/2 c. chopped onion
3 c. canned tomatoes
1 c. water
1 1/2 tbsp. salt
1 tbsp. Worcestershire sauce
2 tsp. sugar
3 c. frozen corn
3 c. frozen lima beans

Shake chicken pieces in flour; saute in hot oil until brown. Add onion; cook until onion is transparent. Add tomatoes, water, seasonings and sugar. Simmer until almost tender. Add corn and limas. Cook until vegetables are tender. Serve hot. Yield: 8 servings.

Mrs. Virginia Johnson, Madelia H. S.
Madelia, Minnesota

CHICKEN-POTATO SOUP

2 potatoes
1/2 onion
1/2 stick margarine
4 tbsp. corn bread mix
1/2 lb. boiled chicken

Cut potatoes and onion into medium pieces. Place potatoes, onion and margarine in covered saucepan; cook until potatoes are done. Remove onion; add corn bread mix and chicken. Heat until thick. Serve hot. Yield: 5 servings.

Mrs. W. J. Tomlinson, Luxora H. S.
Luxora, Arkansas

CREOLE CHICKEN GUMBO

1 fryer or hen
Salt and pepper
Flour
Bacon grease
1 lge. dry onion
3 green onions, finely chopped
4 cloves of garlic
1/2 c. chopped celery
1 hot green pepper
1 green pepper, chopped
1 pt. cut okra
1/4 c. chopped parsley
1/2 tsp. thyme
2 or 3 bay leaves
1 to 2 qt. water

Dredge chicken in seasoned flour. Brown in a small amount of bacon grease. Remove from pan; slowly brown 3 tablespoonfuls flour in 1/2 cup pan drippings, stirring constantly. Add onions, garlic, celery and peppers. Cook for 10 minutes over low heat. Cook okra in a small amount of fat until dry. Add to onion mixture. Add seasonings, water and chicken. Simmer until well done. Yield: 12 servings.

Mrs. Norine R. Edwards, Kilbourne H. S.
Kilbourne, Louisiana

MOM'S HOMEMADE NOODLE SOUP

1/2 lb. chicken pieces
1/2 lb. boiling beef
1 med. onion, chopped
2 stalks celery, chopped
4 tsp. salt
1/2 tsp. pepper
Garlic to taste
Seasoning to taste
3 eggs
Flour

Combine chicken, beef, onion, celery, 1 tablespoonful salt, pepper and seasonings. Cover with cold water; simmer for 5 to 6 hours. Combine eggs, remaining salt and enough flour, about 3 cups, to make a stiff dough. Roll out to a thin sheet; flour lightly. Roll as for jelly roll. Slice into 1/4-inch slices. Drop into boiling soup broth. Cook for 30 minutes or until noodles are tender. Yield: 8 servings.

Mrs. George Raboin, Carney H. S.
Carney, Michigan

CLAM CHOWDER

2 tbsp. butter
2 med. onions, minced
2 c. water
2 med. potatoes, diced
2 tsp. salt
⅛ tsp. pepper
2 7-oz. cans minced clams
3 c. milk

Melt butter in large pan; add onions and cook until yellow. Add water, potatoes, salt and pepper. Bring to a boil. Add clams; simmer for 25 minutes. Add milk; heat to boiling, stirring occasionally. Yield: 8-10 servings.

Mrs. Martha Swingle, Crestview H. S.
Ashland, Ohio

CLAM CHOWDER

6 to 8 lge. clams
2 strips bacon
2 onions, chopped
2 qt. water
1 lge. can stewed tomatoes
2 carrots, diced
2 stalks celery, chopped
½ tsp. thyme
½ tsp. pepper
2 potatoes, diced

Shuck clams, reserving liquid. Fry bacon and onions in small skillet until soft; place in large pot with reserved clam liquid, water, tomatoes, carrots, celery, thyme and pepper. Cook over low heat until vegetables are tender. Dice clams and potatoes; add to chowder before other vegetables are tender. Yield: 8-10 servings.

Mrs. Evelyn Grabowski, Plant City H. S.
Plant City, Florida

CLAM CHOWDER

¼ lb. salt pork, diced
1 lge. onion, minced
3 c. boiling water
3 c. diced potatoes
⅛ tsp. pepper
2 No. 1 cans minced clams
3 c. milk, scalded

Fry salt pork and onion until lightly browned; add water, potatoes and pepper. Boil for 15 minutes or until potatoes are tender. Heat clam liquor and clams to boiling; add with milk to soup mixture. Bring to a boil. Serve hot with crackers. Yield: 6 servings.

Annette Braswell, Monroe Area H. S.
Monroe, Georgia

EASY CLAM CHOWDER

3 or 4 med. potatoes
1 lge. onion
1 sm. can clams
Evaporated milk
3 slices bacon
Salt and pepper to taste

Dice potatoes and onion into 1-inch cubes; add enough salted water to barely cover. Cook until tender. Pour off one-half of water. Mash vegetables with potato masher; add undrained clams and enough milk so that soup has a rather thick consistency. Fry bacon until crisp; crumble. Add bacon bits and fat to chowder. Salt and pepper to taste. Serve hot. Yield: 4 servings.

Helen E. Stanford, Union H. S.
Union, Oregon

OSCAR'S CLAM CHOWDER

1 bunch celery, chopped
1 bunch parsley, chopped
3 med. onions, diced
5 qt. beef stock
1 1-lb. 12-oz. can tomatoes
1 6-oz. can tomato paste
3 lb. potatoes, finely diced
1 bunch carrots, diced and cooked
1 lb. clams, finely chopped
2 tsp. salt
½ tsp. pepper
¼ tsp. nutmeg

Cook celery, parsley and onions in beef stock until tender; add tomatoes, tomato paste, potatoes and carrots. Cook until potatoes are tender. Add clams and seasonings. Simmer, do not boil, for 15 minutes. Serve piping hot. Yield: 5 quarts.

Ruth M. Hitchcock, Sterling H. S.
Somerdale, New Jersey

CRAB STEW

12 live crabs
5 bacon sliced
3 to 4 onions, chopped
1 green pepper, chopped
3 tbsp. cornstarch
2 tbsp. butter
Salt and pepper
1 tbsp. soy sauce

Place crabs in sink; run hot water over crabs to kill them. Clean; use claws and body in stew. Fry bacon in large cooker. Add onions and pepper; fry until onions are clear. Add cornstarch and enough water to thicken into a gravy; add butter. Place crabs in gravy; cook for 30 minutes. Add salt and pepper to taste. Add soy sauce. Yield: 5 servings.

B. J. Womack, Andrew Jackson H. S.
Jacksonville, Florida

OYSTER STEW

1 pt. oysters
Butter or margarine
1 c. cream or top milk
3 c. milk, scalded
Pepper to taste
½ tsp. salt
Dash of paprika

Cook oysters and 3 tablespoonfuls butter in oyster liquid until edges curl. Add cream and milk; heat to boiling. Season; sprinkle with pap-

(Continued on next page)

rika and 2 teaspoonfuls butter. Serve immediately. Yield: 4 servings.

Iona Ross, Freer H. S.
Freer, Texas

OYSTER STEW

1 qt. oysters
1 qt. rich milk
2 tbsp. butter
1 tbsp. minced parsley
Dash of onion salt or juice
Salt and pepper

Strain oyster liquid into saucepan. Heat, but do not boil. Heat milk in double boiler; stir in hot oyster liquid. Add butter, seasonings and oysters. Serve at once, when oysters puff and are crinkled at edges. Yield: 4-6 servings.

Mrs. Fay Taylor, Ingleside H. S.
Ingleside, Texas

SALMON BISQUE

¼ c. butter
⅓ c. finely chopped onion
⅓ c. finely chopped green pepper
½ c. finely chopped celery
3 to 4 tbsp. flour
1 tsp. salt
⅛ tsp. pepper
1 qt. milk
1 7 ¾-oz. can salmon, drained and broken into chunks
2 tbsp. chopped pimento

Melt butter in saucepan. Saute onion, green pepper and celery in butter until lightly browned. Add flour, salt and pepper, mixing to smooth paste. Cook over medium heat for about 1 minute. Remove from heat; add one-half of milk, stirring until blended. Return to heat. Stir constantly until mixture begins to thicken. Add remaining milk. Heat to simmering point; cook for about 5 minutes. Add salmon and pimento. Heat to serving temperature. Yield: 6 servings.

Mrs. Marlo Skurdal, Fisher H. S.
Fisher, Minnesota

SALMON SOUP

1 1-lb. can red salmon
4 tbsp. butter
4 tbsp. catsup
1 qt. milk
Salt and pepper to taste

Flake salmon into saucepan, removing any bones and skin. Add butter. Simmer, stirring occasionally, for 2 or 3 minutes. Stir in catsup and milk. Heat over low to medium heat until hot; do not boil. Salt and pepper to taste. Yield: 3-4 servings.

Mrs. Jacquette K. Robinson, Glenwood H. S.
Glenwood, North Carolina

SHRIMP GUMBO

1 lge. onion, chopped
1 lge. green pepper, chopped
1 lb. fresh okra, chopped
3 cloves of garlic, chopped
1 c. chopped celery
Cooking oil
1 tbsp. (heaping) flour
1 tbsp. sugar
Salt and pepper to taste
2 qt. cold water
1 ½ lb. peeled deveined shrimp

Saute onion, pepper, okra, garlic and celery in oil; remove from pan. Stir in flour, sugar, salt and pepper into pan; cook until dark brown. Add to sauted ingredients and place in large pot. Add cold water and shrimp. Bring to a boil; simmer for 45 minutes to 1 hour. Serve over rice.

Mrs. Becky Edens, Humble H. S.
Humble, Texas

SHRIMP STEW

6 slices salt butts
2 c. peeled cooked or raw shrimp
2 tbsp. flour
Salt and pepper to taste
½ c. catsup

Fry butts; remove from pan. Chip butts. Heat shrimp in grease from butts; add flour and stir well. Add water to cover, chipped butts, salt, pepper and catsup. Stir constantly, until thickened. Simmer until flavors are blended. Yield: 4 servings.

Mrs. Edith L. Barker, Allendale-Fairfax H. S.
Farifax, South Carolina

FISHERMAN'S CHOWDER

1 7-oz. can tuna
1 lge. onion, chopped
2 lge. potatoes, pared and thinly sliced
3 c. water
1 tsp. salt
¼ tsp. oregano
1 can tomato soup
1 tbsp. chopped parsley

Drain oil from tuna; measure 2 teaspoonfuls oil into a large heavy saucepan. Add onion; saute until soft. Stir in potatoes, water, salt and oregano. Cover; cook for 15 minutes or until potatoes are tender. Stir in tomato soup. Flake tuna; add to mixture. Simmer for 5 minutes to blend flavors. Ladle into heated soup cups; sprinkle with parsley. Yield: 6 servings.

J. Marilyn Boyd, Hantsport H. S.
Hantsport, Nova Scotia, Canada

BRUNSWICK STEW

3 squirrel, cut into serving pieces
3 qt. water
¼ c. diced bacon
¼ tsp. cayenne pepper

(Continued on next page)

2 tsp. salt
¼ tsp. black pepper
1 c. chopped onions
4 c. tomatoes
2 c. diced potatoes
2 c. lima beans
2 c. corn

Place squirrel pieces in large kettle; add water. Bring slowly to a boil; reduce heat and simmer for 1 hour and 30 minutes to 2 hours or until squirrel are tender, skimming surface occasionally. Remove meat from bones; return meat to liquid. Add remaining ingredients except corn. Cook for 1 hour. Add corn. Cook for 10 mintues longer. Yield: 6-8 servings.

Mrs. Erlene Dunn, Harper H. S.
Harper, Texas

BURR'S FISH CHOWDER

2 lb. sea bass, cut into large cubes
2 qt. water
1 qt. potato cubes
¼ lb. salt pork, cut into small cubes
2 med. onions
3 to 4 tbsp. flour
1 c. strained tomatoes
Salt and pepper to taste
Cayenne pepper to taste
Dash of Tabasco sauce
Chopped parsley

Wash fish carefully; cover with 1 quart water. Cook until tender; drain, reserving water. Cook potatoes in remaining water; drain, reserving water. Fry salt pork and onions until slightly browned; cover and cook for 10 minutes. Add flour and blend. Slowly add fish water and potato water; bring to a boil. Add tomatoes, fish cubes and potatoes; combine carefully. Season to taste with salt, pepper, cayenne and Tabasco sauce. Serve with parsley. Yield: 8 servings.

Mrs. Doris Burr, Sunset H. S.
Hayward, California

LIVER DUMPLING SOUP

¼ lb. calves liver
⅓ c. fine dry crumbs
2 tbsp. flour
1 tsp. soft butter
½ tsp. grated onion
1 tsp. finely chopped parsley
2 eggs, separated
½ tsp. salt
Dash of nutmeg
1 qt. chicken or beef broth
Fresh parsley

Have butcher put liver through fine grinder twice. Place liver in bowl; stir in crumbs mixed with flour. Let stand for 10 minutes. Add butter, onion, chopped parsley, egg yolks, salt and nutmeg; mix well. Beat egg whites until stiff; carefully fold into meat mixture. Form into balls the size of walnuts. Drop into gently boiling broth. Cover and simmer for 15 minutes. Serve in hot soup bowls; garnish with cut fresh parsley. Yield: 4 servings.

Louise M. Hasbrook, Lincoln Central H. S.
Gruver, Iowa

QUICK MINESTRONE

1 lb. fish fillets, cut into ½-in. pieces
2 10 ¼ or 10 ¾-oz. cans minestrone soup
1 ⅓ c. water
1 8-oz. can tomato sauce
½ tsp. salt
¼ tsp. basil
¼ tsp. oregano
Dash of pepper
Chopped parsley

Combine all ingredients except parsley. Cover; simmer for 10 to 15 minutes or until fish flakes easily when tested with a fork. Garnish with parsley. Yield: 6 servings.

Mrs. Kay Lamb Rushin, Greenville H. S.
Greenville, Mississippi

SEAFOOD GUMBO

1 6-in. slice salt pork
½ can or ½ pkg. okra, sliced
1 onion, chopped
2 tbsp. flour
1 pt. canned tomatoes
1 doz. oysters and liquor
1 ½ qt. boiling water
2 sprigs parsley
1 tsp. salt
1 bay leaf
½ tsp. garlic salt
Dash of black pepper
Dash of cayenne pepper
6 crabs or 1 can crab meat
1 lb. shrimp
1 tbsp. file

Fry salt pork in skillet until crisp. Remove meat; cut into bits. Saute okra in fat. Add chopped onion; fry until tender, stirring constantly. Push vegetables to side of skillet; brown flour. Mix onion and okra into flour; slowly add tomatoes, oyster liquor and boiling water. Add seasonings; stir until smooth. Simmer for 1 hour. Add salt pork, crab meat and shrimp; simmer for a few minutes longer. Add oysters 15 minutes before serving; do not boil. Two minutes before serving, add file. Yield: 6 servings.

Annie G. Childress, Mangham H. S.
Mangham, Louisiana

TURTLE SOUP

1 frozen turtle, cleaned and cut up
3 qt. water
1 tbsp. salt
⅛ tsp. pepper
1 ½ tsp. poultry seasoning
½ tsp. dried parsley flakes
½ bay leaf
½ tsp. celery seed

(Continued on next page)

¼ tsp. paprika
1 tbsp. whole pickling spice bag
3 med. potatoes, diced
2 lge. carrots, diced
1 lge. onion, diced
1 green pepper, diced
1 c. diced celery
1 ½ c. fine noodles, uncooked
1 lge. can mixed vegetables
1 c. tomato juice

Place turtle and water in 6-quart kettle; bring to a boil. Simmer for 3 hours or until tender. When done, lift turtle from broth. Cool slightly; bone. Cut meat into bite-sized pieces. Return meat to broth; add seasonings. Add fresh vegetables; cook for 20 minutes. Add dry noodles; cook for 15 minutes longer or until tender. Add canned vegetables and tomato juice; add more water, if necessary. Remove spice bag before serving. Yield: 8-10 servings.

Mrs. Lois E. Weber, South Central School
Elizabeth, Indiana

BRUNSWICK STEW

7 hens
5 lb. ground pork or unseasoned sausage
7 ½ lb. hamburger
10 lb. potatoes
5 lb. onions
1 gal. cream-style corn
1 gal. lima beans
3 gal. catsup
½ sm. can black pepper
½ sm. can red pepper
2 bottles hot sauce
2 bottles Worcestershire sauce
½ c. vinegar or juice of 6 lemons
Salt to taste

Cook hens; reserve 2 gallons stock. Remove chicken from bones. Grind meats. Grind potatoes, onions, corn and beans. Place reserved stock in a large container or pressure cooker; heat. Add meats; cook for 30 minutes, stirring constantly. Add vegetables and all remaining ingredients; cook until potatoes are done. Yield: 10 gallons.

Mildred Morris, Reeltown H. S.
Notasulga, Alabama

BRUNSWICK STEW

1 lb. sliced fatback
1 lge. hen
2 lb. hamburger
½ c. bacon grease
2 hot green peppers
3 ½ qt. lima beans
1 lge. green cabbage, cut up
4 lge. onions, sliced
½ gal. sliced potatoes
1 ½ doz. ears corn, cut
1 peck peeled tomatoes

Fry fat; add remaining ingredients and enough water to keep from sticking. Cook slowly until meat falls off bones; cook until thick. Remove bones before serving. Yield: 25 servings.

Mrs. Ialeen S. Mode, Franklinton H. S.
Franklinton, North Carolina

HUNTERS STEW

½ lb. salt pork, cubed
½ lb. salami, sliced and cut into ½-in. strips
1 3 to 4-lb. broiler-fryer, cut up
4 carrots, pared
2 leeks or green onions, sliced ½-in. thick
4 sprigs parsley
2 whole cloves
1 bay leaf
¼ tsp. crushed thyme
1 tbsp. salt
½ tsp. pepper
3 beef bouillon cubes
3 c. hot water
1 c. dry white wine
2 10-oz. pkg. frozen California Brussels sprouts
¼ c. flour
¾ c. water

Brown pork and salami in Dutch oven or large saucepan; remove from pan. Brown chicken in the hot drippings; drain off drippings. Return pork and salami to pan. Stir in carrots, leeks, parsley, seasonings, bouillon cubes, hot water and wine. Cover and simmer for 45 minutes or until chicken and vegetables are tender. Add Brussels sprouts. Cover and cook for 10 to 12 minutes longer or until Brussels sprouts are just tender. Blend flour and the 3/4 cup water; stir into stew. Stir over medium heat until slightly thickened. Yield: 6-8 servings.

Photograph for this recipe on page 333.

MEAT SOUP

½ lb. ground lamb
½ lb. ground pork
1 lge. onion, minced
½ tsp. salt
Dash of black pepper
Dash of red pepper
Pinch of nutmeg
2 eggs
Flour
6 c. beef stock
½ c. toasted bread crumbs
2 tbsp. tomato sauce
2 tbsp. chopped parsley

Combine meats, onion, seasonings and eggs; form into small balls. Roll balls in flour; brown in butter. Heat stock; add crumbs, tomato sauce, parsley and meat balls. Simmer for 15 minutes. Yield: 6 servings.

Mrs. Esther M. Hight, Weare, H. S.
Weare, New Hampshire

Outdoor Favorites

CAMPFIRE KITCHEN

½ c. ground beef
2 slices onion
Salt and pepper to taste
1 slice green pepper
½ stalk celery, chopped
¼ c. chopped cabbage
½ med. carrot, grated
1 med. potato, sliced ¼-in. thick
2 tbsp. undiluted cream soup
1 tbsp. water

Shape meat into pattie. Tear two 12-inch square pieces of aluminum foil. Place onion on foil. Add ground beef pattie. Season. Add green pepper, celery and cabbage. Top with carrot and potato. Add soup and water. Wrap tightly. Grill for 1 hour or until done or bake at 350 degrees for 1 hour. Yield: 1 serving.

Marilyn O. Zakariasen, Drumheller H. S.
Drumheller, Alberta, Canada

COFFEE CAN STEW

2 potatoes, diced
1 stalk celery, diced
1 onion, diced
1 carrot, diced
3 tbsp. peas
½ lb. hamburger
3 tbsp. water or pea juice

Combine potatoes, celery, onion, carrot and peas in a 1-pound coffee can. Form hamburger into small balls; place on top of vegetable mixture. Pour water or pea juice into can. Cook in hot coals for 30 to 45 minutes or until done. Yield: 2 servings.

Mrs. Paula Chandler, Westmer H. S.
Joy, Illinois

DELUXE BARBI-BURGERS

2 slices bread
2 lb. ground beef
1 lge. onion, chopped
½ c. chopped green pepper
1 egg
½ c. chili sauce
2 tsp. salt
¼ tsp. pepper
8 hamburger buns, buttered
Garlic salt

Soak bread in water. Squeeze dry; crumble. Combine all ingredients except buns and garlic salt. Shape into eight patties. Broil over charcoal or in oven 6 inches from heat for 5 to 8 minutes on each side. Place on toasted buns seasoned with garlic salt. Top with coleslaw and radish slices, if desired. Yield: 8 servings.

Mrs. Mary Lu Busch, J. E. Murphy H. S.
Hurley, Wisconsin

DILLS BURGER MIX

1 envelope dry onion soup mix
1 lb. lean ground beef
2 eggs

Combine all ingredients; shape into patties 3 inches in diameter. Grill until done or pan-broil. Yield: 4-6 servings.

Mrs. Willa Mae Scroggs, Sylva-Webster H. S.
Sylva, North Carolina

FLANKBURGER

1 flank steak
½ dill pickle
1 egg, beaten
¼ c. cracker crumbs
¼ tsp. liquid smoke
½ tsp. salt

Grind flank steak and dill pickle. Add egg, crumbs and seasonings. Form into four patties; roll in additional cracker crumbs. Broil over hot coals, turning only once. Yield: 4 servings.

Lucy S. Plank, Wheeler H. S.
Fossil, Oregon

GRILLED HAMBURGERS

1 ½ lb. hamburger
1 egg
½ tsp. seasoned salt
½ tsp. salt
½ c. bread crumbs
1 c. grated Cheddar cheese
6 tbsp. catsup

Combine all ingredients except cheese and catsup. Shape into 12 thin patties. Spread catsup on six patties. Sprinkle cheese on remaining patties. Place catsup and cheese sides together. Freeze until coals are hot. Place on greased grill; cook to desired doneness. Yield: 6 servings.

Ellaine B. Scott, DeKalb H. S.
DeKalb, Mississippi

HAMBURGER FILLETS IN SAVORY SAUCE

1 lb. ground beef
½ tsp. salt
¼ tsp. pepper
6 slices bacon
3 tbsp. salad oil
2 tbsp. catsup
1 tbsp. prepared mustard
1 tbsp. Worcestershire sauce
1 tsp. vinegar
Few drops of Tabasco sauce
1 tsp. sugar
1 clove of garlic, chopped

Combine ground beef, salt and pepper. Form into patties; wrap with bacon. Secure with toothpicks. Broil 3 inches from white coals for 6 to 8 minutes; turn. Combine remaining ingredients; sim-

(Continued on next page)

mer for 5 minutes. Spread over patties. Broil for 6 to 8 minutes. Yield: 6 servings.

Mrs. Joanne Odell, Rule H. S.
Knoxville, Tennessee

HAMBURGER IN FOIL

1 lb. hamburger
Salt and pepper
¼ c. chili sauce
1 sm. eggplant, sliced
1 lge. onion, sliced
1 lge. potato, sliced
2 tomatoes, halved crosswise
2 green peppers, cut into halves and seeded

Divide hamburger into four parts. Shape into four thin patties. Place each pattie in center of 10-inch square of foil. Sprinkle with salt and pepper. Sprinkle each with 1 tablespoonful chili sauce. Cover with slices of eggplant, onion, potato, tomato half and green pepper half. Sprinkle again with salt and pepper. Wrap foil securely around hamburger. Roast over hot coals until tender or bake in preheated 375 degree oven for 2 hours. Serve in foil wrappers. Yield: 4 servings.

Mrs. Arthur Ray, Lewis Co. H. S.
Hohenwald, Tennessee

MEXICALI MEAT PIE

6 slices bacon
1 lb. ground beef
1 c. drained whole kernel corn
¼ c. finely chopped green pepper
¼ c. finely chopped onion
¼ c. plus 2 tbsp. corn meal
Oregano
½ tsp. chili powder
1 tsp. salt
⅛ tsp. pepper
1 8-oz. can tomato sauce
1 c. flour
3 to 4 tbsp. cold water
1 egg
¼ c. milk
½ tsp. dry mustard
½ tsp. Worcestershire sauce
1 ½ c. shredded Cheddar cheese
4 stuffed olives, sliced

Fry bacon until crisp; break into large pieces. Chill 1/3 cup drippings until firm. Brown meat in large skillet; drain. Stir in corn, green pepper, onion, 1/4 cup corn meal, 1/2 teaspoonful oregano, chili powder, 1/2 teaspoonful salt, pepper and tomato sauce. Combine flour, 1/8 teaspoonful oregano and 2 tablespoonfuls corn meal. Cut in chilled drippings or shortening until mixture resembles small peas. Sprinkle with cold water, stirring with fork until dough clings together. Form into a ball; flatten to 1/2-inch thick. Smooth edge; roll out on floured surface to circle 1 1/2 inches larger than inverted 9-inch pie pan. Fit into pan. Fold edge to form a standing rim; flute. Fill with meat mixture. Bake at 425 degrees for 25 minutes. Combine egg, milk, remaining salt, mustard, Worcestershire sauce and cheese. Spread on pie; top with bacon and olives. Bake for 5 minutes or until cheese melts. Let stand for 10 minutes before serving. If desired, serve with a tomato sauce. Yield: 6 servings.

Mrs. Mary Ann McColpin, Eisenhower Jr. H. S.
San Antonio, Texas

STEAMED HAMBURGER PILLOWS

½ tsp. salt
Pepper to taste
1 lb. hamburger
4 lge. slices onion

Season meat; shape into four patties. Place patties in center of 12-inch piece of foil; top with onion slice. Wrap securely until meat is airtight. Place on hot grill or over open fire. Cook until done. Yield: 4 servings.

Mrs. Mildred P. Adams, Union H. S.
Benwood, West Virginia

ROYAL BEEF RIBS

2 tbsp. instant minced onion
1 tbsp. brown sugar
1 tsp. monosodium glutamate
1 tbsp. whole mustard seed
2 tsp. paprika
1 tsp. crushed oregano
1 tsp. chili powder
1 tsp. cracked peppercorns
½ tsp. salt
½ tsp. ground cloves
1 bay leaf
1 clove of garlic, minced
1 c. catsup
½ c. water
¼ c. olive or salad oil
¼ c. tarragon vinegar
2 tbsp. wine vinegar
2 tbsp. Worcestershire sauce
2 or 3 drops of liquid smoke
4 to 5 lb. ribs

Combine all ingredients except ribs; stir well. Heat to boiling; simmer gently for 20 to 25 minutes, stirring occasionally. Remove bay leaf. Sprinkle ribs with additional salt; place, bone-side down, on grill away from coals. Add dampened hickory chips to fire carefully. Cook for 3 hours and 30 minutes, basting with sauce the last 30 minutes.

Mrs. Marshall Daniel, Talbot Co. H. S.
Talbotton, Georgia

BARBECUED CHUCK ROAST

½ c. salad oil
½ c. pineapple juice
Juice of 1 lemon
1 tbsp. soy sauce
2 tbsp. Worcestershire sauce
2 cloves of garlic, crushed
¼ tsp. dry mustard
1 4 to 5-lb. 7-bone or round bone chuck roast, 2 to 2 ½-in. thick

(Continued on next page)

Combine oil, pineapple juice, lemon juice, soy sauce, Worcestershire sauce, garlic and mustard; stir well. Pour mixture over roast; cover. Place in refrigerator for 12 to 24 hours; turn occasionally. Let roast stand at room temperature for about 1 hour before placing on grill. When coals are hot, place roast on grill. Cook slowly for 20 to 25 minutes on each side. Brush frequently with remaining marinade. Yield: 5-6 servings.

Susan Holbrook, Blackford H. S.
San Jose, California

BARBECUED CHUCK ROAST

1 chuck roast, 2 ½ to 3-in. thick
½ c. cooking oil
½ c. white vinegar
½ c. catsup
1 tsp. salt
1 tsp. pepper
1 clove of garlic

Punch holes with fork in roast on both sides. Place roast in a large glass enameled pan. Combine all remaining ingredients. Cover roast with sauce; refrigerate for about 12 hours. Pour off excess sauce; reserve sauce for basting. Cook over charcoal, basting occasionally, for 30 minutes on each side. Yield: 5-6 servings.

Mary Lee McComb, Hardee Co. H. S.
Wauchula, Florida

BARBECUED CHUCK ROAST

1 3-lb. chuck roast, 3-in. thick
4 cloves of garlic, minced
4 tbsp. oil
½ tsp. dry mustard
2 tsp. soy sauce
1 tsp. rosemary, crushed
4 tbsp. wine vinegar
½ c. Sauterne or Sherry wine
4 tbsp. catsup
1 tsp. Worcestershire sauce
1 tbsp. steak sauce

Place roast in a crockery bowl. Saute garlic, oil and mustard; add soy sauce and rosemary. Remove from heat; stir in vinegar and wine. Pour mixture over meat. Marinate meat in sauce for 48 hours, turning frequently. Remove meat; place over hot coals. Add catsup, Worcestershire sauce and steak sauce to marinade. Baste meat while cooking. Yield: 8-10 servings.

Sue Filler, Oregon City H. S.
Oregon City, Oregon

BARBECUED POT ROAST

1 4-lb. chuck roast
3 tbsp. flour
1 tsp. brown sugar
1 tsp. salt
½ tsp. dry mustard
¾ c. catsup
2 tbsp. Worcestershire sauce
1 tbsp. vinegar
2 stalks celery, sliced
2 carrots, sliced
1 med. onion, chopped

Brown roast over charcoal. Combine all remaining ingredients. Place part of sauce on piece of heavy foil; place meat on top. Cover with remaining sauce. Seal foil. Bake over hot coals for about 2 hours. Yield: 8-10 servings.

Mildred Christensen, Boscobel H. S.
Boscobel, Wisconsin

BARBECUED ROLLED BEEF ROAST

1 4-lb. rolled chuck, round or rump roast
½ c. chopped onion
½ c. lemon juice
¼ c. salad oil
2 cloves of garlic, minced
2 tsp. prepared mustard
1 tsp. rosemary
½ tsp. salt
½ tsp. pepper

Wipe meat with a damp cloth. Place in large bowl or pan. Combine remaining ingredients; pour over meat. Refrigerate for 24 hours, turning occasionally. Remove from refrigerator 1 to 2 hours before grilling. Grill on rotisserie for 1 hour and 30 minutes to 2 hours, basting often with marinade. Yield: 8 servings.

Naomi Haumont, Bridgeport H. S.
Bridgeport, Nebraska

CHUCK STEAK MARINATE

1 2 ½-lb. chuck roast, 2-in. thick
Meat tenderizer
1 5-oz. bottle soy sauce
¼ c. brown sugar
1 tbsp. lemon juice
¼ c. bourbon
1 tsp. Worcestershire sauce
1 ½ c. water

Sprinkle meat with tenderizer. Let stand. Combine remaining ingredients in 12 x 8 x 2-inch pan. Place roast in marinade; refrigerate for 6 hours, turning once. Grill roast 5-inches from coals for 1 hour, turning 3 times and basting frequently with marinade. Yield: 4 servings.

Patricia A. Jenkins, Leigh H. S.
San Jose, California

GRILLED POT ROAST

1 3 to 5-lb. chuck or round roast, 1 to 2-in thick
Meat tenderizer
6 carrots
6 potatoes
2 med. onions, sliced
1 lge. can mushrooms
¼ c. tomato juice

(Continued on next page)

Sprinkle meat with meat tenderizer; sear over charcoal fire. Season to taste. Place meat on large sheet of aluminum foil; add all remaining ingredients. Seal foil; cook over charcoal until meat is tender. Yield: 6 servings.

Marilou Carlson, Ross Twp. H. S.
Merrillville, Indiana

MARINATED STEAK

1 4 to 5-lb. chuck or sirloin steak, 2-in. thick
1 tsp. garlic salt
1 tsp. unseasoned meat tenderizer
½ c. soy sauce
½ c. water
3 tbsp. wine vinegar
1 tbsp. sugar

Rub meat with garlic salt and meat tenderizer. Pierce meat deeply with fork; let stand for 30 minutes. Combine soy sauce, water, wine vinegar and sugar. Marinate meat in sauce for 4 hours, turning every 30 minutes. Grill over hot coals until of desired doneness. Yield: 8 servings.

Mrs. Eleanor Pritts, Mt. Auburn H. S.
Mt. Auburn, Illinois

GRILLED FLANK STEAK

3 lb. flank steak
Meat tenderizer
Monosodium glutamate
½ c. minced onion
1 c. salad oil
1 c. lemon juice
1 c. red wine vinegar

Sprinkle steak with tenderizer and monosodium glutamate; place in a deep dish or pan. Cover with minced onion; add salad oil, lemon juice and red wine vinegar. Refrigerate for at least 24 hours. Grill slowly for about 10 to 15 minutes per side 2 inches from coals. Cook until done. Yield: 4-6 servings.

Mrs. Don Jackson, Bad Axe H. S.
Bad Axe, Michigan

TERIYAKI BARBECUE

¾ c. vegetable oil
¼ c. soy sauce
¼ c. honey
2 tbsp. vinegar
2 tbsp. chopped onion
1 lge. clove of garlic, minced
1 ½ tsp. ground ginger
1 1 ½-lb. flank steak

Combine oil, soy sauce, honey, vinegar, onion, garlic and ginger. Pour over flank steak. Marinate for 4 hours or longer, turning occasionally. Cook over hot coals for 5 minutes, turning once, until done. Baste occasionally with marinade. Carve into thin slices, cutting on the diagonal from top to bottom of steak. Yield: 4 servings.

Mrs. Jeanette List, Brookpark Jr. H. S.
Grove City, Ohio

BARBECUED FAMILY STEAK

1 round chuck or rump steak, 2-in. thick
Seasoned meat tenderizer
¼ c. minced onion
2 tbsp. oil
8 oz. tomato sauce
1 tbsp. Worcestershire sauce
1 tbsp. brown sugar
½ tsp. oregano
¼ tsp. rosemary
2 drops of Tabasco sauce

Pierce meat with fork; sprinkle with meat tenderizer. Combine all remaining ingredients; simmer for 30 minutes. Cook meat on grill, 2 to 3 inches from coals for 15 to 30 minutes; baste with sauce during last 15 minutes of cooking. Slice meat diagonally; serve with remaining sauce. Yield: 8 servings.

Mrs. Keith Doelker, Manchester H. S.
Manchester, Michigan

BUDGETEER STEAK

4 lb. or 2 round bone shoulder steaks, 1-in. thick
10 sm. cloves of garlic, peeled
Seasoned salt
Pepper
½ c. salad oil
½ c. wine vinegar
1 tbsp. Worcestershire sauce
½ c. chopped celery (opt.)
½ c. chopped onion (opt.)
½ c. chopped green pepper (opt.)

Dot each steak with 5 cloves of garlic. Insert tip of knife in meat; push in garlic clove as knife is removed. Sprinkle steaks generously with seasoned salt and pepper. Combine oil, vinegar and Worcestershire sauce; pour over steak in shallow dish. Refrigerate overnight or let stand for several hours at room temperature, turning occasionally. Grill over hot coals for 15 minutes on each side or until done, basting frequently with marinade. If desired, heat remaining marinade with celery, onion and green pepper; serve with steak. Yield: 12 servings.

Mrs. Norman G. Miller, Petoskey H. S.
Petoskey, Michigan

SAVORY GRILLED STEAK

1 med. round steak, chuck steak or London broil
½ c. wine vinegar
1 tbsp. Worcestershire sauce
1 tsp. monosodium glutamate
1 tsp. seasoned salt
½ tsp. seasoned pepper
1 tsp. brown sugar

(Continued on next page)

Place steak in flat pan; puncture top of steak with tines of fork. Mix remaining ingredients thoroughly; poor one-half of mixture over punctured steak. Let stand for 5 minutes; turn. Puncture turned side; cover with remaining mixture. Let stand for 10 to 15 minutes. Place steak on grill. Cook to desired doneness, turning once. NOTE: Steak may be broiled inside, but part of the flavor is due to the charcoal.

Georgia A. Potterton, Eastern Jr. H. S.
Riverside, Connecticut

TERIYAKI STEAK

½ c. soy sauce
¼ c. brown sugar
1 tsp. dry ginger
2 tbsp. olive oil
½ tsp. monosodium glutamate
2 cloves of garlic, minced
½ c. orange juice
1 ½ lb. top sirloin steak

Combine all ingredients except steak. Mix well. Cut steak into 1 x 1/2-inch pieces. Add to sauce; stir to coat. Let stand for 3 hours. Thread on skewers. Broil over hot coals for 10 to 12 minutes, turning frequently. Baste with marinade. Yield: 5-6 servings.

Sandra Gill, Bruce H. S.
Bruce, Wisconsin

SOUR CREAM STEAK

Salt and pepper to taste
4 T-bone steaks, 1 ½-in. thick
½ c. sour cream

Salt and pepper both sides of steaks; spread each side of steaks with 1 tablespoonful sour cream. Let stand for 2 hours. Charcoal or broil to desired doneness. Yield: 4 servings.

Audrey Rose Johnson, Kickapoo H. S.
Viola, Wisconsin

BEEF KABOBS

¼ c. soy sauce
¾ c. Sherry wine
½ c. salad oil
¾ tsp. powdered ginger
1 tsp. garlic powder
2 tbsp. minced onion
Salt to taste
½ tsp. coarsley ground black pepper
2 lb. stew meat
4 tomatoes, quartered
1 sm. can mushroom caps
Small onions (opt.)
Parboiled potato chunks (opt.)

Combine soy sauce, Sherry, oil, ginger, garlic, onion, salt and pepper. Marinate beef in sauce for 2 hours or longer. Alternate beef with remaining ingredients on skewers. Grill for 15 to 20 minutes or broil for 10 to 15 minutes, brushing with marinade. Serve with rice, if desired. Yield: 4-6 servings.

Marjorie Sellers, Kingsburg H. S.
Kingsburg, California

SHISH KABOBS

1 ½ lb. round steak, cut into 1-in. cubes
1 sm. onion, thinly sliced
1 ½ tsp. salt
¼ tsp. ground pepper
½ tsp. oregano
2 green peppers, cut into 1-in. pieces
1 lge. onion, cut into 1-in. pieces
2 firm tomatoes, cut into 1-in. pieces
Cooking oil

Place steak in a bowl; tuck in small onion slices. Add seasonings. Refrigerate for 1 to 2 hours. Alternate meat cubes, pieces of pepper, large onion pieces and tomato on metal skewers; roll in cooking oil. Broil 3 inches from heat for 15 to 20 minutes. Turn as meat and vegetables brown. Yield: 6 servings.

Mrs. Esther P. Leeds, Piscataquis Comm. H. S.
Guilford, Maine

STEAK KABOBS

2 lb. round steak, 1 ½-in. thick
Meat tenderizer
12 cherry tomatoes
1 4-oz. can mushroom caps, drained
1 green pepper, cut into 1 ½-in. strips
1 1-lb. can boiled onions
½ c. dry white wine
½ c. catsup
1 tbsp. prepared mustard
1 tbsp. Worcestershire sauce
1 clove of garlic, minced
½ tsp. whole rosemary
2 tbsp. brown sugar
2 tbsp. vinegar

Cut meat into 1 1/2-inch cubes; sprinkle with meat tenderizer as directed on bottle. Alternate meat cubes, tomatoes, mushrooms, green pepper and onions on skewers. Combine all remaining ingredients in a jar; shake well to blend. Brush wine sauce over kabobs. Place on grill; broil for 8 to 10 minutes, turning frequently. Heat remaining sauce; serve with kabobs. Yield: 4-6 servings.

Geraldine Luepke, Baldwin-Woodville H. S.
Baldwin, Wisconsin

TERIYAKI

2 tsp. meat tenderizer
1 2-lb. chuck roast, cut into 2-in. cubes
1 clove of garlic
1 tbsp. brown sugar
½ tsp. ground ginger
¼ c. soy sauce
½ tsp. pepper
1 tbsp. cooking oil
2 tbsp. water

(Continued on next page)

Sprinkle tenderizer on each side of roast; let set for 3 hours. Pierce deeply with fork. Set aside at room temperature for 1 hour. Mash garlic and brown sugar to fine pulp; mix with all remaining ingredients in a shallow dish. Marinate meat for 1 hour and 30 minutes to 2 hours, turning occasionally. Grill for about 12 to 15 minutes on each side. Yield: 4-6 servings.

Mrs. Margaret Foil, Pana Jr. H. S.
Pana, Illinois

BARBECUED FILLETS

1 lge. fish fillet
Barbecue sauce
Salt and pepper to taste

Brush fillet generously with barbecue sauce; sprinkle with salt and pepper. Wrap fillet in heavy aluminum foil, using drug store wrap. Place package over hot charcoal fire for 30 minutes, turning frequently. Yield: 1 serving.

Jacqueline Pell Tuttle, Tuckahoe Public School
Southampton, New York

BARBECUED FISH

2 3 to 4-lb. fresh bass or catfish
8 to 10 strips bacon
1 c. bottled barbecue sauce
1 tbsp. finely diced onion
Juice of 1 lemon
Dash of Worcestershire sauce
Dash of Tabasco sauce
Catsup (opt.)

Cut fish crosswise into 1 1/2-inch steaks; wrap each steak with strip of bacon. Tie securely with twine. Place steaks on grill. Combine all remaining ingredients. Baste steaks with mixture, turning occasionally. Grill until done. Yield: 6-8 servings.

Mrs. LaVell Winn, San Marcos H. S.
San Marcos, Texas

CHARCOAL-BROILED SALMON

½ c. melted butter
Juice of 1 lemon
1 clove of garlic, finely chopped
1 5 to 6-lb. salmon
Salt and pepper
1 med. onion, sliced

Combine butter, lemon juice and garlic in saucepan. Clean salmon, removing head and tail. Season inside and out with salt and pepper. Place sliced onion in cavity of fish. Cook over charcoal for 25 to 30 minutes on each side or until salmon flakes easily, basting frequently. Yield: 8-10 servings.

Mattie Finney, Vashon H. S.
Burton, Washington

CHARCOAL-GRILLED RED SNAPPER STEAKS

1 lb. fresh or frozen red snapper steaks or other fish steaks
½ c. melted fat or oil
¼ c. lemon juice
2 tsp. salt
½ tsp. Worcestershire sauce
¼ tsp. white pepper
Dash of liquid hot pepper sauce
Paprika

Thaw frozen steaks. Cut into serving portions; place in well greased, hinged wire grills. Combine remaining ingredients except paprika. Baste fish with sauce; sprinkle with paprika. Cook 4 inches from moderately hot coals for 8 minutes. Baste with sauce and sprinkle with paprika. Turn and cook for 7 to 10 minutes longer or until fish flakes easily when tested with fork. Yield: 6 servings.

Mrs. Molly Fawcett, Katherine Tarver School
Laredo, Texas

BANQUET FRANKS

1 doz. frankfurters
2 c. cracker crumbs
½ c. chopped celery
⅓ c. evaporated milk
¼ tsp. pepper
¼ c. chopped onion
1 tbsp. melted butter
½ tsp. salt
¼ tsp. pepper
¼ c. chopped pimento
¼ c. chopped parsley
1 tbsp. sugar

Split frankfurters lengthwise on one side. Combine remaining ingredients; stuff franks. Wrap in foil. Cook on grill until done. NOTE: May be baked in baking dish, covered, at 350 degrees for 15 minutes. Uncover for 15 minutes. Yield: 6 servings.

Mrs. Doris Arlene Seal Bradley, Kelso H. S.
Kelso, Washington

BARBECUED LEG OF LAMB

½ c. cider vinegar
½ c. apple-mint jelly
1 tbsp. butter or margarine
¼ c. brown sugar
1 tbsp. lemon juice
1 tsp. grated lemon peel
¼ c. white sugar
½ tsp. salt
½ tsp. dry mustard
1 4 to 5-lb. leg of lamb, boned and rolled

Combine vinegar, jelly, margarine, brown sugar, lemon juice and peel in small saucepan. Cook over low heat, stirring frequently, until dissolved. Mix white sugar, salt and mustard; stir into hot mixture. Bring to boil. Remove from heat; cool. Pour cooled sauce over lamb; marinate for about 30 minutes, turning occasionally. Place lamb on spit; cook over hot coals for 1

(Continued on next page)

hour and 30 minutes to 2 hours. Baste with sauce during cooking time. Yield: 6 servings.

Mary A. Buckely, Nort Andover H. S.
North Andover, Massachusetts

HOLLYWOOD LAMB FILET EN BROCHETTE

¾ c. salad oil
½ c. cider vinegar
¼ c. water
¼ c. (firmly packed) dark brown sugar
1 bay leaf
1 tsp. garlic salt
¼ tsp. pepper
6 Hollywood lamb fillets, 1 ½ to 2-in. thick
1 sm. cantaloupe, cut into wedges
2 med. green peppers, cut each into 6 pieces
½ lb. lge. mushrooms

Mix oil, vinegar, water, sugar and seasonings; pour over lamb. Marinate for several hours, turning occasionally. Place lamb on skewers; grill 5 to 6 inches from heat for 10 to 12 minutes per side or until of desired doneness, brushing frequently with marinade. Place cantaloupe and vegetables on skewers; grill for 5 minutes per side, brushing frequently with marinade. Yield: 6 servings.

Photograph for this recipe on back cover.

LAMB CHOPS WATERCRESS BUTTER

6 tbsp. butter or margarine, softened
¼ c. chopped watercress
¼ tsp. marjoram leaves
Dash of onion powder
6 sirloin lamb chops, 1 ½ to 2-in. thick
Salt and pepper

Combine butter, watercress, marjoram and onion powder; mix well. Broil lamb chops 6 to 7 inches from heat for 12 to 15 minutes on each side or until desired degree of doneness. Sprinkle with salt and pepper before turning chops. Serve watercress butter with chops. Yield: 6 servings.

Photograph for this recipe on page 345 .

SHISH KABOB HAWAIIAN

1 c. olive oil
1 c. red wine vinegar
½ c. red wine
¼ c. soy sauce
¼ c. Worcestershire sauce
1 tsp. basil
1 tsp. oregano
1 tsp. tarragon
1 clove of garlic
1 3 to 4-lb. lamb shoulder, cut into 1-in. cubes
Zucchini squash, cut into 1-in. chunks
2 doz. cherry tomatoes, stemmed
Whole fresh mushrooms
Small onions, parboiled
Pineapple chunks

Combine olive oil, vinegar, wine, sauces and seasonings in bowl. Add lamb. Cover bowl tightly; place in refrigerator for 24 hours. Wash vegetables. Arrange vegetables, pineapple and lamb on skewers. Grill until done. Yield: 6 servings.

Mrs. Carol McGee, Yuba City Union H. S.
Yuba City, California

BARBECUED PORK TENDERLOIN

Pork chops
Italian dressing

Place pork tenderloins over slow charcoal fire for 2 hours or until done. Baste often with Italian dressing.

Mrs. Barbara Aud, Highland H. S.
Highland, Illinois

HAM AND CHEESE ROLL-UPS

10 double thin salty crackers
½ tsp. dry mustard
2 hard-cooked eggs, chopped
2 tbsp. grated cheese
2 tbsp. minced green pepper
2 tbsp. minced onion
¾ c. mayonnaise
8 thin slices cooked ham
2 tbsp. melted shortening
2 tsp. bottled steak sauce

Coarsely crush crackers; mix with mustard, eggs, cheese, green pepper and onion. Blend in mayonnaise. Divide mixture evenly on ham slices; roll up and secure with toothpicks which have been soaked in water. Brush with mixture of shortening and steak sauce. Grill over medium heat until heated through. Yield: 4 servings.

Mrs. Mildred G. Grundy, South Middleton H. S.
Boiling Springs, Pennsylvania

BARBECUED CHICKEN

2 fryer or broiler chickens
Salt and pepper to taste
1 lb. margarine
½ c. prepared mustard
½ c. wine vinegar
Paprika to taste

Split chickens lengthwise; sprinkle with salt. Let stand for at least 1 hour. Combine salt to taste and remaining ingredients; cook over low heat for a few minutes. Rinse and drain chicken well. Place on rack over smoldering coals. Sear each side. Cook for 1 hour to 1 hour and 30 minutes or until chickens are golden brown and tender, basting with sauce and turning every 7 to 10 minutes. Yield: 4 servings.

Mrs. Carolyn W. Baxley, Paul Knox Jr. H. S.
North Augusta, South Carolina

BARBECUED CHICKEN

1 c. water
1 pt. vinegar
½ lb. margarine
2 tbsp. salt
3 broiler chickens, cut into halves

Combine all ingredients except chickens; heat until margarine is melted. Place chickens, skin-side up over hot charcoal. Grill for 1 hour and 30 minutes to 2 hours or until tender, turning and basting with vinegar mixture frequently.

BARBECUE SAUCE:

½ lb. margarine
1 c. vinegar
2 c. catsup
Juice of 1 lemon
¼ c. Worcestershire sauce
1 tbsp. Tabasco sauce
1 tbsp. salt
3 tbsp. mustard

Combine all ingredients; simmer for 15 minutes. Baste chickens on each side with sauce just before servings. Yield: 6 servings.

Thrath C. Curry, Carrollton H. S.
Carrollton, Alabama

BARBECUED CHICKEN

6 c. white vinegar
2 c. water
1 ½ lb. margarine
Salt to taste
6 chickens, halved

Combine vinegar, water and margarine; bring to a boil. Salt chickens; place on grill. Spread sauce over chickens. Cook over charcoal for 2 hours to 2 hours and 30 minutes, turning often. Yield: 12 servings.

Mrs. Dorotha Wiseman, Morgan Twp.
Palmyra, Indiana

BARBECUED CHICKEN

3 tbsp. salt
1 pt. cider vinegar
1 c. cooking oil
3 tbsp. salt
1 tsp. Tabasco sauce
6 2-lb. broilers, cut into halves

Mix all ingredients except chickens; bring to boil. Boil for 5 minutes; set aside for 1 hour. Keep sauce warm. Salt chicken halves; let stand for 1 hour. When grill is hot, add chickens, cut-side down. Turn; brush with sauce every 5 minutes. Broil for 1 hour and 30 minutes. Yield: 12 servings.

Mrs. Verna I. Boyd, Pisgah H. S.
Sand Hill, Mississippi

BARBECUED CHICKEN AND SAUCE

1 lb. melted butter
1 bottle Worcestershire sauce
1 bottle catsup
1 c. white vinegar
Juice of 4 lemons
1 tbsp. Tabasco sauce
2 tbsp. prepared mustard
Salt and pepper to taste
2 med. frying chickens, cut into halves lenghtwise

Combine all ingredients except chickens. Place chickens over coals, using a combination of charcoal and mesquite wood. Cook until tender and brown on both sides, basting often with sauce. Yield: 4 servings.

Mrs. Floyd Craig, Divide H. S.
Nolan, Texas

CHICKEN BUNDLE

¼ chicken
2 slices onion
3 slices uncooked summer squash
Pinch of rosemary or oregano
½ tsp. salt
¼ tsp. pepper
1 tbsp. butter
1 tbsp. water

Place chicken quarter on large square of heavy duty aluminum foil. Add vegetables and seasonings. Add butter and water. Fold foil closely around chicken to form a tight package. Cook on grill or over hot coals, turning once every 10 to 15 minutes. Cook for 1 hour. Serve in foil package. Yield: 1 serving.

Mrs. Norine E. Sipe, Goffstown H. S.
Goffstown, New Hampshire

CHICKEN BUNDLES

2 fryer chickens, cut into quarters
8 slices peeled sweet potato
8 slices canned pineapple, drained
8 slices green pepper
½ c. butter
2 tsp. salt
½ tsp. pepper

Place individual portions of chicken, skin-side down, in center of large piece of foil. Top with slice of sweet potato, pineapple and green pepper, 1 tablespoonful butter, 1/4 teaspoonful salt and dash of pepper. Seal foil with double fold seal to make airtight package. Grill over medium heat for 50 minutes, turning once or twice. Unwrap and serve hot. Yield: 8 servings.

Mrs. Ruth Schaffner
Cochrane-Fountain City H. S.
Fountain City, Wisconsin

EASY GRILLED CHICKEN

1 1 to 2 ½-lb. chicken, split in half
¼ tsp. paprika

(Continued on next page)

¼ tsp. salt
¼ tsp. pepper
⅓ c. vegetable oil

Brush chicken with paprika, salt, pepper and oil. Place, cut-side down, on the grill over smoldering coals. Cook for 40 to 50 minutes, turning every 10 minutes. Yield: 4 servings.

Mrs. Imogene Ford Abernathie
Williamsville H. S., Williamsville, Illinois

GRILLED CHICKEN

½ stick melted butter
1 c. vinegar
1 tsp. basil leaves
¼ c. catsup
¼ tsp. Texas Pete hot sauce
1 tbsp. Worcestershire sauce
1 tsp. salt
½ tsp. pepper
1 sm. chicken, cut up

Combine all ingredients except chicken. Marinate chicken in sauce for at least 4 hours or overnight. Place chicken on lighted charcoal grill; cook slowly for 30 to 45 minutes, basting with marinade and turning often. Yield: 3 servings.

Rebecca L. Jones, Greensville Co. H. S.
Emporia, Virginia

HOOSIER BARBECUED CHICKEN

1 ⅛ qt. water
1 c. vinegar
½ c. salt
¼ c. brown sugar
1 ⅛ lb. margarine
½ c. cooking oil
3 tbsp. Worcestershire sauce
1 tsp. pepper (opt.)
6 2-lb. chickens, halved

Mix all ingredients except chickens; bring to a boil and keep warm while using. Dip chickens in sauce; place on grill with skin-sides up. Barbecue over medium to low heat for 2 hours and 30 minutes, turning and basting frequently.

Clara D. Ferguson, Tecumseh H. S.
Lynnville, Indiana

LEMON-BARBECUED CHICKEN

2 tsp. onion powder
2 tsp. crushed sweet basil
½ tsp. thyme
½ tsp. garlic powder
1 c. salad oil
½ c. fresh lemon juice
1 tbsp. salt
1 tsp. paprika
1 frying chicken, cut up

Cpmbine all ingredients, except chicken, in pint jar; shake well. Arrange chicken in glass baking dish; pour on sauce. Cover tightly; marinate for 6 to 8 hours in refrigerator, turning occasionally. Remove from refrigerator 1 hour before grilling. Place chicken on grill, skin-side up. Cook for 20 to 25 minutes, basting often with marinade. Turn; cook for 20 minutes longer. Serve immediately. Yield: 6 servings.

Mrs. Joyce Wisby, West Liberty Comm. School
West Liberty, Iowa

SAUCY BARBECUED CHICKEN

2 2 to 2 ½-lb. broiling chickens, split
1 c. salad oil
¼ c. vinegar
1 tbsp. horseradish
¼ c. chili sauce
½ tsp. dry mustard
1 tsp. salt
½ tsp. onion juice
1 tsp. garlic juice
2 tsp. Worcestershire sauce

Arrange chicken halves in large flat pan. Combine remaining ingredients. Baste chicken, season with additional salt and pepper. Roast at 325 degrees for 1 hour to 1 hour and 30 minutes, turning and basting occasionally. Drain chicken. Place on grill over hot coals. Broil for 30 minutes longer or until well browned, turning and basting frequently with more sauce. Yield: 4 servings.

Mrs. Sara Carnahan, Wamego Rural H. S.
Wamego, Kansas

BARBECUED TURKEY

1 8 to 9-lb. turkey
1 tbsp. salt
1 ½ c. mayonnaise

Wash turkey thoroughly; place salt in cavity of bird. Insert rotisserie into breast and leg area of bird. Secure bird with heavy cord to rotisserie. Place over smoldering briquettes. Cover entire outside of bird with mayonnaise. Turn for at least 30 minutes per pound. Add briquettes as needed, to complete cooking.

Mrs. Bonnie Shaw, Clarkfield Public School
Clarkfield, Minnesota

MARINATED GROUND MEAT

60 lb. ground meat
3 1-lb. 12-oz. jars barbecue sauce
3 ⅓ c. evaporated milk
½ 1-lb. 10-oz. box salt
4 oz. pepper

Place meat in large container. Add barbecue sauce, a small amount at a time, with milk, salt and pepper. Work into meat well. Chill for at least 3 hours or overnight. Shape into patties. Grill until done. Yield: 240 servings.

Aileen Springer, West Columbia Jr. H. S.
West Columbia, Texas

Quick & Easy Favorites

JAPANESE SUKIYAKI

2 lb. beef round or chicken, cut into thin strips
2 tbsp. butter
2 lge. onions, thinly sliced
3 green onions and tops, chopped
1 4-oz. can mushrooms
½ c. thinly sliced bamboo sprouts
½ c. soy sauce
2 tbsp. sugar

Cook meat in butter for about 5 minutes, turning often; add onions, mushrooms and bamboo sprouts. Keep each food separate. Add soy sauce and sugar. Cook for 10 minutes or until meat is tender, turning so that food gets heated evenly. Yield: 6 servings.

Irma Haley, Castleford H. S.
Castleford, Idaho

PEPPER STEAK

1 lb. sirloin or rib, cut into thin slices
2 tbsp. cooking oil
1 lge. green pepper, cut into thin strips
2 scallions, thinly sliced
½ c. very thin diagonally sliced celery
¼ c. unsulphured molasses
2 tbsp. soy sauce
1 tsp. lemon juice
½ tsp. salt
1 tsp. monosodium glutamate
1 tsp. ginger
½ c. water
2 tsp. cornstarch

Brown beef in heated oil in large skillet. Add pepper, scallions and celery. Cook for 3 to 5 minutes, stirring frequently. Stir in unsulphured molasses, soy sauce, lemon juice and seasonings. Blend water and cornstarch; quickly stir into beef mixture. Cover and simmer for 5 minutes. Serve with hot cooked rice. Yield: 4 servings.

Photograph for this recipe on page 355.

BARBECUE HAMBURGER

1 onion, chopped
1 green pepper, chopped
1 c. chopped celery
1 lb. ground beef
1 tbsp. catsup
½ tsp. salt
¼ tsp. pepper
¾ c. barbecue sauce

Brown onion, green pepper and celery. Add ground beef and brown. Add catsup, salt and pepper; mix well. Add barbecue sauce; simmer for 15 minutes. Yield: 6 servings.

Mrs. Pat Vaughan, Fairfield H. S.
Fairfield, Illinois

BEEF GOULASH

1 lb. lean ground beef
1 med. onion, chopped
1 med. green pepper, chopped
1 tsp. salt
¼ tsp. pepper
1 8-oz. can tomato sauce
1 can whole kernel corn

Cook beef, onion and green pepper in skillet until meat changes color; add seasonings and tomato sauce. Cover and simmer for 15 to 20 minutes. Add corn; bring to a boil. Serve immediately. Yield: 6 servings.

Mrs. Mary Ray White, Troup H. S.
Troup, Texas

BEEF-RICE SKILLET

½ green pepper, chopped
1 sm. onion, chopped
1 to 3 tbsp. butter or fat
1 lb. ground chuck
1 can cream of mushroom or celery soup
1 can tomato soup (opt.)
1 soup can water
Salt and pepper to taste
1 c. uncooked instant rice or ½ c. regular rice

Saute green pepper and onion in butter over medium heat; add beef. Brown, stirring to prevent burning. Combine soups, water, salt and pepper; add to meat. Mix well; add rice. Cover tightly; simmer for about 15 minutes or until rice is done. NOTE: Rice may be browned with meat, if desired.

Mrs. Freddie E. Taylor, Dierks H. S.
Dierks, Arkansas
Mrs. Marjorie Balestri, Farwell H. S.
Farwell, Texas

EASY BEEF BARBECUE

3 lb. hamburger
¼ c. chopped onion
2 tbsp. fat
2 ½ tbsp. vinegar
6 tbsp. water
1 bottle catsup
¼ c. brown sugar
2 c. chopped celery
1 tbsp. dry mustard
1 tbsp. salt

Brown hamburger and onion in fat. Add remaining ingredients and simmer until done. Yield: 25 servings.

Sara Thompson, Pineville H. S.
Pineville, Kentucky

BEEF STROGANOFF

½ c. minced onion
¼ c. butter or margarine

(Continued on next page)

1 lb. lean ground beef
1 clove of garlic, minced (opt.)
2 tbsp. flour
1 to 2 tsp. salt
¼ tsp. pepper
¼ tsp. paprika (opt.)
1 can cream of mushroom soup or 1 sm. can mushrooms
1 can cream of chicken soup
1 c. sour cream
2 tbsp. chopped parsley

Cook onion in butter in a heavy skillet; add ground beef. Cook until no longer pink. Add garlic, flour, salt, pepper and paprika. Cover; cook for 5 minutes. Add soups; simmer for 10 minutes longer. Just before serving, add sour cream; stir in well. Sprinkle with parsley. Yield: 5-6 servings.

Mary Ella Porter, Como-Pickton H. S.
Como, Texas
Florence McMullin, Fairdale H. S.
Fairdale, Kentucky

FIFTEEN-MINUTE CASSEROLE

1 lb. ground beef
2 med. onions, chopped
1 lge. can spaghetti
2 6-oz. cans vegetable soup

Brown ground beef and onions in electric frypan at 250 degrees; add spaghetti and soup. Simmer for 5 to 10 minutes. Yield: 4-5 servings.

Mrs. Sandra Ericson, Britton Road Jr. H. S.
Rochester, New York

GRANDMOTHER'S GOULASH

1 onion, minced
1 lb. hamburger
1 10-oz. can tomato soup

Brown onion in fat. Add hamburger; cook until meat is brown and crumbly. Add tomato soup; simmer until flavors are blended. Serve with mashed potatoes, steamed rice or cooked noodles. Yield: 4 servings.

Mrs. Lois E. Pritchard, Consolidated Schools
Susquehanna, Pennsylvania

GROUND BEEF AND SOUR CREAM CASSEROLE

1 c. chopped onions
1 lb. ground beef
Bacon fat
3 c. tomato juice
1 ½ tsp. celery salt
2 tsp. Worcestershire sauce
Dash of pepper
½ 5-oz. pkg. noodles
¼ c. chopped green pepper
1 c. sour cream
1 3-oz. can mushrooms

Brown onions and ground beef in heavy frying pan in a small amount of bacon fat. Combine tomato juice, celery salt, Worcestershire sauce and pepper. Layer noodles over beef. Pour tomato juice over noodles and beef. Cover and simmer for 20 minutes. Add green pepper; cook 10 minutes longer. Combine sour cream and mushrooms; stir into beef mixture. Serve immediately.

Mrs. Mary S. Hatcher, Brooks Co. H. S.
Quitman, Georgia

HAMBURGER CHOP SUEY

½ lb. hamburger
1 sm. onion, chopped
½ c. diced celery
1 c. drained bean sprouts
½ c. beef bouillon
1 sm. can mushrooms, undrained
1 tbsp. cornstarch
¼ c. water

Brown hamburger, onion and celery well; add bean sprouts, bouillon and mushrooms. Simmer for 10 minutes. Add thickening of cornstarch and water; stir. Cook, stirring, for 5 minutes longer. Serve over hot rice. Yield: 6 servings.

Mrs. Keith Van Koevering, Saugatuck H. S.
Saugatuck, Michigan

HAMBURGER-VEGETABLE CASSEROLE

4 oz. noodles
2 stalks celery
2 carrots
1 lb. hamburger
1 onion, minced
2 tsp. salt
½ tsp. pepper
1 tsp. basil
2 c. canned peas, drained
2 c. cream-style corn

Cook noodles, chopped celery and carrots until tender. Brown hamburger and onion; season. Add noodle mixture, peas and corn to hamburger. Simmer for 10 to 15 minutes. Yield: 6 servings.

Sharon Gilley, Bloomer H. S.
Bloomer, Wisconsin

HAMBURGER STROGANOFF

1 lb. ground beef
1 onion, grated
1 can cream of mushroom soup
½ c. sour cream
1 can mushroom pieces (opt.)

Brown hamburger with onion in skillet; add soup and sour cream. Add mushroom pieces. Heat thoroughly. Serve over chow mein noodles. Yield: 4-6 servings.

Mrs. Irma Dixon, Georgetown H. S.
Georgetown, Illinois

ITALIAN GOULASH

½ sm. onion, chopped
½ lb. ground round steak
1 No. 2 can tomato-cheese spaghetti
1 sm. can corn

Saute onion is small amount of fat; add steak. Saute steak. Add all remaining ingredients; season with salt and pepper to taste. Cook until steak is tender. Yield: 6 servings.

Mrs. Nan Dyer, Mission H. S.
Mission, Texas

MEXICANA

1 med. onion, sliced
1 lb. ground beef
1 can corn
Salt and pepper to taste
1 8-oz. can tomato sauce
2 c. cooked rice

Brown onion in hot fat. Break ground beef into small pieces; brown until tender. Add corn, seasonings and tomato sauce; simmer for 10 minutes. Serve with rice. Yield: 4 servings.

Peggy Bryant, Orofino H. S.
Orofino, Idaho

BARBECUED BEEF BURGERS

1 ½ lb. ground beef
½ c. catsup
1 ½ tsp. salt
2 tbsp. chopped green pepper
3 tbsp. chopped onion
1 egg
1 tbsp. Worcestershire sauce
Liquid smoke

Combine all ingredients except liquid smoke. Make into patties. Make hole in top of patties; place liquid smoke in each hole. Let stand for 10 minutes. Broil for 10 minutes on each side. Yield: 6 servings.

Mrs. Mary Margaret Cooley, Sedgwick H. S.
Sedgwick, Kansas

BARBECUED HAMBURGERS

1 lb. hamburger
Salt and pepper to taste
½ c. milk
1 c. bread crumbs
1 egg (opt.)
2 tbsp. sugar
1 tbsp. vinegar
2 tbsp. Worcestershire sauce
1 c. catsup

Mix hamburger with salt, pepper, milk, crumbs and egg. Shape into patties. Brown on each side; drain. Combine sugar, vinegar, Worcestershire sauce and catsup; pour over patties. Simmer for 15 minutes. Yield: 6 servings.

Judith Gress, Moffat Co. H. S.
Craig, Colorado

BARBECUED HAMBURGERS

Salt and pepper to taste
1 ½ lb. ground beef
¼ c. brown sugar
¼ c. vinegar
½ c. catsup
1 tsp. prepared mustard
1 tbsp. Worcestershire sauce

Season ground beef with salt and pepper. Shape into patties; brown in skillet. Mix remaining ingredients; pour over patties. Cover and simmer for 20 minutes. Yield: 6 servings.

Mrs. Marshall J. King, Gatesville H. S.
Gatesville, Texas

CHICKEN-FRIED HAMBURGER

1 lb. hamburger
½ c. milk
½ c. flour
¼ c. fat, melted
Salt and pepper to taste

Shape hamburger into flat patties; chill. Place milk and flour in flat dishes slightly larger than patties. Place each pattie in milk; turn over. Dip into flour. Place patties in hot skillet with melted fat; season. Cook on each side until crispy, flattening as patties cook. Yield: 4-6 servings.

Vera Murphy, Quinter H. S.
Quinter, Kansas

COUNTRY-FRIED STEAK

1 lb. ground beef
Flour
1 tsp. salt
Pepper to taste

Mix beef, 1/4 cup flour, salt and pepper. Roll out on floured board; sprinkle with flour. Cut

(Continued on next page)

into pieces resembling steak. Fry or cook in gravy in oven. Yield: 4 servings.

Mrs. Marjorie West, Northeast H. S.
Meridian, Mississippi

JIFFY BURGER STEAK

1 lge. onion
¼ green pepper
1 lb. hamburger
2 tbsp. dry milk
¼ tsp. salt
⅛ tsp. pepper

Put onion and green pepper through blender; drain. Mix thoroughly with hamburger, milk and seasonings. Divide mixture into two parts; place in saucepan. Flatten into desired shape. Brown meat on both sides. Cover; simmer for 3 minutes. Yield: 2 servings.

Elwanda McCall, Plains H. S.
Plains, Georgia

PIZZA PIE

½ lb. ground beef or sausage
⅓ c. minced onion
2 tbsp. green pepper
½ tsp. salt
1 c. tomato sauce
1 3-oz. can chopped mushrooms
2 tbsp. tomato paste
2 tbsp. sugar
1 c. prepared biscuit mix
⅓ c. milk
½ c. sharp grated cheese

Cook meat until brown; add onion, pepper and salt. Cook for 5 minutes; add remaining ingredients. Cook for a few minutes; simmer for 10 minutes or until thick. Mix biscuit mix and milk; roll to shape of pan. Add mixture to crust. Spread top with grated cheese. Bake at 400 degrees until dough is brown and cheese melted. Cut into wedges and serve. Yield: 4 serving.

Mrs. Ray A. Waters, Sr. H. S.
Texarkana, Arkansas

SCRAMBLE

1 pkg. frozen spinach
1 lb. ground beef
1 sm. onion, chopped
1 sm. can mushroom slices or ¼ lb. sliced fresh mushrooms
3 tbsp. olive oil
Salt and pepper to taste
6 eggs, well beaten

Cook spinach according to package directions. Saute ground beef, onion and mushrooms in olive oil. Season. Add to spinach. Pour into beaten eggs; cook and stir until eggs become firm. Yield: 6 servings.

Mrs. Mitzi Funk, Del Norte Co. H. S.
Crescent City, California

WITCH'S BREW

1 lb. hamburger
1 lge. onion, sliced (opt.)
1 can pork and beans
1 can sliced mushrooms
1 c. catsup or 1 can tomato soup
Salt and pepper to taste

Brown hamburger and onion; stir often to break up hamburger. Add beans, mushrooms, catsup, salt and pepper; blend well. Simmer until ready to serve. Yield: 4 servings.

Mrs. Lena Bell Moore, Peter Soarich H. S.
Vegreville, Alberta, Canada

SALMON OMELET

1 7 ¾-oz. can salmon
6 eggs, separated
1 tbsp. chopped parsley
1 tsp. chopped chives
½ tsp. salt
Dash of oregano
Dash of pepper
2 tbsp. butter or margarine

Drain and flake salmon, reserving liquid. Add enough water to liquid to make 1/3 cup liquid. Beat egg yolks until thick and lemon colored. Add salmon liquid, parsley, chives, salt, oregano, pepper and salmon; mix well. Fold into stiffly beaten egg whites. Pour mixture into a hot buttered 10-inch frying pan; cook over low heat for 3 to 4 minutes or until knife inserted in the center comes out clean. Cut part way through center of omelet; fold in half. Serve immediately on a warm platter. Yield: 6 servings.

Sister M. Claude, O.S.F., St. Francis School
Yazoo City, Mississippi

HOT SEAFOOD SALAD

1 can frozen cream of shrimp soup
¼ c. milk
½ c. chopped celery
¼ c. chopped green pepper
¼ c. chopped onion
1 c. flaked tuna
1 c. cubed Cheddar cheese

Place shrimp soup and milk in boiler over low heat. When soup has melted, add celery, pepper and onion. Stir in tuna and cheese; mix well. Serve hot over toast, toast cups or fili cream puffs, if desired. Yield: 6 servings.

Mrs. Sadie Booker, El Dorado H. S.
El Dorado, Arkansas

TUNA A LA KING IN TOAST CUPS

2 tbsp. chopped green pepper
1 tbsp. butter or margarine
1 can cream of mushroom soup
½ c. milk
1 7-oz. can tuna, drained

(Continued on next page)

2 tbsp. chopped pimento
3 hard-cooked eggs, quartered
12 thin slices bread

Cook green pepper in butter until soft. Mix in mushroom soup, stirring well; add milk. Heat in top of double boiler. Break tuna into chunks; add to soup with pimento and eggs, reserving one egg yolk for garnish. Trim crusts from bread; press each slice of bread into muffin cup. Toast in preheated 375 degree oven for 12 to 15 minutes. Pour tuna-mushroom mixture into toast cups. Garnish with additional pimento and sieved remaining egg yolk. Yield: 5-6 servings.

Mrs. Addie Watson, Webster Co. H. S.
Dixon, Kentucky

TUNA-CHEESE LUNCHEON DISH

1 tbsp. butter
1 tbsp. flour
1 c. milk
1 can cream of mushroom soup
1 can solid pack tuna, drained
½ c. process cheese, diced or coarsely grated
1 can chow mein noodles

Melt butter in saucepan; blend in flour and milk, stirring and cooking until thick. Add soup, tuna and cheese; heat until cheese melts, stirring frequently to prevent scorching. Serve over chow mein noodles. Yield: 4 servings.

Genevieve Kramer, East Chain H. S.
Blue Earth, Minnesota

TUNA SHORTCAKE

1 10½-oz. can cream of mushroom or cream of celery soup
½ c. milk
1 7-oz. can tuna, drained and flaked
1 c. cooked peas
1 tbsp. chopped pimento
Toast

Blend soup and milk; add tuna, peas and pimento. Heat, stirring frequently. Serve over toast. Yield: 4 servings.

Mrs. Sheryl Massey, Morrowville Rural H. S.
Morrowville, Kansas

CREAMED FISH

2 c. cooked fish flakes
1 c. medium white sauce
2 tsp. grated onion
¼ tsp. mace
2 tsp. finely chopped parsley

Combine fish, flakes, white sauce, onion and mace. Heat slowly to serving temperature; add parsley. May be served on toast, rice or baked potato. NOTE: Prepare white sauce using cream or liquid from fish. Yield: 4-5 servings.

Eloise Howerton, Karns H. S.
Knoxville, Tennessee

CRAB MEAT RAREBIT

¾ c. cooked crab meat
2 tbsp. butter
2 tbsp. chopped green pepper
3 tbsp. flour
¼ tsp. dry mustard
¾ tsp. salt
Few grains of pepper
¾ c. tomato juice
¾ c. grated cheese
⅓ c. milk

Remove spine from crab meat. Melt butter; add green pepper and cook for 5 minutes. Blend in flour and seasonings. Gradually add tomato juice; cook, stirring constantly, until thickened. Add cheese and milk, stirring constantly. Fold in crab meat; heat to boiling. Serve in bread croustades, green pepper halves or on toast, if desired. Yield: 6 servings.

Alma E. Leo, Trade H. S. for Girls
Boston, Massachusetts

CREAMED MUSHROOMS AND CRAB MEAT

¾ lb. fresh mushrooms, sliced
1 onion, diced
5 tbsp. butter
3 tbsp. flour
2 c. sour cream
Salt and pepper
¼ tsp. nutmeg
1 lb. fresh crab meat
6 tbsp. Sherry wine

Saute mushrooms and onion in the butter in top pan of chafing dish over hot water. Mix in flour; moisten with sour cream. Season with salt, pepper and nutmeg. Stir in crab meat; heat thoroughly. Stir in the wine; serve on pattie shells or on unbuttered toast, if desired.

Marilyn L. Gies, Olympia H. S.
Olympia, Washington

QUICK 'N' EASY CRAB MEAT

1 to 2 tbsp. butter
1 sm. onion, sliced
1 green pepper, cut into strips
8 oz. frozen canned crab meat, shredded
Salt and pepper to taste

Melt butter in heavy frying pan. Add onion and green pepper. Cover tightly and cook until tender. Add crab meat. Heat thoroughly. Season. Yield: 2-3 servings.

Mrs. Kay Schneider, Ponus Ridge Jr. H. S.
Norwalk, Connecticut

DEVILED CRABS

4 hard-cooked egg yolks, sieved
2 tbsp. flour
2 tbsp. butter
1 c. whole milk or cream
1 can crab meat
1 tbsp. chopped parsley
Dash of salt and pepper
¼ c. bread crumbs

Mix well all ingredients; season to taste. Mix with bread crumbs. Place in buttered baking dish; dot with butter. Bake at 375 degrees until brown. NOTE: May be placed in crab shells.

Ernestina Garcia, San Felipe H. S.
Del Rio, Texas

A LA SHRIMP

3 tbsp. butter
1 sm. green pepper, chopped
1 sm. onion, chopped
½ lb. mushroom caps
3 tbsp. flour
1 ½ tsp. salt
3 tbsp. chopped pimento
1 tsp. chopped parsley
¼ tsp. Tabasco sauce
2 c. cooked shrimp
2 c. milk
1 egg, beaten

Melt butter in frypan; add green pepper, onion and mushrooms. Cook for 5 minutes; add flour, salt, pimento, parsley, Tabasco sauce and shrimp. Heat gently for 2 minutes. Add 1 1/2 cups milk. Cook until thick; add egg mixed with remaining milk. Remove from heat; serve on toast or in toast cups. Garnish with lemon slice. NOTE: Chicken or turkey may be substituted for shrimp. Yield: 6 servings.

Katharine Rigby, Starr-Washington H. S.
Union Furnace, Ohio

CREOLE SHRIMP

3 tbsp. shortening
1 med. onion, sliced
1 med. green pepper, coarsely chopped
2 8-oz. cans tomato sauce
½ bay leaf
½ lb. uncooked shrimp, cleaned
½ tsp. salt
¼ tsp. black pepper
2 ½ c. cooked rice
Cayenne pepper to taste

Melt shortening in a 2-quart saucepan; add onions and green pepper. Saute until tender. Add tomato sauce, bay leaf, shrimp, salt and black pepper; simmer for 15 minutes, stirring occasionally. Remove bay leaf. Add rice; heat to boiling point. Add cayenne pepper. Serve immediately garnished with slices of green pepper, if desired. Yield: 6-8 servings.

Mrs. Frances Fuhrman, Eastern H. S.
Wrightsville, Pennsylvania

CREAMED SHRIMP

4 tbsp. butter
4 tbsp. flour
1 ½ c. cream or half and half
8 tbsp. catsup
4 tbsp. Worcestershire sauce
2 c. cooked or canned shrimp

Melt butter in top of double boiler. Add flour slowly; stir until smooth. Gradually add cream; cook until thickened. Add catsup and Worcestershire sauce; stir to blend. Add shrimp; cook until hot. If sauce becomes too thick, thin with shrimp broth. Serve on crackers, toast or rice. Yield: 6 servings.

Mrs. George Boyens, Many H. S.
Many, Louisiana

CURRIED SHRIMP

½ c. chopped onion
1 tbsp. butter
1 tbsp. flour
1 can frozen cream of shrimp soup
1 c. sour cream
½ tsp. curry powder
2 c. frozen raw shrimp

Saute onion in butter until onion is transparent but not browned. Add flour; mix thoroughly. Add shrimp soup; stir until smooth. Add sour cream and curry powder; stir again until blended. Fold in shrimp; simmer for 10 minutes. Serve over rice with a dash of paprika and slivered almonds, if desired.

Mrs. Pauline Norberg, Parma H. S.
Parma, Idaho

JIFFY SHRIMP CURRY

1 tbsp. butter or margarine
1 can cream of shrimp soup, thawed
1 c. sour cream
2 tbsp. instant minced onion
½ tsp. curry powder
1 5-oz. can tuna

Place butter and soup in skillet. Heat and stir until smooth. Stir in remaining ingredients. Cover; heat until just hot. Serve over rice, if desired. Yield: 4-6 servings.

Mrs. Anita H. Lewis, Oley Valley Area H. S.
Oley, Pennsylvania

QUICK SHRIMP CREOLE

1 med. onion, chopped
1 clove of garlic, minced
1 med. green pepper, chopped
½ c. chopped celery
2 tbsp. oil
1 8-oz. can tomato sauce
¾ c. water
1 lb. fresh shrimp, cleaned and cooked

(Continued on next page)

Cook onion, garlic, green pepper and celery in oil for 5 minutes. Stir in tomato sauce and water; simmer for 10 minutes. Add shrimp and heat throughly. Serve over hot rice, if desired.

Mrs. Walter Holden, Albany H. S.
Albany, Louisiana

SHRIMP AMANDINE

1 1-lb. pkg. cleaned precooked or frozen shrimp
1 c. blanched slivered almonds
½ c. butter or margarine, melted
Dash of pepper
2 tbsp. chopped parsley
Toast points

Thaw frozen shrimp. Saute almonds in butter until lightly browned; remove. Add shrimp; saute until lightly browned. Add seasonings, parsley and almonds. Serve on toast points. Yield: 6 servings.

Ouida M. Shows, Theodore H. S.
Theodore, Alabama

SHRIMP NEWBURG

1 ¾ tbsp. flour
2 tbsp. butter, melted
1 c. half and half
3 tbsp. catsup
¾ tbsp. Worcestershire sauce
½ tsp. dry mustard
1 lb. cooked shrimp
Salt and pepper to taste
Few grains of cayenne pepper
2 tbsp. Sherry (opt.)

Stir flour into butter until blended. Slowly stir in half and half. When sauce is thick, add catsup, Worcestershire sauce and dry mustard. Add cooked shrimp. Stir until shrimp are well heated; season with salt, pepper and cayenne. Before serving, add Sherry. Serve with steamed rice. Yield: 4 servings.

Mrs. Margaret Elliott, Horace Mann Jr. H. S.
Amarillo, Texas

SHRIMP ON PATTIE SHELLS

1 box frozen shrimp
1 c. white wine
½ tsp. salt
¼ tsp. pepper
¼ bay leaf
1 sm. onion, chopped
2 sprigs parsley
2 tbsp. lemon juice
8 bouillon cubes
6 tbsp. flour
1 lb. fresh mushrooms, sliced

Cook shrimp until almost done. Drain, reserving 1 cup liquid. Mix wine, reserved lqiuid, salt, pepper, bay leaf, onion, parsley and lemon juice. Bring to a boil. Simmer for 6 minutes; strain. Dissolve bouillon cubes; stir in flour. Cook until thickened. Add wine sauce and heat. Saute mushrooms lightly. Add mushrooms and shrimp to sauce. Serve on pattie shells or rice, if desired. Yield: 4 servings.

Mary J. Strand, Sr. H. S.
Jamestown, New York

SHRIMP PIE

4 eggs, beaten
1 c. diced celery
½ tsp. salt
1 c. grated cheese
1 ½ c. mayonnaise
1 tsp. Worcestershire sauce
1 lb. shrimp, cooked
1 8-oz. can cream of mushroom soup
¾ c. bread crumbs

Combine eggs with celery, salt, cheese, mayonnaise and Worcestershire sauce; mix well. Add shrimp; pour soup over mixture. Top with crumbs. Bake at 350 degrees until brown. Yield: 4 servings.

Mrs. Kate S. Berry, Latta H. S.
Latta, South Carolina

SHRIMP RAREBIT SANDWICHES

1 tbsp. chopped onion
2 tbsp. chopped green pepper
6 tbsp. butter
1 tbsp. cooked shrimp
1 tbsp. flour
1 c. milk
½ c. Worcestershire sauce
⅛ tsp. dry mustard
⅛ tsp. salt
⅛ tsp. pepper
¼ lb. sharp Cheddar cheese, grated
5 slices toast

Cook onion and green pepper very slowly in 5 tablespoonfuls butter for 5 minutes; add shrimp. Mix carefully with a fork; cook slowly until shrimp are hot. Melt remaining butter; add flour. Add milk gradually, stirring constantly. Add seasonings; cook until thickened, stirring constantly. Add cheese; stir until melted. Serve shrimp on toast with sauce, if desired. Yield: 5 servings.

Catherine Stall, Greenville H. S.
Greenville, Michigan

OLD TRAILS FARM SEAFOOD DISH

2 cans cream of mushroom soup
1 6 ½-oz. can crab meat
1 ½ lb. or 2 cans shrimp
1 10 ½-oz. can clams
Lobster (opt.)
1 4-oz. can mushrooms
Salt and pepper to taste
Paprika

(Continued on next page)

Combine soup, seafood, mushrooms, salt and pepper; add enough paprika to make mixture pink. Serve over hot curried rice, if desired. Yield: 8-10 servings.

Mrs. Louanna Kirkpatrick, Frankfort H. S.
Frankfort, Indiana

HAM A LA KING

4 tbsp. diced onion
½ lb. or 1 6-oz. can mushrooms
2 tbsp. diced celery (opt.)
2 tbsp. diced green pepper (opt.)
4 tbsp. margarine
4 tbsp. cornstarch
½ tsp. salt
¼ tsp. pepper
½ tsp. monosodium glutamate
1 c. milk
1 c. light cream
2 to 2 ½ c. diced cooked ham
2 tsp. pimento
1 c. raw rice, cooked

Saute onion, mushrooms, celery and green pepper in margarine. Make a white sauce of cornstarch, salt, pepper, monosodiumglutamate, milk and cream; add to sauted mixture in skillet. When thickened, add ham and pimento; cook over low heat for 12 to 15 minutes. Serve over steamed rice.

Mrs. E. Ruth Yelvington, Mildred H. S.
Corsicana, Texas

HAM CRESCENT ROLLS

1 c. chopped ham or chicken
2 hard-cooked eggs, chopped
1 sm. onion
1 can cream of mushroom soup
1 pkg. crescent dinner rolls
1 6-oz. can evaporated milk
⅛ tsp. thyme
⅛ tsp. basil
1 8-oz. can peas

Mix ham, eggs and onion with 2 tablespoonfuls soup; spread over triangles of rolls. Roll up; place on baking sheet. Bake at 375 degrees for 10 to 13 minutes. Combine remaining soup and milk, seasonings and peas and heat. Serve over rolls. Yield: 5 servings.

Mrs. Ruth T. Hanegan, Hope H. S.
Hope, Arkansas

MEXICAN SAUSAGE DISH

2 lb. sausage
1 ½ c. chopped onions
1 c. chopped green pepper
1 c. sour cream
2 cans tomatoes
2 tbsp. sugar
1 tsp. salt
1 tsp. chili powder
Cooked macaroni

Brown sausage, onion and green pepper; drain off grease. Add sour cream, tomatoes, sugar, salt, chili powder and macaroni. Cook for 10 minutes, stirring occasionally. Yield: 6 servings.

Mrs. Doran Ingram, Scottsboro H. S.
Scottsboro, Alabama

CHICKEN A LA KING

1 to 1 ½ c. mushrooms
5 tbsp. fat
2 c. cooked white meat of chicken, cut into 1-in. cubes
3 to 8 tbsp. chopped pimento
2 to 6 tbsp. chopped green pepper
½ tsp. salt
Paprika
3 tbsp. flour
3 c. cream, milk or stock
2 egg yolks, slightly beaten

Cook mushrooms for 5 minutes in 3 tablespoonfuls fat. Add chicken with pimento, green pepper, salt and paprika. Make a white sauce with remaining fat, flour and cream. When cooked, pour slowly over egg yolks, stirring. Add chicken mixture to sauce; reheat. Serve on toast, if desired. Yield: 6-8 servings.

Mrs. Naomi N. Risner, Feds Creek H. S.
Feds Creek, Kentucky
Mrs. Frances Bondurant, Cairo H. S.
Cairo, Illinois

CHICKEN A LA KING

¼ c. chicken fat or butter
1 tbsp. minced green pepper
⅓ c. flour
1 ½ c. chicken broth
1 c. milk
½ tsp. salt
⅛ tsp. pepper
2 c. chopped cooked chicken
1 tbsp. minced pimento
2 tbsp. chopped parsley
1 egg

Heat fat in frying pan. Add green pepper and flour. Stir and cook until mixture is light brown. Add chicken broth, milk and seasonings. Stir while cooking. Add chicken, pimento and parsley. Cook until heated through. Beat egg in a bowl. Add a small amount of hot chicken mixture. Mix well; add to remaining chicken. Stir and cook for 3 to 5 minutes or until thickened. Serve at once. Yield: 8 servings.

Agnes Van Oosten, Park H. S.
Livingston, Montana

CHINESE-STYLE CHICKEN

¼ c. chopped onion
2 tbsp. butter or margarine
1 can cream of mushroom soup

(Continued on next page)

½ c. water
2 6-oz. cans boned chicken, diced
1 ¼ c. thinly sliced celery
½ c. salted cashew nuts (opt.)
1 3-oz. can chow mein noodles
1 11-oz. can Mandarin oranges (opt.)
1 tsp. soy sauce

Heat electric skillet to 325 degrees. Lightly brown onion in butter; stir in soup, water, chicken, celery, cashews, 1 cup noodles, 1/4 cup orange segments and soy sauce. Cover and simmer for 10 minutes, stirring occasionally. Garnish top with orange segments arranged in ring; sprinkle with remaining noodles. Cover and heat for 2 minutes. Yield: 4 servings.

Fae M. Briggs, Gary Public School
Gary, South Dakota

LOBSTER AND BEEF TONGUE CASSEROLE

1 c. slivered smoked beef tongue
1 6-oz. can lobster
1 4-oz. can button mushrooms, undrained
1 can cream of mushroom soup
1 can cream of chicken soup
1 tsp. lemon juice
¼ tsp. paprika
½ c. sliced pitted ripe olives
¼ c. chopped pimento
3 c. cooked rice

Combine all ingredients except rice in a saucepan or electric skillet; heat thoroughly. Serve over hot fluffy rice. Garnish with a pimento star or snipped parsley, if desired.

Bliss Maple, Rock Island Sr. H. S.
Rock Island, Illinois

TURKEY-MUSHROOM SUPREME

¼ c. chopped onion
2 tbsp. shortening
1 can cream of mushroom soup
½ c. milk
2 c. diced cooked turkey
2 tbsp. diced pimento
¼ tsp. nutmeg
⅛ tsp. pepper
1 c. canned green beans
3 c. cooked rice

Brown onion in shortening; blend in soup and milk. Add turkey, pimento, nutmeg, pepper and green beans. Heat slowly, stirring often. Serve over hot rice. Yield: 4 servings.

Mrs. Milklos Kaldy, Catholic Central H. S.
Lethbridge, Alberta, Canada

CHILI TWIST

2 c. egg noodles
3 qt. boiling water
1 tbsp. salt
2 15 ½-oz. cans chili con carne
1 tbsp. parsley
½ tsp. sweet basil leaves, crushed
¼ tsp. powdered oregano
18 oz. tomato sauce

Cook noodles in boiling water with salt, uncovered, until tender; drain. Combine with remaining ingredients. Heat thoroughly. Yield: 4-6 servings.

Mrs. Darlene La Borde, Carmichael Jr. H. S.
Richland, Washington

MEAT BALLS SKILLET MEAL

1 egg, beaten
1 ¼ c. milk
⅔ c. bread crumbs
½ tsp. salt
¼ tsp. dry mustard
¼ tsp. celery salt
Few grains of pepper
Few grains of nutmeg
1 ½ tbsp. grated onion
1 ½ c. ground meat
1 pkg. frozen mixed vegetables
1 can cream of mushroom soup

Combine all ingredients except mixed vegetables, soup and 1 cup milk. Shape into small balls, using 1 teaspoonful of mixture for each ball. Roll in flour. Heat small amount of fat; brown meat balls in fat; add mixed vegetables, soup and milk. Heat until mixture steams. Cover; reduce to low heat and cook for 10 minutes. Yield: 6-8 servings.

Betty Henderson, Jordan Jr. H. S.
Sandy, Utah

TURKEY-HAM ROYALE

1 med. onion, minced
4 tbsp. margarine
¼ c. flour
2 tsp. dry mustard
1 tsp. salt
¼ tsp. curry powder
2 tbsp. catsup
½ tsp. Worcestershire sauce
2 ½ c. milk
1 ⅔ c. evaporated milk
2 c. diced cooked turkey or chicken
2 c. diced cooked ham

Saute onion in margarine until golden in large saucepan; remove from heat. Blend in flour, mustard, salt, curry powder, catsup and Worcestershire sauce; gradually stir in milk and evaporated milk. Cook over low heat, stirring constantly, until sauce thickens. Boil for 1 minute; add turkey and ham. Serve over rice, if desired. Yield: 8 servings.

Mrs. Irene Robotham, Bellaire Public School
Bellaire, Michigan

Foreign Favorites

UGALLI (AFRICA)

2 lb. pork, beef or lamb
4 c. finely chopped spinach, cabbage, onions or Swiss chard or combination of vegetables
Salt and pepper to taste
Corn meal mush or corn bread

Brown and cook meat until tender. Add vegetables and seasonings; cook until done. Serve over corn meal mush or corn bread. Yield: 10 servings.

Mrs. Dorothy Lofstrom, St. Peter Jr.-Sr. H. S.
St. Peter, Minnesota

BUBBLE AND SQUEAK (BRITISH ISLES)

4 tsp. salt
2 tsp. pepper
12 slices cold roast beef or 1 cooked chicken, sliced
4 tbsp. butter
1 cabbage, finely chopped and cooked
½ tsp. nutmeg
2 tbsp. vinegar

Mix 2 teaspoonfuls salt and 1 teaspoonful pepper; sprinkle over beef or chicken. Melt 2 tablespoonfuls butter in a skillet. Brown beef or chicken on both sides in the butter. Remove from skillet; set aside in a warm place. Melt remaining butter in skillet; add cabbage, remaining salt, pepper and nutmeg. Cook over medium heat, stirring constantly, until the cabbage is lightly browned. Sprinkle with vinegar; cook for 1 minute longer. Serve with the meat. Yield: 3-4 servings.

Mrs. Jean Mizak, Central H. S.
Bridgeport, Connecticut

CURRIED CHICKEN (CEYLON)

1 to 2 tsp. salt
3 to 5 whole cardamom pods
3 to 5 whole cloves
1 1-in. stick cinnamon
1 ½ tsp. ground coriander
¾ tsp. ground cumin
¾ tsp. ground fennel
½ tsp. chili powder
Dash of turmeric
1 frying chicken, cut up
1 to 2 tbsp. shortening
½ med. onion, chopped
¼ to ½ clove of garlic
2 to 3 bay leaves
1 8-oz. can tomato sauce
½ 6-oz. can tomato paste
½ c. ground nuts
Milk

Combine salt, cardamom, cloves, cinnamon, coriander, cumin, fennel, chili powder and tumeric. Toss chicken with mixture. Heat shortening in large kettle. Add onion, garlic and bay leaves; cook until onion is tender. Add chicken; fry for 2 to 3 minutes. Add tomato sauce, tomato paste, ground nuts and enough milk to almost cover chicken. Bring to boil. Cover; simmer until chicken is tender, stirring occasionally to prevent sticking. Serve hot with rice, if desired. Yield: 8-10 servings.

Mrs. Louise Kregel, Peru Campus H. S.
Peru, Nebraska

CHICKEN AND ALMONDS (CHINA)

1 c. sliced bamboo shoots
1 c. chopped celery
1 c. chopped onions
8 water chestnuts
6 tbsp. oil
½ lb. almonds, blanched
1 lb. cubed uncooked chicken
¾ tsp. salt
2 tbsp. cornstarch
3 tbsp. Chinese or Japanese soy sauce
2 tbsp. Sherry
1 tsp. sugar
¼ c. chicken stock

Saute bamboo shoots, celery, onions and water chestnuts in 3 tablespoonfuls oil. Remove from pan. Brown almonds in deep fat; drain. Dredge chicken cubes with a mixture of salt, cornstarch, soy sauce, Sherry and sugar. Heat pan; add remaining oil. Saute chicken until tender. Add chicken stock to chicken; heat thoroughly. Combine vegetables and almonds with chicken; heat thoroughly. Serve on rice, if desired. Yield: 6 servings.

Mrs. Melba Smith, Grandview H. S.
Grandview, Texas

CHICKEN CHOW MEIN (CHINA)

2 c. chicken broth
1 ½ c. chopped celery
¾ c. chopped onions
⅛ tsp. pepper
2 c. chopped cooked chicken
1 can chop suey vegetables, drained
2 tbsp. cornstarch
3 tbsp. soy sauce

Combine chicken broth, celery, onions and pepper in a 3-quart saucepan; cook until celery and onion are tender. Add chicken and vegetables; stir well. Combine cornstarch and soy sauce; gradually add vegetable mixture, stirring continuously until thickened. Serve over chow mein noodles. Yield: 6 servings.

Mrs. Eva Welch, Beebe H. S.
Beebe, Arkansas

CHOW YOKE--FRIED PORK OR BEEF (CHINA)

1 tbsp. soy sauce
2 tbsp. wine
½ tsp. sugar
Salt to taste
1 lb. pork or beef tenderloin
2 egg whites, slightly beaten
2 tbsp. flour
Fat

(Continued on next page)

Combine soy sauce, wine, sugar and salt. Cut meat into thick 2-inch long strips. Flatten. Soak in soy sauce mixture for 1 hour. Dip strips into egg whites; dredge in flour. Fry in deep fat. Yield: 3 servings.

Avis E. Calgrove, Fort Lupton H. S.
Fort Lupton, Colorado

CRISP WON TAN (CHINA)

3 c. flour
3 tsp. salt
2 eggs, slightly beaten
Warm water
1 lb. ground pork
½ lb. ground raw shrimp
¼ c. water chestnuts
¼ tsp. monosodium glutamate
2 tsp. shoyu sauce

Combine flour, 2 teaspoonfuls salt, eggs and enough warm water to make a stiff dough. Knead well; cover. Let stand in warm place for 1 hour. Roll thinner than paper, using cornstarch to keep from sticking. Cut into 3 1/2-inch squares. Combine remaining ingredients. Pat rounded 1/2 teaspoonful filling in center of each square. Fold diagonally; cross opposite points and press firmly together. Place on paper lightly sprinkled with cornstarch. Do not allow won ton to touch one another. Fry in deep fat at 360 degrees until browned. Drain on paper towels; serve at once.

Donna Jean Pomerenke
Walnut Grove Public School
Walnut Grove, Minnesota

EGG FOO YUNG (CHINA)

1 can Chinese mixed vegetables
6 eggs, well beaten
1 c. chopped chicken
1 med. onion, chopped
½ tsp. salt
¼ tsp. monosodium glutamate
Dash of pepper
Butter

Drain vegetables; reserve 1 2/3 cups liquid for gravy. Combine eggs, vegetables, chicken, onion and seasonings. Melt 1 teaspoonful butter in skillet. Pour one-half of mixture into skillet; cook until set and brown on edges. Turn; brown second side. Repeat with remaining mixture. Serve with Chinese Brown Gravy.

CHINESE BROWN GRAVY:

4 tbsp. bacon drippings
4 tbsp. flour
2 ½ tbsp. soy sauce
1 tsp. brown gravy sauce
Dash of pepper

Melt fat; blend in flour. Add soy sauce, brown gravy sauce, pepper and reserved vegetable liquid. Stir constantly, until smooth and thickened. Yield: 6 servings.

Mrs. Alberta Hawkins, Lakeview H. S.
Battle Creek, Michigan

SHRIMP AND PINEAPPLE (CHINA)

1 lb. shrimp, fresh or frozen
1 No. 2 can pineapple chunks
¼ c. brown sugar
2 tbsp. cornstarch
½ tsp. salt
¼ c. vinegar
1 tbsp. soy sauce
½ tsp. ground ginger
1 green pepper, cut into strips
1 med. onion, cut into rings

Cook shrimp in boiling water for 3 to 5 minutes; clean. Drain pineapple, reserving syrup. Mix brown sugar, cornstarch and salt in saucepan. Add vinegar, soy sauce, ginger and pineapple syrup. Cook until mixture begins to thicken, stirring constantly. Add green pepper strips, onion rings and pineapple chunks; cook for 2 to 3 minutes. Just before serving, add shrimp; bring to a boil. Serve over cooked rice, if desired. Yield: 4 servings.

Grace Norris, Driftwood Jr. H. S.
Hollywood, Florida

SWEET AND SOUR PORK (CHINA)

1 egg, slightly beaten
½ c. sifted flour
½ tsp. salt
½ c. water
1 ½ lb. pork shoulder, cubed
Salad oil
1 can pineapple chunks
½ c. vinegar
2 tbsp. brown sugar
1 tbsp. molasses
2 tbsp. cornstarch
1 tomato, cut into eighths
1 green pepper, diced

Combine egg, flour, salt and 1/4 cup water. Dip pork cubes into batter; cook in 1 inch of salad oil in Dutch oven for 15 minutes or until pork is done. Drain syrup from pineapple, adding enough water to make 1 cup; heat syrup to boiling with vinegar, brown sugar and molasses. Combine cornstarch and remaining cold water; add to sauce. Add pork, pineapple and vegetables; simmer for 10 to 15 minutes. Serve with fluffy rice. Yield: 6 servings.

Mrs. Jane E. Thiesse, Stafford Jr. H. S.
Stafford, Virginia

SWEET AND SOUR PORK (CHINA)

1 egg
½ c. flour
½ tsp. salt
1 c. water
Peanut oil
1 lb. pork loin, cut into ¾-in. cubes
1 tbsp. soy sauce
⅓ c. catsup
½ c. vinegar
¼ c. brown sugar
2 tbsp. cornstarch
1 c. diagonally sliced bamboo shoots
½ c. cubed green pepper
½ c. cubed carrots, parboiled

(Continued on next page)

Combine egg, flour, salt and 1/4 cup water. Heat peanut oil in deep frying pan. Dip pork cubes into batter; drop into boiling oil. Fry until brown; drain on absorbent paper. Combine soy sauce, catsup, vinegar, brown sugar, remaining water and cornstarch. Saute bamboo shoots, green pepper and carrots in a small amount of peanut oil. Add the sauce; cook until thickened. Add pork. Heat and mix well. Yield: 6 servings.

Mrs. Esther Braman, Atlantic H. S.
Atlantic, Iowa

SWEET AND SOUR PORK (CHINA)

3 lge. green peppers
1 lge. can pineapple chunks
1 ½ lb. boneless lean pork
1 egg
2 tbsp. flour
½ tsp. salt
Dash of pepper
¼ c. oil
2 cloves of garlic, crushed
½ c. sugar
2 ½ tbsp. cornstarch
1 c. plus 2 tbsp. chicken stock
½ c. vinegar
2 tsp. soy sauce

Clean peppers and cut into bite-sized chunks. Drop into boiling water; cook for 8 minutes or until tender. Drain well. Drain pineapple well, reserving liquid. Trim all fat from pork; cut into 1/2-inch cubes. Combine egg, flour, salt and pepper; beat well. Pour batter over pork cubes; mix lightly until each piece is coated. Heat oil in heavy skillet; saute crushed garlic until brown. Remove garlic. Add meat to oil, a piece at a time. Cook until golden brown on all sides over moderate heat. Remove from pan and set aside. Pour off all oil remaining in pan except 1 tablespoonful. Mix sugar and cornstarch; add stock, vinegar, pineapple juice and soy sauce. Add to oil in pan slowly. Bring to a simmer, stirring constantly until well blended and thick and clear. Add pineapple chunks, green peppers and browned pork cubes; simmer for 15 minutes. NOTE: Flavor improves as dish stands; may be reheated just before serving. Yield: 6 servings.

Dorothy Moore, The Cecilian Academy
Philadelphia, Pennsylvania

SWEET-SOUR PORK (CHINA)

1 ½ lb. trimmed, boned lean pork shoulder, cut into ½-in. slices
½ tsp. salt
1 tbsp. fat or oil
1 ½ c. water
1 ½ c. undrained pineapple chunks
3 tbsp. brown sugar
¼ tsp. ground ginger (opt.)
3 tbsp. cornstarch
¼ c. cider vinegar
2 tbsp. soy sauce
1 green pepper, cut into strips lengthwise
1 med. onion, thinly sliced
Hot fluffy rice

Cut pork slices into 2-inch long strips. Sprinkle with salt; brown in fat in skillet. Add 3/4 cup water. Cover; simmer for 1 hour. Drain pineapple, reserving 1/2 cup pineapple juice. Add remaining water to the juice; add brown sugar, ginger, cornstarch, vinegar and soy sauce. Pour over meat. Cook until slightly thickened. Add pineapple, green pepper and onion. Bring to boil; cook for 5 minutes. Serve with rice. Yield: 4 servings.

Joanna C. Klock, Monument Valley H. S.
Kayenta, Arizona
Mrs. Beverly A. Reed, Stamford Central School
Stamford, New York

TIN SQAN ROW--SWEET AND SOUR PORK (CHINA)

1 ½ lb. pork chops
1 egg, beaten
1 tbsp. milk
3 tbsp. flour
½ tsp. salt
4 tbsp. vegetable oil
1 clove of garlic, minced
1 c. pineapple chunks
½ c. pineapple syrup
1 lge. carrot, sliced
2 tbsp. vinegar
2 tbsp. soy sauce
1 tbsp. sugar
1 lge. green pepper, cut into eighths
2 tbsp. cornstarch
4 c. hot cooked rice

Remove bones and fat from chops; cut into 1/2-inch strips. Beat egg with milk, flour and salt. Dip meat into egg mixture; saute slowly in 3 tablespoonfuls oil until browned and thoroughly cooked. Saute garlic in remaining oil for 1 minute; add pineapple, syrup, carrot, vinegar, soy sauce and sugar. Simmer for 5 minutes. Add green pepper; cook for 1 minute longer. Add meat. Thicken mixture with cornstarch to which a small amount of water has been added. Serve over rice. Yield: 4 servings.

Mrs. Sherlene Stonner Parson, Basic H. S.
Henderson, Nevada

WALNUT CHICKEN (CHINA)

1 c. coarsly broken walnuts
¼ c. salad oil
2 chicken breasts, boned and cut lengthwise into thin strips
½ tsp. salt
1 c. onion slices
1 ½ c. bias-cut celery slices
1 ¼ c. chicken broth
1 tsp. sugar
1 tbsp. cornstarch
2 tbsp. soy sauce
1 5-oz. can bamboo shoots
1 5-oz. can water chestnuts, sliced

Toast walnuts in hot oil, stirring constantly; remove nuts to paper towels. Place chicken in skillet; sprinkle with salt. Cook, stirring frequently for 5 to 10 minutes or until tender.

(Continued on next page)

Remove chicken; place onions, celery and 1/2 cup chicken broth in skillet. Cook for 5 minutes or until slightly tender. Combine sugar, cornstarch and soy sauce; add remaining chicken broth. Pour over vegetables in skillet. Cook until sauce thickens. Add chicken, bamboo shoots, water chestnuts and walnuts and heat. Serve over fluffy rice, if desired. Yield: 4-6 servings.

Helen R. Moos, Tulare Union H. S.
Tulare, California

FRIKADELLER (DENMARK)

½ lb. veal, finely ground
½ lb. pork, finely ground
1 med. onion, chopped
¼ tsp. white pepper
1 tsp. salt
2 tbsp. flour
1 egg
½ c. warm milk
¼ lb. butter

Combine meats, onion, pepper, salt, flour and egg in a mixing bowl. Add warm milk; mix well. Heat butter in heavy skillet; spoon batter by tablespoonfuls into skillet. Brown patties, turning once. Place browned patties in baking dish. Bake at 300 degrees for 15 minutes. Yield: 4-6 servings.

Emilie Rae Fallstrom, Maplewood Jr. H. S.
North St. Paul, Minnesota

CORNISH PASTIES (ENGLAND)

3 c. flour
Salt
1 tsp. baking powder
¼ c. lard
1 c. (firmly packed) ground suet
Cold water
1 lb. ground steak, cubed
½ lb. lean pork, cubed
Pepper
2 ⅔ c. diced potatoes
1 c. diced carrots or turnips
2 tbsp. minced onion
2 tbsp. butter

Sift dry ingredients including 1 teaspoonful salt; cut in lard. Blend in ground suet. Add enough cold water to make a dough slightly softer than pie crust. Divide dough into four parts. Roll each part into a circle the size of a big dinner plate. Layer meats, seasoned with salt and pepper, potatoes, carrots and onion on half of each circle. Dot with butter. Fold the unfilled crust over the filled side, crimping the edges together. Place in pie pans. Bake at 400 degrees for 30 minutes; reduce heat to 350 degrees. Bake for 1 hour longer. Yield: 4 servings.

Louise Duverney, Elk Rapids Schools
Elk Rapids, Michigan

CORNISH PASTY (ENGLAND)

⅛ lb. suet
1 ½ lb. beef, cut into 1-in. cubes
1 lge. onion, cubed
4 med. potatoes, cubed
4 carrots or 1 rutabaga, cubed
1 tsp. salt
¼ tsp. pepper
Pastry for 2 two-crust pies

Break suet into small pieces; mix suet, meat, vegetables and seasonings. Divide mixture into four parts. Roll pastry into four rounds. Place one-fourth of vegetable-meat mixture on each pastry round. Pull pastry up from each side; pinch together along entire top. Bake at 350 degrees for 1 hour. Yield: 4 servings.

Mrs. Evelyn Hansen, Buffalo H. S.
Buffalo, Minnesota

BOEUF BOURGUIGNON (FRANCE)

1 tsp. butter
1 strip fatback, cut into ½-in. pieces
3 sm. onions, chopped
2 lb. stew beef
½ c. flour
1 bouillon cube
2 c. hot water
2 c. dry cooking wine
¼ tsp. basil or thyme
3 bay leaves
½ tsp. pepper
¼ tsp. salt
6 sm. potatoes
2 to 3 sm. cans mushrooms

Combine butter, fatback and onions in fry pan and onions in frypan; fry until brown. Remove onions and fatback. Place beef in butter; partially brown. Sprinkle meat with flour; stir. Add bouillon cube, hot water, wine, onions and fatback. Add basil, bay leaves and pepper; sprinkle with salt. Bake at 250 degrees for 2 hours and 30 minutes. Add potatoes and mushrooms 30 minutes to 1 hour before removing from oven. Yield: 4 servings.

Roberta E. O'Shields, Dorman H. S.
Spartanburg, South Carolina

CHICKEN DIJON (FRANCE)

2 tbsp. butter
1 2 ½ to 3-lb. broiler, quartered
2 c. dry white wine
¼ tsp. dried tarragon
Pinch of thyme
1 sm. bay leaf
½ tsp. salt
¼ tsp. pepper
2 egg yolks
2 tbsp. sour cream
2 tbsp. Dijon mustard
Pinch of cayenne pepper

Melt butter in frying pan; add chicken and cook until chicken is browned well on both sides. Add wine, tarragon, thyme, bay leaf, salt and pepper. Bring to a boil. Cover and simmer for 45 minutes or until meat is tender. Remove meat to

(Continued on next page)

heated serving dish; keep warm. Discard bay leaf. Blend sauce with egg yolks. Add sour cream, mustard and cayenne pepper. Heat, stirring constantly. Do not boil. Pour over chicken.

Mrs. Marjorie West, Northeast Voc. H. S.
Lauderdale, Mississippi

HAM AU LAIT--HAM BAKED IN MILK (FRANCE)

1 tsp. dry mustard
4 tbsp. brown sugar
1 center slice ham, 2-in. thick
Milk

Mix mustard and brown sugar; spread over ham. Place in casserole; add enough milk to cover. Bake at 300 degrees for 1 hour. Yield: 6 servings.

Mrs. Mildred Burget Nearhoof
Tyrone Area H. S.
Tyrone, Pennsylvania

QUICHE LORRAINE (FRANCE)

CRUST:

⅔ c. sifted flour
⅓ c. corn meal
½ tsp. salt
⅓ c. shortening
2 tbsp. cold water

Sift flour with corn meal and salt; cut in shortening until mixture resembles coarse crumbs. Add water, a tablespoonful at a time, mixing with a fork until just dampened. If necessary, add enough additional cold water to make dough hold together. Form into ball. Roll dough out on lightly floured board or canvas to form 13-inch circle; fit loosely into 9-inch pie plate. Trim crust allowing 1/2 inch beyond rim. Fold edge under and flute.

FILLING:

¼ c. finely chopped onion
1 tbsp. bacon drippings
¼ lb. Swiss cheese, grated
½ lb. sliced bacon, cooked and crumbled
4 eggs
1 pt. half and half or light cream
¾ tsp. salt
⅛ tsp. nutmeg
Dash of cayenne

Saute onion in bacon drippings. Sprinkle cheese onto bottom of pie crust. Combine onion and bacon; sprinkle over cheese. Combine eggs, half and half, salt, nutmeg and cayenne. Beat until thoroughly combined. Pour into unbaked pie crust. Bake in preheated 400 degree oven for 10 minutes. Reduce heat to 350 degrees; continue baking for 30 minutes or until silver knife inserted 1 inch from edge comes out clean. Let stand for 10 minutes before serving. Yield: 4-6 servings.

Mrs. Jean Henkle, Parkway H. S.
Rockford, Ohio

TURKEY CORDON BLEW (FRANCE)

6 turkey fillets
Salt and pepper
Lemon juice
6 slices cooked ham
6 slices Swiss cheese
Flour
1 egg, beaten
2 tbsp. milk
Bread crumbs
6 tbsp. shortening
6 lemon wedges

Cut a deep pocket in each fillet; season with salt and pepper and lemon juice. Stuff the pockets with ham and cheese. Dip into lemon juice, flour, egg-milk mixture and bread crumbs. Chill until crust is firm. Top each fillet with 1 tablespoonful shortening and 1 lemon wedge. Bake at 350 degrees for 1 hour or fry at 350 degrees for 10 minutes. Yield: 6 servings.

Jeraldine Sanders, Dixie H. S.
St. George, Utah

HALUSHKA--PIGS IN THE BLANKET (GERMANY)

8 to 10 lge. cabbage leaves
⅓ c. uncooked rice
1 lb. ground beef
½ lb. pork sausage
¾ tsp. salt
1 ½ tbsp. chopped onion
½ c. sauerkraut

Steam cabbage leaves for 5 minutes. Mix rice with ground beef, sausage, salt, onion and sauerkraut in a medium-sized bowl. Roll a rounded tablespoonful of meat mixture in cabbage leaves. Place rolls in a heavy fry pan; add water. Cover; cook slowly over low heat for 1 hour. Add tomato juice. Cover; cook for 1 hour longer. Sprinkle with pepper and additional salt to taste. Yield: 8-10 servings.

Paula Reister, Enumclaw Jr. H. S.
Enumclaw, Washington

WIENER SCHNITZEL (GERMANY)

4 veal cutlets or 2 lb. veal steak, cut into serving pieces
1 or 2 eggs, well beaten
2 tbsp. milk (opt.)
Bread crumbs
¼ c. butter or margarine

Flatten each cutlet with a meat mallet until very thin. Dip into mixture of egg and milk; roll in bread crumbs. Fry for 10 minutes in butter until brown. Serve with remaining butter as sauce. Sprinkle with lemon juice, if desired. Yield: 4-6 servings.

Mrs. Barbara Hanson, Mayetta H. S.
Mayetta, Kansas
Jacqueline D. Duval, Rothrock Jr.-Sr. H. S.
McVeytown, Pennsylvania
Marion Evans Duncan, Post H. S.
Post, Texas

ARNI SOURBAKIA GREEK LAMB AND BRUSSELS SPROUTS (GREECE)

1 lb. cubed lamb shoulder
1 10-oz. pkg. frozen California Brussels sprouts, thawed
1 sm. onion, sliced
3 tbsp. olive or salad oil
1 tbsp. lemon juice
1 tsp. salt
½ tsp. sweet marjoram or ¼ tsp. oregano
Freshly ground black pepper
2 tomatoes or 8 cherrystone tomatoes

Place lamb, sprouts and onions in large, shallow bowl. Combine oil, lemon juice, salt, marjoram and pepper; pour over lamb mixture. Chill for 4 hours, turning occasionally. Drain, reserving marinade. Set broiler rack or grill 3 to 4 inches from heat source. Broil all except brussels sprouts and onions separately. Broil lamb skewers for 5 to 7 minutes on each side. Combine brussels sprouts and onions on skewers; broil for 3 to 4 minutes on each side. Broil tomato skewers for 2 to 3 minutes on each side. Brush vegetables with marinade during broiling. Yield: 2 servings.

KEFTEDES--HAMBURGERS (GREECE)

1 lb. ground chuck
1 med. onion, chopped
1 c. bread crumbs
2 tbsp. mint leaves, crushed
Juice of 1 lemon
1 No. 2 can tomatoes
Salt and pepper to taste
1 c. flour
1 ½ c. olive oil or shortening

Combine all ingredients except flour and oil. Shape into balls, using 1 tablespoonful mixture for each ball; roll in flour. Shake off excess flour; brown in hot oil. Yield: 5-6 servings.

Mrs. James Franko, James R. Atwater School
Thomaston, Georgia

SAUCIJSJES--PIGS IN BLANKET (HOLLAND)

2 c. flour
1 tsp. salt
2 tsp. baking powder
½ c. lard or vegetable shortening
1 egg, beaten
¾ c. milk and water
1 lb. seasoned pork sausage
½ lb. seasoned ground beef
2 Dutch rusks, crushed
2 tbsp. cream of mushroom soup

Sift dry ingredients; cut in lard. Add egg, milk and water. Roll out into a thin sheet; cut with a small round cutter. Combine sausage, ground beef, rusks and soup; shape into small rolls. Fold each small roll into prepared pastry round. Bake at 350 degrees for 40 minutes.

Phyllis Nagel, Crestwood H. S.
Cresco, Iowa

CHICKEN PAPRIKAS (HUNGARY)

1 to 1 ½ c. chopped onions
Cooking oil
2 tbsp. paprika
1 ½ c. water
½ c. tomato juice
1 tbsp. salt
½ tsp. pepper
2 med. chickens, cut up
Instant flour
½ c. sour cream (opt.)

Fry onions in cooking oil in a large saucepan; add paprika, water, tomato juice, salt, pepper and chicken. Cook for 1 hour and 30 minutes or until chicken is tender. Thicken with flour. Add sour cream, just before serving.

DUMPLINGS:

2 eggs, beaten
2 tsp. cooking oil
3 ½ c. flour
½ tsp. salt
2 c. water

Combine eggs, cooking oil, flour, salt and water; beat until shiny. With a spoon cut off small pieces of dough; drop into boiling salted water. Cook for 10 minutes. Drain and rinse with clear water. Serve with chicken mixture. Yield: 8 servings.

Cathryn M. Koszegi, Stockbridge H. S.
Stockbridge, Michigan

FISH SALAD (NORWAY)

1 c. mayonnaise
Juice of 1 lemon
1 can crab meat
1 can small shrimp
1 lb. codfish or halibut, cooked and flaked
1 pkg. frozen peas, cooked
Chopped chives
Chopped parsley
Sliced hard-cooked eggs
Tomato wedges

Combine all ingredients except eggs and tomatoes; chill for several hours. Serve ice cold garnished with egg slices and tomato wedges. Yield: 6 servings.

Mrs. Nancy LeHew Smithson, Laramie H. S.
Laramie, Wyoming

CHICKEN CURRY (INDIA)

1 3 to 4-lb. chicken, cut into serving pieces
3 tsp. salt
2 tsp. curry powder
½ tsp. saffron
3 med. onions, sliced
1 c. water

Rub chicken with mixture of salt, curry powder and saffron; place in pan. Broil for 5 minutes. Cover with onions; add water. Cover and bake at 375 degrees for 50 minutes. Remove cover and bake 30 minutes longer. Yield: 4-6 servings.

Alice M. Ford, Central H. S.
Cheyenne, Wyoming

CURRY LAMB (INDIA)

2 med. onions, chopped
½ c. melted shortening
1 ½ lb. cubed lamb
Flour
2 tbsp. curry powder
½ tsp. chili powder
1 clove of garlic, diced
Minced parsley
½ tsp. salt
1 green apple, sliced
½ c. grated coconut
1 8-oz. can tomato sauce
¾ c. stock or water
2 c. uncooked rice

Brown onion in melted shortening in 8 to 10-inch skillet. Remove onions. Dust meat with flour; brown in remaining fat. Reduce heat to low. Add curry powder, chili powder, garlic, parsley, salt, sliced apple and coconut. Stir well; add tomato sauce and stock or water. Cover; simmer for 1 hour. Stir occasionally. Reheat fried onions; sprinkle over meat mixture. Serve with rice. Yield: 4-6 servings.

Jo Ann Nicola, Kirkland Jr. H. S.
Kirkland, Washington

LAMB CURRY INDIENNE (INDIA)

1 med. onion, chopped
1 med. green pepper, chopped
2 tbsp. butter or margarine
2 c. cubed cooked lamb
2 ½ c. chicken broth or bouillon
3 tbsp. lemon juice
1 c. prepared mincemeat
1 tbsp. salt
Dash of pepper
1 c. uncooked rice
1 tbsp. curry powder

Brown onion and green pepper in butter until crisp-tender in large skillet. Add lamb, broth, lemon juice, mincemeat, salt and pepper. Bring to a boil; add rice and curry powder. Stir thoroughly. Cover tightly and cook until rice is tender and liquid is absorbed, about 30 minutes. Serve with coconut, diced green pepper, chopped filberts or other condiments. Yield: 4 servings.

Photograph for this recipe on page 365.

GARLIC TRIPE (IRELAND)

1 lb. tripe
Salt and pepper to taste
½ onion
1 c. milk
2 tbsp. chopped onion
1 tbsp. flour
1 tbsp. butter

Cut tripe into bite-sized pieces; place into saucepan. Cover with water; season with salt. Add one-half of an onion. Simmer for 1 hour and 30 minutes; strain off almost all water. Cover with milk; add chopped onion. Season with salt and pepper. Blend flour with small amount of water; stir into milk mixture. Cook until thick. Add butter. Yield: 4 servings.

Martha R. Phillips, Kennet H. S.
Conway, New Hampshire

BUSHILONA--STUFFED ROUND STEAK (ITALY)

1 lge. onion, chopped
¼ c. chopped parsley
¼ c. chopped celery
2 cloves of garlic, minced
½ c. Parmesan cheese
¼ c. dry bread crumbs
2 round steaks, thinly sliced
Salt and pepper to taste
2 6-oz. cans tomato paste
3 tbsp. sugar
1 8-oz. can tomato sauce

Sprinkle onion, parsley, celery, garlic, cheese and crumbs over steaks. Salt and pepper to taste. Roll steaks; tie with twine or secure with poultry pins. Brown evenly in a small amount of hot fat. Remove from fat. Cook tomato paste in hot fat for 5 minutes. Add sugar; cook for 15 minutes. Add tomato sauce; stir thoroughly. Return steaks to skillet, immersing in gravy. Cover; cook for 1 hour and 30 minutes or until tender. Add water if needed. Serve with spaghetti or rice. Yield: 4 servings.

Mrs. Ann Stamps, Pass Christian H. S.
Pass Christian, Mississippi

GALETTE MARINARA--CHICKEN IN MARINADE (ITALY)

¼ c. butter
1 3-lb. frying chicken, cut up
Salt to taste
Flour

Melt butter in 9 x 13 x 2-inch pan. Season chicken with salt; sprinkle with flour. Place in pan. Bake at 450 degrees for 30 to 40 minutes.

MARINARA SAUCE:

1 clove of garlic, minced
¼ c. chopped onion
2 tbsp. oil
1 14½-oz. can tomato puree
1 tsp. salt
½ tsp. oregano
¼ tsp. basil
⅛ tsp. pepper
½ tsp. dill
⅓ c. grated Parmesan cheese

Saute garlic and onion in oil; add remaining ingredients except dill and cheese. Simmer for 15 minutes. Add dill. Spoon over chicken; top with cheese. Bake at 350 degrees for 30 minutes. Yield: 4 servings.

Mrs. Billy Marks, Bodenham H. S.
Pulaski, Tennessee

LASAGNA (ITALY)

1 lge. onion, chopped
1 lb. ground beef
¼ c. oil
1 10-oz. can tomato sauce
½ tsp. sugar
Salt and pepper to taste
⅓ lb. 2-in. wide lasagna noodles
1 8-oz. pkg. sliced Mozzarella cheese
¾ c. grated Parmesan cheese

Brown onion and ground beef in oil; add tomato sauce, sugar, salt and pepper. Cover; cook slowly for 1 hour, stirring frequently. Cook noodles in boiling salted water until just tender; drain and let set in cold water. Drain again. Alternate layers of sauce, noodles, Mozzarella cheese and Parmesan cheese in 9 x 13 x 2-inch pan. Repeat until all ingredients are used. Bake at 325 degrees for 15 to 25 minutes. Yield: 6-12 servings.

Mrs. Shirlee J. Hara, Germantown H. S.
Germantown, Ohio

LASAGNA (ITALY)

1 lge. can plum tomatoes
2 sm. cans tomato sauce
½ c. water
1 tbsp. sugar
Salt and pepper
3 cloves of garlic, chopped
4 tbsp. olive oil
1 ½ lb. sweet Italian sausage
2 sm. cans tomato paste
1 ½ lb. lasagna noodles
1 c. plus 2 tbsp. grated Romano cheese
1 ½ c. cubed Mozzarella cheese
1 ½ lb. Ricotta cheese
1 c. mushrooms, sauted in butter

Simmer plum tomatoes, tomato sauce, water, sugar, salt and pepper to taste for about 1 hour. Brown garlic in olive oil; remove garlic. Brown sausage in garlic oil. Remove sausage; cut into small pieces. Cook tomato paste in remaining oil over high flame stirring to separate mass for 10 minutes. Add tomato paste and olive oil to simmering sauce. Simmer for 1 hour longer. Cook noodles in boiling salted water until tender, drain. Pour 1/2 cup sauce into oblong baking pan; place a layer of noodles, Romano cheese, Mozzarella cheese, Ricotta cheese, sausage and mushrooms. Repeat until all ingredients are used. Top layer should be noodles covered with sauce and grated cheese. Bake at 400 degrees for 20 minutes. Serve hot. Yield: 8-10 servings.

Mrs. Carolyn A. Tibbetts, Oley Valley Area H. S.
Oley, Pennsylvania

LITTLE NOODLE PIZZA (ITALY)

1 lb. ground meat
1 lge. can tomatoes
1 can tomato paste
¼ c. chopped onion
½ tsp. garlic powder
2 tbsp. Italian seasoning
1 tsp. salt
1 4-oz. can mushrooms
1 egg
2 tbsp. water
1 lge. can chow mein noodles
½ lb. grated Mozzarella cheese
Parmesan cheese

Brown meat; add tomatoes, tomato paste, onion, seasonings and mushrooms. Cover and simmer for a few minutes. Beat egg with water; add to noodles. Shape into flat mounds about 3 inches in diameter. Place on well greased baking sheet. Bake at 250 degrees for 15 minutes. Spread meat mixture on rounds. Cover with Mozzarella cheese; top with mushrooms and sprinkle with Parmesan cheese. Bake at 350 degrees until lightly browned and bubbly. Yield: 6 servings.

Dorotha C. Prowell, Hereford H. S.
Hereford, Texas

QUAIETTA (ITALY)

Soft butter
1 slice beef sirloin, cut ½-in. thick
¼ c. chopped fresh parsley
1 clove of garlic, finely chopped
Salt

Spread soft butter over meat. Sprinkle with parsley, garlic and salt. Roll tightly from narrow end. Tie securely with string. Make sure parsley mixture is firmly enclosed. Braise over direct heat, adding water as necessary. May be baked at 250 degrees for several hours. Yield: 4-6 servings.

Martha Jaquish Barocco, Elkland H. S.
Elkland, Pennsylvania

ASPARAGUS AND LAMB ORIENTAL (JAPAN)

1 lb. lamb, cut into long thin strips
¼ c. seasoned flour
2 tbsp. fat or oil
1 sm. clove of garlic, finely minced
1 c. bouillon
2 c. cut or frozen raw asparagus spears, cut into 1-in. pieces
Soy sauce
¼ c. cold water
1 tbsp. cornstarch

Dredge lamb in seasoned flour. Brown in hot fat with garlic. Add bouillon. Cover and simmer for 30 minutes. Add asparagus and 1 teaspoonful soy sauce. Cover. Simmer until asparagus is tender. Combine soy sauce, water and cornstarch. Add to meat mixture. Cook for five minutes. Serve hot over rice, if desired. Yield: 4 servings.

Nina C. Lascari, Vineland H. S.
Vineland, New Jersey

CHICKEN TERIYAKI (JAPAN)

⅓ c. sugar
½ c. soy sauce
Dash of monosodium glutamate
1 fryer, cut up

(Continued on next page)

Combine all ingredients except chicken; pour over chicken. Marinate for several hours or overnight. Place chicken, skin-side down, in baking pan. Bake at 350 degrees for 30 minutes. Baste with marinade. Turn; bake for 30 minutes longer.

Sister M. Aloysius, P.B.V.M., O' Gorman H. S.
Sioux Falls, South Dakota

ORIENTAL STEAK (JAPAN)

2 tbsp. olive oil
2 lb. flank steak, cut into strips
1 clove of garlic
1 tsp. salt
Dash of pepper
¼ c. soy sauce
½ tsp. sugar
2 fresh or canned tomatoes, drained and quartered
2 green peppers, cut into large chunks
1 c. celery, cut into strips
1 can mushrooms
1 can bean sprouts, drained
1 tbsp. cornstarch
¼ c. cold water

Heat oil in large skillet at 350 degrees. Add beef, garlic, salt and pepper. Cook until evenly browned. Season with soy sauce and sugar. Cover tightly. Cook slowly for 5 minutes. Add tomatoes, green pepper, celery and undrained mushrooms. Add bean sprouts. Bring to a boil. Cover; cook briskly for 5 minutes. Combine cornstarch and water. Add to beef mixture. Cook until slightly thickened, stirring occasionally. May be served with steamed rice or fried noodles. Yield: 6 servings.

Mrs. Elizabeth Pottinger, Chilton H. S.
Chilton, Texas

SHRIMP TEMPURA (JAPAN)

2 c. flour
½ c. cornstarch
2 tsp. baking powder
1 tsp. salt
½ tsp. soda
1 egg, slightly beaten
2 lb. jumbo shrimp
Fat
1 tbsp. powdered ginger
¼ clove of garlic, crushed
2 tbsp. sugar
½ c. soy sauce

Mix and sift dry ingredients. Add egg and enough water to make a thin batter. Clean shrimp, leaving on tails. Cut into butterfly shapes. Dip into batter; drain. Fry in deep fat at 375 degrees until golden brown. Drain. Combine remaining ingredients with 1/4 cup water; serve with shrimp. Yield: 6 servings.

Mrs. Nancy Sakurada, Morrill H. S.
Morrill, Nebraska

SPARERIBS (JAPAN)

1 ½ lb. spareribs
Mustard
½ tsp. sage
¼ to ⅓ c. soy sauce

Have butcher crack ribs across once. Cut each sparerib into separate pieces. Spread on both sides with mustard. Place in 1 1/2-quart casserole; sprinkle with a small amount of sage. Pour soy sauce over ribs. Bake, covered, in preheated 375 degree oven for 1 hour and 30 minutes or until meat falls from bones. Turn ribs 30 minutes before end of baking period. Serve with rice. Yield: 4 servings.

Mrs. Margaret D. Miller, Dobbs Ferry H. S.
Dobbs Ferry, New York

SUKIYAKI (JAPAN)

2 4-oz. cans dried bean threads
1 lb. beef tenderloin, sliced paper thin
1 1-lb. can bean sprouts, drained
2 c. diagonally cut green onions, 2-in. long
1 c. diagonally cut celery, 2-in. long
½ c. thinly sliced fresh mushrooms
1 5-oz. can water chestnuts, drained and thinly sliced
1 5-oz. can bamboo shoots, sliced
5 c. small spinach leaves, 2-in. long
2 tbsp. sugar
½ c. soy sauce
1 tsp. monosodium glutamate
Beef stock
Suet

Soak bean threads in cold water for 2 hours; drain. Arrange meat and vegetables on large platter. Combine sugar, soy sauce, monosodium glutamate and beef stock. Preheat 12-inch electric skillet; rub suet over bottom and sides of pan. Render 2 tablespoonfuls fat from suet; remove piece of suet. Add beef; cook briskly, turning constantly with two spoons for 1 to 2 minutes or until brown. Add broth mixture; push meat to side of skillet. Add vegetables; toss and stir vegetables and meat separately for 1 minute. Add bean threads; cook until heated through. Serve over cooked rice with additional soy sauce. Yield: 4 servings.

Mrs. Mazel W. Kemp, Henry Grandy H. S.
Atlanta, Georgia

WALNUT CHICKEN (JAPAN)

1 c. cubed bamboo shoots
1 c. diced celery
1 c. diced onions
8 water chestnuts
6 tbsp. oil
2 c. chopped walnuts or almonds
1 lb. uncooked cubed chicken
¾ tsp. salt
2 tbsp. cornstarch
3 tbsp. soy sauce
2 tbsp. Sherry
1 tsp. sugar
¼ c. soup stock

(Continued on next page)

Saute bamboo shoots, celery, onions and water chestnuts in 3 tablespoonfuls oil; remove from pan. Brown walnuts in pan drippings; remove from pan and drain. Dredge chicken in a mixture of salt, cornstarch, soy sauce, Sherry and sugar. Saute chicken in remaining oil until tender. Add soup stock and heat. Add sauted vegetables and walnuts; serve hot. Yield: 4-6 servings.

Mrs. Mary Jean Earl, Adams City H. S.
Commerce City, Colorado

BARBECUE MEAT (KOREA)

1 2½-lb. rib-eye steak
1 c. shoyu
7 tbsp. sugar
¼ tsp. ajinomoto or monosodium glutamate
2 tbsp. Scotch whisky
2 tbsp. sesame seed oil
1 med. onion, chopped
2 cloves of garlic, chopped
1 piece ginger, 1 x ½-in chopped

Slice partially frozen meat 1/2-inch thick, cutting across grain. Combine remaining ingredients. Add meat. Cover bowl; refrigerate overnight. Turn meat a few hours before cooking. Charcoal or oven-broil until of desired doneness, basting with remaining marinade. NOTE: Sesame seed combined with 2 tablespoonfuls liquid oil may be substituted for sesame oil. Yield: 6 servings.

Sui Inn Nakano, Radford H. S.
Honolulu, Hawaii

BAKED CHICKEN (LEBANON)

2 frying chickens, cut up
1 clove of garlic, mashed
1 12-oz. can tomato paste
1 c. water
1 clove of garlic, mashed
½ tsp. salt
¼ tsp. pepper
1 tbsp. dried mint leaves

Wash chicken pieces; place, skin-side up, in 15 x 10-inch baking pan. Mix garlic, tomato paste, water and seasonings in bowl. Pour sauce over chicken pieces until well covered. Bake at 350 degrees for about 1 hour and 10 minutes. Yield: 8 serbings.

Mrs. Dorothy Huchro, Keene Central School
Keene Valley, New York

DELEH MEHSHI--STUFFED RIBS (LEBANON)

1 lb. lean ground lamb
½ c. washed uncooked rice
3 tbsp. butter
¼ c. pine nuts
Salt and pepper to taste
3 lb. whole lamb ribs

Mix all ingredients except ribs thoroughly in the order given. Separate meat from ribs horizontally, forming a deep pocket. Place stuffing in space between meat and ribs; sew up, closing the opening around ribs. Drop stuffed ribs into pan of slightly salted boiling water to half cover. Steam ribs. Cook, covered, until stuffing and meat are done. Remove ribs from stock; place under broiler until golden brown. Yield: 6-8 servings.

Mrs. Carmen K. Ferris, Consultant
Adult Migrant Education-Homemaking
Texas Education Agency
Austin, Texas

BURRITOS (MEXICO)

½ c. minced onion
2 tbsp. fat, butter or margarine
½ c. chopped green chili
2 ½ c. chopped roast beef
½ tsp. salt
¼ tsp. pepper
¼ tsp. garlic salt
1 c. grated cooked potatoes
½ c. beef gravy or thickened broth
Flour tortillas
Grated cheese

Saute minced onion in fat; add chopped green chili, meat and seasonings. Add potatoes. Add gravy to broth; cook in an open skillet, stirring constantly, until almost dry in appearence. Place 3 tablespoonfuls of meat mixture in a flour tortilla; sprinkle with grated cheese. Roll up into a 2 1/2-inch roll. Place in a baking pan; keep warm until served.

Laura E. Sumner, Cobre H. S.
Bayard, New Mexico

CITY RICE (MEXICO)

1 c. uncooked rice
3 tbsp. olive oil
1 tsp. salt
3 cloves of garlic
3 tomatoes, chopped
2 c. boiling water
1 c. chopped ripe and green olives
2 c. cooked diced pork or chicken

Brown rice in oil; add salt, garlic, tomatoes and boiling water. Simmer for 45 minutes or until done. Add olives and meat. Serve hot. Yield: 6-8 servings.

Augusta Jannett, Yoakum H. S.
Yoakum, Texas

ENCHILADAS (MEXICO)

3 tbsp. flour
3 tbsp. chili powder
4 tbsp. fat
2 c. water
1 can tomato puree
2 cans chili
Salt and pepper (opt.)

(Continued on next page)

Brown flour and chili powder in fat; add water, tomato puree and chili. Season with salt, pepper and garlic, if desired. Simmer slowly for 15 minutes or until slightly thickened. Dip each tortilla into chili mixture; place in flat dish. Sprinkle each tortilla with small amount of grated cheese and chopped onion; roll up. Pour remaining chili mixture over tortillas. Bake at 350 degrees until cheese melts. Yield: 8 servings.

Mrs. Marilynn Collins, Bridgeport H. S.
Bridgeport, Texas

GUISADO (MEXICO)

1 ½ lb. ground round steak
6 tbsp. dry bread crumbs
4 tbsp. grated cheese
Juice of 1 lemon
1 tbsp. parsley
1 egg, beaten
2 tbsp. fat
Flour
1 c. boiling water
1 ½ c. tomato juice
Salt to taste
½ tsp. chili powder
½ c. elbow macaroni, cooked

Combine meat, bread crumbs, cheese, lemon juice, parsley and egg; form into balls the size of large walnuts. Melt fat in heavy fry pan; brown meat balls quickly on all sides. Dredge browned balls in flour; brown again. Add water, tomato juice and salt. Cover; simmer slowly for 2 hours. Add chili powder and macaroni. Serve hot platter; sprinkle with cheese. Yield: 6-8 servings.

Mrs. Jennie J. White, Rosemary School
Rosemary, Alberta, Canada

PORK AND BEANS (MEXICO)

¼ c. chopped onion
½ green pepper, chopped
3 tbsp. shortening
3 tbsp. flour
1 No. 2 can tomatoes, strained
2 c. chopped celery
1 tsp. chili powder
2 tbsp. sugar
⅛ tsp. cayenne pepper
½ tsp. dry mustard
2 tsp. salt
2 tbsp. vinegar
4 No. 2 cans pork and beans

Brown onion and green pepper in shortening; stir in flour. Add tomatoes, celery, seasonings and vinegar; simmer for 35 minutes. Add pork and beans; cook 10 to 15 minutes or bake at 400 degrees for 30 minutes. Yield: 12 servings.

Deanne Tufts, Valley Regional H. S.
Deep River, Connecticut

HOT TAMALE LOAF (MEXICO)

2 med. onions, chopped
3 cloves of garlic
½ lb. bacon, cut up
1 ½ c. milk
2 c. tomatoes
1 ½ c. corn meal
1 c. olives, sliced
1 can whole kernel corn
1 tbsp. salt
1 tbsp. chili powder
Butter
3 eggs, beaten

Fry onions, garlic and meat until brown. Remove garlic. Make a mush of milk, tomatoes and corn meal; add olives, corn, meat mixture, seasonings, a lump of butter and beaten eggs. Place mixture in a baking dish. Bake at 350 degrees for 1 hour. Yield: 6 servings.

Mrs. Rosella F. Lamb, Cowan H. S.
Cowan, Indiana

LUTEFISH (SWEDEN)

6 qt. water
2 tbsp. salt
4 to 5 lb. frozen lutefisk
½ lb. melted butter

Bring water to a brisk boil in a large 6 to 8 quart kettle; add salt. Tie fish loosely in cheesecloth; drop into boiling water. Bring to a boil again and boil for 6 to 8 minutes or until fish will flake. Serve with the melted butter and black pepper, if desired. Yield: 4 servings.

Mrs. Vivian Strand, Chester H. S.
Chester, South Dakota

LOMO SALTADO (PERU)

1 ½ lb. round steak
1 tsp. salt
½ tsp. pepper
¼ c. cooking oil
4 c. cooked French-fried potatoes
½ c. sliced onion
1 chili pepper, chopped
2 lge. tomatoes, peeled and quartered
1 c. cooked green peas

Cut steak into small strips, trimming off any fat; season. Brown steak in oil until of desired doneness. Add french fries, onion and chili pepper; stir to mix. Heat through. Just before serving, add tomatoes and green peas; stir well. Place on platter; serve. Yield: 6 servings.

Mrs. Dona Hatfield, Glynn Academy
Brunswick, Georgia

DUCK SOUP (POLAND)

1 ½ lb. pork rib end roast
3 qt. water
½ lb. to 1 lb. prunes
Flour
1 c. duck or pig blood
2 tbsp. vinegar
1 tbsp. sugar
1 tbsp. salt

(Continued on next page)

Cook pork in water in large pot; when half done, add prunes. Cook until done. Place flour in bowl; add blood to thicken. Gradually add stock to mixture of blood and flour. Slowly add to large pot, stirring continuously. Cook for 15 minutes. Add vinegar, sugar and salt. Serve with boiled potatoes or noodles, if desired. Yield: 10-12 servings.

Lucy B. Skinger, Silas Deane Jr. H. S.
Wethersfield, Connecticut

BEEF STROGANOFF (RUSSIA)

1 lb. lean beef, cut into 3 x ½-in. strips
¼ c. flour
Salt and pepper
¼ c. fat
1 c. hot bouillon
3 tbsp. tomato juice
1 tbsp. prepared mustard
1 tsp. Worcestershire sauce
¾ c. sour cream

Roll beef in flour seasoned with 1/2 teaspoonful salt and 1/8 teaspoonful pepper. Brown in fat; remove meat from skillet. Add hot bouillon to skillet; bring to boil. Add tomato juice, mustard, Worcestershire sauce, sour cream and salt and pepper to taste. Bring to boil again; add meat. Simmer for 20 to 25 minutes or until meat is tender. Serve on rice or noodles, if desired. Yield: 3-4 servings.

Mrs. Helen J. Watson, Lakeview H. S.
Winter Garden, Florida

CAUCASIAN SHASHLIK (RUSSIA)

2 lb. lamb, loin or shoulder
1 tsp. salt
1 c. chopped onions
1 clove of garlic, finely chopped
½ tsp. coarse black pepper
½ c. lemon juice
½ c. red wine
¼ c. olive oil

Cut meat into 1-inch cubes. Place in glass bowl or earthenware dish; sprinkle with salt, chopped onions, garlic and pepper. Add lemon juice, wine and oil. Let stand for 4 to 6 hours or overnight. Drain; place meat on skewers. Broil for 15 to 20 minutes or until all sides are browned. Serve immediately. Serve with rice if desired. Yield: 4-6 servings.

Connie E. Davenport, Jefferson H. S.
Cedar Rapids, Iowa

NOODLES STROGANOFF (RUSSIA)

½ c. minced onion
1 8-oz. can sliced mushrooms
2 tbsp. butter or margarine
1 lb. ground beef
2 tbsp. flour
1 tsp. salt
¼ tsp. pepper
1 can cream of chicken soup
1 c. milk
1 pkg. Noodles Romanoff
Parsley

Saute onion and mushrooms in butter over medium heat. Add meat and brown. Stir in flour, salt, pepper and soup; simmer, uncovered, for 10 minutes. Stir in milk and package of sour cream-cheese sauce mix from Noodles Romanoff. Heat through. Garnish with parsley. Serve over noodles cooked according to package directions. Yield: 4 servings.

Verda Rex, Fielding H. S.
Paris, Idaho

EMPANADAS CHICAS--MEAT PIES (SPAIN)

FILLING:

3 c. chopped green peppers
Dash of pepper
2 med. onions, chopped
3 tbsp. oil
1 tsp. salt
1 c. chorisos or pepperoni
1 c. chopped cooked ham
1 c. chopped cooked chicken breasts
½ c. sliced stuffed olives

Combine green peppers, pepper, onions, oil, salt and chorisos; cook until peppers are tender. Add remaining ingredients; mix well.

DOUGH:

1 pkg. granulated yeast
1 ¼ c. lukewarm water
5 ½ c. sifted flour
1 tsp. salt
3 tbsp. oil
Sesame seed

Dissolve yeast in 1/4 cup lukewarm water. Sift 4 cups flour and salt into medium mixing bowl; add oil, remaining water and yeast mixture. Beat for 5 minutes with spoon until smooth. Brush with oil; let rise until doubled in bulk. Knead with hand; add remaining flour. Work until dough is smooth. Grease top of dough; turn over and grease other side of dough. Let rise until almost doubled in bulk. Divide into four pieces. Divide each piece into three pieces. Roll out on floured board into 5 or 6-inch circle. Place 2 heaping tablespoonfuls of filling on one-half of each circle. Fold over; seal with fork. Prick top in several places. Place on greased baking pan. Brush top with milk; sprinkle with sesame seed. Bake at 400 degrees for 25 minutes. Yield: 12 servings.

Mrs. Audessa Wright, Stoco H. S.
Coal City, West Virginia

KOTTBULLAR (SWEDEN)

1 lb. ground beef
¼ c. fine dry bread crumbs
⅔ c. chopped onions

(Continued on next page)

1 tsp. salt
Dash of pepper
2/3 c. evaporated milk
2 tbsp. butter
2 beef bouillon cubes
1 1/2 c. boiling water
1/3 c. flour
1/2 tsp. allspice
1 c. evaporated milk
1 tbsp. lemon juice

Combine ground beef, bread crumbs, onions, salt, pepper and milk; shape into balls. Brown in butter. Dissolve bouillon cubes in 1 cup boiling water; pour over meat balls. Bring to a boil over medium heat. Cover; simmer for 15 minutes. Remove from heat; sprinkle with flour and allspice. Gradually stir in evaporated milk and remaining water. Cook, uncovered, over low heat, stirring occasionally, until sauce is thickened. Stir in lemon juice.

POPPY SEED-NOODLES:

1 8-oz. pkg. noodles, cooked and drained
2 tbsp. butter
1 tsp. poppy seed

Toss noodles with butter and poppy seed. Serve with meat balls.

LaVonne Wiener, Rock Valley Comm. School
Rock Valley, Iowa

POTATO SAUSAGE (SWEDEN)

1 to 2 lb. ground beef
1 lb. ground pork
2 to 3 lb. potatoes, coarsely ground
1 lge. onion, coarsely ground
Salt and pepper to taste
1/2 tsp. allspice
1/2 c. water
Sausage casings

Combine all ingredients; fill casings with mixture. Cook slowly for 45 minutes to 1 hour in boiling water.

Mrs. Erna Peterson, Rush City Public School
Rush City, Minnesota
Leona Matson, Barstow H. S.
Barstow, California

MILD CURRY (THAILAND)

1 whole fresh coconut
12 serving pieces chicken
4 potatoes, peeled and quartered
1 tbsp. curry powder
2 tsp. salt
1 tsp. sugar
1 tsp. monosodium glutamate

Place coconut in oven. Bake at 350 degrees until shell cracks. Remove shell. Puncture coconut meat; drain, reserving liquid. Discard coconut meat. Add water to coconut liquid to equal 6 cups liquid. Add chicken and potatoes; simmer, uncovered, for 1 hour. Remove from heat. Combine 3 tablespoonfuls liquid from mixture with curry powder, salt, sugar and monosodium glutamate; stir into chicken mixture. Cook for about 10 minutes longer. Yield: 6 servings.

Mrs. Hope Atkinson McCuskey, Titusville H. S.
Titusville, Florida

BAKED STUFFED FISH (UKRAINE)

1 3-lb. fish, cleaned
Salt and pepper
1 med. onion, chopped
1/2 c. diced celery
1 c. sliced mushrooms
Butter
2 c. soft bread crumbs
2 tbsp. chopped parsley
1/4 tsp. savory seasoning
2 tbsp. water
Paprika
Flour

Sprinkle fish lightly inside and outside with salt. Cook onion, celery and mushrooms in 1/2 cup butter until tender. Combine with remaining ingredients except flour; season to taste. Fill fish cavity with stuffing. Sew opening with a needle and coarse thread. Brush fish generously with soft butter or oil; coat with flour. Sprinkle with paprika. Cut three or four gashes in skin on both sides of the fish to prevent cracking. Place fish in a pan lined with greased paper. Bake at 450 degrees for 10 minutes per inch of stuffed thickness. Baste several times with a mixture of 2 parts of water and one part of butter or oil. Place fish on a hot platter; remove thread. Garnish with sprigs of parsley and lemon slices, if desired. Yield: 6 servings.

Mrs. Lillian Meronyk
New Myrnam School No. 4364
Myrnam, Alberta, Canada

RIZOTA--CHICKEN WITH RICE (YUGOSLAVIA)

4 tbsp. butter or bacon drippings
1/2 c. finely chopped onion
1/2 fryer, cut up
1/2 tsp. salt
6 whole cloves
3 c. boiling water
2 tsp. salt
1/2 c. cooked tomatoes
1 1/2 c. uncooked long grain rice
Grated Parmesan cheese

Melt butter in large skillet. Add onion; brown well. Add chicken, salt and cloves. Brown chicken well. Cover and cook over low heat until tender, stirring occasionally. Add boiling water, salt and tomatoes. Add rice; cook over low heat without stirring for 15 minutes or until rice is done. Leave skillet partially covered. If more water is needed, add 1/4 cup boiling water; cook for 5 minutes longer. If too moist, remove cover; let moisture cook off. Serve sprinkled with Parmesan cheese. Yield: 3-4 servings.

Mrs. Isabel Qualls, Hudson H. S.
Hudson, Wisconsin

INDEX

FRP ® INC

FRP creates successful connections between organizations and individuals through custom books.

Favorite Recipes Press, an imprint of FRP, Inc., located in Nashville, Tennessee, is one of the nation's best-known and most-respected cookbook companies. Favorite Recipes Press began by publishing cookbooks for its parent company, Southwestern/Great American, in 1961. FRP, Inc., is now a wholly owned subsidiary of the Southwestern/Great American family of companies, and under the Favorite Recipes Press imprint has produced hundreds of custom cookbook titles for nonprofit organizations, companies, and individuals.

Other FRP, Inc., imprints include

 BECKON BOOKS

CommunityClassics®

Additional titles published by FRP, Inc., are

Recipes Worth Sharing

The Hunter's Table

More Recipes Worth Sharing

The Illustrated Encyclopedia of American Cooking

Cooking Up a Classic Christmas

Almost Homemade

The Vintner's Table

Junior Leagues In the Kitchen with Kids: Everyday Recipes & Activities for Healthy Living

To learn more about custom books, visit our Web site, www.frpbooks.com.